Ulan Bator

CYPRUS

SINAI

The Gulf

PAKISTAN

KOREA

Hanoi

HONG KONG

MALAYA

BRUNEI

Singapore

INDIAN

OCEAN

ZAIRE

ZIMBABWE

MAURITIUS

CRAFTSMEN OF THE ARMY

VOLUME II

FIELD MARSHAL HIS ROYAL HIGHNESS
THE PRINCE PHILIP, DUKE OF EDINBURGH
KG KT OM GBE AC QSO

Colonel in Chief
Corps of Royal Electrical and Mechanical Engineers

CRAFTSMEN OF THE ARMY

VOLUME II

The Story of
The Royal Electrical and Mechanical Engineers
1969–1992

Compiled by
Brigadier J M Kneen BA CEng FIMechE FIMgt
(late Corps of Royal Electrical and Mechanical Engineers)
and
Brigadier D J Sutton OBE FCIT
(late Royal Corps of Transport)

With a Foreword by
Field Marshal The Lord Vincent GBE KCB DSO

Leo Cooper · London

Corps of Royal Electrical and Mechanical Engineers
1996

ACKNOWLEDGEMENTS

The permission of the *Soldier* magazine to publish
many of the photographs in this book
is gratefully acknowledged.
The permission to publish quotations from *Storm Command*
by General Sir Peter de la Billière KCB KBE DSO MC
is gratefully acknowledged

The help of The Royal School of Artillery, Larkhill
is gratefully acknowledged

The pencil drawings in this book were produced
by students of the School of Illustration,
Bournemouth and Poole College of Art and Design
whose help is gratefully acknowledged.
The artists are listed on page 690

ISBN 0-85052-549-7

A CIP record of this book is available from
The British Library

First Published in Great Britain 1996
by the Corps of Royal Electrical and Mechanical Engineers
Arborfield Berkshire
and
LEO COOPER
an imprint of
Pen and Sword Books Ltd
47 Church Street, Barnsley, South Yorkshire S70 2BR
Designed and produced by John Mitchell
Typeset by Bexhill Phototypesetters
Printed in Great Britain
by Redwood Books Ltd

FOREWORD

I have served alongside the Corps of Royal Electrical and Mechanical Engineers for many years and became a Colonel Commandant in 1981. In all this time I have taken a very close interest in the work of the Corps and its widespread activities and achievements many of which I have seen at first hand. As Field Marshal The Viscount Montgomery of Alamein wrote in Volume I of this history, REME has kept 'the Punch in the Army's Fist' from its formation in 1942 right through to the victory in the Gulf War in 1991 and beyond. All through these years, REME has a proud record of operational support to the British Army through its wide range of engineering activities, whilst never forgetting that REME soldiers also have to match the rest of the Army in military skills.

However, this proud record does not just end there. The Corps has always been at the forefront of new developments and forward thinking within the Army through its innovative training methods, its pro-active approach to the ever-increasing pressure on very scarce manpower and cash resources and its application of modern management techniques to activities behind the front line.

The strength of the Corps lies in its members, those who have kept the weapons and equipment of the British Army functioning in all parts of the world and displayed ingenuity, resourcefulness and considerable soldierly skills. This is the second part of their story – a story which covers the ever-increasing sophistication of equipment issued to the Army and its associated support.

Vincent of Coleshill

Field Marshal The Lord Vincent GBE KCB DSO

PREFACE

Volume I of Craftsmen of the Army, the story of the Corps of Royal Electrical and Mechanical Engineers, was first published in 1970 and proved so popular that there have been four reprints. This book, Volume II, continues the story and generally covers the period from 1969 to 1992, the 50th Anniversary of REME. Where it has seemed sensible, however, to complete a story with a major impact on Corps affairs, it has been allowed to overrun slightly.

As you would expect, the book contains plenty of meat for the serious reader and traces the mounting complexity and cost of the support of the Army's weapon systems, fighting and logistic vehicles, electronic equipment and aircraft. But it also has a human aspect recording the names of many officers and soldiers who played key roles. The book also records the major contribution made by the Corps to adventurous training and sport.

No one person wrote Volume II but, like Volume I, it is the result of much labour by many serving and retired members of the Corps who freely contributed from papers, reports, personal knowledge and experience of events. When Brigadier Michael Kneen embarked on the task of compiling it in 1987, he estimated a more modest work. Little did he realise just how much was worth recording! In 1990 he was joined by Brigadier John Sutton OBE (late Royal Corps of Transport), an established author of military history who has developed the sound initial structure into this book. The Corps is indebted to them and also to those who contributed to the story and criticised the many drafts of the text.

The progress of the book has been in the hands of a Steering Committee presided over by the several Commandants of the REME Training Centre (later Group) at Arborfield. Also Brigadier Martyn Clark, initially as Corps Secretary and latterly as a volunteer, has been responsible for all the business management and a leading light not only in the detailed editing of the text but in the conduct of much research. Colonel David Axson, having taken over as Corps Secretary, has worked tirelessly to prepare the final text and to see the project through to a successful conclusion. Major Mike Martin has been a constant help, supported by the typewriting skills of Mrs Audrey Thurston and Mrs Dorothy Ingram. Captain Eddie Thomas REME (V) spent much time in the closing stages finding suitable photographs, formatting the text for printing and preparing the index.

I am certain that the reader will find the book of great interest and a pleasure to read.

M S Heath

Major General M S Heath CB CBE
Representative Colonel Commandant
Corps of Royal Electrical and Mechanical Engineers

CONTENTS

ANNEXES

Chapter

MAPS

CHAPTER 1

INTRODUCTION

Background · Military Commitments · Ending of the Cold War · Logistic Studies · The Effects of Ministry of Defence Committees · Training · British Army of the Rhine · Northern Ireland · REME in the Reserve Army · Servicewomen in REME · REME Regimental Activities · Sport and Adventurous Training · The 50th Anniversary

BACKGROUND

This second volume of Craftsmen of the Army takes the continuing story of The Corps of Royal Electrical and Mechanical Engineers from 1969 until towards the end of 1992 when celebrations were held to mark the 50th Anniversary of the formation of the Corps. The first volume published in 1970 told the story of the Corps in war and peace from its formation on 1 October 1942 – 'born in the bleakest days of the Second World War' – through its formative years of growing strength and experience.

In his Epilogue to Volume 1, Major General Peter Girling, then the Director of Electrical and Mechanical Engineering (Army), outlined many of the important characteristics essential to the Corps in carrying out its task. He concluded that REME could have every confidence in its future in a changing world, if it followed the precept – 'above all of keeping an eye on the ball – the fitness for operations of the Army's equipment'. How well this has been achieved can be judged from the narrative in the chapters which follow. In some cases the opportunity has also been taken to include some of those overall activities of the Corps and its units which had to be omitted from Volume 1, but which are now recorded to complete the story.

This volume covers all aspects of the Corps at work and recreation in many places, and under many conditions that tested both physical and mental abilities to the full. It also illustrates the constant endeavours and technical skills of the Corps that were needed to meet the ever-present challenges in providing the Army with sustained and effective equipment support, in peace and war.

During the period now covered, a succession of major national and world events inevitably produced substantial effects on our national defence policy – some good, some bad, and some to have momentous consequences. Many resulting decisions and their implementation were to have a direct impact on the work of the Corps, particularly those involving military operations, advancing technical knowledge, and the efforts to contain the costs of equipment support. This opening chapter highlights the more significant national, international, political and military occurrences in the time scale, and their consequences of relevance to the function of the Corps. It provides an introduction to all REME's extensive activities which are described in detail in the succeeding chapters.

A number of acronyms inevitably occur in a work of this nature: they are explained in the Glossary.

MILITARY COMMITMENTS

Until almost the end of the period covered, the successful deterrence provided by NATO for the defence of the Western World required that the strength and effectiveness of BAOR should be fully maintained. There was, however, a progressive reduction in our colonial interests and commitments, resulting in the withdrawal of our forces from many overseas garrisons, leaving only minor garrisons requiring greatly reduced but nevertheless essential support. However, commitments still arose outside Europe both within our own responsibilities, or as part of United Nations Forces, and these ranged from major operations to the provision of peace-keeping forces. REME played an exacting part in all these actions, which involved an extended use of their resources, and the employment of technical skills across the whole range of equipment support. Threats to one of our remaining overseas territories brought about the Falklands War in 1982, when we were as a nation singly involved, and in 1990, the invasion of Kuwait by Iraq led in 1991 to the Gulf War, when we were in a coalition with our Allies under the aegis of the UN. There our Forces played a major role in the defeat of Iraq and the restoration of Kuwait, and the Corps made a very significant contribution in their support. Since both these actions are covered by complete chapters, 11 and 12 respectively, no attempt is made in this chapter at further introduction, but both must be seen as landmarks in the struggle to achieve equipment reliability. The mounting of the Gulf War as it affected BAOR, from where most of our ground troops and equipment were provided, is additionally described in Chapter 6, and other activities overseas are covered in detail in Chapter 9.

ENDING OF THE COLD WAR

The greatest effect on defence policy, however, was to be made by the ending of the Cold War resulting from the astonishing and unexpected revolt of the Eastern Pact countries during 1989–90, the collapse of communism and moves towards democracy in the Soviet Union, the removal of the Berlin Wall, and German reunification. These events led to a need for the complete restructuring of NATO and its role and responsibilities, the manifestations of which are still evolving as this volume is published. They have, however, already had a profound effect on our own forces, and some of the resulting changes, where they are clearly definable at this stage, are covered in appropriate chapters.

The Wall comes down

Apart from the effects of direct military involvement by British forces in this period, either in conflict or as a deterrent, the Government's defence policy was a reflection of many political and economic factors. Changes of government, an oil crisis in the Middle East, high inflation, recession, and meeting the requirements of changing social habits and attitudes, are just some that played a part in prompting the search within our forces for greater economies and technical innovations. The rolc of the Corps in this situation was vital in the provision of the most cost-effective equipment support for the Army, and it affected all aspects of its functions, organization, manpower and training. The evidence of this will become apparent throughout the book.

LOGISTIC STUDIES

From the early Seventies onwards, the effort required for 'keeping an eye on the ball' was bedevilled by the distractions of the Army's need for continuous examinations into the size and structure of the Army, and the cost of logistic and equipment support. Such examinations were mainly in the shape of Ministry of Defence studies by various committees. These could be frustrating as they sometimes diverted effort away from current problems, which notably included the reliability of equipment, and the end advantages were not always at the time clearly visible. The effects of the findings of these committees were Army-wide and ultimately influenced the organization and all the activities of REME. Because of the wide implications of these studies, the effects are described over a number of chapters. Apart from the studies initiated as a result of Government requirements, the Corps carried out its own continuous assessments of its role, and the cost-effectiveness of, and improvements to, its engineering support. Much was made possible by the introduction of new technology to assess and progress the workload. These internal advances, added to the Ministerial studies, meant that across the years the whole concept of Equipment Management was examined, and this led progressively to an increase in the reliability and cost-effectiveness of Army equipment, and the enhanced ability of REME to support it.

There were, as a result of all these studies, extensive changes in both the control of major equipments at all levels of the Staff, and in engineering supervision at equipment procurement level. The Corps reinforced its position as part of the equipment staff chain, and its engineering resources were deployed to provide the total quality control of equipment support from 'conception to the grave'. The responsibilities of REME were necessarily and satisfactorily widened, but at the same time the overall need for financial stringency placed a great strain on all involved in producing practical results. The overall effect on the Corps of all the major changes in Army reorganization at the highest level is considered in Chapter 2, together with details of the working of the various Ministry committees which produced any of these changes. These are introduced in the paragraphs which follow.

THE EFFECTS OF MINISTRY OF DEFENCE COMMITTEES

There were in the period covered by this volume three major Ministry committees, and a small number on the periphery, whose studies and recommendations as a whole were to have an effect on the working of the Corps. Of the three major committees, two were directed Army-wide, and one specifically at REME. All three are described in brief outline below, and the details and effects are to be found in the later relevant chapters – 2, 3, 4 and 5 – Higher Management, Equipment Branches, Army Aviation and Training respectively. In addition to these studies, following the ending of the Cold War, the Government's overall study of the strength and composition of all three Services, known as Options for Change, was introduced to Parliament in 1991. Where final decisions resulting from this study have been made and put into effect, these are considered in appropriate chapters.

The Somerville Committee

The Logistic Reorganization Committee set up in 1974, under the chairmanship of Major General R M Somerville (late RA), then the Vice Quartermaster General at MOD, was the first in the series of studies dealing with reorganizations specifically to achieve economies in the management of logistics in the Army. There had already been in 1965 one major reorganization of all the logistic corps, as a result of the findings of the McLeod Committee. This dealt with the functioning of the logistic system, and was the first such reorganization since the formation of REME in 1942. It resulted in the formation of the Royal Corps of Transport, which was established from the transport element of the Royal Army Service Corps and the transportation and movements elements of the Royal Engineers. The Royal Army Ordnance Corps took over the supplies, barracks and Staff Clerk functions of the RASC. The resulting effect on REME was small, as basically its tasks were to remain the same, but some first-line repair responsibilities were taken over from the Royal Engineers. First-line repair of radios not owned by Royal Signals was subsequently taken over by REME as a result of the recommendations of the Odling Committee which looked specifically at repair of telecommunications equipment.

The aim of the Somerville Committee was to find savings in manpower, and therefore money, and was established against the background of the 1974 Defence Review requiring a cut of 15,000 men over a period of ten years. Although the Committee considered the option of establishing a single logistic corps, this was discarded in favour of more centralized management and a recommendation for the retention of individual corps functions in their existing form for at least ten years. As a result of its recommendations, the Logistic Executive (Army) was formed at Andover from the staffs of the Quartermaster

General and the directorates of RCT, RAOC and REME to provide a central focus of logistic management. Major changes were made in the employment and role of Staff and Service officers at all levels of this Headquarters. This established a requirement for more officers from the logistic corps to fill staff appointments concerned with all aspects of logistic management and was for REME an important step forward in greater responsibility in this area. Seven separate organizations came together and, although there was to be a 20% cut in the strength of the combined staffs, much greater efficiency was expected to result, as they would have closer working contacts. Details of the important changes in organization and responsibilities for REME that the establishment of LE(A) was to produce are related in Chapters 2, 3, and 7 – The Higher Management of the Corps, The Work of the Equipment Branches and REME in the United Kingdom.

Tickell Committee

In 1976 the Ministry of Defence established the REME Manpower Review Committee, under Major General M E Tickell (late RE), specifically to investigate the strength of REME. At that time there was concern in MOD that REME, because of its potentially increasing support load, was likely to expand to exceed 10% of the strength of the Army. This situation would be contrary to the MOD policy of cutting the administrative tail in order to increase the ratio of teeth arms. It was considered that there could be a requirement for several hundred more REME soldiers in the field army due to the introduction of more complicated army helicopters, such as the LYNX, as well as new technically sophisticated ground equipment. The aim was to find savings elsewhere within REME's resources to offset this probable requirement.

The Tickell Committee recommended several specific savings in REME manpower in the field, in the Training Organization, and, leaving no stone unturned, in the Staff Band. After further studies by DGEME and his own staff, somewhat larger numbers were found. A further recommendation to help achieve these savings was that old equipment should not be retained in service without a realistic appraisal of the manpower penalty for keeping it serviceable. Of even greater importance, however, was the effect that the Committee's recommendations were to have in increasing the involvement of DGEME in the principles of equipment design and modifications. This was very much in line with REME's own wish for a more effective part in equipment management, in order to maximise the utilization of the workforce, improve reliability and give better value for money. The necessity for large increases in REME military manpower, which had been forecast in 1976 due to the introduction of the LYNX helicopter into the Army Air Corps, had not materialized by 1978, mainly because savings were achieved as the result of a REME study by Brigadier John Boast. Support to the Army Air Corps, though, still took some 10% of the Corps' manpower and required highly skilled technicians, so that it was a vital area to consider in balancing overall savings. Since the Sixties, the technical sophistication of aircraft with the Army Air Corps had increased dramatically, and Chapter 4 considers the overall support that was provided in relation to the new developments. The effectiveness of this support is well illustrated in Chapters 6, 10, 11 and 12, – BAOR, Northern Ireland, the Falklands Campaign, and the Gulf War respectively.

By 1978 REME military manpower had fallen to below the critical 10% of the Army's manpower, and stood at 9.6%. However, the problem still existed, and by 1980 DGEME had found less than half the savings he was still required to make, mainly due to opposition to further cuts by theatre commanders. At this stage the second and third set of outstanding reductions were abandoned. It had also proved to be impossible to make the headway expected in achieving more emphasis on technical production and less on military duties, which was a recommendation of the Committee. This was mainly because senior field commanders understandably required all logistic units to complete their mandatory individual military training programmes. It was considered essential for REME units to carry out their normal field exercises so that they could train to move, communicate, deploy and defend themselves in war. The repair and recovery of A vehicles well forward on the battlefield also clearly emphasized the need for effective military training for REME tradesmen and units, and this need was later reinforced by the experience of the Gulf operations.

Finally, the Tickell Committee in one of its general conclusions recognized the truth of the long-held REME belief that the load on REME would tend to expand unless the inevitable increase in the complexity of Army equipment was matched by its greater reliability. This need is borne out in the chapters that follow and is exemplified by the experiences of equipment performance in the Falklands Campaign and the Gulf War, and the actions required by REME to produce the essential support against this background. Fortunately, however, at the time of publication of this volume, many of the requirements to remedy this situation have been put in place and the problems and their solutions are described in the chapters that follow. This has proved a most rewarding development for the Corps and, although the way to success was tortuous, the eventual result was eminently satisfactory.

The Logistic Support Review

This, the third major study considered in this volume, was the most far-reaching in its decisions. These affected all the logistic corps and overran into Options for Change studies, affecting not only the whole Army but the other two Services as well. The study, prompted by the Master General of the Ordnance and the Quartermaster General, was based on the premise that the logistic support for the Army could be achieved at less cost and more efficiently. In December 1990, the main basic recommendation of the Logistic Support Committee headed by Major General A N Carlier (late RE), was that there should be only two corps involved in logistic support. These were to be concerned with Service Support and Equipment Support. The detailed considerations, recommendations and effects on REME are given in Chapter 2 – The Higher Management of the Corps. REME, though, was to remain as a single corps, retaining its title, and the effects of this study, although involving major reorganizations and some reductions in manpower, were not as dramatic as for other logistic corps. Many of these lost their single identities and were amalgamated into one corps – The Royal Logistic Corps. The essential prize, however, which REME gained and had striven for over many years, met the vital requirement for the Army as a whole. This was the recognition of the need to establish a single organization under the Quartermaster General for Equipment Support, and in April 1992 the Equipment Support Organization (ESO) was formed.

Chapter 3 describes the responsibilities and work of the REME Equipment Branches, and how through them the equipment engineering support resources of the Corps were organized and controlled, and responded to all the changes that occurred as a result of the studies outlined above. The Equipment Branches, with their agencies, initially formed part of Technical Group REME. In 1992, after several reorganizations, described in the chapter, they were part of the Directorate General of Equipment Support. Over the years they had carried the responsibility for implementing the engineering support policy formulated by the then REME Directorate, and ultimately its successor ESO, and can claim credit for much of the success of achieving higher standards of equipment reliability.

TRAINING

Technical training was the linchpin for the success of REME tradesmen in the field, to attain the very highest standards required in the support of the multiplicity and complexity of equipment brought into service. This training took place within the REME training units at Arborfield, Bordon and Middle Wallop and the Army Apprentices Colleges. Subsequent continuation training took place within all REME units. A very important element of officers' technical training was also carried out within the training organization. The need for cost-effectiveness in training was just as essential as in other fields of economy throughout the Army, and the work of all the committees described in outline above had an effect on these establishments in varying degrees to achieve this aim.

Changes over the years covered by this volume were quite considerable, not only to effect economies, but to balance this need against the increasing technical knowledge required for supporting new equipment. Chapter 5 draws together all aspects of training of both officers and soldiers and describes all the steps taken to produce a satisfactory balance of requirements.

BRITISH ARMY OF THE RHINE

Nowhere were the effects of changes in role, organization and equipment in the Army during this period to be felt more than in the British Army of the Rhine, where much of the expensive and complex equipment of the Army was located. At the latter end of the period BAOR's participation in the Gulf War provided confirmation, if this was needed, of the effectiveness of our Army in Germany, even though it was to be deployed in a totally unexpected role. It also served to highlight the continuing problems that the Corps had faced over the intervening years in providing, within overall economic constraints, a high standard of equipment support. Not only was there the ever-increasing technological demand of sophisticated new equipments, but the reliability of some was suspect, and spares were restricted because of economies. The implications of the working of the Ministry committees

and the important changes stemming from them, as they affected BAOR, are covered in Chapter 6.

With the demise of National Service in the Sixties the Corps in the Seventies was already fast gaining experience in how to recruit, train and retain a professional Corps of Regular officers and soldiers with all the varied skills required for the changes in this essential equipment support. This was of immense importance for BAOR, as such skills included those needed for the complete modernization of its armoured vehicle fleet. This included the replacement of the CENTURION tank by the CHIEFTAIN, and the introduction of the tracked FV432 armoured personnel carrier in large numbers to replace a wide range of wheeled armoured vehicles. The Army Air Corps too was being re-equipped with new aircraft which were far more technically advanced than those in service in the Sixties and, again, the GAZELLE and the LYNX helicopters required new skills of equipment support from the Corps. All the new equipment in BAOR for which REME provided this enhanced support is described in Chapters 4 and 6 – REME Support to Army Aviation and BAOR.

NORTHERN IRELAND

A resurgence of IRA violence in Northern Ireland began in 1969, making great demands on the Army. REME was fully involved from the beginning, using resources, as with the other Arms and Services, both from UK and BAOR. The Army presence in Northern Ireland varied in strength from about 3,000 in 1969 to almost 17,000, including UDR, in 1989. By that time the strength of REME in the province was 433 all ranks. The overall strength varied slightly over the years up to the present day, as the threat to security altered with political initiatives or changes in terrorist activities. Despite many efforts to achieve a peaceful settlement in Northern Ireland the problems are still unresolved as this volume is completed. The task for the Corps, however, was clearly established from early on, this being the essential requirement for the maintenance of additional aircraft, ground equipment, and, particularly, elderly armoured personnel carriers requiring special treatment. This situation gave scope for considerable engineering resourcefulness and the solving of problems that did not arise elsewhere. It was a task often carried out under difficult conditions, with individual skills and initiative being of great importance. It also proved the wisdom of the high standard of military as well as trade training that the Corps insisted upon. The overall situation and the work of the Corps in Northern Ireland in providing this valuable support is fully described in Chapter 10. The means of providing the contribution for this support from BAOR is also covered in Chapter 6, and from UK in Chapter 7.

REME IN THE RESERVE ARMY

Over the years covered by this volume the Reserve Army, with its vital role to play in backing up the Regular Army, changed its title several times, in conformity with Defence Policy. Now once again clearly named the Territorial Army, many of the influences that have affected the Regular Army have caused similar changes in the TA in the matters of role, organization, equipment and training. REME in the Reserve Army was not excepted from these changes, but, despite them, has continued to perform an essential role to the same high standards in carrying out very much the same tasks as its Regular counterpart. It has a long history of support to units of both the Reserve Army and, in its mobilization roles, the Regular Army. In all its many activities REME TA is very much an integral part of the Corps. This was particularly so in training in Germany for its vital NATO role of reinforcing REME Regular units, and the provision of complete units for some tasks. This always meant the closest co-operation on exercises in Germany, and engendered the true Corps spirit of co-operation. Some of the history of REME TA together with details of roles, organization and training is told in Chapter 8 – REME in the Reserve Army.

SERVICEWOMEN IN REME

One social factor that was to have a noticeable effect on all three Services during the period covered by this volume was a reflection of the changing role of women in society generally. More and more women were successfully entering fields of employment hitherto considered to be largely the preserves of men, and taking on skills and holding appointments that were previously considered by many to be not suitable to their sex. There was too an acceptance that women and men could be more closely integrated at work. In the case of the Army, women have been employed in its ranks on mechanical tasks in some strength since the First World War. Then, members of the First Aid Nursing Yeomanry, the FANYs, and the Women's Legion were in all-women units driving ambulances and staff cars, and served with distinction on active service in France and Belgium. No regular cadre for servicewomen was, however, created between the wars, and when the Second World War started there were initially, as far as women were concerned, only volunteers. These were members of the Auxiliary Territorial Service, which was formed in 1938 with a recruitment strength of 20,000, and who were mobilized in 1939. From 1941, however, conscription of women started, and by the end of the war they had a strength of 215,000 and were employed in 124 trades. They filled a vital role not only in the duties which they carried out, but also meeting the major requirement of releasing men for duties then considered unsuitable for women.

As a result of the wide-ranging tasks so successfully undertaken by women during the Second World War, the attitude towards their employment in the Services was beginning to change dramatically, and after the war it was decided that women were to take a permanent place in the Regular Army. In 1949 the ATS was accordingly re-named Women's Royal Army Corps, but not all the wartime trades were retained. However, all ranks were to serve in a wide range of non-field force units and headquarters, but retaining their own WRAC cap badge wherever they served. In REME, over the years, women were successfully employed in many of the less physically demanding technical trades, often on permanent attachment, but still retaining their WRAC badges. A number of WRAC officers who possessed engineering degrees also served with the Corps in engineering appointments. Until the Seventies women were normally in WRAC units, or sub-units of mixed units, and integration within sub-units was minimal. WRAC officers did not then command mixed units, but this was soon to change, and by the Eighties female officers were eligible for command of mixed units and sub-units: despite some doubts being expressed, integration was under way.

REME also started to receive female officers with engineering degrees, from the integrated courses at the Royal Military Academy, Sandhurst, for permanent employment with the Corps, although still badged WRAC. In 1990 the WRAC was disbanded and became part of the Adjutant General's Corps. WRAC officers and women on permanent attachment, where suitably qualified, were re-badged in the regiment or corps in which they were serving. The fourteen engineering-trained officers employed with the Corps were re-badged REME, and this was followed in 1992 with the re-badging of ninety-nine tradeswomen. These women could now serve in units in an equal role with their male counterparts and would receive the same training, and could be armed. With the change of cap badge the women serving in the Corps were firmly part of the team in every respect. The overall story of this successful ongoing process of recruitment and integration of women into the Corps is told in Chapters 8 and 13 – REME in the Reserve Army and REME Regimental Activities. In the remaining chapters, servicewomen in REME are given the same appropriate mention as their male counterparts, according to the task and occasion, in their fully integrated role in the Corps.

REME REGIMENTAL ACTIVITIES

This simple title heading to Chapter 13 encompasses a very wide range of subjects which affect to a greater or lesser extent every single member of the Corps of whatever rank. The chapter deals with every facet of Corps domestic policy and activity, and over the years the regimental structure of the Corps has changed to keep pace with the many other general changes affecting its function and organization. Despite all these changes the momentum of activities has not diminished and indeed, in some spheres such as benevolence, has accelerated to keep pace with increased need. In others, the range of activities supported has been widened, particularly to meet new challenges in adventurous training. Examples of all these are contained in the chapter.

During the years covered by this volume the Corps has been exceedingly fortunate to have Field Marshal His Royal Highness The Prince Philip, Duke of Edinburgh, KG KT OM GBE AC QSO as Colonel in Chief. Prince Philip was appointed by Her Majesty The Queen to succeed Her Royal Highness The Princess Marina, Duchess of Kent CI GCVO GBE when she died in 1968. His great interest in the Corps and his frequent visits to units both at home and abroad have been a source of tremendous encouragement and pride to the Corps. Many officers and soldiers and their families have had the opportunity to meet him over the years and have been inspired by his knowledge and understanding of the work of the Corps and its members. In addition to those in Chapter 13, details of some of his extensive visits to the Corps are also to be found in Chapters 6 and 8 – BAOR and Reserve Army.

SPORT AND ADVENTUROUS TRAINING

As mentioned at the beginning of this chapter some activities were not able to be fully described in Volume 1, and sport and adventurous training are two of these elements which are now covered in this volume. The Corps has a fine reputation for sporting achievements and the whole of Chapter 14 is now devoted to this important part in the life of the Corps. The chapter, in addition to covering the ever-widening range of sports and adventurous training in the time frame of this volume, also describes many of the achievements from the earliest days of the Corps.

THE 50TH ANNIVERSARY OF THE CORPS

The year 1992 was the occasion of the 50th Anniversary of the formation of REME and celebrations in many different forms took place throughout the Corps. The various occasions were an opportunity not only for the members of the Corps to enjoy the fruits of their labour, but also to display to the remainder of the Army and general public a panorama of their wide-ranging achievements and skills. It had indeed been a very eventful and impressive fifty years, and certainly an anniversary that all could proudly celebrate. In addition to details contained in Chapter 13 of those activities within and emanating from UK, the BAOR major celebratory REME 50 event is described in Chapter 6. The thread of success running through all the chapters that follow provides fitting cause for celebration by the Corps after fifty years. They also contain a message of hope for the coming years of even greater accomplishment and the ability to surmount the inevitable problems with which it will be faced. History has a habit of repeating itself.

CHAPTER 2

THE HIGHER MANAGEMENT OF THE CORPS

Introduction · The Corps Directorate · Channels of Responsibility · Organization and Control of Technical Resources up to 1977 · Merger of REME Directorate and REME Support Group in 1977 · The QMG Directive – 1988 · Development of UK Static REME Organization · Management Information Systems · The REME Contribution to the Procurement Process · Logistic Support Review 1990–1991 · Conclusion

INTRODUCTION

This chapter is concerned with the overall direction of the Corps stemming from the Director of the Corps – DEME(A), later becoming DGEME and then DGES(A) – and his Staff at the REME Directorate. It covers a period of considerable and accelerating change in the Army brought about by military and political situations world-wide. These not only affected the size and disposition of our Forces as some risks diminished, but also brought about the need to effect economies within them to contain the rising costs of high technology. Throughout the chapter there runs the thread of change, with almost unending studies designed to achieve the best possible organizations to meet the new operational concepts and technological advances in the most economical and effective manner. The Director was involved in all these studies.

Many of the reorganizations, spreading from the Directorate throughout the whole Corps, during this period led to some economies being achieved by the comparatively simple process of cutting manpower, though not without pain to those personally involved. However, by far the most important changes concerned with reorganizations were designed to effect economies by improving the management of the Army's equipment. It is in this field that REME can claim to have achieved great success. The way to this success was complex and at times not without acrimony. It involved every aspect of the Corps' responsibility and the difficult balancing required between Engineering and Staff functioning at the highest level. The fact that the Corps maintained throughout the period the highest pitch of engineering support to the Army, in such differing conditions as Northern Ireland, the Falklands Campaign and the Gulf War, is indicative of the abilities of those responsible in maintaining the Corps' impetus during this time of intricate change and reorganization. The importance of the resourcefulness and skills of those facing the burden of implementing these changes in the field is only touched on in this chapter but their success story is related in detail in subsequent chapters.

THE CORPS DIRECTORATE

At the beginning of the Seventies the Director of the Corps – DEME(A) – was located with his Directorate in London. A charter reflected his recently acquired responsibility to the Vice Chief of the General Staff and the Master General of the Ordnance, in addition to the Quartermaster General, for the provision of an Army Department focus for equipment reliability matters, excluding ammunition. Officially the Directorate was outside the Ministry of Defence, but in practice it continued to function very much as part of it, as it had been until 1964, when the Nye Committee, chaired by Lieutenant General Sir Archibald Nye GCSI GCMG GCIE KCB KBE MC, on the organization of the War Office, had led to the separation from it of the Arms and Services Directors. Some Arms Directors had moved out of London, but the Service

Directors had stayed there, DEME (A) moving his Directorate in October 1964, from its wartime birthplace in Golden Cross House, off Trafalgar Square, to First Avenue House, High Holborn (on the site of the Victorian First Avenue Hotel). There it remained until 1977 when the Logistic Executive (Army) was formed.

The process by which successive Directors of the Corps discharged their responsibilities, including those encompassing the REME contribution to the procurement process, the base repair organization and the management information systems, is described in this chapter. Prior to 1977 the Directorate, at First Avenue House, was divided into those staff branches covering the manpower, training and organization under the one star DDEME(A) and the engineering staff branches under DDEME(Tech)(A), the latter being retitled DDEME(Engineering Policy)(A) in mid-1974. In addition during the Sixties there had been a third brigadier, separately appointed as the Inspector of REME. The transition in 1977 of this organization into the Logistic Executive (Army) is described later.

Outside the Directorate there were the engineering equipment branches of Technical Group REME, such as Electronics Branch or Vehicles and Weapons Branch located respectively with the Research and Development Establishments at Malvern and Chertsey. These were the executive agencies or engineering support units which executed the policies developed by the Directorate's engineering staff branches. The work of these agencies is described in Chapter 3.

The REME Data Centre at Woolwich was a unit controlled by the Directorate and responsible for producing Feedback of Repair Workshop and Reliability Data (FORWARD) printouts of management information and equipment engineering information. This was used by the Higher Management of the Corps and by REME staff and units world-wide.

CHANNELS OF RESPONSIBILITY

The Director exercised his responsibilities outside the MOD, whilst in London and subsequently (from 1977) in the LE(A) in Andover, through senior REME officers at home and abroad. There were DEMEs in theatres overseas and DDEMEs in Home Commands. The surviving appointments overseas later became Commanders Maintenance and, in the UK, Chief Electrical and Mechanical Engineer at HQ United Kingdom Land Forces when this HQ was set up as described in Chapter 7. This latter appointment reduced in rank to Colonel in 1982 as a staff officer (DACOS), seven years passing before it became a Commander Maintenance. The senior REME appointments overseas had broadly similar responsibilities to their commanders and their headquarters staff as the DEME (A) or DGEME had to the QMG and his staff.

DGEME was also responsible to C-in-C UKLF through Commander Training and Arms Directors for the implementation of special-to-service REME training policy in REME training units within its Individual Training Organization (ITO): in REME's case, commanded by the two brigadiers at HQ REME Training Centre, Arborfield and the School of Electrical and Mechanical Engineering, Bordon.

In 1970 the Corps had four main elements in the UK, which were:

- Technical Group REME, which is included in this and the following chapter. Technical Group became REME Support Group but its HQ and title disappeared with the formation of the LE(A).
- The REME training organization, which is the subject of Chapter 5.
- The Command support organization of static workshops and the field force, which is the subject of Chapter 7.
- The TAVR which reverted to the title TA, and which is the subject of Chapter 8.

ORGANIZATION AND CONTROL OF TECHNICAL RESOURCES UP TO 1977

Technical Group REME formed on 1 April 1960, as recorded in Volume I, from the Base Workshop Group at Feltham and REME Technical Services at Chislehurst. Its headquarters was at Woolwich and it controlled the functional activities in the engineering services, management services and base repair areas. Within the organization there were five central workshops, and in addition the Group had functional control through two CREMEs of the direct support given to the Base Organization RAOC by a Stores Inspection Branch and three vehicle depot workshops. It also had units established in the Royal Radar Establishment (RRE) at Malvern and the Signals Research and Development Establishment (SRDE) at Christchurch (later combined at Malvern as the Royal Signals and Radar Establishment). Although the main parts of Vehicles Branch and Weapons Branch were in Woolwich, there were elements with the Fighting Vehicles Research and Development Establishment (FVRDE) at Chertsey (later the Military Vehicles Engineering Establishment (MVEE)) and the Royal Armament Research and Development Establishment (RARDE) at Fort Halstead. The Army Scaling Authority was being formed at Woolwich early in 1969 and the REME Data Centre had been opened in October 1967 with the first phase of the FORWARD project nearly complete. The five central workshops had a full programme of work for some years ahead and a sizeable overload was passed each year to the command workshops and to a contract repair organization run by the Group.

Technical Group was responsible for the engineering support of all equipment of REME concern with the exception of aircraft which were supported by the Aircraft Technical Services Unit (ATSU) at Middle Wallop, the home of the Army Air Corps. ATSU reported to the Chief Aircraft Engineer (CAE) at Middle Wallop, who in turn reported to EME 9 at HQ DEME(A). REME support for Army Aviation is the subject of Chapter 4. The organization of Technical Group in 1973 is given at Annex A.

Base Repairs

Base repairs were carried out mainly in the five central workshops but some also in command workshops, planned and co-ordinated by HQ Technical Group Production Wing. The central workshops carried out more than 3,500 programmes a year to meet the needs of the Equipment Management Staff and Ordnance. Responsibility for base repairs was transferred to HQ DGEME at LE(A), Andover in 1977 when HQ REME Support Group, as Technical Group had become, was disbanded.

Contract Repairs

Contract Repair Branch, part of Production Wing at Woolwich, arranged for work to be carried out in civilian workshops. The branch had been transferred in 1964 from the former Ministry of Supply as Vehicle Contract Repair Branch. Before long its headquarters staff was halved, the annual value of its contracts was quadrupled and its activities were extended in support of UK Command Workshops to include more than vehicles. By 1971/72 it was arranging 18,000 jobs a year, spread over 1,200 contractors including Fazakerley Engineering Company in Liverpool. This firm occupied Government premises but was entirely manned and managed by civilian contract. Contract Repair Branch not only arranged for part of the overload from central workshops to be put out to contract but was responsible for arranging unit and field repairs throughout the UK to fill the gaps in capacity in the command workshop organization.

Vehicle Depot Workshops

The period of run-down in the RAOC Vehicle Organization in the late sixties and early seventies had led to the closure of the depots at Marchington, Feltham and Irvine. By 1973 the three REME Workshops at the RAOC Vehicle Depots, under the control of CREME Vehicle Organization RAOC at Chilwell, were 91 at Hilton, 93 at Ashchurch and 96 at Ludgershall. They carried out work on Royal Navy and Royal Air Force transport, as well as Army vehicles.

Equipment Engineering

By 1970 the Corps had established engineering branches or Maintenance Advisory Groups (MAGs) at the principal Research and Development (R&D) establishments. Radar Branch was with the RRE at Malvern; Telecommunications Branch was with the SRDE at Christchurch and Vehicle Investigation Branch, which had been formed in 1969, was with the FVRDE, later renamed the MVEE, at Chertsey. Weapons Branch at Woolwich had a MAG with the RARDE at Fort Halstead; Vehicles Branch, which was also at Woolwich, had three MAGs at FVRDE Chertsey and a MAG at the Military Engineering Experimental Establishment (MEXE) at Christchurch.

The Corps was also represented at the principal defence contractors such as the British Aircraft Corporation, Stevenage, and at the Royal Small Arms Factory, Enfield. Major General Vic Hayward, when

Fording trials at Instow

Commandant of Technical Group, wished to strengthen the REME presence and influence at MVEE and this was achieved in 1972 when Vehicles Branch moved from Woolwich into specially built accommodation within the MVEE perimeter and amalgamated with Vehicle Investigation Branch. This branch also took Fording Trials Branch at Instow in Devon under its control.

Fleet Repair Branch at Portsmouth carried out maritime base repair planning and the maritime technical function corresponding to the other equipment engineering branches. Base repairs to craft were handled by the Royal Navy and Civilian Contractors.

All the engineering Branches were tasked by the Chief Equipment Engineer (CEE) at HQ Technical Group and reported on these tasks directly to the staff engineering branches EME 7 and EME 8 at DEME (A)'s Directorate. The CEE monitored progress to ensure that they were carried out efficiently and on time, so that, for example, Electrical and Mechanical Engineering Regulations (EMERs) were ready to accompany new equipment into service.

Publications

Publications Branch at Woolwich took over printing, storage and distribution of EMERs from various Government agencies and private contractors in 1969. It was concentrated in one building and produced up to 14 million pages a year. The REME Data Centre computer was used as an aid to distribution, helping to speed up the supply of the correct EMERs to all units who needed them. In 1974 it became the REME Publications Centre and by 1990 it had become the Land Systems Technical Publications Authority with a wider Defence remit. In 1978 the EMER system sponsored by the Corps since 1942, user handbooks, illustrated parts catalogues and servicing schedules were all replaced by a new system of Army Equipment Support Publications (AESPs) for which REME assumed management responsibility. The increased responsibilities after 1977 owed much to Lieutenant Colonel Dennis French who developed the AESP system.

Scaling

The Army Scaling Authority was formed in 1967 after Scales M (mechanical) Branch moved from Chilwell to join Scales E (electrical) Branch at Woolwich. The Authority was tied into the RAOC computer with a direct line to the Central Inventory Control Point RAOC at Bicester in 1972. It was responsible for writing initial scales of spares for new equipment repaired by REME, except aircraft. It worked closely with REME Data Centre at Woolwich which was developing a system to produce information on the use of spare parts for comparison with the initial scale. ASA, after amalgamating with the Army Cataloguing Authority in 1990, became the Army Scaling and Cataloguing Authority.

Quality

At Woolwich there was a Chief Quality Engineer, a lieutenant colonel, responsible for the technical efficiency of the Stores Inspection Branch, running the Calibration Centre and its teams, and also the Specialist Equipment Examination Team. CREME Stores Inspection Branch, also a lieutenant colonel, was established at the HQ of the Commandant Base Organization RAOC at Didcot and controlled Stores Inspection Detachments at each Central Ordnance Depot RAOC.

Productivity Agreements

Colonel Roy Knowles negotiated the first Productivity Agreement (PA) in a Ministry of Defence Establishment at 38 Central Workshop, Chilwell, in 1968. The PA made use of the workshop's new labour control procedure using local work measurement, and later a simpler version was adopted elsewhere known as Type 1. Colonel Knowles was awarded the CBE for his work on these agreements.

Within five years nearly all major UK static workshops had such agreements producing really significant results in increased output with only a limited increase in cost. Much better labour relations prevailed, resulting in the ability to recruit younger men. There was an immense amount of detailed work such as work measurement on the shop floor, negotiation and discussion with MOD and the Trade Unions, as well as analysis of the mass of information produced by the complicated budgetary control system. This produced information for use in the control of resources known as the Management Information and Accounting System (MIAS). It was designed by a firm of management consultants, Cooper Brothers, and installed at 38 Central Workshop in 1966 and in other workshops in the early Seventies. The first new Type 2 PA was signed at 34 Central Workshop, Donnington, in 1975. In 1991 the Corps was still using the Type 2 PA. 34 Base Workshop had a modified version of the original which aimed to reduce some generous allowances; no change to the Type 2 PA was expected. The story of MIAS and PAs was well told in the REME Journal for 1976.

Management Services Wing

In mid-1970 the Management Services Wing was established with the Brigadier Management Services at its head, the first officer being Brigadier Hugh Macdonald-Smith who later became DEME(A) and the first DGEME. Later in the same year the Senior Management Accountant, a Lieutenant Colonel RAPC, joined him in Woolwich to control the work of the RAPC accountants in workshops concerned with MIAS. Much progress was made in simplifying and improving MIAS during the period 1971–73 when Major General Vic Hayward was Commandant. A benefit of the MIAS budgetary control system was that it enabled the workshop commanders to obtain delegated financial powers beyond the wildest dreams of the commanders ten years earlier. As a result it was possible for them to buy workshop plant and machinery costing many thousands of pounds when necessary. The value of these improved powers of local purchase was demonstrated when Technical Group took on the up-armouring of the Humber armoured personnel carriers known as 'Pigs' for Northern Ireland, and was able to complete the programme in a much shorter time than industry could achieve. (The details of this project are given in Chapter 10.) By the Nineties MIAS had been somewhat superseded by ARROW (ADP Assistance to REME and RAOC in Workshops) and the Management Accountants Computer System in base and district workshops. The principle of collecting data from the same sources as with MIAS remained, but the information was more refined.

Creation of REME Support Group

At the beginning of the Seventies the Commandant of Technical Group REME had been Major General Vic Hayward. He was followed in the appointment by Major General Vincent Metcalfe who had been in charge of the FORWARD project at the REME Data Centre in Woolwich from 1966 to 1969. He decided that the time had come for a fundamental review of the whole organization that he now commanded. A good starting point was a new name and since General Metcalfe considered that the current one did not give the right impression vis-a-vis the abilities of the whole Corps in technical matters, and furthermore did not embrace the new management function of the Corps, he cast around for ideas on change. His own choice was REME Support Group, which was well received by his own officers, who were also in favour of the overall change, and was agreed by DEME(A). The new renamed organization came into effect on 1 June 1974. As illustrated in Annex B, the Group was divided into four Wings:

- Resources and Administration Wing
- Engineering Technology Wing
- Management and Information Systems Wing
- Production Management Wing

All units of the Group reported direct to the head of one of the three functional Wings who were ranked as brigadiers. Among the units created out of headquarters staffs was Workshop Technology Branch, which provided a focus for the assessment and procurement of the tools and equipment needs of both static and field force units of the Corps and filled a serious gap in Corps organization. General Metcalfe subsequently wrote: 'It was a great pleasure when, as Commander REME Support Group, I was able to present the new organization to my five predecessors during a visit they made to Woolwich on 24 June 1974 – and something of a relief to receive their approval of the new name!' The Group settled down quickly to the new organization and responsibilities and the benefits soon became apparent. But even with its new name the Group was not to last much longer.

Logistic Reorganization

In the mid-Seventies many reviews and cuts were being made. To achieve further economies in manpower the QMG was implementing 'Lean Look' cuts which focused attention on the civilian complement of the static workshops in the UK. The Corps was also subjected to a close examination by the Tickell Committee in the UK and in BAOR as described in Chapter 6. Lieutenant General Sir Hugh Beach was examining the RCT, RAOC and REME in a committee scrutinizing the selection, training and appointment of officers in these corps and their eventual suitability for the highest appointments on the Q staff. The QMG and his staff were also looking to achieve greater efficiency by co-locating the Directorates and staff of his logistic services, and studies by the Logistic Reorganization Committee headed by VQMG (the 'Somerville Committee'), as indicated in Chapter 1, led to the establishment in 1977 of the Logistic Executive (Army) at Andover. This required the amalgamation of HQ DGEME and HQ REME Support Group within it, with the loss of a two star appointment. The new organization of the Group, which had already been implemented, made this transition much easier than it would otherwise have been and it fell to Major General Derek Walker to see it through before his appointment was abolished.

MERGER OF REME DIRECTORATE AND REME SUPPORT GROUP – 1977

The Somerville Committee had led in 1975 to the formation of a Logistic Executive Working Party, the eight members of which included Colonel Martyn Clark from the Directorate of Equipment Management and Lieutenant Colonel Peter Crooks representing DEME(A). The Working Party was to make detailed proposals for the formation of the Logistic Executive, including the recommendation of a suitable location. Manpower savings of 10% were to be made upon its initial establishment, and a further 10% after four years. In the event RAF Bicester and RAF Andover were the two locations short-listed, the latter proving to be the most suitable. The Army Establishments Committee formally approved the LE(A) establishment in November 1976, and 4 April 1977 was fixed for its formation. All units of REME Support Group were informed in February 1977 of the outline organization of the new LE(A) and of the absorption of REME Support Group into it as part of the REME Directorate. The new title of the Head of Corps as a Director General at two star level was in line with the other Service Directors, but at the same time the DGEME took on additional responsibility for equipment management. In general Directors in the Ministry of Defence were to become one star appointments and the DDEME(A) thus became DEME (Organization & Training) and Inspector of REME, retaining responsibility for the EME 1 and EME 2 branches; similarly the Brigadier ManIS at REME Support Group took up the new appointment of DEME (ManIS), with the newly formed branches EME 11 to 14. The Commander of REME Support Group was redesignated as Director of Equipment Engineering (DEE), a two star appointment which remained with Major General Walker; under him three one star DDEEs were formed from the former DDEME (Engineering Policy)(A) and the Technical Group appointments of Brigadier Engineering Technology and Brigadier Production Management. Several branches of LE(A) were set up at Andover from 6 July 1977, with others following in August and September, the remainder joining up towards the end of the year with the final move on 13 December, the organization at this time being as shown at Annex C.

At the time of the move to Andover, Brigadier Tony Palmer (later DGEME) was DEME (Organization & Training), and recalls one of the hi-tech problems of amalgamating and settling in:

'The area allocated for the offices of Major General Derek Walker (DEE – still then a two star appointment) and myself and our PAs was a large open office, located over the front entrance of the main building and previously occupied by several RAF officers. Panels were erected and, hey presto, we all had our individual offices. It was quite a cold winter and the central heating was full on but my office was terribly hot even with the windows wide open. I decided some temperature changes were necessary and in conjunction with the PSA got my office down to a very comfortable temperature. The next morning was bitterly cold and at around 10 am into my office stepped a blue and shivering General. Thanks to my efforts to make myself comfortable the temperature in his office was below freezing. I have no doubt this happened all over the building as the shape and size of offices changed to suit the Army with total disregard to the heating system.'

HQ REME Support Group ceased to operate as a headquarters from 31 August 1977, and was disbanded by the end of the year. The Commander became Director Equipment Engineering in the Logistic Executive from 1 September, to be downgraded to one star in May 1979, as were the second two star appointments in RCT and RAOC. Those units which had been under the functional command or technical control of HQ REME Support Group became LE(A) units under control of HQ DGEME. LE(A) REME units in 1977 thus included Equipment Branches, Central Workshops, Vehicle Depot Workshops and other REME units.

When the LE(A) was established a Staff organization was formed in addition to the Services' directorates, with a Chief of Staff Logistics (COSLOG) – then Major General T S C Streatfeild (late RA) with a number of Q Staff Officers. COSLOG exercised responsibility on behalf of the QMG in the Staff policy functioning of the Service Directorates of RCT, RAOC and REME at LE(A) and provided the day to day consultative Staff link for those Services with the QMG and his Staff at MOD in London. Some though regarded the imposition of his Staff link with misgivings, and there is no doubt that since ultimately the Services had to deal directly with the QMG Staff at MOD on many functional aspects it could complicate decision making. This aspect as far as the REME Directorate was concerned and the ultimate change in the Staff organization in LE(A) is discussed later in this chapter.

The organization of the REME Directorate at LE(A) consisted of five divisions. These were Organization and Training, Management and Information Systems, two Equipment Management and Engineering Support divisions, and Production. DEME (Org & Trg) reported direct to DGEME and was concerned with civilian and military manpower, training and organization, and Corps matters as a whole; he was also Inspector of REME. DEME (ManIS) reported direct to DGEME on management techniques, policy, ADP, technical publications and management systems; he also acted as a consultant to the Corps and had functional command of the REME Data Centre, Publications Centre and the Methods Engineering Unit (UK). The remaining three divisions reported to DGEME through the Director of Equipment Engineering (DEE) who had functional command or gave technical direction to twenty-one major units including five central workshops, the major equipment engineering branches, the Army Scaling Authority, Aircraft Branch and the Field Repair Contract Support Unit.

Two divisions under DDEE 1 (with branches EME 8 and 10) and DDEE 2 (EME 7 and 9) were concerned with the development and provision of engineering support for all Army equipment of DGEME's concern. They provided the in-service Equipment Management for specific equipments such as A Vehicles, towed artillery, aircraft, electronics and guided weapon equipments. These two divisions also provided the Chairman of the Maintenance Support committees and Repair Planning sub-committees. The third division under DDEE 3 (with branches EME 4 and 5) controlled and planned the loading of base repair work in the UK static workshops and the contract repair facilities in conjunction with others concerned.

Following an inspection of the REME Directorate by the Inspectorate of Establishments (Army) in 1979, DEE was abolished and the three deputy directors (brigadiers) became Directors in their own right as DEE 1, DEE 2 and D Prod E. DEME (Man IS) became DEME (Man S).

Evolution of Equipment Management

Before the changeover, DDEME (Eng Pol)(A) and his staff had maintained links with the Directorate of Equipment Management to ensure that engineering support policy met the Staff Requirements. These activities, enlarged to include such matters as the Equipment Management Policy Statement (EMPS), were taken on by the LE(A) nominated equipment managers, in conjunction with the small COSLOG staff at Andover.

From the formation of the LE(A) DDEE 1 and 2 controlled not only their staff engineering branches but also the respective former Support Group technical branches (including the MAGs). Thus there was in the DGEME Directorate both a staff function and a command function. As an example, DDEE 1 had line manager/command responsibility for various technical branches such as Telecommunications and Radar Branch as well as taking on the existing staff responsibilities in the previous organization which had been carried out by DDEME (Eng Pol) (A). DDEE 1 and 2 also inherited several disparate tasks which came with the demise of Support Group, such as the Army Scaling Authority and Workshop Technology Branch. These changes enabled them to establish manpower cover much more readily for project work and made the total equipment management task that much easier. Having the small COSLOG staff at Andover provided consultation on the spot, effectively enabling day to day work to go ahead smoothly. There was now little need at one star level to have any dealings with the QMG's office in London, though there were some who did not accept such advantages in the reorganization as being of overall benefit to the Corps. This aspect is examined later.

By 1978 the newly established LE(A) at Andover was finding its feet. Its formation had required major changes in the way that the Q Staff functioned in relation to the three major Q Services, RCT, RAOC and REME, and in the organization of the Service Directorates. These were quite apart from the effects of moving out of London, away from the 'centre'. REME in particular was affected by the new organization, bringing together as it did staff and functional responsibilities within the Directorate, and increased involvement, with all its complexities, of equipment management. It was a considerable achievement that all was brought together so smoothly.

However, because of the very nature of the changes there were, not surprisingly, still doubts amongst some of those who had grown used to the well established and structured concept of the central hierarchical control by MOD Staff Branches: in this case the Director of Equipment Management (D of E Man) and his staff.

It was undoubtedly the case that there were divisions between the Staff and Services which were real in terms of power, patronage and responsibility. Not everybody in the REME engineering branches viewed the changes and the widening spectrum of responsibility with total acclaim. Their concern was focused on whether adequate authority would be given to them to match their increased responsibilities and whether they would be empowered with full Staff status in their resulting decision making. On the other hand there was also concern that the assumption of the Staff mantle for equipment management and the operational and political imperatives that this involved, would dominate the work of the engineering branches at the expense of engineering planning and development. The effect could be that acute short-term equipment management issues would take priority over the long-term engineering work necessary to develop equipment quality, performance and reliability.

The engineering branch, EME 7, now included responsibility for both equipment management and engineering support for A vehicles and guns, and engineering support only for B vehicles, small arms, C vehicles, railway equipment and ships. Responsibility for equipment management in these latter five areas was divided between RE, RCT and RAOC.

Within eighteen months of taking on equipment management it became clear that engineering branches EME 7, EME 8 and EME 9 were heavily overloaded. EME 7 and EME 8 each covered a very wide range of equipment, both in-service and under development. REME staff officers were frequently drawn between the competing demands of in-service and therefore immediate problems on the one hand and pressing requirements for considered judgement and advice in relation to new equipment projects on the other. These pressures demanded excessively long hours of work and tended to be concentrated on the officers dealing with armoured and electronic weapons and communications systems. It was in these areas that the highest priorities were sought, both from field commanders wishing to keep their combat availabilities high and from those at an elevated level in MOD who were sensitive to the overall strategic, financial and political implications and responsibilities to NATO. The MOD sought to establish individual new projects as 'top priority' and indeed the mere fact of the growth of the Warsaw Pact armour and missile strengths and the necessary response by NATO inevitably demanded high priority. The clash of competing priorities was further compounded by the very different perspectives and perceptions demanded when considering 'in-service' and 'project' equipments.

A good example of the dilemma facing REME staff officers in dealing with conflicting priorities was the experience of Lieutenant Colonel Dennis Bingham, who was SO1(W) EME 7a when confronted with such a problem. He was the Equipment Manager for A Vehicles and as such was responsible for the 'in-service' management of CHIEFTAIN, CENTURION, CVR(T), FV600, FV430, FERRET, STALWART, Humber 1 Ton (Pig), M Series and LANCE. The major retrofit programme of the Improved Fire Control System (IFCS) to CHIEFTAIN and the programmes to counter stress corrosion cracking of the CVR fleet were also his 'in-service' equipment management responsibility. On the 'project' side of his job his responsibilities for A Vehicles included being the Engineering Support Planning Officer for the MBT80, with major engineering input to the proposal for an aluminium armoured hull.

Other such responsibilities included involvement in the gas turbine versus the piston engine debate, CHALLENGER Tank, MCV80, Tracked RAPIER running gear, Multiple Launch Rocket System (MLRS), Thermal Observation and Gunnery Sight (TOGS), and IFCS improvements. With this plethora of responsibility towards both 'in-service' and 'projects' and the balancing of priorities between the two it was not surprising that there were conflicts in the application of equipment management. This is well brought out in the example that follows.

The particular difficulty that faced Dennis Bingham and which had to be successfully overcome, in spite of the sort of complexities outlined above, concerned the IFCS retrofit programme for CHIEFTAIN. The effects which subsequently arose from the implementation of this programme, led to a major examination of how best the Directorate could be organized in future to deal with such problems. At this time the threat to NATO from the Warsaw Pact countries was considered sufficiently serious to drive the 'in-service' CHIEFTAIN retrofit programme through, irrespective of its effect on the current development 'projects' programme. The retrofit programme was therefore carried out concurrently with the development programme and resulted in the first fifty CHIEFTAINS having six different build standards. These projects, and there were others affecting EME 8 and EME 9, had considerable operational, political and financial implications. The consequential studies to try to obviate complications in future programmes were of great importance to REME in relation to equipment management.

The two ideas considered in the REME Directorate to cope with the sort of problems outlined above were either to separate the responsibility for 'in-service' and 'new projects' by establishing a new branch (EME 6) responsible only for major equipment projects, or to strengthen the engineering branches by adding dedicated Engineering Support Planning Officers (ESPOs) to support Project Managers for major 'new projects'. The first idea undoubtedly gave strength to the formal recognition of the dual role of DGEME towards the Quartermaster General and the Master General of the Ordnance, with their respective responsibilities for 'in-service' and 'new projects'. However, at this time the decisions resulting from Exercise 'Lean Look' were being implemented, including the reduction in MOD Staff and clearly on these grounds alone, the introduction of a new branch would be difficult. In the event, also because there was seldom a clear line between 'in-service' and 'new projects' (particularly for evolutionary equipment systems) and control might therefore be difficult, the idea of EME 6 was dropped. The second idea was, however, adopted and dedicated ESPOs were duly appointed at Lieutenant Colonel level for CHALLENGER, MCV80 (later WARRIOR), MLRS, SP70, and PTARMIGAN, and the concept of dedicated ESPOs soon proved its worth. In 1986 this principle moved to the world of Aircraft Engineering when Lieutenant Colonel Rob Preece became ESPO Light Attack Helicopter (LAH), having cut his teeth as ESPO WARRIOR.

The appointments of ESPOs was an important step in establishing the proper basis for REME input of informed engineering and logistic support from the start of the development of a project. They ensured that the whole weight of REME expertise and experience in the field of engineering and logistics was incorporated in the project. This would help to ensure that when the new equipment came into service it would be of the greatest possible asset to the user and require the least possible maintenance by REME. The achievement of this situation would provide an essential indication of the effectiveness of the equipment.

During the early period of LE(A), when its new organization was under self-examination, the Corps went through a period of indecision as to where it placed 'engineering' as such in its overall priorities. Within the Directorate, DEME (Org & Trg) was acknowledged as 'primus inter pares' and accorded the general status of Chief of Staff to DGEME, acting as his deputy when necessary. This gave rise to a feeling, rightly or wrongly, that organization, manpower and training matters had superior status to the purely engineering functions of the engineering branches, which had previously formed part of the REME Support Group. It suggested that there was still an attitude of 'bridge' and 'engine room' which had existed in the Directorate in the early Sixties when located in Golden Cross House. It was argued that the primary attention and priorities of the Directorate should be focused on engineering and equipment management policies and that these priorities should be absolute and visible. It appeared to some that they were neither.

However, a change in this long-established system and the views held about it were certainly neither quick nor easy to bring about, the more so because of the abolition of the two star appointment of DEE in 1979, and the position then of COSLOG in the staff and engineering chain. The introduction of staff responsibility into the engineering branches inevitably meant that COSLOG could be as well informed on some engineering and equipment management matters as the DGEME, and at times, when the DGEME was attending to matters on the ground in his wide parish, could even be one step ahead in the game! This situation took time to resolve, but resolved it was, as the equipment management powers of DGEME were gradually extended over the next few years, as is described later in this chapter.

Brigadier Geoffrey Atkinson wrote of his time as DEE 2 at the Logistic Executive 1981–83, when the search by the Corps for better equipment management was being pursued against a background of entrenched systems that stultified progress:

'We rationalized further by running down Woolwich to create Vehicles and Weapons Branch at Chertsey and moving Maritime Branch to join its RCT customers at Gosport. Both these moves made sense. EME 7 had already successfully taken on the equipment management function for A vehicles, guns and related equipment including, for instance, generators and sights. Vehicle fleet management and planning for modification programmes were also undertaken in the branch. This involved very close liaison with the MOD PE and Ordnance branches. The former held the money and purchased major equipments and major enhancement kits, such as the Thermal Observation and Gunnery Sight; the latter obtained other items and handled and issued most stores. Major problems were the unreliability of the Combat Engineer Tractor, Tank Laser Sight and the CHIEFTAIN L60 engine (still after 20 years!). All involved combinations of design faults, poor build standards and spares shortages. A major hindrance to improvement was the inability to get to the root cause of a major equipment problem and to take rapid redesign and procurement action to resolve it. This reflected a situation caused by the many agencies involved, all with conflicting priorities. I, as the engineering director and fleet manager, had no money at all and precious little authority. PE Project Managers, R&D Establishments, manufacturers and sub-contractors, REME Equipment Branches, Ordnance Branches and Finance Branches all had a different master – a recipe for disaster; it is a wonder we achieved anything.'

1981 was the time of a moratorium imposed by the Government on equipment expenditure. It was necessary for DGEME to warn VQMG and MGO at MOD that the effect of the moratorium on equipment availability would be long-lasting. Even though there had been some recent relaxation, many important combat system spares demands from the previous August still remained frozen. REME advice to the Staff was that activity levels would have to be reduced forthwith to avoid a run on spares. As a result, training activity levels for the whole of 1981, for tanks and other combat equipment, were severely reduced. These reductions were a serious blow to the field force, and the reduced level of its effectiveness and morale were in marked contrast to those apparent with the training levels of only a few years earlier.

By the end of 1983 the introduction of cash limits, the demise of supplementary estimates, the need to reduce inflation, and a Conservative Government determined to control Government expenditure more closely led to a watershed in the way that logistic support was provided and managed. 'Management by Exception', sometimes equated to 'Management by Neglect', did not suffice in the new culture of pro-active management. Compelling reasons for greater financial control to be exercised included the escalating costs of military hardware at the 'frontiers of technology' and the constant trend towards more complex systems which competed in budgets with military pay, conditions of service, accommodation, etc. Critical questions were being asked as to whether more economies could be squeezed from the Army's logistic support organization. The whole structure of this organization, the manpower employed and indeed the role of the Logistic Executive itself was called into question and studied at length. These studies are considered later in this chapter.

Fortunately at ground level there were brighter spots of which the successful operation of the Engineering Support Project Officers (ESPOs) mentioned earlier was one. They had been introduced for CHALLENGER, MCV 80 (later WARRIOR), MLRS, etc. They not only did a good job in relation to getting reliability and maintainability built in and setting up the repair pools, manuals, spares and tools needed, but with their existence it became possible to start to introduce cross-disciplinary equipment management committees to achieve overall compatibility of equipments. For example, the lieutenant colonel in EME 7 responsible for heavy A vehicles would expect to call on the grade 2 or 3 experts from EME 8 branches who dealt with night sights or radio fits for consultation. Similarly, the EME 8 committee for RAPIER would have expert advice from the vehicle representative from EME 7.

EME 9 and Aircraft Branch were rather different in character. EME 9 dealt with the RAF branches and the air side of PE. Things worked rather better in this area probably because the RAF, and for that matter the RN, were always equipment-orientated and very conscious of spares support. In this respect the RN support from Fleetlands for major overhauls was very good and well linked to our system. The Equipment branches, Vehicles, Weapons, Maritime and Aircraft, together with the ESPOs and Maintenance Advisory Groups (MAGs), also did a very good job in their various fields.

Brigadier Atkinson, before going to Andover as DEE 2, was DDEME, (later titled CCREME) in 1(BR) Corps, and through a series of study periods and wide consultation had secured agreement by 1981 to the concept of the combined repair and recovery vehicle, the ARRV, at both tank and APC level. This concept had been developed over the previous two years as part of a range of studies undertaken by the newly formed REME Combat Development Cell at Arborfield. During the next two years at Andover, with Brigadier Martyn Clark as DEME (Org & Trg) and EME 2 in the lead, the concept was accepted as Army policy. Subsequently, in Brigadier Atkinson's last few days as DEE 2, he saw the CHALLENGER ARRV Staff Requirement through the WEPC. As a result, in the winter of 1990/91, the first few ARRVs were available to support our Forces for the war in the Gulf. This particular development period of ten years emphasizes the long lead time for such major equipments, and the extended equipment management support that is necessary.

Brigadier Atkinson later wrote of his experiences as DEE 2 and his final remarks were:

'A very good example of the difficulties which DGEME and his Directors had in the initial setting-up of engineering support for major new projects was the complexity of introduction of base repair facilities for CHALLENGER tanks in BAOR. HQ DGEME was responsible for procuring special jigs and tools through the Project Manager; 23 Base Workshop at Wetter was responsible for planning and initiating bids for Works Services; HQ BAOR controlled the finance for Works Services and allocated priorities for construction work, which had to be let through the German works organization.

'Inevitably the priorities, contracts, financial approvals and eventual completion dates could not be properly managed by any single person or agency and the chance of meeting one in-service date was virtually zero. I know that successive DGEMEs have argued for total responsibility for engineering support, whether in mainland Europe or UK, but without success. It really was a very inefficient way of trying to run very major support programmes.'

The Director of Army Management Audit (DAMA) reviewed the organization and establishment of LE(A) again in 1986, resulting in an overall reduction of staff and minor transfers between branches. In 1989, though, the first steps towards a systems engineering approach were taken. A new multi-cap badge branch, EME 6, was established in April 1989 which became responsible for operational command, control, communications and information systems (CIS). This branch was at first under DEME (Man S), but later came under DEE 1 and contained RA and R SIGNALS Staff. This result of many months of hard work involving much discussion and decision-making was approved by the Army Establishments Committee in June 1990 and came into force that August, as shown in Annex D. As part of the change DEME (Man S) was retitled Director Engineering Policy (Army) (D Eng Pol(A)).

Logistic Support Planning

In 1984 MGO and QMG sponsored a joint study into the Commissioning and Support of Equipment (CASE) because of growing concerns about the lack of logistic support influence in the procurement cycle. One major conclusion of the study was that a new staff should be set up in London comprising Logistic Support Planning Officers who would provide input to the Operational Requirements staff and to the Procurement Executive during the early stages of equipment development. A one star Director of Support Planning (Army) was established on QMG's staff, the manpower for the Directorate being found mainly from the disestablished COSLOG in LE(A). The role of DSP(A) was to conduct initial support planning for all new equipment projects. The CASE Study was led by Colonel Mike Heath, then Colonel (W) MGO

Secretariat. Early tasks were the introduction of logistic support annexes into Staff Requirements, the setting up of QMG equipment reviews, the formulation of equipment management policy and the introduction of equipment management training for senior officers. Later, the Directorate laid the groundwork for the introduction of Integrated Logistic Support into new equipment projects.

Although not a REME Directorate, a number of staff who served under DSP(A) were, in fact, REME officers and had a major part to play in the procurement of supportable equipment. Indeed of the four directors who served in the post, two were late REME officers. In 1992, under the Logistic Support Review reorganizations, covered later in this chapter, the Directorate was amalgamated with D Eng Pol (A) and reformed in Andover as the Directorate of Equipment Support 2 (DES 2). The last DSP(A) and first DES 2 was Brigadier Robert Shields, son of Major General Ronnie Shields who was Commandant Technical Group REME until 1965. As it turned out, he and his branch were to be responsible for a development of engineering policy more rapid than anyone would have believed possible in earlier years.

New Management Strategy

A further very important step was the introduction by MOD of a management system to replace the 'management by exception' philosophy. It introduced a Corporate Plan to highlight the logistic implications of General Staff operational decisions and to control the Army's logistic services. The system ensured that the General Staff were made aware of the consequences of their decisions on logistic matters and the risks which they might decide to accept in making them. Much detailed work went into setting up the QMG's Logistic Management Board, the QMG's Corporate Plan, the computer-based Financial and Management Information System and the Management Boards of LE(A) Directors General. Corporate objectives were published and Directors General of the Logistic Services responded within their own functional objectives. Reviews of major projects were also introduced to brief the QMG on logistic progress and prospects.

The REME Management Board was chaired by DGEME with the five one star directors as members (no stand-ins were permitted) and met quarterly prior to the meeting of the QMG's Logistic Management Board. Subordinate to the DGEME's Board were various policy committees chaired by the DGEME and lower level committees chaired by the one star directors.

The organization to operate Corporate Planning was established in 1986 when the then Quartermaster General, Lieutenant General Sir Richard Trant, applied it to his area of responsibility, partly in response to the Thatcher Government's Financial Management Initiative (FMI) of

1982 and partly because of the need to respond to the reorganization of MOD in 1985. The QMG's Corporate Planning Unit (CPU) became responsible for Corporate Planning and the associated Financial Management Information System (FMIS). The MOD's New Management Strategy (NMS) was launched in a Defence Council Instruction in October 1987. It was to affect dramatically the way in which the MOD conducted its business, with its primary aim to get better value for money.

Corporate Planning in the QMG's area of responsibility was a systematic approach to the management of logistic support. It aimed to adopt the most cost-effective strategy to meet all future demands whilst retaining the flexibility to operate in peace or war. It endeavoured to increase efficiency and productivity without detriment to operational effectiveness and it encouraged long-term planning rather than crisis management. A fundamental feature was the monitoring of plans using FMIS to provide the information required. Its aim was to produce a more cost-conscious businesslike approach to management. The management of maintenance support provided by REME, including equipment management where applicable, was one of the eight functional areas. The functional directors such as DGEME had Functional Planning Units (FPUs) to develop their plans and to operate and develop the inputs to the FMIS and to the lower level systems supporting the functional plans. The strategic objective, or statement of intent, was to achieve a 20% improvement in performance against a 10% reduction in resources during the five year period 1986–1991.

The pursuit of the Holy Grail of getting more for less continued. Performance as far as the Corps was concerned was measured in terms of reduced repair costs, including better base workshop utilization, against the increasing size of the Army's equipment fleet. Several indicators were developed to compare demand and output, including the percentage equipment availability achieved, compared with that required by the EMPS and the actual base repair load in man-hours compared with the planned load. Within the REME Directorate at Andover two principal branches were formed to deal with the functional changes that were necessary for the New Management Strategy. They were EME 3, headed by a Grade 7 Civil Servant, to provide financial advice and manage the new Higher Level Budget and the Functional Planning Unit formed alongside the Secretariat to deal with the vehicle fleet and the maintenance functional plan.

When the Government launched FMI to improve the allocation, management and control of resources, the MOD already had in the form of the Long Term Costing (LTC) a well established process to allocate financial resources in all areas. In response to FMI the MOD produced two new main budgetary systems – Staff Responsibility Budgets

(SRBs) and Executive Responsibility Budgets (ERBs). In addition there was a top management information system (MINIS).

The new budgetary regime covered operational and maintenance expenditure across the operational and support areas of responsibility with a hierarchy of budgets based on the ERB in support areas. It was decided that 1 April 1991 would be the target date for full implementation of the new budgetary system which was subject to an annual cycle of Performance Review and Objectives Setting Exercise (PROSE). DGEME was required to submit Quarterly Reports in standard format which reported progress since the start of the year and shorter Monthly Digests to cover those months when the full Quarterly Report was not submitted. Discussions between the QMG and DGEME took place following the submission of each Quarterly Report. Information for the Quarterly Report was provided by FMIS from the figures entered on their own computer by the DGEME's FPU.

THE QMG DIRECTIVE – 1988

In 1988 the Quartermaster General issued a new Directive to DGEME. This was felt to be necessary at this stage to bring together in one document the results of all the changes that had affected DGEME's responsibilities over recent years. These changes were the effects of wide-ranging reorganizations both in Corps and Staff functions, the implementation of the recommendations of various MOD committees and the pressure of the initiatives that had been instigated by the Corps. This new Directive made clear the responsibilities of DGEME, as Head of the Corps, to the QMG, and also set out the responsibilities towards a wide range of Senior Staff Officers, Headquarters and other organizations. These included all Army Board Members, including the Master General of the Ordnance (MGO), the Deputy Chief of Defence Staff (Systems), the Commander in Chief United Kingdom Land Forces, and other Services and civilian agencies. Finally, it appointed DGEME to various committees such as the Defence Maintenance Committee, the Army Doctrine Committee (Logistics) and the Logistic Management Board. Some of the more important effects of this Directive confirmed the responsibilities of DGEME for:

- The implementation of the Maintenance Functional Plan as part of QMG's Corporate Plan.
- Developing, implementing and monitoring engineering support policy for Army equipment. Determining and implementing the policy for the management of equipment for which he was the designated equipment manager.
- The provision of advice on technical and special-to-service matters relating to in-service equipment support.

- The development of Logistic Executive (Army) as a focus for Army equipment support.
- Developing management information systems applicable to repair and associated resources.
- The control and development of productivity agreements in REME civilian-manned workshops in conjunction with civilian management branches.
- The provision of advice on electrical, electronic, mechanical and aeronautical engineering matters.
- The provision of advice on the assessment and improvement of reliability and maintainability of military equipment of MGO's concern and providing the focus for reliability and maintainability engineering matters.
- The framing of reliability and maintainability requirements for new equipment and the assessment of those qualities on equipment entering service.
- The sponsorship, as delegated equipment sponsors, of general purpose test equipment, recovery equipment, repair vehicles and workshop machine tools required by the Army.
- Engineering support, including management aspects, for the modification of in-service equipment for which REME had a repair responsibility.

DEVELOPMENT OF UK STATIC REME ORGANIZATION

In September 1967 Colonel Alex McKay, later to be DEME(A), had written a paper as ADEME EME 2 on 'Proposals for the Reorganization of REME Command Workshops in the UK' which explained very clearly why it was necessary to have a major reorganization. The DDEME of each UK Command had been asked for a report on the future requirement for second-line repair support in the light of various factors such as the re-organization and re-equipping of the Reserve Army, the re-deployment of Regular Army units from overseas to the UK, the most economic method of repair and the scope for extending contract repair. The proposals included closing some workshops and ending the independent status of a few and making them detachments of others. It also involved reducing the strengths of some workshops and amalgamating others to make a saving against establishments of nearly 40 military and more than 1,100 civilians. In practice the Corps lost over 400 civilians and most of the balance was made up from vacant posts.

Features of the plan were to reduce base repair in command workshops and limit base repair programme work to four command workshops only. The field repair of small arms and machine guns, instruments and telecommunications equipments was to be concentrated wherever possible in one workshop in each Command. Field repair cells were to be set up in the central workshops in Bicester, Chilwell, Donnington and Old Dalby, to economize in repair support and eliminate some command workshop detachments adjacent to central workshops. Closure of command workshop detachments would enable buildings and land to be given up.

FAIR VALUE Studies

The 1974 Defence Review had required cuts of £4,700M over a nine-year period with a reduction in Army manpower of 15,000 military posts and 11,000 civilian posts. Further cuts of £110M were announced in April 1975, followed by £670M in March 1976. The proposals, known as FAIR VALUE, required a cut of 5,400 civilians from the QMG's department of which 1,600 would be REME posts. Following these proposals, the QMG decided in 1975 to carry out a series of FAIR VALUE studies to find these savings. In view of previous economies and reductions in manpower in static installations, it became obvious that a major restructuring of the logistic base organization would be needed to save overhead costs, if the targets were to be achieved. The Army Board accepted that some lowering of standards had to be accepted and that some logistic risks should be taken.

A review of all REME UK activities in detail was carried out by Commander REME Support Group, then Major General Derek Walker, the last Commander of the Group, and CEME UKLF. It was realized at once that there was little scope for reductions in equipment engineering branches, support planning or in the provision of engineering services such as spares scaling and publications, there being a heavy backlog of work in many of these branches. Workshop Technology Branch for example was becoming more and more involved in workshop processes and repair techniques, especially where unusual engineering problems arose in service, stemming from the use of new materials in Army equipments. Attention therefore focused on central and command workshops. The main REME proposals were to close 32 Central Workshop at Bicester, except for a small garrison workshop, and to close six detachments of command workshops. Two of the three vehicle depot workshops at Ashchurch and Ludgershall, in common with the RAOC plan to close their depots there, were to be closed, involving a considerable manpower saving. The Fording Trials Branch at Instow was to be closed, following a threat of this that had existed for some years. Its fate was sealed when it was decided that the capability for future across-the-beach wading would be restricted to the Royal Marine Commandos. Overall, in addition to the closing of establishments, there were also to be cuts in various management posts. A study had been made in 1974 to see if it would be economical to bring back more base repair work from BAOR, but this proved to be impracticable because of handling and transport costs or because of the small numbers of spare equipments in repair pools. Furthermore the operations staff at HQ BAOR required that armoured vehicles remained in Germany for base repair, so that in an emergency they could be made ready in a shorter time than if they were in the UK.

At the time of the FAIR VALUE studies the two largest central workshops were 34 at Donnington with a strength of 1,081 and 38 at Chilwell with 1,052. It was decided that it was not feasible to close or reduce either of them but that they both had the potential to accept larger loads. The workshop at Newark, with a strength of 245, repaired radio and line equipment and was to be responsible for some of the CLANSMAN range base repair, and that at Old Dalby, with a strength of 576, to repair mainly GW equipment and radars. Both had very specialized repair facilities and employed skilled men and women who would be hard to replace elsewhere, so both were spared as a possible source of major FAIR VALUE savings. It was also concluded that there was no scope for any significant transfer of the contract repair element of programme work to REME workshops.

The effects of the various studies and planned economies were wide-ranging, but spread over several years. In July 1977 the separate Radar and Telecommunications Branches in DGEME Directorate amalgamated to form Electronics Branch. In 1978 Fording Trials Branch at Instow disbanded, together with 32 Central Workshop which amalgamated with 43 Command Workshop. The Bicester Detachment of 43 Command Workshop remained. The Army Equipment Calibration Centre disbanded in June 1979 and reorganized with 35 Central Workshop. Again at DGEME Directorate, Weapons Branch disbanded in October 1982, with Vehicles Branch under DEE 2 retitled Vehicles and Weapons Branch.

Static Workshop Review

The FAIR VALUE studies were not the end of the story. The Static Workshop Review (SWR) soon followed. In 1981, following an examination by the Parliamentary Accounts Committee of the Comptroller and Auditor General's report on the cost of overhaul in central and command workshops, a study was sponsored by DASD to examine the balance of static workshop repair activity in UK and BAOR between REME and industry. The aim of the study was to make recommendations to achieve the maximum possible manpower and financial savings whilst retaining the operational capability considered essential. The study team was headed by DEME (Man S), Brigadier Derek Richardson. The interim report was submitted to VQMG in March 1982 and examined by VQMG and AUS(A/Q) who were broadly content with its findings, but requested qualifications on various points. The final report made twenty-seven recommendations which included:

- In BAOR 23 Base Workshop should be retained in its base repair role and 37 (Rhine) Workshop should be retained for both base repair and Command work.
- In UK 33 Central Workshop at Newark should be closed, whilst 34 Central Workshop at Donnington should be retained.
- 35 Central Workshop at Old Dalby should be expanded to take on the specialized work then carried out at 33 Central Workshop.
- 38 Central Workshop at Chilwell should be closed with transfer of work to Bicester, Bovington and Donnington. 18 Command Workshop at Bovington should become centrally controlled and undertake base repair of tanks and CVR(T) based in UK.
- 30 Command Workshop at Mill Hill should be closed and the repair load transferred to the workshops at Aldershot, Colchester and Ashford.

The above recommendations and others were considered at Ministerial level and the proposals were announced in Parliament on 28 June 1984. A Ministerial statement on 20 December 1984 announced full implementation of the proposals over a two- to three-year period. One effect was that more B and C Vehicle assemblies for base repair were to be back-loaded from BAOR to UK to be included with those UK equipments repaired by contract. The amount of UK contract base repair was to be doubled from 18% to 36% of arisings. As a result of the SWR the Corps lost over 600 UK civilians. On 1 April 1985 four base workshops were formed from 34 and 35 Central, 18 Command and the Bicester detachment of 43 Command Workshop, the latter becoming 32 Base Workshop. All other command workshops became district workshops. In May 1986 DGEME reported that there had been a good response from industry to the requirement to increase contracted base repair work from 18% to 36% and that some large contracts had been placed at very competitive prices. The Fazakerley Engineering Company at Liverpool, a Government-owned but contractor-operated facility, which amongst other things had carried out in-depth repairs to STALWARTs, was closed on 31 December 1985. 33 Central Workshop at Newark closed in March 1987. In June 1987 DGEME reported that plans to double the amount of contract base repair work had been delayed, but by April 1988 it had risen to the planned 36%. DGEME was able to report that implementation of the SWR would be completed by 31 March 1989 with the closure of 38 Central Workshop. Subsequently the closure of 30 District Workshop at Mill Hill was postponed until March 1990.

Early 1990s Rationalization

Following the end of the Cold War and the massive reductions planned for the Army, over-capacity in the static workshop organization swiftly became apparent. On taking up his post as Director of Production Engineering in 1991, Brigadier Jim Drew set in hand an in-depth study and Investment Appraisal to define the way ahead. 37 (Rhine) Workshop had already closed but, despite this, there was insufficient projected workload to utilize existing facilities both in UK and BAOR. Sadly, the decision had to be taken to close 39 District Workshop at Bridgend, 41 District Workshop in York and 42 District Workshop in Liverpool. These workshops were all to close by 31 March 1993. Equally sad was the decision to close 23 Base Workshop in Wetter; our largest workshop with an impressive production capability and fine history was to be lost by 31 March 1994. Then all base repair for the Army would be effected in mainland UK for the first time since the Army could remember.

The Future

With the recent history of strategic change it would be a wise man who could predict the future with any certainty. As this volume closes all remaining static workshops were being subjected to market testing. The competition would decide the size and shape of our future non-deployable workshops and who operated them, the prime aim being to deliver as good a service (if not better) at best value for money.

MANAGEMENT INFORMATION SYSTEMS

Several Data Systems were developed at the REME Data Centre, Woolwich, for the Corps over the years, of which only the most important are mentioned in the following paragraphs. The REME Data Centre at Woolwich had been opened in October 1967 and, as described in the first volume, its main task was to develop and implement the FORWARD engineering and management information system. Throughout the period covered by this volume it remained the focal point in the Corps for the development of computer-based information systems and for large-scale automatic data processing (ADP). Originally equipped with an ICL 1904 computer, the ADP capacity was enhanced in 1971 with the addition of an ICL 1903 machine. Both machines were replaced in 1974 by a more powerful ICL 1904S central processor with peripheral equipment added a year later. The punched card machines used for data input were replaced by key-to-disc machines so that the Centre now had a modern installation with processing capacity well able to cope with the load at that time. However, ADP techniques and equipment were changing rapidly and interest was growing in the possibility of putting data into the data bank and interrogating it from remote points. This concept was demonstrated at DGEME's Study Period 1974, when a terminal in the conference hall at Arborfield was linked via a communications satellite to a computer in the USA and used to interrogate and manipulate FORWARD data previously stored in the computer's memory. The Data Centre's capability for remote working in this way, previously very limited, was considerably increased in 1984 with the arrival of an ICL 2966 replacement.

In parallel with the growth of central ADP facilities, the appearance of low-cost microcomputers in the eighties led to a spread of computing equipment elsewhere in the Corps. The Data Centre established a Small Systems Group as the focus for developing many small systems and as a source of advice for those being developed on a self-help basis. Colonel Ken Osman (the first officer who had served in a junior capacity in the Data Centre a generation earlier to return as its commanding officer), writing in 1989, claimed, 'This area of REME Information Technology (IT) can be considered a genuine success story. At the beginning of 1989 there was still a potential backlog of over 100 Small Systems projects'. There were, however, considerable delays in deciding on a replacement for the FORWARD system and in introducing ADP facilities into field workshops and LADs. To a large extent this was due to procrastination and changes of direction outside Corps control, but for some time it led to a reduction in Data Centre staffing and to a certain amount of frustration.

A more optimistic outlook began to emerge in the second half of the eighties, and illustrative of this was an extension to the Data Centre building opened by Major General John Boyne, DGEME, in October 1986. However, at the same time the Q Information Technology (Q IT) Strategy Study was taking shape and a number of new IT projects were included in the Army IT Strategy. The Directorate of Logistic Information Systems (Army) was established and took over the control of the REME Data Centre. There were some major shortcomings in the Q IT strategy and it was not until 1992 that the way ahead became clear. FORWARD, which was ahead of its time in 1967, was now providing little benefit to REME compared with the effort required for data acquisition, and reporting for FORWARD Main was therefore stopped in late 1992.

FORWARD

Major General Vincent Metcalfe was chairman of the DEME ADP Policy Steering Committee from 1970 until 1976, during which time detailed responsibility for the project was held in turn by Colonels Jim Hillier,

Peter Mayes and Gerry Beswick. He wrote later of his rapid realization of the pressing need for machinery for consultation on the system within the Corps so that it could be developed to meet the true needs as far as this was technically feasible. This necessary communication was achieved by the establishment in March 1967 of nine FORWARD Advisory Committees. Each dealt with a specific area such as field workshops, training, spares scaling, aircraft etc. Each committee was chaired by a colonel and members were drawn from those currently concerned with the particular aspect to be covered and from the Data Centre. It proved to be a most successful means of assimilating ideas.

When FORWARD was introduced into units in the Sixties there had been considerable comment at all levels in the field from time to time, particularly in BAOR, on the additional workload produced by the reporting procedures involved in the system. General Metcalfe later wrote in reply to these criticisms:

'We were very conscious that the reporting effort required of units (particularly first line) was not inconsiderable and must be justifiable. Reductions were made by introducing an ADP version of the stores demand form (so that manual transcription was no longer required) and in 1975 the number of equipment categories was doubled to six. In addition the Coding Panel reviewed the equipment categories each year and downgraded wherever possible.' . . . Looking back in 1989 General Metcalfe again wrote. *'We were well aware that the FORWARD concept had some serious limitations and that some were fundamental, whilst others could be tackled during development. But we were also aware that the system had considerable potential for growing into a powerful information source and that we were in fact blazing the trail of systems analysing equipment maintenance data.'*

At the start there had been ADP limitations and it took many hours to insert new data each week and many more to extract a month's output. Programming was slow before a high-level language (COBOL) was adopted and there were never enough analysts and programmers available.

Even after considerable development the basic FORWARD system was not capable of giving information about equipment reliability except in the most general sense. There was a growing need to monitor and measure reliability parameters more precisely, and to specify reliability of new equipment in numerical terms. Equally important was the need to monitor reliability during development and the early service life of new equipments, whilst funds were still available for improvements to be made. The Data Centre played an important role in the reliability studies of SCORPION, RAPIER and SWINGFIRE. These studies were particularly noteworthy, monitoring being carried out with the appropriate engineering branches through which the results were fed to the R & D establishments concerned. The expertise and practical experience gained by the Corps in this work was second to none. General Metcalfe was invited to give an account of it to a Reliability and Maintainability Symposium at Las Vegas, Nevada, during January 1976. The paper was well received in spite of, or perhaps because of, the early hour of its delivery! The provision of spares usage data to the Army Scaling Authority was one of the prime aims of FORWARD, and its achievements therefore gave it high priority in view of the potential for financial savings. For this purpose usage rates were produced in the accepted manner of usage per 100 equipments per year and compared with the authorized scale – at first manually but later on the computer.

FORWARD also increased the Corps' involvement in equipment management. Two notable examples were the derivation of optimum repair limits for the B Vehicle Casting System and the REME contribution to the RAOC inventory control system VESPER. Information was produced on the rates at which equipments were declared BLR, BER or BR and a joint VESPER team was set up in 1970.

FORWARD had three basic limitations so far as workshop management was concerned. Firstly, it did not cover base repair except in a very limited sense. Secondly, it collected data on completed jobs only, ignoring work in progress. Thirdly, and not least, input data was sent by post as was the output – the whole process usually taking several weeks. A study made by the Field Workshop Advisory Committee of the acceptability of proposals from the Data Centre led to the introduction of an Inspection Return reporting the condition of equipment found during periodic unit inspections and a much improved Job Report which led to more useful outputs from the Data Centre. The next development was an analysis of labour utilization and availability of direct and indirect labour, with the aim of setting theatre standards. In HQ DEME a Standing Committee on Labour Utilization was set up followed by a Military Manpower Activity Study in 1972. As a result of the findings, REME establishments no longer needed to be based on rule of thumb estimates of man-hours per soldier tradesman per year.

Concluding Remarks on FORWARD

Major General Vincent Metcalfe writing in 1989 said:

'The FORWARD system went through a period of continuous development for a number of years. There was no comprehensive "Rule Book" to be computerized and contributions came in from many quarters. New ground was being broken all the time and this fired the imagination of all concerned. In retrospect the pace of development was remarkable. The limitations of the basic concept were recognized from the outset. Some were overcome but others were more fundamental and would have to await advances in computer technology for their solution. In the area of equipment reliability, the system proved to have less potential for development than had been envisaged. The Treasury had to be convinced that the money being saved by the project covered the cost of the Data Centre. In April 1971 a paper entitled "Cost Benefit Analysis of the REME Data Centre" was produced with the Data Centre contributing its costs and external managers producing evidence of the benefits. The Treasury (at least) were convinced!

'The use of FORWARD information gathered pace as familiarity with it grew. There was a shift of emphasis from the regular issue of standard outputs to special issues and interrogation of the data bank on request. In the year 1975–76 423 special outputs were produced, in an average response time of five days, for 260 customers; 505 interrogations were completed of which 255 were for customers outside the Corps. Lack of factual information was no longer an acceptable excuse for management indecision!'

At the end of the Eighties FORWARD was still the only source of historical equipment management and engineering information, and about ninety ad-hoc queries every month indicated that more use was being made of FORWARD than many people realized. FORWARD was still operating in 1992, twenty-five years after its beginning in 1967 – something that was possibly not envisaged by its founders at the time.

FORWARD (Air)

When FORWARD was implemented its application to aircraft had been excluded, and there was pressure from the RAF for the Corps to use their system which was under development at that time. The RAF system had little potential for producing management information and it relied on a central staff to code the reports and was therefore expensive in man-power. The decision was taken to extend FORWARD to army aircraft and this improved system became known as FORWARD (Air). Aircraft engineers were already used to detailed recording of all work done so that a more detailed job report was not unacceptable to them. The new system was output-orientated from the beginning, and the FORWARD (Air) Advisory Committee drew up the ADP Requirement Document detailing the twelve or so outputs to be produced initially. Reporting began in January 1971 and the list of these outputs was produced in November. Development continued until the agreed requirement had been met.

The Chief Aircraft Engineer's confidence in the completeness and accuracy of the FORWARD (Air) Data Bank was made clear at the DEME(A) Study Period in 1974 when Colonel Gerry Beswick, OC Data Centre, reported that the CAE was able to rely on an interrogation to make a policy decision after a recent helicopter crash in Northern Ireland. The CAE had requested a print of all aircraft with a particular modified tail rotor drive shaft coupling and he received this information within twenty-four hours. This thereby avoided the need for a lengthy grounding and the physical inspection of all SCOUTs which would have cost about £10,000 at that time. FORWARD (Air) was inherently accurate and actively used to monitor the maintenance man hours per flying hour and to analyse the figures to identify areas for improvement.

At the end of the Eighties and the beginning of the Nineties information from FORWARD (Air) was still in great demand. In August 1986 it supplied data to Hunting Engineering Ltd for the LYNX and GAZELLE Life Cycle Engineering Cost Study. The information required was considerable and it was supplied well into 1987. During 1990 information was assembled in aid of the Attack Helicopter. A request for information on turn-round times of major servicing and other work carried out in second-line workshops was made in 1991 to help with the planning of a new workshop. A new database system for FORWARD (Air) was being set up in 1991 to process data more quickly and make outputs more up to date. It became possible to interrogate the data base direct from the FORWARD (Air) desk in Aircraft Branch.

ADP in Large Static Workshops

In 1975 the Corps called in a firm of management consultants to make recommendations for the use of ADP in the Eighties. One study was concerned with large static workshops, and it was learned that RAOC was looking into ADP applications for RAOC Stores Sections in support of static workshops. This led to a joint Full Study by both Corps – thus ARROW was born. (ADP Assistance to RAOC and REME Operations in Workshops). The Full Study Report was approved in 1978, and the main equipment was delivered to 34 Central Workshop in 1980. By 1985 the system had main modules providing Automated Spares Demanding and Control, Job Cards and Progress Information, Payroll incorporating the

Productivity Scheme, Management Information on Spares and Job Activity. By 1991 modules on Job Time Recording, Engineering Outputs and an interface with FORWARD had been added and implemented in every static workshop. ARROW communicated with external systems, such as the RAOC Stores System via an automated demand link, with FORWARD for engineering data, and with CPRO Cheadle Hulme for civilian pay data. Following its success in 34 Central Workshop, the system was put into two base workshops and two district workshops in 1986–87 and into three district workshops and 46 Northern Ireland Workshop in 1988.

ADP for First and Second Line Units

During 1979–80 a FORWARD review confirmed the need for the higher management information (HMIS) provided by FORWARD and recognized the need for relevant and timely information at unit level which gave rise to the First Line Operating System (FLOS) and Computer Assistance to the Production and Stores System (CAPSS) which were ADP systems for first and second line units respectively. They provided direct read-out availability and reliability data across the fleet.

In 1988 FLOS, having been tested successfully and being ready for implementation, was absorbed into a new project called UNICOM developed by a team at Worthy Down. CAPSS was tested in 7 Armoured Workshop in 1985 but did not work successfully with the RAOC stores system COFFER; it was replaced in 1989 by CARRIFF which provided CAPSS facilities in workshops and a replacement for the RAOC system.

The closure of FORWARD in 1992 and delays in the development of UNICOM left a potential gap. The First Line Equipment Management Information System (FEMIS) was procured and deployed in haste to first-line units in 1992 as an interim information and data recording system. At the same time the Battlefield Equipment Reliability Return (BERR) was deployed to the field force and headquarters to monitor reliability and availability information. At MOD level the data was to be held by the Central Army Equipment Support data Analysis and Retrieval system (CAESAR) which was set up at Andover. The framework was, therefore, established to gain user confidence in a new reporting system and to provide some experience before the introduction of UNICOM.

THE REME CONTRIBUTION TO THE PROCUREMENT PROCESS

The establishment of the Procurement Executive in the Ministry of Defence after the 1971 White Paper 'Government Organization for Defence Procurement and Civil Aerospace' (known as the Rayner Report) led to the growing power of the London-based project managers with their financial accountability. This gave rise to a feeling that REME was gradually losing its influence in Research and Development (R & D) establishments. DEME (A) therefore published a paper 'The REME Contribution to Equipment Procurement' for submission to the QMG and the MGO. This important paper, written by Lieutenant Colonel Bob Alexander, contained several positive proposals including recognition of REME as the link between the designer and the user as well as early and continuous REME participation in projects. The proposals were accepted and implemented.

The need for a new weapon system usually arose because the existing system was wearing out or because its performance was inadequate to meet new operational requirements. A sponsor in the MOD would produce a concept generally in the form of a General Staff Target (GST). Feasibility Studies were carried out by the Procurement Executive MOD (PE), with R & D establishment or industry. The recommendations and probable cost of procurement were sent to MOD(A) where, if all went well, the Equipment Sponsor would produce a General Staff Requirement (GSR), a much more specific document than the GST. The draft GSR paper was then circulated round MOD, including EME branches, for comment. Provided that technical progress and cost control were acceptable, the project would be approved for Full Development. The aim of the Corps in this process was to advise upon and influence the design and development of the system so that when it came into service it was the greatest possible asset to the user and the least possible liability to REME in carrying out its maintenance function.

This latter requirement was of particular importance, as the extent of REME's maintenance effort was also a measure of the equipment's reliability.

At the GST stage, when the Procurement Executive appointed a Project Manager, the REME Directorate appointed an Engineering Support Planning Officer (ESPO) whose task it was to achieve this aim. At the same time a Maintenance Advisory Group (MAG) was identified to support the ESPO. An outline Target Repair Policy had to be included in the GST so that its feasibility would be examined during the Feasibility Study. The MAG would get involved directly with the competing contractors, explaining in detail what REME repair policies meant and what REME might wish to see for that project. The MAG would be involved in some depth with the Project Manager when MOD (PE) received the Feasibility Study Reports from industry, assessing REME aspects of the proposals. The next stage was to draft the GSR, the main body of which has been described as the 'Project Manager's Shopping List'. The Corps had to make sure that anything it wanted was in that main body and that it was correct; otherwise what was bought would also be wrong. Once the GSR had been approved and funded the Technical Requirement was drafted, spelling out in considerable technical detail and depth exactly what was to be procured. This document was an inherent part of the contract and was the most important document in the procurement.

In the days of cost-plus development contracts it was no problem to get a change or modification in the design to make maintenance easier, and the contractor would accept it and get paid for it. In the Eighties the Secretary of State for Defence, Mr Michael Heseltine, set in train a policy to get better value for money for the tax-payer with more competition and Fixed Price Contracts. A Fixed Price Contract required the Army to specify exactly what was wanted in terms of reliability and maintainability. There was an impasse if REME subsequently asked for design changes for which the contractor required more money than provided for in the Fixed Price.

It became Government policy in the Eighties to devolve more responsibility for development from MOD R & D establishments to industry. Contracts became increasingly let to Prime Contractors, who had much more project control delegated to them and were largely autonomous in the control of cash and technical progress. They alone selected the sub-contractors and controlled access to them with the result that access to industry by MAGs and Test Package Evaluation and Acceptance Teams (TPEATs) became much more difficult. The trend from Cost Plus to Fixed Price made it more important than ever to get the Technical Requirement or specification complete and correct, as this was the binding contractual document. During the drafting stages REME would ensure that the Target Repair Policy was spelled out in detail, that the General Purpose Test Equipment (GPTE) or General Purpose Automatic Test Equipment (GPATE) requirements were specified, as were the Maintenance Software Policy requirements and the Reliability and Maintainability requirements. Close liaison was maintained with the R & D establishment to ensure that this happened.

Space does not permit a record of the ADP systems and procedures which enabled DGEME to achieve 'Contracting for Reliability'. Nevertheless, the driving force at this stage in the late Eighties was Brigadier Sam Webber. Emphasis was placed on clear unambiguous specifications and assessment methods which were contractually binding. This, combined with progress assessed at project milestones, enabled REME to get on and do it. Early examples of such a contract are the High Velocity Missile System (HVM), the Air Defence Alerting Device(ADAD) and the Manportable Surveillance and Target Acquisition Radar (MSTAR). By 1990 it had become the norm for new development contracts to bind contractors to achieving their reliability predictions, and if they failed they had to rectify the shortfall at their expense. In the late Eighties contracting for the Q Readiness Date was brought in, starting with the Field Standard C RAPIER ground to air missile, followed by others in the electronics, vehicles and weapons areas. From its introduction the Army would only accept and pay for deliveries of equipment which included, for example, a battery's worth of fire units, a battery's worth of first- and second-line test equipment and tools, a battery's worth of first- and second-line spares and publications. The contractor was not paid for the second battery's equipment until all the first battery's requirements had been delivered and paid for. This was first achieved with RAPIER.

In 1989 the support contribution to procurement took on a more structured and formal role upon the adoption of Integrated Logistic Support (ILS), an American-proved process, to Project BOWMAN – the successor to the CLANSMAN radio system. The ILS Manager worked in the Project Office for the Project Manager to assist him in procuring suitable equipment. The approach of ILS was for both the Contractor and MOD (PE) to complete a full and formal Logistic Support Analysis (LSA) and use this to influence design at an early stage, with the desired end result of reducing life-cycle costs. The introduction of ILS was sponsored by DSP(A)'s staff, Colonel QMG 4, firstly Colonel Philip Corp, and subsequently Colonel Peter Gange. DSP (A) also sponsored the ILS manager and team members. The first ever ILS Manager for the Army was Lieutenant Colonel Brian Hutchins who played a key role in developing the methodology.

LOGISTIC SUPPORT REVIEW 1990–1991.

The Logistic Support Review (LSR) of 1990–91 was the most wide-ranging review of the QMG's organization and responsibilities since before the First World War. The Review reflected a perception that logistic support to the Army could be provided more economically and more efficiently; in particular that two basic tasks (equipment support and supply/distribution) were being handled by three Corps. The low availability of important armoured vehicle fleets had acted as a catalyst for this review. The initial study had been put in hand in 1989 before the major initiative involving the whole Army – 'Options for Change'. It had arisen from a brief introductory QMG/MGO interface study conducted by the DSP(A) Brigadier Mike Heath.

The terms of reference for the LSR were drawn up by the Army Board, and the team led by Major General A N Carlier (late RE) included Colonel Tony Millington (EME 2). They gave an oral report of their interim findings to the Army Board in December 1990. They made a large number of recommendations and their final report was endorsed by the Executive Committee of the Army Board (ECAB) in June 1991. The major recommendations were:

- That there should be a two-corps structure for logistics responsible for Service Support and Equipment Support (ES). This would exist throughout the chain of command from MOD(A) down to units.
- That there should be one Director General responsible for Service Support and one for Equipment Support.
- That the G4 staff system should incorporate these new functional activities.
- That QMG and the majority of his London staff should be re-located to Andover.
- That an implementation plan should be prepared.

Service support was to include transport, movement, supply, catering, postal and pioneer functions and was to be provided from a new Corps, The Royal Logistic Corps, formed from the RCT, RAOC, ACC, the RE Postal and Courier Service and the RPC. This was put into effect under the Government's 'Options for Change', published as a White Paper in November 1991.

An LSR Implementation Team was formed to deal with the ES element of the LSR and produced an implementation plan that was endorsed by the Executive Committee of the Army Board in January 1992. This plan detailed how HQ DGEME was to be organized and how RAOC materiel posts were to be embedded in all REME staff organizations from MOD down to brigade level to form a broad-based Equipment Support Organization (ESO) from April 1992. It also outlined follow-on studies which included a complete review of repair polices and the REME field force organization, a review of MGO/QMG interface responsibilities, and a re-examination of the REME/R SIGNALS repair interface. However, the most immediate impact upon REME from the LSR was the formation of the ESO.

The Equipment Support pillar of QMG's new logistic organization was based principally upon REME's core activities of inspection, repair, recovery, modification and equipment management, but it also included additional key equipment support responsibilities that had previously been carried out within different functional chains of command. In particular the responsibility for technical spares management and procurement was to be part of the ESO. For the first time, therefore, a single focus was created which aligned the responsibility and accountability for the Army's key equipment support activities.

DGEME became the Director General of Equipment Support (Army) (DGES(A)), on 6 April 92 in recognition of his wider functional responsibilities as head of the ESO. At the same time HQ DGEME was renamed the Directorate General of Equipment Support (Army) (DGES(A)) within the embryonic HQ QMG that was to replace the Logistic Executive (Army) at Andover from September 1992. This new multi-cap badge MOD Directorate contained 127 military and 300 civilian posts with over 50% of the military staff being non-REME. The DGES(A) operating budget exceeded £500M in its first year.

Major General Mike Heath coined the term 'Equipment Support Organization' to reflect the fact that it now included many non-REME elements. Although less than half the ES military posts in the Andover Headquarters (by this time renamed HQ QMG) were REME, the ESO nevertheless remained predominantly manned and led by REME. The principal imports came from elements of the Directorate of Support Planning (Army), the Directorate of Supply Management (Army), Quartermaster Finance (Logistic Executive), and RE, R SIGNALS and RCT staffs. The main exports were the Directorate of Production Engineering, which became a stand-alone organization under the Commander Army Static Workshops (previously the Director of Production Engineering), the REME Small Systems Group and the General Purpose Test Equipment Section. This was a most significant achievement, bringing together all Army equipment management staffs, and aligning supply management and equipment management to a single point of responsibility. From REME's point of view, creating an equipment support policy focus for DGES(A) was also the attainment of an ideal that had for so long eluded those in the Corps who saw the tremendous overall value that there was in total equipment management. It was indeed a great leap forward and of much potential benefit to both the operational effectiveness of equipment and its economic life expectancy.

Under its Director General the organization of DGES(A) was established with five one star Directors of Equipment Support (DES) and a Grade 6 civilian Head of Equipment Support Finance and Secretariat (Hd of ES(F&S)). The responsibilities of each of the one star Directors is given at Annex E.

The Directorate of Production Engineering formerly controlled the base workshops in the UK. Within the space of twelve months it was to change its title twice. A further policy change (separate from but related to the Logistic Support Review) saw all district workshops moved from the control of HQ UKLF to the Directorate on 1 April 1992. The Directorate's title changed to HQ Army Static Workshops to reflect the new arrangements, and its changed status from a Ministry of Defence staff directorate to a 'below the line' organization removed from the MOD Headquarters. The Director, Brigadier Jim Drew, became Commander Army Static Workshops, and with the magic word 'command' came the entitlement to a staff car and the gnashing of his brother brigadiers' teeth.

There followed a year of intense development work within the Headquarters to prepare the Army Static Workshops for launch as a Defence Agency. The business was analysed in depth, blocks to progress identified and enhanced delegations defined and then negotiated. SWOT analyses, brainstorming and many other management techniques were fully deployed to define where the organization should be three years ahead and, equally important, how it was going to get there. Many people were involved in this work but chief amongst them were Brigadier Jim Drew, the agency Chief Executive designate, Grant Morris and Bob Nunn (respectively Grade 6 and 7 civil servants). This work was all distilled into the Agency Framework Document (in effect a 'contract') and the Agency Corporate Plan which charted targets for the next five years. The final step was the formal launch of the Army Base Repair Organization Defence (ABRO) Agency in the House of Commons on 31 March 1993 by Mr Archie Hamilton, MP (Minister for the Armed Forces).

On 16 April 1993 Mr Hamilton joined many guests at 18 Base Workshop for a launch PR day which was a huge success. Following the speeches there was an impressive drive past of REME armoured vehicles down the ages drawn mainly from the REME Museum's Historic Vehicle Fleet; bringing up the rear was the nostalgic sight of a Mark 5 tank from the 1918 era.

And so the ABRO was firmly on its way as an agency. It had much to keep it busy. The implementation of the closure programme whilst keeping the production programme to plan, and restructuring its Headquarters to enable it to discharge its new responsibilities, featured large in its activities. Overshadowing all of this, though, was the massive programme of market testing on which the Agency embarked. Being the

Mr Archie Hamilton at 18 Base Workshop for the Launch of ABRO

first of its kind, the 18 Base Workshop pilot scheme hit all manner of new and difficult problems. Employment law, spares pricing, Intellectual Property Rights, terminal redundancy provision and works services, to name a few, all brought major difficulties. They were all resolved and early June 1993 saw invitations to tender to nine companies selected to bid, plus the In-House team. Tenders were returned on 30 September and then began the major task of tender evaluation.

Despite these extensive changes, the formation of DGES(A) was seen very much as an enabling strategy. Studies into Post Design Services recommended the transfer of these responsibilities from MGO to QMG. Equipment support managers would, therefore, be responsible for the design sponsorship of in-service equipments and the procurement of modifications. There were further moves to give equipment support managers greater responsibility over defining which spares should be procured for their range of equipments. It was also being suggested that ILS managers should report to the main equipment directors rather than to DES 2. All these moves would lead to the creation of Multi-Disciplinary Groups to be responsible for the procurement of equipment support as part of a through-life equipment business. Further studies resulted in the delegation of administrative B vehicle procurement to DES 5.

The formation of DGES(A) also led to some significant changes to the number of technical branches and authorities that had been under the command of HQ DGEME (commonly referred to as 'below-the-line' units). The post-LSR 'below-the-line' organization expanded to include the ES Small Systems Group, Royal Engineers Technical Services (RETS), the Vehicle Spares and Technical Equipments Divisions and the Army Static Workshop Organization. The latter organization was considerably larger than previously, due to the transfer of the control of all District Workshops from HQ UKLF in April 1992.

CONCLUSION

Back in the Sixties considerable effort had been spent on promoting awareness of the dire consequences, both operational and logistic, of introducing unreliable equipment into Army service. The early years of CHIEFTAIN, RAPIER and SCOUT were painful, but not untypical, examples of the lack of investment in reliability at the design stage. Unfortunately, but perhaps not surprisingly, things got better only very slowly. The urge to get new equipment into service 'on-cost and on-time', the continued separation of capital and maintenance expenditure, successive financial and staff cutbacks and the ever-growing complexity of new weapons all seemed to conspire against significant achievement in this field.

Eventually, however, the patient work of many years began to show results. By the late Eighties reliability had achieved a remarkably high political profile throughout the MOD and there was growing evidence that some new systems, particularly in the electronics area, were markedly better than their predecessors. REME could take much credit for their part in this saga. The Corps was well represented on CODERM – the Tri-Service Reliability Committee which had done much to stimulate top-level interest and provide guidance, training and documentation. Within the Land Systems area, ESPOs, MAGs, EME 10 and many others, at Andover and elsewhere, had fought to get the message across in Staff Requirements, Project Meetings and other such places. All of that said, much still remained to be done and the vision of uniform and high levels of equipment reliability throughout the Army remained elusive, though the situation was progressively improving. Brigadier Webber's contribution, as DEE 1 from 1986–1991, to the Army's perception of the importance of reliability and maintainability, to its long-term benefit, was recognized by his appointment to CBE in the 1990 New Year Honours List. In particular he had ensured that full attention would henceforth be given to all aspects of an equipment from the very inception of development, with suppliers being obliged contractually to meet carefully specified criteria. By 1990 Integrated Logistic Support was seen as the route to fully effective and economical support systems. The creation of a multi-disciplinary Equipment Support Organization as a result of the 1991 Logistic Support Review was a major advance towards aligning authority with responsibility for the availability of the Army's equipment, and the prospect of adding PDS and administrative B vehicle procurement to the portfolio of the ESO promised to develop this further. The results of the many studies, re-organizations and technical advances were at last beginning to bear fruit.

Annex A

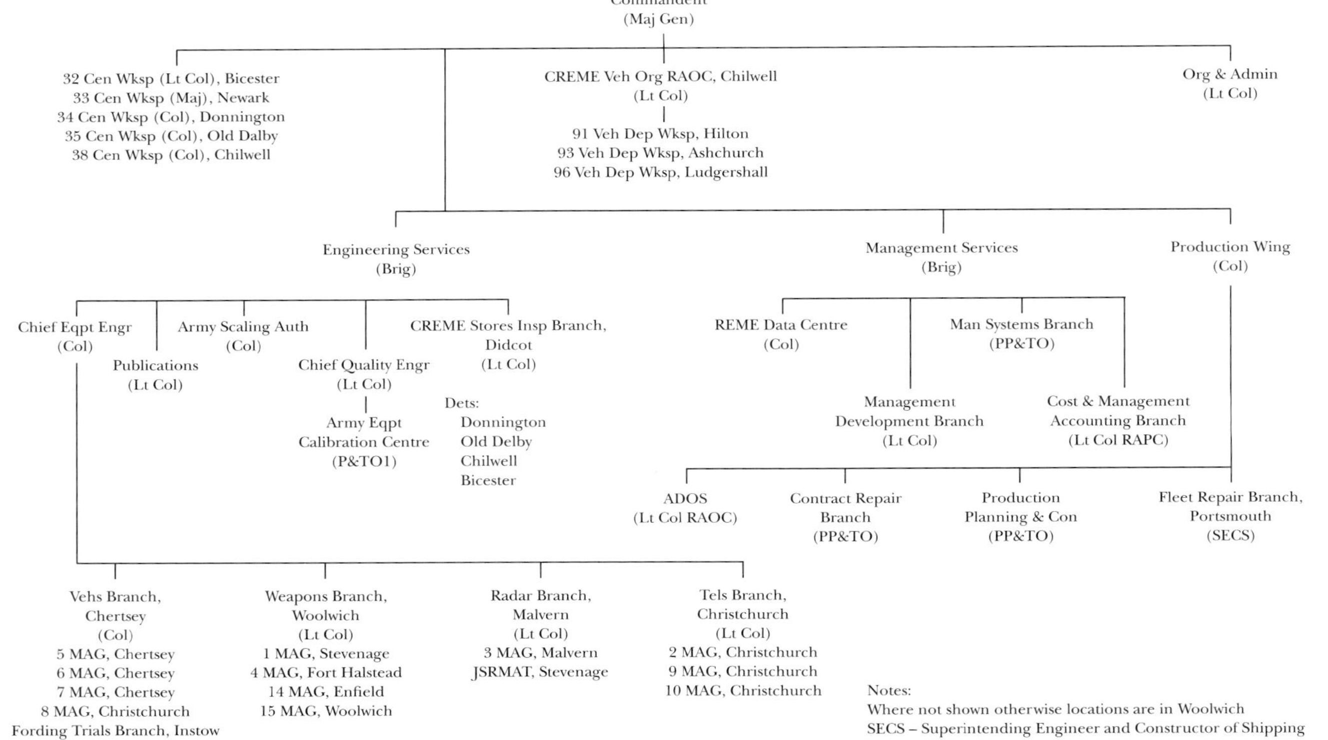
ORGANIZATION OF TECHNICAL GROUP REME 1973
Commandent
(Maj Gen)
32 Cen Wksp (Lt Col), Bicester
33 Cen Wksp (Maj), Newark
34 Cen Wksp (Col), Donnington
35 Cen Wksp (Col), Old Dalby
38 Cen Wksp (Col), Chilwell
CREME Veh Org RAOC, Chilwell
(Lt Col)
91 Veh Dep Wksp, Hilton
93 Veh Dep Wksp, Ashchurch
96 Veh Dep Wksp, Ludgershall
Org & Admin
(Lt Col)
Engineering Services
(Brig)
Management Services
(Brig)
Production Wing
(Col)
Chief Eqpt Engr
(Col)
Publications
(Lt Col)
Army Scaling Auth
(Col)
Chief Quality Engr
(Lt Col)
Army Eqpt
Calibration Centre
(P&TO1)
CREME Stores Insp Branch,
Didcot
(Lt Col)
Dets:
Donnington
Old Delby
Chilwell
Bicester
REME Data Centre
(Col)
Man Systems Branch
(PP&TO)
Management
Development Branch
(Lt Col)
Cost & Management
Accounting Branch
(Lt Col RAPC)
ADOS
(Lt Col RAOC)
Contract Repair
Branch
(PP&TO)
Production
Planning & Con
(PP&TO)
Fleet Repair Branch,
Portsmouth
(SECS)
Vehs Branch,
Chertsey
(Col)
5 MAG, Chertsey
6 MAG, Chertsey
7 MAG, Chertsey
8 MAG, Christchurch
Fording Trials Branch, Instow
Weapons Branch,
Woolwich
(Lt Col)
1 MAG, Stevenage
4 MAG, Fort Halstead
14 MAG, Enfield
15 MAG, Woolwich
Radar Branch,
Malvern
(Lt Col)
3 MAG, Malvern
JSRMAT, Stevenage
Tels Branch,
Christchurch
(Lt Col)
2 MAG, Christchurch
9 MAG, Christchurch
10 MAG, Christchurch
Notes:
Where not shown otherwise locations are in Woolwich
SECS – Superintending Engineer and Constructor of Shipping

Annex B

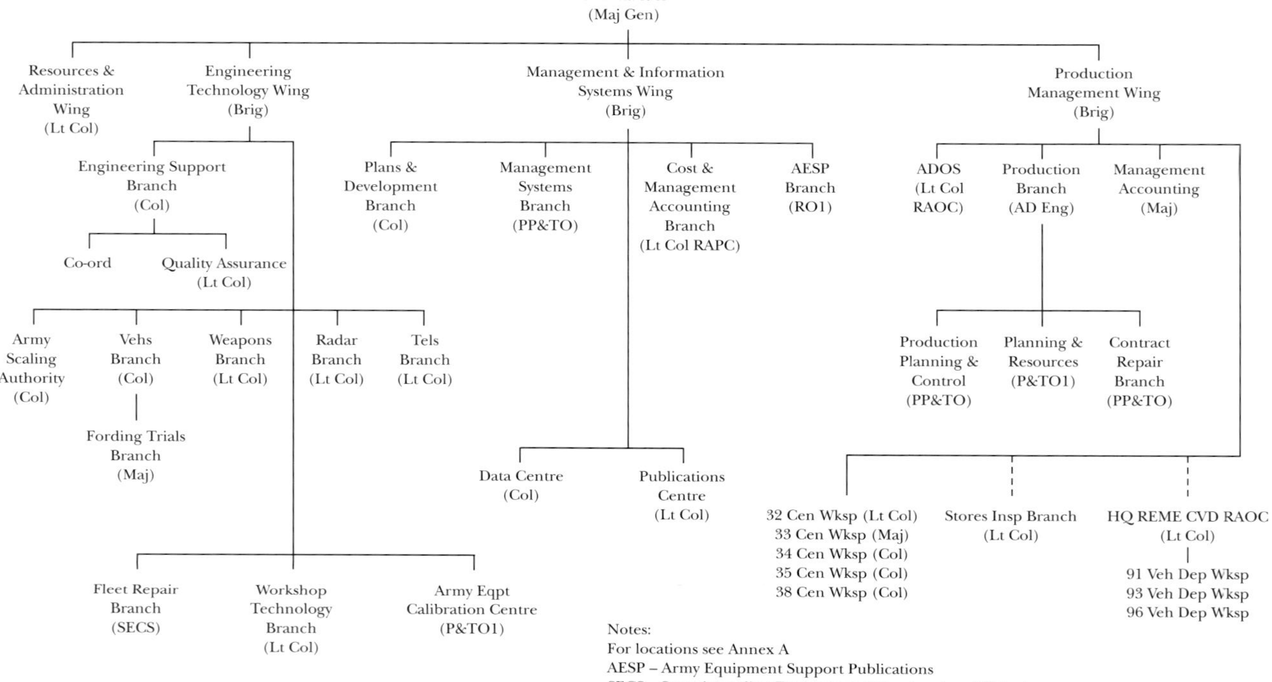
ORGANIZATION OF REME SUPPORT GROUP 1974
Commander (Maj Gen)
Resources & Administration Wing (Lt Col)
Engineering Technology Wing (Brig)
Management & Information Systems Wing (Brig)
Production Management Wing (Brig)
Engineering Support Branch (Col)
Co-ord
Quality Assurance (Lt Col)
Army Scaling Authority (Col)
Vehs Branch (Col)
Fording Trials Branch (Maj)
Weapons Branch (Lt Col)
Radar Branch (Lt Col)
Tels Branch (Lt Col)
Fleet Repair Branch (SECS)
Workshop Technology Branch (Lt Col)
Army Eqpt Calibration Centre (P&TO1)
Plans & Development Branch (Col)
Management Systems Branch (PP&TO)
Cost & Management Accounting Branch (Lt Col RAPC)
AESP Branch (RO1)
Data Centre (Col)
Publications Centre (Lt Col)
ADOS (Lt Col RAOC)
Production Branch (AD Eng)
Management Accounting (Maj)
Production Planning & Control (PP&TO)
Planning & Resources (P&TO1)
Contract Repair Branch (PP&TO)
32 Cen Wksp (Lt Col)
33 Cen Wksp (Maj)
34 Cen Wksp (Col)
35 Cen Wksp (Col)
38 Cen Wksp (Col)
Stores Insp Branch (Lt Col)
HQ REME CVD RAOC (Lt Col)
91 Veh Dep Wksp
93 Veh Dep Wksp
96 Veh Dep Wksp
Notes:
For locations see Annex A
AESP – Army Equipment Support Publications
SECS – Superintending Engineer and Constructor of Shipping

Annex C

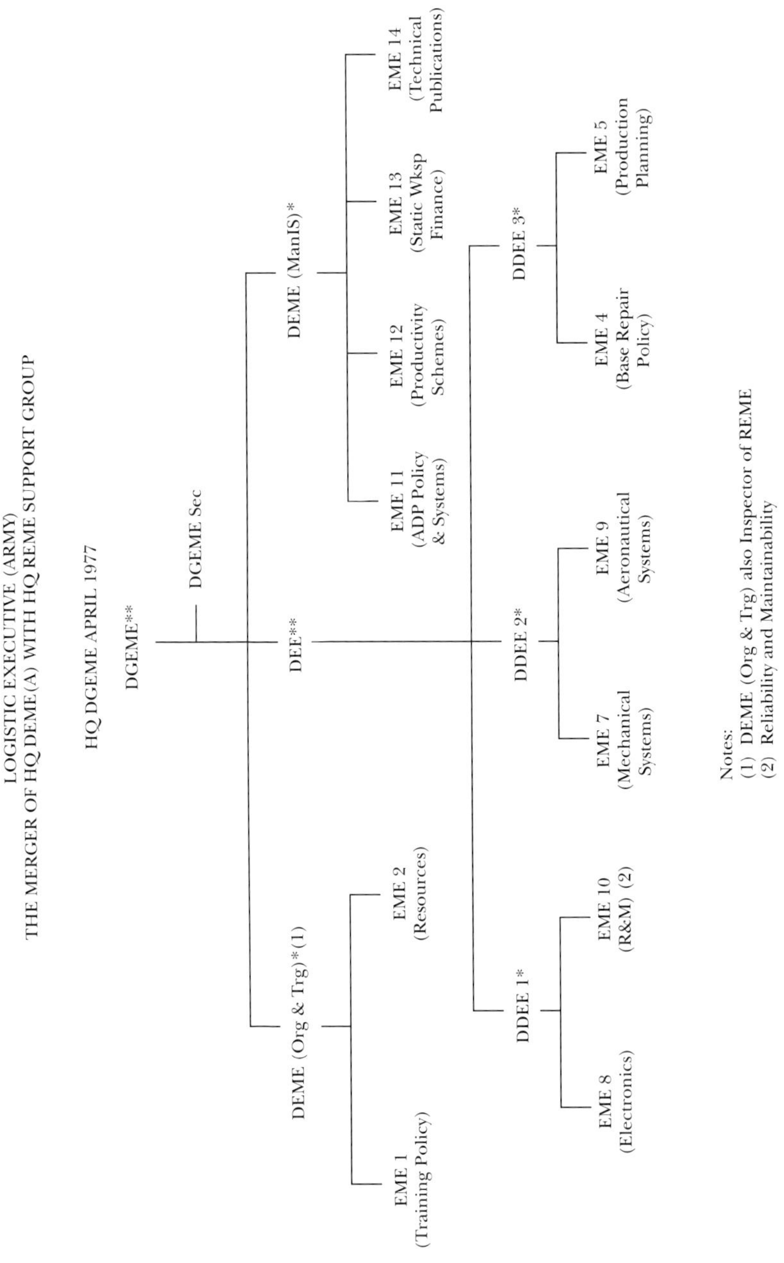

LOGISTIC EXECUTIVE (ARMY)
THE MERGER OF HQ DEME(A) WITH HQ REME SUPPORT GROUP

HQ DGEME APRIL 1977

- DGEME**
  - DGEME Sec
  - DEME (Org & Trg)*(1)
    - EME 1 (Training Policy)
    - EME 2 (Resources)
  - DEE**
    - DDEE 1*
      - EME 8 (Electronics)
      - EME 10 (R&M) (2)
    - DDEE 2*
      - EME 7 (Mechanical Systems)
      - EME 9 (Aeronautical Systems)
    - DDEE 3*
      - EME 4 (Base Repair Policy)
      - EME 5 (Production Planning)
  - DEME (ManIS)*
    - EME 11 (ADP Policy & Systems)
    - EME 12 (Productivity Schemes)
    - EME 13 (Static Wksp Finance)
    - EME 14 (Technical Publications)

Notes:
(1) DEME (Org & Trg) also Inspector of REME
(2) Reliability and Maintainability

Annex D

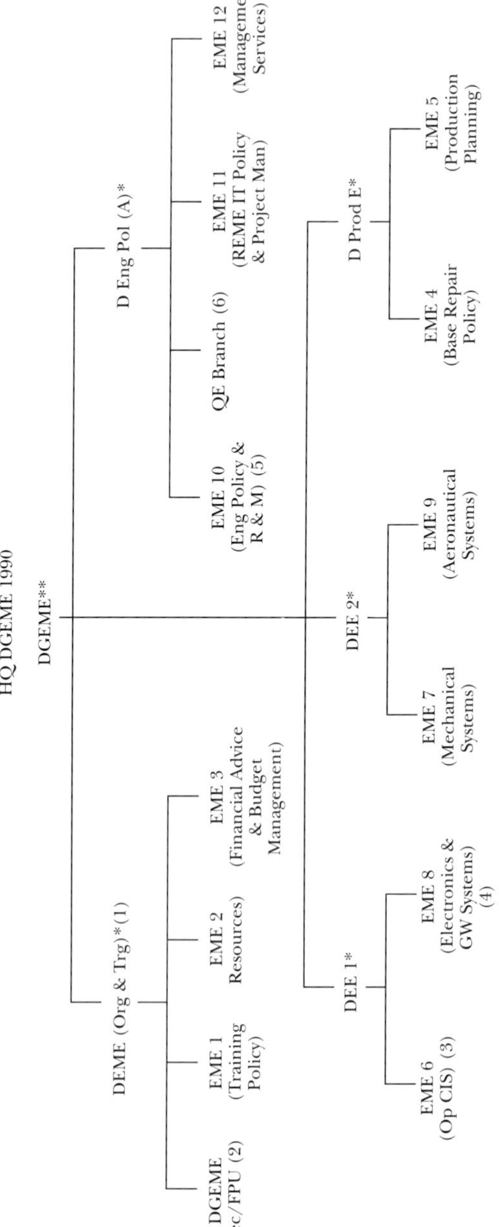

Notes:
(1) DEME (Org & Trg) also Inspector of REME
(2) FPU – Functional Planning Unit
(3) Operational CIS – PTARMIGAN, WAVELL
(4) Including RAPIER
(5) R&M – Reliability and Maintainability
(6) QE – Quality Engineering

Annex E

ORGANIZATION OF DGES (A) FROM 6 APRIL 1992
RESPONSIBILITIES OF ONE STAR DIRECTORS.

DES 1 – (Brigadier)

ES 11. Organization and Deployment; Planning & Resources.
ES 12. Secretariat; Corporate Planning; Training Policy; Civilian Management.

DES 2 – (Brigadier)

ES 21. ES and Information Systems Policy; Reliability; Availability; Maintainability; Durability; Health & Safety.
ES 22. ES Plans; Integrated Logistic Support (ILS) Projects; Development and Management.
ES 23. ES Services: Total Quality Management (TQM); ES Publications; Projects Procedures Cell (PCC) and Standards.

DES 3 – (Brigadier)

ES 31. Communications Equipments and Command and Information Systems: Equipment Support.
ES 32. Guided Weapons and General Electronics (including Test Equipment and Radar): Equipment Support.
ES 33. Army and RM Aircraft: Engineering Authority; Equipment Support.

DES 4 – (Brigadier)

ES 41. A Vehicles and Workshop Equipment: Equipment Support.
ES 42. Weapons, C, E and R Vehicles, Engineer, Marine and Railway Equipment: Equipment Support.

DES 5 – (Brigadier)

ES 51. Planning and Budgets.
ES 52. B and P Vehicles and General Mechanical Equipment: Equipment Support.
ES 53. Technical Spares Procurement.

Head of ES (F & S) (Civil Servant, Grade 6)

ES 61. Finance and Secretariat.
ES 62. DGES (A) Higher Level Budget (HLB).
ES 63. Individual Training Organization (ITO) Intermediate Higher Level Budget (IHLB).

CHAPTER 3

THE WORK OF THE EQUIPMENT BRANCHES

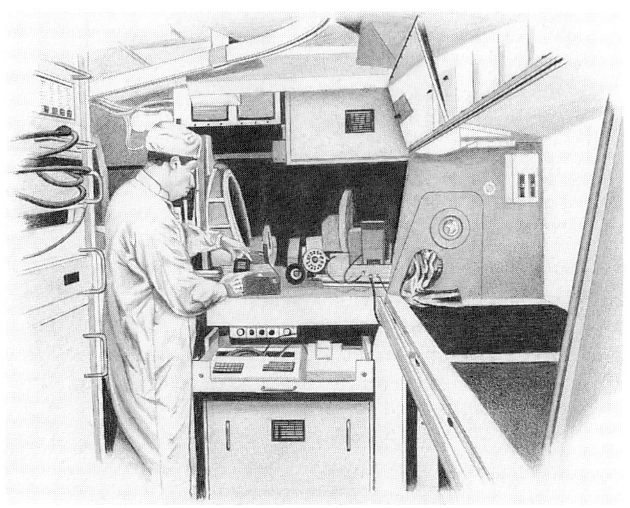

Introduction · Vehicles and Weapons Branch · Electronics Branch · Maritime Branch · Conclusion

INTRODUCTION

This chapter describes the work of the equipment branches which until 1977 were the executive agencies or engineering support units of Technical Group REME, subsequently REME Support Group, and thereafter were responsible to the appropriate directors in the Logistic Executive (Army) at Andover. The work of Aircraft Branch is included in Chapter 4.

The seven equipment branches, other than Aircraft Branch, at the beginning of the period covered by this volume were:

- Vehicles Branch at Woolwich, with Maintenance Advisory Groups (MAGs) at the Fighting Vehicles Research and Development Establishment at Chertsey and the Military Engineering Experimental Establishment at Christchurch.
- Vehicle Investigation Branch with the Fighting Vehicles Research and Development Establishment at Chertsey.

- Weapons Branch at Woolwich with a MAG at the Royal Armament Research and Development Establishment at Fort Halstead.
- Radar Branch with the Royal Radar Establishment at Malvern with the Joint Services Reliability and Maintainability Advisory Team and a MAG at British Aerospace, Stevenage.
- Telecommunications Branch with the Signals Research and Development Establishment at Christchurch.
- Fleet Repair Branch at Portsmouth.
- Fording Trials Branch at Instow.

Fording Trials Branch was absorbed by Vehicles Branch in 1972. The outline organization of the equipment branches within Technical Group REME in 1973 is given in Annex A to Chapter 2.

The Chief Equipment Engineer at HQ REME Technical Group, under the Brigadier Engineering Services, was responsible for controlling the equipment branches and for their completion of work on time. The branches also gave technical information and advice direct to EME 7 and EME 8 at the EME Directorate in London. When the Research and Development establishments at Christchurch and Malvern were rationalized (to become the Royal Signals and Radar Establishment), the two equipment branches concerned amalgamated at Malvern in 1977 to form Telecommunications and Radar Branch, later designated as Electronics Branch in January 1983. Similarly, in December 1982 one branch, Vehicles and Weapons, was formed at Chertsey by the amalgamation of the two separate branches concerned. When the new Logistic Executive (Army) was set up at Andover in 1977 HQ REME Support Group, as Technical Group had been renamed in 1974, was disbanded. Thereafter the engineering branches came directly under the two Deputy Directors (later Directors) of Equipment Engineering 1 and 2, at HQ DGEME LE(A) as shown in Annex C to Chapter 2.

Neither Technical Group nor subsequently REME Support Group were responsible for Army aircraft. Aircraft Branch at Middle Wallop, (formerly Aircraft Technical Services Unit) was the engineering equipment branch for Army aircraft and was responsible to the Chief Aircraft Engineer at Middle Wallop. He in turn reported to EME 9, the engneering staff branch, firstly of DEME(A) until 1977, and subsequently of DGEME in LE(A) and then (as ES 33) of DGES(A).

In 1988 the DGEME's charter, described in Chapter 2, laid down responsibilities to the QMG for 'developing, implementing and monitoring engineering support policy for Army equipment' and also 'the provision of advice on technical and special to service matters relating to in-service equipment support'. DGEME was responsible to the MGO for 'the provision of advice to MOD (Procurement Executive) and defence contractors on the assessment and improvement of reliability and maintainability of military equipment of his concern and providing the Army focus for reliability and maintainability engineering matters'.

These responsibilities were reflected in the charters for the equipment staff branches and their individual Maintenance Advisory Groups (MAGs). The role of a MAG was 'to advise the Engineering Support Planning Officer (ESPO) and/or the DGEME engineering branch and equipment designers on aspects of in-service maintenance and reliability to influence design such that equipment entering service is the greatest possible asset to the user and the least possible logistic commitment'. The MAG was the engineering liaison and advisory link between the REME Directorate and the establishments and organizations responsible for research, design, development and production of new equipments.

For many years the influence of MAGs on reliability and maintainability was important though not spectacular, but nevertheless this influence often resulted in considerable design changes. Until the early Eighties MAGs maintained a meticulous and persistent process of close, but not always harmonious, liaison with the design and technical authorities, resulting in the production of full Ease of Maintenance Assessments (EMA) for each new project. By the end of the Eighties, and after the issue of the QMG's Directive in 1988, the position of the MAGs was greatly strengthened and the increased influence that REME were to have in the field of equipment management is explained in Chapter 2.

Rapid advances in technology, especially in electronics, made it necessary for some MAGs to specialize and others to take a systems approach to major projects. Multi-national collaboration, which became more common, had its effect on MAG work. The most important change in the role and method of operation of MAGs was due to the arrival of competitive tendering and fixed price contracts for new equipments. This required much more effort in the earliest phases of a project, including precisely worded contracts. Many Army equipments had achieved long service lives with few reliability and maintainability problems. Some though, like the Infantry Radar No 14 (ZB 298), earned a reputation for unreliability, lost the user's confidence and were therefore under-used. In contrast, the MILAN anti-tank guided weapon system was a good weapon system, but again procured without UK MAG involvement. However, replacement of a failed graticule lamp in the tracker assembly required breaking the assembly's hermetic seal, which then needed eight day's work to complete the resealing procedure; MAG involvement at an early development stage would have spotted this problem.

Brigadier Sam Webber claimed in an article in the 1987 REME Journal that the main reason for the pursuit of reliability is not its cost-effectiveness, the saving in whole-life cost, as many people considered, but the availability of weapon systems to the user when they are needed in war. He pointed out that 'in the next, short, war, we cannot afford, operationally, to have downtime to any significant degree. We cannot afford to have equipment suicide'. He went on to say that even very reliable equipment would fail sooner or later, and it was then that the importance of maintainability would be demonstrated as faulty equipment was quickly repaired and returned to the user. Older readers may remember the days of the thermionic valve and the steady progress made since then towards solid state electronic chips with their greater reliability and physical robustness. REME staff in MAGs had met design engineers who saw their prime job as being only that of making the equipment work, rather than that of also making it testable or maintainable. The Corps put in a great effort to obtain reliability and maintainability in new equipment. If this did not produce all the results which REME would have liked, it was because more authority was needed to withhold payment for new equipments, until stated and agreed requirements had been met. It must be admitted, though, that exactly what was wanted in an equipment was not always clearly specified, and this had to be remedied, as indeed it later was.

The Work of EME 10b

Since ultimately, with whichever equipment they were involved, all the Equipment Branches were concerned with the achievement of equipment reliability, it is appropriate here to spotlight the work of EME 10b at the EME Directorate and the part it played in this process. The task of EME 10b was to act as the Army focus for all aspects of reliability and maintainability (R & M). This entailed specifying the R & M needs of each new project at the earliest possible stage – notably in General Staff Requirements – and then monitoring progress throughout the procurement cycle. The final act in this cycle was to measure equipment reliability in the hands of troops.

Until the early Eighties the combination of engineering policy branch staff cuts, and a lack of senior Army interest in reliability, had prevented the effective application of reliability engineering by EME 10b into the design and procurement process. At this time, however, there was a growing realization across all three Services, but predominantly in Royal Navy and Royal Air Force circles, that the intrinsic unreliability of the equipment inventory was operationally unacceptable. Put another way, high reliability was a 'force multiplier'. The Committee for Defence Reliability and Maintainability (CODERM) was the Tri-Service reliability focus and by the mid-Eighties it had succeeded in raising the case and status for achieving maximum reliability of equipment to a very high level, with Parliamentary Questions and National Audit Office reviews. REME officers played a significant part in all this activity, whether working alongside RN and RAF representatives in the CODERM Secretariat in London, or from Andover, where Colonel EME 10 and his staff were based.

Also by the mid-Eighties there was a new and very positive attitude towards reliability. From this new baseline, and with better staffing levels, EME 10b began to have a significant impact on the Army equipment procurement process. They inserted stiff requirements in GSRs to produce reliable and maintainable equipments, and became increasingly adept at following them through the complexities of the procurement system.

A major weakness in arguing for better reliability had always been the lack of worthwhile statistics on the performance of in-service equipment. EME 10b eventually succeeded in developing a simple and effective system, known as BERR (Battle-winning Equipment Reliability Return) which provided convincing information. In 1992, EME 10b became ES 21b and handed on a creditable reputation as the Army centre of reliability expertise.

VEHICLES AND WEAPONS BRANCH

Vehicles and Weapons Branch can trace its origins to the Maintenance Technique Development Establishment REME, formed at Arborfield in 1947, and Standards and Modifications Branch of REME Technical Services at Chislehurst, Kent. These later moved to Woolwich as part of Technical Group REME and amalgamated to form Vehicles Branch REME. An organization called Military Services had been at the Fighting Vehicles Research and Development Establishment (FVRDE) Chertsey since the Forties and was joined in 1967 by the A and B Vehicle Defects and Modification Sections of the branches at Technical Group REME. In 1970 this organization was renamed Vehicle Investigation Branch REME, and in 1972 the vehicle aspects of Vehicles Branch REME and Vehicle Investigation Branch REME were combined at Chertsey. Later Workshop Technology Branch took over some functions from Vehicles Branch. In 1982 Weapons Branch was disbanded, the conventional weapons work being transferred to a new Vehicles and Weapons Branch REME. Guided Weapons work went to Electronics Branch REME. Individual MAGs remained at Woolwich to ensure continuity of staff with specialist expertise.

In 1984 Vehicles and Weapons Branch took on the task of assessing field force tools and equipment from Workshop Technology Branch and in 1989, when Workshop Technology Branch was disbanded, Workshop Equipment Group and Workshop Processes Group became part of Vehicles and Weapons Branch, but remained at Woolwich. After all these amalgamations, with 8 MAG (C Vehicles) at Christchurch and 18 MAG (SP 70 Howitzer) at Fort Halstead, Vehicles and Weapons Branch had a geographic spread to match its range of responsibilities. 15 MAG, which covered medical and dental equipment, also remained at Woolwich, but was transferred to Electronics Branch REME. The organization of the branch in 1989 is given at Annex A.

Most MAGs were responsible for an equipment for its whole life, from 'cradle to the grave', including work on in-service defects and proposed modifications. This, though, did not go far enough. The ideal, yet to be achieved, was for responsibility to be extended to 'conception to the grave'. The traditional MAGs dealt with the workload from B Vehicles, C Vehicles, Mechanical Handling Equipment and most of the conventional weapons. In addition MAGs were formed to deal with specific new equipments such as the SHIR tank, one version of which was later adapted for British army service as CHALLENGER (17 MAG) and a new self-propelled gun (18 MAG). A MAG would normally consist of six to eight experienced artificers led by a major. There might also be several civilian P&TO grades and an HPTO specifically responsible for defects and modifications. A case in point was 6 MAG which was responsible for all B vehicles in service with the Army and RAF. This was commanded by a Squadron Leader RAF who had a REME team of one officer and seven artificers, an RAF team of one officer and eight RAF chief technicians and a civilian team of two HPTOs and six P&TOs.

To chronicle the work of Vehicles and Weapons Branch and its predecessors in full would demand a volume in itself, but examples in the following pages give a flavour of what has been achieved.

CHIEFTAIN Engine

The CHIEFTAIN L60 engine had never been completely satisfactory in its early years of service because of the various technical problems described in Chapter 6. Vehicles Branch carried out a detailed study of these problems and made a significant contribution to their solution through a programme of reliability improvements led by Major Reg Pearce which were introduced into service in 1978–80.

L60 Power Pack

One of the problems successfully solved concerned the engine cooling fan hubs. These were connected to, and lubricated by, the main engine lubrication system, and the oil feed pipes to the hub passed across the front of the cooling group, very close to the right hand belt tensioner. Failure or loosening of the tensioner allowed the pulley to damage one of the feed pipes, resulting in severe loss of oil. This was followed frequently by main engine failure. To overcome this fault, Vehicles and Weapons Branch proposed the removal of the oil feed system and the introduction of grease-filled hubs. The tensioner assembly was also improved. Trials at BATUS in Canada in 1981–82 and with the RAC Demonstration Squadron proved the modification to be successful. It then was agreed by Leyland and a Modification Instruction was issued.

Armoured Recovery Vehicles

5 MAG was deeply involved in the CHIEFTAIN ARV project, including a redesign of a prototype which led to considerable improvements in layout, maintainability, performance and reliability. Major advantages of the CHIEFTAIN ARV compared with the CENTURION ARV were the front-mounted 30 ton capstan main winch instead of a drum winch at the rear, and a $3\frac{1}{2}$ ton auxiliary winch to pull out the main winch rope. Two ARV prototypes were built by the Royal Ordnance Factory, Leeds, in the late Sixties. Military Vehicles and Engineering Establishment (MVEE – the revised title for FVRDE), Chertsey, Vehicles Branch, 5 MAG, and tradesmen on loan from SEME Bordon, carried out a great amount of work before the first vehicle went to SEME in 1971 for User Trials. The second prototype, partly redesigned, went to SEME in 1972 and completed its trials in a few months. This subject is described in detail in an interesting article by Major Ralph Mealor and Major David Axson in the REME Journal of 1974.

Armoured Repair and Recovery Vehicles

Hydraulic systems for armoured recovery vehicles are complex, but the original designs for both the CHIEFTAIN ARV and CHALLENGER ARRV nevertheless paid too little attention to the needs of those who were to maintain them. Insistence by the MAG led to the redesign in 1971 of the CHIEFTAIN ARV hydraulics. This involved rationalizing the system and the replacement of much piping and a series of individual components with a purpose-built valve-block. This single assembly eliminated numerous connectors and seals. Some years later the initial design of the hydraulic system for the CHALLENGER ARRV showed similar problems. Some pumps were virtually hidden and even minor work on a pump required removal of a hydraulic tank and the main winch for access. The early involvement of the MAG led to a better hydraulic design and relocation of a gearbox. In 1990 both development and user trials of the CHALLENGER ARRV were progressing satisfactorily; the vehicle was accepted for Army service and performed outstandingly well in the Gulf War. The user trials were conducted under the direction of Major Ray Gatward who was subsequently awarded the MBE for this work.

WARRIOR Infantry Combat Vehicle

Warrior

A very successful attachment to a contractor's factory was that of an Artificer Sergeant Major (ASM) assigned to give advice on the WARRIOR Mechanized Infantry Combat Vehicle project. The contractor, who won a development contract in 1979, did not accept at first that there was anything for the ASM to do. However, their experience with AFVs, especially APCs, had been diluted since they produced the FV 430 series and before long the Warrant Officer proved invaluable to them with his own up-to-date expertise. This was so much so that when he became due for a career posting some four years later the Managing Director made pleas to the Director General of Fighting Vehicles and Engineer Equipment for him to stay. The Warrant Officer, ASM R A Skinner, was awarded the MBE in 1988 for his work on this project.

The WARRIOR hull was constructed from aluminium armour fitted with a steel turret, on which was mounted a 30mm RARDEN gun and a 7.62mm Hughes chain gun. In 1988 the first armoured infantry battalion to be equipped was the 1st Battalion Grenadier Guards at Münster in BAOR, which carried out a full reliability trial in the first year of service. Two variants were developed for the Royal Artillery – an Observation Post Vehicle and Battery Command Post. These had advanced sights and electronic equipment, including the new Battlefield Target Acquisition and Engagement System (BATES).

The original concept for the WARRIOR power pack lower mountings required removal of four securing bolts behind an access cover beneath the hull to free the power pack. This required someone slim to crawl under the belly plate of the vehicle on flat ground, with preferably not too much mud! 5 MAG suggested a single screw-activated vice clamp system which could be operated from the side of the vehicle. This reduced the time to change a power pack in the field and removed the need to crawl underneath the vehicle. WARRIOR had two variants for use by REME in the field. Both these vehicle types were extensively trialled by Vehicles and Weapons Branch during 1986–88, under the direction of Major Peter Ellis. WARRIOR (Repair) mounted a Coles crane and was designed for the REME squadron and company fitter sections in the CHALLENGER tank regiments and the WARRIOR infantry battalions. It could also provide FRG support from armoured workshops, towing a purpose-built trailer carrying a spare power pack. WARRIOR (Recovery) had the same crane and had a double capstan winch and recovery spade to provide recovery support for the infantry battalions equipped with WARRIOR. Production vehicles for these battalions arrived in BAOR in 1989 and 1990 and were well received.

Bulk Handling System (DROPS)

One of the most notable examples of how REME contributed to defence procurement was illustrated by 6 MAG's substantial achievements during the project development of the Demountable Rack Off-Loading and Pick-up System (DROPS). This project was a vehicle-based bulk handling system to be used by the RCT for the planned outloading and resupply of ammunition, mines and explosives in NW Europe and, on an improved medium mobility chassis, for the RA to supply ammunition from a divisional supply area to gun positions. It involved mounting pallets or containers on 'flatracks' which could be transferred from a vehicle or trailer to the ground (or vice versa) by means of a Load Handling System (LHS). It also interfaced with a system for loading 'flatracks' onto or off railway wagons known as the Simple Rail Transfer Equipment (SRTE). Once the contracts for the validation equipment had been placed, 6 MAG was actively engaged with the manufacturers while the validation models were being built. On MAG advice many product improvements were made, such as the introduction of automatic brake slack adjusters, air driers on the vehicles, and extended oil change intervals. Further improvements made were the reduction of 'plumbing' and manual over-ride on the LHS, removal of all working parts and stowage lockers from the 'flatracks', the redesign of the engine installation to ease removal and integration of the SRTE hydraulic system. The hydraulic oil change interval was also extended from six months to two years, which at 120 litres per equipment, was a big saving in oil, as well as servicing time. This system was to be extensively used by the RCT in the Gulf War, described in Chapter 12, and proved the great value of 6 MAG's contribution to its effectiveness.

DROPS

Turret Systems

Since it was formed in 1967 under Captain Jim Barnett, 7 MAG had always dealt with turret systems. Major Robin Loader controlled the MAG over the period 1980–92 during which time projects included the computer-controlled Improved Fire Control System (IFCS), the Thermal Observation and Gunnery Sight (TOGS) and the Multiple Launch Rocket System (MLRS). The original target ranging for the CHIEFTAIN tank was a coaxially mounted 0.50 inch Browning machine gun. This was replaced in the early Seventies with a laser ranging system and towards the end of the Seventies the Improved Fire Control System (IFCS) was introduced. The final CHIEFTAIN turret enhancements were made in the late Eighties with additional turret armour and the TOGS, which had earlier been fitted to some of the CHALLENGERs issued to seven armoured regiments over the period 1983–1989. The early CHALLENGERs lacked the TOGS system but some 120 were retrofitted; more than 100 of them at 7 Armoured Workshop in Fallingbostel and the remainder in the UK at 18 Base Workshop. The line at 7 Armoured Workshop was run by Captain Bob Pollin who had previously been involved in the EMA of the system at Vehicles and Weapons Branch.

For the retrofitting of TOGS new tools in the form of specialized welding equipment and a plasma cutter were procured and the necessary fresh skills required to operate the equipment were learned. This specialized equipment proved to be vital for the reshaping and modification of metal work to accept the TOGS systems. Some forty-five tanks required modifying in this manner.

The initial teething and setting-up problems for the REME production team in BAOR were resolved by AQMS Ian Smith, an Artificer Telecommunications (reporting direct to the Commanding Officer, Lieutenant Colonel Philip Corp). He interpreted the ROF Leeds blueprints and retrofitted the first pilot CHALLENGER. The first tank was completed by the production team with great enthusiasm, and formally handed over to the Commanding Officer of The Royal Hussars in the presence of the Commander 1st (British) Corps, Lieutenant General Sir Brian Kenny. The full strength of the team involved in this task was over forty, including men on loan from LADs. The complexity of the task can be judged from the fact that it took about three months per vehicle from initial inspection to completion of the full retrofit.

The work involved external fitting of a sighting head and cooling pack, and included some drilling of armour. Internally, much of the turret had to be stripped out and seventeen extra black boxes, together with a mass of cables, fitted into an already crowded turret. A concurrent but unrelated modification entailed fitting a new NBC filtration pack with its controls and sensors. The task required mainly control equipment technicians, instrument technicians, gun fitters and metalsmiths. For each tank the task was broken down into stages, each having several activities.

Each activity had to be signed off by the tradesman responsible, then countersigned by an inspector before the next stage could begin. During the commissioning, a technician from the regiment receiving the tank sat in with the inspector, so achieving familiarity with, and confidence in, the product. This meticulous approach to quality minimised the problems of the lack of continuity with military tradesmen and paid dividends in customer satisfaction. Thirty months after the first tank was handed over, the last one was delivered, three months ahead of schedule. This was perhaps the largest and most complex task ever undertaken by a second-line workshop. For his work on this project ASM Smith, as he had become, was awarded the MBE; he was subsequently commissioned.

7 MAG was particularly successful in conducting a reliability assessment of the CHALLENGER tank fire control computer interface unit No 6. The failure rate of the computer system was a major cause for concern, but it appeared impossible to prove, without doubt, that the reliability of the unit was below that originally required from the manufacturer. 7 MAG made a detailed study in close co-operation with Swansea University, using an advanced form of Weibull Analysis, and a census of all equipment in service. The evidence of poor reliability was so strong that MGO was able to approach the manufacturer who took action which resulted in the saving of many thousands of pounds and introduced a more reliable unit into service.

7 MAG also carried out much effective work to bring into service the American-designed MLRS which was used to devastating effect in the Gulf War.

Power Pack Repair Facilities

CHALLENGER and WARRIOR power packs were larger and more complex than those of the CHIEFTAIN tanks and the FV432 APCs. It was decided that the power pack repair 'barns' in the armoured workshop MRGs, based on aged 10 ton trucks, were no longer adequate for the

Power Pack Repair Facility

long term. Vehicles and Weapons Branch, commanded by Colonel David Axson, was given the task in 1984 of finding a solution. Project CAPTURE was born, with Major Jim Walker masterminding the engineering proposals. A concept based on a 20 foot ISO container, with a side extension that almost doubled the floor area, was devised. Power packs were handled on special splitter frames mounted on air skates. The Branch built one concept demonstrator that was trialled in 6 Armoured Workshop in 1987. In the meantime, variations of the 'barns' were built and trialled in 5 Armoured and 7 Armoured Workshops during 1984–85 and were introduced into MRGs supporting CHALLENGER as an interim measure. These were still labour-intensive, slow to erect and take down, and did not provide satisfactory working conditions. The Vehicles and Weapons Branch concept provided the basis for a Minor Equipment Requirement for a purpose-designed facility; this proceeded as far as competitive tendering before falling victim to MOD financial savings measures.

At the start of the Gulf War in 1991 the inadequacy of the 'barns' in the desert was painfully obvious and the Containerized Power Pack Repair Facility was hastily revived, based on the best tender submitted in 1987. The contractor produced one fully containerized facility comprising three repair bays, a run-up bay and a stores/logistic bay. With air conditioning, light and soundproofing, power tools and recycling of washing solution and coolant, this facility provided a substantial improvement in productivity and working conditions. It was unfortunately not completed in time to see service in the Gulf, but later in 1991–92 it was extensively trialled – again in 6 Armoured Workshop.

Wheeled Recovery Vehicles

6 MAG was closely involved in the development of the Foden 6 × 6 Wheeled Recovery Vehicle. This was an important improvement to REME's capability, and the background to its introduction is of some interest. At the end of the Sixties REME operated three types of medium and heavy recovery vehicle. These were the ageing Scammell 6 × 6 medium recovery, the AEC 6 × 6 medium recovery and the Leyland 6 × 6 heavy recovery. It was decided that a single type of vehicle, capable of supporting all in-service wheeled B vehicles up to and including the Tractor and Limber Foden 6 × 6 FH70, should be procured. It was later required to support the new DROPS vehicles.

In 1971 SEME Bordon was given the task of carrying out a trial using a Volvo vehicle fitted with an EKA recovery system which had been vigorously promoted in BAOR. This trial proved that the EKA equipment was superior to those in service at the time; it provided a supported tow, which could be rigged in a fraction of the time for a suspended tow. As it was the policy to buy British, whenever possible, a search began for a vehicle that could carry the EKA recovery gear. The first phase of fleet modernization was a 'commercial' procurement of 130 Scammell Crusader 6 × 4 vehicles with the standard EKA equipment. These were deployed to Line of Communication and static units. In 1975–76 a feasibility study was carried out on the Foden 6 × 6 chassis used on the Tractor and Limber for FH70 and the 16 tonne Medium Mobility Load Carrier (MMLC). This study concluded that the basic vehicle was suitable and would give the added advantage of in-service commonality.

Prince Philip is shown the Foden by Corporal Brooke. Colonel David Axson looks on.

Unfortunately, at this stage, Foden Ltd went into receivership. In 1980 after lengthy negotiations the company became a division of Paccar and the project began to move forward. Four FH70 Tractor and Limber vehicles were converted to the recovery role, utilizing an improved recovery package of British design, developed by EKA and manufactured in the UK. Following a successful mating of the two systems, a further three purpose-built vehicles were tried out. This culminated in the production of 336 Foden 6 × 6 Recovery Vehicles, the first three of which were used for confirmatory trials. Vehicles and Weapons Branch was involved at many stages of the Foden development, including the User Trial, the EMA, and the Reliability and Maintenance Study. Its influence on the final product was substantial, not only in ensuring that the equipment could fulfil its intended role and be maintained in the field, but in promoting crew comfort and safety. A few typical examples to illustrate these points are:

- The original brakes quickly became inefficient and dangerous because of mud and water contamination. Overall efficiency was improved and maintained by more effective sealing of the components and the fitting of automatic slack adjusters.

- Road lights, floodlighting and illumination of controls were all considered inadequate and were improved by the contractor.
- There was a danger of the operator's feet being trapped when slewing and a foot rail was fitted.

In all, thirty-four unsatisfactory features were identified in the EMA alone. Twenty-nine of these were modified or redesigned. During service, the Foden Recovery Vehicle proved to be reliable, flexible and simple to operate, despite its relative complexity, and the merit of the contribution by MAGs was once again confirmed.

Small Arms

The 25 years from 1967 to 1992 saw significant changes in the small arms and machine guns issued to and maintained by the Army. NATO's love affair with the 7.62 × 51mm cartridge proved short-lived. In the late Sixties the rather worrying decision by the Americans to adopt the 5.56mm M16 family of weapons, against NATO standardization agreements, led to much discussion and debate. Extensive trials followed, leading to the adoption of a second NATO standard, the Belgian 5.56mm SS109 cartridge. This had a steel core to its bullet, which aided penetration and the destruction of the target. It was felt by some that the old 7.62mm round was unnecessarily powerful and heavy for the modern battlefield, where most engagements were at 300 metres or less. The 7.62 calibre round was retained for use in some machine guns where heavy sustained support fire might be required and also for specialized sniper rifle ammunition.

Britain followed the NATO lead in adopting the 5.56mm round, and the SA80 weapon system developed by Royal Ordnance to meet this requirement began its user trials in 1981. After several delays, mainly due to production difficulties, L85 Individual Weapons and L86 Light Support Weapons were issued to line units in 1986. The adoption of the SA80 had considerable influence on the day-to-day work of unit armourers, as its modern construction reduced the amount of detailed fitting and 'fettling' required, compared with its predecessors. Stoning of bents, repairs to wooden furniture and the tightening of rivets were becoming lost arts, as repairs were in the main reduced to component replacements or write-off.

There were other more complex weapon systems which came under the armourers' wing during the second twenty-five years of the Corps' life. These helped to redress the loss of specific armourer skills already mentioned and maintained job satisfaction. Probably the most notable newcomer was the Hughes Chain Gun, built in the UK under licence by Royal Ordnance for use in some AFVs. This weapon was a complete departure from the gas-operated machine guns previously in service with the Army, as it required an external electrical power source to function the gun. Gas stoppages became a thing of the past, a particular advantage when the gun is turret-mounted, and space to carry out necessary drills is at a premium. The design concept of the chain gun meant that armourers were given a new breed of faults to diagnose and repair, usually on a firing point, with frustrated crew members offering 'helpful' advice at opportune moments!

Another change to the armourers' repair repertoire came in the form of the RARDEN 30mm cannon. This gained its name from the Royal Armament Research and Development Establishment, Fort Halstead and the Royal Small Arms Factory, Enfield who collaborated in the design of the weapon in the early Sixties. Accuracy was the primary design requirement and this was achieved at the expense of a high rate of fire. RARDEN was fitted to FOX, SCIMITAR, FV432 and WARRIOR, but despite this armoured environment the repair responsibility was given to the armourer rather than the gun fitter. This served to increase armourer manning levels when armoured infantry replaced mechanized battalions, as RARDENs fitted to their WARRIORs required very careful and detailed maintenance. If handled without due care and attention, this weapon had the capability to punish the clumsy or faint-hearted.

At the other end of the repair spectrum the armourer also gained the evolutionary L96 Accuracy International PM sniper rifle. Like the SA80, this suffered from several production problems in its early life, but since the late Eighties it well and truly replaced the 19th Century design of the old L42. The use of high-impact plastic furniture on this and other small arms meant the removal of repairs to wooden furniture from all armourer training: yet another sign of the times.

From 1967–92 a great deal of development took place in the field of anti-tank weapons. Armourers had to maintain a variety of equipments, from the 120mm BAT family to the 66mm American Light Anti-tank Weapon. In 1987 the Army took delivery of the first of a new breed, the LAW 80. This 'fire and throw away' weapon was developed by Hunting Engineering and placed great emphasis on accuracy. To that end it combined a 9mm five-round spotting rifle with the 94mm main armament. Its 500 metre range, allied to a far higher hit-probability, represented a considerable advance in British anti-tank weapons. Experience gained in the maintenance of the trainer versions ensured that the armourer could, if called upon, help out with the real thing in an emergency.

Armourers continued to demonstrate their resourcefulness and adaptability maintaining the Army's ever-changing array of weapons from the freezing conditions of northern Norway to the jungles of central America and from the Falklands to the Gulf. Operating in these theatres tested the armourer's 'Mr Fixit' reputation to the extreme, and it was a matter of great pride that units operated on the premise 'when in doubt, call the armourer out'.

SA80 System Performance in the Gulf

When operating in desert conditions sand will always get into small arms, no matter how hard individual users try to prevent it. Both versions of the SA80, the Infantry Weapon and Light Support Weapon, suffered from well publicized sand ingress problems in the Gulf. Although not exceptional, compared with other small arms used under similar conditions, these led to a lowering of confidence by a significant number of troops issued with them and in the consequent failure of the weapons to function at an acceptable level. This lack of confidence varied, depending on both the unit and the individual questioned. At the time of the Gulf War, though, full familiarization of the weapon had not been achieved, and there is no doubt that, after approximately eighteen months in service, the SA80 was still in the transition phase when the war started.

From the armourer's point of view SA80 must be declared a success in the Gulf. Only one Defect Report concerning SA80 was received by Vehicles and Weapons Branch and that highlighted sand ingress rather than pure mechanical failure. It is not suggested by this that armourers were not kept fully employed in the Gulf; they were. Many long hours were spent repairing weapons. However, the majority of component replacements were considered 'fair wear and tear'. Considering the substantial amount of ammunition that had been expended, this result was not abnormal. There was the known problem of the fracturing of firing-pin tips, but this was not attributable to the theatre of operations and had been identified as a production quality problem. This particular failure, however, did not significantly affect the overall stoppage rate.

The users were also suspicious of the reliability of the Royal Ordnance Radway Green magazines and preferred to use the Colt M16 version, but there was little evidence to support this suspicion. There was, however, a great deal of evidence to back up the users' dislike of the cleaning kit, which left much to be desired in certain areas. To resolve these shortcomings various parts of the cleaning kit were subsequently replaced. The bayonet was also subject to criticism, as a substantial number suffered from broken tips, and the scabbard, sharpening stone and wire cutters were also found to be inadequate. Despite these problems, the bayonet was still highly prized by the infantry.

Although there was little evidence that the SA80 suffered greater problems than the weapons used by our allies, a House of Commons enquiry was held into the performance of the weapon. Vehicles and Weapons Branch provided a considerable amount of data for this enquiry which found that, in most cases, the fault which had occurred had already been identified and modification action taken.

ELECTRONICS BRANCH

In common with Vehicles and Weapons Branch, Electronics Branch was the product of reorganization, in this case the merger of Radar Branch and Telecommunications Branch and its detailed organization varied according to the projects in hand. In 1989 Electronics Branch was divided into four divisions with a mixture of MAGs and MSGs as shown at Annex A.

2 MAG was responsible for reliability and maintenance aspects of combat net radio, first at Christchurch when it was still part of Telecommunications Branch and then from 1977 at Malvern. The staff by then had been reduced from nearly forty military and civilians down to fourteen. They designed a test kit for Pye Commercial Radios which cut repair time by 50%, and saw the end of the old LARKSPUR range of radios and the introduction of the new CLANSMAN system. The hardware of the related seventy-seven Field Test Consoles had been delivered, but the abrupt withdrawal of the Honeywell company from the contract left the machines without any controlling software. With no previous experience in this field, within two years personnel of 2 MAG had written, proven and produced the software for the entire CLANSMAN range. Sadly their efforts – particularly those of ASM Reader and Staff Sergeant May – went largely unrecognized. 2 and 10 MAGs were involved with the Automatic Test Equipment (ATE) for CLANSMAN at field and base level. 2 MAG wrote the field test specifications and 10 MAG wrote the Honeywell Field ATE Test Packages, the computer software tailored for testing specific equipments. Major (Retd) Bill Meadows designed and built an alternative Test Rig Electronic which was widely used in the field for both LARKSPUR and CLANSMAN.

An early success for 3 MAG was the acceptance of sixty-five of their sixty-six suggestions to improve the FOX Night Sight. 9 MAG helped to obtain teleprinter equipment which was strikingly easier to dismantle than that originally presented to them. Digital facsimile equipment which was more reliable was also introduced and was well received by the users, partly due to modifications recommended and made before delivery. In 1989 this section of 9 MAG was headed by a R SIGNALS officer with a Foreman of Signals as an assistant project officer.

Another interesting area concerned Close Air Defence Weapon Systems. 1 MAG, initially in Woolwich and later at Malvern, worked closely with Short Brothers at Belfast, who developed and manufactured BLOWPIPE, JAVELIN and High Velocity Missile Systems. A change from contract repair to REME repair required a new look at this aspect of REME's task: for instance the aiming unit covers on JAVELIN were glued on to reduce weight, making it difficult in the field for a technician to carry out repairs, as it was necessary to heat up and prise off the cover. The MAG obtained covers that were sealed and screwed on and thus easier to deal with.

PTARMIGAN and RAPIER were two major systems of great operational importance, using advanced electronic technology. Because of this, REME involvement with them is described in some depth in the following paragraphs.

PTARMIGAN

PTARMIGAN replaced BRUIN as the Area Communications system providing secure communications to staff users down to brigade level. It was the largest mobile computer-aided communications system ever used by the British Army and was able to act as the bearer for WAVELL and other computer-based command, control and information systems. The main development contract was placed in 1973 when 9 MAG was part of Telecommunications Branch at Christchurch. The ESPO was Lieutenant Colonel Bob Alexander and the OIC 9 MAG was Major Peter Ost; they had four artificers with the contractors in 1974. Most of the work in those days consisted of commenting on vast numbers of draft specifications and working papers. The volume of paper was legendary, the Manual of Standards alone amounting to eight to ten well-filled EMER binders. The MAG had to answer many questions from the contractors such as ‘What’s in a Tels toolkit?’, ‘What’s an LAD?’, as well as general questions about lines of repair, repair trucks, forward repair teams and so on. In 1976 it was considered essential to define clearly what was meant by a ‘module’, since the PTARMIGAN repair philosophy was that the equipment was to be repaired by the operator replacing a spare module, to be carried on the vehicle. The definition was said to be still the subject of argument in 1982!

In 1981 and 1982 the major production contracts were let to the prime contractor and seven major sub-contractors. Following this, a series of sales demonstrations were run at short notice in 1984 and 1985 on behalf of the prime contractor, who was interested in selling the PTARMIGAN system to the US Army. This required fielding and demonstrating a divisional slice of PTARMIGAN in UK, and later in BAOR, before full logistical support was available – causing major problems for R SIGNALS, REME and the Communications Installation and Advisory Team (CIAT) in BAOR. Although the demonstration was successful, the US Army unfortunately decided to buy a cheaper and arguably less capable system from another country.

PTARMIGAN had two significant new areas of involvement for REME. Firstly, it was a distributed software-controlled communications system, which was the first system to be deployed throughout the whole of 1st (British) Corps. Secondly, the installation of PTARMIGAN into divisional signals regiments required major REME involvement in units in the field where installation work was carried out by teams of REME and R SIGNALS technicians, assisted by contractor working parties, working under QMG's staff direction on behalf of the MGO. Previously systems deployed in the Corps area could be bounded within a regiment/battalion or battery/squadron/company. In particular, maintenance and modifications had been relatively simple to control. With PTARMIGAN deployed across the whole Corps area and the Rear Combat Zone, great care and control was required to maintain the integrity of the system.

Modifications affecting operational software had to be implemented at the same time across the complete fleet. There had been three such system-level modifications by 1989 and they all required meticulous attention to detail to co-ordinate the contractor's working parties, establish build standards and distribute modification kits. This was necessary to ensure that the system was non-operational for the minimum time and this had to be kept secret.

The second new area of involvement was the installation of PTARMIGAN into Armoured Staff Vehicles in 1(BR) Corps. The CIAT (at that time an abbreviation for the CLANSMAN Installation and Advisory Team) had proved invaluable in helping units to replace LARKSPUR radios with CLANSMAN in 1977–1982, and proved beyond any doubt the value of an expert mobile team which could go anywhere in BAOR to give help with communications vehicle installations. The team was retitled Communications Installation and Advisory Team and given the task of co-ordinating the installation of PTARMIGAN into ASVs starting with 1st Armoured Division in 1984. The procurement of such equipment traditionally included installation, usually at the contractor's premises. With PTARMIGAN the QMG took on this major task, CIAT at one time having one officer and ninety soldiers from R SIGNALS, RAOC and REME. Almost all the first-class metalsmiths in the armoured workshops in BAOR were seconded to CIAT. This involvement with installation led to a dialogue between MGO and DGEME staff over the 'Offer and Accept' procedure. This was to agree that REME would not accept an installation task until the details of the work involved were known, so that a considered judgement could be made. The major difficulties arose through delivery of incomplete installations from the UK contractors and the frustrations of being unable to complete a task because a bracket or cable was lacking. This made great demands on the initiative of the CIAT members and the leadership of their officer. That they overcame their difficulties magnificently was reflected not only in the success of the system when installed, but in the award of the MBE in 1986 to Major Alan Morton.

RAPIER

In 1989 Colonel Andrew Platt recalled the evaluation trials in the early days of RAPIER development carried out by 21 Joint Services Trials Unit which had formed up at Ty Croes in Anglesey in 1966:

'21 JSTU complete with operators, trials controllers, administrators and a team of sixteen technicians, comprising REME, RAF and RAEME, flew out to Australia in October 1967. They took with them two sets of RAPIER ground equipments. British Aircraft Corporation established a base at the Weapons Research Establishment at Salisbury near Adelaide in South Australia to provide contractor support. Major John Drennan REME was the senior engineer, based at WRE Salisbury, and Captain Trevor Elkins, followed by Captain Andrew Platt, successively ran Launch Area 9 on Range E as the site and trials engineers. This was in the desert about 10 miles from the Range Head, and some 30 miles from the village of Woomera. The RAPIER equipment was totally cocooned in instrumentation cables leading to a monitoring room underground, itself linked to the Range Control building. There were as many faults in this complex equipment as there were on the RAPIER system itself. We had telemetry heads on the missiles as well, and thus we knew exactly what had gone wrong during a firing. We tested the weapon system to the limits of its specified performance, against trials objectives set by scientists in the Ministry of Technology.

'It has to be said that there were huge problems to start with. It took nearly a year before the first successful guided missile left the launcher. It was, however, a

spectacular missile fired at a Meteor Jet aircraft, and it gave the team and the sponsors some hope for the future. Nevertheless, there were some very bleak times, long hours, disappointments and many very clever scientists and engineers, some flown in from England, scratching their heads in their efforts to make the system work. Modifications were generated at an alarming rate, all carefully documented with defect reports and considered by a local modification committee. In the two and a half years that I served with 21 JSTU they numbered several thousand and were all later incorporated in the production weapon system. It was a very exciting raw engineering job, encouraged by the occasional successful firing. When we finally left Woomera in September 1969 we had fired 69 missiles. During the testing of the missile war heads, we once shot down a brace of Meteor Jets before lunch!

'Once the firing trials were successfully completed, the team carried out hot and wet environmental trials at RAF Tengah in Singapore and returned to the UK in October 1970 to the Royal Aircraft Establishment, Aberporth. Here work was starting on preparations for a sales drive at Whitesands in the USA, in which REME technicians were again indispensable.'

In October 1973 the RAPIER Cold Trials Unit was formed, an Army/RAF unit under Squadron Leader Jack Churcher with Captain Jim McLaughlan as OC Engineering Section. The aim was to show that the RAPIER missile system worked at 30°C below freezing. After two weeks of preparation the team, including Staff Sergeant K A Brown of 12th Light Air Defence Regiment Workshop, went to MVEE Chertsey. There they found in the cold chamber that their cold-weather clothing enabled them to work at thirty degrees below, provided that they did not absent-mindedly tap a screwdriver against the tongue, when, as one sergeant found out, it sticks! Under somewhat contrasting conditions, REME also helped the manufacturer's sales teams sell RAPIER to several countries – eg Brunei, Switzerland and Turkey.

Further development of the RAPIER system followed. The introduction of optical RAPIER in 1973, and the DN 181 Tracker Radar in 1978, went to form blindfire units at Field Standard A, to give capability in poor weather and at night. During the years 1981–83 all Field Standard A units were improved by cutting down the false alarm rate. More development work during the years 1975–89 provided a new system with improved resistance to electronic counter-measures, a better all-weather radar, better and more ready-to-fire missiles, and further development of BITE, the built-in test equipment. Introduction of Tracked RAPIER in 1983 was followed by development over the years 1983–89 with various improvements. The first Field Standard B2 equipment came into Army service in 1988, with an improved launcher, and electro-optical tracker. This provided improved reliability and reduced interference, with better deployment and reaction times. Operation was simplified and was less subject to clutter, rain, and bright sky backgrounds. BITE gave it a fault diagnosis and continuous monitoring facility.

The Joint Services Reliability and Maintainability Advisory Team (JSRMAT), co-located with British Aerospace at Stevenage in Hertfordshire, was responsible for MAG activities for the RAPIER ground-to-air missile system which was first used on operations in the Falkland Islands in 1982. JSRMAT carried out ease of maintenance appraisals as early as possible in project development, so giving the project manager an early indication of the development of his project. It also gave the designer the confidence that his design was acceptable, provided that he implemented the Ease of Maintenance Assessment (EMA) recommendations. JSRMAT had long advocated the use of Close Monitoring Teams (CMT) in equipment trials as the eyes and ears of the MOD on the ground, providing useful data for the Project Manager independently of the contractor. The CMT report was one of the factors that caused delay to the In-Service Date by highlighting the fact that the specification for reliability had clearly not been met for the RAPIER Field Standard B2 developed over the years 1975–88. The contractor offered to hold a reliability demonstration and again the CMT took an active part in collecting data for MOD (PE). Further modifications and design changes were incorporated at the contractor's expense, which otherwise the MOD would have had to pay for had it gone into service on time without the Team's scrutiny.

The RAPIER Test Package Evaluation Acceptance Team (TPEAT) was one of the first specialist maintenance software teams, having been set up in 1981 in a form which lasted throughout the Eighties. The Team evaluated test packages being introduced during conversion of the RAPIER Electronic Repair Vehicle (ERV) from a tape-driven to disk-driven system. At the start TPEAT access to contractors was very good, but after the introduction of fixed price contracts the contractor's immediate reaction was to limit severely TPEAT access and influence. An example was the Tracked RAPIER Mark 1A contract. This virtually excluded TPEAT activity during development, which led to its only formal involvement being a post-production evaluation of prime run tests, in which the system had to perform for a specified time without any recorded failure. There was no attempt to evaluate the diagnostic capabilities. Test packages for nineteen separate applications were assessed of which nine were shown to be unsatisfactory for a variety of reasons, including design and manufacturing errors in the software and hardware. Many lessons were learned, including the important one that design errors could be corrected and desirable changes made more easily and more cheaply during the early stages than at the end of a project. By 1989 a reasonable compromise had been reached, but the era of fixed price contracts still created problems if the writing of the contract was not sufficiently specific and tight.

Thermal Imaging

The successful development of cadmium mercury telluride in the early Seventies enabled a completely new class of day and night surveillance equipment to be developed which was independent of the level of visible light or any artificial illumination. It made use of the inherent infra-red radiation of a scene (ie the heat emitted by all objects) from which a cadmium mercury telluride detector produced an electrical output which, after processing, could be used to drive devices such as light-emitting diodes to compose an image. The system performance was superior to both passive optical image intensifier sights and active infra-red devices which were in common use before thermal imaging development. The MOD decided to develop thermal imaging sights to see through battlefield smoke, haze, mist, camouflage and darkness. This was to include the Thermal Observation and Gunnery Sight, the RAPIER System Thermal Imaging, and a Thermal Imaging system for PHOENIX, the remotely piloted vehicle operated by locating batteries RA. To enable the Corps to maintain the common modules and their parent thermal imaging systems the General Purpose Thermal Imaging Repair Facility (GPTIRF) was developed. This ensured repair at second line with a minimum number of Centrally Repairable Modules (CENTREMS) and items requiring contractor maintenance.

3 MAG access to the contractor designing the day and night sight for the WARRIOR Infantry Combat Vehicle was actively opposed by the prime contractor for the complete vehicle, with the result that the MAG was not involved until about three years after development had taken place. Eventually major deficiencies were found in aspects of maintenance, test equipment and technical publications, in addition to the sight failing to achieve its required range performance. Another sight manufacturer had to be found to ensure that WARRIOR had a satisfactory sight on entering service. The new sight had MAG involvement from the design stage and there was full liaison with design and development teams. During the Ease of Maintenance Assessment the sight was assessed as an acceptable commitment for REME maintenance, and in the user trials the indicated range performance exceeded the General Staff Requirement. The sight came into service.

Automatic Test Equipment

The origin of Corps interest in automatic test equipment is to be found almost a decade before the period covered by this volume begins, but unfortunately this was not described in Volume I of 'Craftsmen of the Army'. Since this initial interest provides the background to what became an extremely relevant and important subject, it is now included here.

In the early Sixties the increasing quantity, variety and complexity of electronic equipment planned to enter service in the next ten to fifteen years became a cause of concern. In addition to the traditional areas of communications and weapon systems, electronics were to be used in new fields such as infra-red weapon sights, fire control computers, battlefield surveillance, reconnaissance drones and aircraft navigation systems. Three main problems were identified. First, the sheer quantity and variety of this equipment, if supported by traditional methods, would bring with it a huge increase in the variety and quantity of test equipment required for the diagnosis of faults, functional testing after repair and testing to field and base specification standards. All this equipment would be very costly to develop, produce and maintain. This led to the second problem. Traditional methods of support would require highly skilled technicians specializing in a number of discrete equipment areas. They would be difficult to recruit and take a long time to train. Even if these problems could be surmounted, there was a third problem facing not only the Corps but user Arms as well. At this stage the benefit of higher reliability through the adoption of large-scale integrated circuitry had not yet been achieved, and the growth in complexity was so great that reliability of complete equipments was dropping. Also, the time required to test an equipment after repair was rising and the point was reached where, for the larger systems, there was the likelihood of a new fault occurring whilst testing an equipment following the repair of a previous fault! Lieutenant Colonel Roy Knowles was later to point out that 'Unless this trend is arrested, functional testing could become an interminable procedure – like painting the Forth Bridge'.

In this period the British Liaison Officer at Redstone Arsenal in the United States was Lieutenant Colonel Denis Blackman, and his remit was to alert the Corps to developments of interest. Thus it was that when Colonel Peathey-Johns (then ADEME EME 8) visited the USA in 1961 he learned of a development programme to produce a computer-controlled automatic test equipment capable of diagnosing faults in a range of different systems and testing them at high speed after repair. On his return he tasked Lieutenant Colonel Vincent Metcalfe (who had recently joined EME 8 to lead the section developing support for guided weapon systems) to write a one-page General Staff Target (GST) calling for the development of such an equipment which he saw as going a long way to alleviate the problems referred to above.

Lieutenant Colonel Metcalfe takes up the story:

'I thought this was a tall order and I decided to get some more information first from Denis Blackman and then write a longer paper to circulate to interested departments in the War Office. This paper was circulated in March 1962 and, having been generally welcomed, the GST was produced in January 1963 and submitted to the Ministry of Aviation (at that time the department responsible for equipment procurement) with a request that a feasibility study be undertaken. However, my involvement with the project which I had christened Multi-System Automatic Test Equipment (MATE), was soon to be terminated. P-J (as we knew

him) had spotted a gap in the Ministry of Aviation organization: no one was responsible for sponsoring the development of general purpose test equipment. He was successful in getting this responsibility delegated to DEME and a Lieutenant Colonel was added to the staff of EME 8 to discharge it. Thus in June 1963 Lieutenant Colonel Roy Knowles, who had been dealing with electronic test problems as OC Radar Branch at Malvern for the previous two years, joined EME 8 with responsibility to plan and arrange procurement of test equipment for the Army. He took over the MATE project and was to become an acknowledged authority on the subject of automatic test equipment.'

In the Sixties experience in the development and operation of ATE was confined to the USA and there was widespread scepticism about the concept throughout UK industry, and indeed within the British Armed Services. The immediate task was to generate interest and to persuade designers, producers and operators of complex equipment that test automation was essential to achieve failure diagnosis with the accuracy and speed necessary to meet operational requirements using the available technical manpower resources. Following a series of discussions with the defence ministries, R & D establishments and industry, a symposium was sponsored by DEME and held at Arborfield in May 1964, involving the Ministry of Aviation, selected manufacturers and representatives of the user Arms. This event resulted in a major breakthrough, with authority being given for a formal feasibility study to be undertaken. A Project Team was formed consisting of Mr Wiatr and Mr Frost from the Signals Research and Development Establishment at Christchurch representing the Ministry of Aviation, and Lieutenant Colonel Roy Knowles representing DEME. Feasibility Study contracts were placed with four companies; Hawker Siddeley Dynamics, British Aerospace, Honeywell (UK) and Elliot Instruments.

The Project Team conducted an in-depth study of ATE developments in the USA, in addition to controlling progress on the study contracts. The contractors were tasked with making separate practical proposals for the development of an automatic test system capable of dealing with the first- and second-line test requirements of most, if not all, electronic equipment in the field army.

There were many problems to be solved and difficulties to be overcome. In the technical area the interface between an automatic test system and equipments which had been, or were being, designed without automatic testing in mind presented particularly difficult problems. The contractors involved had considerable expertise in paper tape controlled automation but, in spite of pressure exerted by the Project Team, were reluctant to enter into the field of computer control (compact solid-state computers being still in the early stages of commercial availability). Interest by all three Services in the project but fundamental differences in their requirements also complicated progress; but general purpose test equipment was nevertheless a matter for joint Service procurement. Both the Royal Navy and the RAF favoured single equipment test facilities suited to static central maintenance bases, to which failed equipments could be returned for repair. The Army needed to take test facilities to failed equipments in the field, and therefore required a mobile system with multi-equipment testing capabilities. Despite these problems the feasibility study was completed early in 1965 and comprehensive reports and recommendations were presented at a high-level policy meeting held at MOD in April. It attracted considerable interest and support; the concept of automatic testing was accepted and the existence of the basic technology was established. However, it was decided that the development at that time of a multi-purpose test system in a form suitable for use in the field would involve an unacceptably large-scale and costly programme. The fundamental problem therefore remained: if no further progress was to be made in developing MATE, then weapon development authorities could not include it in their planning, and if they could not do this, then the development of MATE would never be possible. This was a classic 'Catch 22' situation.

MATE (GST 3618) was suspended following a paper by Major Rob Calderwood on its over-complexity and the vast range of adaptors required to support the variety of analogue equipments and their servo-mechanisms, together with limited use by each individual customer. MATE was, however, resurrected in 1977 by Mr Alan Johnson of 10 MAG. He, with OIC 10 MAG, saw that the growing commonality of digital electronic systems and lack of mechanical interfaces offered scope for a digital MATE. This was pursued by EME 8 in 1978–80 as a DGEME-sponsored GSR 3618 which became DIANA, a digital and analogue test facility. A similar commonality, based on the Thermal Imaging Common Modules, led to the concept of GPTIRF mentioned in the preceding section. This was treated as a separate Staff Requirement and was readily accepted in 1980 by the Weapons Equipment Policy Committee, which could see its application as the solution to two other projects laid before it: the Thermal Observation and Gunnery Sight and the Thermal Imaging Common Module System.

Although MATE was not to be realized, the project made a significant contribution to progress in the automation of test equipment and produced a number of positive results. The companies who participated in the feasibility study went on to develop automatic testers and, as more powerful and reliable small computers became available, many others followed. It can be said with certainty that REME played an important role in the early development of this industrial achievement. For the Army, sound foundations had been laid for the subsequent introduction of automatic testing for a wide range of electronically controlled weapons, telecommunications equipment and RAPIER.

The requirement for RAPIER ATE arose from the need to ensure high operational availability from a complex equipment. This required repairs to be carried out at unit workshop level, making some method of automatically diagnosing faults necessary. As a result, two ATE systems were introduced in the Seventies: a Land Rover-based Forward Repair and Test Vehicle to repair RAPIER at Battery Fitter Section level and a 4 ton truck-mounted Electronic Repair Vehicle for field repair at the main section of the Regimental Workshop. Both ATE systems were similar in their electronics but differed mechanically.

Although many problems had to be overcome during development, both DIANA and GPTIRF entered service in 1989, but initially they were unable to support many of their intended customers because the necessary application test packages (ATPs) were not available. The availability of ATPs for DIANA and GPTIRF improved during 1990 and 1991; by the autumn of 1991 ATPs had been issued to support Single Channel Radio Access (Terminal) and the Multiple Launch Rocket System. With GPTIRF the improvement was not as swift, and ATPs were still lacking when Iraq invaded Kuwait in August 1990. As a result GPTIRF was subject to intense activity to provide capability for Operation GRANBY. REME worked long hours, as did the contractors, to install ATPs direct from the production line into 7 Armoured Workshop's two GPTIRFs prior to shipping them to Saudi Arabia. After 6 and 11 Armoured Workshops were sent to the Gulf there was a total of seven DIANAs and four GPTIRFs deployed on Operation GRANBY.

A General Purpose Base ATE was proposed in 1979 to support equipments not covered by DIANA, and was targeted for CHIEFTAIN IFCS, RAPIER DN181 and MILAN base repair at 35 Base Workshop, due to a proliferation of Special to System Test Equipment within the Workshop. Membrain, a subsidiary of Schlumberger, won the contract with a development of their MB7700 series ATE used in the PTARMIGAN ERV, following an initial study by three contractors. This ATE was deployed to 35 Base Workshop in late 1981 and put into service in 1982. In 1989 one of the experts wrote 'all the projects targeted at the ATE have had tortuous paths to tread and indeed some have failed'. However, the problems were addressed and, increasingly into the Nineties, ATE was being utilized effectively in the workshop.

In 1980–81 Lieutenant Colonel Pat Hemsley, OC Telecommunications Division of Telecommunications and Radar Branch, wrote a paper reviewing the general principles of software, its characteristics and general management, and the existing practices of RN, RAF, R SIGNALS and REME. He proposed a Software Division be formed at Telecommunications and Radar Branch, having a Software MAG with specialist software teams and a Software Techniques Group. The specialist software teams were to be attached to existing specialist equipment MAGs and Test Package Evaluation and Acceptance Teams (TPEATs) were to be established. These would provide a means of evaluating the software for test systems throughout the software life cycle in order to ensure that ATPs were reliable and helped rather than hindered the user. In the event Lieutenant Colonel Hemsley's proposal was implemented in the more restricted field of maintenance software, leaving aside the broader issues of operating systems. The adopted title was Maintenance Software Division.

To conclude, REME had taken the lead in seeking to introduce ATE as soon as possible but the twenty-five-year history of ATE in REME up to 1989 had not been a great success story. There were many reasons, but the lack of experience of all concerned at the start was the main one. Many of the problems encountered while trying to bring ATE and the test packages into service were not foreseen and were underestimated. However, the difficulties would have been far greater without Maintenance Software Division and TPEATs identifying problems at the earliest possible time, and thereby keeping them to a minimum. By 1989 the future looked far better as the Corps had learned from experience how to specify accurately REME ATE test package requirements, and MOD (PE) learned how to procure test packages to meet these requirements. Industry, too, had become more experienced in the development of ATE and test packages requested from them.

Logistic Support Modelling

A logistic support model was first introduced into Telecommunications Branch in the Seventies. It was based on work undertaken by Lieutenant Colonel Ron Middleton and recommended, on purely cost grounds, the most economic repair option at Base level. The options available were: repair by REME, repair by contractor, or discard. This model became known as 'REPOL', and was adopted by Telecommunications and Radar (now Electronics) Branch on amalgamation.

During the mid-1980s it was considered that, with continual improvements being made in the capability to diagnose and therefore repair at Field level, a new model should be developed to address this level of repair. The improvements in capability were, in the main, brought about by the introduction of ATE systems. By 1989 the new model was completed and was given the name 'REPDIS'. With this model it was now possible to formulate a cost-based 'repair or discard' policy at Field level as well as a Base analysis similar to REPOL. In developing REPDIS the opportunity was taken to consider some more obscure (but important) costs than were considered by REPOL. This led to a very comprehensive modelling facility used regularly by MAGs as an input to their Ease of Maintenance Assessments.

MARITIME BRANCH

Introduction

The history of Fleet Repair Branch, later Maritime Branch, was not covered in the first volume. The Branch had been in existence in one form or another since December 1890 when Mr James Hay became the Superintending Engineer and Constructor of Shipping (SECS) and took over the construction of War Department vessels from an Admiralty Overseer. In 1951 the Fleet Repair Unit REME was formed and it was fully civilianized in 1961, having in 1960 been renamed Fleet Repair Branch (FRB) when it became a part of Technical Group. In 1969 there was a technical staff of fifteen, of whom the SECS was Mr Alan Blight, who had been appointed in 1968. He later published two very interesting articles on the maintenance of the Army Fleet: 'Fleet Repair Through the Ages' in the REME Journal for 1976 and 'Marine Engineering in the Army Navy' in the Journal of Naval Engineering December 1985.

At the beginning of the Seventies the RCT had more than one hundred craft including eleven Landing Craft Tank, twelve Ramped Powered Lighters, General Service Launches, Harbour Launches and forty-seven other craft. There were also over four hundred MEXEFLOTE pontoons and other equipments. MEXEFLOTE steel pontoons could be connected together to provide Class 60 rafts, causeways and floating platforms. They were accepted into service in the period 1969–71. REME was responsible for the repair of all these craft which included the basic condition of the craft, the integrity of the structure and the reliability of the machinery and installed equipment. A continuous survey system was introduced in the Sixties and was still operating at the start of the Nineties.

In the Sixties there was one Assistant Superintending Engineer and Constructor of Shipping (ASECS) and two overseers for the vessels at Singapore and in the Gulf, and one ASECS in both Hong Kong and Malta. The SECS and his HQ staff were based in Hilsea Lines at Portsmouth.

Rationalization

In 1967 it was decided to rationalize Water Transport and from April 1969 the Navy Department assumed responsibility for major repairs and refits of Army marine craft operated by the RCT, which were then deployed in Cyprus, Hong Kong, Malta, the Gulf and Singapore. The effect of the 1969 rationalization was that the Naval Dockyard was transferred to commercial hands. The Royal Navy then set up a Naval Contracts Department to be responsible for all contract repairs. As far as RCT vessels were concerned FRB still retained responsibility for their survey and condition, and the production of specifications for contract repair. This arrangement, which also covered the Gulf, continued until the Army left Singapore in 1971. In Hong Kong, however, the Royal Navy had no facilities for repairs of small craft, and the first- and second-line work was carried out by the RCT Squadron Workshop backed up by local contract repair controlled by FRB. In Cyprus there was no change and FRB retained its responsibilities unaltered into the Nineties. In Malta a Royal Navy Contracts Section was set up when the Dockyard was transferred to commercial hands and this continued until Army vessels were run down there in 1970. In the UK the Navy began to undertake major repairs and all scheduled refits. They also undertook all emergency repairs beyond REME resources and routine slipping of vessels beyond Army resources, although FRB continued to oversee the work. The refits were carried out in Royal Dockyards or by civilian contractors overseen by Naval staff with FRB providing technical liaison.

From 1969 FRB ceased to be the design authority for all Army vessels, this responsibility being transferred to the Navy except for vessels built before 1970. In 1977 Fleet Repair Branch was renamed Maritime Branch.

There was a major change of policy in 1983 when the task of carrying out 'overseeing' duties was transferred back from the Royal Navy to the Army, which was welcomed as a sensible change, and which also brought greater job satisfaction to the Branch technical staff. The Branch moved that year, after twenty-one years at Hilsea, into temporary accommodation at St George Barracks at Gosport for six years. A further study, 'Rationalization of Water Transport' in 1987, resulted in the management of the Ammunition Vessel *St George* and the range clearance fleet operated by 18 Maritime Squadron RCT being transferred to the Navy. This reduced the size of the RCT fleet to fifty-five vessels and small craft, plus 421 MEXEFLOTE pontoons and associated equipment. Maritime Branch moved out of its temporary accommodation in 1989, this time into two misappropriated Married Officers' quarters, which were also only a temporary home. There it stayed until September 1991 when it moved into permanent accommodation suitably located in McMullen Barracks, at Marchwood Military Port, Southampton.

New Equipment

During the years 1969–71 the MEXEFLOTE pontoons and ancillary equipment were accepted into service, together with five 47 foot Workboats Mark II and six 41 foot Command and Control Launches (CCLs). The CCLs were the first vessels in the Army fleet to be constructed from glass reinforced plastic. The new Workboats, however, were of all-welded steel construction; three of these were still in service at Marchwood Military Port in the Nineties.

Between September 1974 and August 1975 FRB completed fifteen design projects, including the design of a special roll-on/roll-off pontoon for Marchwood Military Port. In Cyprus the permanent slipway and trolley for locally based vessels at the Akrotiri mole in the Western Sovereign Base Area was designed, together with a MAXI-MEXEFLOTE raft and docking blocks to refit a Ramped Powered Lighter (RPL) in Cyprus before the new slipway was available.

The twelve years 1977–89 saw 80% of the RCT Fleet renewed. Two Landing Craft Logistic, *Ardennes* and *Arakan*, came into service in 1977 to replace the Landing Craft Tank. The Ammunition Vessel HMAV *St George* was built in 1981 to replace a Landing Ship Tank. A new class of 15 metre Range Safety Craft was procured and two new 24 metre Range Safety Craft were built for operations in Cyprus and the Hebrides. Four Landing Craft Vehicle and Personnel were obtained for UK, Belize and the Falklands. Nine Ramped Craft Logistic (RCL) were procured for UK, Cyprus and Hong Kong as well as eight new harbour launches.

In 1982 the two prototype RCLs, *Arromanches* and *Antwerp*, two Workboats Mark II, a harbour launch and five MEXEFLOTE rafts were sent to the Falklands on Operation CORPORATE where they played a very important role in ship-to-shore transfer of men and equipment. Maintenance support was provided by a Naval party operating from a Depot repair vessel.

Overseas Visits

In the mid-Seventies new overseas commitments arose even as many other overseas stations closed. MEXEFLOTE pontoons were deployed to Masirah and Salala in Oman and RPLs were deployed to Belize in Central America. ASECS from Marchwood was required to undertake surveys and oversee repairs. The survey and repair task in Belize was especially demanding and is described in Chapter 9. Although in the late Eighties facilities in Belize were much improved, it was still necessary to return RPLs to the UK for a Periodic Survey and refit. After the campaign in 1982 Maritime Branch staff also visited the Falklands as necessary to advise on technical matters.

The Nineties

Mr Alan Blight retired in 1989 after twenty-one years as Superintending Engineer and Constructor of Shipping – perhaps the longest time any one man has held such a responsible post since the Corps was formed. The new SECS was Mr Michael Warner whose former post as Deputy was abolished. The Branch continued to provide engineering support world-wide for the RCT fleet. In this task it was helped both by 17 Port and Maritime Workshop at Marchwood, with its excellent new facilities, and by civilian contractors. This provided a very efficient balance of resources, attaining an 87% availability of vessels for operational use. Two typical contrasting examples of tasks carried out were the refitting in 1991, in a Scottish yard, of the Landing Craft Logistic HMAV *Arakan* and that of the Ramped Powered Lighter, RCTV *Forth*, which was towed to Penzance to be refitted and then sent back to Belize. Other work included a contract to repair eighty MEXEFLOTE pontoons. The Branch drawing office helped MOD (Navy) in 1991 with an inclining experiment and weighing of a 47 foot Workboat Mark II which was then to be redesigned to improve its habitability and fire-fighting capability.

The strength of the Maritime Branch over the years was based on a small, enthusiastic and professional team, much helped by unusual continuity in their appointments, who travelled the world to ensure that the RCT fleet was maintained in a safe and seaworthy condition. In this task they succeeded admirably.

CONCLUSION

There is no doubt that the skill, determination, hard work and persuasiveness of so many officers, soldiers and civilians in the equipment branches and MAGs made a major contribution to the reliability and maintainability of new Army equipment during nearly a quarter of a century. Ever more complicated and effective weapons and equipment were brought into service and eventually came under their scrutiny from their conception. The aim of equipment reliability involvement from 'conception to the grave' had been achieved. Without the work of the equipment branches the policies and plans made by higher authorities in the MOD and at LE(A) would not have been so fruitful and the high quality of military equipment might not have been so well demonstrated in the Falklands, the Gulf and in Northern Ireland, when put to the ultimate test.

Annex A

EQUIPMENT BRANCH ORGANIZATION IN 1989

Vehicles and Weapons Branch – Chertsey

5 MAG	Chertsey	A Vehicles.
6 MAG	Chertsey	B Vehicles and RAF Mechanical Transport.
7 MAG	Chertsey	Turret Systems and MLRS.
8 MAG	Christchurch	Plant, Mechanical Handling Equipment and Bridging.
11 MAG	Chertsey	Container Bodies, Generators, Field Force Tools and Miscellaneous Equipment.
14 MAG	Woolwich	SA & MG and Gun Systems.
16 MSG	Chertsey	Light A Vehicles Defects and Modifications.
17 MAG	Chertsey	CHALLENGER MBT.
18 MAG	Fort Halstead	Self-Propelled Artillery.
19 MSG	Chertsey	Heavy A Vehicles Defects and Modifications.
RT&R Group	Chertsey	Reliability, Trials and Recovery.
Workshop Equipment Group.	Woolwich	Workshop Plant and Equipment.
Workshop Process Group	Woolwich	Workshop Materials, Processes and Techniques.
REME Special Trials Group	Chertsey	Short-Term Cover for User Trials of CHALLENGER ARRV.

Electronics Branch – Malvern

Division 1

30 MSG	Malvern	Maintenance Software, Control of the Army ATE Support Centre.
31 MSG	Malvern	R&M and GPTE.
35 MSG	Malvern	IT Development and Operation, Drawing Office.

Division 2

JSRMAT	Stevenage	Rapier Field Standard C Hardware and Software.
20 MAG	Filton	Rapier Field Standard C Software.
34 MSG	Malvern	PDS Rapier Equipment.
36 MSG	Malvern	Rapier Spares and Publications.
38 MSG	Malvern	Rapier Modifications.

Division 3

1 MAG	Woolwich	Guided Weapons and Close Air Defence Weapon Systems.
3 MAG	Malvern	Night Vision, Thermal Imaging and OE Projects.
9 MAG	Blandford	WAVELL, PTARMIGAN, Electronic Warfare and Battlefield ADP.

Division 4

2 MAG	Malvern	Communications Equipment and Cipher.
4 MAG	Malvern	Radar Systems and Area Communications.
15 MAG	Woolwich	Medical and Dental Equipment.
32 MSG	Malvern	Vehicle Communications Installations.

CHAPTER 4

REME SUPPORT TO ARMY AVIATION

Introduction · Army Aircraft Changes over the Years ·
Aircraft Engine and Avionics Technical Development ·
Development of Aircraft: the REME Contribution ·
Development of REME Support ·
Detection and Prevention of Premature Failure · Servicing Philosophy ·
Battle Damage Repairs · Accident Investigation and Flight Safety ·
Regimental Matters · Honours and Awards · Conclusion

INTRODUCTION

Volume 1 described how in 1958 REME took over responsibility from the RAF for first- and second-line servicing of Army aircraft. This followed the decision in 1957 that the Army Air Corps should assume responsibility for manning and operating single-engined unarmed light aircraft of all-up weight not exceeding 4,000 pounds, used in air observation post (AOP) and light liaison roles. Development of the part played by REME in Army aviation in the years covered by this volume is one of the greatest success stories in the Corps' history to date.

ARMY AIRCRAFT CHANGES OVER THE YEARS

There were progressive major changes to Army aircraft over the years from 1958 onwards. Their weight, engine power and technical complexity, including communications equipment and weapon systems that were subsequently introduced, all developed to an astonishing degree. The Corps played an increasingly important part in these developments, as new aircraft were introduced into the Army Air Corps, some of which are described in outline in the following paragraphs.

The SIOUX AH Mark 1 had an all-up weight of 2,950 pounds. It was a military version of a Bell Agusta with a distinctive two-bladed main rotor and two-bladed tail rotor powered by a 265 BHP piston engine. It was progressively replaced by the GAZELLE AH Mark 1 from 1973 to 1978.

The ALOUETTE AH Mark 2 was a French Sud Aviation 460 SHP turbine engine three-bladed main rotor machine with an all-up weight of 3,300 pounds. The fleet was initially deployed in UK and BAOR but eventually concentrated in Cyprus. It was withdrawn from service in December 1988 and replaced by the GAZELLE AH Mark 1.

The BEAVER AL Mark 1 was a De Havilland (Canada) single-engine, high wing, five-seater monoplane with a nine-cylinder radial piston engine. It first entered service in 1961 and was used particularly in the Far East, including operations in the Brunei campaign. There was also a liaison flight in BAOR. The aircraft at BATUS in Canada was sold in October 1985, leaving one in Northern Ireland for air reconnaissance and one at Middle Wallop for pilot training. BEAVER was withdrawn in 1989 and replaced by the ISLANDER.

The SCOUT AH Mark 1 came into service in 1962. It was a five-seater used for liaison, designed by Saunders Roe and powered by a 685 SHP Bristol Siddeley Nimbus turbine engine. It was given an anti-tank role in 1969 when it was fitted with the Nord Aviation SS11 wire-guided missile system and the Avimo Ferranti 120 roof-mounted optically stabilised sight. The latter produced for REME their aviation baptism in problems of misting, vibration, windscreen wiping and washing and failure to track. The anti-tank missile was fired in action for the first time in the Falklands in 1982 against Argentinian ground installations. The already established pintle-mounted GPMG was also used in the Falklands campaign. IS duties in Hong Kong required SCOUTS to fly over water for long periods so they were modified to use flotation equipment in 1971. The SS11 missile system, less the sight,was declared obsolete in 1987.

The GAZELLE AH Mark 1 came into service in 1973 having started life as the Sud-Aviation SA 340. The maximum all-up weight was 3,750 pounds and the maximum engine power from the Turbomeca Astazou engine, produced jointly by the French and Rolls Royce, was 600 SHP.

The AGUSTA 109A was basically an eight-seater helicopter but had a variety of seat configurations. It had an all-up weight of 5,400 pounds and was fitted with a 400 SHP Allison engine. The first two were captured in the Falklands and a further two were purchased later.

The LYNX was the replacement for the SCOUT and a product of the Anglo-French helicopter project which also produced the GAZELLE and PUMA. The LYNX AH Mark 1 with an all-up weight of 9,600 pounds was fitted with two Rolls Royce Gem engines (the Army's first twin-engined helicopter) each of 900 SHP. In 1985 the requirement was confirmed to improve the battlefield capability and agility of the LYNX Mark 1 by introducing more powerful Gem engines, a three-pinion main rotor gearbox, reverse direction tail rotor and structural strengthening. This increased the all-up weight from 9,600 pounds to 10,750 pounds and improved directional control of the aircraft. The new standard became the LYNX Mark 7 and a rolling modification programme at RNAY Fleetlands commenced in January 1987, with the first LYNX Mark 7 entering service in 1988. The LYNX AH Mark 9 or Light Battlefield Helicopter (LBH) based on the LYNX Mark 7 filled the requirement for greater airmobility on the battlefield which was highlighted by exercises held in BAOR in 1984. Some of the main differences between the Mark 9 and Mark 7 aircraft were a wheeled undercarriage and associated hydraulics instead of skids; secure speech fitted as standard; no built-in ATGW system; fitment facility for GPMG and replacement of main rotor blades with composite blades with an improved new design for their shaping. The first aircraft were in service in 1990 with 9 Regiment AAC – the dedicated AAC regiment of 24 Airmobile Brigade. A total of twenty-four LBH were required, sixteen of which were to be new build by Westland and eight to be conversions from Mark 7 reserve aircraft.

The Pilatus Britten-Norman ISLANDER was a conventional twin-prop, high-wing monoplane of all-metal construction with a fixed tricycle type undercarriage powered by two 320 SHP Allison gas turbine turbo-prop engines. Its main role was reconnaissance in Northern Ireland. REME maintained the five aircraft at first line, including engine changes, but all other work was undertaken by the manufacturer.

AIRCRAFT ENGINE AND AVIONICS TECHNICAL DEVELOPMENTS

Engines in Army aircraft have come a long way from the AUSTER Mark 6 with its simple upside-down, normally aspirated, four cylinder petrol De Havilland Gypsy engine, developing about 180 BHP. The same engine was enhanced by using fuel injection to produce 215 BHP in the SKEETER helicopter delivered by Saunders Roe in 1958. The SIOUX helicopter had a turbo-charged Lycoming 265 BHP engine. The REME technicians maintaining this engine found themselves introduced to the Turbomeca Artouste 460 SHP and Bristol Siddeley Nimbus 685 SHP turbine engines, both coming from the same French family, but with very different reliability and appearance. The former was used in the ALOUETTE helicopter and the latter in the SCOUT. The Nimbus engine suffered from problems that were never fully cured. A third member of this French family, the Astazou 600 SHP engine, fitted to the GAZELLE, proved to be a very reliable engine, but it too had its problems. The introduction of the LYNX into service in 1978 marked the Army's first twin-engined helicopter and its first modular designed engine. All seven modules of the Rolls Royce Gem could be changed at second-line aircraft workshops and repaired engines could be checked for performance on their semi-portable test bed facility. Problems with the Gem engine resulted in an average engine removal rate more than three times anticipated. As a result Rolls Royce produced a package of modifications to put into the engines which were then given intensive flying trials in Northern Ireland. These trials were known as the 'Gem Fleet Leader Programme'. The trials from mid-1985 to early 1987 produced a dramatic reduction in engine removals and improved oil consumption. The improved engines were subsequently fitted to the LYNX Mark 7 and Mark 9.

The greatest aviation technical developments in the twenty-five years with which this volume is concerned, have occurred in the field of avionics. Avionics, which includes weapon systems, has continued to be the maintenance responsibility of just one widely skilled avionics trade discipline. Space precludes the listing of all the items which have come into service and the problems resulting from trying to fit them into already crowded cockpit displays and aircraft equipment bays, or finding places on the aircraft for the many, often conflicting, requirements for aerials. Among these major avionics items, though, have been the SS11 and TOW weapon systems, tactical navigation systems, radar altimeters, automatic flight control systems, UHF homing, sonar locator beacons, laser range finding systems and various automatic test equipments and weapon training equipments.

There have always been some installations under development with many more under evaluation, often for specialist use with the Royal Marines or in Northern Ireland. Many of these concerned radios or navigation equipment and were introduced under operational emergency conditions. The increased avionics content of the aircraft has exacerbated such problems as electromagnetic interference between equipments. This has made the installation of additional equipment increasingly difficult. The increased avionics workload and the limited manpower available made the use of automatic test equipment (ATE) attractive, but progress was limited because of high development costs in producing ATE for relatively small numbers of equipments and the need for updating as equipments were modified. A main area of REME involvement was in obtaining ATE for aircraft radios but, as RAF interest was limited, joint development was not feasible.

DEVELOPMENT OF AIRCRAFT – THE REME CONTRIBUTION

REME involvement in the management of aircraft development projects has always been one of deep commitment and strong links have been generated with the aircraft industry, particularly Westland Helicopters Ltd of Yeovil and Rolls Royce, Leavesden. REME officers have served in the Procurement Executive in the Directorate of Helicopter Projects and the Directorate of Air Armaments, managing not only Army helicopter projects, but also those of the RN and RAF. EME 9, then the aircraft engineering policy branch in HQ DGEME, ensured that developments were in line with maintenance policies, with Aircraft Branch and its Maintenance Advisory Groups carrying out the detailed work.

Maintenance Advisory Groups (MAGs)

Aircraft MAGs were formed to deal with the full support of aircraft on the same basis as MAGs concerned with vehicles and weapons. This included support for aircraft weapons and ground support and test equipments. All aircraft MAGs came under the direct command of Aircraft Branch REME (and its different titles between 1958 and 1977). 12 MAG was permanent and responsible for carrying out technical evaluations of proposed aircraft, avionic and ground maintenance equipment. It developed equipment and techniques to meet present and future maintenance requirements. It also undertook limited research and development of maintenance and test equipment to prototype stage, in co-operation with service departments and industry. Other MAGs were formed when needed to cover the efficient technical introduction into service of new aircraft types. For instance 11 MAG was formed in 1967, based in France to cover GAZELLE and disbanded in 1974. 13 MAG was formed at Yeovil in 1969 for LYNX and again in 1987 to cover the introduction of the Light Attack Helicopter (LAH) and fortuitously, as it proved, the ISLANDER. Examples of particular tasks carried out by all the MAGs are given later in the chapter under the aircraft with which they were concerned. 12 MAG in its permanent capacity, though, was of particular importance to Army aviation, and the illustrative examples given below of the continuous work undertaken by this MAG emphasizes the importance of that work.

- Following the introduction of the LYNX with the TOW anti-tank missile in the late Seventies, there was a need to extend the range at which the GAZELLE in a reconnaissance role could detect a potential target. Ferranti used the core of their AFB 120 sight as the basis for the GAZELLE Observation Aid (GOA). Development began in 1980, field trials were carried out on major exercises in BAOR in 1983 and the equipment was introduced into service in 1985. The Observation Aid Test Set (OATS) was developed as a second-line test facility and became the first benchtop computer-driven test set used in Army Aviation maintenance. AQMS Dennis of 12 MAG did a great deal of work helping to develop usable software and preparing the Air Publications.
- The Rotortuner 5JS Rotor Track, Balance and Vibration Analysis Equipment was introduced into the Army as the definitive rotor track and balance and vibration analysis equipment for use on all helicopter types. The equipment was a software-driven, lightweight portable item which employed an active infra-red linescan camera to provide a 24-hour capability to measure rotor tip position. It was able to accept vibration data from up to eight accelerometers. The data gathered was processed and displayed as track/balance with recommended maintenance actions and vibration signatures showing frequency and amplitude. In 1987 12 MAG was made responsible for the introduction of the equipment into service. This was an exacting task requiring activity in many fields other than the usual ease of maintenance assessment and included such requirements as the preparation of aircraft operating procedures. By 1989 the operator had a totally objective 'state of the art' equipment which offered the capability for balancing and analysing other rotating systems. During this progression the scene was set for the creation of an excellent data base against which to make engineering decisions.
- The decision to enhance the TOW helicopter anti-tank missile with a Thermal Imager was made in 1983, the aim being to achieve a 24-hour anti-tank role capability with the added bonus of better performance in poor visibility. By 1988 two missiles were successfully fired at Shoeburyness by AAC gunners using the TOW Thermal Imager (TOWTI) sight. Trials took place in the early Nineties, followed by deployment, which was completed in BAOR in 1992 and in the UK during 1993. Thermal Imager repairs were undertaken in the General Purpose Thermal Imaging Repair Facility, deployed in each Aircraft Workshop. 12 MAG was also involved, in parallel with the TI enhancement, with further improvements to the TOW

system, giving an Overfly Top Attack capability and Electro-Optical Counter-Counter-Measures.

- In 1985 a project was started to provide Army Aviation with a self-loading helicopter transporter, which was not dependent on a crane, and the specification was written with advice from 12 MAG. By 1987 the first trailer was at Middle Wallop for trials with LYNX, GAZELLE, SCOUT and AGUSTA 109A helicopters, to assess the capability of the semi-trailer to load and unload them itself. The success of these trials resulted in seven trailers being brought into service with 70 and 71 Aircraft Workshops in 1988–89.

The SCOUT

In 1962, the first SCOUT (XP 855) was accepted into service with due VIP ceremony and great publicity, and was the subject of the front cover of 'The Craftsman' in May 1963. One hour after taking off for its acceptance air test, after an apparent engine failure at a critical height for autorotation, the aircraft crashed and was a complete write-off. Only the considerable skill of the pilot, and the all-metal main rotor blades then fitted, prevented the aircraft from rolling over on landing, and saved the occupants from serious injury. One was the engineering officer, Captain Brian Porter, who survived to become the Chief Aircraft Engineer more than 20 years later. The established cause of the engine failure was the shearing of the splines on the engine accessories driving shaft, because they had not been case-hardened after being machined to size.

One winter's afternoon, during the period in 1969 when the Nimbus engine in the SCOUT helicopter was prone to shed a free turbine blade, a Royal Air Force officer in BAOR on exchange duties at Detmold was piloting 1(BR) Corps Commander, Lieutenant General 'Tubby' Butler, to his residence at Spearhead House after a sortie in his SCOUT. The General was an enthusiast for flying and kept his own log book recording his flying hours. He was well aware of the overall performance of all types of helicopter in his Corps at that time, including the Nimbus turbine blade problem. The pilot was about to land the SCOUT with the skids just above the lawn of Spearhead House when there was a 'ping' (the General's word) followed by a vibration. The aircraft touched down instantly and the pilot ran down the engine. The General guessed what had happened and sympathized with the pilot who had to leave the SCOUT on the lawn and return to Detmold by road.

The CREME Aviation, Lieutenant Colonel Keith Tweed, and the Rolls Royce representative at Detmold soon arrived at Spearhead House to find that the engine was already receiving a close investigation. The General was standing on the top of a step ladder peering up the Nimbus tail pipe and pointed out to CREME the marks made on the casing by the departing blade. He said he would have found the blade but for 'this bloody snow'. It was clear from the footmarks that he had in fact already made a search. After confirming that the General's diagnosis appeared to be correct the visitors were invited to tea. The cucumber sandwiches were accompanied by various observations pulling the leg of the Rolls Royce man about the relative merits of the SCOUT with its Nimbus engine and that of its competitors.

Repairs to the Scout helicopter

Throughout its life the SCOUT aircraft has presented REME aircraft engineers and technicians with a succession of challenges. The history of the Nimbus engine has been one of a sequence of problems, solutions, and yet more problems. Main and tail rotor blades have also given rise to many modifications to improve flight safety, reliability and aircraft handling characteristics. REME technicians became familiar with the latest crack detection systems, and most adept at finding cracks before in-flight difficulties arose. Despite these many and continuing problems the aircraft became 'a marvellous and well-loved' workhorse for the AAC, giving distinguished service throughout the Falklands War. The aircraft remains in limited service with the Army in Hong Kong and the TA Squadron at Netheravon. As the TA SCOUTs swooped over Tidworth golf course on a Saturday morning, Major General Dennis Shaw (a former DGEME), happy in retirement, but disturbed in the middle of a crucial putt, was often heard to murmur that it really was time for the SCOUTs to retire!

The GAZELLE

The GAZELLE AH Mark 1 came into service in 1973 as the result of the Anglo-French helicopter collaborative project. 11 MAG under Major Tony Davies was responsible for providing maintenance advice to the Project Manager during the development phase. Captain George Southon was the engineering member of the Intensive Flying Trials Unit (IFTU) formed in May 1973. Lieutenant Colonel Stuart Smith was serving in EME 9 when the GSR was prepared, became DPO Gazelle in the Ministry of Technology and was 'hoist with his own petard' when he became CAE at the time of the Intensive Flying Trials.

Gazelle fitted with SNEB rockets

Over 660,000 hours were flown with the GAZELLE between 1973 and 1989 and, although it looked almost the same in 1989 as in 1973, a considerable number of changes had been made, many of them resulting from the 5,000 defect reports raised upon it. Nearly 1,000 modifications were carried out, including a better 'fenestron' (shrouded fan) tail rotor system; a turbine uprated from 600 to 640 SHP; an uprated main rotor head; new radio and navigational equipment and the GAZELLE Observation Aid (GOA). Its all-up weight increased from 3,750 pounds to 4,190 pounds and the major servicing cycle was raised by stages from 1,200 to 3,200 flying hours, or every 10 years.

The GAZELLE was fitted to take SNEB rockets during the Falklands campaign. An account by Captain Larry Rotchell, OC 3 Commando Brigade Air Squadron LAD, who travelled out to Ascension Island by sea with the Task Force in April 1982, gives an idea of the scene on Ascension Island and the work speedily undertaken there before sailing on to the Falklands:-

'As I landed from our ship by helicopter at Wideawake airfield with Sergeant Middleton RAOC, who was responsible for FAACO, we were confronted with a mountain of spares five metres wide and running the length of the airstrip. The RAF had, over the previous few days, been dumping the stores straight from their transport aircraft with no receipt system having been established. As a result our spares and SNEB Systems were mixed up in this mountain along with the remainder of the Task Force's goodies! We organized a small team of storemen and technicians to extricate anything with our name on it. Some sets of GAZELLE

Storesbooms were found with new holes drilled in them (for our SNEBs?). A box of SNEB rockets and some boxes with SNEB pods were uncovered and finally a modified armaments box was discovered. That same afternoon we assembled the SNEB System and one of our pet "Greenies" – Sergeant Gilbert – wired up and modified the system. A way of setting up the sights was devised and the mysteries of how to arm and disarm the pods was worked out. A GAZELLE was launched – with me in the back – to trial the SNEBs. They worked! – although not very accurately. The next day we found the fitting instructions in another SNEB pod box!'

Since the Falklands War the GAZELLE not only continued to be the main liaison aircraft of the Army, but was also deployed all around the world in permanent detachments to Belize, Cyprus, and Brunei and on exercises to the United States, Canada, Kenya, Turkey, Denmark and Norway. It defied those critics who saw it on arrival as a cheap and cheerful French civilian aircraft, unlikely to stand up to the rigours of Army use. It continued to withstand high-level use in Northern Ireland and in the Middle East during the Gulf War. Problems were few – clutch balancing, jet pipe deflector cracking, and the behaviour of the fenestron, which required continued investigation, being the more complex. Much of REME's success with GAZELLE was due to the high standard of engineering in second-line workshops, and the strength of the support provided by EME 9 and Aircraft Branch. This success story provided a fitting farewell for that well-known character of REME Aviation, Mr Peter Jupp, who was with Aircraft Branch, Westlands, and finally on the GAZELLE desk in EME 9, completing thirty-four years of civilian service to Army aircraft.

The LYNX

The LYNX first appeared in BAOR in 1972 during its initial Westland flight trials. 11 MAG based at Westland's Yeovil plant under Major Rob Preece provided all maintainability advice during development. Captain Ian Garrow was OC of the IFTU LAD which did sterling work keeping four aircraft flying during the eight months of the LAD's existence from May 1977. During this time the four LYNX flew a total of 1,344 hours, although for some of this period only three were flying after one caught fire. However, the future was not to be easy, as

Aircraft Technician working on a Lynx Mark 7

instead of the maintenance load coming down from 12.5 to 11.3 man-hours per flying hour, as anticipated in 1976, the world-wide figure was 17 in 1985 and only by April 1989 had it had fallen to 15. The major problems which arose in service did not show themselves during its early life in the intensive flying trials. Between its introduction in 1978 and the spring of 1989 5,000 avionic-related and 3,000 mechanical defect reports had been raised, prompting many of the 555 modifications to the LYNX Mark 1 and 385 airframe modifications to the Gem engine.

Defect Reports were raised whenever an item failed in service either through a high rate of wear, material failure or malfunction, and a normal defect report would be carefully assessed by an equipment specialist. Early in an aircraft's life each new report would be particularly scrutinized to see if the defect was due to normal or excess wear, whether the failure was serious, if a change in the servicing cycle was necessary or whether some other action was necessary. Significant defects were progressed through meetings with the staff of the Design Authority, the Engineering Authority, the Procurement Executive and fellow users until modifications were accepted.

The modifications could vary from minor design changes embodied during new manufacture or overhaul to a mid-life update such as the LYNX AH Mark 7. The Corps was involved in the meetings when the changes were proposed, in the trial fits, in vetting leaflets and arranging programmes of embodiment and then monitoring the effect of the modification. All this work by so many in REME Aviation resulted in the major servicing cycle being doubled from 1,200 to 2,400 flying hours. The all-up weight increased from 8,650 to 9,600 pounds and the whole LYNX fleet had flown almost 200,000 hours by early 1989.

LYNX AH Mark 7 was the first new mark Army helicopter brought into service as a result of a major mid-life improvement to its performance specification. This came about through a 1983 MOD paper to remedy shortfalls in performance due to increases in the all-up weight and a change of role to include the TOW missile system. The LYNX Improvement Programme (with the curious acronym LIMP) increased the all-up weight from 9,600 to 10,750 pounds, increased engine power from 900 to 1,120 SHP and strengthened the transmission system and tail fuselage to cope with the increased power (the inadequate structural strength of the tailboom had been a serious problem on the Mark 1). The first Mark 7s entered service in mid-1988 and proved to be an immediate success. The Lynx Mark 1 had a number of problems over the eleven years 1978–1989, two of the main ones being:

- Freewheel slippage of the main rotor gearbox and what is known as 4R vibration induced through the rotorhead by the rotation of the four main rotor blades. This first began to be serious in 1982 after four years operational service and from then on more

A woman Aircraft Technician working on a Lynx

and more aircraft began to exceed the limit. There was no clear indication as to the primary cause. The evidence was often conflicting and there was no credible fault diagnosis system. The result was that many maintenance hours were wasted and expensive spares used before an aircraft could be cleared below the permitted vibration limit. 75% of the LYNX fleet exceeded the specified vibration limits for normal flight operations by 1985. The solution was found when the known problem of the loss of the pre-load on the top bearing of the main rotor gearbox was established as the primary cause of excessive 4R vibration. The pre-load was then restored with a Westland Helicopter Ltd approved scheme to fit larger shims. This outcome was substantially due to the commendable persistence of several key REME personalities in Army Aviation who had long suspected the cause.

- Erosion pitting and cracking of the metal leading edge of the main rotor blades was a constant problem. At specified periods blades were returned to second-line workshops for monotonous work, taking an average of eight hours per blade (32 hours per set), blending out by hand erosion pits down to a minimum metal wall thickness determined by using an ultrasonic digital thickness gauge. Protective strips for the leading edge were tested without success. An improved corrosion check and caulking technique was carried out on all the Army's blades by Westlands, but the discovery of a crack in a similarly treated Royal Navy LYNX blade in 1988 meant that all the Army's blades had to be returned to Westlands for a re-work to an improved standard. In the meantime REME carried out visual inspections of the blades every four hours and a Non-Destructive Testing inspection of the critical area every fifteen flying hours. The OC was explaining to a VIP who was visiting the Rotor Blade Bay in 70 Aircraft Workshop: 'General, these men are rubbing down the blades – the weight and balance of the blades is crucial.' The General showed interest. 'Yes, obviously. What does a blade weigh?' 'I'm not absolutely sure Sir, ASM what does a blade weigh?' The ASM too was 'not absolutely sure'. However, the RSM was hovering in the background and interjected, 'A blade weighs 82 pounds, Sir'.

> The General replied, 'Thank you. Are you a technical man?' The RSM replied, 'No Sir, I'm the RSM.' The General asked, 'Then how do you know what a blade weighs?'. The RSM answered, 'It's printed on the side of the blade, Sir,' – to which there could be no answer!

13 MAG carried out a Preliminary Ease of Maintenance Assessment of the LYNX Battlefield Helicopter in 1989 and in August made a formal presentation on reliability, maintenance, vulnerability, airworthiness and life cycle costs to the MOD, the manufacturers and other interested parties. Various shortfalls in the design were identified. Three new services to the hydraulic system were accepted and embodied, as were six system layout changes. A similar exercise was undertaken on the avionics. The two most important items were the survivability of the Cockpit Voice Recorder in an area of high risk after an accident and compatibility between the passenger/aircrew telephone equipment and the Wide Band Secure Speech amplifier. 13 MAG submitted proposals for a design change.

In May 1990 a formal presentation was also made by 13 MAG to Westland's Composite Main Rotor Blade design team and other members of Westland's advanced technology department to explain to them the environment in which REME would maintain these blades on operations. Damage assessment and repair, including Battle Damage Repair, was still unresolved at that time. 13 MAG was given the task of investigating and validating Ground Support Equipment, both new and existing, that would be required to support the LYNX Mark 7 in service. It became apparent that more work was required on supportability and maintainability aspects of the aircraft. Most of the problems identified concerned the yaw control system and these were highlighted to the Ministry and to Industry. The 13 MAG task was then expanded to include all aspects of the Mark 7 modification including technical publications and the Flight Test Schedule. The investigations which followed proved the need for further airframe modifications, as well as changes to maintenance procedures and publications.

The ISLANDER

The introduction into service of the ISLANDER AL Mark 1 to replace the BEAVER aircraft was another task undertaken at short notice by the hard-pressed REME Staff. Simplified support procedures were agreed as the way to proceed, after consultation with EME 9 and Aircraft Branch, and liaison was quickly established with

The Islander on observation duties in Northern Ireland

the Procurement Executive, the publications specialists and the RAF spares management branches. Once support policies were decided, 13 MAG was set to work to consider the maintenance aspects. This task was carried out in conjunction with the Engineering Services Group of Aircraft Branch REME and included a complete package of Air Publications, the identification and procurement of Ground Support Equipment, procurement and manufacture of specialist role handling equipment, design and manufacture of Special to Type Tools and spares scaling for avionics, airframes and engines. There were many visits to Pilatus Britten-Norman Ltd during this process and the liaison with various service and civilian agencies involved in the project was considerable before the first aircraft was delivered to 13 MAG for acceptance checks in February 1989. Following these checks, the aircraft was issued in March 1989 to 1 Flight Northern Ireland for operational duties.

The AGUSTA

Colonel Mike Newby described the AGUSTA 109A project:

The Agusta 109A

'The necessary committee was formed to manage the project led by EME 9 with significant contributions from Commander Maintenance (Aviation) and the whole range of MOD PE Branches. Alan Mann Helicopters (AMH), the UK agent for the aircraft type, was contracted to bring the two captured aircraft from the Falklands Campaign to an acceptable standard and two new aircraft were purchased from Agusta in Italy. The short time frame allowed little time for the full procurement system to operate, so special systems were instituted for spares, publications and technical bulletins. It was agreed that second-line repairs would be carried out by AMH for the aircraft, Hants & Sussex Aviation Ltd for the engine, and the manufacturers for avionic components. The Project Office was immersed in Italian clearance documentation that, when translated, allowed a Controller Aircraft Release to be given. Many hours of hectic work resulted in the first aircraft being flown on 18 June 1984, with delivery to the Flight in October. The aircraft subsequently proved well up to its demanding users' requirements. It was easy to maintain and had remarkably few problems. Technicians have required little extra training and the original support system has been easily adapted to meet the in-service long-term system. Overall a most successful venture that demonstrated REME flexibility at its best.'

DEVELOPMENT OF REME SUPPORT

In 1967 during the expansion of Army Aviation through the integration of aircraft into major units there were some thirty AAC flights and forty-eight integrated air troops and platoons, all with attached REME soldiers. There were also six second-line aircraft workshops around the world, including Aden, Malaya and Singapore. Every divisional headquarters had an aircraft engineer (AE) who was a major and each Theatre had a Senior Aircraft Engineer (SAE) who was a lieutenant colonel.

In the EME Directorate in 1967 the staff branch responsible for aircraft engineering policy and equipment management was EME 9, which by then was firmly established. Aircraft Servicing Branch was responsible for providing a comprehensive central engineering support service for EME 9 and all aviation units. This Branch was retitled Aircraft Technical Services Unit in 1969 and Aircraft Branch REME in 1977. The primary responsibilities of EME 9 and Aircraft Branch were still the same in 1990, but the scope and complexity of the work carried out was much greater. In 1966–79 the Chief Aircraft Engineer (CAE), Colonel Jim Armstrong, was on the establishment of the Army Air Corps Centre, Middle Wallop, responsible to DEME(A) for ensuring the implementation of aviation engineering policy, advising on the engineering support required and acting as DEME's staff adviser to the Brigadier Army Air Corps. By 1990 the CAE's role was almost the same, although he was by now the DGEME's staff adviser to the Director Army Air Corps and also Commanding Officer of Aircraft Branch. The first CAE to have this dual role was Colonel Frank Morgan in 1974.

In 1968 the policy of expansion through integration was cancelled due to Defence cuts. By 1 September 1969 most aviation units were re-centralized into Aviation Squadrons, each with its own LAD commanded by a captain. Royal Marine units followed this policy in 1971 and four Royal Armoured Corps Air Squadrons were all absorbed into the AAC by 1975.

Colonel Mike Newby recalled that in 1968, while still a young captain on his RYO training course, he was surprised to be told that he was to attend the first RYO Officers' Long Aeronautical Engineering (OLAE) course. This would be followed by a posting to an Aviation Squadron LAD which would be formed by amalgamating the Armoured Regiment flights in BAOR into two units each of twelve aircraft. After another six months' training split between the Royal Naval Engineering College, Manadon, and Middle Wallop he had reason to think that his training cycle was complete, but his first appointment held many more lessons:

'Having survived this ordeal, I was sent off to BAOR to form my LAD. Soltau was the chosen site for 657 Squadron AAC and a flight of six ALOUETTEs were

already in location. To these were to be added a flight of six SIOUX culled from two of the cavalry regiments in 7 Armoured Brigade. Similar exercises took place throughout each BAOR brigade and a series of squadrons were created. After the inevitable teething problems with vehicles, AF G1098, FAMTO, FAACO et al, everything except aircraft, the LAD and its parent squadron settled down to a constant round of exercises to shake it out at all levels. OC LAD quickly became expert at leading the echelon convoy and setting up defensive locations. Just when all was looking good the decision came to change the ALOUETTE for the SCOUT as well as key personnel, artificers and technicians.

'Exchanging one aircraft between units is bad enough, but six was a different story and generated a far more complex situation, with a lot of hard work involved in bedding down new aircraft and the team to support them. The Divisional Aircraft Engineer was kept busy answering the inevitable stream of calls from the Commander REME Aviation at Corps HQ while we coped with the new problems of the SCOUT. The CO of the Aviation Regiment appeared, and was inevitably an ex-Gunner, and the Squadrons were full of a happy mix of young officer pilots and experienced Sergeants, with a closely integrated REME element. It all worked surprisingly well. Twenty years on the Squadron Commander retired as a Brigadier AAC, one of the flight commanders was Chief of Staff to DAAC and the OC LAD became Colonel EME 9.'

The Senior Aircraft Engineers in UK and BAOR, the latter being a CREME, subsequently became Commanders Maintenance (Aviation) in line with their colleagues in divisions and corps troops in BAOR. By 1989 there were no Divisional AEs (majors) and there were only nine units with attached REME soldiers, five LADs, five regimental workshops and two second-line workshops. These establishments were still well distributed around the world with elements in UK, BAOR, Cyprus, Hong Kong, Belize and Canada (BATUS). In 1976 the decision was taken to establish AAC regiments in their own right, each with two squadrons in a single location, together with a supporting LAD to be commanded by a Major in place of the Divisional Aircraft Engineer.

In 1977, when the Logistic Executive (Army) was set up at Andover and the REME Directorate moved from London, there was on the establishment a Director of Equipment Engineering (DEE). He had, among others, two Deputy Directors (including DDEE 2) responsible for the development and provision of engineering support for all army equipment of the DGEME's concern. Together they also provided the in-service equipment management, inherited from the Director of Equipment Management, for specific equipments including aircraft. In 1979 a new organization was recommended for DGEME; DEE was abolished and DDEE 2 became DEE 2 at the head of the chain of engineering control shown at Annex A. In 1992 EME 9 became ES 33, responsible to DES 3.

Changes also affected BAOR: 73 Aircraft Workshop, Celle was absorbed in 1977 into 71 Aircraft Workshop, Detmold, to provide one major second-line aircraft workshop in that theatre. In 1980 in UK 70 Aircraft Workshop, Middle Wallop, ceased to be responsible for first- and second-line maintenance of all training aircraft based there, the work being handed over progressively to Bristow Helicopters Ltd. The military manpower saved was used to provide additional technicians in other maintenance units, required because of the introduction of the LYNX, which was far more complex to maintain than previous Army helicopters.

Colonel John Tinkler, writing in 1989, recalled his time as Colonel EME 9 1980–1983:

'Apart from the paramount need for flight safety, our principal objectives were to improve the reliability and maintainability of the helicopters making up the major part of the aircraft fleet, namely the SCOUT, GAZELLE and, in particular, the LYNX. From information obtained from FORWARD (Air) which, unlike its predecessor in the other engineering fields, was inherently accurate and actively used, we constantly monitored the maintenance man-hours per flying hour, and analysed the figures to identify areas for improvement. In the case of LYNX one of the first actions we took was to reduce its routine servicing. We believed that they were being over-serviced, particularly in BAOR where the flying rates were comparatively low. We decided virtually to double the intervals between the periodic servicings and introduced a policy of "check" servicings based on flying hours rather than time intervals, although time did have to be taken into account if flying rates fell too low. This was one of the most important decisions made at that time.'

HQ REME (Aviation) UK was formed at Netheravon in 1984 with Lieutenant Colonel Mike Newby as the first Commander Maintenance (Aviation) UK. His responsibilities included all aircraft in the UK, including Northern Ireland, together with the Falkland Islands, Cyprus and Belize. Responsibility for aircraft in Brunei and Hong Kong was taken on from CAE later.

An important change was made in 1986 in Northern Ireland when it was decided to make resident all aircraft operating from there, instead of having a roulement squadron from UK or BAOR at Aldergrove for four months. At the same time all the aircraft maintenance elements in the Province, including the second-line support element from 70 Aircraft Workshop, Middle Wallop, and 71 Aircraft Workshop, Detmold, were combined to form the NI Regiment AAC Workshop REME.

Following trials by 6 Airmobile Brigade, 1988 saw another major change, when it was decided to give 24 Brigade an airmobile role in BAOR, and to establish its own dedicated 9 Regiment AAC with two of its three squadrons equipped with LYNX helicopters. The supporting regimental workshop, commanded by Major James Crawford, a qualified helicopter pilot, evolved from 657 Squadron AAC LAD from June 1989.

The total maintenance of Army and Royal Marine aircraft remained a tri-service responsibility during the period covered by this chapter, the Royal Navy and Royal Air Force providing REME with an excellent service. REME carried out first- and second-line maintenance and recovery, whilst the Royal Navy provided most of the third- and fourth-line maintenance and recovery as well as damage categorization. This they effected through the Mobile Aircraft Repair Transport and Salvage Unit and aircraft storage at RNAY Wroughton. This support should have included avionics and armaments equipment, but in practice the RN had problems in providing this service on equipment unique to the Army, such as the TOW missile system. Support for this equipment, all the Army's fixed wing avionic equipment and all other equipment held in common by Army and RAF was generally provided by the RAF. In Hong Kong, however, all major servicings and engine overhauls, together with some limited field repair, was undertaken by HAECO, the Hong Kong Aircraft Engineering Company, thus eliminating the need to ship aircraft back to the United Kingdom. HAECO was situated on Kai Tak airport and covered the locally based AAC aircraft including those rotated on 1,200 flying hours detachments to Brunei, and some contract work on BELL helicopters of the Royal Brunei Armed Forces. Liaison with HAECO was effected by an Engineering Control Unit consisting of an ASM and two clerks co-located with the Composite Ordnance Depot in Blackdown Barracks, Kowloon. HAECO carried out its first major service of an Army aircraft, an AUSTER, in 1963 and the association was to come to an end in servicing a SCOUT in 1993.

Ground support equipment was maintained by REME at first and second line, but by the RAF at third and fourth line, the RAF having supplied 95% of this equipment. Spares, scaled by Aircraft Branch, were provisioned by RAF through Aircraft Support Units RAOC. The RAF, through their Central Servicing Development Establishment (CSDE) at Swanton Morley, were responsible for the maintenance and calibration of all aircraft integrity monitoring equipment as well as the preparation, issue and periodic review of aircraft servicing schedules.

In 1989 there were more than seventy posts for REME aircraft engineers, more than 160 for aircraft artificers and almost 1,000 for technicians. In round terms 10% of the Corps (which was itself about 10% of the Army) provided support for Army Aviation. In BAOR 71 Aircraft Workshop at Detmold supported sixty-seven GAZELLE and fifty-three LYNX helicopters with eleven officers, twenty-six artificers and 238 other soldiers of whom 196 were technicians. Despite the fact that the LYNX helicopter was much more complicated, in 1989 there were still only two technician trades – the Aircraft Technician and the Avionic Technician. The former covered air-frames and engines, whilst the latter was responsible for all aircraft electrics, instruments, communications, navigational aids and sighting systems, including thermal imaging weapon systems. Both trades offered promotion to artificer in the same disciplines. As in the rest of the Corps these men had to be soldiers first and technicians second. This policy proved its worth in Northern Ireland and in the Falklands Campaign in 1982, but it was estimated that only 56% of their time was then available for work on aircraft.

The depth of maintenance work at first line was limited by manpower and the scaling of special tools and equipment rather than by the time a task would take. The two second-line aircraft workshops, 70 at Middle Wallop supporting UKLF and 71 at Detmold supporting BAOR, deployed forward repair teams to first-line units to undertake major assembly changes in situ and support them during exercises. The LYNX required just over sixteen maintenance man-hours for every one flying hour and the GAZELLE required nearly eight. REME support, though, had been planned on just over eleven hours for the LYNX and less than six for the GAZELLE. Even so, the sixteen and eight maintenance hours did not include the time involved in second-line major servicings for LYNX and GAZELLE. These had been transferred in 1986 to the Naval Aircraft Repair Organization (NARO) and to a civilian contractor to reduce overstretch in the REME system. NARO also carried out modification programmes due to lack of capacity in the REME system.

All the work carried out at first and second line was recorded by technicians on dual purpose Job/ADP Report Forms and the data was fed back to the REME Data Centre at Woolwich. This formed the basis for the FORWARD (Air) management information system which had started operating in October 1969. It was a parallel ADP system to that operated by REME for other equipments outlined in Chapter 2. Aircraft management and engineering information based on this data was then made available to authorized units. In peacetime each aircraft had a Daily Flight Servicing (DFS) which was mandatory before the first flight in any 24-hour period and which remained valid for 24 hours; and also a Technical Flight Servicing (TFS) which was undertaken every 7 days or 25 flying hours, whichever was the sooner, provided that it was not invalidated by other maintenance work during this period. The DFS was carried out by REME or authorized aircrew but the TFS could only be undertaken by REME. Scheduled servicing was based on flying hours. In war the policy was to put into use 'contingency servicing' which reduced the depth of maintenance required, which in theory enabled the same number of technicians to support greatly increased flying rates and carry out battle damage repair tasks.

DETECTION AND PREVENTION OF PREMATURE FAILURE

The emphasis on time-controlled replacement and overhaul of major assemblies was gradually changed by REME over some twenty years or more to Equipment Health Monitoring (EHM) systems which, instead, enabled the detection of early signs of failure.

Spectrometric Oil Analysis Programmes (SOAP), Early Failure Detection (EFD), which included magnetic chip collection and filter wash analysis, and Vibration Analysis were used regularly to monitor the wear of aircraft engines and helicopter gear-boxes. Perhaps the greatest success that the Corps had with EFD was in keeping the GAZELLE helicopter fleet flying when the French had grounded all their aircraft because the Astazou engine developed gear failure problems. Very careful inspection for the very fine tell-tale slivers of metal after every flight made sure that not one of our engines or aircraft was lost. In 1989 this method was still regarded as being the quickest and most efficient way of determining potential failure of a component. Until 1986 oil samples were sent from the field to the laboratories at Harefield, and thereafter to the Naval Aircraft Materials Laboratory at RNAY Fleetlands, for analysis using an Atomic Absorption Spectrometer. The results were fed into a computer to produce trend/wear graphs for the component.

SOAP was complementary to EFD, which proved to be the more effective, but close monitoring over the years established when SOAP could be most useful. Since 1987 it has been used in monitoring the wear in main rotor gear-box top bearings, giving advance warning of loss of pre-load on the bearing which had proved so significant in the serious LYNX 4R vibration problem. Gone are the days when REME monitored vibration 'by the seat of one's pants' and tracked rotor blades using a hand-held flag. The work to bring in the Rotortuner 5 JS has already been described. Aircraft Branch in 1989 had a powerful computer capable of holding all the vibration records of Army and Royal Marine helicopters, from which it was possible to study trends and reassess vibration limits as a constant process for reducing wear throughout the aircraft. This reduced maintenance, saved running costs and ultimately made more aircraft available.

Non-destructive testing (NDT) progressed tremendously over the years from the use of the eyeball, aided only by oil and chalk, through dye penetrants, to ultrasonics and X-rays. Viewing equipment had progressed by 1989 from the torch and dental mirror used with a magnifying glass to Aircraft Branch's flexible fibre optic equipment coupled to a camera and video screen, enabling photographs to be taken of any suspect damage. The RAF provided NDT schemes to meet REME requirements through their specialist unit at Brize Norton, where REME had two senior NCO technicians on permanent detachment.

SERVICING PHILOSOPHY

DGEME was the engineering authority for all Army aircraft except the CHIPMUNK throughout the period of this volume. The Army policy for first- and second-line maintenance was set out for each type of helicopter in the Equipment Management Policy Statement (EMPS), and included the requirement for all aircraft to achieve a guideline availability figure of 66%.

The maintenance system has already been described briefly. Preventative maintenance, embracing all technical work undertaken at regular intervals, was carried out at first- and second-line through Flight and Scheduled Servicings in accordance with instructions issued in the form of Servicing Schedules, Servicing Instructions and Preliminary Instructions. The Flight Servicing System was simplified in 1987 to help redress the tendency to over-service aircraft and to provide greater flexibility for aircrew to look after their own aircraft on operations and exercises. This simplified system was introduced in November 1987 for world-wide implementation by 1 January 1988. There was some resistance to the change and initial scepticism, but it proved to be a great success. For a period between 1981 and 1985 all major servicings had been related to calendar months. However, such a system produced severe management problems in trying to accommodate the variety of flying rates of operational aircraft and, after this period, scheduled servicing was all based on flying hours.

Until 1987 scheduled second-line servicing on LYNX and GAZELLE operational aircraft was only carried out by REME, but as a result of a DGLP(A) study in 1985 into REME technician support for Army Aviation carried out under Colonel Brian Porter, Chief Aircraft Engineer, major servicing on the GAZELLE and LYNX was transferred to contractors. Servicing for a few was retained to give REME technicians in-depth experience in servicing these aircraft. Based on the experience of the previous seven years, a major revision of the LYNX Servicing Schedule was also carried out in 1985 by Aircraft Branch, with the help of the CSDE at RAF Swanton Morley. It was implemented from 1 January 1986, with the express aim of reducing unnecessary maintenance and the premature removal of part-worn items.

BATTLE DAMAGE REPAIRS

Battle Damage Repair (BDR) in Army Aviation is defined as 'the best possible repair that can be carried out taking into account the time and resources available, the environment and the operational requirement'.

Repairs to dynamic components are complicated by vibration, flight load and aerodynamic considerations. There must be a high degree of confidence in the repairs, since proving them can only be carried out by flying the helicopters and applying flight loads. A failed repair might well kill the crew and destroy the helicopter. Among the many repair techniques taught are those for all electric cabling and a system using a pin and pin sockets embedded in a quick-curing compound to make new plugs. It was always a matter of amusement that the BDR plug was better electrically and more durable than the correct item, as it is almost indestructible!

A range of techniques was developed to repair fuel, hydraulics, pitot static and pneumatic pipes, flying control rods, twisted steel control cables and aircraft structures. These techniques made quite significant repairs possible in a short time with very limited resources. Aviation BDR has to be an extension of the strict engineering discipline applied to aircraft in peacetime by authorizing the use of tools, techniques, repair materials and relaxed limits which would be inappropriate in peacetime but are necessary in war in order to keep equipments fit in the hands of the user. There is no room in aviation for 'bodging' and Aviation BDR has therefore to be formalized and to an imposed standard.

A major investment in BDR was made in 1981, involving training; production of technical publications and the purchase of tools and equipment. This preparation proved invaluable in the Falklands Campaign in 1982 when repairs to perspex canopies and small arms damage were undertaken. The difficulty in giving realistic BDR training was that it was not possible to practise the techniques on unit aircraft in peacetime and lack of money prevented the provision of complete equipments with functioning avionic, electrical and weapon systems. Nevertheless, training was given on upgrading and artificer courses at the Aircraft Engineering Training Wing. This instruction took place jointly with RN staff at HMS *Daedalus* which had excellent facilities, including those for NBC training. The RAF Battle Damage Repair Flights, RAF Abingdon, provided courses for unit instructors and assessors

ACCIDENT INVESTIGATION AND FLIGHT SAFETY

In 1969 an Accident Investigation and Flight Safety Section was formed in Aircraft Technical Services Unit under Major Jim Whelans, a former RAF engineer officer. Aircraft Branch contained an Aircraft Accident Investigation and Flight Safety Group to investigate aircraft accidents involving Army aircraft, in order to find the cause or causes so as to prevent further accidents of the same nature. The Group was also adviser to the President of the accident Board of Inquiry and responsible for mounting and running a good flight safety campaign. The Group came under the direct command of the Chief Aircraft Engineer but was located with Aviation Standards Branch within the Headquarters of the Director Army Air Corps. It was led by a REME major known as the

Accident Investigator and Flight Safety Officer (AIFSO), and helped by an ASM. On appointment these officers attended the Accident Investigators Course at the Cranfield College of Aeronautics, the same course that members of the Department of Transport Aircraft Accident Investigation Branch (AAIB) attended. This course not only provided invaluable instruction in the techniques of investigating accidents but provided useful contacts throughout the aircraft accident investigation world.

The procedure for investigating an accident was basically the same for a civil or a military aircraft, but there was a fundamental difference in the investigation. This was because the civil investigation was only concerned with establishing the cause or causes, whereas the military inquiry was also responsible for determining whether or not any person involved in the maintenance or operation of the aircraft had been negligent.

The AIFSO required a free exchange of information between the operators, maintainers and flight safety officers throughout Army Aviation in order to run a good flight safety campaign. Most of this information from the field force came to him in accident, incident and servicing error reports. Using this information he produced flight safety posters with the help of the Central Graphics Office in London. He also produced flight safety bulletins which highlighted operation and maintenance errors. It was essential to guarantee that the identity of the individual or unit concerned was not divulged if there was to be a free flow of information. Other sources of valuable information were FORWARD (Air) and technical defect reports. A very good exchange of information with the Royal Navy and Royal Air Force accident and flight safety groups was maintained, especially for common aircraft such as LYNX and GAZELLE helicopters. In the years 1967 to 1988 inclusive, the Army Air Corps had 208 accidents, only thirty-nine of which were due to technical causes, including failure of a component and servicing errors. In nine of those years there were none due to technical causes at all. Two interesting articles on this subject by Lieutenant Colonel I A Garrow appeared in the REME Journal in 1987 and 1988.

REGIMENTAL MATTERS

Following the success of the Falklands Campaign in 1982, the Commanding Officer of 70 Aircraft Workshop, Lieutenant Colonel Brian Porter, was directed by Brigadier Army Air Corps UKLF to nominate individuals for honours in view of the outstanding contribution made by the Workshop in supporting the campaign. The Commanding Officer felt that it was inappropriate to single out individuals in this case and asked whether it was possible to honour the Workshop. As a result, during a ceremony at Middle Wallop in August 1983, 70 Aircraft Workshop became the first unit to be awarded the Director Army Air Corps' Commendation.

ASM Ashton was awarded The Queen's Commendation for Valuable Services in the Air in 1986 – the first ever awarded to a REME pilot. He was an Artificer Aircraft at Middle Wallop in 1985, flying several types of aircraft, including LYNX, as the workshop test pilot. He had many hundreds of hours flying experience, in addition to flying as a test pilot. His flying experience and engineering skills were used to great benefit, particularly towards the resolution of chronic aircraft transmission problems.

On Friday 25 September 1987 the Army Air Corps Centre, Middle Wallop, at a ceremony in which they were represented by detachments from Depot Regiment AAC, 70 Aircraft Workshop and Aircraft Engineering Training Wing, was granted the Freedom of the Test Valley. This was followed in January 1988 by another significant event, when the achievements of the Aircraft Engineering Training Wing were recognized by it being formally re-titled the School of Aeronautical Engineering.

70 Aircraft Workshop also celebrated an important milestone with its Silver Jubilee in the autumn of 1989. Two anecdotes illustrate the quality of the young technicians who have served in it over the years. The Commander in Chief UKLF was being shown round the Avionics Bay at 70 Aircraft Workshop when he saw a lance corporal sitting on a high stool working on a radio on the bench in front of him. The General approached him and asked what he was doing. The lance corporal who was soldering a joint deep inside the radio set, his head bent low over the set and concentrating very intently, did not respond. The General asked him again what he was doing and again there was no response. Several feet began to shuffle a little as embarrassment began to show on some of the faces around. The young lance corporal very carefully replaced his electric soldering iron back on its holder, got down from his stool, turned to the General and, standing very correctly to attention, said, 'Please excuse me for not answering straight away but I had just got my soldering iron on a very inaccessible joint on the set.' A few seconds later there were two heads bent low over the radio set, the General in

discussion with the lance corporal. The General left the Avionics Bay most impressed by the standard of young REME technicians.

The Inspector of REME, well known for his ebullient manner, was also touring 70 Aircraft Workshop when he spotted a very recently qualified lance corporal technician who had just started his continuation training. The Brigadier approached and questioned him. 'Hello young man, what are you doing?' 'I am wire locking this nut, Sir'. 'Good, well that's easy enough, isn't it?' There was a pause while the lance corporal laid down his pliers, stood up and faced the Inspector most respectfully. 'No Sir, it is not "easy enough". In fact it's very difficult. If I don't do it very carefully, the only thing easy about it is getting it wrong!' Looking crestfallen, the Inspector replied 'I know, but you did learn how to do it during training, didn't you?' 'Oh yes, Sir. Don't worry. I shall do it right.' 'Good man!'

CONCLUSION

Army Aviation by the Nineties had advanced very considerably since the decision in 1957 that the Army should man single-engined unarmed aircraft with a maximum all-up weight of 4,000 pounds. The engineering provided by the REME aircraft engineers, artificers and technicians, supported by many others, had responded well to the growing demands of ever more complex aircraft and the sophisticated systems fitted to them. This sophistication is epitomized by the introduction of the LYNX AH Mark 7 with its twin-turbine engines of more than 1,100 shaft horsepower each, and an all-up weight of nearly 11,000 pounds, when fitted for anti-tank guided missiles.

Annex A

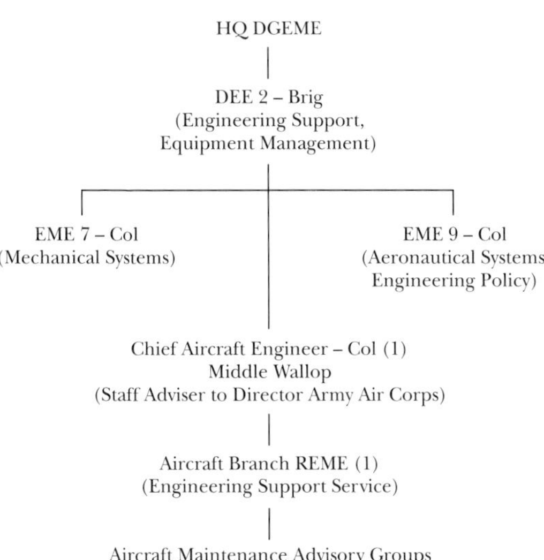

Note:
(1) CAE, located at Middle Wallop, was also CO Aircraft Branch until 1995 when the responsibilities were transferred to Colonel ES33.

CHAPTER 5

TRAINING

Introduction · Organization of REME Training ·
Milestones in REME Training · The REME Officers School ·
The School of Electronic Engineering ·
The School of Electrical and Mechanical Engineering ·
The School of Aeronautical Engineering ·
The Army Apprentices Colleges and Princess Marina College ·
The Training Battalion and Depot REME ·
Links with the Engineering Profession · Adventurous Training

INTRODUCTION

The Corps has always been in the forefront of technical training and its very life has depended on recruiting men and women for training in the ever-increasing complex technology of Army equipment. The complexity of a CHALLENGER tank with its electronics and thermal imaging equipment, the RAPIER Air Defence Missile System and the LYNX and GAZELLE helicopters are but some examples of such technology. Throughout this period the Corps was under relentless pressure to keep down its share of the Army's manpower, reduce training times to a minimum and ensure that its tradesmen could perform their tasks thoroughly and quickly under all conditions. These conditions varied considerably between those found in barracks, on the training areas of Germany and Canada, or in operations in Northern Ireland, the Falklands and the Gulf War.

ORGANIZATION OF REME TRAINING

Training policy was the responsibility of the DDEME(A) at the DEME (A) Directorate in London at First Avenue House, and later of the DEME (Organization and Training) at HQ DGEME at Andover. Following the establishment of the HQ QMG at Andover in 1992 this latter appointment was redesignated DES 1. The implementation of training policy was the responsibility of the two brigadiers commanding the training organizations at Arborfield and Bordon. HQ REME Training Centre at Arborfield was responsible for the REME Officers School, the School of Electronic Engineering (SEE), the Army Apprentices College (later Princess Marina College), the Training Battalion and Depot REME all at Arborfield, and the Aircraft Engineering Training Wing (AETW) (later the School of Aeronautical Engineering) at Middle Wallop. The School of Electrical and Mechanical Engineering (SEME) at Bordon was responsible for electrical and mechanical training.

HQ REME TA at Bordon was responsible for arranging training for Sponsored (later renamed Specialist) units, although much of the individual training was carried out at the REME Officers School, the School of Electronic Engineering and at the School of Electrical and Mechanical Engineering.

Colonel Geoffrey Atkinson was ADEME of the training branch EME 1/3 in 1975–76. In 1990 he recalled:

'The drive for more cost-effective training was my own particular crusade and I tried to change the emphasis from a preponderance of equipment training to basic skill training using high population equipment as teaching aids. This was supplemented by specialist training on complex items whilst getting rid of overlap on, and repetition of, upgrading and artificer courses. We tried to get relevant City and Guilds of London Institute (CGLI) and Business and Technician Education Council (BTEC) recognition for our courses with a minimum of additional content. We began moving the mechanical artificer courses towards the Higher National Certificate (HNC), and to bring them up to the standard of the electronic and aircraft streams. At the same time I tried to contain the length of the artificer courses. All of this was an uphill battle. Units tended to complain that newly joined soldiers were not experts in everything, which of course they were not meant

to be! We tried to reduce the proportion of time spent in training in the first three years in order to maximize the time spent in operational units and then to invest further training in the long-service man. All this may sound familiar in the Eighties and early Nineties but it was thought rather revolutionary in the Seventies.

'Much effort went into writing of specific training objectives and enabling objectives, the design of multiple choice questions, computer-marking techniques and testing against the criteria. It became a little bit of a fetish but was a well- meaning attempt to keep up with the best educational and training practice.

'We were concerned by over-civilianization of the instructional staff in the schools. It was acceptable up to a point, and we had some very excellent and dedicated individuals, but balance was important in injecting the realism of the field force into the instruction as well as providing good experience for artificers in instructing. We were really saved by the fact that many of the civilian instructors were ex-military themselves, although they did get out of date gradually.'

MILESTONES IN REME TRAINING

There were many developments in REME training in the years covered by this volume and some of the more important of these are outlined in the next few pages. These show the changes which took place as a result of both Army-wide and internal Corps studies and affected the whole spectrum of training of all ranks in the Corps.

Trade Structure

In the years 1970–79 a new Vehicle Mechanic trade structure was introduced and the skills of the Fitter Turner were taken on by the Armourers and Gun Fitters; the latter were to be divided into AFV and Field. The syllabus for several trades was revised, including Radar Technicians and Instrument Technicians. A review of Clerks and Storemen was also carried out, and Storeman training moved from the RAOC at Deepcut to SEME at Bordon, which now managed the training of both Clerks and Storemen. In 1981 Armourer and Gun Fitter apprenticeships were started again due to the lack of adult entrants. A further development occurred in 1983 when it was decided that all REME junior soldiers should go to Princess Marina College and be given a trade. A review of radar, control equipment, instrument and vehicle electrical trades was also undertaken. The trade of Master Welder was introduced over this same period because of a need for more specialized welding skills.

In 1984 Commander Training Establishments was appointed in HQ UKLF to control the Individual Training Organization (ITO) and all TA training units. The following year he was redesignated Commander

Training and Arms Directors and became responsible for the training budget. The next development was the Vertical Study of 1986 to look at reorganization of the ITO and REME career structures. Its aim was to identify what REME wanted, and then to design a suitable structure. In 1988, although generally favourable to REME methods, the Study proposed that Vehicle Mechanics A and B should amalgamate, and this was agreed in 1989. A validation report on Metalsmith problems was produced over the same period.

Training Development

In 1978 a Training Development Cell (TDC) was set up in HQ DGEME EME 1 with a staff of three officers headed by a lieutenant colonel. They began a general review of the technical training of REME soldiers. In 1981 they recommended an update of basic electronics training and pointed to the need for systems training rather than a system technician; instrument technicians were to be taught mechanical aspects at SEME and electronics at SEE. In 1987 the cell was heavily involved with the Vertical Study set up to look at the ITO reorganization and there was a considerable increase in its responsibilities. The following year they turned their attention to Battle Damage Repair. In 1990 the TDC expanded into the Training Development Team (TDT) with the task of applying the Systems Approach to Training to REME individual training. This had hitherto been carried out in training units, together with the functions of external validation and the production of training objectives, and all were now centralized in the TDT. At this time the Team also moved to Moat House, Arborfield.

As a result of a Corps initiative instrument technicians were added to the two-year apprenticeships at Princess Marina College. Later, in 1985, following an external study, it was decided that RAMC and RAOC Juniors should go there as well from May 1990. In 1986, following the trend towards centralized training of common trades, training of Clerks, except for Special to REME training, moved from SEME to the RAPC at Worthy Down, and in 1989 this was followed by the ending of REME Junior Leader training.

Job Evaluation

In parallel with the reviews of the form that training should take and the subsequent changes to trade-training structures, a great effort was put into Job Evaluation and the resultant Pay Banding. This inevitably produced not only successes but also disappointments for those who were not up-banded despite expectations, or for those who were down-banded. For example, in 1970 the Metalsmith was downgraded from Group A to Group B. In the same year Recovery Mechanics were left in Group B, whereas comparable tradesmen in other arms moved up to Group A.

However, eleven years later, in 1981, corporal and sergeant Metalsmiths went up one pay band and staff sergeants went up two bands. In 1983 sergeant, staff sergeant and WO2 Recovery Mechanics were upgraded one band. In 1984 it was the turn of staff sergeant Vehicle Electricians, together with sergeant and staff sergeant Armourers, to go up one band, but a job evaluation that year downgraded seven artificer trades in the rank of staff sergeant from Band 7 to Band 6. The same year brought good fortune to the WO1 Shipwright who was upgraded from Band 6 to Band 7. This process continued in 1988 with corporal Gun Fitters and Vehicle Mechanics A and B upgraded from Band 2 to 3; the sergeants in these trades advanced from Band 5 to 6.

Review of Artificer Training

In 1970 there was a shortage of artificers in Aircraft, Electrical Control, Radar and Vehicle trade disciplines. The shortage of electro-mechanical artificers in 1971 was so great that candidates were allowed to take the qualifying mathematics examination a second time. In 1976 a review of artificer selection, training and employment was instigated, with the aim of providing a base on which SEE and SEME would build. There were, as one might expect, mixed views on this subject, but by 1977 there was no longer a critical shortage of artificers. However, there was still a need to examine the long-term selection and training of artificers. To this end in 1978 an Artificer Review Steering Committee was established and in the following year job analysis questionnaires were issued. In 1980 briefing teams visited all units and began a study looking into Artificer selection. In 1983 the overall review was completed and the findings accepted by DGEME. As a result course syllabi for artificers were revised and course lengths reduced. In addition, more emphasis was to be placed on initiative, intellect, leadership and management in the selection and training of artificers.

Civilian Qualifications

In 1977 it was decided that the Technician Education Council (TEC) qualifications should replace the City and Guilds of London Institute (CGLI) qualifications for technicians, and from 1978 TEC certificates and diplomas were awarded to apprentice aircraft and electronic technicians.

Overseas Students

Many hundreds of students from overseas were trained at SEME and SEE under arrangements made by the Ministry of Defence. In the Seventies, when so many tanks were being sold to Iran, special arrangements were made to train Iranians in support of Millbank Technical Services, the Ministry of Defence sales arm. REME support to Iran is described in Chapter 9.

REME Officers School, Arborfield

THE REME OFFICERS SCHOOL

Introduction

The REME Officers School at Arborfield can trace its history back to 1942 when it was decided to provide courses at Arborfield for wartime officers, covering REME organization. In 1950 a Management Wing, which was one of the first of its kind in the UK, was added to the School. During the Fifties and early Sixties courses were provided for young National Service Officers as well as for Regular Young Officers, covering the organization and operation of REME in the field. Courses were also run for majors and captains on military and management subjects, and the Senior Management Course was introduced as early as 1952.

Recruitment and Selection of REME Officers

Potential officers were brought to the attention of the Corps Recruiting Liaison Staff by various means. Schools and University Liaison Officers played an important part in this recruiting and, as well as press advertising and direct civilian enquiries, about eighty REME presentations were given each year to schools and universities. Commanding Officers of REME units also recommended soldiers for commissions.

Once a potential officer was identified he was invited to Arborfield for interview: this was a two-way passage of information. If the outcome was satisfactory the candidate visited an active REME unit to find out more about life in the Corps for himself. If the candidate then applied for a commission he was given two days of briefing at Arborfield and Bordon before going to the Regular Commissions Board (RCB) at Westbury. Success at the RCB would be followed by two years in training at The Royal Military Academy, Sandhurst. Other suitable cadets at Sandhurst were found by the REME representative there who would get to know suitably qualified cadets, many of them from Welbeck College. He would meet them informally and encourage them to find out more about the Corps and to make it their choice.

From the mid-Fifties until his transfer to Regimental Headquarters in the early Nineties, there was an officer in the REME Officers School designated 'R1'. He had prime responsibility for seeing that the training of young officers of the Corps at the School, and their practical engineering training elsewhere, was properly co-ordinated with their education at The Royal Military College of Science (RMCS) at Shrivenham or university. Another task of the R1 was to administer all sponsored undergraduates, and this continued until the early Eighties when the responsibility was transferred to the Corps Recruiting Staff. Later in the Eighties the R1 also became responsible for direct entry undergraduates. These responsibilities extended to making arrangements for those whose academic attainments were not up to expectations but who, with encouragement (and sometimes both stick and carrot) would succeed and become valuable officers. This took place against a background of major changes, including the reduction in the length of courses at Sandhurst.

Having obtained the REME quota from PB21, the REME officer-manning branch of the Ministry of Defence, the R1 and the Sandhurst representative would produce a selection of candidates for the DGEME Selection Board. This was chaired by the Commandant REME Training Centre with the Commandant REME Officers School and R1 as members. The R1 was also the Secretary of the Board. The Board would interview the candidates and select those thought fit for DGEME's approval.

At the start of the Eighties, during one such process of selection, a young assistant Recruiting Liaison Officer was sent down to Wokingham railway station to meet twenty-five hopefuls coming on a Potential Officers' Familiarization visit. He collected twenty-six and on the way back in the bus he pointed out: 'On your left School of Electronic Engineering, on your right REME Officers School, here we are at West Court Officers' Mess'. He took them in for a beer at the bar, then into dinner and finally back to the bar. By this time the Liaison Officer had identified No 26 and asked him if he was meant to be on the

Familiarization visit. 'No Sir,' came the answer, 'I'm a new recruit in 26 Platoon at the Training Battalion.' An NCO was summoned from the Training Battalion to hurry him back down the West Court drive. Looking back wistfully over his shoulder No 26 was heard to say, 'I thought it was a bit soft for my first day.'

Regular Young Officers Training

The first volume indicated that a high proportion of young career REME officers came through Welbeck College before going to The Royal Military Academy, Sandhurst. They had to be capable of reading for a degree which was normally achieved at the RMCS, but a few went up to Cambridge University. They all required professional engineering training and were encouraged to become members of the professional engineering institutions.

One of the reasons for shortening the course at Sandhurst from two years to the Standard Military Course of twenty-six weeks was that so many young men preferred to go through Mons Officer Cadet School at Aldershot, obtain a Short Service Commission and after one year apply for a Regular Commission. In 1970 and 1971 almost three-quarters of the officer cadets wanting to join the Royal Armoured Corps and Infantry went through Mons. Many of these could have gone to Sandhurst but preferred the shorter path through Mons.

Lieutenant Colonel David Crook recalled that, when a subaltern himself, he and another young REME officer went to commiserate with a University Cadet who had failed at Shrivenham and had been rusticated to Mons Officer Cadet School:

'We asked at the CSM's office as to his whereabouts and the CSM, a tall imposing Coldstream Guardsman, hedged a little. He explained that his cadets got the run-around during their first few weeks of training and were not normally available for social visits. We said that we were aware of this as it had been the same when we were at Sandhurst. The CSM braced a little at this and asked, "Were at Sandhurst, Sirs?". When we confirmed our attendance at that august establishment, he braced even more and threw us an extremely smart salute saying, "You've been deceiving me, gentlemen. I thought I was talking to two scruffy young civilians – I now find that I'm talking to two scruffy young officers – you'll find him playing hockey on the hockey pitch if you're quick!"'

One of the consequences of the Army Restructuring Plan of 1974 was the need to cut down on the number of young REME officers attending courses at the expense of filling posts in units. The DGEME's Regular Young Officers Training Advisory Board once more reviewed the skills and experience a young officer should have on completion of all his academic, military and special-to-arm training to meet the needs of the Corps from 1979 onwards. Another reason for a review was the change in

the requirements of the engineering institutions for corporate membership. The main change resulting from this review was the introduction of a fourteen-week General Engineering Practice Course to initiate young officers in engineering practices used in the Corps, and to familiarize them with common equipments and repair techniques in the field force. It took place at SEME Bordon, SEE Arborfield and AETW (as SAE Middle Wallop was still called at that time).

In addition to the course change, the policy on the subaltern's first posting also changed: instead of this being an attachment to a Corps or teeth-arm unit, the posting was to be to an established subaltern's appointment in a field force REME unit, lasting for ten to sixteen months depending on when the officer left Sandhurst. During the second long vacation from university the RYO was encouraged to take up an adventurous training pursuit. Post-graduate training was also made the same for all disciplines, consisting of the REME Captains course, an equipment updating course and a three month industrial training attachment. The R1 was in touch with the training managers of nearly one hundred firms on the Officers' School books.

Despite these decisions the duration of formal training was still three years and eight months. The revised training programme was first applied to officers commissioned from Sandhurst in March 1978. The illustration shows what was required; the height of each step represents the length of the course.

There were, over the years, big reductions in the length of practical training in civilian engineering works given to Regular Young Officers. The changes in the RYO training cycle were reviewed by Major Stephen Abate in the 1979 REME Journal. Beyond the confines of the cycle were the long specialist courses, loaded to suit the Corps' employment needs. The Officers' Long Electronic Engineering Course was continued but the Officers' Long Mechanical Engineering Course was abolished by 1980, and Automatic Data Processing (ADP) was introduced as the fourth REME officer discipline.

There was an almost non-stop review of young officer training in the Eighties. In 1981 a working party looked into the qualifications necessary for Regular Career Officers. In 1982 they concluded that the minimum academic standard for the RYO was a degree from the RMCS. In 1983 the Corps advanced the case for a common first year for the engineering subjects at Shrivenham, which was to be reviewed in 1984. This year was also marked by the success of Second Lieutenant Richard Mitchell in winning the Sword of Honour at the RMA Sandhurst. Five years later it was to be the turn of a woman officer serving with the Corps to gain an award there, and in April 1988 Second Lieutenant Elaine Roberts WRAC/REME won the Sash of Honour. Two years later all women officers in the Corps ceased to be part of the WRAC and became REME-badged.

General Sir Frank Kitson presents the Sword of Honour to Second Lieutenant Mitchell

At the end of 1984 a Review of Officer Training and Education (ROTE) started to look into Sandhurst and Staff Training. Mr Anthony Frodsham CBE, who had been Director General of the Engineering Employers Federation 1975–82, also carried out a review of 'The Provision of Engineer Officers in the Armed Forces' from January to December 1983. He visited forty-five establishments in the UK and several abroad, including 7 Armoured and 71 Aircraft Workshops in BAOR. He talked to well over a thousand engineer officers, including many junior ones. His report made more than forty recommendations on recruitment, training and employment. Among these were that RMCS Shrivenham should continue, and a variety of measures should be taken at Welbeck College, including the appointment of a military headmaster. It was also recommended that REME should consider taking a few exceptional officer candidates without formal engineering qualifications, but this recommendation was not implemented; the DGEME confirmed the need for a graduate engineer Regular career structure. In due course, however, a military headmaster was appointed to Welbeck, but he was followed again in 1990 by a civilian headmaster, Mr Ken Jones. In the same year the Training Development Team reviewed RYO training under the Systems Approach to Training.

During the late Eighties the Workshop Practice and Engineering Practice courses which involved bench fitting were abolished, as this became included in degree courses, and the industrial attachments also changed their emphasis from 'Cook's Tours' round the works to more intensive project work. The introduction, though, of a summer camp break in Cyprus for first-year degree officers strangely proved to be far more popular with the officers and lifted their morale.

In 1989 it was decided that Army Entrants from the ranks already in the service could be accepted for a commission provided that they would study for a Higher National Certificate (HNC) as a minimum qualification. This enabled officers who failed to obtain a degree at Shrivenham to continue serving in the Corps provided they obtained this qualification. Also about this time the Standard Military Course at Sandhurst was increased from two terms to three terms, which was one of the recommendations of the ROTE study mentioned earlier.

RYO 100 Course was dined into the Corps in September 1989. Two members of RYO 1 attended, including Major General John Homan. The RYO Training Pattern was accredited with the five engineering institutions – Electrical Engineers, Electronic and Radio Engineers, Mechanical Engineers, Production Engineers and the Royal Aeronautical Society. Appropriately, at this dinner, the Worshipful Company of Engineers presented their first award for the 'best young REME Officer completing training during the year', which was Captain Iain Clyde.

The first Army Entrants to be commissioned entered the REME Training Cycle at this time, and the first academic enhancement package at Reading College of Technology started in September 1991, followed by the first special HNC course in September 1992.

Management Training

In 1968 the REME Officers School started the REME Supervisory Management Courses for non-industrial civilian PTO grades. In the early Seventies senior NCOs became eligible for these courses. This set a trend for other courses which started to have military and civilian students of officer and NCO grades. Following the 1971 Industrial Relations Act and the 1974 Health and Safety at Work Act, appropriate courses were run at the School to make officers aware of the implications of these two Acts.

Another innovation in the early Seventies was to introduce short courses for senior officers. At first they were one week long, designed to update officers on new developments in the Corps. Eventually they were reduced to one- and two-day briefings held at six-monthly intervals and attended by officers from other Arms and Services. These briefings formed an open forum for new ideas and thinking and proved useful for launching Responsibility Budgets and QMG's Corporate Plan.

In 1982 the Management and Military Wings of the REME Officers School combined to form one Instructional Wing and in the same year the Corps Recruiting Officer became part of the School. A year later the Artificer Command and Field Course was introduced for all artificers as part of their courses at the three trade schools, SAE, SEE and SEME, and Territorial Army artificers attended the first two weeks of this course.

The most radical change in management training during the years covered by this volume concerned the Senior Management Course. A pilot study in 1988 replaced it by a series of short courses in Engineering Resources Management. A detailed structured survey of the training required was conducted by questionnaire and interview as part of this study, and as a result courses of two to ten days were introduced. Nearly 1,000 officers attended the Senior Management Course at the Officers School, including students from other arms and services and from countries all over the world. Brigadier Dick Chown was attending a reception in Stockholm when he was surprised to be asked by a Swedish general how the course was progressing. The general had attended the Senior Management Course as a major some years before. A reunion was later arranged at West Court for the general to meet staff and students again, including Major Pat Stafford and Mr Ken Casey who were DS for his course.

The School maintained a close liaison with civilian institutions, centres of learning and military establishments to ensure that its teaching was up-to-date and it gave presentations and briefings to courses at other Schools. An interesting exercise at the School in 1974 started with a request from Millbank Technical Services (MTS) that 44 Senior Management Course should conduct a project to build a base workshop for Iran. This became part of the twelve-week course. The aim of the exercise was to design, staff and equip a workshop to overhaul British equipment purchased by the Imperial Iranian Ground Forces. The size of the fleet to be supported was said in the instructions to be 750 CHIEFTAIN tanks and 350 SCORPION CVR(T). MTS support for Iran is described in Chapter 9. Two framed artist's impressions of the workshop which 44 Senior Management Course designed were presented by them to the School where they now hang.

Following the Logistic Support Review a fundamental redesign of all courses was undertaken to reflect the resulting new role of the Corps, and from 1 April 1992 the School was redesignated the School of Equipment Support (Army) (SES(A)).

THE SCHOOL OF ELECTRONIC ENGINEERING

Introduction

The School of Electronic Engineering which was opened on 1 April 1961 heralded a totally new approach to the training of electronic technicians and artificers. Following the pioneering work of the Electronic Training Investigation Team in the late Fifties training was structured into a common module of fundamental mathematics, electrical and electronic science studies, followed by the teaching of the specialist techniques employed by a generic range of equipments such as radar or telecommunications and concluding with practical training on the military hardware and a trade test. Over the past thirty years electronics had advanced at an amazing rate and, in order to keep pace, courses and teaching methods were frequently modified. The secret of the School's success lay mainly in its ability to explain complex and abstract concepts in easily understood language and demonstrations.

Basic Electronics
The Basic Electronics training in the Sixties catered for the mainly thermionic valve-driven equipments of that era, together with the principles of alternating and direct current circuits and associated machines. With the advent of semi-conductors the basic course was redesigned, with teaching based on a 'whole to part' concept using a transistorized radio transmitter/receiver system. Students were shown the 'whole' equipment which was broken down to modular circuits and taught to component level. In the early Eighties the course introduced digital electronic theory and the microprocessor became the main teaching aid. By 1985 most new military electronic systems used digital technology and the micro-computing training was extended to include the theory of in-built automatic test and diagnostic systems. This marked the end of the 'whole to part' training concept and a modular building block course evolved, laying the foundation for an understanding of complex circuits with each block interacting. This Basic Electronics course, if successfully completed as a whole, qualified students for an Ordinary Certificate Award by the Technician Education Council. However, a part failure on the course denied them the certificate, and in 1990 the course was further modified to cater for the increasing number of students who needed improved mathematics and general science training. This not only gave greater emphasis to the engineering applications of computers but then presented the opportunity to acquire a unit-based civilian qualification under the auspices of the (by then) BTEC. Throughout all this period hand and bench fitting skills were taught in order to instil into students high standards of practical repair and quality control, and the ability to improvise battle damage repair.

Upgrading and Artificers
The upgrading and artificer courses were conducted along complementary lines. The policy was to complement the basic course with a series of building blocks which aimed to make the technician more versatile in the field and to give him a broader technical base and the ability to supervise. The artificer courses had the additional aims of ensuring that the student could play his part in the work of MAGs, other technical departments and as an instructor. From 1966 artificer courses had qualified students for a HNC and, with the constant advancement of the science of electronics, approval was given in 1983 by the BTEC for a revised project-based course at Higher Diploma Level.

Techniques and Equipment
On the techniques and equipment side of the School the pace of change was driven by the Army's equipment programme. The large, cumbersome CORPORAL and SAGW missile systems and associated radars were replaced by compact and sophisticated systems such as RAPIER, and

much manual testing gave way to tape-driven automatic test equipments. The LARKSPUR range of radios was replaced by CLANSMAN, again with its associated automatic testing; these automatic systems eased the technician's prime role in repairing customer equipment but created a new problem in the maintenance of the test system itself. The Eighties saw many developments to RAPIER, including the introduction of the tracked version with enhanced built-in testing, and a new towed version which controlled the missile in flight by a thermal imaging as opposed to an optical sight. In the same decade the CHIEFTAIN and CHALLENGER main battle tanks were equipped with thermal imaging (TI). This posed additional training and repair problems, as did the introduction of the two general purpose repair facilities, one which supported thermal imaging equipments (GPTIRF) and the other new digitally based electronic equipments (DIANA). Both equipments aimed to eliminate the plethora of specialist repair vehicles and were designed to conduct, with the aid of the appropriate test package software, a specification test on a faulty line replaceable unit (LRU) or 'black box'. Whilst the conduct of the test was relatively simple, the support of the test equipment was not.

Instructor and Student working in GPTIRF

Multiple Launch Rocket System

By 1990 training on the Multiple Launch Rocket System (MLRS) and Battlefield Artillery Target Engagement System (BATES) had been introduced and plans were well in hand for courses on RAPIER Field Standard C and the tank to replace CHIEFTAIN, as well as many other smaller equipments.

From the early Sixties many changes took place, but the fundamental task of producing a highly skilled technician able to diagnose failures and apply the necessary repair never ceased, despite rapid technological enhancements.

Contract Training in SEE and Princess Marina College

No account of the history of SEE would be complete without brief mention of the study initiated by Commander Training and Arms Directors into the feasibility of placing some technical training to contract. As a result it was decided to place a contract for the trade training of apprentices in Princess Marina College, some of the technical training in SEE, and for training support services in both establishments. Lieutenant Colonel Neil Kenyon, who had been Chief Instructor in SEE, drafted the Statement of Requirement which was issued in September 1989. In September 1990 a three-year contract was awarded to SERCo, which started on 25 March 1991. This contract, except for the earlier example of The Royal Military College of Science, was the first in the Army individual training organization.

Twenty-First Anniversary of SEE

A reunion of founder members and former commandants was held on 23 April 1982 to celebrate the twenty-first anniversary of the SEE, which had been formed by amalgamating 3 (Telecommunications) Training Battalion and 5 (Radar) Training Battalion. They were welcomed by the current staff and taken on a tour of the School. The tour was followed by lunch in the Officers' Mess and then there was a tree-planting ceremony. That evening the final SEE Officers' Mess party was held before amalgamating with Princess Marina College Officers' Mess.

Students at A Vehicles Branch SEME

THE SCHOOL OF ELECTRICAL AND MECHANICAL ENGINEERING

Introduction

SEME at Bordon was formed by the amalgamation of 4 (Armament) Training Battalion and 6 (Vehicle) Training Battalion on 17 March 1961. SEME was responsible for adult training in all electrical and mechanical trades, whilst junior training in these trades was carried out at the new Apprentices School which had opened at Carlisle in 1959. In the Sixties this school was placed under the command of the Brigadier at Bordon. SEME was also responsible for the selection of soldiers for artificer training in all disciplines. In the early Seventies SEME made a major contribution to the technical training of young officers by adjusting their training to enable them to start regimental duty six months earlier than previously.

Artificer Selection

The artificer selection system was restructured completely in the years 1970–72 to ensure that candidates were tested under mental and physical stress. The system was based on that of the Regular Commissions Board, but adapted to meet the special needs of the Corps. Studies were undertaken which included a thorough review of artificer selection, training and employment. A job analysis of all artificer disciplines was carried out and job descriptions and training objectives were prepared for all artificer courses. In 1981 the Artificer Selection Board moved in Bordon from Louisburg Barracks to Canada Hutments where indoor testing and administration was established. At the same time a new outdoor testing area was set up in the woods next to the newly built Prince Philip barracks, close to the existing assault course. Ten years later the board was able to concentrate its activities by vacating Canada Hutments in favour of the defunct Sandes Home premises.

Artificer Training

External qualifications in the form of CGLI certificates were first awarded to SEME-trained artificers in 1972. The examinations were set, marked and certificated by the SEME City and Guilds Office, later called the Awards Office. The first courses received the CGLI 255 Part 1 Mechanical Engineering Technician Certificate. By 1976 Parts 2 and 3 had been added; an artificer could qualify for a CGLI Full Technological Certificate (FTC). With an FTC the status of Technician Engineer was made possible for selected 'fast stream' artificers together with corporate membership of appropriate institutions. In 1981 SEME changed over to the Technician Education Council (TEC) National Certificate Scheme. (TEC became the Business and Technician Education Council (BTEC) later). Following changes made by the Engineering Council in 1987 and in line with Army policy in regard to the membership of civilian and professional bodies all SEME artificer BTEC programmes were reviewed. The new programmes were designed to ensure that all SEME artificer graduates were qualified to receive professional recognition in the UK and European engineering fields.

Military training for artificers was carried out in Havannah Barracks Bordon (later in June 1984 named Prince Philip Barracks by General Sir Richard Trant, Quartermaster General) until 1976 when it moved to Louisburg Barracks and in 1980 to the Training Battalion and Depot REME at Arborfield.

Trade Training

In the early Eighties there was a complete change in teaching philosophy in that the Vehicle Technology Branch ceased teaching specific equipments and started teaching automotive technology. The aim was to give the student a much broader knowledge base and prepare him in greater depth to deal with a much wider range of equipments. A battle damage repair module was introduced into class 1 and artificer career courses in 1986.

Milestones in training in the A Vehicle Branch were the first equipment courses for CVR(T) in 1973, CHALLENGER MBT in 1982, Tracked RAPIER 1983, WARRIOR 1987 and MLRS 1990. Milestones in recovery, driving and maintenance were the introduction of Foden GS Recovery Vehicle into career training courses in 1986, CHALLENGER and WARRIOR driving and maintenance to career courses in 1989 and the reintroduction of the CENTURION driving and maintenance to recovery mechanic training in 1989, following the re-introduction of the CENTURION ARV. In 1990 WARRIOR (Recovery) courses were introduced for recovery mechanics.

Continuous progress was also made in the standards of trade training throughout the Seventies and Eighties. Significant improvements were made in the training of welders and sheet metal workers, fitters, armourers, gun fitters, instrument technicians and electricians.

In 1988 a CHALLENGER familiarization package containing fourteen video-taped lessons, an audio-tape and other material was introduced as a prerequisite for students attending CHALLENGER equipment courses. Also in 1988, the move to rationalize common trades in the Army continued with the cessation of Driver trade training in the Corps and the transfer of all REME drivers to RCT. In 1989 WARRIOR computer-based training began for vehicle mechanic and electrician courses.

British Petroleum Buildacar Competition

SEME planned and carried out this competition, giving it contact with schools all over the country. The Buildacar competition has been described as the backbone of BP's long-running Challenge to Youth programme; it was sponsored jointly by BP and REME, starting in 1972. In 1974 twenty-five schools took part, the Chairman of the organizing committee being Colonel Derek Gardiner, who was a member of BP's staff and the senior REME TAVR officer. The judges included the Chairman of the Automobile Division of the Institution of Mechanical Engineers, the Director of the Motor Industry

REME Apprentices in the BP Buildacar Competition

Research Association, the Editor of a motoring magazine and a teacher of automobile engineering. A team of military and civilian scrutineers tested, recorded and marked all measurable features of the cars on the first day (a Saturday) for the judges to consider on the second day; together with their own observations, this enabled the judges to select six cars. The Sunday was an open day at SEME for a large crowd of schoolboys, their parents and others to watch a display of the cars in action and a drive past of SEME's vehicles. The first prize in 1974 was won by Cranleigh School which received a British Leyland minibus and a silver trophy. The three winning cars were put on show at the 1974 Motor Show.

In 1986 the prizes were presented by Mr Peter Bottomley MP, of the Department of Transport, who said: 'this event has been a remarkable demonstration of the learning experience, education and engineering'. The winning car was made by Shelley High School from Huddersfield. BP also sponsored a 'Build a Robot' competition, held at Arborfield in 1983 and 1985. It was for entrants from schools and was paid for by BP but with help from SEE, including the judging.

SEME Rebuild

SEME Officers' Mess under construction

General Sir Hugh Beach, Representative Colonel Commandant, opened the new SEME Officers' Mess on 19 May 1979 in the presence of senior REME officers and representatives of the architects and contractors. The building was believed to be the first officers' mess to be built specifically for REME. It was built in a Scandinavian style with an imposing entrance hall forty feet high, with exposed beams, and a gallery from which the REME Staff Band played for the occasion. Three wings radiated from the entrance hall to provide the living accommodation. The mess was the first building to be completed in the general rebuilding of the SEME barracks at Bordon. In 1984 the mess was named the Havannah Officers' Mess, thus perpetuating the name originally given to the set of barracks built in 1935 and temporarily lost at the inception of Prince Philip Barracks. The Warrant Officers and Sergeants occupied the old officers' mess, and SEME Regimental HQ had a new building. The wooden 'spider' huts of Martinique Barracks had been associated with the Corps since 1945 after their wartime occupation by 1 Canadian Base Workshop. The Workshop had left Bordon in July 1945, their workshop area being divided between RAOC and 3 Central Workshop. When the latter disbanded in 1953 its technical accommodation was taken over by 6 (Vehicle) Training Battalion which was in Havannah Barracks. About this time 4 (Armament) Training Battalion came from Blackdown to Martinique Barracks. The barracks were finally given up in 1982 and a farewell parade was held on 5 May, followed by a march to Havannah Barracks led by the REME Staff Band. The Corps was fortunate in having Major General Denys Wood in the appointment of Director of Army Quartering, 1975–1978, whilst the initial rebuilding work for SEME was taking place.

SEME Twenty-First Anniversary

The twenty-first anniversary of the formation of SEME was celebrated on 25 February 1982 with a reunion of former members of the military and civilian staff, including Major General Pat Lee, DGEME, and six former commandants. A parade was followed by a presentation of the antecedents of SEME and progress made at SEME during twenty-one years. Accommodation in Havannah Barracks and all departments were open for the visitors to tour before lunch in the Officers' and Sergeants' Messes. In the afternoon there were football and hockey matches and one of the best rugger matches seen at Bordon for a long time when the SEME XV played a touring RNZEME team.

THE SCHOOL OF AERONAUTICAL ENGINEERING

The Beginning

The story of the Corps' support to Army Aviation and the development from the simple, light and unarmed aircraft with which the Army Air Corps was equipped in the Fifties to those such as the sophisticated LYNX and GAZELLE helicopters of the Eighties and Nineties, is related in Chapter 4.

The Aircraft Trades School started at Middle Wallop in 1957 and became the Technical Training Branch, Technical Wing REME in 1958. In 1964 it became the Aircraft Engineering Training Wing (AETW) and remained so until 1 January 1988 when it was retitled School of Aeronautical Engineering, and a parade was held at Middle Wallop with the Corps Band in attendance to celebrate the occasion. In the early days three separate trades were involved in what later became known as avionics – electricians, instrument mechanics and radio mechanics. They came from the corresponding mainstream REME trades and were all trained on aircraft during a six week conversion course at Middle Wallop. They were supervised in the field, and their work was oversigned, by Aircraft Mechanics (Airframes and Engines) who were mostly converted vehicle mechanics. The aircraft on which they worked – the AUSTER fixed wing and SKEETER helicopter – had relatively simple systems. The AUSTER did not have an electrical engine starter and the electrical generation and distribution systems were not as complex as many family cars have today. Flight instruments were simple suction-driven devices and radios were not very different from their ground-based contemporaries.

Auster

The electrical and radio tradesmen took on a secondary role in first-line units because the simple equipment which they supported could be bay-serviced or repaired at second line. This took these tradesmen away from mainstream aircraft operations and gave them an image of being 'backroom boys'. The airframes and engines tradesmen assumed control of flight and squadron operations, although they were often junior to the senior electrical and radio men. This was because dependency on avionic equipment was very low and, if the airframes and engines were serviceable, the aircraft had a 95% chance of completing their mission. The secondary role of the electrical and radio tradesmen lasted for many years.

When more complicated aircraft like the BEAVER fixed-wing and the SCOUT and SIOUX helicopters were introduced, the airframes and engines men could no longer supervise the other three trades. This had the effect of drawing the electrical and radio tradesmen into the centre of first-line operations working on the flight line.

The Sixties

In the early Sixties Artificers (Electrical Control) and Artificers (Telecommunications) were given conversion training to become Artificers EIR (Electrics, Instruments and Radio). In 1963 Electrics and Instruments were combined at the basic level, but Radio trade training remained separate. A few years later selected students from SEE were sent to Middle Wallop for comprehensive equipment training for the combined trade of EIR Technician; the total training time at SEE and Middle Wallop was sixty-five weeks.

The Avionics Technician

From 1968 conversion training from other trades ended and in 1972 the EIR trade was renamed Avionics Technician. It was not until the mid-Seventies that the Avionics trade became as important operationally as the Aircraft trade. This was due to the introduction of the LYNX helicopter which was very dependent for stable flight on an Automatic Flight Control System. The LYNX pushed avionics technology into the front rank of importance and the Aircraft tradesmen now had to rely heavily on the Avionics men to ensure that the aircraft was fit for flight. Further complications in its support were an airborne navigation system using a gyromagnetic compass and a Doppler system to calculate speed, drift and track. To these were later added the Tube-launched, Optically-tracked and Wire-guided (TOW) anti-tank missile based on a micro-processor using infra-red guidance for the missile. The avionics trade was responsible for all TOW servicing, and in the Seventies and Eighties the role at first line expanded tremendously with the avionics artificers sometimes running the squadron fitter sections.

The Training Challenge

The challenge to SAE was to keep up with the rapidly developing technology and train technicians to keep the aircraft flying. Over a period of twenty-five years the basic Aircraft Technician course increased by ten weeks to forty-two weeks and the basic Avionics course increased by eighteen weeks to fifty-eight weeks. There was a big investment in high-quality training aids which were made available prior to the operational equipment going into service in the field: for example the first production LYNX Mark 7 was issued to SAE. In 1984, personal microcomputers were also provided for students on these courses. The association of the Officers Long Aircraft Engineering (OLAE) course with the Royal Navy Engineering College, Manadon, ceased in 1978 when all officer training was based at Middle Wallop. During 1978 LYNX and TOW training was included in SAE courses and in October 1979 the LYNX Engineering Systems Simulator was provided for the school.

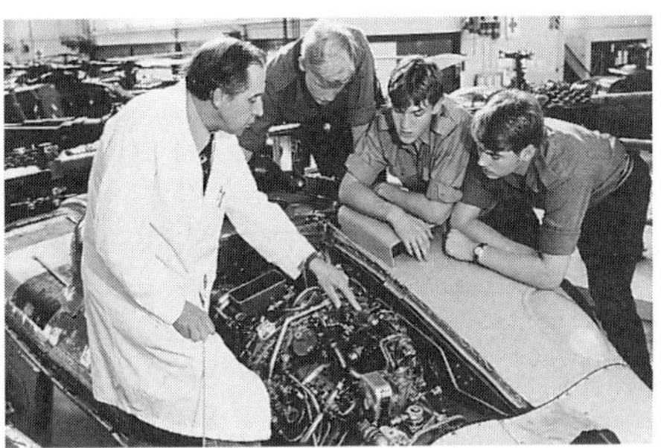

Technicians in training – Middle Wallop

Battle Damage Training

Formal training was given at AETW to Class 1 technicians, artificers and aeronautical engineering officers in the skills of battle damage assessment and repair. There had to be a high level of confidence built into battle damage repairs since proving could only be carried out by applying loads in flight, and failure might have led to loss of life or aircraft. The success of the training and techniques was shown in the Falklands in 1982.

Review for the Eighties

In 1979 a formal study was made into the training of technicians. This involved looking at FORWARD (Air) data over an eight-month period, doing a field survey in which all technicians itemized their work over ten days, and visits to units by AETW to question officers, senior ranks and technicians. A paper was written for DGEME and the outcome by 1982 was that adult avionic technicians were specifically selected for that trade on joining the Army. They started their technical training at Middle Wallop before going to SEE for a shorter basic electronics course which they could then relate to aircraft. Technician Education Council (TEC) Aerospace Programme A9 was to be adopted in place of the former City and Guilds of London Institute and Higher National Certificates. Apprentice training was also brought into line with the adult entry training.

ARMY APPRENTICES COLLEGES AND PRINCESS MARINA COLLEGE

Early Days

There is almost no mention of the early life of the Army Apprentices Schools and Colleges in the first volume – probably because they did not come under the direct control of the DEME until the mid-Sixties, shortly after the appointment of the first REME commandants at Arborfield and Carlisle. The history of Arborfield, however, goes back to the Thirties.

Building of the Army Technical School (Boys) at Arborfield began in 1938 on the site of the remount depot, and in May 1939 the School was ready for its first intake of 400 boys – badged RAOC. In January 1942 the first intake to be badged General Service Corps arrived, but when REME was formed in October the RAOC boys were re-badged REME. From April to September 1944 the boys were dispersed all over England as Arborfield became a concentration area for troops assembling for the invasion of Normandy. On 1 February 1947 the School became an Army Apprentices School, and the Army Apprentices School cap badge, worn by many thousands of Army apprentices, was first worn at Arborfield in August 1947.

Opening of Carlisle

In 1959 a new Army Apprentices School was opened at Carlisle, making four in all, the other two being Chepstow and Harrogate. The first apprentices went to Hadrian's Camp at Carlisle in January 1960 and Arborfield then ceased to train armourers, fitters and gun fitters. Over 200 apprentices moved from Arborfield to Carlisle, leaving Arborfield to concentrate on vehicle mechanics, the electrician and electronic trades. Armourers, gun fitters, instrument technicians and vehicle mechanics were trained at Carlisle. It was decided then to give vehicle mechanics two weeks' driving instruction in their eighth term and a full week's military training in their fourth and eighth terms.

REME Control

The first REME commandant at Arborfield, Colonel Joe Dobie, arrived at the end of 1962, whilst the first REME commandant at Carlisle was Colonel Bill Kinchin who arrived in 1964. In August 1965 the control and sponsorship of the two Schools was transferred from the Inspector of Boys Training (Army) to the DEME. On 1 September 1966 both schools changed their name to Army Apprentices College and all apprentices adopted the REME cap badge. Towards the end of 1966 it was decided that vehicle mechanics would no longer be trained at Arborfield and that the final phase of equipment training for other trades would take place in the appropriate adult schools – SEE and AETW. It was also agreed that all the training courses at Carlisle would be shortened from three years to two years and that larger intakes of vehicle mechanics should be trained there but that instrument technicians would be trained elsewhere. In April 1967 the first Arborfield apprentices to complete their Ordinary National Certificate (ONC) passed out, having been taught the whole course in the College.

Closure of Carlisle

In 1968 the MOD announced that the Army Apprentices College Carlisle was to close in 1969. In its nine years it had trained 2,378 apprentices. Amongst its many sporting successes the College won the Army Swimming (Senior) Team Championships three years running in 1966, 1967 and 1968.

One consequence of the closure was that vehicle mechanic recruiting started again at Arborfield, but for a two-year course with instructors, apprentices and training equipment coming from Carlisle. The last of the three-year vehicle mechanics passed out in the spring of 1969. To mark the amalgamation a set of wrought-iron gates was erected in July 1969 near the main entrance incorporating the famous Hadrian eagles and regimental badges of the Carlisle staff. The College's new mascot, Midge, a Shetland pony, was on parade for the first time at the Passing Out Parade in December 1969. The first of the two-year vehicle mechanics passed out in April 1970, having spent their first year at Carlisle. The technicians' courses were reduced from nine terms to eight terms. Major Percy Chivers' renown for designing and constructing wrought-iron gates received further recognition when the College produced a set for the Army's Tweseldown race course at Aldershot, and also acquired the main entrance gates from Carlisle which he had made whilst there.

City and Guilds

In the early Seventies the City and Guilds examination was introduced for all disciplines to match the three intakes each year, and to bring about a close relationship with the adult schools. At the same time closer attention was paid to the education system in support of technical training. September 1973 marked the arrival of the first intake who had all stayed on at school until their sixteenth birthday. In 1975, after discussions with the CGLI, the National Craftsman's Certificate was introduced for vehicle mechanics – a nationally recognized qualification.

AT Sergeant Adrian Wood receives the Award of Honour from the Colonel in Chief

Visit of HRH Prince Philip

His Royal Highness Prince Philip visited the Army Apprentices College in December 1974 for the Passing Out Parade with Captain Andy Platt on duty accompanying him as his Equerry. The visit started when he personally landed his helicopter on the cricket field outside Hazebrouck Officers' Mess, with a red carpet stretching all the way from the cricket square to the Mess. He was in very good form, as was illustrated by some of his remarks during the visit. As he stood on the saluting dais waiting for the March Past he asked Colonel Keith Tweed, the Commandant, what that old corrugated iron building was at the far end of the square. It was explained that it was the college gymnasium and it was there that he would be addressing the College and presenting prizes later on, to which he retorted, 'I hope it lasts until then'! At the event in the gymnasium he presented a number of half-pint pewter tankards, which he clearly did not think were very large. As he presented the prizes he announced, 'Here is your prize, and here is your egg cup!' – much to the delight of the audience.

Review of Apprentice Training

A review of apprentice training took place in 1974 and 1975 to examine the implications of the Technician Education Council (TEC) requirements; the introduction of the Director of Army Training Common Military Syllabus; rationalization of workshop practice; introduction of a new basic electronics course and coordination with SEE and AETW over the submission to the TEC of certificate and diploma programmes to replace the existing CGLI Technician Certificate and ONC in Engineering.

In June 1976 Colonel Barrie Keast became the first Arborfield apprentice to return as Commandant. The new TEC courses were launched in September 1977 for aircraft and electronic apprentices. A seven-term TEC Certificate course was introduced for selected vehicle mechanics in September 1979.

Renaming – Princess Marina College

The College was renamed Princess Marina College on 1 June 1981 to commemorate the first Colonel in Chief of the Corps, 1963–68: HRH The Princess Marina, Duchess of Kent. Later, in 1989, the College was to celebrate the golden jubilee of apprentice training in Arborfield with a Jubilee Passing Out Parade and Reunion.

New seven-term diploma courses started in September 1981 and weapons apprentices were re-introduced, none having been trained since Carlisle was closed in 1969. Armourers and gun fitter apprentices started a six-term CGLI apprenticeship followed by a twelve-week course at SEME.

Move to New Barracks

Aerial view of Princess Marina College

The move to the new buildings close to SEE at Arborfield began in March 1981 with the move of the Electronics Wing. The final move from the forty-two-year-old wood and corrugated iron huts took place in July, but the Aircraft Wing remained in the old Bailleul Barracks until September 1985. Most of the 1,000 inhabitants of the college and their equipment moved to their new location in only two weeks. The apprentices concerned are unlikely to forget helping to move the library of 10,000 books in what seemed almost as many heavy boxes! HRH Prince Philip opened the new buildings on 15 April 1982 and a plaque in the main entrance hall commemorates the occasion. Representatives of the Worshipful Company of Turners, who have maintained such close relations with the Corps since shortly after it was formed in 1942, visited the College on 20 October 1982. Later, at the end of the decade, the Company generously decided to make an annual award of their Silver Medal, a monetary award and a certificate to the apprentice who achieved the highest standard of craft skills during his training.

1983 saw the arrival of one-year apprentices when the REME company at the RAOC Apprentices College at Deepcut closed, and at this time seven-term apprenticeships were reduced to six terms. Three ex-apprentices were commissioned from The Royal Military Academy Sandhurst in December 1983 – Richard Mitchell who won the Sword of Honour, Alan Powell who won the Anson Memorial Prize and Paul Martin. 1985 began well when another ex-apprentice, Brigadier G B Berragan, was selected to be the Director General of Ordnance Services at the Logistic Executive (Army), Andover.

In May the RAMC/RADC Junior Leaders came from their closing facility at Mytchett. So by the mid-Eighties there were again three cap badges worn by the apprentices, as there had been in 1939. Further information about the Apprentices Colleges may be found in the REME Journal in articles by Brigadier Mike Kneen in 1970 about Carlisle and Captain D B Richards in 1984 about Princess Marina College.

THE TRAINING BATTALION AND DEPOT REME

Military Training

The responsibility for military training of adult recruits for REME at the Depot REME, as it was then named, started on 5 January 1961. The Depot had moved to Poperinghe Barracks, Arborfield, from Otley, Yorkshire, in October 1948. In 1967 it was renamed Training Battalion and Depot REME, which better reflected its training role. The famous old wooden hutted 'spider' barracks at this late stage in their life were unfortunately prone to catching fire, and in May 1961 the Sergeants' Mess was burnt to the ground and in 1963 a recruit hut was burnt with much loss of kit, both fires happily without casualties. The drill square, however, was indestructible, as any recruit would testify, and was famous for its electricity grid pylon landmark. The East Gymnasium too was well known to hundreds of officers who came to DME/DEME(A) Study Periods there year after year. This era was to come to an end, however, in October 1977, when the newly built Rowcroft Barracks were ready for occupation, and Poperinghe Barracks passed into history. A full and amusing account of life in Poperinghe Barracks from 1948 to 1977 is given in 'The Chronicle of Poperinghe' by Captain Geoff Beere who served there as a CSM, twice as RSM and finally as a Captain. Further information is given in the REME Journal for 1979 in an article by Lieutenant Colonel Chris Derbyshire.

After the Sergeants' Mess fire

The Move to Rowcroft Barracks

The last Battalion parade in Poperinghe Barracks took place on 26 August 1977 and was reviewed by Major General Derek Walker,

Commander REME Support Group. On 13 September the Quartermaster took over the new Rowcroft Barracks and during the next month the heavy equipments and office furniture were moved. The main move to the new Rowcroft Barracks at the opposite end of Arborfield Garrison took place on 13 October 1977. It was a beautiful day and it was decided that the Battalion would march to its new home with the REME Staff Band leading the way, followed by B Company commanded by Major John Norman. Led by the Band, the Battalion marched in the sunshine in a circle around the REME Training Centre and the REME Officers School and then up the road into the new Barracks, where the sunlit red brick buildings blended in so well with the oak trees around them and the red clay soil of the Arborfield countryside.

The Battalion was well pleased with its new accommodation which was spacious and especially well laid out for the recruits. Each barrack block of several rooms for eight men each shared common facilities of lounge, ablution block and a cleaning area – very different from the old crowded wooden spiders of Poperinghe. A particular feature was the exceptionally well-designed Sergeants' Mess. Other assets were the drill shed with a training theatre and a purpose-built band block, whose inner walls had offset bricks. These the rock-climbing enthusiasts were very keen to practise on, despite the disapproval of the Director of Music.

Major John Norman leads the march out of Poperinghe Barracks

The barracks were officially opened on 27 April 1978 by HRH Prince Philip, with a Battalion parade, a tour of the barracks and the unveiling of a plaque. While visiting the Sergeants' Mess the Prince realized there were others in the building whom he had not met who, because of lack of space, had not been allowed to join the official ceremonies. He asked Lieutenant Colonel Chris Derbyshire if there was anybody whom he had not seen, upon which the CO opened a door on to a surprised audience. They set aside their refreshments and expressed their pleasure at the informal way in which Prince Philip joined them. The final event was lunch at West Court where he met all the Battalion officers and their wives. The next month the Battalion further celebrated by winning eight trophies, including the Major Units team championship, at the REME Corps Small Arms Meeting; Staff Sergeant Walshaw's four trophies included the Rowcroft Cup which seemed very appropriate.

Military Training

1973–76 were active years in the Training Battalion, providing milestones in REME military training. A working party had been set up to look into the RD/GD role and there was another working party looking into the military training of REME soldiers. Lieutenant Colonel Peter Crooks, chairman of both, had recently completed a tour as CO of the Training Battalion and Depot. The Crooks Report, and the Director of Army Training's new directive 'Shoot to Kill', resulted in a revised Common Military Syllabus and a complete restructuring of all REME military training courses. The Recruit Syllabus was lengthened from six to eleven and a half weeks. The former Military Training Certificates 1, 2 and 3 were abolished, and a Basic Military Certificate course covered the MTC 3 as well as the Common Military Syllabus and Corps requirements. A Junior Military Certificate course for two weeks for potential junior NCOs, to give them some leadership training and more military skills, and a Senior Military Certificate course of five weeks, were introduced. All these courses in future would take place at the Training Battalion to ensure a uniform high standard. Revisions were made in 1982 to improve these courses.

In 1981–82 the Training Battalion had a recruit intake of only 256, including six Sappers. In the next two years the allocations were 1,033 and 1,200 with the prospect of 1,400 in 1984–85. Platoon staffing and even finding enough bedspaces was an interesting and continuing problem for the CO, Lieutenant Colonel Roger Bellis. A problem of a different nature faced Lieutenant Colonel Roddy Mullin who was CO in the period 1984–87, when the recruit course was issued with a new Army boot which replaced the old directly-moulded sole boot. It produced foot problems because the recruits could not get their boots broken in quickly enough. Athletic training shoes or 'trainers' were issued instead because the new boots could not be used to the full for some activities. It was also noticed at this time that some recruits were arriving very unfit, and that this appeared attributable to lack of physical activity at school. This was well within the capacity of the Battalion to put right and at the end of their courses recruits were in every way fit for the tasks ahead.

During the period 1988–91 the New Management Strategy (NMS) formulated within the MOD during Mr Michael Heseltine's period as Secretary of State for Defence began to be implemented in the Training Battalion, and the unit charter was formally accepted. Budgets took on increasing importance but without much delegation of powers to deal with the mass of detail. There were annual rounds of saving measures, including a spending moratorium and efficiency measures, which were usually small percentage cuts perceived to be arbitrary in nature. This new MOD policy required that services such as catering and cleaning were performed by civilian contractors. The exceptions were the Battalion's regimental restaurant catering and the cleaning of the soldiers' lines.

At this time the tasks of the Battalion included:

- Military training for up to 1,024 adult recruits per year, split between two companies. There were sixteen platoons in each company, every platoon holding thirty-two students on a ten-week course following the Common Military Syllabus. The capacity could be increased to 1,280 recruits per year.
- Military, regimental and leadership training and assessment of 560 potential senior NCOs per year in fourteen platoons, each of forty students on a five-week course.
- Military, regimental and leadership training and assessment for 200 potential artificers per year on five courses, each of forty students for eight weeks.
- Selection, training and upgrading of all Regimental Duty personnel.
- Administration of all unit staff and students and the REME Staff Band.
- Administration of all REME officers and soldiers who were not on the held strength of another unit such as those on civilian courses, in transit, pending Court appearances, absentees from overseas and personnel to be discharged.

1988 and 1989 were two very important years in the life of the Training Battalion. In these years training in the Battalion was reviewed by Commander Training and Arms Directors (CTAD) Inspectorate. The report on the REME Individual Training Organization (ITO) was half an inch thick. Essentially, it recommended the introduction of a Systems Approach to Training using a procedure called the Mellor Loop, which CTAD had identified as the way ahead for all Army training establishments. The Mellor Loop was named after Brigadier Derrick Mellor, who, after a distinguished career in the Corps, was Director Technical Training and Inspector of Boys Training at the Ministry of Defence 1966–69. As far as REME was concerned CTAD's Review and Monitoring Programme generated several training action plans in the Training Battalion and required other significant changes. In the summer of 1988 the number of courses was at an all-time high, but the number of trained instructors had sunk to an all-time low. Over a hundred recruits were sent to Catterick to be trained by R SIGNALS. In addition, Corporal instructors were posted in at short notice from the whole Corps and from other Arms, but several courses had to be cancelled. A major internal training programme started to improve the instructional quality of the NCOs and the training qualifications of the Officers and Warrant Officers. Steps were taken to ensure that all the courses were relevant and challenging. Infantry instructors were employed in the recruit platoons – one by one they asked to transfer to REME. Much attention was paid to the military and leadership training given to the Corporals and Artificer students.

A New Decade

The revised Common Military Syllabus for Recruits was introduced in 1990. This was a ten-week course which was introduced against a background of the largest number of recruits ever taken on at Rowcroft Barracks and an eighteen-month delay in the issue of the new SA80 rifle. The Kohima remedial training platoon was conceived to help those recruits who were not so physically and mentally robust as the training staff would have liked. The closure of the Army Personnel Selection Centre (APSC) in March 1990 gave Kohima platoon an unexpected boost – it was soon the size of a normal training platoon.

In 1990, also, HQ DGEME commissioned a study of artificer non-technical training which resulted in the last of the eight-week Artificer Military Training courses ending in February 1991 to be replaced with a revised five-week course. The study was carried out by the new Training Development Team (TDT) and the Battalion.

The introduction of PAMPAS – Personnel Administration Microcomputer System – for documentation and pay led to the Unit Administration Office, headed by the Paymaster, going about the business of the Depot function in a new way and providing a service to HQ REME Training Centre, the REME Officers School and several minor units. A constant problem, though, remained the high degree of civilian and military undermanning.

Closure of Training Battalion and Depot

In May 1991 a severe reduction in the budget allocation for HQ REME Training Centre forced it to consider major cuts in its training commitment. This led to the early implementation of a Training Base Review recommendation that the Training Battalion and Depot REME basic recruit training be transferred to one of the four (later five) units earmarked to become an Army Training Regiment. This enabled the unit to be closed, with the shedding of other tasks.

A Company of the Battalion, which had carried out the military and leadership training of REME potential senior NCOs and artificers, the selection, training and up-grading of all NCOs employed on the REME Regimental Duty Roll, and the sponsorship of all REME Junior Military Certificate courses run by the major REME units in the field force, moved to SEME in October 1991.

B and C Companies were the adult recruit training companies. The final intakes of Burma and Tobruk platoons of B Company completed training in December 1991, whilst C Company was disbanded. The last CO of the Training Battalion and Depot was Lieutenant Colonel Martin Bowles and the last RSM WO1 S M Green, with the final parade on disbandment being reviewed by Major General Mike Heath, DGEME. In January 1992 B Company moved to the Guards Depot, Pirbright, where it was redesignated Rowcroft Company, and an impressive memorial sundial was placed outside the Battalion Headquarters in Rowcroft Barracks to commemorate the thirty productive years that the unit had spent in Arborfield.

The HQ and Depot Company that remained was responsible for the drafting, holding, release and administration of the Depot, including all REME officers and soldiers on the unit strength and those not on the strength of any other unit. It was also responsible for the administration and command of the REME Staff Band and the administration of the Garrison Physical and Recreational Training Centre and West Court Officers' Mess. Also in January 1992 the Depot REME moved to a location within Princess Marina College as an independent unit under command of the Regimental Colonel.

LINKS WITH THE ENGINEERING PROFESSION

The Corps has always sought to ensure its recognition as a significant element of the nation's engineering profession, taking appropriate steps to achieve relevant qualifications and participating in its corporate activities. In particular members of the Corps always played a prominent part in the activities of professional engineering institutions with which the Corps was associated. For example, in December 1971, at a joint meeting of the Institution of Electrical Engineers and the REME Institution, Major General Peter Girling, DEME(A) presented a paper for discussion – 'A Systems Approach to the Provision of Engineering Support for Army Equipment'. In the mid-Seventies, Major General Alex McKay, DEME(A), also had the honour of delivering the James Clayton lecture to the Institution of Mechanical Engineers. His paper described the contribution made by the Corps towards improving the reliability and maintainability of Army equipment based on knowledge of its operating environment and on the Corps' whole-life approach to the provision of engineering support. The paper was printed in the REME Journal for 1976.

Senior members of the Corps also served on the Councils, and as officers to the Institutions. Major General Sir Leonard Atkinson was President of the Institution of Electronic and Radio Engineers in 1968–69, for many years a member of the Council of Engineering Institutions, becoming Chairman in 1974, and continued this interest on the formation of the Engineering Council. From 1976–1987, Major General Alex McKay was Secretary of the Institution of Mechanical Engineers. In more recent times Major General Malcolm Hutchinson was for three years the first President of the Institution of Electronics and Electrical Incorporated Engineers and a member of the Engineering Council; he was also a member of Sir John Fairclough's working party set up in 1992 to examine the unification of the Engineering profession. Other posts as chief executive have, inter alia, been held by Lieutenant Colonel Alan Stroud (Institute of Road Transport Engineers) and Brigadier Peter Crooks (Institution of Production Engineers, later Institution of Manufacturing Engineers); the latter was succeeded by Brigadier Gordon Rawlins who continued the Institution's merger into the Institution of Electrical Engineers where he became a deputy secretary. Many others have held various significant posts in engineering and quality assurance organizations.

There were links, too, with many hundreds of individual engineers who served in the Corps during the Second World War or as National Servicemen after the war. Some of them achieved fame in civil life in positions of great responsibility such as: Sir Denis Rooke, Chairman of British Gas, a Fellow of the Royal Society and President of the Fellowship of Engineering; Sir Terence Beckett, Chairman of the Ford Motor Company Ltd and Director General of the Confederation of British Industries; Sir David Plastow, Chairman and Chief Executive of Vickers; Lord Stokes of Leyland, Chairman and Chief Executive of British Leyland Motor Corporation and President of the Institution of Mechanical Engineers; Professor Tom Patten, eminent Ocean Engineering Consultant; Ewen McEwen, Vice Chairman (Engineering) Joseph Lucas Ltd and President of the Institution of Mechanical Engineers; Alastair Paterson, Senior Partner Bullen and Partners, Consulting Engineers, President of the Institution of Structural Engineers and of the Institution of Civil Engineers; Sir George Jefferson, Chairman and Chief Executive Dynamics Group British Aerospace and in the Eighties the first Chairman of the privatized British Telecommunications; Sir Robert Scholey, Chairman of British Steel.

Finniston Committee

Major General Hugh Macdonald-Smith both before and after his retirement from the Active List was a member of the Government Committee of Inquiry into the Engineering Profession 1977–79, under the chairmanship of Sir Montague (Monty) Finniston FRS. Although members of the committee took part as individuals, and not as representatives, it nevertheless showed the high standing of the Corps in the engineering profession that the Director General was invited to be a member of the committee which made eighty important and far-reaching recommendations in their report which was published in 1980. The recommendations, which included the supply and employment of engineers, a system of statutory registration of qualifications and the role of the Institutions, led to the formation of the Engineering Council.

The Engineering Council

The Engineering Council was established by Royal Charter in 1981 to advance education in and promote the science and practice of engineering with a view to improving the efficiency of UK industry. The Council controlled and granted engineering qualifications in three grades – Engineering Technician, Incorporated Engineer and Chartered Engineer. Each grade required qualification by education, training and responsible experience. The Engineering Council negotiated for those who had Chartered Engineer (CEng) status in the UK to be eligible for the title 'European Engineer' (EurIng). The Council was active in promoting good relevant education for engineers and promoting awareness of what engineering is in schools, polytechnics and universities and maintaining a register of many thousands of engineers and technicians and the standards associated with it. Colonel Denis Filer TD was the Director General of the Engineering Council from 1988. He was a former Colonel REME TA – the senior active TA post in the Corps.

The Armed Services were jointly an Industrial Affiliate to the Engineering Council, which allowed the Army and the Corps to express their views on engineering in the same way as many major companies in the UK. Individual officers of the Corps could influence their own professional institution, if they took an active part in local branches or served on their councils. The major engineering institutions had long accredited REME Young Officer training as meeting their requirements for Corporate Membership. After graduating and completing RYO training young officers only needed to get the necessary experience in a responsible engineering post before they could apply to become Chartered Engineers. One of the aims of the REME Institution Technical Sub-Committee was to encourage close relations between the Corps and the many professional engineering institutions and bodies and to promote the standing of the Corps throughout the profession.

Members of the Corps who were qualified by education, training and experience could apply for membership of their professional institutions and for registration with the Engineering Council as Engineering Technician, Incorporated Engineer or Chartered Engineer. Such qualifications were recognized in civilian life by employers and were likely to become more important throughout the European Community after 1992.

The Fellowship of Engineering

Major General Tony Palmer, with a team of officers and senior ranks, gave a presentation to the Fellowship of Engineering in February 1984 with the title 'Education and Training in the Corps of Royal Electrical and Mechanical Engineers'. HRH Prince Philip took the Chair, being the Senior Fellow of the Fellowship and Colonel in Chief of the Corps. A few members of the Corps have been elected Fellows since the Fellowship came into being in 1976 and held its inaugural meeting at Buckingham Palace. It is a senior learned society which exists to work for and reflect excellence in engineering in a similar role to that which the Royal Society plays for science. It was founded with 126 Founder Fellows, half of them those engineers who were Fellows of the Royal Society and half of them chartered engineers who were considered to be the most eminent in the profession. The President in 1987 was Sir Denis Rooke CBE FRS FEng, Chairman of British Gas plc who served in the Corps from 1944 to 1949 in the UK and India. The Executive Secretary for several years was Brigadier Geoffrey Atkinson, followed by Brigadier John Appleton. It became The Royal Academy of Engineering in 1992.

The City Livery Companies

The ancient craft and trade guilds in the City of London in days long ago contributed armed men to keep watch in the City, so being linked with auxiliary forces from very early days. From the 14th to the 18th century the livery companies controlled the City and Royal Charters were granted to many of them. Since the 19th century the City companies have used their considerable resources to support and encourage general and technical education, industrial research and craft skill. The City and Guilds of London Institute founded in 1878 clearly shows its origin in its title.

The Corps has had a long relationship with two City of London livery companies, the Worshipful Company of Turners and the Worshipful Company of Armourers and Brasiers. In the Eighties a liaison was gradually being established with the newly formed Worshipful Company of Engineers.

The Worshipful Company of Turners has a history extending over many centuries in the City of London. From the middle of the 19th century the Turners encouraged trade skills and awarded prizes for competition between apprentices throughout the country and presented lathes to schools and training establishments. They later extended their encouragement to the metal trades in general and to mechanical engineering design. The Company was quick to respond in February 1943 to the formation of REME in October 1942 by presenting Major General Rowcroft with a silver porringer, now in West Court, and their Honorary Freedom. They presented the Corps with an illuminated inscription recording the Turners' appreciation of the Corps' contribution in the Second World War. They have adopted REME TA units and in

1954 presented a shield which is competed for by those units; it is often presented personally by the Master. They also make an annual award to the Princess Marina College apprentice who achieves the highest standard of craft skills during his training. A number of REME officers have become Liverymen, and invitations are exchanged to Livery Dinners and Corps Dinners.

The Worshipful Company of Turners, including three former Directors of the Corps, Major General Sir Leslie Tyler, Major General Sir Leonard Atkinson and Major General Peter Girling, visited SEE on 8 November 1984 where they saw the latest electronic equipment in service in the Army including CLANSMAN Automatic Test Equipment, CHALLENGER and CHIEFTAIN tanks, Towed and Tracked RAPIER air defence missile systems, JAVELIN, MILAN and Thermal Imagers. Major General Sir Leslie Tyler was Master of the Company of Turners 1982–83 and Major General Sir Leonard Atkinson was Master 1987–88.

The Worshipful Company of Armourers and Brasiers dates from the 14th century. The Company awarded a silver medal for the best all-round performance by an armourer in the annual REME Skill-at-Arms meeting, awarded for the first time in 1956, and in 1990 a bronze medallion plus £200 for the best weapons artificer student in each training year. The Master and the Clerk are invited by tradition to attend the Corps meeting and present the medal. Exchanges of invitations to Livery and Corps dinners are made.

The Worshipful Company of Engineers was formed in 1983. They soon approached the engineering Corps of the Army to establish links. In 1991 they made their first awards to the Corps to Captain Iain Clyde and Staff Sergeant Beckwith, an Artificer Avionics. The awards are made annually for the best performance in young officer and artificer training. Membership of the Company of Engineers, 94th in order of precedence of City Livery Companies, was confined to those who were Fellows of one of the chartered engineering institutions, unlike other Livery Companies where membership may include other City professions such as bankers and stockbrokers and not just the profession implied in the title of the Company. As a guild the Company is concerned with apprentices, craftsmen and technicians – hence the two awards to members of our Corps. In 1992, in appreciation of their close association, the officers of the Corps presented the Company with a set of silver wine goblets.

Army Engineering Symposium

The Director of Army Recruiting (DAR) sponsored a two-day symposium every two or three years from the early Seventies, to which he invited leading members of the engineering profession, professors and members of engineering departments of universities, polytechnics and colleges of higher education. The aim was to show them the training and employment of graduate engineers in RE, R SIGNALS and REME.

The idea had begun in the late Sixties when a University Symposium had been held at Arborfield for university staff without representatives from the profession outside. The engineering symposia usually included about fifty Army hosts and one hundred guests; twenty-five for each of the three Corps and the DAR. A typical symposium took place at the School of Signals at Blandford in 1981, where the guests were shown the range and sophistication of military equipment and told about the training and employment of graduate engineers in the three engineering Corps. REME gave a formal presentation and mounted equipment displays including GAZELLE helicopter and CHIEFTAIN ARV repairs, and also CLANSMAN Automatic Test Equipment and RAPIER repair vehicles in operation. The Corps invited representatives from the National Advisory Centre on Careers for Women; by 1990 there were ten lady officers in the Corps as full members of REME – no longer WRAC.

In 1983 a similar event was held at The Royal School of Military Engineering at Chatham followed by a REME presentation to the Southern Branch of the Institution of Mechanical Engineers at Croydon. In 1985 the Symposium was held at Arborfield with the latest equipment from Vehicles and Weapons Branch, SEE, SEME and AETW.

ADVENTUROUS TRAINING

Adventurous training expeditions fall into the categories of both training and sport, and examples are included not only in this chapter but also in Chapter 14, Corps Sports, to give an indication of the wide range of activities that are an essential part of the life of officers and soldiers in the Corps. All such expeditions are designed to increase self-reliance, self-discipline, fitness and teamwork under arduous and interesting conditions.

The Rory Cape Award

Captain Rory Cape achieved more in his short life than many men have done in a lifetime; he died when only 30 years old. He had reached, when still very young, the quarter-finals of the British Amateur Boxing Association Championships and was the Corps Boxing Champion at his weight for many years. He was a fine tennis player and a regular competitor in the Corps Championships. He took a great part in adventurous and mountaineering activities. When still under training as a young officer he undertook an arduous expedition down the Fish River in a very desolate part of South West Africa. He went on a Royal Marines expedition to the Himalayas while serving as BEME 3 Commando Brigade in Singapore, where he climbed some hitherto unclimbed peaks. He and the leader of the expedition, Lieutenant Stuart Rose RM, were the first to reach the summit of the Menthosa Peak. At the time of his death in 1972 he had been selected for the Services Expedition to climb Mount

McKinley in Alaska in 1973 and for the Mount Everest expedition planned for 1975.

The Rory Cape Memorial Trophy

After his death his family approached the DEME(A) with a very generous offer to donate to the Corps a large sum of money to be used to encourage adventurous and enterprising activities. After consultation, the Corps initiated the Rory Cape Award to be presented annually to the officer or soldier who had made the most outstanding contribution to such activities during the previous year. Some years later Mr and Mrs Harms presented a further sum of money for the Rory Cape Fund. The award has only been made in years in which an activity of the highest merit has taken place. Three early winners of the Award were Lieutenant Colonel John Peacock in 1974 for a climbing expedition to Nuptse, Staff Sergeant David Leslie in 1975 in recognition of his notable achievements as Mate of *Great Britain II* in the Financial Times Clipper Race around the world, and Captain Pat Gunson, REME TAVR, in 1976 for his outstanding performance on the Army Mountaineering Expedition to Mount Everest.

So many expeditions in so many parts of the world have been undertaken by the Corps that it is not possible to describe them all in this chapter. Two typical expeditions have therefore been chosen from the middle of the Seventies as good examples. The first is a brief account of an expedition to Africa in 1974–75 involving five REME NCOs; the second, to South America, involved five young REME officers on a reconnaissance in 1973, and three officers, two warrant officers and a sergeant on the main expedition in 1977. Finally, Exercise Master Craftsman, part of the REME 50 activities in 1992, is a fitting story to end the Adventurous Training section.

Staff Sergeant David Leslie at the helm and Lance Corporal Shepard. Round the World Race 1975

Zaire River Expedition 1974–1975

Staff Sergeant L Winterburn, Sergeant Malcolm Pace, Sergeant Ben Cartwright and Sergeant Brian Hammond joined the main party of the 1974–75 Zaire River expedition in London in October 1974. Lieutenant Colonel John Blashford-Snell RE led the expedition which was to attempt the first navigation of the renamed Congo River from its source to the sea while making some scientific surveys on the way. The Zaire River is more than 2,700 miles long, flowing from near the border of Zambia to the Atlantic Ocean, crossing the equator twice; its volume is second only to the River Amazon.

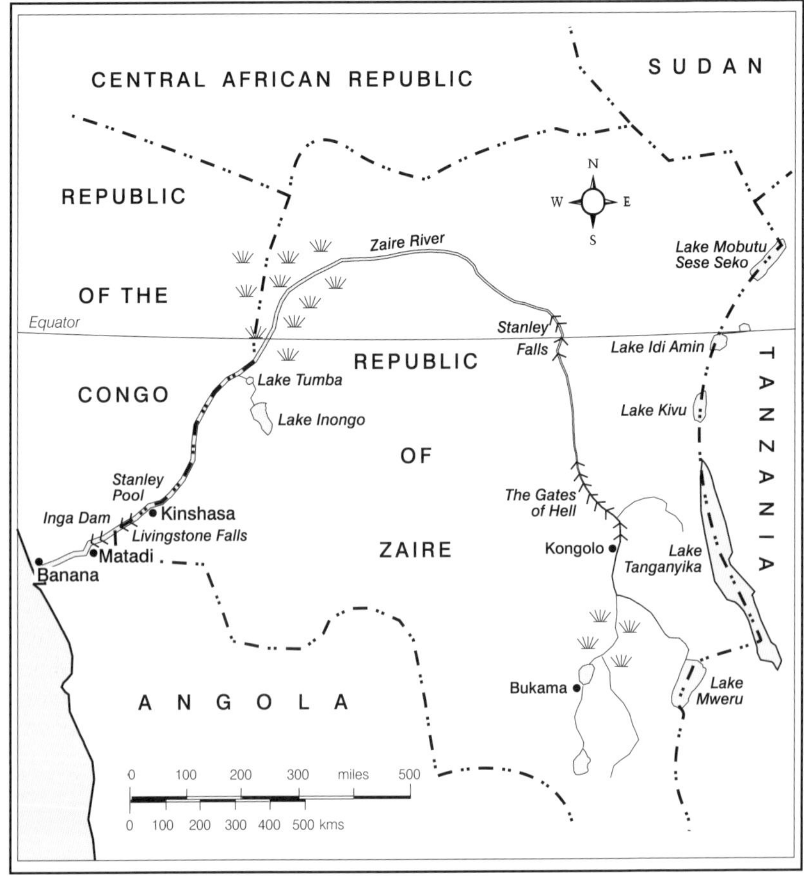

The planning of the expedition took three years, during which special inflatable boats were developed to withstand the pounding from rocks and rushing water. At the time these boats were the largest in the world – 40 foot long and 15 foot wide. The expedition had a Beaver aircraft and eight ex-Army Land Rovers; Staff Sergeant Sandy Donald, another REME member, came with the Beaver. On 27 October the main boat party of some 70 people set out from Bukama in three giant craft and two Avon inflatable reconnaissance boats for Kongolo. Staff Sergeant Winterburn and Sergeant Cartwright were to drive overland – 800 miles that took them seven days over rough tracks and through the northern part of the Upemba Game Park across mountains to the north-east of Bukama. At Kongolo Staff Sergeant Winterburn joined the boats as 'chief engineer' to look after the powerful steering outboard motors on which the crews' lives would depend. He joined in time to shoot the 'Gates of Hell' rapids which are about one mile long. That night they camped under the hills from which Stanley had first seen the Congo a century earlier. A few days later they navigated a five-mile stretch of rapids which include the Stanley Falls. The river narrowed from a mile to 200 yards, running very fast: one minute they were riding the crest of a wave and the next they were side-on to a fifteen foot drop into a boiling, frothing pit. As the boat crashed down the stern went under and the water cut out the engine; the boat could not be steered and was sent swirling around a large whirlpool. Two fifty-gallon fuel tanks broke loose and threatened to crush the helmsman. After about two minutes which seemed like two hours they were hurled into calmer water where a quick spray from the ever-ready combat fluid started the engine and they were ready to help the following boats. The locals told them it was the first time that anybody had gone over the Tshunga Falls and come out alive. On 24 November they crossed the Equator going north. On 5 December they started on the 1,000-mile stretch to Kinshasa which had no rapids but 300 miles of mosquito swamps. The most dangerous part of the journey was still to come, the thirty-two cataracts of the Livingstone Falls between Kinshasa and the port of Matadi 200 miles away. The crews were cut down from fourteen to six because of the increased danger. There was a long stretch with twelve-foot waves pounding over the rocks or large waves and deep holes in an otherwise smooth surface, caused by huge underwater boulders or giant whirlpools. At one whirlpool which was fifty yards across the boat did a 'wall of death' run round the rim. They reached the Atlantic port of Banana on 19 January 1975 to be greeted by a crowd of dancing girls in grass skirts! They had navigated the whole river apart from an impassable stretch around the Inga Dam. A full account may be read in the 1976 REME Journal.

Colombian Amazonas Expedition 1977
The Amazonas Expedition was an Anglo-Colombian scientific expedition sponsored by the Corps and supported by the Armies of both countries, which spent four months in a remote part of the Amazon Basin of Colombia, South America.

Prior to that, in 1973 a three-month logistic reconnaissance had been carried out, following an invitation from Colombia, by five REME officers, Adrian Goldsack, Charles Hutchinson, Peter Jackson, John Saunders and Ray Slater during their summer vacation from The Royal Military College of Science. The young officers reported that 'for exhilaration and sheer excitement it would be hard to beat that of negotiating the rapids of the Rio Caqueta in a 40hp outboard-assisted dugout Indian canoe'. One of the largest tributaries of the Amazon River, it is compressed as it passes Angostura into one quarter of its normal width, transforming it into a mill-race of deep water, a thing of treacherous ridges, troughs and whirlpools. Their task was to travel the Caqueta and the entire length of the Rio Putamayo until it joined the River Amazon in Brazil and then to travel up the Amazon to Leticia. An important result of the reconnaissance was to recommend Araracuara as an ideal base camp for the main expedition; a very remote place on the Rio Caqueta

– the 'Siberia of Columbia'.

In 1974 the Corps agreed to sponsor the major follow-up expedition planned for 1976 but which eventually took place in 1977. The Army role was to provide logistic support so that scientists could concentrate on archaeological, environmental and medical work. The expedition leader was Captain John Saunders, who later received the Rory Cape Award for his dedication and drive. Other REME members of the expedition were Captains Stuart Cameron and Adrian Goldsack, WO1 Gordon Sands, WO2 Geoff Tancred and Sergeant Ian Tutt.

Lieutenant Adrian Goldsack on the Anglo-Colombian Expedition

Exercise Master Craftsman 1992

Exercise Master Craftsman was an exceptionally large adventurous training exercise held as part of the REME 50 celebrations. It started on 27 February 1992 with Exercise Rowcroft Ride when a team of six cyclists rode from Arborfield to Andover where they handed over two Talismans to DGES(A), Major General Mike Heath. The team of six included Brigadier Bob Cooper, the Arborfield Garrison Commander and apprentices Mike Thompson and Steve Nelson-Jones from Princess Marina College. Each talisman was a caduceus(a small carrier or ancient herald's wand) manufactured by 14 (Berlin) Field Workshop in a Corps-wide competition to create a talisman representative of the Corps' engineering expertise. One, in nickel silver, would be presented to the Canadian Land Electrical and Mechanical Engineers, the second (in brass and mahogany) returned for display in the Corps Museum.

Exercise Tope's Tab required a running team from the REME Wing Royal School of Artillery to take

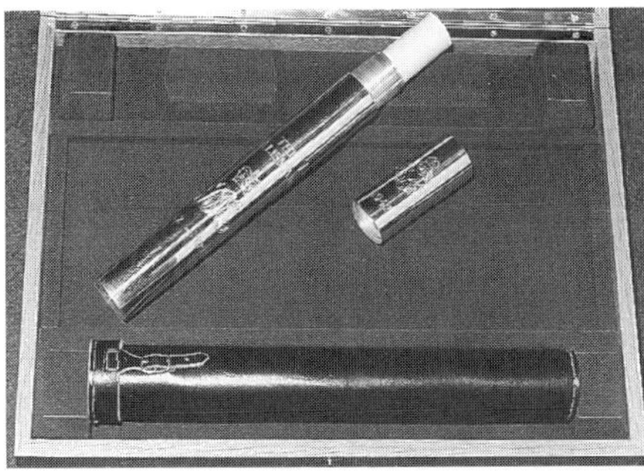

The Talisman

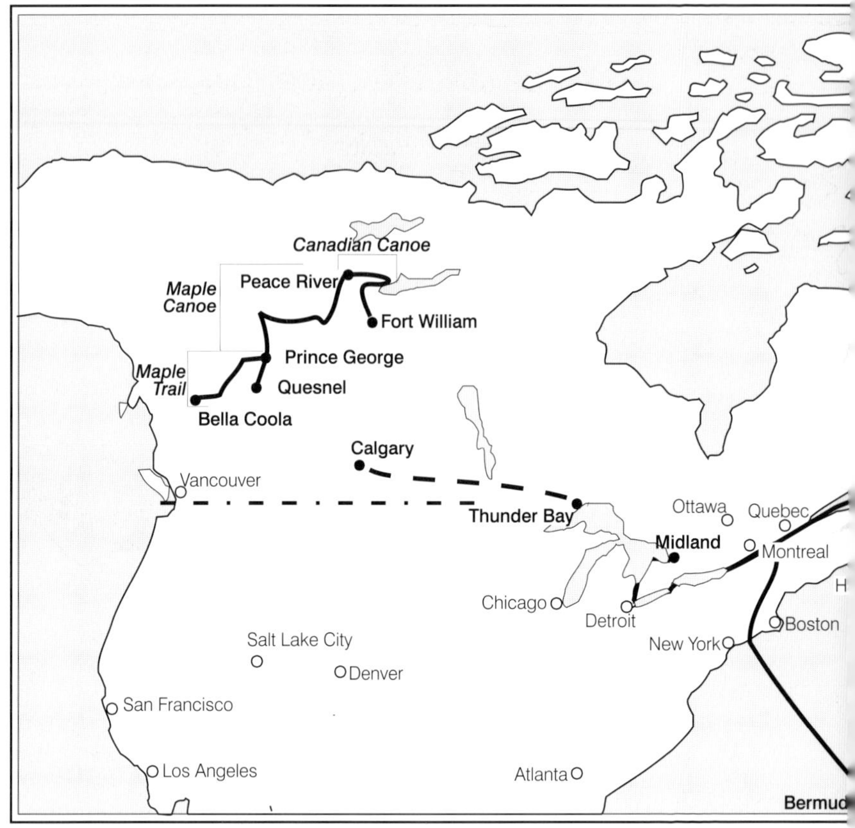

the scrolls signed by DGES(A) and placed inside the caducei the 51 miles from Andover to Marchwood Military Port near Southampton. On arrival Major Peter Storey and CSM Neil Denton handed them over to the Skipper of Master Craftsman, Staff Sergeant Nigel Rennie, who was also from REME Wing RSA. Two of the fourteen runners, Staff Sergeant George Hughes and Corporal John Hubbard, made a quick change of clothes as they were to sail on the first leg of the next phase on the yacht *Master Craftsman*.

This phase was the major exercise Maple Sail which started as planned at 1700 hours on 27 February. The yacht *Master Craftsman* was a 39 foot Westerly Sealord which had been converted for the exercise by a hard-working team at 17 Port and Maritime Workshop. The Exercise involved thirteen crews of ten sailing for about two weeks each (except for the last leg) from Marchwood to the Great Lakes calling at Plymouth, the Azores, Bermuda, New York, West Point, Kingston, Midland,

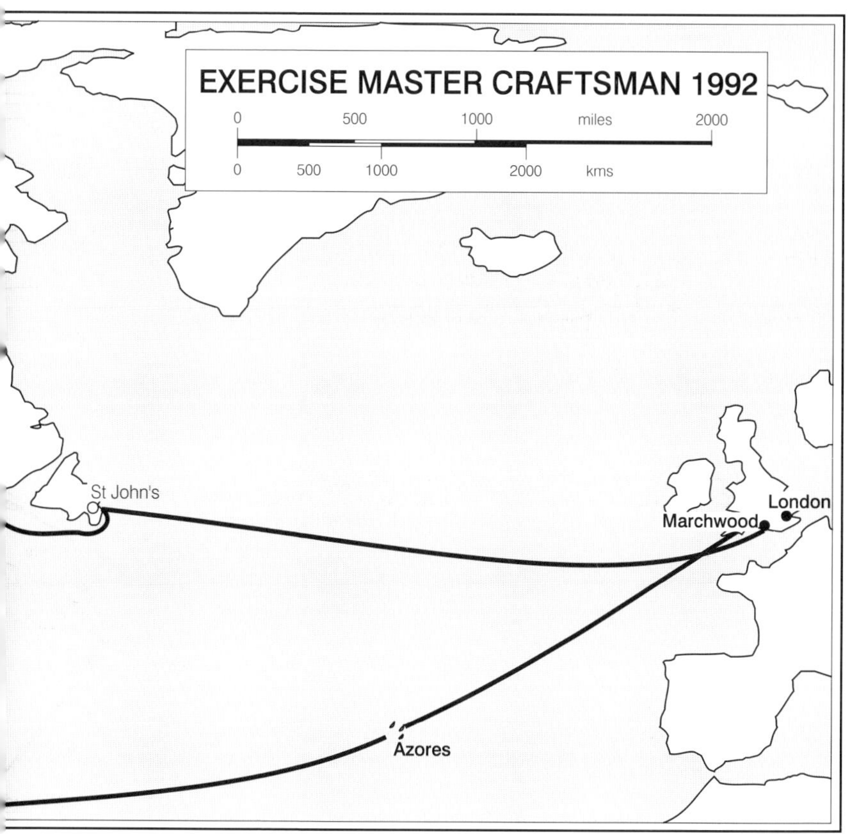

Thunder Bay, Trenton, Montreal, Quebec, St John's Newfoundland and back to Marchwood.

Staff Sergeant Rennie and his crew, mainly from the REME Wing RSA and SEME, met several problems on their leg to the Azores including beating into gale force winds and very rough seas. Damage to the new sails and the hull when they were nearly half way to the Azores was judged to be so hazardous that they returned to Plymouth for inspection and repair, having sailed nearly 1,500 miles by 14 March. After repairs Staff Sergeant Rennie sailed on 16 March with a new crew, largely from 7 Armoured Workshop, with Mr Chris Penfold as Mate. They arrived in the Azores in less than ten days after covering 1,417 miles. The most exciting event this time was the appearance of a forty-five foot whale right under their bow.

The third crew, under ASM Barry Wickett and Mate Mr John Redpath, sailed from the Azores to Bermuda experiencing a storm lasting two days and sailing under 'bare poles'. On the twelfth day they sailed 187 miles in 24 hours.

The fourth crew came from NIEW, SEME and SES(A) with Lieutenant Colonel Alastair Campbell as Skipper. They sailed from Bermuda to New York between 24 April and 7 May. One night was marked by gale force winds and gusts up to 40 knots, causing broken rigging and disintegration of the Autogen wind generator blades. They arrived in New York on the eleventh day and two days later motored up the Hudson River for fifty miles, there being no wind, to West Point Military Academy, having sailed nearly 1,200 miles.

Captain Cameron Ferguson was Skipper for Leg 5 from New York to Kingston, Ontario, via the canal systems and the St Lawrence River. En route they arrived in Old Montreal in time for its 350th anniversary celebrations, with *Master Craftsman* dressed overall. The crew came from NIEW, 50 Missile Regiment Workshop and 12 Armoured Workshop, and were delighted to join in the party spirit of the City, with the public taking a great interest in their vessel and its activities. They sailed on past the Thousand Islands into Lake Ontario to The Royal Military College Kingston on 21 May.

The sixth crew, with Skipper Colonel Jeremy Towler and Mate Colonel David Axson, was found from SEME, SEE and Canada. This leg took them from Kingston to Midland, Georgian Bay (on Lake Huron) a distance of 800 miles. This included the Welland Canal to get round the Niagara Falls into Lake Erie. They enjoyed an excellent beat to the Detroit River, followed by another excellent sail across Lake Huron.

Leg 7 was from Midland to Thunder Bay on the west shore of Lake Huron. Skipper Colonel Geoffrey Simpson, with Mr Jim Green as Mate, took the crew found from Princess Marina College through seventy miles of foggy weather; the radar did not work and the Global Positioning System (GPS) which had become known as Tim the Trimble played up too, but fortunately the automatic fog horn worked well. After lightning which seemed to be aimed at them and pouring rain, their best sail of the leg took place as they creamed along with ten foot waves to Thunder Bay. They had sailed 635 miles on the largest expanse of fresh water in the world.

The eighth crew with Lieutenant Colonel Robert East as Skipper and Major Greg Collins as Mate came back from Thunder Bay to Midland in the last ten days of June, arriving 2 July with the air and water temperature on Lake Superior only 4°C. This leg included many hours of motoring across glass smooth water – 101 miles on one day thanks to their Perkins engine. They covered 700 miles in all, across some of the finest cruising waters in the world, made even more memorable by the warm hospitality on shore.

While Leg 5 was under way, the Talismans were handed over at Montreal by Captain Cameron Ferguson to Captain Bob Hambly who took them by air to Calgary. There they were married up with the canoeing exercises, Exercise Canadian Canoe (13 May – 22 June) and Exercise Maple Canoe (22 June – 22 July). These set out to follow the outward route pioneered in 1792 by Sir Alexandra Mackenzie, the first non-native to cross the North American continent. Exercise Canadian Canoe took fourteen canoeists, ten British and four Canadian, from Fort McMurray on the Athabasca River to Fort Vermilion on the Peace River. Faced with the daunting nature of the task after leaving Lake Athabasca, involving two days paddling against the flow of the Peace River, continuity was broken by overland movement from the Peace Point to Peace River town; from there a reversal of direction gave a downstream passage of some 160 miles to complete the leg at Fort Vermilion. Exercise Maple Canoe, the seven aluminium canoes freshly crewed with an identical number of British and Canadians, then progressed upstream to Peace River and so on to reach and pass through two-thirds of Lake Williston, a feat never achieved before, during which three canoes, to survive storm-driven waves, had to be lashed together, followed by a strenuous twenty-eight-mile portage from Summit Lake across to the Fraser River. They then faced fierce rapids and white water at nearly every bend to the final destination at Quesnel. Both expeditions were extremely challenging, each covering some 600 miles, with many nights spent in spectacular wilderness in which a wide variety of wild life was seen, including beavers, black bears and golden eagles. The two exercises were led by Lieutenant Jim Legard and Captain Dean Critchley respectively, whilst on land Captain Bob Hambly's support team covered 2,000 miles or more.

The canoe expeditions were followed by Exercise Maple Trail 22 July – 22 August. It was necessary to run all three expeditions concurrently with Exercise Maple Sail in order to achieve a co-ordinated finale at Arborfield. For Maple Trail eight REME team members from several units, including Brigadier Bob Cooper (Commander Arborfield Garrison) and four Canadians with a support team of two, Captain Bob Hambly and AQMS Dave Stubbington, trekked from Quesnel, British Columbia, on the Fraser River, to Bella Coola sixty-five miles from the Pacific coast. They followed 168 miles of ancient Indian trade trails in the steps of the last stages of Sir Alexander Mackenzie's epic journey through the Rainbow Mountain Range to the Bella Coola Valley, now named the Alexander Mackenzie Heritage Trail. In the first half of the trek temperatures had been as high as 35 degrees centigrade, but it was superb wilderness country where they saw caribou, black bears, bald eagles, beavers and ospreys. On 11 August they climbed the highest peak in the area, Mount Mackenzie 2,146m. At Bella Coola they were met by Colonel Murray Johnston, Colonel Commandant of our allied Canadian Corps – Land Electrical and Mechanical Engineers – who congratulated them on their achievement.

Meanwhile during the first two weeks of July, Exercise Maple Sail Leg 9 had taken the Skipper, Major Paul Musgrove, and the Mate, Corporal Nigel Broadbent, from 17 Port and Maritime Workshop, with the crew from 3 Regiment AAC Workshop and one Canadian, from Midland harbour 800 miles back to Kingston on Lake Ontario across Lake Huron and Lake Erie and through the Welland Canal. Despite unfavourable winds on Lake Huron, a thick pea-soup fog and cracked engine mountings, they reached Kingston on time on 16 July.

Lieutenant Colonel Peter Jaram, Electronics Branch, was Skipper for Leg 10 from Kingston to Trenton 17 July – 25 July with a crew of nine, including several from Electronics Branch, one brave woman, Mrs Eileen Simpson, a French Canadian, and two cadets from Welbeck College. They enjoyed good sailing conditions including a brilliantly clear starlit night sail and excellent food, not least that produced by the French Canadian Dominic Plourde and Corporal Chris Ginger of Electronics Branch, arriving at Trenton on 24 July.

On 2 August Lieutenant Colonel Larry Le Var, Skipper, and Staff Sergeant Miles Kennah, Mate, with a crew including two Canadians set sail on Leg 11 from Trenton to Quebec via New York State and Montreal. They reached Cape Vincent in New York State USA the next day, where the Immigration Officer, presented with a NATO Movement order made out for Exercise Maple Sail, exclaimed, 'I sure as hell haven't seen one of those before!' Nevertheless he let them in. Thirty-seven changes of course to clear the Thousand Islands, down the St Lawrence Seaway through the locks and lakes brought them to the old harbour at Montreal – virtually in the middle of the city on a lively waterfront. Major Giles Roberge, who accompanied them from 202 Depot Workshop, Montreal, surprised the harbour master at the port of Sorel when a British Army yacht asked him for a berth on the VHF in fluent French. The voyage ended by sailing into Quebec past the Heights of Abraham, made famous by General Wolfe.

Colonel Andy Platt then took over the yacht for Leg 12 to St John's, Newfoundland, with Lieutenant Colonel Chris Deacon as Mate. They left Quebec going down the St Lawrence on a warm sultry evening in a beautiful sunset. The currents were complicated and strong, the flood tide opposing and overcoming the underlying flow from the Great Lakes. The crew saw many whales in the river, but one morning visibility was very poor and they could only hear the whales blowing all round them – their advice was to keep the echo sounder transmitting so that the whales would be aware of the boat! On 20 August they sailed for Prince Edward Island. Leaving there on the 23rd they were entertained by a most spectacular display of Northern Lights appearing as curtains of greenish light, thin and misty, punctuated by streaks of light shooting out from the north, giving the impression of a rapid movement towards the North Pole. On 25 August they hurtled through the Cabot Strait on a hot sunny morning flying the spinnaker for the first time and reaching a speed of 9.5 knots, but by 2200 hrs they were beating into a rough sea in very unpleasant, cold, wet conditions.

By Saturday afternoon 29 August they were round the south corner of Newfoundland despite a very uncomfortable bumpy sea, arriving at St John's in fog the next morning. They had covered 1,252 miles with some excellent sail training in a wide range of wind and weather in unfamiliar and hostile waters. Brigadier General Fischer, the Canadian Director General of LEME, hosted a reception when the Skipper handed over the Talisman, and the Canadian Talisman, an astrolabe, which was a copy of a mariner's astrolabe dating from 1603, was handed over to Staff Sergeant Dickie Boast, the Skipper for the last leg across the Atlantic. With Colonel John Peacock as Mate, they left on 3 September taking a south-easterly course to the Gulf Stream, then turning north-east, eventually arriving in England after a trip in a 39 foot yacht which many sailors would consider the highlight of their sailing career. When no ship had been seen for several days it was a real morale booster to have a school of dolphins stay with the yacht for several hours. After fifteen days at sea a storm hit them; during the night the wind and waves increased and the least amount of sail was used. In the early morning a wave struck the yacht broadside so hard that the keel was forced over, causing the mast to hit the water. Good preparations had ensured that the sea did not enter and *Master Craftsman* righted herself immediately. The Canadian crew member Gordon Goddard was laid low with what turned out to be severe appendicitis, and on arrival at Falmouth he was taken to Truro Hospital for an operation.

A flotilla of yachts from the REME Yacht Club met *Master Craftsman* in the Solent on Saturday 26 September. The Talisman was transferred to a Laser 2 dinghy crewed by Sergeant McIntyre and AT Dunkley in Osborne Bay and taken to the Hamble River. There it was transferred to a

The Talisman leaves Master Craftsman. *Apprentice Tradesman Dunkley and Sergeant McIntyre*

Corporal Flynn with the Talisman in the River Hamble

Corporal Flynn hands over the Talisman to Major General Mike Heath

windsurfer sailed by Corporal Flynn who in turn handed it to Major General Mike Heath, Admiral of the REME Yacht Club, safely back on UK soil. On arrival at Marchwood on 28 September, *Master Craftsman* had sailed nearly 16,000 miles.

On 1 October 1992, the 50th Anniversary day, *Master Craftsman,* dressed overall, was on a transporter at Arborfield. The band played and a big crowd assembled in the sunshine outside the Bailleul Sergeants' Mess. The REME free fall parachutists dropped from an assortment of aircraft including a 1942 Tiger Moth. Awards and presentations were made, including Colonel Murray Johnston presenting the astrolabe from LEME to REME. Corps guests from the Commonwealth and industry who had helped with Exercise *Master Craftsman* mingled with Chelsea Pensioners and REME men and women to listen to speeches from Major General Mike Heath, DGES(A), and Colonel Murray Johnston. So ended the Corps' biggest and most demanding adventurous training exercise.

Full details may be read in the pages of 'The Craftsman' in 1992 and 1993 and in the published story that can be found in the Corps Archives.

CHAPTER 6

BAOR

INTRODUCTION

The first volume of Craftsmen of the Army covered the story of REME in BAOR up to the late Sixties, when the MOD was already seriously considering a major workshop reorganization in the theatre as part of a drive to effect overall Army economies. One proposal was that 23 Base Workshop at Wetter and 37 (Rhine) Workshop at Moenchengladbach should close, but after a detailed financial and engineering assessment by BAOR staffs these proposals were seen to be fallacious and the Workshops remained open. This decision removed one complication for REME from the many subsequent reorganizations in BAOR; to achieve economies and adapt to the introduction of new equipment. Solving the organizational and equipment management problems involved in these changes was to become an increasingly challenging part of life for REME in BAOR in the Seventies and Eighties.

From the Seventies to the early Nineties BAOR, with our responsibilities to NATO, continued to be the largest commitment for the British Army. The latter part of this period saw the removal of the Berlin Wall, the ending of the Cold War and the re-unification of Germany. This commitment to the Central Front has been reflected in REME's deployed strength in BAOR, some 6,000 all ranks in the Seventies, – and the matching organization necessary to meet their manifold tasks in Germany over the years. A measure of the size of the REME maintenance commitment can be gathered from the number of vehicles for which REME was responsible that were in BAOR in the Seventies. Whilst sheer numbers do not indicate the extent of the technical engineering problems, which are discussed later in this chapter, they nevertheless give some idea of the extensive involvement of the Corps in the support of BAOR and the vital nature of its role. Including reserves, there were some 600 main battle tanks with a further 3,000 A vehicles, ranging from reconnaissance vehicles to armoured personnel carriers. B vehicles, ranging from tank transporters to Land Rovers, numbered over 50,000 while C vehicles, from heavy plant to mine clearance and bridging tanks, constituted a further 2,000.

While vehicles of every description formed the major part of REME support, maintaining the equipment of the RA was a considerable commitment. Weapons varied in type, calibre and means of traction, with increasingly complex supporting equipment. For the Corps, this required different additional engineering management and technical skills. So too did the support for the R SIGNALS and the AAC. The introduction of new ranges of more complex radio equipment was extensive, with maintenance and major developments of new systems requiring more sophisticated backing. Helicopters in service were also increasing in number, size and complexity, and their specialized electronic and armament equipments extended the skills required in their maintenance. For all these tasks in the Seventies, across the whole range of equipment support, the Corps had deployed throughout the Theatre up to twenty workshops. Of these, two were base workshops and others specialized in specific types of repair, such as aircraft and electronics. In addition, each major unit had its own LAD or regimental workshop, whilst other smaller units had individual REME-attached tradesmen.

FV434 lifting an FV432 Power Pack

The introduction of the CHIEFTAIN tank to replace the CENTURION at the end of the Sixties started an era of organizational and technical change for REME in BAOR. The tracked FV432 Armoured Personnel Carrier for the infantry was also brought into service in large numbers. Included in this range was the REME 'fitters' vehicle', the FV434 which replaced the wartime half-track, with the various innovative local designs of lifting gear which had been introduced over the years. The arrival of the new tanks and APCs led to a revision in the organization and tactics of the brigades in 1(BR) Corps. The initial changes were followed by even more dramatic organizations and subsequent reorganizations of divisions and brigades both in the Seventies and the Eighties, resulting from the Army Restructuring Plan. Each change meant not only that there had to be a corresponding reorganization of REME units to provide the best possible operational support in the field, but also that this support, with all its implications, should be essentially cost-effective in peacetime.

Apart from these changing commitments for the Corps, the implementation of the recommendations of the Odling Committee resulted in REME taking over from the R SIGNALS the first-line repair of telecommunications equipment. The exception to this was those equipments owned and operated by the R SIGNALS. The introduction of the new CLANSMAN radio sets, followed by the PTARMIGAN computer-aided trunk communication system, posed challenging problems for those concerned with telecommunications; the implications for REME are outlined in later paragraphs.

This chapter can only briefly illustrate the overall activities of REME in BAOR during the period covered by this book, but it shows clearly how the Corps met the challenges of the management of new equipment, and the relentless organizational and operational changes that invariably accompanied them. It also provides a glimpse of the life of the officers and soldiers of REME in BAOR, whose skills and sustained efforts provided support of the highest standard.

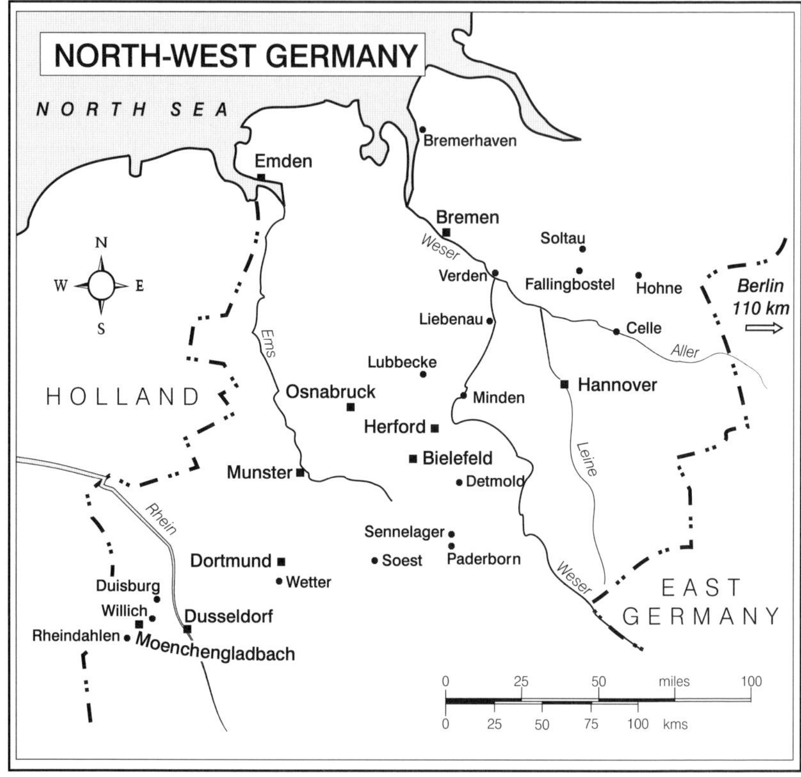

ORGANIZATION OF REME SUPPORT FOR 1(BR) CORPS

The major organizational question for REME as 1970 approached was how best to support the brigades in 1(BR) Corps, each now containing two armoured regiments and two mechanized infantry battalions, and known as square brigades. The armoured regiments were equipped with the new CHIEFTAIN tanks and the infantry battalions with FV432 APCs. REME support for these brigades presented a number of crucial problems which had to be solved if the brigades were to receive properly balanced maintenance support. The best possible means of providing such support for these brigades required a careful assessment of the conflicting problems existing in peace and those likely to occur in war. It was a fact of life that, in arriving at ideal procedures for a war situation, peacetime constraints, had to be taken into consideration. No solutions were entirely clear-cut; overlap in both constraints and the time scale involved in solving the problems was inevitable. How these problems were gradually solved, albeit with some agonizing and compromise, will emerge in the next few paragraphs.

Some of the crucial factors were the correct division of resources between first- and second-line repair; whether fluid movement on the battlefield allowed enough time for forward repair and how the difficulties of supporting battle groups (whose composition could alter rapidly under battle conditions) could be overcome.

However, one fact established by 1970 was that forward repair by the replacement of power packs was the right way to support mechanized formations. The use of power packs in CHIEFTAIN tanks and the FV430 series of vehicles speeded up major assembly exchange times, and work started on the development of platforms for the subsequent repair of power packs in the Main Repair Groups (MRG) of armoured and infantry workshops. The organizations of Main Repair Groups and Forward Repair Groups (FRG) were now reflecting this concept, as were first-line support capabilities within units.

1st Division carried out trials in 1969 with the square brigade, and this organization was adopted throughout 1(BR)Corps in 1970. At this stage 1st Division had 7 Armoured Workshop, commanded by a Lieutenant Colonel, to support the armoured brigade, and 11 Infantry Workshop, which was smaller and commanded by a major, to support the infantry brigade. A similar situation existed in other divisions in 1(BR) Corps. REME support to square brigades, each balanced in armour and infantry, now required balanced workshops, which would all be called field workshops.

The policy of balanced field workshops was to meet the operational need in war, but it produced substantial difficulties in operating within peacetime constraints. Not the least of these was the question of available suitable accommodation for these workshops close to the square brigades which they were to support. It did not, for example in the case of 1st Division, seem sensible to reduce the size of the larger 7 Armoured Workshop, which had a good site close to its division's armoured regiments, and to increase the size of the smaller 11 Infantry Workshop which was in a congested location about 50 miles away from the armoured regiments that it should now support. There seemed to be a strong case that things should stay as they were in peacetime, particularly as in war these workshops would be split into MRGs and FRGs to meet the operational requirement. However, it was decided by DEME(A) that, despite these difficulties, the operational needs should prevail, and that a policy of balanced field workshops commanded by majors should be implemented as soon as possible. It was not until 1974 that this was largely achieved, but lack of suitable accommodation in the right places still precluded total balancing, even at that stage.

ECONOMY MEASURES

By the early Seventies the effects of an overall shortage of soldiers in BAOR were becoming more and more marked, and REME was no exception. One such effect was that an enormous backlog of uncompleted modifications to equipment built up in BAOR, growing steadily to exceed four million man-hours of work. This situation was also exacerbated by a shortage of spares, mainly due to industrial problems in the UK. The consequence was that equipment of units throughout BAOR, which could neither be manned nor maintained by the users, was put into care and preservation. Another effect was that REME soldiers were required to work excessive hours to support the maintenance load. Although properly employed at their trades, the overstretch was at the expense of their military training and the overall quality of their lives.

In 1972–73 track mileage restrictions and other economy measures, imposed by MOD on BAOR, affected training, although at unit and brigade level it remained reasonably well sustained, and these economies were mainly applied to higher formation training. LADs, unit workshops and FRGs were able to carry out almost as much training as before, but it was difficult to train MRGs without divisional exercises and, apart from a major NBC trial held by 4th Division, these did not take place. However, by careful and thorough planning, HQ BAOR EME Directorate was able to help the overall situation by ensuring that there was only a minimal effect on the part played by REME in maintaining the operational efficiency of 1(BR) Corps. Such steps as placing the emphasis on reclamation and repair, rather than exchange of parts, helped limit the effect of the shortage of spares. Less strict inspection standards and better progressive Periodic REME Examinations (PRE) eliminated the typical surge in stores demands which PREs normally involved. Value Engineering, which had been introduced into 23 Base Workshop in 1972, was also now proving its worth and the man-hours required for the base overhaul of a CHIEFTAIN tank, for example, were reduced by 20%.

Individual units, including REME workshops, were able to continue their unit training, often in US Army training areas, which made an interesting change from those in the BAOR area, many of which became all too familiar to the units who trained there. On one such occasion in the mid-Seventies, 7 Armoured Workshop went to Wildflecken and their

American hosts, as usual, made them feel very welcome in their inimitable hospitable manner. In return for this hospitality the OC workshop decided to lay on the mother of all barbecues. The centre-piece would be the spit-roasting of a complete pig. The cooks claimed that they were equal to this task, and prepared a bed of glowing charcoal sufficient to autofrettage a gun barrel. The spit was no challenge for the metalsmiths. The great moment came, the pig was hoisted aboard to cheers, and slowly rotated: too slowly as it turned out, as it started off upside down, and several gallons of rendered-down fat collected inside the carcass. On further rotation, this fat decanted onto the hot charcoal and burst into flames which compared favourably with a Ruhr steel works' blast furnace. Sadly the pig was located for its culinary debut in a marquee, which proved to be equally inflammable. All might still have been well, certainly for those fond of crackling, if an enthusiastic fire-fighter, lacking culinary taste, had not tried to put out the ensuing blaze with a chemical fire extinguisher! Fortunately there still remained plenty of 'bratties' and hamburgers, which proved the basis for a good party, and the Americans did not seem to mind about their marquee.

As pressure to reduce the cost of maintaining BAOR continued, plans for economies were examined throughout 1975. This resulted in cuts which were concentrated in units outside the command of 1(BR) Corps, particularly in 60 Station Workshop in Belgium. There were also disbandments of units; 40 Army Support Regiment RE at Willich which held stocks of 1944–45 bridging was one such unit. Both 23 Base Workshop and 37 (Rhine) Workshop were also considered for closure, as they had been in 1966–67. Once again the capital cost of providing base facilities in the UK proved to be a major obstacle, and the Commander-in-Chief BAOR was firmly opposed to having his equipment moved out of the theatre for base repair.

A feature of life throughout the Army in the Seventies, which continued unabated in the Eighties, was the number of efficiency studies and cost-cutting exercises which took place; REME in BAOR did not escape this process. There was an increasing use of civilian consultants in these reviews and there were studies to obtain objectivity and avoid inertia, sometimes known as status quo-itis.

ARMY RESTRUCTURING

Chapter 1 described in outline how the Corps and the Army as a whole were affected by the recommendations of various committees which had examined the structure of the Army. These covered the management of logistic support, the role of each major logistic corps and the manpower specifically required by REME to meet future tasks. The recommendations in the reports of these committees had a direct effect on REME in BAOR. Outline organization diagrams of 1(BR)Corps REME, before, during and after restructuring are given at the end of this chapter at Annexes A, B, C and D.

The 1974 Defence White Paper confirmed that NATO was the United Kingdom's primary defence commitment. In the MOD there was concern that it might not prove possible in future to maintain the force levels required for NATO as well as the other commitments still existing. There were three main problems. First, how to limit expenditure on defence to a reasonable share of the Gross Domestic Product. Second, sustaining the level of recruiting as, for demographic reasons, fewer young men and women of recruiting age would become available each year. Third, the means of providing enough fighting soldiers from within a smaller army to sustain the same operational tasks. A major study into these and associated problems was set up by the MOD. It was anticipated that some small overall savings could be expected from within the remaining overseas stations such as Belize, Cyprus and Malta; the commitment to Northern Ireland, however, was not to be taken into account in the study.

The Army Restructuring Plan (ARP), as the study was titled, was prepared in the MOD under the leadership of a small group of senior officers in great secrecy and, consequently, with limited overall consultation. One of these senior officers was the Director of Army Recruiting, who had, coincidentally, as his staff officer for this important Army-wide task Major Jim Drew REME. A team presentation of the model organization formulated for the ARP was given to a small group of senior officers in the War Room of HQ 1(BR)Corps early in August 1974. The model envisaged a corps of four divisions with appropriate supporting elements. The brigade level of command was to be removed, and there would be fewer units of regimental size, but each of them would have more and larger sub-units. Each division would have five major teeth-arm units, producing a total of twenty combat teams formed from varying combinations of armour, infantry and supporting arms, as required for particular operations.

For logistic support it was proposed that each major logistic corps would have only one unit in each division. In REME's case there would be one workshop battalion and the CREME of the division would also be the workshop commander. It was then necessary for REME and the other logistic Corps to consider how this organization and allocation of manpower and equipment in the ARP would work in relation to the responsibilities in their own Corps. HQ REME 1(BR)Corps set to work to solve their particular problems involved in implementing the plan, and to ensure that the proposed organization would function and provide the necessary support. There was little room for manoeuvre within the proposals, and the solution required any previous shortcomings in equipment and manpower to be discounted. Any increase of either resource in any particular part of the plan had to be offset by reductions elsewhere in the organization.

The Corps Commander required that as much as possible of the considerable volume of staff work necessary to plan the implementation of the ARP should be concentrated in his headquarters. HQ REME at 1(BR)Corps, taking on their share of this commitment, had few staff available to study all the implications of the plan, and formulate a new organization. However, with the help of an additional officer from HQ BAOR, Major Ted Walder, the new organization and establishments of personnel and equipment were thrashed out amid the inevitable changes and conflictions in such a far-reaching plan. In the end sensible solutions were achieved, for what seemed at first to be intractable problems.

Paper studies of the ARP went on throughout the autumn and winter of 1974 and various exercises were held in the spring and summer of 1975 to test aspects of the plan. Of course there was always the problem of time and space on exercises in the field. On one such exercise it had been decided to speed up the action by having one real hour represent two exercise hours, but to avoid impossible situations and exhaustion of headquarters on the exercise, every other move of units dictated by the tactical situation was to be notional only. Unfortunately this important fact did not reach the staff of HQ 7 Field Workshop, who consequently found that no sooner had they arrived at a location and set themselves up than they were told to move on again. After two days of packing,

moving and setting-up, the Workshop was exhausted. When Major James Johnston, the Officer Commanding, felt that he had cause to complain to the divisional headquarters he was berated for moving so often. However, once all had been revealed and good humour restored, the time warp was removed and the workshop allowed to rest.

Fortunately, not all activities on exercises were as onerous, and unit exercises between formation exercises sometimes gave opportunities for more relaxed interludes in the intensive exercise programme. Some soldiers' wives were suspicious, despite protestations from their husbands to the contrary, that exercises were a planned means of escape by males. The soldiers could enjoy the great outdoors, free from household chores, whilst their wives guarded the married quarters. One workshop commander, Major Mike Heath, in consultation with his wife, decided that a party of wives should be taken out to a unit exercise location. Each wife could then see for herself how stoically borne were her husband's, much boasted-about, privations in the field. When the wives' coach arrived at the exercise location, the husbands' stories of hardship rather lost credibility. It was a beautiful day, and the ACC cooks had provided an al fresco spread, as only they can. It was more like a garden party than a field workshop location, where only the men were dowdily dressed. Nevertheless, the ladies were impressed and very pleased to see their husbands again; rather too much so in fact. Several couples set off into deep cover. One telecommunications technician took his wife to show her his box-bodied repair vehicle. While inside, the door unaccountably jammed. They were unfortunately locked inside for over an hour! This brief taste of freedom was soon over, and the workshop quickly returned to its less colourful but more serious tasks on major formation exercises.

The Command Post Exercises which had taken place were followed by full-scale exercises in the autumn of 1975 to test the ARP plans, and were known as WIDE HORIZON. REME workshops and LADs were made up to the proposed ARP establishments by combining units and attaching men and equipment from units not taking part in the exercise. In 4th Division elements of 4 and 5 Field Workshops combined to make up the newly designated workshop battalion. This title, however, did not last for long and was later changed to armoured workshop, a name which was to be retained into the Nineties. The proposed REME organization and associated second-line resources revealed weaknesses; many were corrected without too much difficulty, while others proved more obstinate. One major weakness was a lack of recovery vehicles, especially of ARVs, in REME units. Another, touched on earlier in this chapter, which had been of concern to REME since the introduction of battle groups, was that many of the teeth-arm unit attachments to battle groups brought equipment with them for which the supporting parent battle group LAD lacked spares. This lack of flexibility in support was proving difficult to overcome, since it was not feasible to scale LADs with spares for every contingency. It was a problem that was not to be solved over the next few years and continued to be a headache to all REME officers in the divisions from LAD EME up to the divisional CREME.

The exercises also highlighted the problems of command and control, both in the broader aspects of overall operational command and in parallel problems for REME. For the latter, the valued Brigade Electrical and Mechanical Engineers (BEMEs) had been abolished, together with the brigade headquarters, and one Lieutenant Colonel had to double up as both CREME and commander of the only workshop battalion. These reductions seriously weakened technical control. At the highest level, with the loss of brigade headquarters, it was found impossible for divisional headquarters to command directly five or more battle groups. In place of brigade headquarters therefore, intermediate headquarters known as Task Force Headquarters were introduced. At first they were only to be used for specific tasks on operations, but later they became permanent, and the commanders filled the role of garrison commanders in the BAOR static chain in peacetime.

2nd Division became the first restructured armoured division on 1 September 1976, and demonstrated its capabilities on Exercise SPEARPOINT 76. However, at this stage the Division still did not have its final order of battle completed and, for the exercise, units were brought up to strength by the addition of armoured squadrons and infantry companies from other divisions. Completion of 2nd Division's reorganization was to take place in 1977. However, Exercise SPEARPOINT 76 was to bring out many lessons that affected the operation of the divisional REME in the field before this reorganization.

Although on maps, with chinagraph pencils, regrouping of units within battle groups seemed a straightforward matter, actual implementation on the ground brought out the practical difficulties involved, and rapid tactical movement caused confusion for some units when trying to maintain contact with their REME repair and recovery teams. Exercise SPEARPOINT 76 emphasized this sort of problem. It was not always easy, for example, to maintain the right order of road movement.

12 Armoured Workshop at work in the field

Some armoured and infantry unit vehicles which broke down became stranded, because their REME LAD was ahead of them on the road instead of behind them where they should have been.

Speed of deployment produced other problems too within workshops. Lieutenant Colonel John Tinkler, as CREME, noted that, a few days after the end of SPEARPOINT 76, the CO of a field ambulance in the Division telephoned his Headquarters to find out whether there was any news of his Land Rover which had gone into the armoured workshop for repair during the exercise. Enquiries were made with 6 and 12 Field Workshops which had formed the composite armoured workshop, but even after a search was instigated there was no trace of the Land Rover's existence. A few days later a German farmer phoned the Military Police to ask whether they wanted the vehicles that had been left in his barn. It transpired that it had been used as an Equipment Collecting Point and when the MRG moved quickly some vehicles had been left behind and forgotten. Needless to say, the Land Rover belonging to the CO of the field ambulance was one of those that could now be reunited with its rightful owner.

No vehicles were known to have been mislaid because they were too well camouflaged, but there was always great emphasis throughout BAOR on camouflaging vehicles in the field. This was a particular problem for REME units which had to be able to deploy into both wooded and urban environments. On one occasion Major Mike Heath, commanding 7 Armoured Workshop, remembered being located in a delightful village south of Hannover where they were well received. A recovery vehicle, cunningly disguized as a large shrubbery, crouched against the wall of a charming little house in the centre of the village. Although hours of effort had effectively hidden its identity, the result was, it had to be admitted, not very attractive. This clearly discomfited the good hausfrau who decided that beauty and recovery vehicles were incompatible and, when the crew's backs were turned for a moment, brought out half-a-dozen potted geraniums and placed them artistically round the edge of the camouflage netting.

At the same time as the reorganization of the Divisional REME in 2nd Division was taking place, changes in the organization and nomenclature of other REME units were being implemented. 73 Aircraft Workshop left Celle in January 1977 and amalgamated with 71 Aircraft Workshop at Detmold, while 19 Corps Electronic Workshop at Duisburg was closed in June, leaving 20 Corps Electronic Workshop in Minden as the only electronic workshop in the Corps. 1(BR)Corps Artillery was concentrated into an Artillery Division, but did not have any REME representation at its headquarters; it was dependent on HQ REME 1(BR) Corps Troops to provide this service. 5 Field Workshop at Soest became 5 Armoured Workshop in support of 3rd Division, which had moved from the Strategic Reserve in UK to become an armoured division in BAOR.

The process of change continued and fortunately some, but regrettably not all, of the initial unsatisfactory proposals affecting REME were rescinded. By 1978 there were 1st, 2nd, 3rd and 4th Armoured Divisions each with one armoured workshop – 7, 12, 5 and 4 respectively. CREMEs and their staff were now retained separately from the establishment of the armoured workshops and this gave considerable satisfaction to all concerned. CREME Corps Troops remained, but the appointments of CREME (Air) BAOR and CO 71 Aircraft Workshop at Detmold were combined in what was now the only aircraft workshop remaining in BAOR. The BEMEs had been early victims of reorganization, but subsequent exercises pointed to the clear need for an experienced officer at what was now the Task Force level. It was not therefore surprising that Task Force EMEs (TFEMEs) had to be found. The solution however was an unsatisfactory expedient, and achieved simply by requiring the armoured workshops to provide them as an additional commitment.

1981 saw another major change in the structure of 1(BR)Corps, with the acclaimed re-introduction of the brigade organization within the divisions. Major Peter Besgrove, then Deputy Chief of Staff of 6 Armoured Brigade in Soest, remembers the relief throughout 1(BR) Corps among his fellow DCOSs when each of the reformed brigades received a REME major, a warrant officer and clerk as full-time members of the brigade staff. The BEME and his staff were back at last. However, as was touched on earlier, there still remained for REME a complex situation arising from the unsuitability of the peacetime locations of some workshops in relation to the units that they supported. After the brigade reorganization took place, there was for operational reasons a switch of brigades between divisions, and these changes unfortunately perpetuated an already difficult accommodation situation for some workshops, which affected the support of their brigades. The complexity of this situation is illustrated by the REME problems within 3rd Armoured Division during the years 1981–83. Lieutenant Colonel Bryan Fleming was the CREME (shortly to be re-designated Commander Maintenance) during the time that the overall organizational changes were taking place.

Before the changes 3rd Armoured Division had 33 Armoured Brigade at Paderborn and 6 Armoured Brigade at Soest. After the change it retained 6 Armoured Brigade at Soest, but lost 33 Armoured Brigade at Paderborn to 4th Armoured Division, gaining instead 4 Armoured Brigade at Munster from 2nd Armoured Division. However, even the retention of 6 Armoured Brigade was not to be as straightforward as it might seem, as this Brigade converted to an Airmobile Brigade on 1 January 1983; consequently it again required different REME support. In October 1981 REME in 3rd Division had 5 Armoured Workshop at Soest commanded by Lieutenant Colonel David Axson supporting the whole division. It provided two Main Repair Groups and two Forward Repair Groups. When 4 Armoured Brigade joined the Division it was supported by 6 Armoured Workshop, which had one MRG and one FRG in unsatisfactory accommodation in Munster, lacking cranes, storage space and adequate heating. (Even by 1985 living accommodation still remained so poor that the GOC wrote personally to the Corps Commander and Commander in Chief BAOR to try to speed up the planned improvements.)

Since, even before the change of Brigades, there was no suitable accommodation for an armoured workshop in Paderborn, it was decided to continue to support 33 Armoured Brigade – now in 4th Armoured Division – with 5 Armoured Workshop at Soest. Major Besgrove took over command from Lieutenant Colonel Axson, and the Workshop was reduced to one MRG and one FRG. The remainder of the men and equipment were then redeployed to an expanded 6 Armoured Workshop split between Munster and Soest. The workshop complications in 3rd Armoured Division caused by inadequate accommodation and unsuitable locations on the reorganization of its brigades were now to be perpetuated in 4th Armoured Division.

In 1982 accommodation for a large armoured workshop had not yet been found, and the situation was still fraught. The now newly titled Commander Maintenance 4th Armoured Division was understandably expressing his discontent at having 5 Armoured Workshop still in Soest, now supporting his division, but located in the 3rd Armoured Division Area. In the case of 3rd Armoured Division, however, it was fortunate that some accommodation occupied by the RAOC could be released in Soest for use by REME. This enabled 6 Armoured Workshop in Munster to expand to a large workshop, albeit in two locations. Headquarters and A Company were established at Munster and B Company in Soest alongside 5 Armoured Workshop in the same barracks, and sharing some facilities. This spread of technical command and control gave the first CO, Lieutenant Colonel Ewan Curphey, a very demanding task. Two years later it proved possible to remedy this unsatisfactory arrangement by forming two small armoured workshops from 6 Armoured. At Munster 6 Armoured Workshop was re-established as a small armoured workshop, while 11 Armoured Workshop was formed at Soest, replacing B Company of 6 Armoured, and supporting 6 Airmobile Brigade on light scales.

On 22 May 1985 11 Armoured Workshop held a formation parade at Soest with the REME Staff Band in attendance. The salute was taken by Brigadier Chris Tyler, Commander Maintenance 1(BR) Corps, who was accompanied by his father Major General Sir Leslie Tyler, a former Colonel Commandant of the Corps. Brigadier Andrew MacLauchlan, Commander Maintenance BAOR, and a former OC of the earlier 11 Field Workshop, was also present. The ceremony was somewhat dampened by the Westfalen weather; during the parade the rain was so heavy that the parade ground was flooded, the soldiers marching through nearly ankle-deep water. However, the sense of occasion prevailed and 11 Armoured Workshop was well and truly launched.

The two new OCs – Major Andrew Figgures at 6 Armoured Workshop in Munster, and Major Richard Rickard at 11 Armoured Workshop in Soest, with their staffs, were still faced with many months of hard work in their units, dividing up their establishments and unit equipment, and forming a new RAOC Stores Platoon at Soest. This task was not made easier by the fact that, contrary to a previous MOD decision, the new CHALLENGER tanks were now to be deployed in 3rd Armoured Division as well as 1st Armoured Division, both in advance of the availability of the special tools, spares and transport essential for their proper support. This entailed a great deal of extra organization and work by RAOC and REME to ensure that the best possible support under the circumstances could be provided. The situation was made worse by the fact that, even in 1986, 3rd Armoured Division still had many CENTURION ARVs to support CHIEFTAIN, and now CHALLENGER, tanks. These ARVs were by now not particularly reliable, spares were hard to come by and their extravagant operation on petrol, as distinct from the diesel-engined tanks that they were required to support, posed additional logistic problems.

In 1985 and 1986 most first- and second-line REME units in 3rd Armoured Division had 10% or more of their manpower away from their units on detached duty. They had detachments in Canada at BATUS, Northern Ireland and the Falkland Islands, while in BAOR teams were deployed outside the Division installing the PTARMIGAN communications system and carrying out CHALLENGER tank modifications. This threw an additional strain on the remaining artificers and tradesmen in LADs and workshops; overwork became a cause for concern. In January 1986 the GOC 3rd Armoured Division, Major General D J Ramsbotham, prompted by Lieutenant Colonel Peter Gibson, his Commander Maintenance, issued a paper in which he stressed the need to reduce the overstretch on REME soldiers and improve their quality of life. He said that this should be achieved by all units improving the care of their equipment, reducing additional commitments imposed on REME, and by lending manpower to help their LADs when they were working extended hours. He also directed his brigade commanders and their commanding officers to implement an Equipment Management and Husbandry plan, produced by his Commander Maintenance.

Although second-line workshops and LADs in BAOR had so much excellent and expensive new equipment by the mid-Eighties, with well trained and motivated officers, artificers and other skilled tradesmen, some weaknesses were still apparent. There was still a shortage of radios, especially for recovery tasks, and it was not possible to produce all the expensive specialist repair facilities such as automatic test equipment (eg DIANA, GPTIRF) and associated Application Test Packages (ATP), partly due to funding and partly due to development difficulties. With so many complicated new weapons, optical and electronic sights and surveillance devices, some FRGs lacked the sort of repair vehicles they would have liked or might have needed. Continuing cuts in civilian staffs, and the imposition of fuel restrictions meant that MRGs, FRGs and LADs were not able to carry out their own field training properly, in addition to giving the repair and recovery support to teeth-arm units in barracks and for their training in the field. By the late Eighties, though, there were fewer formation exercises in Germany because of growing political and environmental pressures on the use of land for training, easing some of REME's problems in this respect.

1988 saw the last divisional formation exercise of 1(BR)Corps when 3rd Armoured Division deployed on Exercise IRON HAMMER. It was the first time that both CHALLENGER and WARRIOR had been deployed at this level. The Commander Maintenance 3rd Armoured Division, Lieutenant Colonel Peter Besgrove, recalled that no one could have foreseen that so many of the REME lessons learned on the exercise were to be put to good use in the Gulf three years later. While the trial WARRIOR Repair and Recovery Vehicles on the exercise proved to be excellent in support of WARRIOR, the speed of operational movement now possible confirmed the need for a CHALLENGER Repair and Recovery Vehicle.

Secure and dedicated REME communications were proved essential if the FRGs and MRGs were to operate at their best. HQ REME 3rd Armoured Division had managed to equip all REME units on IRON HAMMER with the latest PTARMIGAN secure communications. It was the first time that many in REME had access to such excellent communications. They so improved operational procedures that all WARRIOR and all CHALLENGER, less two tanks, were available to cross the Divisional start line for the final counter-stroke operation at the end of three weeks hard exercising.

Challenger in the Gulf with extra fuel tanks

Another REME success was the in-house design, development and trial of external fuel tanks for CHALLENGER. The CHALLENGERs of 17th/21st Lancers were fitted with extra fuel tanks to increase the operating range of the tanks. The fuel tank design and build was largely the work of Major Andrew Burch and his team at 6 Armoured Workshop, helped by HQ REME 3rd Armoured Division. The trial was an outstanding success and all CHALLENGERs in the Gulf were subsequently fitted with fuel tanks to this design, which has also been included on the new CHALLENGER 2 tank.

By 1989 it could be said that, despite the problems that there had been, and some that inevitably still remained, the REME service to all those that it supported in BAOR had never been better.

TICKELL COMMITTEE

The work of the Tickell Committee was outlined in Chapter 1. The Committee visited BAOR under their Chairman, Major General M E Tickell, during his appointment as Commandant of The Royal Military College of Science, Shrivenham. They took evidence and examined REME's role in BAOR, their commitments and their deployment, in great detail. Their overall aim was to recommend how the REME share of Army military manpower could be restricted to 9% instead of the 10% or more which it seemed to be about to reach. 1(BR) Corps, having so many of the Army's armoured fighting vehicles and a wide range of complex equipment, weapons and other vehicles, employed more than half of all REME's trained soldiers. 1(BR) Corps was thus vulnerable to a large share of any cuts which were to be made in the Army overall.

The Tickell Committee could not have appeared at a worse time. REME in BAOR were just completing the draft establishments to meet the Army Restructuring Plan after two years of hard work and field trials. All this now had to be re-examined to provide evidence for the Committee, and to identify the implications in peace and war of any cuts which the Committee might propose. It was a daunting task.

The first visit of the Committee to BAOR was followed by a draft report containing radical proposals for reorganization of REME in 1(BR) Corps. This report was unacceptable to the Corps Commander, and the Committee paid a second visit to the Corps during Exercise SPEARPOINT 76. This was followed by a long period of gestation; the final ruling of the Army Board on the Tickell Committee recommendations did not come until 1978. This involved the cutting of sixty specific military posts in BAOR, followed by a further 200, which were to be identified by DGEME after further studies. All the posts specified by the Army Board in the first cuts were to come from telecommunications technician posts in LADs and unit workshops of radio users. This was based on the assumption that the new CLANSMAN range of radio sets would not require REME technicians for first-line work, as unit inspection and very limited repair would be the user's responsibility. By 1979 BAOR was of the opinion that most of the military posts that were to be abolished would have to be replaced by an equivalent number of civilian posts, because the anticipated equipment repair load was not in fact expected to decrease.

The new Conservative Government of Mrs Thatcher (elected in the summer of 1979) announced, that in accordance with NATO policy it would increase defence spending by 3% per annum in real terms, much of which would be spent on new equipment, but that it would impose cuts in public expenditure. This resulted in mandatory civil labour cuts for REME BAOR of 2% in 1979, and a further 5% in 1980. There was the prospect of more cuts to follow, and it was represented to the Army Board that REME BAOR could not continue to give acceptable support if subjected both to the Tickell Committee's recommended military cuts and to civilian cuts. The Army Board agreed that no further Tickell cuts in the military strength should be made, but that those cuts already implemented should not be restored.

The civilian cuts were to be achieved by a freeze on recruiting, always a most unsatisfactory method, and produced an imbalance of trades in the labour force. By 1980 it was no longer possible to avoid the closure of a station workshop in 1(BR)Corps area, and 59 Station Workshop at Liebenau was closed in March 1981. It had previously been the home of 32 Armoured Workshop, a site occupied by REME since the early Fifties, with a particularly fine officers' mess in the Schloss, surrounded by a magnificent garden. Major General James Johnston recalls that, when he was Adjutant to CREME 1st Division, 59 Station Workshop had lost the mess but still kept the vegetable garden, which was seen as a market garden on a semi-professional basis. It provided a valuable, unofficial, monthly income to CREME's fund for the benefit of REME soldiers in 1st Division as a whole. The Workshop had over the years given valuable support to 7th Armoured Division, and later 1st Division with its HQ at Verden. The civilian staff had seen many changes in their time and, with their military colleagues, had given loyal and unstinting service in overcoming the many problems with which they had been faced.

During the late Seventies and early Eighties most of the German civilians who had come to work in REME workshops soon after the end of the Second World War retired. These men and women had mostly had war service and then given many years of loyal and dedicated service, maintaining and repairing our vehicles and other equipment to a very high standard. They had kept up to date with knowledge of new equipment through in-job training given by REME artificers. By the end of the Eighties this was not so easy for the newer generation of German civilians now having to cope with more complicated equipment and technical instructions, often written only in English. There were fewer REME artificers in the civilian workshops to give guidance and training to the workforce who were having, as a result, to learn the hard way without formal training.

THE MANAGEMENT INFORMATION SYSTEM – FORWARD

In the late Sixties a management information system known as FORWARD was introduced into BAOR using the ADP systems that had become available to REME, as described in Chapter 2. This required the field workshops and LADs to provide the newly established REME Data Centre at Woolwich with accounting and equipment information. The system was intended to enable management to assess more effectively equipment reliability and the general cost effectiveness of repair.

Over several years in the Seventies the field workshops and LADs in BAOR built up doubts about the value of sending all the FORWARD data to Woolwich. The amount of time and labour put into all the form-filling and dispatching by post was questioned. Nevertheless, the system was tolerated whilst REME was still learning about accountability in the new age of ADP. Those formation commanders in BAOR who became acquainted with the system also had reservations about its value in relation to manpower effort. At the end of 1978 the GOC 4th Armoured Division threatened to stop FORWARD reporting in his REME units, to save effort and manpower. The Commander in Chief BAOR, on hearing of this, also found little to commend the FORWARD system. Fortunately, by this time HQ DGEME had begun a two-stage study which was to placate those who mistrusted this advanced technical system still in its experimental stages. The study was aimed at seeking instant relief for units in the field and then re-assessing the whole system. As a result, the reporting load was eased in 1979 by reducing the list of information to be reported on and reporting on only a 10% sample of large vehicle fleets. An additional help was that almost all reporting by tradesmen attached to units without LADs was stopped.

EQUIPMENT MANAGEMENT

In the Sixties the Army, especially in BAOR, developed with increasing rapidity into a force which had far more new and complex equipment than ever before. The importance of the efficient management of this multiplicity of sophisticated and expensive equipment was recognized by MOD, in making a branch of the Q Staff responsible for equipment management. This was later to have a profound effect on the responsibilities and organization of REME.

Experience in BAOR in the early Seventies led REME to use mathematical models to predict base overhaul loadings and the number of major assemblies required to support specific training exercises, with considerable accuracy. This convinced, in practical terms, both the G and Q Staffs of the importance of equipment management and the need to rationalize the responsibilities of all those concerned. The problem of defining and implementing such responsibilities was not straightforward and there were a number of interested parties involved across the board at MOD. Their involvement covered such disparate matters as operations, finance, provisioning, maintenance, and the supply of spares. The fact, for instance, that the ability of RAOC to supply spares to REME workshops as required and the capacity of REME to carry out repairs were inter-related led to long discussions between RAOC and REME staffs on their respective management responsibilities. These were clearly matters that needed resolving and answers to the problems were not going to come easily.

The Staff sought advice from everyone and there was no reluctance on anyone's part to provide it! It required much effort by EME Directorate to turn the resulting confusion into a logical method of dealing with the equipment management problems. To this end, REME in BAOR took on responsibility for in-service development of equipment in addition to its traditional repair function. This increasing responsibility covered such equipment as the CHIEFTAIN tank L60 engine, the CVR(T), the Nimbus engine fitted to the SCOUT helicopter, and the M2 Amphibious Bridge. These commitments were taken on as part of REME responsibilities, without any extra manpower being provided. By 1980, REME in BAOR had already accepted cuts in military and civilian staff, whilst supporting much more complicated equipment and in larger numbers than their predecessors ten or twenty years earlier could ever have imagined.

Following the establishment of the LE(A) at Andover in 1977, many of the responsibility problems were resolved. The responsibilities of the Q (Equipment Management) staff were transferred to the Heads of Service with the major interest in the equipment concerned; RAOC becoming responsible for B vehicles and REME for A vehicles. In BAOR, EME Directorate took over the staff responsibility for A vehicles and telecommunications, which formalized what in practice had been going on for some years. The workload in EME Directorate was recognized and five posts were re-established as Weapons Staff appointments and two staff captain posts were added. These were not all initially found from REME; one was filled by an Infantry officer responsible for electronics and one by a Gunner officer dealing with A vehicles. At lower headquarters in BAOR the Q Staff remained responsible for equipment management, but in 1980 EME Branch 1(BR)Corps took over the staff responsibility for equipment information and monitoring which had previously lain with the Q Staff. This change enabled EME Branch to be more effective in solving equipment management problems and, in conjunction with Ordnance Branch, with the provision of major assemblies and stores.

ARMOURED VEHICLES

Main Battle Tanks

Of the many new equipments and weapons issued to BAOR in this period, there were few that caused major problems. But with the large quantities and technical sophistication involved there were bound to be exceptions to the high quality generally experienced. The problems associated with the CHIEFTAIN main battle tank fell into this category. The CHIEFTAIN was driven by an opposed-piston compression-ignition engine known as the L60. It was designed as a multi-fuel engine, but in practice was adjusted to use only diesel fuel. The General Staff Requirement (GSR) stipulated that the tank should achieve 2,500 miles as a Mean Mileage Between Failures (MMBF), and the logistic planning was based on 2,000 miles MMBF. These mileages were about twice those of the CENTURION tank which the CHIEFTAIN replaced, and the L60 engine was mounted in a power pack which could be changed far more rapidly than that of the CENTURION. The anticipated reliability and quicker engine changes of the CHIEFTAIN were expected to increase the number of fit tanks in the users' hands at any one time, and to reduce the workload on REME and thus its manpower requirement. This in turn was calculated to improve the operational capability of 1(BR) Corps, and to increase the 'teeth-to-tail' ratio between fighting arms and supporting services. However, these expectations were not to be fulfilled without a very difficult struggle.

In July 1969 The Blues and Royals, who had recently joined 4th Division, were on their initial field training with their CHIEFTAIN tanks in the Soltau training area when they experienced major engine failures in the L60 engine. Forty engines failed in ten days, much to everyone's amazement and consternation, and ultimately presented a huge workload for 4 Armoured Workshop. The Artificer from 20 Armoured Brigade who initially was sent to investigate later wrote that, as the helicopter in which he was travelling arrived at Soltau, there were tanks to be seen littered all round the training area. Preliminary investigation showed that prolonged dry weather with high temperatures had changed the usually muddy earth into powder and dust, which was ingested into the engines through the air filters. British Leyland sent engineers to BAOR to investigate the problem and as a result a new filter material was introduced, with improved sealing round the filter body. Although this proved successful, the filter required constant washing and, if this was not carried out, premature engine failure resulted.

The problem of the engine failures of the tanks of The Blues and Royals was only the start of a long saga of engine unreliability in the CHIEFTAIN tank. Initially the experts suspected that uneven metering and atomization of the diesel fuel was a major cause of the high failure rate. REME Technical Services BAOR studied test equipment available to analyse the fuel injection equipment (FIE) of the L60 engine and they recommended a new test kit. Calibrated injectors and master pumps on FIE pump test beds were introduced into workshops, which soon became expert in this subject. Despite this effort, the failures continued and other causes were sought. Attention turned to the sealing of the cylinder liners in the engine blocks. This had long been an area of concern because of coolant loss and overheating, but it was to be some time before a modification to solve this problem proved satisfactory.

Prediction of the failure rate of the L60 engine, to enable repair support to be planned, was essential if operational and training viability was to be maintained. Colonel Douggie Templeton had pioneered the use of advanced statistical techniques in the prediction of failures while he was at EME Directorate HQ BAOR. He was helped in this task by Major Mike Kinshott, who collated the information and plotted the graphs. These techniques proved to be indispensable during the period of the L60 failures, as it enabled REME Technical Services BAOR to have a data cell and a history card for each L60 engine in BAOR. Brigadier Sam Lecky, DEME BAOR at the time, described the statistics produced by the data cell as probably the most valuable that he had ever had, because they enabled REME to support training exercises by predicting engine failures, forecasting the number of engines required for specific training and to make plans for base overhaul. The data was also invaluable to Vehicles Branch REME and the Military Vehicles and Engineering Establishment (MVEE) in assessing the L60 engine's performance during the many modifications that it underwent during its service.

In 1973 an epidemic of fractures of the rear gear casing added to the problems of the L60 engine. For some time the toothed rubber fan belts which drove the twin cooling fans had been breaking, but they were replaced with a stronger belt which did not break; now the casing of the rear gearbox, which drove the belt, started to break. Fan belts being cheaper and easier to replace than gearbox casings, it was decided to weaken the new and stronger fan belts by drilling holes in them so that they should be the weak link! The defect was ultimately found to lie in the sprag clutches in the hubs of each of the two cooling fans. Modified clutches and stronger rear gear casings overcame the problem towards the end of the decade, but the L60 engine was still causing concern because failures were not always limited to pistons, liners and cylinder blocks. It developed a dangerous habit of running away and disintegrating with explosive force, especially when on workshop test beds. In May 1978 an L60 engine ran away in a purpose-built test shop at 5 Armoured Workshop at Soest. It seized up and stopped, but the vibration had loosened a fuel pipe which allowed diesel fuel to splash on to a very hot part of the engine, so creating a vaporized fuel cloud. This exploded, destroying the test shop and damaging other workshop buildings, fortunately without loss of life or serious injury. Major General James Johnston later recalled:

'At the time I was taking over as CREME 3rd Armoured Division from Lieutenant Colonel George Briggs. We were that day in the Divisional Headquarters at Korbecke and he had just told me, correctly, how smoothly everything had been going. Suddenly there was a dull thud in the distance, to which we paid little attention. Ten minutes later the telephone rang and George's face changed dramatically!'

Other similar L60 incidents, though not so sensational, occurred, but fortunately also caused no loss of life.

It took until the end of 1980 before it could be said that the L60 engine was nearly as reliable as the original GSR had specified. Amongst other important modifications, a new method of fitting the cylinder liners in the engine blocks solved the continuing problem of coolant loss. The first Mark 11A engine came out of 23 Base Workshop in February 1979 and 600 Mark 11A/13A modified engines had been fitted by April 1981. During this long period of improvement to the L60 engine, 23 Base Workshop had built several prototype engines and prototype power packs. They designed the tools and jigs to bore the L60 blocks to the high degree of accuracy required and, during ten years of too few spares and too small a repair pool, managed to keep up with the failure rate in the field and the demand for modified replacement engines.

In April 1982 DGEME's Liaison Letter could report on the modified L60 engine: 'The Mark 11/13A build standard has fulfilled its early promise of improved reliability, mean miles between failure (to base level) being approximately 2,200 miles'. Colonel James Johnston expressed the REME BAOR opinion in the 1982 REME Journal, that poor design and insufficient proving were the root causes of the CHIEFTAIN tank taking over ten years to reach the automotive reliability of the CENTURION. The design authority had refused to recognize until some time after acceptance into service that its unreliability was such as to seriously prejudice operational capability.

Recovery of MBTs

Recovery and subsequent repair by REME of MBTs and other armoured vehicles that had broken down due to mechanical failure could be difficult and time-consuming. However, the recovery of MBTs that had become bogged down due to terrain and weather conditions presented a different range of recovery problems to be overcome, and it could take very much longer to actually remove a vehicle from the battlefield. In

December 1984 1st Armoured Division was involved in a formation exercise – STAG RAT – that led to the testing of major recovery under exceptionally wet and therefore boggy conditions. The exercise involved a fighting withdrawal, and movement over the potentially marshy Stellings Moor area, a few kilometres south of Zeven. By 4 December there were twenty-one armoured vehicles bogged down in a sixteen-square-kilometre area, waiting for REME assistance.

Main Battle Tank recovery

The area of this recovery nightmare was flat and wooded in parts, but consisted largely of peat-base scrub with tracks cutting through, just wider than a MBT. These tracks had the appearance of being firm going. However, they were only sand on top of the underlying peat, and in this instance, whilst two or three of these fifty ton tanks had passed through successfully, the fourth had caused the track to collapse, and the MBT to be bogged down. The soft nature of the ground made conventional recovery very difficult, and it was almost impossible to get a good anchor position. This was partly why initial attempts by units using their own Armoured Recovery Vehicles (ARVs) failed, often causing the ARVs themselves to become bogged. It was difficult to pull the casualties back onto the tracks, as once they were off the track and into a rut or ditch alongside, there was not enough resistance in the ground to force the vehicle back onto the track. There was thus a requirement for lift, as well as pull, with many of the casualties.

The overall recovery plan for the situation that faced 1st Armoured Division REME was to recover, first, the easiest recoverable casualties within the constraints of the RE assistance that was available. In practice this meant that some six vehicles, which required little or no RE assistance, were cleared within the first few days. Thereafter, all casualties required considerable RE effort before REME could effect recovery. The approach roads had to be prepared to allow ARVs access to the casualties, then hard-standing pads had to be made, from which the ARVs could pull with their winches. It commonly took several day's preparation for each pull, and this included building up the roads with hard-core, and then overlaying with trackway or pierced steel plank. The RE trackway proved adequate for the positioning of the ARVs, providing the ARV spade was not used or, if it was, it was supported on a series of railway sleepers. This sometimes made it difficult to provide a good anchor and so for each pull the minimum was two ARVs connected in train (the last pull made having two ARVs and two CETs connected in train). Attempts to hasten this rather long and laborious process usually met with failure and the bogging-down of more ARVs! Movement of ARVs was therefore quickly banned on all except a few main routes into the area.

One third of the bogged casualties were ARVs. This would seem to reflect badly on ARV crews and it was undoubtedly true that in two or three cases the crews, in their enthusiasm, had driven in their ARVs without adequate reconnaissance and had fallen into the same 'traps' as the MBTs. The lesson that ARV crews should get out of their vehicles and reconnoitre on foot to assess a task before positioning their ARV, was duly re-learned. What was certainly true was that learning the lesson during training was the right time to have done so, even if the consequences were somewhat tedious. In any case, with conditions as they were, some ARVs were liable to become casualties, as it was clearly the crews' duty to make some attempt at recovery with the resources that they had, particularly under tactical pressure and at night.

On this particular exercise the Bundeswehr were also taking part and were very willing and keen to help, but occasionally their enthusiasm had to be restrained. The German LEOPARD ARVs were superior under these conditions to the CHIEFTAIN/CENTURION ARVs, and they were put to good use on jobs where they performed better. The LEOPARD ARV was lighter, approximately forty-five tons, and had a much reduced ground pressure. This enabled it, with its greater power, also to travel along the tracks at high speed, which seemed to be an advantage in avoiding bogging. Its other advantages were that it had, at forty tonnes, a greater winch pull; the spade used as an anchor gave a greater vertical component lift, and the vehicle mounted a front twenty tonne lift crane giving a useful lift/pull capability.

Finally, the extended period of this recovery, under extremely cold conditions, meant that eventually the problem of frozen solid mud on the tracks and hulls of the vehicles had to be overcome before they could be driven away. This mud had to be burned off with petrol, but it was recognized that the use of small charges of plastic explosive for this purpose should be explored.

On Exercise STAG RAT the extensive recovery task involved, apart from the tactical lessons, gave much valuable recovery training. The old lesson of 'time spent on recce' was reinforced, and it was clear that many of the ARV casualties were caused by hasty attempts at night to carry out recovery.

APCs

Another major equipment problem in BAOR during the Seventies concerned the F432 infantry tracked armoured personnel carrier, which, with its many variants, was one of the most numerous new equipments in this decade. Several serious, but apparently inexplicable, traffic accidents involving FV432s occurred. The cause was eventually found to be cracked steering brake drums due to oil holes with insufficient chamfers around the drum circumference acting as stress raisers. Later on, similar cracks were found around the hub securing bolt holes. Steering brake drums soon cluttered the workshop floors throughout BAOR and workshop staff became crack-detection experts, often helped by REME aircraft engineers and technicians who were familiar with the techniques. A regular programme of thorough visual inspections of steering brake drums was introduced, together with a speed limit on the vehicles, until an 'interim' drum was available. 5 Field Workshop at Soest became the BAOR workshop responsible for the reclamation and repair of the steering brake drums, and all were sent there for inspection and repair. This concentrated the expertise and achieved engineering economy.

CVR(T)

The excellent new Combat Vehicle Reconnaissance (Tracked) (CVR(T)) was introduced into BAOR from 1973, with many variants, to replace the SARACEN and SALADIN fleet of six-wheel vehicles. The reduction in weight of the vehicles, achieved by using an aluminium alloy hull, made them fast for tracked vehicles, but in 1974 cracks were found in this armour in the UK. As a result, a long series of fleet inspections took place in BAOR. The resulting diagnosis was stress-corrosion cracking. Aluminium alloys were known to be susceptible to stress-corrosion cracking, so the vital question for REME was whether the CVR(T) was fit or unfit for operations and to advise accordingly. After much investigation DEME BAOR was able to advise the Commander in Chief that the CVR(T) was operationally fit. The question was never raised again, which said much for the thoroughness of the engineers who investigated the cracks and made the diagnosis.

In 1975 hairline cracks were found in the turrets of the SCORPION variant of the CVR(T) in two regiments. The question was then whether the turrets were fit enough to have their guns fired. The turrets were stripped and dye penetrant applied to detect any cracks. Decisions were then made on which CVR(T)s the guns could be fired without repair to the turrets, and records were kept. At about this time a serious crack was found in the belly plate of a CVR(T) which raised doubts about the wading capability of the fleet, so another fleet inspection took place to decide whether any remedial action was necessary.

By 1978 the Design Authority and the Project Manager had decided that stress corrosion cracking in the hull of the CVR(T) was not as serious in its practical effects as they had feared. Nevertheless, it was decided that the whole fleet should go through 23 Base Workshop on a programme to remedy any defects that had already occurred and reduce any potential future defects to a minimum. New repair methods were introduced, including special aluminium armour welding, fitting reinforcing plates, metal stitching and stress-relieving by shot peening.

Power Pack Repair

The development of AFV power pack repair platforms took ten years and involved considering many different designs, and changing operational concepts. Forward repair of tanks and other tracked vehicles became much quicker with the ability to exchange power packs, but this left the problems of where and how to repair the damaged power pack once removed from the AFV. The most effective place was found to be at the Main Repair Group (MRG) of the second-line workshop. Repair usually required replacing the engine within the pack. Some believed that power packs should be repaired on mobile platforms equipped for the task and able to move if necessary with the MRG, even before the repairs were completed. This conformed to the concept of mobile warfare. Others believed that power packs should be repaired on the ground. This option offered easier access and more working space than repair platforms. The use of repair platforms also had the disadvantage that they would possibly become filled with stripped power packs which could not be worked on due to lack of spares.

Power Pack Repair in NBC conditions

By 1970 most second-line workshops had produced their own design of power pack platforms, mainly on 10 ton trucks, but sometimes on trailers. One of the first designs on a 10 ton truck was produced in 1971 by 37 (Rhine) Workshop, Moenchengladbach in collaboration with 7

Armoured Workshop. By 1978 there was wide experience of power pack repair under all conditions, on a variety of platforms, and DDEME 1(BR)Corps decided that the time had come to standardize on one design. Many in REME in BAOR had contributed in some way to the design of the final model, based on a 10 ton truck chassis with integral crane. This was made by 37 (Rhine) Workshop, and was subsequently issued to all armoured workshops. It was not the final answer, however, as the introduction of the CHALLENGER tank presented different problems and prompted a further interim design based on the new 8 tonne vehicles, with the power packs now being repaired on the ground. This was to be replaced by the CAPTURE containerized system described in Chapter 3.

RAPIER Surface to Air Missiles

In 1975, with the arrival of 12th Light Air Defence Regiment, RAPIER Surface-to-Air Missiles were introduced to BAOR. RAPIER replaced the ageing Second World War L40/70 Gun systems and, eventually, the THUNDERBIRD 2 of 36th Heavy Air Defence Regiment. The 'state-of-the-art' RAPIER systems brought many new problems for REME. Maintenance and fault diagnosis relied upon automatic test equipment, but, particularly at first line, the Forward Repair and Test Vehicle (FRTV) proved unreliable and there was a severe shortage of certain critical spares. Centralization of repair facilities and specialization in unit workshops were both used in the attempt to keep these problems to manageable proportions. The equipment and its REME support proved their ultimate ability in both the Falklands and Gulf Wars.

Rapier in action

COMMUNICATION SYSTEMS

CLANSMAN Radio Installation

In 1976 planning started in BAOR for the replacement of the existing range of radios with the new CLANSMAN range. The changeover was not just a simple one-for-one swap of radios but required major alterations to wiring harnesses and the installations themselves. A team of forty REME craftsmen, mostly from 1(BR)Corps, together with R SIGNALS and RAOC representatives, was set up. REME staff at all levels, especially in HQ BAOR, were involved in the planning. 23 Base

Workshop manufactured many items for the installation kits because UK manufacturers failed to deliver in time.

REME Technical Services BAOR were responsible for the administration of the Clansman Installation and Advisory Team (CIAT) and for the execution of the work. This had to be arranged to cause as little disruption as possible to user unit training and to retain operational effectiveness. It was decided that CIAT would fit all the A vehicle radios in BAOR and that user units would replace the radios in their B vehicles, with supervision and advice from CIAT. The team began its conversion programme in 1977 with 2nd Armoured Division. By 1980 installation was complete in three of the four armoured divisions, and subsequently in 3rd Armoured Division, the Artillery Division and Corps Troops.

PTARMIGAN Communications System

The development of PTARMIGAN is described in Chapter 3. At the end of 1984, after trials on Salisbury Plain, the system replaced the BRUIN system as the area communications system in BAOR. PTARMIGAN was to provide secure communications between headquarters, down to brigade level. The PTARMIGAN and WAVELL System Support Team, which included two REME Telecommunications Artificers, was deployed on its arrival. Unfortunately PTARMIGAN came initially without many of the necessary tools, test equipment and documentation; this caused complications for all those concerned in the setting-up and maintenance of the system. The former Clansman Installation Advisory Team became the Communications Installation Advisory Team (CIAT) and, together with part of REME Technical Services BAOR, was heavily involved with a modification programme to re-configure the Armoured Staff Vehicles (FV436) for the new equipment, and to design and implement several installations in other vehicles. A major problem for REME in the early years of PTARMIGAN was maintaining the system generators, with few spares and no documentation. LADs had to carry out improvised repairs and search local garages and other equipment in service for spares. Many of the generator electronic black boxes and sub-assemblies, intended for contract repair or discard, had to be repaired in BAOR to avoid long delays in achieving serviceability, and 20 Electronic Workshop was given this task.

PTARMIGAN became the largest ever British Army mobile computer-aided communications system and acted as a bearer for WAVELL and other computer-based Command and Control Information Systems. The way in which PTARMIGAN had been installed in Armoured Staff Vehicles, without causing undue detriment to the operational readiness of BAOR, brought much well-deserved credit to those who had planned it and carried it out to overcome the many inevitable difficulties which arose.

ARMY AVIATION

The overall story of the development of REME engineering support for Army Aviation, also covering the technical details of aircraft and their maintenance, is given in Chapter 4. The following paragraphs, and those covered in the Operation GRANBY section later, give particular examples of the part played by REME in support of Army Aviation in BAOR.

The reorganization of Army Aviation in BAOR took place towards the end of the Sixties and was completed in 1970. HQ 1(BR)Corps and each of its divisions and brigades had an Army Air Corps squadron, each squadron having its own LAD REME. Each division had a divisional Aircraft Engineer on the staff of the divisional Commander REME, who also had responsibilities to the divisional Commander Army Aviation. As one might expect, there were some forthright arguments over the location of the divisional aircraft engineer and his responsibilities to the two commanders – both Lieutenant Colonels. These arguments were clearly constructive, as a practical solution was arrived at allowing CREME's officer to work with, and undoubtedly for, the Commander Army Aviation who possessed the aircraft.

In the Sixties helicopters were still relatively few in numbers and were still regarded as an exceptional form of personal transport, and their allocation, even for senior officers, by no means certain. This led to unforeseen incidents when 'haves' and 'have nots' became too obvious. Such was an occasion when Major General Peter Girling, DEME (A), was visiting REME units in BAOR in 1969. Those officers arranging his programme had tried to obtain a helicopter for his longer journeys, but were unsuccessful in their bid and travel by car was a necessity. For the visit to his unit, Major John Bidgood, OC 1(BR)Corps Troops Workshop had arranged an impressive scripted demonstration in the field for the DEME (A). The participants were well into their parts when in the distance a faint buzz was heard which developed into the all-prevailing noise of a SIOUX helicopter, which landed nearby, completely drowning all proceedings. The demonstration came to an abrupt halt. The SIOUX was then surrounded by a throng of gesticulating senior officers urging the pilot to switch off his engine, which he was not technically permitted to do until on the ground for some minutes. At this stage out of the SIOUX passenger seat climbed one sheepish LAD commander, Captain Jim Drew, OC of the 5th Royal Inniskilling Dragoon Guards LAD. He explained, with some difficulty, to a sceptical audience, that he had come to check the progress on a SALADIN AFV in the workshop for repair, and had to travel by helicopter to keep up the airframe flying hours to even out service intervals. Twenty minutes later the demonstration was able to re-start, but the grounded DEME's reaction cannot be recorded live!

About this time the Commander Aviation BAOR moved from the airfield at Detmold to HQ 1(BR)Corps at Bielefeld, as did CREME (Army Aviation). CREME commanded the two second line aircraft workshops, 71 Aircraft Workshop at Detmold and 73 Aircraft Workshop at Celle, each of which had a major as OC. Both of these workshops had a static element and a mobile element, which could put out Mobile Servicing and Repair Detachments (MSRDs) for second-line aircraft support in the field for divisions and brigades.

During the Seventies the aircraft in service in BAOR were mainly SCOUT and SIOUX helicopters, though there were also a few BEAVER fixed-wing aircraft. In 1978 BAOR received the new LYNX helicopter, which was, compared to previous Army aircraft, a very complex machine. Six LYNX were issued to each of five AAC squadrons in 1981 to replace their SCOUTs, and the first TOW anti-tank missiles were fitted. The major servicing pattern for the LYNX was at the same time changed from a flying- hour basis to a calendar basis, but no change was made in minor servicing. This system later reverted to a flying-hours basis because of severe management problems experienced in trying to absorb the varying flying rates of operational units into the calendar system. The LYNX TOW programme was completed in 1984 and, by then, 71 Aircraft Workshop had seventy-two GAZELLE and sixty LYNX ATGW aircraft to support with five GAZELLE detached to BATUS in Canada.

By 1980 71 Aircraft Workshop at Detmold had become a major unit with a strength of over three hundred, with CREME (Aviation) as CO, and included on its strength 2 Aircraft Support Unit RAOC. In 1981 the rebuild of the accommodation of the unit was finished and on 5 March 1981 the opening ceremony was performed by Brigadier Geoffrey Atkinson CCREME 1(BR)Corps. The first woman aircraft engineer, Lieutenant Sharon Dearle, arrived at 71 Aircraft Workshop in 1983. Next year she was OC 655 Squadron AAC LAD in Ballykelly, Northern Ireland, where she was Mentioned in Despatches.

During the unit's annual training camp in May 1983 there was an extended period at NBC State Red. Everyone had spent a night in full NBC kit and had been subjected to simulated liquid chemical agents dropped from the air. The padre, Bill Robson, was undaunted by this inconvenient situation and decided to hold Holy Communion whilst the alert was still in progress and all were clad in their respirators and NBC suits. To make himself heard through his respirator he used a loud-hailer clipped to his belt and his communion wafers were contained in a small Tupperware box placed inside a green metal case. The service began with one verse of the hymn 'Onward Christian Soldiers' which the congregation sang well, despite their respirators, while doubtless also praying for a happy release from those encumbrances.

In 1985 Advanced Workshop Detachments (AWDs) were deployed to the LADs to assist in remedying some of the problems outlined in a DGLP(A) study led by Colonel Brian Porter, the Chief Aircraft Engineer, which had examined the REME manpower implications for the operation of the LYNX helicopter, including the work overstretch of aircraft technicians. This study covered reliability and maintenance problems, the effect of increased avionic and weapon equipment fitted to helicopters, the results of extended flying hours with increasing use of night vision aids and the lack of AAC manpower to fully carry out some of their allotted tasks.

On 1 October 1986 the changes in the establishments recommended by the DGLP(A) study were introduced. Fifty-seven technicians from second-line aircraft workshops were transferred to first line with the AAC squadrons, to maintain LYNX and GAZELLE helicopters within units. Major Servicing on both aircraft was passed to the Naval Aircraft Repair Organization and civilian contractors, and 1, 3 and 4 Regiment AAC LADs, having taken on limited second-line capability for changing major aircraft assemblies, were re-designated Regimental Workshops.

B AND C VEHICLES

Behind every successful man can be found a successful woman and vice versa. Similarly, following every 'battle-winning' A vehicle (successful or not!) there follows a faithful band of B and C vehicles spread amongst every sort of unit. In January 1992 there were still some 31,000 of these often unsung heroes in BAOR, some dating back to the Fifties, and still providing useful service thanks to the efforts of their users and REME LADs and workshops in providing effective maintenance. The newer members of the fleet include the most modern high-technology B vehicles, such as the DROPS MMLC vehicles, still making their debut in BAOR after initial and rapid deployment to the Gulf on Operation GRANBY in October 1990, with the RCT and their associated LADs.

DROPS offloading a Power Pack Repair Container

Casting Policy

Prior to the early Sixties most B and C vehicles and other technical equipments were subject to in-house base overhaul, and pictures of the time show workshops full of long lines of trucks in various stages of stripping and rebuild. This began to be seen as an uneconomical way of doing business and a system was introduced whereby repair cost limits were applied to these equipments. If the estimated repair costs exceeded the repair limit, then the equipment would be disposed of or 'cast', a term dating back to when horses and mules that were no longer fit for work in the Army were cast or destroyed and their carcasses sold.

When the casting policy was first introduced by the War Office in July 1961 repair limits were calculated by a simple linear depreciation of the equipment's value over each year of its life until, at the end of the assumed useful life, the repair limit became zero. This rather simplistic approach failed to take account of a number of factors, including usage, individual repair history, modification state, theatre of employment, etc. It was therefore necessary to refine the calculation of repair limits and a mathematical model, known as the Casting Model, was developed. This took into account such factors as the age of the equipment, cost of the replacement item, cost of spares, repair hour's rate, repair data from FORWARD, and the resale price of the cast equipment. Following development work carried out by the Data Centre during the late Sixties and early Seventies, the new Casting Model was taken into use in 1974. However, the computer operating system which ran the model became out of date and could not be supported beyond 1992. A new mathematical model was being devised for this time, to run under a modern supportable operating system.

There were two exceptions to the casting procedure, which were still applicable in 1992. The Resale Range, such as cars and other commercial vehicles, were put up for sale at a predetermined point in their lives, regardless of mileage and condition, and the Special to Cast Range, expensive specialist vehicles (such as recovery vehicles, fuel tankers and tank transporters), which were subject to Mid-Life Refurbishment during the mid-third period of their normal overall life of twenty years. This repair, normally undertaken in a base workshop or under contract, was designed to bring the vehicle back to 80% of its new condition, and thus improve its availability and reliability for the remainder of its life.

Casting was carried out by committees at Command/Theatre level, chaired by the Theatre Equipment Manager, with members from G4 and Finance Branches. In making their decision as to whether or not to cast an equipment, these committees needed to take account of a number of factors, such as the availability of a replacement, the state of the equipment and its repair history, and the availability of spares and repair facilities. In earlier years it would have been quite exceptional for a committee not to cast an equipment put up to them for disposal. However, in the years leading up to 1992, under-funding for replacement equipments led to a situation where certain operationally-vital-equipments had to be repaired uneconomically, and this trend looked likely to continue into the foreseeable future.

Design Changes

The twenty years to 1992 saw increased use of the Commercial Livery (CL) vehicle, and these gave useful service in less demanding General Service (GS) roles. At that stage their future in a smaller and more compact Army was unknown.

The use of the Manufacturer's Warranty for vehicle life was also the subject of much change. The trend was towards more meaningful and usable warranties, an essential of which was a workable dealer network, regardless of the theatre in which the vehicle was used. Latterly, much work was done in this connection, with the result that the warranty was made effectively operable. So much so that a complaint from one supporting regimental workshop commander was that the warranty worked so well that his tradesmen were gaining no experience on their new vehicles after twelve months of use – a complaint difficult to answer!

Concepts for B Vehicles changed greatly over the twenty years from the Seventies. In REME's own fleet of specialist vehicles particularly, the arrival of the container body greatly simplified support and maintainability of the vast and complex range of specialized vehicles of the units which they supported. Also, the demize of the rugged Austin K9 'Tels Wagon' and the Bedford RL 'Machy Wagon' gave way to the age of the specialist Container Body (CB), which has become vital to support modern complex equipments. The most significant gain became the ability to cast and replace the flatbed, whilst retaining the expensive CB.

The wheeled recovery vehicle also progressed greatly over the same period. The Leyland Heavy Recovery Vehicle, renowned for its noisy-revving petrol engine and numerous gear changes which resulted in little noticeable forward progress, was to disappear. In the early Seventies the Scammell CRUSADER entered service, the first Army recovery vehicle to be fitted with the EKA arm. EKA is the name of the Swedish company which invented the hydraulically-operated beam to which is attached a cross frame, which in turn is secured to the axle or chassis of the vehicle to be recovered. This enabled a more rapid hook- up of the casualty, and without the need for crane and A frame. The CRUSADER was, however, a CL variant and as such was a low-mobility vehicle suitable mainly for road use. At the same time the AEC Medium Recovery vehicle entered service. This, while more reliable, was eventually replaced by the Foden, which had the advantage of both the EKA concept and the conventional hydraulic crane. It is hoped that it will survive well into the twenty-first century.

The tank transporter took a quantum leap forward with the arrival of the Scammell COMMANDER in 1984. The faithful but vintage MIGHTY ANTAR, in service with the major users, the RCT Tank Transporter Regiments, since the Fifties, was finally laid to rest as the high-technology COMMANDER replaced it. The 650 BHP CV 12 TCE Perkins engine of the COMMANDER, driven through a semi-automatic gearbox, greatly speeded up transit times, with considerably less fatigue to its crew. Cab comforts included double-bunk beds and a boiling vessel. Both were a great asset when the vehicles were deployed during the Gulf War. Not without its teething problems, it reached in the early Nineties that flat part of its reliability curve, normally associated with an occasional sports afternoon being possible for the Regimental Workshop!

All the design changes evolved over the years have been beneficial to both user and maintainer, but possibly the biggest step forward was the introduction of the tilt cab. Those involved with the maintenance of vehicles who are old enough to recall carrying out plug and points changes to the trusty Bedford RL will remember the crushed-chest syndrome resulting from being draped over the seat, legs hanging out of the cab, with head and arms resting on a very warm engine. The first vehicle fitted with a tilt cab was the Foden 16 tonne in the early Seventies, and this was followed by the Bedford 8 tonne and 14 tonne. In 1990 and 1991 the Leyland/DAF MMLC DROPS and the 4 tonne appeared. The new designs greatly improved the lot of the mechanic. The gradual change from petrol engines to diesel right down to the light B vehicle fleet again reduced maintenance, and in most cases improved reliability. The heavy and medium fleets saw a dramatic improvement to power by the introduction of the turbo diesel. Vehicle electrics became electronics with the advent of the alternator, transistorized control boxes and ignition systems. Black box technology came of age, possibly at the expense of repair by repair. Air brake technology was a continuing success story, the third line-system, air dryers to replace anti-freezers, and plastic air lines to replace steel. All have made for more reliable systems over the years.

Possibly one of the most difficult changes was the arrival of metric fasteners. Those in the past who memorized AF and Whitworth spanner and socket sizes suddenly had to bring the metric size into the equation. The basic vehicle mechanic's toolbox underwent numerous changes, usually involving an increase in weight. It is not recorded whether it ever weighed as much as the tradesman carrying it, but it certainly seemed to.

Management of B vehicles remained largely unchanged during the period, with the casting system still being the backbone of economical repair. 1985 saw the introduction of the first contract hire fleet in BAOR, when the Mercedes Tractor and a King trailer were taken into the light A vehicle fleet for the movement of light A vehicles. This was followed in

1990 by the Grade B staff car fleet at Rheindahlen and Bielefeld. It was expected that the contract hire of certain B vehicles would increase in the future.

The most significant change to BAOR repair policy was the closure of 37 (Rhine) Workshop on 31 March 1992. The workshop used to undertake both third-line repairs to B vehicles as well as a great many B Vehicle Engine and Major Assembly base repair programmes, together with FV432 base repair in latter years. The greater part of the base repair workload was transferred back to the UK, while third-line repair went out to contract under the newly formed Contract Repair Branch operating from HQ BAOR, and which started up operations in April 1991. CRB was then expanding and producing an alternative to conventional 'in-house' repairs. It was capable of providing all levels of repair for B vehicles, including In-Depth Repair, and it was hoped that it would expand to provide an exchange service for suitable minor assemblies, windscreen glass and other services.

IMPACT OF NORTHERN IRELAND ON BAOR

BAOR had been able to concentrate for many years on its NATO task, as part of the deterrent forces defending Western Europe, in the face of a potential threat from the Warsaw Pact forces. The importance of this role had been emphasized by Russian military action in Czechoslovakia in 1968. The withdrawal from former Imperial outposts in Africa and Asia had little effect on BAOR. Events in Northern Ireland in 1969 and 1970 had only a marginal effect. In 1971, two years after the renewal of the trouble in Ulster, this was to change and BAOR began to play an important reinforcement role in providing both units and individuals for the force there. Six major units from 1st Division were initially required for a four-month tour in the infantry role; by 1972 ten major units were involved.

The major units each took fifteen to twenty REME soldiers from their unit workshop or LAD to work at their trade, but before long the adaptable, intelligent REME tradesmen were being employed in other roles where there were deficiencies, and found themselves as infantrymen or as intelligence collators. From 1972 up until 1980 about 40% of each LAD in BAOR was going to Northern Ireland with their parent units, and most were not being employed at their trade. The remainder, left behind in Germany, were overstretched in maintain ing their unit's BAOR equipment to the standard that they aimed to reach.

By mid-1972 the second-line workshop load in Northern Ireland exceeded the capacity of the resources of United Kingdom Land Forces (UKLF). BAOR sent thirty-one individual tradesmen to Northern Ireland that July to work in the Saracen (Armoured Personnel Carrier)

Workshop. They were replaced in November by a platoon of the same strength from 1 Field Workshop who, together with the UKLF element, formed the Armoured Personnel Carrier Workshop Northern Ireland. Experience with this workshop, and the effect that the Army Restructuring Plan was having on UKLF's ability to provide continuously an adequate number of REME personnel, led to the formation of a Northern Ireland Roulement Workshop. This could be manned completely by either UKLF or BAOR for a tour, but by BAOR for five times in every seven tours. 11 Field Workshop was the first to take on this task and in 1976 provided 150 all ranks. By 1980, the requirement had risen to six officers and 166 soldiers. Also, the composite AAC Squadron in Northern Ireland, provided from BAOR, was supported by about half of its associated LAD, together with individual technicians from 71 Aircraft Workshop. By the end of 1984, because of the length of time that soldiers were not available to their units in BAOR, the overall effect of the BAOR REME support provided for Northern Ireland was that all REME units in 1(BR)Corps were undermanned.

Although an emergency tour in Northern Ireland, known as Operation BANNER, was only for a period of four months, it meant in practice, allowing for special training before going and leave afterwards, that an individual soldier was away from his unit for seven months. The effect of this absence on the second-line workshop left in BAOR was serious, because the numbers required in particular trades in Northern Ireland sometimes took an undue share of the workshop strength, as the very young and inexperienced could not be sent. However, the best junior NCOs who had to go to Northern Ireland received excellent training and experience as a result of their tours. The part played by all REME soldiers from BAOR sent to Northern Ireland is described in Chapter 10.

The commanders of the rear parties of units left in BAOR had their problems too. They had to continue to maintain REME support, sometimes for formation exercises, despite having sent key tradesmen and their more experienced soldiers to Northern Ireland. They also had the very important task of ensuring that the soldiers' families left behind in BAOR were properly cared for. There was no doubt, though, that this experience was to prove invaluable when the time came to implement Operation GRANBY, described later in this Chapter.

NEW EQUIPMENT IN THE EIGHTIES

During the Eighties BAOR continued to receive excellent new sophisticated equipment, which REME had to learn to keep in battle-winning condition and compete with the teething problems that inevitably arose. This is discussed in detail in relevant sections of this chapter, and is summarized here. New equipment included the

CHALLENGER main battle tank, the WARRIOR infantry combat vehicle, the tracked vehicle version of the RAPIER air defence ground-to-air missile system, the PTARMIGAN communication system, and the LYNX helicopter TOW (Tube-launched, Optically-tracked, Wire-guided) anti-tank guided weapon. The new weapons included, or were supported by, several optical and electronic devices.

New REME equipment to assist the workshops in their increasingly complex tasks included the CHIEFTAIN Armoured Recovery and Repair Vehicle (ARRV), the Foden 6 × 6 recovery vehicle to replace the Leyland Heavy and AEC Medium Recovery Vehicles, as well as specialist repair and test facilities such as CLANSMAN radio electronic repair vehicles (ERV), SWINGFIRE ERV, Combined Sight Repair Vehicle and Fuel Injection Equipment (FIE) Repair Container. The new tank weaponry also required its own special test equipment including DIANA, (the General Purpose Digital Test and Diagnostic Facility), and the General Purpose Thermal Imaging Repair Facility (GPTIRF), complete with Application Test Packages. Added to the wide range of equipment necessary for the repair of CHIEFTAIN and CHALLENGER tanks, these particular items were concerned with the all- weather, day-and-night direct-fire facility, Thermal Observation and Gunnery Sight (TOGS).

CHALLENGER Main Battle Tank

In the early Seventies the Government of Iran placed an order in Britain for main battle tanks. Part of this order was under development when the Shah was deposed. This type was subsequently to replace the CHIEFTAIN in the British Army and to be known as the CHALLENGER. The tank mounted the same 120mm gun as the CHIEFTAIN, but it had some major overall advantages when compared with the CHIEFTAIN, which had been developed in the Sixties and brought into service in the Seventies. The new tank had Chobham armour, a totally new power pack, and a hydrogas suspension system, which gave it a major improvement in operational performance. This design was rapidly adapted for British Army service, and the tanks were issued to seven armoured regiments over the period 1983–1989.

The early CHALLENGER models lacked TOGS. To remedy this about one hundred tanks of 1st Armoured Division were retrofitted at 7 Armoured Workshop, Fallingbostel. This considerable task was organized there by AQMS Ian Smith who was awarded the MBE for his work. The power pack in the CHALLENGER tank consisted of a Rolls Royce CV12 turbocharged diesel engine, a gearbox fitted with hydrostatic steering and integral main vehicle brakes, a cooling group and a fan group. The power pack could neither be lifted nor carried by the FV434 repair vehicle which supported the CHIEFTAIN tank, so the CHIEFTAIN ARV was converted to the repair role by adding an excellent Atlas crane and power pack carrying-frame, after which it was redesignated Armoured Repair and Recovery Vehicle (ARRV). Fourteen CHALLENGER tanks belonging to the Royal Hussars in Fallingbostel carried out successful troop trials in 1983–84, culminating in Exercise LIONHEART in 1984. They covered 20,000 kilometres and were supported by two CHIEFTAIN ARRV. Issues of the tanks continued and in 1989 the Queen's Own Hussars became the seventh and last regiment of the programme to be equipped with CHALLENGER 1.

WARRIOR Infantry Combat Vehicle

WARRIOR was the name given to the Mechanized Infantry Combat Vehicle in the final stages of its development in 1985. The 1st Battalion Grenadier Guards received the first WARRIOR in BAOR at Munster in 1987, the fleet for troop trials growing until they were fully equipped by the In-Service Date of April 1988. An in-service reliability study took place from April 1988 to March 1989, at the same time as the troop trial. Although some defects were found, the equipment proved to be a great success. By mid-summer 1989 three infantry battalions had been equipped, with a few of the variants already in service. REME also received their supporting vehicles and four recovery vehicles per battalion.

23 BASE WORKSHOP

In the late Sixties the workload at Wetter consisted of CENTURION tanks and its variants, wheeled SARACENs, SALADINs and FERRETs. The CENTURIONs and SALADINs were coming to the end of their lives and being replaced by CHIEFTAIN tanks and the FV432 range of tracked vehicles. The workload during 1968–70 also included some vehicles of American manufacture belonging to the Canadian Brigade at Soest. The detachment of 4 Field Workshop RCEME, which had been attached to 23 Base Workshop since 1952 and had been responsible for the base overhaul of AFVs and B vehicles belonging to the Canadian Brigade, moved with its parent workshop when the brigade moved to Laar in Baden in 1972.

The new generation of armoured vehicles being introduced into BAOR, described earlier, replaced many traditional mechanical components with electronic or hydraulic systems. The methods of repair and replacement had to be completely reassessed and staff trained in the new systems. As both the scale and scope of the armoured vehicle load increased it was necessary both to minimize the repair time and usage of spares. As a result, 'Value Engineering', subsequently called 'Economic Base Repair', was introduced in 1972. This enabled the man-hour content for the base overhaul of CHIEFTAIN tanks to be reduced by 20%, while still achieving the base overhaul standard.

In 1972 the last of the base overhauls of CENTURION tanks was completed, 2,259 tanks having passed through the workshop during the programme. In the same year the 1,000th FERRET Scout Car to receive a base overhaul left the workshop. As the programmes continued, in 1975 the 1,000th FV432 was completed, and in 1980 Lieutenant General Sir Peter Leng, Commander 1(BR)Corps, drove the 2,000th off the production line. In 1981 his successor, Lieutenant General Sir Nigel Bagnall, drove off the 1,000th CHIEFTAIN. Base overhaul of the SCORPION started in 1979, followed by SPARTAN in 1982, and in 1984, the Combat Engineer Tractor which, like the CVR(T), had an aluminium hull. The remainder of the CVR(T) range – SULTAN, STRIKER, SAMARITAN, and SAMSON – followed, all being rebuilt on the same assembly line. In 1987, the base repairs for most FV430 series were transferred to 37 (Rhine) Workshop at Moenchengladbach, to make room for the base repair to WARRIOR at 23 Base Workshop. By then, 23 Base Workshop had overhauled 4,400 FV430 series vehicles at Wetter.

Major modifications to AFVs were sometimes required to be made more quickly than would be possible if they awaited the normal base repair programme. 23 Base Workshop frequently established a retrofit modification line in parallel with the base repair line, for unit equipments. In 1973 the first such line was set up for CHIEFTAIN tank major sighting and automotive modifications. In 1977 the fitting of a new NBC pack began, and in the early Eighties trials of a new Muzzle Reference System and an Improved Fire Control System (IFCS) were carried out. This led to the fitting of these systems to some 775 guns of CHIEFTAN tanks, the last one being completed in 1986. IFCS was a digital computer-based fire-control system, providing an automatic laying facility for the main weapon. This was followed immediately by the up-armouring of 480 CHIEFTAINs. The up-armouring included welding additional armoured plate to the turret armour with a thick rubber buffer placed between the turret and the new armour. Another important programme still in progress in 1990 was fitting TOGS. A separate programme was the fitting of the CLANSMAN communication harness in place of LARKSPUR in 527 CHIEFTAINs.

Between 1983 and 1988 sixty-nine CHIEFTAIN ARVs were converted to ARRVs by the addition of a 7 tonne hydraulic Atlas crane to lift the CHALLENGER power pack, weighing 5.5 tonnes, in the field. To achieve this it was necessary for the hull to be stripped, placed in a turn-over stand, cut and welded. Other modification programmes included equipments such as the M109 155mm self-propelled gun, the CHIEFTAIN L60 engine, the CHIEFTAIN Armoured Vehicle Launched Bridge and the Combat Engineer Tractor. Although the base overhaul of CHALLENGER tanks did not start until 1990, major assemblies had been repaired for several years before this, and a dedicated test house had been built in 1986 for the CHALLENGER transmission (TN37), with a special clean repair facility for the assembly of its hydraulic steering unit.

An unusual programme also began in 1990 when 23 Base Workshop

First overhauled Challenger

won a competitive contract to modify the Multiple Launch Rocket System (MLRS) vehicles on receipt direct from the manufacturers and prior to issue to the British Army.

In addition to their base repairs and modification programmes, the workshop manufactured spares and components for the field force, and carried out emergency modifications such as the refurbishment of tank engine air filters. The same ingenuity as was required for emergency modifications was required to reclaim components economically and overcome spares shortages within the workshop. During the late Eighties there was a marked deterioration in the availability of spares which, despite all efforts by the workshop, led to programme stoppages. For the first time ever a major overhaul line, that for the CHALLENGER, came to a complete halt for lack of spares, very soon after it started in 1990. This situation was to affect the mounting of Operation GRANBY discussed in the next section.

MOUNTING OF OPERATION GRANBY

Operation GRANBY was the code name given in August 1990 to the sending of British Forces to the Middle East, as part of an international coalition. This action resulted from the invasion of Kuwait by Iraq on 2 August 1990, and the initial aim of the overall Force was to prevent further incursions by Iraq, particularly against Saudi Arabia. The subsequent air and sea operations against Iraq from January 1991, followed by the land battle in February, were carried out as a result of the UN Security Council Resolution 678 of 29 November 1990.

The initial build-up and preparations affecting REME from September 1990, both within the Middle East and elsewhere, but excluding those preparations carried out within BAOR prior to the dispatch of their major elements of the Land Force, are described in Chapter 12 – Operation GRANBY. The activities of the Corps during the land battle to free Kuwait, which started on 24 February 1991, and the recovery phase from March 1991, are also covered in that chapter. The following paragraphs in this Chapter, however, cover the specific activities carried out within Germany by REME from August 1990, in the preparation and despatch, in its two phases, of the main Land Force elements provided from BAOR. All activities on their arrival in the Middle East are also described in Chapter 12.

Because the bulk of the British Land Forces under Operation GRANBY was found from BAOR, the overall impact in Germany was very considerable. As in the case of the Falklands Campaign, there was no contingency plan in existence for the operation that confronted those involved. In BAOR operations outside Europe were never contemplated, and indeed only became remotely feasible with the ending of the Cold War and consensus within NATO. Thus, the Government announcement on 14 September 1990 that 7 Armoured Brigade Group would be sent to the Middle East was a realization of the unexpected. The complexities involved in the successful deployment of such a Force were a unique test of the skills inherent in BAOR. Logistics, more than ever, though not always given due recognition, particularly by the media, were to play a major part in the despatch of the Force from Germany. REME's contribution in this phase of the operation was of paramount importance, particularly as there had been some relaxation of the operational readiness state of equipment since the ending of the Cold War.

In September 1990 the Force initially mounted consisted of 7 Armoured Brigade Group, but ultimately it was enlarged to divisional size consisting of HQ 1st Armoured Division with 4 and 7 Armoured Brigades. The Division deployed with significantly more than a full divisional slice of supporting Arms and Logistic Units, with their REME support. In the event, Operation GRANBY took place in two phases, GRANBY 1 and GRANBY 1.5. The expansion of the Force from the original one brigade to divisional strength was named GRANBY 1.5 with true British logic, since, before the increase in the size of the Force had been decided, GRANBY 2, 3 and 4 were already in the planning stage to cover the roulement of 7 Armoured Brigade Group and the logistic support elements. The force deployed for GRANBY 1.5 was almost twice the size of that involved for GRANBY 1, with corresponding logistic complexities. In the preparation for the two phases, there was a considerable overlapping of the deployment of resources, and a switching of both men and equipment between units. There was a particular necessity for this action within REME units, and the high standard of support provided to the Force in the Gulf is a tribute to the skills of all those involved in these complicated initial processes.

REME Participation – Operation GRANBY 1

On 14 September 1990 the Government announced that 7 Armoured Brigade Group, commanded by Brigadier Patrick Cordingley, would move from Germany to the Gulf to join recently increased RN and RAF units already in the area. This announcement of the introduction of a land force set the scene for a period of intense activity within BAOR. The Brigade Group was to consist of 9,500 men and women, 117 Challenger tanks, 101 Warrior infantry fighting vehicles, an armoured reconnaissance squadron and twenty-eight M109 self-propelled guns, all backed up by their War Maintenance Reserves. They would be supported by two engineer regiments, two transport regiments, two ordnance battalions, two armoured workshops and other specialist units. The move of the Brigade Group to the Gulf was accomplished by late October 1990, and the following paragraphs indicate by examples the extent of the essential support provided by REME, not only from the accompanying workshops and LADs, but also the many others in the Corps who contributed in the preparations necessary to deploy this force from BAOR.

Before the major involvement of REME units in BAOR, covert planning had already started in the main HQs in BAOR – JHQ at Rheindahlen, and 1(BR) Corps at Bielefeld. As always on these occasions, not every individual involved can be in the best possible place to take up their duties at very short notice when the whistle is blown. Lieutenant Colonel Alastair Campbell, then SO1 Maint/E Man HQ BAOR, experienced this situation when his participation in Operation GRANBY began in earnest. A keen yachtsman, on 15 September he was ten nautical miles north of Kiel in the south-west Baltic, racing the new BKYC Hallberg Rassy 29 in the inter-divisional regatta. It was Day 4 of the event and his yacht was lying second, cross- tacking for the first windward mark, when the VHF radio 'crackled': 'Urgent message – Skipper of *Widgeon* – report back to Kiel immediately.' His yacht was reluctantly retired, and two hours later at Kiel he was being briefed by the duty NCO, who told him that he was to return to Rheindahlen immediately to attend a briefing at 2300 hours that night by the Commander Maintenance, Brigadier Mike Heath, at the house of his deputy, Colonel Keith Palmer. There then started an astonishing ten days of non-stop activity. After a tedious six and a half hours' drive back to Rheindahlen in a mini-bus, he was told that he was to leave the following day for Saudi Arabia, as part of a covert reconnaissance team of twelve. The team was to include Commander 7 Armoured Brigade (Brigadier

Patrick Cordingley), COS 1(BR)Corps (Brigadier Mike Walker), and Commander Force Maintenance Area (Colonel Martin White, at that time a staff officer in HQ BAOR). His task on the reconnaissance was to propose the Equipment Management and Maintenance plans with locations and facilities for the British Land Forces.

On the afternoon of Sunday, 16 September, following inoculations, issue of weapons and desert kit, which included NBC suits, Lieutenant Colonel Campbell flew with the team in a VC10 from RAF Wildenrath to Saudi Arabia. The team was accompanied by a somewhat covert Foreign Office official and a general, who were to square the presence of the team with the Saudi Arabians and the Americans. This took three days, during which time the team was holed up, incognito, in the Intercontinental Hotel in Riyadh, and was getting used to the 'dry' surroundings. Eventually it was agreed that the British should come under command of the US Marines, and the team could venture out to do its reconnaissance. Lieutenant Colonel Campbell takes up his story:

'The RAF provided a HERCULES aircraft from those already in the area, for the ground reconnaissance. We needed a port and an air head somewhere in the north-east and, having looked briefly at Dhahran, settled on Al Jubayl. Both these ports were being used by US Forces. We were on the ground for half a day only, but I managed to talk a British expatriate into driving me into the desert to have a look at the terrain on which we would have to train, and eventually advance to contact.

'We had many briefings from, and visits to, US Marine HQs and units, and I spent a lot of time with the US Maintenance Battalions. Real estate in the port area was a big problem. There was a custom-built dock with eight giant warehouses, but the scale of the US logistic effort was enormous and clearly dovetailing of shipping and its clearance was going to be a difficult task. I bid for one warehouse in which to do the desert modifications for CHALLENGER MBTs and WARRIOR MCVs, and managed to book two sites for MRGs. Distances, though, were much greater than we were used to in BAOR, and maintenance of MSRs and repair and recovery support would be a tough job.

'We started our Recce Report back at the hotel in Riyadh, and continued it in the HERCULES in which we flew back to UK via Cyprus on 23 September. The report had to be delivered to the Commander-in-Chief JHQ UK, Air Chief Marshal Sir Patrick Hine, on our return. It was completed in the HERCULES during our fifteen-hour flight by Commander Medical, Colonel Lou Lillywhite, on his lap-top computer, and briefed to the High Command at High Wycombe the next day.

'Then it was back to BAOR and on with frantic preparations. The planned FMA organization was set up in an empty building in JHQ BAOR and people to fill the establishment started to arrive from all over BAOR as well as UK, on an ad hoc basis. I left the BAOR equipment preparation to my successor in Maint/E

Man HQ BAOR, and concentrated on building up the Maint/E Man organization in the FMA for Saudi Arabia, in my new appointment as SO1 Maint/E Man FMA. After debriefing Comd Maint, I went to Fallingbostel to liaise with HQ 7 Armoured Brigade and 7 Armoured Workshop, and within eight days was flying back to Al Jubayl on the FMA pre-advance party. The initial Maint/E Man presence in the FMA was to be one lieutenant colonel, three majors and one sergeant clerk. In the event five men gradually expanded as the scale of the task became more apparent, and eventually we were to be forty-five military and thirty-five civilian defence contractors.

'I had done some calculations in August 1990 on what engines and major assemblies would be required to sustain a 1,000 kilometres of training and 30 days of operational stocks for the Force. For three armoured regiments equipped with CHALLENGER plus one infantry battalion with WARRIOR the bill was horrendous. MDBF statistics were available for WARRIOR in BAOR intensive use. Figures for CHALLENGER were derived from a CHALLENGER/CHIEFTAIN comparison in BAOR multiplied by a factor of 2.5, which was the BATUS differential. The figures were disputed, but eventually agreed. To support 7 Armoured Brigade would take all existing stocks, plus about 50–75% of the E & MAs of the equipment left in BAOR.

'A package of desertization modifications was designed for CHALLENGER and WARRIOR, mainly air filtration plus up-armouring. These modifications, however, would not be ready to fit in BAOR and would have to be sent out by air, to meet the tanks that had arrived in Saudi Arabia by sea; hence the requirement for the defence contractors, and the warehouse in which to undertake the modifications. I recommended that two MRGs be sent out as part of the REME element, both CHALLENGER/WARRIOR equipment proficient. In the event, 7 Armoured Workshop, which comprised one MRG which was proficient in this type of equipment, and another proficient only on 432/CHIEFTAIN, were tasked.

'The Operational Commander was most concerned about the vulnerability of all his armour being held at the dockside on arrival, for the desertization modifications. However, he accepted that, if equipment went directly into the safety of the desert unmodified, it would fail within 50 kilometres of motoring. Faced with this dilemma, he gave me a maximum period of 24 hours in which to desertize each squadron of tanks at the dockside.'

Since all the REME activities in the Gulf from the arrival of the Force there, including those in the FMA, are contained in Chapter 12 (Operation GRANBY), it is appropriate at this stage to leave Lieutenant Colonel Campbell, newly arrived with the pre-advance party of the FMA at Al Jubayl, and to return to the continuing preparations in BAOR to launch the remainder of the Force. These preparations were frenetic, and we take up the story at HQ 1(BR)Corps with Major Gill Prowse, REME, the SO2 G4(E Man), who was the equipment manager, coordinating equipment information from below, and disseminating from above. The next level upwards was at HQ BAOR which she describes as being where the 'real' (theatre) equipment managers sat. She continues in her own words, which provide an insight into the pace and extent of the work and the personal views of a Grade 2 Staff Officer who was totally involved in the equipment preparations:

'Part of my job normally was to monitor equipment availability on a monthly basis and brief it to the Corps Commander. This task was the key in the initial equipment planning stages and highlighted the need for accurate and timely equipment availability reporting. Around the beginning of August, I was asked for advice on lots of different "what if?" options should we have to send a Force to the Gulf. At first it seemed highly unlikely that anyone would go, particularly as the Out Of Area Brigade in UK was also being considered. Personally, I had to temper what I read in the Press with what I heard at work, and to make educated guesses as to the way forward. My comments on equipments were, on the whole, pessimistic, because so few of them had been brought into service Q Ready. The Operations Staff therefore had a difficult task listening to both me and the hierarchy, who were very optimistic. My answers had a common theme to them, and the phrase, "lack of spares, hence unsupportable", was heard frequently. As plans developed comments became more specialized and operational decisions such as regimental and formation coherence had to be considered as well. We were concerned about such things as recent defects on CHALLENGER, modifications to WARRIOR, and the use of totally new equipments such as DROPS and MLRS.

'Once we knew that a Force was to go, and we knew before the components of the Force did, we had to get all the armoured vehicles of the right type in the one place, fully operational and supported at all levels by the right spares. The RAC said that only Mark 2 CHALLENGERs should go, and there were just enough for two regiments' worth, but they were scattered around the Corps. It was difficult to keep the proposed deployments secret when all Mark 2 tanks had to be made fully operational as soon as possible. A problem that cropped up at this stage, and stayed with us for some time, was the reluctance of some units to help others by giving up equipment which they cherished. It was particularly acute across divisional boundaries, and we at Corps HQ spent endless hours on the phone persuading people why they should help, be it by giving up their equipment or helping to make it good, so to speak. There were problems for specialist units such as the tank transporter squadrons RCT, which had to move all the tanks between units, transport them to the ports, and then get ready to go themselves. Finally, they had to be got to the Gulf before the tanks, so that they could move them from the port when they got there.

'We knew that we should have to cannibalize equipment, in some cases to make an equipment fully operational in the first place, and in others to ensure that there were enough spares to accompany the complete equipments. We thought it prudent to take extra CHALLENGER spares. There was no visibility of spares and we had to ask units through their quartermasters what spares they had, and this meant

Part of the cannibalized fleet

that we had to trust to the integrity of people. The cannibalization had to be documented and it was not easy making the decision as to which tanks should be cannibalized first. Some items, particularly the Line Replacable Units in the turret, were common to both CHALLENGER and CHIEFTAIN, and so all the CHIEFTAIN regiments became involved as well. Then we needed REME manpower to do the cannibalization, and this required to be specially organized, and initially was done with undue haste.

'We had started planning using current unit establishments to work from. However, the establishments were written for a general war in Europe and not a limited war in hot sandy desert conditions. Commanders' whims at all levels had to be coped with, and we had to sort out the real necessities from the desirables and plain padding. Giving units in 7 Armoured Brigade exactly what they asked for had lots of knock-on effects; depriving others and rendering them non-operational; increased costs when we were not sure who would pay; and the fact that extra equipment could sometimes mean extra manpower. Also, not the least of our endeavours was trying to keep something up our sleeves in case one brigade was not enough for the ultimate task, as indeed proved to be the case. The list of operational requirements grew daily, and G3 OR were another branch thrust into the limelight.

'Our office had to try to match assets with liabilities for 7 Armoured Brigade. The requirements rarely stood still but we had to monitor progress and report on a daily basis. We also monitored progress towards fully operational 100% availability, which was our desired start state. I was a briefer at the morning conferences. Many equipments became personally known to us, such as the rogue

tank that could not shoot straight! Once all the tanks had been made fully operational they had to go to the ranges. This too involved considerable effort, more spares and more REME manpower. There was also not a little frustration, when time was of the essence, because the Germans for various reasons would not allow range firing on a Sunday.

'Our days were spent talking up and down the chain of command, trying to be honest brokers, grilling formations beneath us for a justification, and then in turn begging superiors to support our requests. We wrote many justifications, and of course after the reconnaissances the goal posts moved again. Night shifts started in September and were spent in consolidating the moves of equipment; writing signals to units organizing more moves; checking that moves had taken place; sorting out paperwork; and endeavouring to help the few remaining units who were trying to be just a little bit normal.

'We had just finished organizing the deployment of 7 Armoured Brigade when further planning became necessary. Firstly to replace 7 Armoured Brigade on roulement after six months (which mainly involved manpower) and then to provide additional troops as well as replace that brigade. It was soon realized that both could not be done, and as the broader situation was changing anyway, the option of sending a division, ie an additional brigade and a divisional HQ, soon became the preferred option. It was indeed fortunate that we knew that another brigade was to go before 7 Armoured Brigade had actually left. Gradually more and more people became involved, the net was cast wider, and those who had initially been untouched were gathered in. Rules changed, standards were lowered, eg Mark 1 tanks could now go, and work on equipment was now being done all over the place. This ranged through unit lines, workshops and the port, and still plans had to be made for a workshop to be set up at Al Jubayl. After the decision to increase the strength of the Force, it was decided to establish a Staff Headquarters in Saudi Arabia, and this took away important personalities in the Equipment area, particularly from HQ BAOR.

'As the ships began to sail the workload lessened and the nightshift stopped, but there was still plenty of work to be done. There were many major assemblies to be stripped out of a wide range of vehicles, as it was not just tanks that had been affected by the cannibalization programme. A repair loop had to be set up for the base repair of assemblies, which was very complex, and to this day I do not know how effective it was. There was a great deal of tidying up to be done, equipment censuses to carry out to see what we had left in 1(BR)Corps, and the imposition of some new monitoring systems. Many lessons were learned after this operation, some new, some old. If enough had been in place to begin with, and equipments had been brought into service Q Ready, then the whole Corps would not have been rendered non-operational as a result of deploying one of its divisions out of the Theatre. In my humble opinion, not enough importance had been attached to logistics. This resulted in the sort of problems that occurred when subordinate HQs would only do as G3 Ops told them rather than accept instructions direct from G4. The interaction between G3 and G4 seemed to get less, further up the chain of command. The fact that we had both functional and operational chains of

command meant a certain amount of conflict, although it had the advantage of spreading information a lot more quickly'.

Major Gill Prowse, married to Captain Dennis Prowse REME, gave birth to their baby on 31 January 1991, having worked at her demanding and responsible job well into her entitled maternity leave. She made a valuable contribution to the complex task of equipment management for the launching of the Force from BAOR and was later awarded the MBE for her overall work whilst in HQ 1(BR)Corps. Captain Dennis Prowse, at the time of GRANBY, was OC 10 Regiment Group RCT Workshop, and himself heavily involved in the preparation stage in BAOR, prior to going to the Gulf with his Regimental Workshop in October.

Throughout BAOR REME units were preparing to deploy to the Gulf, whilst others were heavily involved in helping with the preparation of equipments of units of all arms and services, who were also being deployed under GRANBY 1. Some examples of both these categories, which are typical of the wide-ranging activities involved, are given in outline below.

7 Armoured Workshop

7 Armoured Workshop at Fallingbostel, commanded by Lieutenant Colonel Rod Croucher, and consisting of two MRGs and one FRG, was the REME support element for 7 Armoured Brigade. The news that they were to go to the Gulf could not have been more directly received by the whole workshop, since all available personnel were paraded outside RHQ at 1530 on 14 September to listen avidly to the Government announcement on Radio 4 through the shop-floor 'boogie box' set up for the occasion. Earlier that day, though, information was already coming through more normal channels and the planning for deployment to the Gulf had begun for the workshop. Thereafter there was no doubt about the extent of their involvement, and by the following day hectic preparations were well under way. To enable these preparations to go ahead unhindered by the normal routine workload, a detachment from 11 Armoured Workshop at Soest was to move into one of the MRG workshop hangers at Fallingbostel to take on this task, being then blissfully unaware that they too would later deploy to the Gulf under GRANBY 1.5.

By 1200 hrs on 18 September, MRG 7B had vacated their hanger and other accommodation for 11 Armoured Workshop detachment to move into, and were well under way with their own preparations for deployment. The issue of 'dog tags' and the signing of will forms which these preparations included, and concern for the well-being of their families to be left in Germany, and their reactions, brought home to many the reality of the situation – it was not just another exercise, they were going to war! Many of the wives were to help in supporting the unit's preparations, but, although separation was nothing new to them, the Media did little to allay their fears that their husbands were about to face situations that they had not known before. Support was of great importance.

MRG 7B's own vehicles, of which there were some 125 prime movers and 70 trailers, were prepared for all emergencies, such aids as Thomas bins were welded on, and emergency vehicle boxes gathered together to provide a 'quick fix' in the event of break-down, and a degree of self-sufficiency. An interesting record maintained by platoon commander Lieutenant Alan Dale of all the O Groups held in the MRG from 14 September until the end of the campaign shows the remarkable diversity and comprehensiveness of the information received, orders given, and actions resulting, both in the preparation stage in BAOR and in the Gulf. AQMS John Uttley obviously got his priorities right when, on Day 1, with his usual foresight, he produced a fridge to be installed in a vehicle; later this proved invaluable, even without a stock of German beer! At least it brought back memories. However, in everyone's mind was the great emphasis now to be placed on individual military training and fitness for the whole workshop, and this was continuous and testing up to the time of departure for the Gulf. It was of particular importance with the number of individual reinforcements being received, in order to bring everyone up to the same high standard.

The war establishment of 7 Armoured Workshop was 595 all ranks, at which strength it deployed to the Gulf. Between 14 September and 11 October, when deployment started, it received 150 reinforcements from some fifty different units, not only to make up the normal peacetime deficiencies, but also to replace those men in the unit who were not medically fit for service in the Gulf. Some key personnel were in the latter category and were difficult to replace. Another problem was the disparity in military skills amongst the reinforcements, some coming from LADs where more emphasis tended to be placed on technical rather than military skills. For the Gulf operation, the balance of sub-units within the workshop had to be changed to provide two balanced MRGs – MRG 7A and 7B and one enhanced FRG 7, as opposed to two different MRGs and two FRGs, normally 'tailored' to support the different ORBATs of 7 and 22 Armoured Brigades supported in BAOR. MRG 7B was commanded by Major David Bowhay and 7A by an Australian attached officer, Major Chris Cromack RAEME, who was subsequently awarded the MBE for his services in the Gulf. FRG 7 was commanded by Captain Mark Hygate, followed by Captain John Ellis.

Both MRGs were as identical as possible with an establishment and manning level of seven officers and 221 soldiers. Both were organized into functional groupings and consisted of a small HQ, an administrative platoon, a power pack platoon, a vehicles and general platoon, an optronics platoon and an RAOC stores platoon. It was of major importance on the technical side to ensure that special tools and test equipment were brought up to establishment, and there was some concern about the chaotic state of optronic repair facilities, particularly with regard to the range and number of modification states of Application Test Packages and Electronic Repair Vehicles (ERVs).

ASM Collins and Sergeant Brazier on arrival in the desert

On 6 October the Workshop's vehicles were moved to Hamburg and, with a boat party, were loaded onto USS *Guyanne* for shipment to the Gulf. Major General Dennis Shaw, DGEME, visited the workshop early on 10 October, and then went on to visit LADs of Brigade units. The advance party of the Workshop left by air between 11 – 13 October, and the remainder of the Workshop between 17 and 23 October, confident that they could do all that was required of them.

Meanwhile, those REME units with direct responsibilities for the support of the regiments or battalions to which they were attached were ensuring that their equipments met the highest standards of reliability. Such a unit was The Queen's Royal Irish Hussars LAD in Fallingbostel. Captain Paul Armstrong, ASM Collins and all the LAD were very busy indeed. The strength of the LAD grew from 86 to 120 in a little over a week, as individual reinforcements arrived from all over BAOR and were integrated into the unit. The LAD worked round the clock to prepare their CHALLENGER tanks and other vehicles of the Regiment, including their own, and bring them up to operational readiness before shipment by ferry to the Gulf. Once the vehicles had been shipped, the personnel of the LAD, as with all other units, were totally involved with intensive personal training, NBC, first aid, fitness and weapon training. On 26 October the last men flew to Al Jubayl to join up with their equipment. They were to work non-stop from their arrival there to restore the vehicles to standard, following the effects of the sea voyage, and to implement the desertization programme described in Chapter 12.

The wide-ranging preparations by REME units included those for the AAC. 71 Aircraft Workshop was warned on 14 September 1990 to prepare ten LYNX and eleven GAZELLE helicopters for possible deployment on Operation GRANBY and to prepare an MRG to deploy in support of 659 Squadron AAC. A rigorous training programme began for the soldiers who were to be deployed to the Gulf, whilst the remaining technicians worked an average of eighteen hours a day to prepare the aircraft, reinforced by a team from 70 Aircraft Workshop. The LYNX required modifications, thorough checks and servicing to raise the aircraft to the highest possible standard. The GAZELLEs required armoured seats, modifications (including sand filters) and servicing. The LYNX flew to RAF Wildenrath for painting and the GAZELLEs were sprayed at 71 Aircraft Workshop. Wives brought in refreshments to their rarely seen husbands and one, Mrs Sue Beck, helped to mask up the GAZELLEs ready for spraying. The ten LYNX in their new desert colours went to Soltau ranges for TOW live firing on 24 September. Final rectifications were completed for the LYNX and GAZELLE on 25 and 26 September respectively.

Lynx being prepared for re-spray

The MRG, one officer and forty soldiers with their twenty-six vehicles, was prepared from scratch in five days. Part of the MRG was the Forward Stores Group (FSG) RAOC which was required for scaling, demanding and loading of the aircraft stores. It was a big disappointment when, being ready to go on 26 September, they did not deploy with 7 Armoured Brigade. However, their time was yet to come on GRANBY 1.5.

5 Armoured Workshop at Soest, in a supporting role, provided more than thirty men for REME units going to the Gulf on GRANBY 1. These were mainly for 7 Armoured Workshop, but some were also to reinforce LADs. The workshop also provided three Power Pack Repair and Run Up vehicles, the DIANA and FIE Repair Containers as well as several other vehicles and equipment for 7 Armoured Workshop. These men and vehicles left 5 Armoured Workshop on 18 September with a rousing send-off from the OC, Major Peter Sharpe, and the remainder of the

unit left behind. Several more soldiers, plus two ARRVs and IFCS and GPTIRF electronic repair vehicles, went to 11 Armoured Workshop, acting at first as an FRG at Fallingbostel to support training and live firing as part of the build-up. Support was also given at Sennelager ranges, at firing camps and at Bremerhaven, the port of embarkation.

Those of 5 Armoured Workshop who remained at Soest after they had provided the Operation GRANBY 1 reinforcements were far from idle, as CHALLENGER power packs were required for the War Maintenance Reserve (WMR) and many of these had to be stripped so that the engines and gearboxes could be separated and sent back to 23 Base Workshop at Wetter. This was done on two lines working twelve-hour shifts, and without their own power pack vehicles, splitter frames and many of the experienced tradesmen who had already gone to 7 Armoured Workshop. Nevertheless, thirty-two packs were processed in an exhausting few days in September, a further example of the diverse and considerable contribution which the workshop made in support of GRANBY 1. This support was to be increased even more for GRANBY 1.5.

REME Participation – Operation GRANBY 1.5

By mid-October all REME units in support of 7 Armoured Brigade were established in Saudi Arabia and fully involved in their initial role of preparing the brigade equipment for desert training and, ultimately, combat. To reach this stage had required a tremendous effort by all ranks, and this was to be sustained in BAOR when GRANBY 1.5 was announced. Much had been learned from the deployment of 7 Armoured Brigade by all those involved, both in headquarters and units, but many of the same sort of problems remained. Again, as for GRANBY 1, REME units consisted of a variety of workshops and LADs, but the spread of types was now wider as the size of the Force had increased. Examples of these units, and their activities in overcoming the problems with which they were faced in their preparations, are outlined in the paragraphs that follow.

The UK Government announced on 22 November 1990 that it would send HQ 1st (British) Armoured Division, commanded by Major General Rupert Smith, and 4 Armoured Brigade, commanded by Brigadier Christopher Hammerbeck from BAOR, with additional supporting troops to increase the UK land force in the Gulf to divisional strength with all necessary backing.

1st (British) Armoured Division was to be operationally ready by the end of January 1991. The Division, including 7 Armoured Brigade already on the ground, would have 28,000 men and women, of whom 2,500 would be REME. (There were to be a further 936 REME in the support echelons including the FMA already established). The division would be equipped with 176 CHALLENGER main battle tanks, 316 WARRIOR infantry combat vehicles, seventy-nine M109 and M110 self-propelled guns, plus their War Maintenance Reserves, as well as sixteen Multiple Launch Rocket Systems (MLRS), an armoured reconnaissance regiment, anti-tank helicopters, three engineer regiments plus one RAPIER composite air defence regiment and two JAVELIN air defence batteries. For logistic support there were five transport regiments, two ordnance battalions, three armoured workshops and other specialist units. In addition there would be four field hospitals with 1,600 beds. The division was supported by RN SEA KING and RAF CHINOOK and PUMA helicopters.

The Commander Maintenance 1st Armoured Division was Lieutenant Colonel Andy Ashley, who took up his appointment in November 1990, just after the Divisional Commander had returned from his reconnaissance in Saudi Arabia, and work had already started on the preparations for GRANBY 1.5. Lieutenant Colonel Ashley's assessment from the REME point of view was that the scale of the operation would require the lines of communication within the Division to be kept as short as possible and that there would undoubtedly be a greater requirement for movement. One effect on REME with this increased movement would be that the amount of static time for a Divisional MRG would be reduced, and therefore the production rate correspondingly less than would be achieved in BAOR. There was also the probability of a shortfall of capacity and it was clear that this would be best met by including power pack and electronic repair in the MRG, which was being included in the ORBAT for the FMA as a B vehicle repair workshop. Fortuitously, this solution was already being formulated by those in the FMA who had arrived in the Gulf and saw the problem in the same light.

It was when the Commander Maintenance 1st Armoured Division issued his first Maintenance Operation Order that he realized that there was to be a problem over the operational and functional command and control net for REME in the Gulf. At that time, though, he was not aware of some of the planning that was taking place at a higher level and was to change the structure. His order was made in the clear knowledge that 1st Division was to have under command the FMA, now established at Al Jubayl. He was disconcerted to find that, two days after issuing his order, the FMA and MRG 6 were removed to the command of British Forces Middle East in Riyadh. The subsequent complexities for REME command and control, stemming from the organizations established in the Gulf, and that were of necessity somewhat at variance from those experienced in BAOR, were to present an element of vexatiousness that kept everybody on their toes to the end of the campaign. Because of these complexities a Commander Maintenance Middle East was despatched to the Gulf just before Christmas 1990. However, these problems, as for many others, were patiently overcome with skill and dedication both during the mounting stage of GRANBY 1.5 in BAOR and after the marrying-up of the whole Division in the Gulf in January

1991. On arrival there, the Division would have three phases of activity – deployment, training and battle. Lieutenant Colonel Ashley, prior to flying to the Gulf, had been heavily involved at Verden in the continuous detailed planning for the REME support of the Division in these phases, (described in Chapter 12). The remaining REME units providing this support were carrying out a variety of hectic preparations prior to leaving for the Gulf.

After 7 Armoured Brigade left for the Gulf 1st Battalion, The Royal Scots (The Royal Regiment) at Werl became part of 4 Armoured Brigade. The battalion was soon joined by The Queen's Company, 1st Battalion, Grenadier Guards. The Queen's Company Fitter Section, under Staff Sergeant Bob Cooley, came under the wing of The Royal Scots LAD, and started their GRANBY tour by commuting to Werl in late November to prepare a company's worth of WARRIORs for deployment with The Royal Scots.

The LAD, under Captain Martin Court, and with ASM Ivor Knighton, moved into overdrive to get the battalion's equipment prepared ready to move to the Gulf, and the more immediate pre-Gulf firing camp at Hohne. The days and nights were taken up with armament inspections, WARRIOR gearbox modifications and a spray-painting programme. After the vehicles left for the Gulf in the best possible condition, and their technical task was temporarily removed, the emphasis was on attaining a high standard of physical fitness for those personnel to follow by air. There was early morning PT in the gymnasium, the trek there inevitably being made in the dark, in German winter conditions with rain or slushy snow underfoot. At the end of a useful day's training there was another bout of PT. At this stage the thought of some Middle East sunshine, but not the rain, was encouraging. This training continued until 19 December when the LAD main party left for the Gulf. The last flight was on 28 December, the ASM extending his colour service so that he could be on it and go to the Gulf with the LAD.

3rd Battalion, The Royal Regiment of Fusiliers LAD at Hemer had enough of their share of emergencies and changes of plan in meeting the Gulf requirements to keep Captain Richard Welsh and ASM Wright on their toes. The whole LAD was totally involved with Operation GRANBY 1 and 1.5 preparations in BAOR. The battalion gave up much of its equipment and time for 7 Armoured Brigade. No sooner had 7 Armoured Brigade left for the Gulf than work started to rebuild and retrain to provide Battle Casualty Replacements for GRANBY 1 or to go out on GRANBY 2, then being planned for the relief of those who went out to the Gulf under GRANBY 1.

One day, which the whole LAD will always remember, the CO called everyone together – the message was GRANBY 1.5. Days suddenly became twenty-eight hours long, and 3rd Royal Tank Regiment LAD and 26 Engineer Regiment Workshop sent men to help 3 RRF LAD meet their loading deadline. The Fusiliers were to re-form and were placed on 14 days' notice to deploy to the Gulf. One company of the 1st Battalion, Grenadier Guards, and men from 1st Battalion, the Queen's Own Highlanders (Seaforths and Camerons), brought the battalion up to establishment for operations in the Gulf. After a gunnery camp at Hohne for the WARRIOR crews and other training at Hohne/Soltau and Sennelager with fog, rain and even snow on the desert-coloured WARRIORs, the A vehicles were loaded at Emden onto ferries in the first week of December. Captain Welsh, the OC LAD, flew out to Al Jubayl on 12 December and the whole battalion was complete there by 2 January.

The Queen's Own Highlanders LAD advance party, including ASM Terry Scanlon, flew out to the Gulf in December, while the main party ensured that the vehicles and equipment were loaded onto their allotted ships. The LAD main party expected to fly out on 21 December – then the move was suddenly cancelled and reinforcements returned to their units. Early in the New Year, Battalion HQ and Echelon sections of the LAD were given the task of providing the command and support element of the newly formed Armoured Delivery Group LAD under Captain Alex Tucker, responsible for the repair of 250 WMR equipments. Soon they were in Baldrick Lines, Al Jubayl!

Trial loading a Galaxy

4 Regiment Army Air Corps Workshop had spent a month preparing aircraft for 659 Squadron AAC, as did 71 Aircraft Workshop, for Operation GRANBY 1, but then they were told that they were not required as the American forces had plenty of helicopters in Saudi Arabia. Suddenly Op GRANBY 1.5 was announced and the regiment was to go, joined by reinforcements from 661 Squadron AAC from Hildesheim, including their REME tradesmen. The Workshop received reinforcements from 1 and 3 Regiment AAC Workshops. 71 Aircraft Workshop painted the aircraft and started the modifications programme. The workshop then sent a loading team to put two GAZELLEs into each of several HERCULES from RAF Gutersloh. The OC and fitter section also left for Saudi Arabia by air to meet them on arrival. ASM Frank Summers took forty technicians to the American air base at Ramstein to find out how many helicopters would fit into two C5 GALAXYs, and they managed to put six LYNX or GAZELLEs into each GALAXY before returning to Detmold. Soon a number of BELFASTs turned up at Gutersloh so another team went there to see how many helicopters could be loaded into them – they found that only two LYNX and a GAZELLE could be loaded, the width of the skids preventing a third LYNX

going in. The last BELFAST was loaded on Christmas Eve, and most of the workshop flew out on 27 – 28 December and the last few on 2 January.

The announcement in the middle of November of Operation GRANBY 1.5 brought 71 Aircraft Workshop at Detmold the challenge to prepare, within ten days, twenty LYNX and twenty GAZELLE helicopters fully modified and clear of servicings, together with a few other tasks such as a live firing exercise and the preparation of the MRG for deployment. Manpower began to arrive next morning from other workshops and LADs, followed rapidly by eight aircraft and fourteen more the next day. The vehicles had to be prepared and painted for embarkation within seven days.

The aircraft were given an in-flight inspection and vibration check to assess flying faults. Just as the workshop were processing more air tests than ever before achieved, and so more aircraft were moving in and out of the hangar, the snow came down and then froze, followed by the hangar heating failing! Everything else went well – even a new paint-spray booth was built for the LYNX desert colours. In the midst of all this activity a LYNX double engine change was carried out in a hurry between touch-down and take-off and a LYNX gearbox was changed overnight. The TOW anti-tank missile systems were thoroughly checked and prepared for live firing. The first eight GAZELLEs went off to Gutersloh for loading into RAF HERCULES by 4 Regiment AAC Workshop and next day fourteen LYNX and four GAZELLEs went to the American base at Ramstein to be loaded into C5 GALAXYs.

12th Air Defence Regiment Workshop at Dortmund were warned for Operation GRANBY 1.5 on 15 November. The regiment's own equipment was considered unsuitable for the Gulf, so 12th and 22nd Air Defence Regiment Workshops were soon busy getting the latter's RAPIER Field Standard B1 equipment and Tracked Mark 1A ready for operations. Experts from British Aerospace came to BAOR for a month, incorporating many modifications during which process the Tracked RAPIERs were almost completely rebuilt. In the meantime the workshop prepared themselves and the rest of the regiment's equipment for the Gulf, helped by 61 Station Workshop.

After many rumours and counter-rumours, 5 Armoured Workshop at Soest received orders on 15 November to provide men and fifty-five vehicles for GRANBY 1.5. Almost eighty men were sent as reinforcements, mainly to 6 Armoured Workshop and 11 Armoured Workshop, but also a few to other units. All the specialized technical vehicles were deployed on Operations GRANBY 1 and 1.5. The most remarkable sight in 5 Armoured Workshop at this time was the ever-growing stack of 270 packing cases received from the UK, 23 Base Workshop and 37 (Rhine) Workshop, made for sending major assemblies to the Gulf. When the pile was at its highest, orders were received to preserve the pinewood boxes against termites in the Gulf – some of the boxes cost £2,000 – which would have necessitated covering over 8,000 square metres with toxic preservative. Fortunately at the last moment the order was cancelled!

Local manufacture at Soest included WARRIOR heat shields, GPMG mounts and sand ladders, as well as storage trays and boxes. Three command posts were fitted out; two had heaters for cold nights in the desert and air conditioners for hot days! The Optronics Platoon deployed men to Fallingbostel for firing camp support and helped contractors at Soest to uplift GPTIRF equipments for 6, 11 and 12 Armoured Workshops. Four armourers went back to the ranges at Sennelager to support units and Battle Casualty Replacements undertaking their training 20 November – 21 December, during which over 1,100 troops used the range to fire almost every type of small arm, mortar and anti-tank weapon. The workshop also provided support for the Gulf driving school set up by 3rd Armoured Division. At 1400 hours on 20 December 11 Armoured Workshop telephoned to say that they had sent all their drivers on leave but had just been told that they had to get their vehicles to Bremerhaven that night! Despite having stood everyone down at 1230 hours, 5 Armoured Workshop found sufficient drivers to deliver the 11 Armoured Workshop's vehicles for them. Such was the unstinting support between REME units.

'Packing Case City'

The German civilian detachment worked much overtime and remained cheerful despite the frequent moving of the goalposts – one foreman remarked that sending the Afrika Korps would have been easier! The reality of all this activity, however, was brought home to all when a very Scottish voice on the telephone one day asked the Workshop office for the use of a grinding machine; when asked what he wanted it for he replied 'To sharpen 800 bayonets, Sir'!

6 Armoured Workshop deployed thirty-five men, mainly FRG and most of them to 7 Armoured Workshop, on GRANBY 1 and fifty men plus vehicles to 11 Armoured Workshop on GRANBY 1.5 to deploy in December or early January. On the day on which the men were due to leave, 6 Armoured Workshop was itself earmarked for GRANBY 1.5 (some four weeks later than other units). The men on loan to 11 Armoured Workshop were returned, but not the vehicles. The workshop had to be brought up to strength in men and vehicles, trained and documented to go to the Gulf in early January. Eighty men arrived from all over BAOR equipped, vaccinated and trained in time for Christmas

leave. Vehicles were collected and sprayed in desert colours just in time to go to the docks at Emden. The last of the soldiers arrived in the Gulf on 7 January making the unit up to a strength of seven officers and 221 soldiers.

23 Base Workshop at Wetter had an important role to play in preparing equipment for the Gulf. There was the immediate rush of work to provide vehicles and equipment to support 7 Armoured Brigade GRANBY 1 and then the prolonged effort to support 1st Armoured Division and GRANBY 1.5. At that time there was a general shortage of fit major assemblies in BAOR, due to limited repair pools and shortages of base spares. It was decided to cannibalize some equipments to provide major assemblies and power packs to form a reserve to support 7 Armoured Brigade. These assemblies would be passed through 23 Base Workshop for repair, preservation and packing prior to carriage to the Gulf. It was necessary to cancel leave of military personnel and UK based civilians, and a number of the German civilians responded by voluntarily cancelling their holidays. A drive was also made to fill some existing gaps in the civil labour force, so that a sustained effort by the Workshop could be maintained. There was pressure on storage facilities, and areas and buildings were cleared to receive major assemblies, and tentage was erected for extra storage. Additional equipment was bid for, to expand CHALLENGER CV12 engine and TN37 gearbox facilities, and overtime working began on the overhaul of items required by 7 Armoured Brigade.

The first few assemblies taken out of vehicles arrived on 14 September; work started over the weekend 15 – 16 September and the inflow of assemblies became a torrent by the end of the first week. Tank stripping was stopped and the labour put onto Operation GRANBY work. During a period of three weeks 870 engines and major assemblies were despatched from the Workshop, including fifty-one CHALLENGER engines. The production rate for the base overhaul of CHALLENGER engines was increased by a factor of six compared with the pre-GRANBY rate. At the same time the throughput time for a CHALLENGER engine, which in September was between fifty and sixty days, mainly due to spares shortages, was down to twenty-five days and still falling by December. This considerable improvement was due to a combination of some vigorous back-stripping, and after some delay a much better supply of spares than anyone could ever remember. However, the shortage of some modification kits was a further bar to progress. Seventy-four CHALLENGER engines were base overhauled during the period 1 October – 4 January, whilst a further fifty-eight had lesser repairs and/or modifications carried out before being dispatched during the same period. By 4 January 2,238 major assemblies had been inspected, repaired and despatched to support GRANBY, a tremendous effort by all concerned.

The aid of both 37 (Rhine) Workshop at Moenchengladbach and HQ Engineer Support Group at Willich was obtained to refurbish wooden boxes for all the extra assemblies, because the numbers required were far beyond the capacity of the carpenters' shop at Wetter to complete in the time available. Orders were placed in England for new boxes which arrived without internal furniture and external metal work, all of which was made and fitted at Wetter. There were so many that the area around the helicopter LZ plus the tennis court had to be used.

Fifty-six power packs, including, thirty-six CHALLENGER power packs, were despatched within three weeks. The power packs had to be inspected and repaired which often meant replacing one of the major assemblies within it. When it had been repaired, the power pack was run-up outside on one of the power pack trolleys. It says much for the inhabitants of Wetter and their relationship with the workshop that there were no complaints about the noise, even when the packs were run-up on Sunday afternoon.

MLRS in action

There were no boxes for power packs so transportation frames with shock-absorbing mounts were built and the packs were then sealed in large plastic foil or polythene bags. The CHALLENGER CV12 power packs were fractionally wider than the containers, so they were loaded with the slight projections marked rather than removing the cooling group, which would have meant extra work at both ends of the journey. The first sixteen containers were despatched on the night 26 – 27 September and 141 power packs were despatched by 4 January.

Three CHALLENGER tanks going through the workshop for specified base repairs were completed by 12 October, and fourteen more, including seven complete base overhauls, were completed by 4 January. Ten Multiple Launch Rocket Systems (MLRS) went through the workshop for accelerated conversion between 8 October and 4 January. The spectacular sight of the rockets being fired and their trails in the sky was a familiar scene to millions of TV viewers during the land war that followed in February.

The workshop provided a special Electronic Repair Vehicle for 7 Armoured Workshop for the repair of High Pressure Pure Air systems in support of TOGS, and trained a Sergeant from 7 Armoured Workshop by 21 September. A second TOGS Hot Rig Vehicle was provided by fitting out a vehicle with the technical equipment, bench and fittings. It was handed over, complete and tested, to two technicians from 7 Armoured

Workshop by 29 September. A third ERV from 5 Armoured Workshop was refurbished.

The total support of the UK-based and German civilians and the Unit Works Council ensured that all the activities that the workshop undertook in this period were completed on time, and to the highest standards. Essential production staff worked twelve hours a day, seven days a week until late November when it was reduced to ten hours a day six days a week, as the long hours without a rest day were starting to have an adverse effect on the workforce. Work went on over the Christmas period and by the end of December the German civilian employees had worked a total of 58,469 hours of overtime on GRANBY.

37 (Rhine) Workshop did not just provide assemblies and packing cases for GRANBY, it also provided its Commanding Officer to become Commander Maintenance Middle East. During November 1990 it had become clear to Commander Maintenance BAOR and to DGEME that a senior REME officer was needed at the British Headquarters at Riyadh to coordinate the equipment support activities in the Middle East theatre. Rumours abounded as to who that officer might be, but time passed and no announcement was made. On 4 December 1990 Rhine Workshop was hosting Commander Maintenance BAOR's annual conference which the DGEME, Major General Dennis Shaw, was attending. At the mid-morning coffee break he took the workshop commander, Colonel Peter Gibson, to one side and said, 'Peter, there is something I want you to do for me.' Thinking that the request referred to a quick repair to the General's staff car, or some other simple task, Colonel Gibson gave the reply, 'Of course, what do you need?' He was a little taken aback to discover that he was being asked to go to the Gulf in seven days time as the REME commander. It actually took a further two weeks for the final decision to be made by the QMG, on the need for Heads of Services at HQ Middle East, and it was not until 23 December that Colonel Gibson finally said farewell to his workshop and flew to Riyadh, via Al Jubayl, to join the staff of Lieutenant General Sir Peter de la Billière, the Commander British Forces Middle East.

Return of Equipment to BAOR

At the end of the war in the Gulf an all important task was the return and refurbishment of all the equipments that had been sent with the Force from BAOR. A Port Task Group was established at Emden for the purpose of unloading the shipping used for conveying them, and processing vehicles through to their unit locations. A Port Workshop Detachment established from within BAOR operated for four months, from 13 April to 12 August 1991, to support the Port Task Group; it was located in three of the many car-parks normally used by Volkswagen. Half the eighty personnel for the detachment were provided by 1 Corps Troops Workshop whilst the remainder did a month's tour and were found from other workshops in 1(BR) Corps.

The work at Emden involved the recovery from ships' holds of some nine thousand vehicles from thirty-two ships and their inspection and repair to enable them to be driven back to their units. Some vehicles required considerable recovery effort and the detachment had a strong recovery section, including an ARRV and Foden recovery vehicles. 124 Recovery Company (V) helped in the tasks. Although something of a contrast to the activities at the port six months earlier, the task was an essential element in the restoration of BAOR's equipment to an acceptable condition.

The strain on the REME resources in BAOR in mounting GRANBY 1 and 1.5 during the period from September 1990 – January 1992 was considerable, but it is a matter of great satisfaction that everything that was required of the Corps was achieved within the imposed constraints. Much has been made earlier in this chapter, and elsewhere in this volume, of the vital importance of Equipment Management, and the necessity to have reliability built into equipments from the onset of their life. Certainly within BAOR, GRANBY underlined the problems of unreliability, the inadequacy of spares backing and the overall importance of logistics. Regrettably the media, whose role in the Gulf War became a major factor for consideration by Commanders, failed to give logistics and those involved the place in history which they deserve. The fact that the Force was launched from BAOR with its equipment in the high state of readiness that was achieved, owes much to those responsible for the logistics that enabled it to happen. There were still many problems to be faced in the desert, but the Corps was to continue the processes started so well in Germany. The story of this continuing support of the Force is related in Chapter 12.

ANGLO-GERMAN RELATIONS

Achieving good Anglo-German relations played an important part in the life of the British Army in Germany, and continues to do so. For REME, as a major employer of German labour, it was not only essential that a good relationship existed in the workshops that employed this labour, but also that friendship should extend to the towns in which the units were located, and from which their labour came. Apart from good working relationships on the shop floor and with the Works Councils, the wider activities therefore included sporting and social events with local organizations. Some REME workshops remained in the same location for many years, unlike armoured or infantry regiments which moved complete at the end of their normal BAOR tours. REME officers and soldiers moved as individuals, but the workshops remained in situ, even if their titles changed with the innumerable reorganizations that took place. Close, friendly relationships were built up with the local Stadt and people, and this was recognized over the years by various ceremonies and exchanges of awards, some of which are recounted in the following paragraphs.

The path to attainment of good relations was not always easy, and was often complicated by language and social and age differences. Sometimes the Germans understood us all too well, whilst on other occasions language difficulties produced unexpected effects. British Army officers in Germany are often dog lovers personified, and dogs of all shapes and sizes are to be seen both at places of work and on exercise, at the heels of their owners, welcoming their lavish attentions. This does not pass without notice, and caused one German at a function to remark to a senior REME officer's wife that, should he be reincarnated, he would like it to be as a British Army officer or, failing that, a British Army officer's dog, which had the best life of all.

Although a lot of effort went into encouraging German language training, few officers and soldiers reached the fluency necessary to talk 'off the cuff' at German functions, and the aid of translators had to be sought. One now very senior REME officer was asked to talk at a gathering with the dignitaries of a Stadt and found it necessary, with reluctance, to write his speech in English, and got his German PA to translate it. When he gave the speech, his understanding of the translation was insufficient for him to put the appropriate emphasis on the words. He was therefore reduced to putting emphasis on every word equally. The effect was almost identical to a Nuremburg rally, but it obviously went down well in the Rathaus. When he glanced at the Burgermeister at the end, he noticed that he was weeping, and at first thought that it was with laughter. A second glance, though, confirmed that the Burgermeister was indeed sincerely shedding tears. What the speaker had accidentally produced was the most moving German oratory!

Of course, regrettably, though perhaps fortuitously, many more Germans spoke much better English than those in the British Army spoke German. Hopefully, in the changing European political climate, we might improve on the German lead. The Germans certainly appreciated the efforts of our trying to speak their language, even if those efforts were not always entirely successful. The same senior officer, having discarded his interpreter, was trying out his German at a friend's dinner party in Fallingbostel, where he was introduced to the local Pastor and his wife. The time came to go into dinner, and noting that the house was none too warm, and that the Pastor's wife was wearing an off the shoulder gown, thought to offer to fetch her shawl. He began in German, 'Sind sie kalt?' (are you cold?). The Pastor's wife went bright scarlet and scuttled away into dinner. The Pastor laughed and said to our senior officer's wife, in excellent English, 'Does your husband realize what he just said to my wife? He asked her if she is frigid!'

A large number of more formal occasions took place over the years, and these were both popular and rewarding for both the Germans and the Corps units that participated. A selection of some of the more noteworthy of these events is given in the following paragraphs. Germany, unlike Britain, did not have the tradition of awarding the freedom of a city or town to a regiment or other military unit, but after eighteen years in Fallingbostel the goodwill existing between 7 Armoured Workshop and the Town was recognized by a ceremony on 30 November 1969 to establish a Partnershaft. Lieutenant Colonel Derek Cash, then commanding the workshop, took part in the ceremony in front of the Rathaus which was attended by many civilian and military notables. The workshop was presented with a scroll and pewter plate to mark the occasion.

Nearly twelve years later, on 17 October 1981, the Germans, by then having decided that some British traditions were well worth following, granted the Freedom of Fallingbostel to 7 Armoured Workshop. The Burgermeister in his speech said, '7 Armoured Workshop REME is heartily welcomed and invited to march through the town on ceremonial occasions with bayonets fixed, drums beating and music playing'. The Freedom was marked by the presentation of a scroll and a Coat of Arms of Fallingbostel town. Major General Sam Lecky, who had served in the workshop in 1947 and commanded it from 1963 to 1965, presented a silver salver to the Burgermeister on behalf of the Corps.

On 10 November 1973, the Burgermeister of Minden granted the Freedom of Entry to 11 Field Workshop, then commanded by Major Romney Higson. The workshop had been established at Minden since June 1952. Major General Peter Girling, as the Representative Colonel Commandant, received the Scroll from the Burgermeister and presented the Stadt with a silver salver on behalf of the Corps. During the march past to exercise 'The Right of Entry', a very narrow one-way street was supposed to have been cleared of traffic by the civilian police so that the workshop could march and drive along it the 'wrong way'. Corporal Ray Flatman driving a machinery wagon nudged a miscreant German car very lightly and was promptly fined DM10. by a policeman spectator who had clearly got neither sense of occasion nor discretion. The DM10 was later refunded and honour was satisfied. At the Rathaus reception a magnificent Coat of Arms carved from solid oak, one metre high and weighing seventy-four kilograms, was presented to the Workshop. The Stadt was given a cast REME badge set in the triangle of 1st Division and made of polished mahogany.

The general goodwill surrounding this freedom is emphasized by an extract from the minutes of the Town Council of Minden for 4 October 1973. It is recorded that the main committee had voted unanimously on 9 August 1973 to recommend the Town Council to present the freedom of the town and so 'express the appreciation, trustworthiness and friendship which has built up between the Citizens and the Soldiers'. Prince Philip, Colonel in Chief, sent a message to the Representative Colonel Commandant to say, 'I am very glad to hear of the continuing friendship between the Town of Minden and 11 Field Workshop REME. The Honour of Freedom of Entry to Minden does you great credit and I am sure that my pleasure in this tribute will be shared throughout the Corps.' The Workshop exercised its right again in November 1977 under command of Major Paul Wessendorf before its amalgamation with 7 Field Workshop on 17 December 1977 to form 7 Armoured Workshop.

Four months later on 21 April 1978 it was the turn of 14 (Berlin) Field Workshop to be given the Freedom of the Borough of Spandau, at a ceremony that took place in the Spandau Citadel in the presence of the GOC Berlin and DEME BAOR, Brigadier Derrick Ballard. They were presented with the Freedom Scroll together with a fine wood carving of the Spandau Coat of Arms and in return the Corps presented Spandau with a silver salver. In 1985 the Workshop celebrated its 40th Anniversary at the Spandau location, which was part of the original Spandau machine-gun factory.

Next year, on 23 May 1979, the Town of Wetter awarded 23 Base Workshop with the Freedom of Wetter. The ceremony included a parade and march past of the small military staff, and also representatives of the British and German civilian staff. That year Herr Hen Reinup, a senior clerk, was awarded an Honorary BEM. This workshop took on its first German workers in Wetter on 24 July 1945 and celebrated its Silver Jubilee in 1970. In 1972 it had been granted the privilege of displaying the Wetter Coat of Arms, adjacent to the Corps emblem, over the main entrance to the Workshop.

The Freedom of Detmold was granted to 4 Armoured Workshop on 3 June 1982 after 25 years in Detmold. The celebrations had begun on the previous Sunday with a service in the Garrison Church sponsored by the Workshop at which a section of the REME Staff Band played. On Wednesday evening 2 June the whole Band Beat Retreat in the Schlosspark with an excellent display. It was not without its moments of apprehension, however, as Major General Sam Lecky, then Representative Colonel Commandant and present at the ceremony, recalls:

'It was a delightful balmy evening with a truly lovely setting, the home of Prince and Princess Armin of Lippe. As we all settled down to enjoy the Band's usual immaculate performance, the peace of the evening was rudely shattered by a dozen young people with long hair and beads who came prancing in amongst the bandsmen to disrupt the performance. The Drum Major and his cohorts ignored the invading throng with quiet dignity despite murmurs of disapproval from the watching population. The marching and counter-marching continued with the invaders becoming increasingly objectionable, but the Band played on. My feeling of helplessness grew – how could we intervene on behalf of the Band? I need not have worried, for the resourcefulness of the Corps noted for its adaptability was ever present in the Band. With a skill born more out of frustration than anger, the trombone player caught one youth after another a sharp crack with his slide. A defeated and dishevelled enemy withdrew to the applause of the audience, and the REME Staff Band marched triumphantly on to the conclusion of its performance, full of pride and not a little satisfaction.'

Major General Lecky and Herr Vogt take the salute

The Detmold Freedom Parade took place the next morning in the magnificent Schlosspark in blazing sunshine. Three companies and the REME Staff Band were on parade and the Burgermeister, Herr Vogt, presented the Freedom Scroll to Major General Lecky, who in turn presented the Burgermeister with an engraved silver salver on behalf of the Corps. The parade was followed by a march through Detmold 'with bayonets fixed and bands playing', after which there was a reception in the Town Hall for the senior military guests, including six former commanding officers, the workshop officers and their ladies. A Silver Jubilee Ball was held that evening at the Falkenkrug Guest House in Detmold for all ranks of the Workshop, as well as many military and German civilian guests.

ANNIVERSARIES

37 (Rhine) Workshop

37 (Rhine) Workshop celebrated its 25th Anniversary in October 1973 with a Families Open Day. The REME Staff Band struck a happy note with their marching and concert music, after which they marched through the workshop with the visitors falling in behind. The celebrations had opened with Colonel Philip Andrews addressing the guests in German, to their obvious delight. The Oberburgermeister of Moenchengladbach replied, and unveiled a plaque marking the occasion. The Workshop had opened in 1948 in bomb-damaged, unheated and badly-lit buildings, the German workers being compensated for the conditions with a daily bowl of hot soup nicknamed 'calves teeth', probably due to the small quantity of meat in it.

HM The Queen's Silver Jubilee Parade

HM the Queen's Silver Jubilee Parade

On 7 July 1977 HM the Queen's Silver Jubilee Parade took place at Sennelager in the presence of HM The Queen. More than 600 vehicles, mostly tracked, took part, twenty-one of which were REME-manned, carrying two REME officers and sixty-four soldiers. The mechanical fitness of all the vehicles was apparent, and this was a credit to REME and the support given by 4th Armoured Division REME at Sennelager. The parade was seen by millions on TV, being one of the highlights of that summer of Jubilee celebrations.

60 Station Workshop – Olen

60 Station Workshop at Olen in Belgium celebrated its 30th Anniversary in April 1983 with a reception for 430 guests to which the local Belgian MP, three Burgermeisters and British officials from Brussels and Antwerp were invited. Twenty-one employees received 30-Year Certificates and there were parties for the workshop employees and children from a local orphanage. In 1986 this Workshop contributed to British exports by preparing three Land Rovers for loan service with the Antwerp Police, painted in their white and blue colours, fitting Makrolon kits as well as special lights and sirens. The vehicles were subsequently bought by the City of Antwerp for permanent use.

23 Base Workshop – Wetter

Prince Philip's visit

23 Base Workshop at Wetter, the largest of all REME workshops, celebrated its 40th anniversary in 1985, the major event that year being the visit of HRH Prince Philip, the Colonel in Chief, on 21 and 22 April. The actual anniversary of the day on which the workshop site had been taken over from the American Forces in 1945 was on 2 July, which was celebrated with a Jubilee Ball in the Officers Mess. The remaining celebrations were held over more than a week in September. In 1985 the workshop employed thirteen REME officers, twenty senior ranks, nine UK-based civilians and 1,700 local civilians, compared with 700 military and 2,500 civilians in the early days. By 1985 there were second and third generation employees, 175 who had more than 30 years service and fifteen who had been employed since 1945. In March 1985, a nineteen-year-old electronic apprentice had been placed second in his trade in a competition for the whole of North Rhine Westphalia. This all says much for the training and management at Wetter, in a country with such a prosperous engineering industry as Germany in the Seventies and Eighties.

The programme at Wetter for the 40th Anniversary was even more ambitious than the celebrations that had taken place for the 25th Anniversary in 1970. A very enterprising programme was drawn up and agreed by Brigadier Philip Winchcombe and the Chairman of the Works Council, the Works Council having been raising funds for the programme for many years. Everyone was involved, employees, pensioners, relatives, friends and other residents of Wetter. A souvenir brochure with a message from the Commander in Chief, General Sir Nigel Bagnall, beer mugs, glasses, plates, and first day postal covers were produced to mark the celebrations. These began on Friday 13 September with a brilliant reception at the Rathaus, after which there was a Rock Night for the young and a formal dinner in the Officers' Mess. On the Saturday 12,000 visitors came to an open day, and on Sunday the Commander entertained the German Managers and their Wives. On Monday 600 Pensioners came to a reunion.

During the remainder of the week at Wetter lunches, football matches, social evenings, Beating Retreat and an Officers' Mess Reception were held. The climax was reached on Friday night with the largest dance ever held in Wetter, which was repeated on Saturday with another 2,150 guests. One thousand children and older people also enjoyed a childrens' party on the Saturday, with a Turkish and Portuguese ethnic folklore afternoon. During all these celebrations more than 20,000 Germans came to the various activities, which raised £2,000 for British and German charities. Just after the year end the Embassy in Bonn announced the award of an Honorary MBE to Herr Paul Kapnobur, the Senior German Manager who had retired in 1985 after working for REME since 1951.

REME 50th Anniversary Parade, Sennelager, 9 May 1992

On 4 September 1991 the REME 50 Project Team was born, its purpose in life being to plan and organize the BAOR Parade for REME's 50th Anniversary, under the direction of Brigadier Murray Wildman (Commander ES 1(BR) Corps). The team was established in suitable Project 50 offices and began work immediately on what was to be a major task and ultimately a gratifying experience. The team consisted of three officers and a warrant officer all of whom at the time of starting were unsuspecting of the extent to which all their energies, talents and powers of persuasion were to be tested over the next nine months. Captain Graham Belgum, full of bright ideas, having just completed the Junior Command and Staff Course at Warminster, was the Project Leader, Captain Mike Pendlington was the 2IC and alleged slave driver, and Second Lieutenant Lee Saunders was the Project Officer and, as befitted his rank, was kept fully occupied by everybody. Fortunately he also had time to record the activities of the team and the ultimate success of the Parade. AQMS Ivan Mungroo, from 32nd Heavy Regiment Workshop, spared whilst the unit was awaiting re-equipping with MLRS, was the Project QM miracle-worker. The team was also joined by Corporal Mick Robson, who was to be the Chief Clerk and, with Corporal Bill Greenhill and Lance Corporal Liz Moss to assist, coped admirably with all aspects of running a very busy office involved with every REME unit in BAOR, and a wide range of military and civilian organizations.

The march-past

The Parade, to be held on 9 May 1992 at Sennelager, was to consist of both foot and mounted elements, and was to be reviewed by the Chief of the Defence Staff, Field Marshal Sir Richard Vincent, a former Colonel Commandant of the Corps, in the presence of some 4,500 spectators. There was also to be a large static display drawn from military and civilian sources. The scope was both substantial and diverse, and the logistics, particularly because of the wide geographic spread of the troops and equipment, presented many interesting problems for the Project Team. The Foot Parade was to be found from some 600 officers, senior NCOs and soldiers in REME units all over BAOR, together with the Corps Staff Band from UK, and the Parade would be commanded by Lieutenant Colonel Mike Huntley, with the Parade RSM, WO1 (RSM) Graham Matthews. Eight half-companies of soldiers were to be drawn from HQ Equipment Support 4th Armoured Division, 1 Corps Troops Workshop, 4, 6, 7, 11 and 12 Armoured Workshops, 20 Electronic Workshop, 71 Aircraft Workshop, The Royal Scots Dragoon Guards LAD, The Queen's Royal Irish Hussars LAD, 9th/12th Royal Lancers LAD, 1st Battalion, The Cheshire Regiment LAD, and 1, 3 and 4 Regiments Army Air Corps Workshops.

The Mounted Parade was to be comprised of thirty-one tracked and thirty wheeled repair/recovery vehicles drawn from thirty units, and included two new CHALLENGER Armoured Repair and Recovery Vehicles (CRARRV) specially obtained from UK six months ahead of schedule, and to be named at the Parade by the CDS. In addition there was to be a fly-past by six LYNX and three GAZELLE helicopters of 3 Regiment AAC, flown by REME pilots.

The drive-past

The Static Display was to cover over 200 acres, with seven individual displays to consist of: The History of the Corps; Twenty-five in-service REME repair and recovery vehicles; REME in the Nineties; REME and Industry; REME on Operation GRANBY; 5 Armoured Workshop MRG and 71 Aircraft Workshop MRG, both deployed as in the field. The REME and Industry stand was to consist of two marquees including a 600-square metre display by Volkswagen, illustrating pictorially and with period and modern vehicles how a REME unit led by Major Ivan Hirst occupied the destroyed VW factory at Wolfsburg after the Second World War, and gradually re-built it. In 1949 the factory was handed back to the German authorities, a solid platform for today's international company having been established.

The second marquee would consist of nine civilian companies which had worked closely with the Corps, and illustrated this with individual pictorial displays. The Companies who would be represented were: British Aerospace (manufacturers of RAPIER); Unipower (previously known as Scammell); Rolls Royce (Aeronautical section); Perkins Engines (manufacturers of diesel engines for such vehicles as

CHALLENGER and WARRIOR); Vickers (manufacturers of CHALLENGER ARRV); Racal Automation (manufacturers of the DIANA and GPTIRF); DAF Trucks (manufacturers of DROPS and 4 Tonne vehicles); David Brown Vehicle Transmissions (manufacturers of transmissions for CHALLENGER); and GKN Defence (manufacturers of the 432 and WARRIOR families of vehicles).

By the beginning of May the Project Team was established at Windmill Camp, Sennelager, and starting to put into effect the results of their planning. A site company began the building of the site; a security platoon began the task of securing and patrolling the area; and the static displays, with the many military and civilian agencies who were to play vital roles in the REME 50 Project, began to set up and prepare for 9 May.

When 9 May 1992 finally dawned, all had been perfected for REME 50 except the one thing not in the hands of all those now poised for the start of the parade – the weather. At 0600 hours the sky was clear and cloud-free, and the Services Sound and Vision Corporation who were to film the event, and the British Forces Broadcasting Service who were to broadcast it live, were hopeful of ideal conditions, as indeed were all the participants. But it was not to be, and by 0900 hours as the spectators started to arrive, there was a deluge, which continued until and beyond the arrival of the Chief of the Defence Staff to review the parade. The whole parade, although by now seriously wet, were not to be intimidated by the weather, and the foot parade proceeded to show what they were made of, producing a parade of which the Corps could be very proud. At its conclusion, after the eight drenched half-companies marched proudly off followed by the Corps band, the Vehicle Parade swept in from their standing position to roar past the CDS and the spectators. The helicopter fly-past followed immediately, with the aircraft trailing smoke in the Corps colours, and a Corps flag specially manufactured for the occasion by 23 Base Workshop.

At midday Field Marshal Vincent led the walk to lunch, followed by 4,500 wet and cold soldiers, families and guests. Here at least, in the marquees, they were able to shelter from the rain which was still falling, and after lunch and a few glasses of REME 50 wine, people began to feel better. It was at that point that the monsoon finally died down, and the CDS spent the afternoon viewing the whole of the static display, and talked to the soldiers, those guests who remained despite their cold and dampness, and the manufacturers' representatives. Also during this walkabout, at a simple naming ceremony, he gave the type name RHINO to the new CHALLENGER ARRV.

The day ended after tea, with a hastily re-scheduled Parachute Display by the Corps Parachute Team, followed by the Craftsman's Cup Tug-of-War competition which was won by 1 Armoured Divisional Transport Regiment Workshop. Finally there was a presentation to the Field Marshal of a special commemorative REME 50 Rose Bowl. It had been a great and memorable day, and a fitting tribute to all those members of the Corps who had served it so well since its birth almost fifty years earlier.

The day would not be complete though without returning to the REME 50 Project Team who had seen their nine-month task brought to a very satisfactory conclusion. It was an exhausted and relieved Team which left the Windmill site, Sennelager, that night, carrying out its own recovery of a little collection of 5.5 kilometres of rope, 2,500 pickets, 1,200 metres of carpet, 1 kilometre of Class 30 Trackway, 24 spectator stands, 9,000 square metres of tentage and more than 60,000 items of crockery and cutlery – perhaps not the most exciting recovery task but certainly one that symbolized a job well done!

VISITS BY THE COLONEL IN CHIEF

Our Colonel in Chief, Field Marshal His Royal Highness The Prince Philip, Duke of Edinburgh, has paid many visits to REME in BAOR over the years. The first visit was in 1970. Brigadier Geoffrey Atkinson recalls that when he was commanding 7 Armoured Workshop as a Lieutenant Colonel, Prince Philip visited his unit in Fallingbostel:

'After much argument about the programme and the attendant VIPs, the then Representative Colonel Commandant, Major General Ronnie Shields, was in attendance. HRH had travelled up from Minden on the Royal Train overnight, having attended a guest night in the REME Minden Mess the previous evening where he had signed the Visitors' Book. Whilst HRH was being shown round the main A Vehicle Shop by the ASM, Mr Johnstone, the rest of us were walking down the main aisle in a crocodile. General Ronnie spotted the RAOC Staff Sergeant photographer and said to him, "Weren't you at the dinner in Minden last night and did you get any good photographs?" To which the answer was, "Yes, and I did not." Somewhat taken aback, General Ronnie asked him why, to which the response was, "Because you stood in the . . . way, Sir". Just at the critical moment when Prince Philip raised the pen to sign the Visitors' Book, the Representative Colonel Commandant had stepped in front of the camera – hence the extremely uncompromising remark made by the Staff Sergeant the following morning, to which there was no answer!'

Prince Philip on this occasion also visited REME units deployed in the field and the German Army airfield at Celle where he saw 73 Field Workshop (Aircraft) and 712 Mobile Servicing and Repair Detachment from 71 Field Workshop (Aircraft) Detmold.

In 1976 Prince Philip visited BAOR REME units in the field during Exercise SPEARPOINT, on this occasion flying his own helicopter. He was able to take lunch in a nearby Schloss with a number of REME officers. As always on these visits, the Colonel in Chief took a close interest in all that he saw, speaking to many officers and soldiers and to German civilians in their own language. These visits always proved stimulating to the units he visited and instilled a great sense of pride in all ranks.

Prince Philip's visit on 21 April 1985 to 23 Base Workshop in their 40th Anniversary year was an honour that was tremendously appreciated by all those that were involved in the celebrations that year, already described earlier. On this memorable visit the Colonel in Chief arrived piloting a WESSEX helicopter and stayed the night at Brigadier Philip Winchcombe's house where a dinner party was held for HRH that evening. The guests included Brigadier Andrew MacLauchlan, Commander Maintenance BAOR, Herr Schmid, Burgermeister of Wetter, Herr Reiber, Stadtdirektor of Wetter and Herr Sticht and Herr Howe, both managers in the Workshop. The next morning Prince Philip signed the Golden Book of Wetter, which, exceptionally, was brought to the Workshop for the Ceremony on this very special occasion. HRH then toured the Workshop, meeting and talking to the civilian employees in excellent German, and seeing the overhaul of CHIEFTAIN tanks and other armoured vehicles. When speaking to Herr Samm, a Foreman in the Tank Assembly Shop, Prince Philip asked him what he did before working for 23 Base Workshop. Herr Samm explained that he was a soldier, who voluntarily joined the Navy when he was 17. Realizing that he had found a fellow sailor, HRH told him that he had joined the Navy because he did not want to walk, to which Herr Samm responded by saying that he had joined because he knew that the food was better. On being asked how old he was he replied, '60 years, so I still have to work another three years before I can retire'. HRH replied, 'You are in a better position than me because you yourself can decide when to retire!' This drew laughter all round and Prince Philip moved on to the next point of interest. This was the floodmark 15 feet high on the doorway of the RAOC Stores Section marking the level reached by the water after the breaching of the Mohne Dam more than thirty miles away, by the RAF 'Dambusters' in 1943. HRH then talked to the officers and senior ranks and their wives over a cup of coffee, before leaving for the workshop helipad. Here he met German civilians informally on a walkabout and talked to British schoolchildren waving their Union Jacks. He then flew his helicopter away to Dusseldorf to return to UK. Everyone had 'a really great day' as one young German put it.

AMENITIES AND SPORTS

Two interesting features of amenities and sports in BAOR over the period were the setting-up of the REME Hotel in Wertach, Southern Germany and the development of the REME ski huts. The hotel did well, largely due to the enthusiastic and energetic management by HQ REME 1st Armoured Division in Verden, who also operated one of the ski huts. This ski hut provided facilities for all REME in BAOR for Exercise SNOW QUEEN ski training in winter and adventure training activities during the rest of the year. It was near Gunzesried-Säge where the annual REME ski meeting was held. The second ski hut at Moosbach was run by 71 Aircraft Workshop and concentrated on Exercise SNOW QUEEN. In 1988 it was decided to leave these two ski huts and to concentrate the REME effort on Berghaus Lieb, previously used by the Royal Military Police, which was in Gunzesried-Säge and had several advantages.

REME BAOR were also responsible for the development of bobsleighing as a new REME sport, which started in 1986 when REME teams competed in the 1986–87 British Four-Man Championship (Best Novices), the Army Novice Championship, the Army Two-Man Championship and the Inter-Services Championship (Best Novice). This was an impressive start. In 1987–88 the REME teams came eighth in the British Two- and Four-Man Championships, won the Army Junior Championship, and finished second in the Army Novices Championship. The REME No 1 bob came a close second to the 2 RTR crew in the Army Championship – 2 RTR representing Great Britain at the Calgary Olympics. The driver of the No 2 REME bob won the best 'Maiden'. All five REME contestants were selected to represent the Army in the Inter-Services Championship where we once again won the Novice Driver Prize. The Chairman of REME Bobsleigh, writing from HQ REME 4th Armoured Division in March 1988, described bobsleighing in the following words: 'It is extremely dangerous and demands a very high degree of fitness. Those that complete even one season will have experienced excitement and danger unrivalled by most other sports'. The REME team that year was made up entirely of corporals and lance corporals. In their first two years the REME bobsleigh teams achieved outstanding success, and the complete story is told in Chapter 14.

CONCLUSION

This period in BAOR was one of continuous change and, whichever touched upon REME, the Corps' response was one of the utmost effectiveness despite the difficulties that these changes brought. In particular, the great influx of new, highly technical and complex equipment of all sorts into the British Army in Germany was coupled with a reduction in manpower and many reorganizations. These presented problems to REME that required all the high technical skills possessed by all ranks of the Corps and the outstanding managerial techniques that REME were able to produce, to overcome them. Notwithstanding these challenges, the excellent training and high morale of its soldiers have stood them in good stead. This has enabled them to give the excellent quality of support always expected of them, both within BAOR and on external operations mounted from BAOR, notably in Northern Ireland and the Middle East.

Annex A

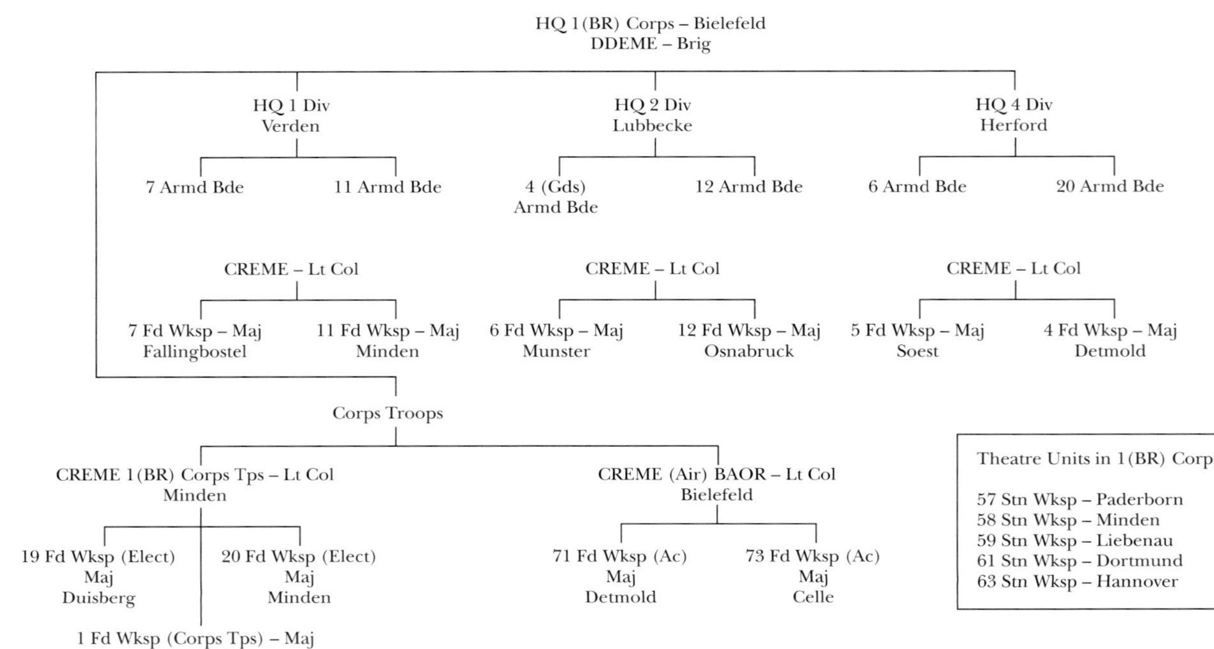
OUTLINE ORGANIZATION OF 1 (BR) CORPS PRIOR TO ARMY RESTRUCTURING PLAN 1976
HQ 1 (BR) Corps – Bielefeld
DDEME – Brig
HQ 1 Div
Verden
7 Armd Bde
11 Armd Bde
CREME – Lt Col
7 Fd Wksp – Maj
Fallingbostel
11 Fd Wksp – Maj
Minden
HQ 2 Div
Lubbecke
4 (Gds)
Armd Bde
12 Armd Bde
CREME – Lt Col
6 Fd Wksp – Maj
Munster
12 Fd Wksp – Maj
Osnabruck
HQ 4 Div
Herford
6 Armd Bde
20 Armd Bde
CREME – Lt Col
5 Fd Wksp – Maj
Soest
4 Fd Wksp – Maj
Detmold
Corps Troops
CREME 1 (BR) Corps Tps – Lt Col
Minden
19 Fd Wksp (Elect)
Maj
Duisberg
20 Fd Wksp (Elect)
Maj
Minden
1 Fd Wksp (Corps Tps) – Maj
Bielefeld
CREME (Air) BAOR – Lt Col
Bielefeld
71 Fd Wksp (Ac)
Maj
Detmold
73 Fd Wksp (Ac)
Maj
Celle
Theatre Units in 1 (BR) Corps
57 Stn Wksp – Paderborn
58 Stn Wksp – Minden
59 Stn Wksp – Liebenau
61 Stn Wksp – Dortmund
63 Stn Wksp – Hannover

Annex B

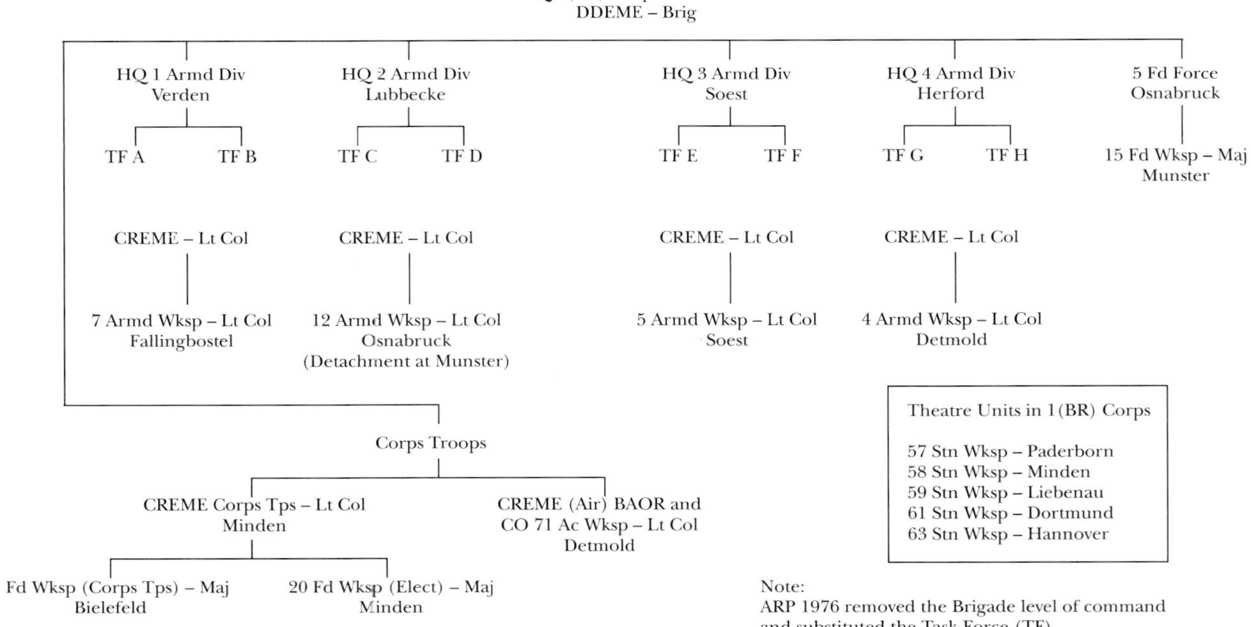
OUTLINE ORGANIZATION OF 1 (BR) CORPS POST ARMY RESTRUCTURING PLAN 1976
HQ 1 (BR) Corps – Bielefeld
DDEME – Brig
HQ 1 Armd Div
Verden
TF A
TF B
CREME – Lt Col
7 Armd Wksp – Lt Col
Fallingbostel
HQ 2 Armd Div
Lubbecke
TF C
TF D
CREME – Lt Col
12 Armd Wksp – Lt Col
Osnabruck
(Detachment at Munster)
HQ 3 Armd Div
Soest
TF E
TF F
CREME – Lt Col
5 Armd Wksp – Lt Col
Soest
HQ 4 Armd Div
Herford
TF G
TF H
CREME – Lt Col
4 Armd Wksp – Lt Col
Detmold
5 Fd Force
Osnabruck
15 Fd Wksp – Maj
Munster
Corps Troops
CREME Corps Tps – Lt Col
Minden
1 Fd Wksp (Corps Tps) – Maj
Bielefeld
20 Fd Wksp (Elect) – Maj
Minden
CREME (Air) BAOR and
CO 71 Ac Wksp – Lt Col
Detmold
Theatre Units in 1 (BR) Corps
57 Stn Wksp – Paderborn
58 Stn Wksp – Minden
59 Stn Wksp – Liebenau
61 Stn Wksp – Dortmund
63 Stn Wksp – Hannover
Note:
ARP 1976 removed the Brigade level of command
and substituted the Task Force (TF)

Annex C

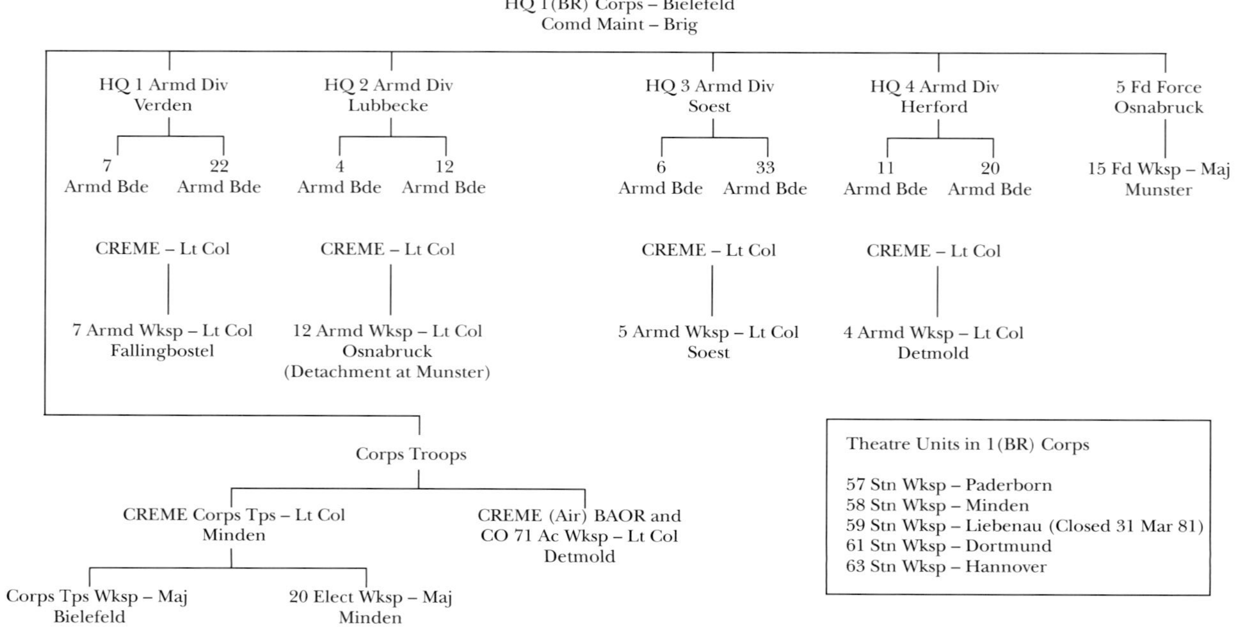
OUTLINE ORGANIZATION OF 1 (BR) CORPS IN 1981
HQ 1 (BR) Corps – Bielefeld
Comd Maint – Brig
HQ 1 Armd Div
Verden
7 Armd Bde
22 Armd Bde
CREME – Lt Col
7 Armd Wksp – Lt Col
Fallingbostel
HQ 2 Armd Div
Lubbecke
4 Armd Bde
12 Armd Bde
CREME – Lt Col
12 Armd Wksp – Lt Col
Osnabruck
(Detachment at Munster)
HQ 3 Armd Div
Soest
6 Armd Bde
33 Armd Bde
CREME – Lt Col
5 Armd Wksp – Lt Col
Soest
HQ 4 Armd Div
Herford
11 Armd Bde
20 Armd Bde
CREME – Lt Col
4 Armd Wksp – Lt Col
Detmold
5 Fd Force
Osnabruck
15 Fd Wksp – Maj
Munster
Corps Troops
CREME Corps Tps – Lt Col
Minden
CREME (Air) BAOR and
CO 71 Ac Wksp – Lt Col
Detmold
1 Corps Tps Wksp – Maj
Bielefeld
20 Elect Wksp – Maj
Minden
Theatre Units in 1 (BR) Corps
57 Stn Wksp – Paderborn
58 Stn Wksp – Minden
59 Stn Wksp – Liebenau (Closed 31 Mar 81)
61 Stn Wksp – Dortmund
63 Stn Wksp – Hannover

Annex D

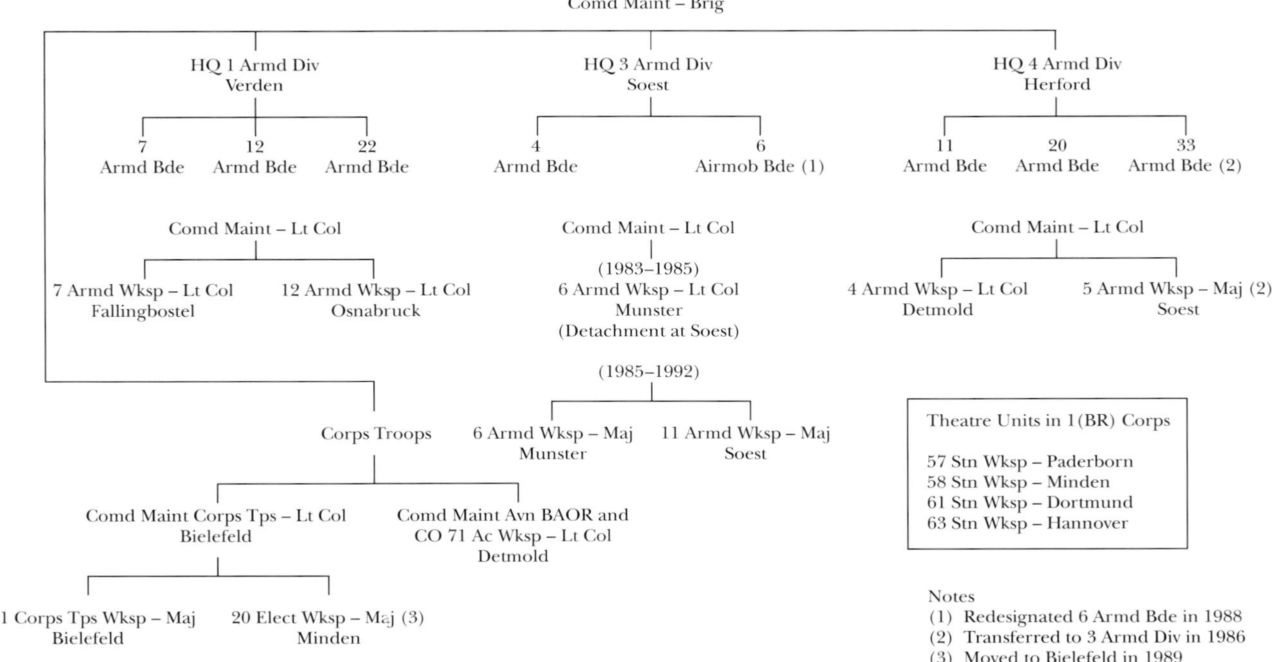
OUTLINE ORGANIZATION OF 1 (BR) CORPS 1983–1992
HQ 1 (BR) Corps – Bielefeld
Comd Maint – Brig
HQ 1 Armd Div
Verden
7
Armd Bde
12
Armd Bde
22
Armd Bde
Comd Maint – Lt Col
7 Armd Wksp – Lt Col
Fallingbostel
12 Armd Wksp – Lt Col
Osnabruck
HQ 3 Armd Div
Soest
4
Armd Bde
6
Airmob Bde (1)
Comd Maint – Lt Col
(1983–1985)
6 Armd Wksp – Lt Col
Munster
(Detachment at Soest)
(1985–1992)
6 Armd Wksp – Maj
Munster
11 Armd Wksp – Maj
Soest
HQ 4 Armd Div
Herford
11
Armd Bde
20
Armd Bde
33
Armd Bde (2)
Comd Maint – Lt Col
4 Armd Wksp – Lt Col
Detmold
5 Armd Wksp – Maj (2)
Soest
Corps Troops
Comd Maint Corps Tps – Lt Col
Bielefeld
1 Corps Tps Wksp – Maj
Bielefeld
20 Elect Wksp – Maj (3)
Minden
Comd Maint Avn BAOR and
CO 71 Ac Wksp – Lt Col
Detmold
Theatre Units in 1 (BR) Corps
57 Stn Wksp – Paderborn
58 Stn Wksp – Minden
61 Stn Wksp – Dortmund
63 Stn Wksp – Hannover
Notes
(1) Redesignated 6 Armd Bde in 1988
(2) Transferred to 3 Armd Div in 1986
(3) Moved to Bielefeld in 1989

CHAPTER 7

REME IN THE UNITED KINGDOM

Introduction ·
Army Strategic Command ·
REME in the Static Chain of Command ·
United Kingdom Land Forces
– REME Command and Control in UKLF, Army Restructuring Plan 1974–75, REME in the Field Force after Restructuring, Operations, Overseas Exercises, Belize, UK Static Workshops, Introduction of the New Management Strategy, The District Review.
Command and District Workshops ·
Other Organizations · Conclusion

INTRODUCTION

REME support to units in the United Kingdom was provided by workshops and LADs spread between the static army formations forming the UK base and those elements of the Field Force located in UK. These diverse units were, according to their role, under the functional control of appropriate HQ organizations existing at the time. Over the years there were major changes to these higher formations which affected the command and control of all UK-based REME units. There were also fundamental reorganizations within the MOD and LE(A) which affected technical control and the division of responsibilities between the Staff concerned with Equipment Management and REME technical staff. This latter development is covered in Chapters 2 and 3. The effects of these changes in MOD extended throughout the UK command chain and were reflected in reorganizations of the various HQs and the units which they commanded. These changes are linked together in this chapter.

The REME workshops in the static chain initially consisted of Central Workshops, RAOC Vehicle Depot Workshops and Command and District

Workshops. Central and Vehicle Depot Workshops formed part of Technical Group REME, later REME Support Group, eventually absorbed into the Logistic Executive (Army). Command or District Workshops were under the technical control of the senior REME officer of the Command (until 1972) or District in which they were located.

Field Workshops and LADs varied in their organizations according to the role of their Field Force formation and were under the technical control of the senior REME officer in that formation.

ARMY STRATEGIC COMMAND

Army Strategic Command (STRATCO) was formed on 1 April 1968, as a result of the Government's policy decision of that year that Britain's future defence effort would be concentrated mainly in Europe and the North Atlantic area. No special capability was to be maintained for use outside Europe once withdrawal from Singapore, Malaysia and the Gulf was complete. The new Command was formed at Wilton, near Salisbury, mainly from the existing staff of HQ Southern Command then located there. At the same time a new HQ Southern Command was formed at Hounslow, Middlesex, by the amalgamation of HQ Eastern and Southern Commands to cover their combined geographical responsibilities. HQs Northern and Western Command remained at York and Chester respectively, and Scotland and Northern Ireland became independent Districts.

As shown in Annex A, HQ Army Strategic Command commanded all Field Force troops in the UK less 6 Brigade (which belonged to BAOR), battalions on public duties and battalions placed under command of HQ Scotland. The Command consisted of the airportable 3rd Division (with 5, 19 and 24 Infantry Brigades and 16 Parachute Brigade), 5th Division (with 2, 8 and 39 Infantry Brigades) and a Support Echelon. Each of these formations had their own integral REME support. Brigadier Lionel Libby, the last DDEME of Southern Command, became the first DDEME of Army Strategic Command.

Role of Army Strategic Command

In the words of Lieutenant General Sir John Mogg, the Commander in Chief, STRATCO was formed 'to raise the standard and training of field force units to ensure any force sent abroad is correctly prepared, equipped and mounted to carry out its task speedily and successfully'. To this end STRATCO had three main roles:

- Support to NATO anywhere from Northern Norway, on the northern flank, to Turkey on the southern flank.
- Internal security world-wide.
- Limited war operations in conjunction with Allies.

The previous support for such roles from British bases overseas was generally no longer available. Thus logistic support from elements of the Support Echelon, which included the allocated field workshops and LADs, became increasingly important.

From 1969 the prime role of 3rd Division was to form the main land component of the UK Mobile Force, with the task of reinforcing NATO forces in Europe. By 1970 the three infantry brigades of 3rd Division had all been redesignated 'Airportable' and 16 Parachute Brigade had been put under the direct command of STRATCO.

REME in the Field Force

The units in brigades had attached tradesmen, LADs or regimental workshops, as appropriate. Each infantry brigade in 3rd Division had a supporting airportable infantry workshop, later redesignated 'field workshop (airportable)'. These were 3, 8, and 15 Field Workshops (Airportable), located adjacent to their brigades. Divisional troops had 10 Divisional Support Workshop in which the Division's heavy repair resources were concentrated. The Support Echelon included 9 Force Workshop which was formed in 1969 and also some T & AVR REME, including HQ REME Force Troops. A mobile element of 70 Aircraft Workshop at Middle Wallop provided second-line aircraft support on exercises and operations. There were, however, no organic second-line REME units in 5th Division, which was a formation consisting of infantry, with few supporting arms, and no logistic units.

The airportable infantry workshops had several airportable platoons which operated in the field mainly from Land Rovers and trailers. Workshop equipment was mounted on trailers equipped with shelters, and modified Land Rovers and Bedford light recovery tractors were used for recovery. A vehicles had to be repaired in the Divisional Support Workshop, which provided forward repair teams for both wheeled and tracked A vehicles. This workshop also had two airportable platoons. From 1967 16 Parachute Brigade no longer had a separate brigade workshop, the workshop becoming part of the 1st Parachute Logistic Regiment. This Regiment was formed in 1967 from 63 Parachute Squadron RCT, 16 Parachute Ordnance Field Park RAOC, 16 Parachute Workshop REME and some LADs. The reason for its formation was primarily the need to save manpower and vehicles within the brigade, without resorting to major cuts in the parachute battalions.

Major Martyn Clark, commanding the workshop at the time, remembered the determination of the Brigade Commander, Brigadier A H Farrar-Hockley, in pushing the concept through. A logistic regiment was trialled in late July 1967, dropping and exercising in the Mull of Kintyre with Major Clark in command. He recalled the near demise of two future generals, let alone himself and the pilot, when, with the Brigadier and the Brigade Major, Major Peter Chiswell, their helicopter broke through an 11,000-volt power line 200 feet up during some tactical flying.

'Fortunately we came down the right way up and survived the impact; parachute fitness then paid off as the BM and I set off on a cross-country run to search for help from some inevitably power-less cottages. The 'Scottish Daily Mail' produced suitably dramatic headlines! Back at Aldershot we had to demonstrate the potential savings in the proposed regiment, to a staff delegation. We lined up impressively on the square in our three independent units, complete with transport, and on the word of command we doubled and drove forward to form a single logistic regiment. To our rear, groups of men and vehicles stood fast – these being the savings convincingly demonstrated!'

Within weeks the incipient regiment was in routine operation, and after trials and further cuts it was officially formed on 31 March 1969 with a strength of sixteen officers and 181 soldiers – a saving of nearly 50%. The CO, 2IC and Adjutant were selected from officers of RCT, RAOC and REME. On operations the Logistic Regiment provided the Brigade Maintenance Area Command Post, taking under command for defence and movement the Parachute Field Ambulance and B echelons of other brigade units. A clear advantage was that the RHQ concentrating the expertise available in carrying out all common tasks such as pay, documentation, stores accounting, catering and regimental training, allowing the three squadrons to concentrate on their specialized skills. The Workshop Squadron had four officers and forty-nine soldiers to carry out unit repairs for brigade units without attached REME support, and field repairs for all the brigade's parachute scales of equipment. The OC Workshop Squadron acted as BEME. The Squadron wore the traditional red beret and the maroon and light blue lanyard awarded to 16 Parachute Workshop after the Suez operation in 1956, as a battle honour for outstanding technical and tactical performance.

In 1969 units of Army Strategic Command took part in fifty-five exercises overseas. Over the remaining period covered by this volume there was to be a gradual reduction in scope, but they would still provide an immense challenge for REME. REME tradesmen could find themselves as far east as Fiji, west as British Columbia, north as the Arctic Circle or south as New Zealand. Some idea of the Corps' involvement in these exercises is given later in this chapter.

Units of 3rd Division all carried out four-month tours in Northern Ireland, except for the workshops which carried out six-month tours. 15 Infantry Workshop was the first to carry out such a tour, on the outbreak of violence in August 1969. This support for Northern Ireland is described in Chapter 10.

REME IN THE STATIC CHAIN OF COMMAND

Until 1972, when the recommendations on the future Command structure in the UK by the Stainforth Committee were implemented, REME static support in UK, as illustrated in the adjacent map was divided between those workshops which came under command of Technical Group REME (later REME Support Group), and those under the technical control of senior REME officers in Commands. The former consisted of the Central Workshops, 32 at Bicester, 33 at Newark, 34 at Donnington, 35 at Old Dalby and 38 at Chilwell. These carried out base repairs for both field force and static units, and special engineering requirements. Also under command of Technical Group were the Vehicle Depot Workshops, 91 at Hilton, 93 at Ashchurch and 96 at Ludgershall. Repairs beyond the capacity of static units were carried out

Sergeant David Robb adjusts USN 501 Drone in 35 Central Workshop

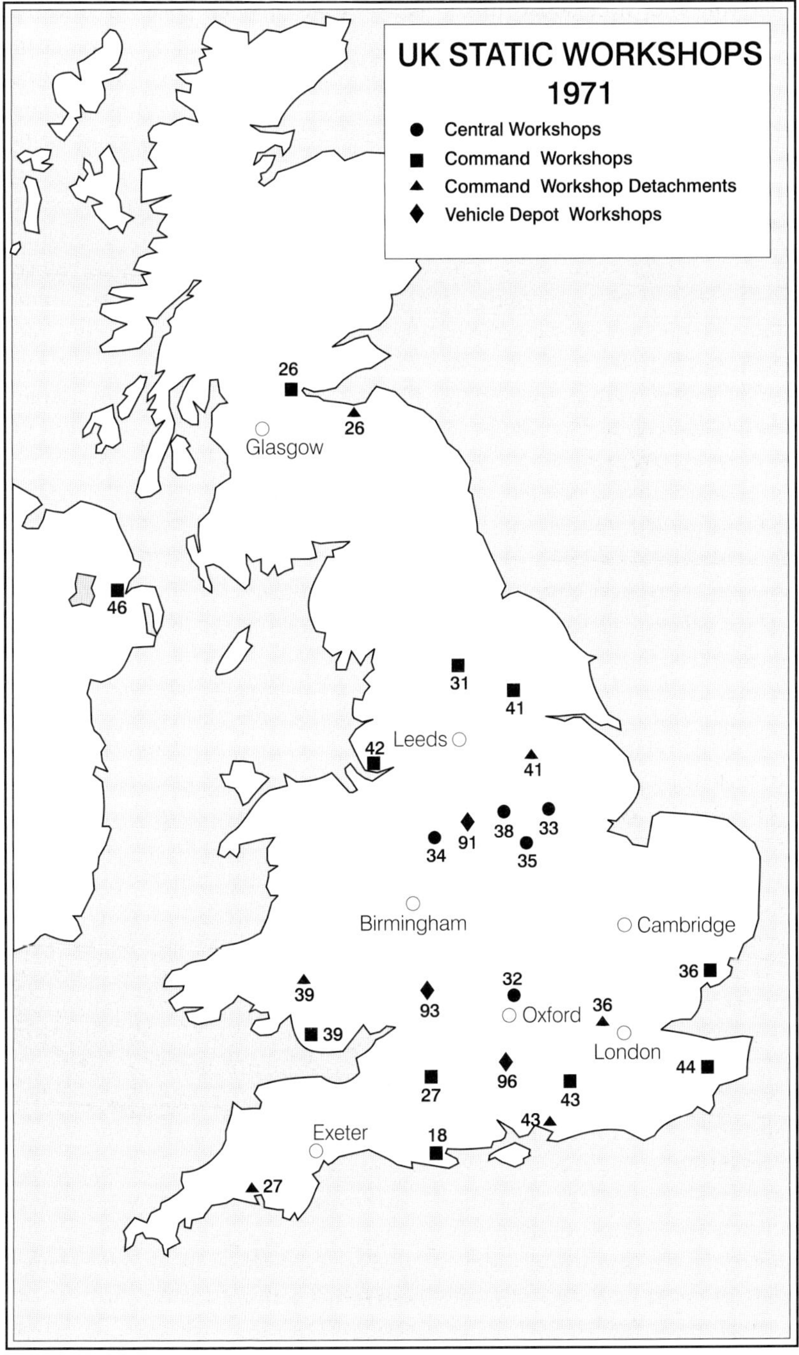
UK STATIC WORKSHOPS
1971
Central Workshops
Command Workshops
Command Workshop Detachments
Vehicle Depot Workshops
26
26
Glasgow
46
31
41
Leeds
42
41
38
33
91
34
35
Birmingham
Cambridge
36
32
39
93
Oxford
36
39
London
44
96
27
43
43
Exeter
18
27

by command workshops, which also provided an overload capacity for field workshops in their area. Their organization is set out at Annex B.

UNITED KINGDOM LAND FORCES

Army Strategic Command was replaced on 1 April 1972 by UK Land Forces (UKLF) as the result of UKFCSS. The geographic Home Command HQs were abolished and replaced by ten Districts. The operational elements of UKLF were:

- 3rd Division (until 1976 when it moved to become an armoured division in BAOR).
- UK Mobile Force (Land) (UKMF) (L) complete with its Logistic Support Force, which included the Reserve Army element.
- Allied Command Europe Mobile Force (Land) (AMF(L)).
- UK Joint Airborne Task Force.
- Combined Amphibious Task Force.
- Home Defence Forces.

REME Command and Control in UKLF

With the abolition of Command HQs under the Stainforth proposals all REME production resources in UK (outside those provided by Technical Group workshops) were put under the higher management of one HQ for the first time. Command workshops, however, retained their titles until 1985. Brigadier Arthur Reading, formerly DDEME Strategic Command, became Chief Electrical and Mechanical Engineer (CEME) UKLF, controlling these resources. His responsibilities covered:

- REME support to Field Force formations and units in UK.
- UK Land Forces, which had CREMEs in Districts and Scotland, and included Command Workshops.
- Territorial Army in UK.
- REME support for overseas detachments, including Belize.
- REME support for Suffield training area in Canada.
- REME support for formation exercises in Norway.
- Sponsorship of REME adventurous training activities including the Rory Cape Award.

The CEME had no responsibilities for the technical control of REME units from UKLF whilst they were serving in Northern Ireland.

In 1972 UKLF had overseas detachments in Thailand, Malaysia, Singapore, the Gulf, East Africa, West Africa, Naples, Gibraltar, Oslo, Caribbean, Central America and Suffield. AAC units too were widely spread, in Belize, Cyprus, Hong Kong and Suffield, and the Senior Aircraft Engineer at UKLF was heavily involved with their REME support. Visits to these detachments, and to REME units throughout UK with their large civilian element, were an important part of the duties of CEME. The strength of the UK REME civilian workforce at this stage was 4,270, and CEME was involved with those employed in workshops other than those of Technical Group.

Sergeant Keith Pannell with a Malaysian colleague

Although there were ten Districts within the United Kingdom six CREMEs shared the work as follows:

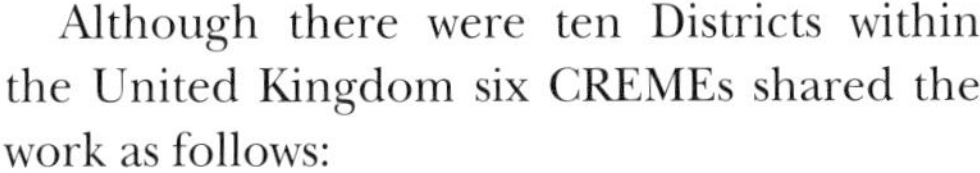

• South East and London Districts	Colonel.
• North East and Eastern Districts	Colonel.
• South West District	Colonel.
• North West and West Midland Districts and Wales	Lieutenant Colonel.
• Scotland	Lieutenant Colonel.
• Northern Ireland	Lieutenant Colonel.

After Brigadier Joe Rayment took over from Brigadier Tony Hughes as CEME in 1978 the grouping of Districts was changed to distribute the work more evenly and to provide closer REME advice especially to commanders with large field forces. These changes coincided with HQ South West District moving from Taunton to Bulford. Also at this time, despite the general emphasis on shrinking the REME organization, there was a need to reverse some cuts, and 39 Command Workshop at Bridgend, due for closure, was an example. The GOC Wales, Major General A G E Stewart-Cox, represented that there was a requirement to retain a workshop within his command to meet support requirements, instead of depending on a detachment of 42 Command Workshop at Liverpool. This was supported by CEME, who made a successful case for the reinstatement of 39 Command Workshop. The District changes resulted in some CREMEs being regrouped as follows:

- North East and North West Districts — Colonel.
- South West and Western Districts and Wales — Colonel.
- Eastern District — Lieutenant Colonel.

The organization of REME TA, and appointments to senior posts in units were the responsibility of CEME. In 1979 the units sponsored by HQ REME TA, which had previously reported direct to DGEME, joined the TA units in the Districts as part of the UKLF Order of Battle. This was a significant improvement, since it removed the anomaly whereby some TA on an operation could be reporting direct to DGEME rather than to CEME.

In 1982 a pointer to the future occurred when an adjustment within the staff functions of HQ UKLF was made: EME Branch became a logistics staff branch with the title of G4 Maint. This was headed by a REME DACOS in the rank of Colonel, whose title subsequently changed twice; firstly to Commander Maintenance, and then in 1992 to Commander Equipment Support. These changes were part of the pattern that evolved from the early Eighties, affecting the Corps as its enhanced responsibilities for equipment support gained impetus. Some of these changes were generated from overall Army studies, and many from initiatives taken by the Corps in seeking to achieve better equipment management. These are discussed in Chapter 2, and in later paragraphs in this chapter, as they affected UKLF.

Perhaps an indication of the atmosphere pervading HQ UKLF at the time is illustrated by the direction given to the new ACOS G1/G4, Brigadier Dennis Shaw, by the C-in-C of the day: 'I want to hear your proposals for replacing that organization at Andover [the Logistic Executive] – three SO 2s and a clutch of staff assistants should do!' There was clearly an element of mischief in this remark but also an underlying serious intent.

Army Restructuring Plan 1974–75

The background to the Army Restructuring Plan 1974–75 and its effect within BAOR have already been explained in Chapter 6. On the whole the effects on our force in the UK were less dramatic, although the change of role of 3rd Division and the removal of the brigade level of command did lead to a reappraisal of REME manpower and its utilization. The role of the Army in the UK, after this restructuring, was recast:

- To provide formations, units and individuals needed to put NATO headquarters and BAOR on a war footing. To this end Field Forces were formed.

- To provide a reinforcement capability for Allied Command Europe (ACE) ie troops deployed direct to Supreme Allied Commander Europe and not to BAOR: the equivalent of the old-style airportable brigade group. The role of the Special Air Service and the British component of the ACE Mobile Force (Land) remained unchanged.
- To secure the UK base and to provide the forces and structure for home defence.

District HQs assumed increased responsibility and for some of them this included functions previously carried out by those brigade HQs which were disbanded. Units within a District boundary, whether Regular or TA, were under that District's command. Logistic support was provided for each formation consistent with its role, and included much more use of the TA than before.

REME in the Field Force after Restructuring

The overall REME tasks within units in the Field Force remained the same after restructuring, and the establishments of LADs and regimental workshops were simply adjusted to meet changed holdings of vehicles, weapons and equipment. However, at second-line level after restructuring, only two full-size Regular field workshops remained in UKLF: 3 Field Workshop and 8 Field Workshop. 9 and 10 Field Workshops were reduced to small regular cadres to be supplemented on mobilization by Territorial Army soldiers. There was also a small AMF(L) Workshop which was part of the Logistic Support Battalion AMF(L). CREMEs of appropriate Districts also took over the responsibilities of the former CREME 3rd Division.

There were some more involved changes such as that affecting 15 Infantry Workshop (Airportable), which had been raised at Plymouth in December 1967 and which, with changes of name, had supported 24 Infantry Brigade. It moved to Munster in BAOR in 1977 after six years in Catterick. In Germany the Workshop supported 5 Field Force, returning in 1983 to Catterick, where it supported 2nd Infantry Division with an establishment of 60% Regular and 40% TA soldiers.

The Corps was also responsible for the provision of 29th Commando Regiment RA LAD and for some of the personnel of the workshop and LAD of the Commando Logistic Regiment Royal Marines, both of which formed part of 3 Commando Brigade. In the Commando Brigade, unlike in the conventional Army logistic system, all logistic elements, including the workshop, were coordinated within the Brigade's Logistic

Regiment after its formation at Stonehouse Barracks, Plymouth, in January 1972. REME tradesmen also formed 3 Commando Brigade Air Squadron LAD and the small workshop attached to 59 Independent Commando Squadron RE. All were later to be involved in the Falklands Campaign described in Chapter 11. The first OC of the Logistic Regiment Workshop Squadron was Captain Rory Cape, whose premature death later that year was to be commemorated in the Corps' principal adventurous training award described in Chapter 5.

The REME involvement in the Commando Logistic Regiment was in the form of attached officers and tradesmen in the Workshop Squadron located at Coypool, with the OC, 2IC, troop officers and a small number of tradesmen being REME, the remainder RM. In addition to the Workshop, the Regiment had an integral LAD to support its own equipment and vehicles. This was commanded by a REME captain, all the tradesmen being RM. The Regiment was commanded in turn by a Royal Marine officer and an Army officer. Lieutenant Colonel Dennis Shaw commanded from 1975 to 1978, a period which included nine weeks when the Regiment – considerably reinforced – provided an emergency fire service for the West Midlands Metropolitan County during the firemen's strike in late 1977. This was hardly the best preparation for their annual deployment to Norway a couple of months later!

Selection for Commando Forces

Operations

During the period covered by this volume two major overseas operations took place. In both, CORPORATE – The Falklands Campaign in 1982, and GRANBY – The Gulf War in 1991, REME units in the Field Force and the static chain of UKLF played their full part. In CORPORATE the Land Forces were found from within UKLF and the operation was mounted from UK, whereas for GRANBY, although the bulk of the units deployed came from BAOR, much support activity took place in the UK. REME activities in these operations are described fully in Chapters 6, 11, and 12.

Operation HAVEN followed immediately after the Gulf War in April 1991. This was a humanitarian operation mounted to help alleviate the suffering of the Kurds in north Iraq and south-east Turkey. Their plight was a result of Saddam Hussein's aggressive policies towards the Kurds, which had not diminished as a result of the Gulf War. The United States forces were also involved in this operation, which they nicknamed PROVIDE COMFORT and were later to be most generous in their support of the British element to make their life more comfortable under difficult conditions. As part of 3 Commando Brigade, the Commando Logistic Regiment played an important part in this operation, which required a major logistic effort.

The Brigade's role in the operation developed into the double task of securing an area in Kurdistan, and of bringing the Kurds out of the mountains and setting up 'Safe Haven' camps to maintain them. The initial move of the Brigade was by air, and on 20 April an advance party from the Commando Logistic Regiment was established at what was to become the initial Brigade Maintenance Area at Silopi in south-east Turkey. The LAD at this stage was heavily involved at Coypool with the normal problems of priority of movement of vehicles and stores by air. The fact that a Foden recovery vehicle would not fit into a HERCULES aircraft, and that the Regiment's vehicles were to be used both to establish an Advanced Logistic Group and in a troop-carrying role with 40 Commando, provided the LAD with plenty to think about. In the event the LAD worked shifts to provide all the support that was needed for the preparation of the Regiment's own vehicles for the initial air move and subsequently the sea tail. The first element of the sea tail sailed on 23 April for the port of Iskenderun in Turkey, from where it was some 650 kilometres drive to Silopi.

By mid-May the Workshop Squadron had moved forward to Sirsenk, then the location for the Logistic Task Group. This was ultimately to be the Brigade Maintenance Area, from where 40 and 45 Commando RM would continue to be supported in their operations until their task ended a month later. It was an operation which again tested the ingenuity and skills of all those providing support. Although in the event the operation did not require offensive action, full logistic support for that eventuality was required under difficult conditions of terrain, climate and threats of attack. The REME personnel who took part gained much from the experience.

Overseas Exercises

Over the years REME units in STRATCO, and later UKLF, were involved in exercises and the maintenance of detachments overseas. Exercises varied in size, from major unit to formation, and the potential use of a wide variety of equipment, both old and very new, required a high degree of flexibility from the Corps in providing the essential support. As with operations, climatic conditions, terrain, and spares availability were ever-present problems and this support was always challenging to the individual skills of REME soldiers. There was always the opportunity to practice their skills and ingenuity on 'repair by repair' when spares were not available, and when operating under exceptional working conditions. Examples of some of these exercises and detachment areas and the varying conditions encountered are given in the following paragraphs.

Macedonia

In September 1971 HELLENIC EXPRESS 71 was a major exercise to practise both the Land and Air elements of the ACE Mobile Force, held on NATO's southern flank in the Greek/Turkish Thrace region of north-eastern Greece bordering Bulgaria. The exercise was based on Thessaloniki, planned by the Supreme Hellene Armed Forces Command and jointly directed by CINCSOUTH and CINCENT. AMF(L) was commanded by the Italian General Gobbi and consisted of an Italian Alpine battalion (Bersaglieri), a German parachute battalion and an American and a British infantry battalion. The REME contribution to the multinational logistic support was provided by 9 Field Workshop and the LAD of 27 Regiment RCT, co-located with US Army and Bundeswehr workshop elements. The exercise terminated with a parade of all participants in Serrai. DDEME STRATCO, Brigadier Arthur Reading, attended all briefings throughout; he recalls that the exercise took place during the period of martial law that followed the deposition four years earlier of King Constantine by a group of Colonels. The Regent, HE General George Zoetakis, hosted the exercise as head of state, whilst members of the junta were present at most exercise briefings.

Norway

Exercises in the north of Norway by AMF(L) always had that extra touch of realism provided by the Arctic conditions and the proximity to the Soviet border during the Cold War period. In the late Seventies, when Brigadier Joe Rayment was the CEME, the AMF(L) Workshop was commanded by Major Alan Sharman. Under Arctic conditions special drills were necessary in the

BV 206 engine change

Workshop to prevent frostbite in the fingers of tradesmen working on vehicles and equipment in the open. Bare fingers were often essential for difficult assembly tasks and so the length of working time allowed between 'warm-ups' had to be controlled to avoid frostbite. These precautions necessarily resulted in a slow-down in work rates and productivity.

Canada and USA

The British Army Training Unit at Suffield (BATUS), in Canada, controlled a major training area with a permanent staff, the weather presented a more extreme range of conditions than those found in Germany, from hot in the summer to very cold in the winter, when the conditions were similar to those in Norway. During one visit by Brigadier Rayment an armoured regiment was deployed at night for a live-firing demonstration. The firepower of this concentration of 120mm guns at night was anticipated to be impressive and an array of visitors was assembled by helicopters far out into the training area. Mother nature had other ideas, and a gigantic storm blew up just as the demonstration started. The thunder and lighting outclassed all the gunnery efforts and not one gun was seen nor heard by anybody. The helicopters for the return of the visitors to base were not only grounded but had all their plastic cockpit domes cracked by the hail. 'Natural causes' had provided another task for REME. The visitors had to return to base in transport less susceptible to climatic conditions – 4 tonners, which crunched their way back to base across the hail-covered plain.

At the end of each BATUS training season REME went to work refurbishing the tanks, vehicles and equipment for the next year.CHIEFTAINs were parked in the open throughout the bitter winter, and this was satisfactory unless the Chinook, a freak and transient warm wind, blew in from the Pacific. When this happened the snow and ice around the tank tracks melted, only to freeze again more solidly a few hours later, when the tanks became literally frozen to the spot. This prevented them from being moved normally until they thawed out in the Spring and added an additional support hazard.

9 Field Workshop, based in Bordon, was one REME unit to exercise in a different part of Canada. As a result of the Army Restructuring Plan, mentioned earlier in this chapter, 9 Field Workshop became an unusual unit. Although a Regular field workshop, commanded by a Regular officer, it was manned by only a small nucleus of Regular Army tradesmen, the main element of the workforce being provided from the TA. These would only materialize in the event of mobilization, and in its peacetime role the Workshop had only a very limited unit dependency. It

was thus in an ideal position to provide second-line support for B vehicles of UKLF units exercising out of theatre.

One such series of live-firing exercises, for UK based non-mechanized infantry with support elements, had started in the early Seventies. These exercises were carried out in Wainwright, Canada, during the summer months and in various locations in southern USA during the winter. They were named Exercise POND JUMP WEST and TRUMPET DANCE respectively, and relied to a large extent on the hire of host-nation equipment. In 1979, in an effort to reduce costs, a large permanent fleet of B vehicles and a battery of 105mm light guns for use on both exercises in turn were shipped to Canada. A twelve-man team, led by an artificer staff sergeant and consisting of REME tradesmen plus two RAOC storemen, was detached from 9 Field Workshop to provide second-line support.

Major assemblies were collected from BATUS 350 miles south of Wainwright and the team purchased 110V power tools locally. Beside supporting the successive units during their exercises, they also carried out short refurbishment programmes between unit changes. At the end of the summer exercise period all equipments were inspected and repaired by an enhanced team of seventeen tradesmen, which was also provided by 9 Field Workshop. In Canada this work had to be completed to meet a tight deadline for return movement to the USA. This was to avoid subjecting the equipment, which was stored in the open, to the onset of the harsh Canadian winter, and possibly prevent its removal under the sort of conditions experienced at BATUS. This cold was a sharp contrast to the sweltering heat of the Alberta prairies during the summer exercises. Even so, as at BATUS, extremely low temperatures were experienced, down to –42°C, before all equipment was cleared on railflats to Fort Campbell in Kentucky, before the winter really set in.

At the end of the Exercise TRUMPET DANCE series in USA a further inspection and repair programme was carried out before moving the equipment back to Canada. All of this work was completed with the nearest RAOC spares depot 4,000 miles away in the UK, and no local Rover agencies in Kentucky. 'Repair by repair' became the norm, with the vehicle mechanics regularly stripping gearboxes down to the last gearwheel and bush. The Americans, who were always helpful, nevertheless found it difficult to understand the versatility of the REME team, and the wide responsibilities that it accepted at a much lower rank level than in the US Army. On the other hand the team were impressed when unofficial attachments were organized: on such occasions they enjoyed the experience of working with the American automotive specialists who worked on all the systems of any one equipment.

At any one time 9 Field Workshop had soldiers detached to Kenya,

Canada, USA and Belize, and the experience gained by young soldiers under the varying conditions would stand them in good stead for the future.

Denmark

3 Field Workshop was doubly fortunate in that its exercises outside UK took place in either Denmark or Schleswig-Holstein: well away from the normal British exercise areas. They therefore found the local people very much more welcoming and cooperative. For instance, Major John Palmer, on Exercise BOLD GANNET in Denmark in 1984, spotted an ideal workshop location in a factory manufacturing prefabricated warehouses. Although some of the factory would be perfect for the workshop, it was clearly a very busy operation. Approaching the manager for help in finding accommodation, he expected a fairly dusty reply, but instead was told, 'If we want you to protect us we must help you to train'. Tons of concrete sections were moved to accommodate the Workshop and production in both the factory and the Workshop continued side by side for over a week. Despite the disruption which the Workshop must have caused, its soldiers enjoyed the use of all the facilities throughout their stay and were treated to a party when they left.

On the same exercise the Workshop was visited by GOC South West District, Major General B M Lane. He arrived by helicopter and set off round the Workshop at best Light Infantry pace. Half-way round he ordered an RAOC soldier to simulate having stomach pains, and turning to Company Sergeant Major Anderson told him to let him know when the casualty arrived at the Field Hospital, also on the exercise. (The General had previously visited the Field Hospital and found it short of business!) At the end of his visit General Lane was returned to the helicopter landing strip, but found no helicopter. CSM Anderson, recognizing an emergency, albeit an exercise one, had 'hijacked' it for the casualty. It was some moments before the Workshop knew whether the GOC was impressed and amused or just plain furious. Fortunately he saw the funny side. CSM Anderson did not see the funny side the next morning when he was paraded in front of the OC, given a dressing-down and told that he would never make RSM. He felt somewhat better though when told that the reason was because news of his commissioning had just come through!

The return journey from this exercise was not without incident. One subaltern, who shall remain nameless, had not impressed during the exercise so was detailed by the OC to organize and lead the trip home. The OC tucked his vehicle into the first packet of the convoy, and promptly fell into a well earned sleep. He awoke to find the subaltern trying to turn the packet round (trailers and all) on a railway platform, without waking the OC. The more amusing side was the sight of some very cross Gunners whose packet had somehow got into the Workshop convoy and followed mindlessly onto the platform.

Belize

In contrast to the areas which had extremes of climate, Belize was always hot and humid and provided a daunting jungle in which to train, as well as being a political danger spot. REME tradesmen could be found in the remotest corners cheerfully carrying out their support tasks. CEME on one visit arrived at a pinnacle of rock standing out above the jungle. Here an infantry detachment was located overlooking an Army camp in Guatemala, their subject of scrutiny. The only way to reach this detachment was by helicopter, for the jungle was quite impenetrable for many miles. At the location he met a REME tradesman servicing night binoculars for the surveillance section manning the position. The tradesman hoped that his work, inspected by the Brigadier, would be of sufficiently high calibre to enable him to risk asking the Brigadier for a lift back to civilization in his helicopter. It was, and he got his lift.

The jungle was certainly not always 'user friendly' and contained a variety of fauna of which perhaps the most horrifying was the land crab. These flesh-eating scavengers were quite aggressive. Captain Tom Wilton, making a routine visit to Belize from the staff of Brigadier Tony Hughes (then the CEME UKLF), was thrown from a truck on one of the exceptionally rough tracks and broke his neck. The Warrant Officer in charge of the Belize Workshop, ASM Goat, refused to leave him to seek help, in spite of being forcefully ordered to do so by Captain Wilton. What Captain Wilton could not see, fortunately, as he lay paralysed, was a circle of crabs, only being prevented from closing in for a meal by the perambulation of the ASM! It was some hours later that a vehicle came by and Captain Wilton was transported to Belize City, and then by air to the United States hospital in Panama for treatment.

UK Static Workshops

In 1972 CEME UKLF, Brigadier Arthur Reading, started to review his resources and workload to improve their balance. This review eventually became part of the 1976 FAIR VALUE studies described in Chapter 2. In April 1977 three civilian workshop detachments, at Coypool and Taunton (27 Command Workshop) and Killingworth (31 Command Workshop), were closed. By then the UKLF REME civilian workforce had fallen to 3,320.

In 1978 a review of the pay of skilled Civil Service industrial tradesmen compared with local jobbing engineering organizations revealed an unsatisfactory situation which was affecting civilian recruiting. It was at its worst at 43 Command Workshop at Aldershot where only three civilian vehicle mechanics remained. CEME UKLF, Brigadier Joe Rayment, was forced to deploy twenty military vehicle mechanics from field force units to keep the workshop viable. This situation was improved when, towards the end of 1978, work-measured productivity schemes were cleared for introduction into command workshops, providing the possibility for employees to earn up to 30% of basic pay as a productivity bonus. This had a salutary effect on pay, recruiting and productivity in command workshops. Economic pressures, however, worked both ways: in 1982 to make savings it was necessary to close the detachment of 41 Command Workshop at Gainsborough and to alienate the site. It had operated the only REME fuel tanker de-gasification system in the country and it was the only REME unit in the UK certified for 'hot work' on fuel tankers.

The REME Static Workshop Review described in Chapter 2 finally received ministerial approval in November 1984 (taking effect from April 1985) after three years of study, discussion and consultation. The review, sponsored by the QMG, set out to rationalize the base repair facilities and commitments in the UK. The effect on UKLF was that:

18 Command Workshop

- Most of the UKLF command workshops lost their base repair commitments and were retitled District Workshops.
- 18 Command Workshop became 18 Base Workshop.
- The Bicester detachment of 43 Command Workshop became 32 Base Workshop.
- The strength of the REME civilian force directly controlled by DACOS G4 Maint, HQ UKLF, on behalf of DGEME, was reduced to 2,240.

Introduction of the New Management Strategy

In the late Eighties UKLF was again being studied, this time by a team of consultants from a civilian firm – Price Waterhouse. They examined the way in which Executive Responsibility Budgets (ERBs) and the New Management Strategy (NMS) could be extended, and be introduced across the whole of the UKLF district structure. At this time the only units in UKLF operating to formal budgetary procedures were the District Workshops and some RAOC depots, most of which were operating full-cost ERBs, and had been doing so for some years.

The Consultants' report recognized that at HQ UKLF both the senior REME and RAOC officers had considerable financial responsibilities, and recommended that on financial grounds alone these two posts should be at one star level. However, on political grounds this recommendation was not viewed favourably by HQ UKLF and was not pursued. Nevertheless, the Consultants' finding that the DACOS titles were inappropriate for the heads of the three principal logistic corps at the HQ, and recommendation that they should once again revert to being functional commanders, was accepted. The new titles were taken into use on 1 April 1989.

The principal result of the Consultants' report was that a Top Level Budget (TLB) was set up for Commander in Chief UKLF, with the Commander UK Field Army and the Inspector General of Doctrine and Training (IGDT) each having a Higher Level Budget (HLB). Each District GOC became an Intermediate Higher Level Budget (IHLB) holder within Commander Field Army's HLB, with the various Arms and Services Directors General (including DGEME) and Directors having training IHLBs within IGDT's HLB.

As part of the work carried out in setting up the UKLF budgetary structure, all UKLF units were classified as either district or theatre troops and, depending upon their classification, financial control of these units fell to the appropriate district IHLB, or the Field Army HLB. There was much discussion over the classification into which logistic units would fall, since whoever held the budget would effectively have total control of the resources that would be allocated for these units. The situation was complicated by the fact that the Quartermaster General, who was technically responsible for the support to UKLF given by these units, including REME workshops, was not going to be in their budgetary chain.

Ultimately, after considerable debate, REME field workshops were classified as district units and resourced by the district IHLBs, whilst the nine district workshops, 70 Aircraft Workshop, 17 Port and Maritime Workshop, and the Engineer Resources Workshop were classified as theatre units. In spite of resistance from district staffs, the district workshops and the three specialist workshops were grouped together in a Maintenance IHLB run by Commander Maintenance HQ UKLF, which was part of the Field Army HLB.

The Maintenance IHLB was set up on 1 April 1989. It was the only full-cost budget within the Field Army HLB, its value being about £80M with some £50M of this being a cash resource. On 1 October 1989 the cash and manpower resources for the civilian element of the UKLF REME static workshops were transferred from the DGEME's element of the QMG's budget to the Commander in Chief UKLF's TLB.

The District Review

After budgets had been set up in each district as a result of the New Management Strategy the continued pressure for cost-effectiveness resulted in yet another study being initiated. Its aim was to reduce the number of districts in Great Britain from nine to four – Scotland, Wales and West, Eastern, and Southern. Considerable heat was generated by the proposal to absorb London District into the new Southern District, and in the event London District retained its independent status.

The plan to form these much larger districts had a significant impact on the existing REME support organization. Support for the original nine districts was based on a mixture of field force units, backed up by the static district workshops, whilst the DGEME controlled base workshops. This arrangement effectively provided at least one static workshop in each district. However, as explained earlier, some districts shared Commanders Maintenance and maintenance staffs. REME support to UKLF units lacked representation at BEME level, particularly for TA units whose military maintenance manpower had been replaced by civilian tradesmen, who were difficult to recruit and retain in some areas.

The reorganized four large districts plus London District meant that the already heavily pruned maintenance staffs were even more stretched, and REME advice and management was at an unacceptably low level. As a result of this situation the then Commander Maintenance UKLF, Colonel Brian Ross, took steps to redress some of the staffing deficiencies. His efforts were successful and it was agreed that each district would have an autonomous Commander Maintenance and staff, and each of the regional brigades would have a BEME. This was achieved after much blood, mainly that of Lieutenant Colonel Bill Harrison, SO1 Maintenance UKLF, had been spilled on the carpet of HQ UKLF's Establishment Committee room, in successfully wresting an additional slice of REME manpower from UKLF's total manpower ceiling.

In June 1991 Colonel Tony Millington took over the reins as Commander Maintenance at HQ UKLF. He came fresh from being a member of the Army's Logistic Support Review, described as the most wide-ranging consideration of QMG's organization since the Esher Report of 1904, so was well placed to embark upon the period of significant change then under way.

The UKLF district restructuring was in process and this was to realign the Command's boundaries. At the same time 'Drawdown' was being planned, which was to create wider responsibility for REME staffs throughout UKLF. This was coupled with the need to restructure them into the new Equipment Support (ES) Branches and organization, consequent upon the recommendations of the Logistic Support Review. The background to this review is largely covered in Chapters 2 and 3. The role and command arrangements for the UKLF static district workshops were also being examined in depth.

In the event the command and the budgets of all the UKLF district workshops were transferred from UKLF's control to that of QMG in April 1992, with the UKLF requirements to be managed from then on by way of a Service Level Agreement developed and run by the new ES Branch at UKLF. Thus the district workshops together with the base workshops already in QMG's area were concentrated under one management focus for efficiency. At the same time rationalization meant that the closure of 39 (Bridgend), 41 (Strensall) and 42 (Liverpool) District Workshops would take place by March 1993. Under DGES(A), the remaining workshops were to be transformed into a Defence Support Agency in 1993 and would be subject to a progressive programme of market testing. UKLF would remain a principal customer through the medium of the Service Level Agreement.

Following the recommendations of the Logistic Support Review the ES Branch at UKLF was formed at the same time as HQ QMG on 6 April 1992. Commander Maintenance became Commander Equipment Support, controlling all the Theatre's equipment support, with management of most technical equipment and supply management aspects of technical material concentrated in the Branch. This had expanded accordingly with the addition of several key equipment and supply management posts, the role and responsibilities of the Branch increasing significantly. Similarly, adjustments were to be made to form the ES structures down the chain of command to UKLF districts, the newly formed 3rd (UK) Division and to several brigade headquarters. The new structure is outlined in the diagram at Annex C.

It was proposed that from 1993, the second-line REME support to the UK Field Army, in particular, would undergo radical change in line with revised REME support policies. REME battalions would be formed, predominantly to support the 1st (UK) Armoured Division in Germany (1, 2, and 3 Battalions REME). 6 Battalion REME would be formed in support of 3rd (UK) Division with its Close Support Companies at Tidworth (3 Field Workshop) and Catterick (15 Field Workshop), and its HQ and GS Company (9 Field Workshop) at Bordon. 7 Battalion would also form at Wattisham later to support the aircraft of 1st (UK) Armoured Division,

3rd (UK) Division and 24 Airmobile Brigade. Four new REME TA battalions were planned to be formed, largely from existing TA Units – 101 and 103 in support of 1st and 3rd Divisions respectively, 102 for the L of C and 104 from the Specialist TA for UK Home Defence. It was to be the most significant change in the Corps ORBAT for some considerable time.

In 1992, as well as managing the complicated series of reorganizations originating from the Logistic Support Review and Options for Change, UKLF mounted two significant UN operational deployments in the former Yugoslavia – HANWOOD and GRAPPLE. The latter deployment in November 1992 included twelve REME officers and 325 REME soldiers in support of 1st Battalion, The Cheshire Regiment battle group and the UN humanitarian aid programme. The REME contribution to GRAPPLE on roulement was to become a continuing commitment.

COMMAND AND DISTRICT WORKSHOPS

It is not possible in this volume to consider the many aspects of all the individual workshops in the static chain. The achievements of some are mentioned in other chapters, where more appropriate to events, and those described briefly in the following paragraphs are a selection of others that are typical. Some have had long histories, stretching back to the predecessors of the Corps, and some detail of these has been included to show the development of the Corps in this particular area of support. By the completion date of this volume some will have already passed into history, while others will have undergone changes in role or will be under scrutiny for further possible revision. Certainly all, whatever their past or future, will be worthy of recognition as providers of support in the highest traditions of the Corps.

Command Workshop Organization

The command workshop organization in 1967, prior to many proposals for economies and reduction, is given in Annex B. The changes, culminating in the Static Workshop Review, are covered in Chapter 2. In the mid-Eighties the surviving command workshops became district workshops. Some workshops such as 31 District Workshop at Catterick and 36 District Workshop at Colchester reduced their civilian strength by 50% in the twenty years 1969–1989. 39 Command Workshop at Bridgend in 1969 had three detachments at Long Marston, Hereford and Sennybridge, and in the Seventies had an important task to support RAF St Athan with second- and third-line repairs until the RAF obtained their own repair facilities. In 1973 the Workshop itself became a detachment of 42 Command Workshop, Liverpool, but in 1979 reverted to its old name again. In 1985 it became a District Workshop and by the end of the decade it had retained only one of the three detachments, at Sennybridge, and a small mainly first-line repair facility in Cardiff.

43 District Workshop

Room could not be found in Volume 1 for the story of this, the oldest REME workshop, but it is now appropriate to relate some of its earlier history. The workshop started at Aldershot in 1857, in the time of the predecessors of REME, and was housed in temporary wooden structures erected on heathland bought by the Government. Its task was to repair guns, limbers, saddlery and wagons. The first permanent workshop was built in 1879 in the Ordnance Stores Depot in Aldershot. In 1902 the War Office bought the first military car, a four-seater Panhard for the GOC Aldershot, Major General Sir John French. Mechanization of the Army was becoming established, and the role of those supporting it was emerging.

The First World War, 1914–18, had led to a great increase in Army mechanization, which then continued to gain momentum. By 1929 a bigger and better equipped workshop, entitled Aldershot Area Workshop RAOC, was needed where the 1st Division was located and the first building, later known as the West Hangar, was erected on the Ordnance Road site. In those days tank parts were difficult to obtain, a situation not unfamiliar even in the 1990s! Components were therefore built up, sleeved, bushed, re-installed or locally manufactured. Blacksmiths, general fitters, machinists, and welders were in great demand for these processes.

In 1941, during the Second World War, a new tank workshop, later known as the East Hangar, was erected. The workshop strength grew to 1500 military and civilians which it maintained for ten years. Up until the war only time-served apprentices were employed, but 80% of the civilian staff were then called up for the armed forces. The new wartime employees were directed labour who at first required much training and supervision. It became 13 Command Workshop REME in 1942 when REME was formed; in common with other command workshops it was re-numbered in 1962 to 43 Command Workshop. The outbreak of war in Korea in 1950 brought many busy months for the workshop which overhauled, modified and converted CENTURION and CHURCHILL tanks. It designed and produced a stop-gap CENTURION ARV Mark 1 (Aldershot Pattern), the first batch of which was rushed to Korea in 1952. For the Suez operation in 1956, there was a requirement to work round the clock to prepare CENTURION tanks for wading in an assault sea landing.

The work on a wide range of special equipments for operations

Conversion to a mobile fish-and-chip van for the troops in Northern Ireland

continued in the Seventies and Eighties. In the Seventies the workshop was producing such contrasting requirements as Land Rover protection kits and mobile fish-and-chip wagons for the troops in Northern Ireland, whilst in 1982 all the stops were pulled out in preparation for the Falklands Campaign. A number of other workshops in the UK were equally involved in supporting the campaign: the overall role of REME in the Falklands is dealt with in Chapter 11. In Aldershot the Workshop's task was to winterize the Land Rovers of 5 Infantry Brigade and convert a large number of them to Command Posts. Many rough-terrain trolleys were manufactured as well as equipment for medical units and mobile HQs.

By 1985, when its redesignation to a District Workshop was made, the unit's strength had fallen to below 300 military and civilians. There was, however, an expansion in electronic engineering and the opening of a new air-conditioned optronics workshop. Over many years this workshop, located at 'the Home of the British Army', has carried out many varied support tasks with great dedication, using its skilled manpower to maximum effect. The Static Workshops Engineering Display, part of the REME Museum collection, is situated in the Workshop, a singular testimony to its long and interesting history.

41 District Workshop

102 Company Workshop was formed from 18 Battalion RAOC when REME was created in 1942. From June 1943 it was under the command of Lieutenant Colonel R W Wilkinson DLI, a TA officer, who continued to command it until it became 4 Command Workshop in 1944, and its first REME commanding officer arrived. Lieutenant Colonel Wilkinson transferred to REME in 1946 and later in the Fifties became well known to many REME officers and soldiers as Commanding Officer of 2 Training Battalion at Honiton. He was subsequently the very efficient Mess Secretary at West Court Officers' Mess. Meanwhile the workshop which he had commanded twenty years earlier had become 41 Command Workshop, and in 1967 moved from the York Tram Sheds at Fulford and Ordnance Road to Strensall on the edge of the MOD range. It became 41 District Workshop in 1986 and was to be closed finally in 1993.

27 District Workshop

A workshop existed at Warminster before the formation of the Corps in 1942, a detachment of the Central Ordnance Depot Tidworth having been established there in workshop accommodation in 1939. It had then about 125 civilians to maintain the vehicles and equipment of the 2nd and 3rd Battalions of the Royal Tank Corps (2nd and 3rd Royal Tank Regiments from 4 April 1939) stationed there. Subsequently an RAOC field workshop took over the premises before moving to France in 1940, and this was followed after Dunkirk by the 1st Armoured Division Workshop RAOC, a unit with a strength of some 350. In October 1940 about forty men were posted out to form the basis of the 2nd Armoured Division Workshop at Northampton, which in turn a month later formed the nucleus of 7th Armoured Division Workshop at Aldershot. By the summer of 1941 the 1st Division was training on Salisbury Plain, preparing for an active role in support of the 8th Army in North Africa, and recovery and repair support was provided by the Warminster Depot Detachment. Later it became host to 1st Guards Armoured Division Workshop which became REME in 1942, and as the war developed the workshop site at Warminster was extended.

The workshop premises at Warminster were taken over in 1943 by the United States Army and handed back in 1945. At this stage an initial occupation by four sub-workshops soon developed into the formal status of a command workshop, becoming 27 Command Workshop. It was then some 360 strong, including 125 civilians. By 1959 that strength had increased to about 1,200, of whom 500 were civilian but, soon after, the strength diminished with the ending of National Service and other overall force reductions. This resulted in insufficient manpower to guard the unit's barracks at Boreham Fields, and until 1965 the troops were temporarily housed in the School of Infantry barracks. The original barracks were then enlarged for the School of Infantry Demonstration Battalion, renamed Battlesbury Barracks, and the workshop personnel moved back. Two years later, just before the beginning of the period covered by this volume, the strength of the Workshop was a mere seven officers and four soldiers, and dependent for its production on the civilian element of 504. Detachments were maintained variously at Shrivenham, Tidworth and Taunton. Administrative and technical modernization programmes were implemented during the Seventies and Eighties, and in 1985 the title was changed to 27 District Workshop, when the Blandford Detachment was also taken over from 18 Command Workshop at Bovington.

In 1992, the Corps' 50th Anniversary year, in recognition of its long and friendly association with the town of Warminster, the Workshop was honoured by the granting of the 'Liberty of Warminster'. This 'Liberty', equating in significance and purpose to a 'Freedom' proclaimed by the Freemen of a borough or city, was the first such honour of a Regular Army REME unit stationed in the UK. A guard of forty-five men – nearly three-quarters of its posted strength – marched through the town in the presence of Major General J M Brockbank, Vice Lord Lieutenant of Wiltshire, and Major General Dennis Shaw as Representative Colonel Commandant. The Lady Mayor presented a scroll, in response to which the Corps presented an engraved silver Elizabethan alms dish.

Over its life in various guises, the Warminster workshop had fluctuated substantially in strength and composition: typical of the adjustments that such static workshops routinely experienced in their geographical roles in meeting the local demands on their resources. General repairs to all varieties of soft-skinned vehicles, telecommunications equipment, armaments, instruments and so on were enhanced by support to a wide variety of A vehicles (both tracked and wheeled) used by the School of Infantry, which included many prototype and range target vehicles not in general issue. Base repair of all variants of the CENTURION was undertaken from 1977, the 100th major rebuild of a variant being achieved in August 1982. Ten years later 261 CENTURIONs had been overhauled when this work came to an end, to be replaced in September 1992 by the overhaul of CHIEFTAIN variants.

30 District Workshop

30 District Workshop, Mill Hill, London, which closed in March 1990, started life before the Second World War in Regents Park Barracks, London. In 1939 it opened on land at Bittacy Hill Farm, Mill Hill, but its buildings were not completed until 1940. From April 1941 until the end of the war the Mill Hill Workshops RAOC and its REME successor was commanded by Lieutenant Colonel Claude Tofield. The transition to REME was effected on 1 October 1942, when 1 Battalion REME was formed under the command of Lieutenant Colonel C N R Kirkpatrick KOSB; it is believed to have remained in existence until 1945, providing regimental administrative command. On that day a grand ceremonial parade was held, the march past being led by the full Middlesex Regiment Band and the salute taken by Major General A R Valon, Colonel Commandant. The Battalion was to act also as a holding unit, enabling drafts to be assembled during which the men could be usefully employed at their trades in the Workshop. The conflict of administrative and technical priorities, given the coexistence of 1 Battalion and 10 Command Workshops (as the working unit became), was to some extent resolved by the early promotion of Tofield to Colonel.

The Workshop prepared equipment for armoured units earmarked for the 1942 landings in North Africa and later prepared amphibious tanks for the invasion of Normandy in 1944. During this period the unit's War Diaries make frequent mention of the 'Dig for Victory' campaign, exploiting over six acres for growing fruit and vegetables; in 1942 production totalled over sixteen tons.

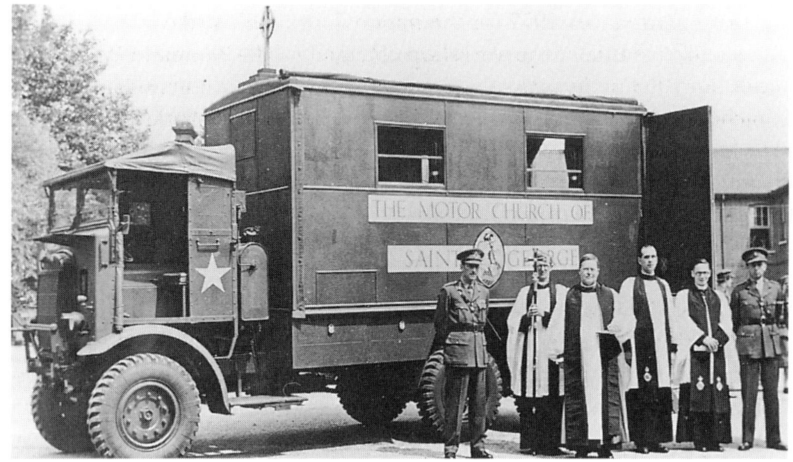

Dedication of a Mobile Church by the Archbishop of Canterbury

In the spring of 1944, before the invasion of Normandy the Workshop made two mobile churches for OVERLORD. These were dedicated by the Archbishop of Canterbury, the Most Reverend Frederick Temple, in the presence of the Chaplain General, the DME, Brigadier Caffyn DDME 21st Army Group and chaplains of the invasion force. It being the era of the V1 flying bomb, suitable slit trenches had to be dug – for which special provision had to be made for the particularly generously sized Archbishop! After the invasion the workshop became responsible for the repair of armoured vehicles from 21st Army Group.

In 1958 the Workshop was given the interesting task of preparing vehicles and equipment for Sir Vivian Fuchs' and Sir Edmund Hillary's Commonwealth Trans-Antarctic Expedition. One member of the twelve-man party was AQMS Roy Homard REME who went as the advance party engineer and drove the SNO-CAT 'County of Kent' for two thousand miles across the continent, thus certainly confirming his engineering skills. Another 'extramural activity,' providing evidence of its versatility, was the major part the workshop played in supporting the Royal Tournament at Earls Court stadium, making special models, stands and recruiting displays. In 1974, a particularly spectacular contribution was the design and construction of two ships with sails 60 feet high, which could fold up into the roof of the Earls Court stadium. A major routine problem lay in keeping the pre-First World War 13-pounder QF guns serviceable for the King's Troop Royal Horse Artillery, all spares clearly requiring local manufacture. Other special tasks included the support programme for the 'Green Goddess' fire engines brought back into service in November 1977 for the national firemen's strike.

In 1962 the title of the workshop changed to 30 Command Workshop, until in 1968 it became a detachment of 36 Command Workshop, Colchester. In 1973 it reverted to being 30 Command Workshop. For the last five years of its existence it was to be 30 District Workshop, and, on closing, all could look back on its achievements over fifty years with a great deal of satisfaction.

26 District Workshop

This Workshop, based at Stirling in Scotland, was formed in 1942 as 26 Command Workshop. There remained a sizeable REME personnel presence throughout the period of National Service, with soldiers being accommodated in the vicinity of Stirling Castle. With the demise of National Service the military establishment gradually reduced, until by 1971 there were three officers, a warrant officer and a staff sergeant in the unit, the remainder of the work-force being civilians. It was planned that by 1994 there would be no military personnel in the unit.

The Workshop was fortunate to have an interesting Officers' Mess at Carlton House, Stirling. This was originally an RAOC Officers' Mess, and became a combined RAOC/REME Officers' Mess on the formation of REME. It was a delightful Victorian building with a charming garden, and well remembered by all those officers fortunate enough to be located in Stirling, for its enormous Victorian baths, complete with brass taps, in which one could float. Unfortunately the Mess was designated for closure in early 1994 because of the reduction in the number of officers in the area, and the sad demise of stately tubbing would remain only a symbolic reminder that change is all-pervasive.

The unit was scheduled to become an Army Base Repair Organization Workshop in April 1993, located on its original site at Forthside, Stirling, with a function to provide an element of unit repair, and field repair for designated units in Scotland, both Regular and TA. The Workshop, when this decision was made, was headed by the first Civil Servant to be in charge of the unit, Mr Tom Tudhope, and comprised 165 industrial and non-industrial staff. It was also one of the workshops designated for

Market Testing, a process soon to be implemented whereby civilian industry would be able to compete for the work.

OTHER ORGANIZATIONS

REME Wing, The Royal School of Artillery, Larkhill

Until 1958 there were many and disparate REME sections operating at Larkhill, including REME specialist advisers to the Gunnery, Equipment and Observation Wings of the School. Immediately after the Second World War the RA Workshop was taken over by REME and in 1952 the small Vehicle and General Workshop was transferred to the Corps. The REME Guided Weapons Workshop was established in 1956 to support the CORPORAL surface-to-surface system.

In 1958 the then Commandant, Brigadier A J C Block, suggested to the DDEME Southern Command, Brigadier Mike Scott, that all the REME functions should be brought together under one command, and in 1961 the School of Artillery, Larkhill, Workshop was formed as an independent command under a lieutenant colonel, responsible to the Commandant. In 1965 the Workshop became REME Wing and in 1971 it expanded further to become a colonel's command of some 400 when the School of Artillery, Manorbier amalgamated with Larkhill to become the Royal School of Artillery (RSA), Larkhill, and the new Air Defence Wing was formed. The LAD of the School Support Regiment (later to become 14th Regiment RA) remained independent of REME Wing until 1982.

At its height in 1983 the REME Wing comprised two production companies under a lieutenant colonel production manager. Also under the lieutenant colonel, second-in-command, were sections for trials, management services, quality control and administration. The production companies were E Company (RAPIER, DRONE, SWINGFIRE and E Workshop); and M Company (A, B and Weapons Workshops).

Over the years the military strength of the Wing declined; production became concentrated in A, B and E workshops under a major and in 1989 the commanding officer's post reverted to a lieutenant colonel. In 1994 the Director Royal Artillery was to move from Woolwich to Larkhill and to embrace the Projects Wing of the RSA, and REME was to continue providing trials support to the renamed Artillery Developments Division.

REME Wing RA Ranges Hebrides

A unique REME organization in UKLF was located in Scotland with the Royal Artillery ranges on St Kilda, Outer Hebrides, and titled REME

Wing Royal Artillery Ranges, Hebrides. There was a REME supporting presence on the Ranges since the rangehead equipment for the CORPORAL missile firings was installed in 1957–58, and this was developed to the larger REME Wing organization in 1971, when the first Commanding Officer was Lieutenant Colonel John Peacock.

RAPIER trials were conducted on the range in the Seventies, and the deep-range facilities were brought on line by the early Eighties. The REME Wing was gradually replaced by the expansion of civilian contracts, until in April 1992 the Thorn EMI General Support Contract expired and the maintenance of all instrumentation deemed 'mature' passed to HQ QMG. From December 1992 all instrumentation maintenance work was on contract with a small residual uniformed REME and MOD civilian presence in a support and monitoring function.

17 Port and Maritime Workshop

The unit title of this Workshop in the early Seventies was 17 Field Workshop (Maritime) REME. Based at Marchwood, it also maintained a Detachment Workshop at HM Gunwharf, Portsmouth which was manned mainly by civilian staff, the Officer in Charge being a Technical Grade (HPTO). The detachment was able to provide marine engine support to various range safety craft employed around UK coastal ranges and also the vessels on the dependency of 20 Regiment RCT.

The Marchwood Workshop provided marine engineering support to the vessels of 17 Port and Maritime Regiment RCT and also the cargo-handling equipment of Marchwood Military Port. Support to port and maritime activities in Belize was provided throughout the Eighties and early Nineties. The Workshop was also heavily involved in the support of the CORPORATE and GRANBY Operations, both in the mounting phase, particularly for CORPORATE, and in providing detachments in the Falklands and Saudi Arabia to support port and maritime activities. More details of the tasks and involvement of this Workshop are to be found in Chapters 3, 11 and 12.

CONCLUSION

This chapter has shown that the elements of the Corps based in the UK during the period covered by this volume were involved in the whole spectrum of Corps activities, both in the static chain of the Home Base and in the Field Army. It was a period of great change affecting every element from those responsible for the higher direction at MOD level down through the chain of command to the smallest REME detachment. Throughout the period the aim of the Corps was to provide the best possible equipment support for the Army, and this had to start in the UK. It could not be achieved without the introduction of a more balanced staff for equipment management, streamlining of organizations and higher performance and cost effectiveness, and these were all achieved in the period. Those in the UK were the first to feel the effect of these overall changes, even before the more dramatic implications of the ending of the Cold War. Some changes such as the increased responsibility for equipment management were particularly gratifying to the Corps, whilst others involving the loss of old- established static workshops were a sad reminder of the cost of progress. The REME organization in the UK responded well to these many changes, without faltering in their support. Some of the changes were soon well tested by operational involvement, and at the beginning of the Nineties REME in the UK, with its new responsibilities and organizations, was poised to provide even more effective maintenance support for the Army.

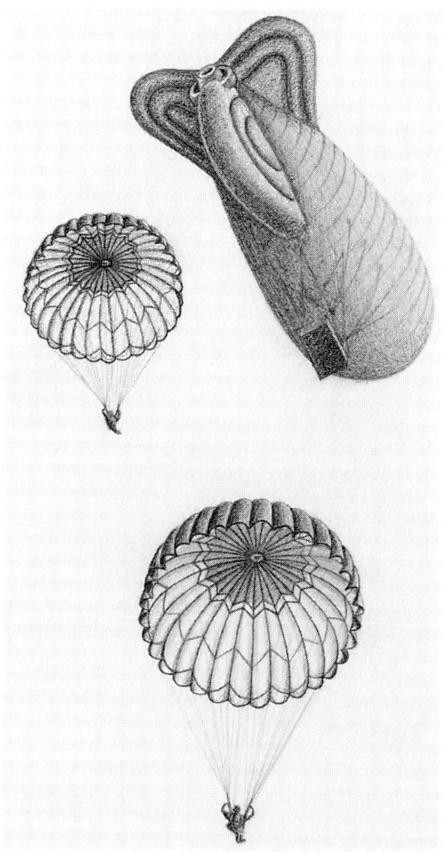

Annex A

ARMY STRATEGIC COMMAND 1968–1972

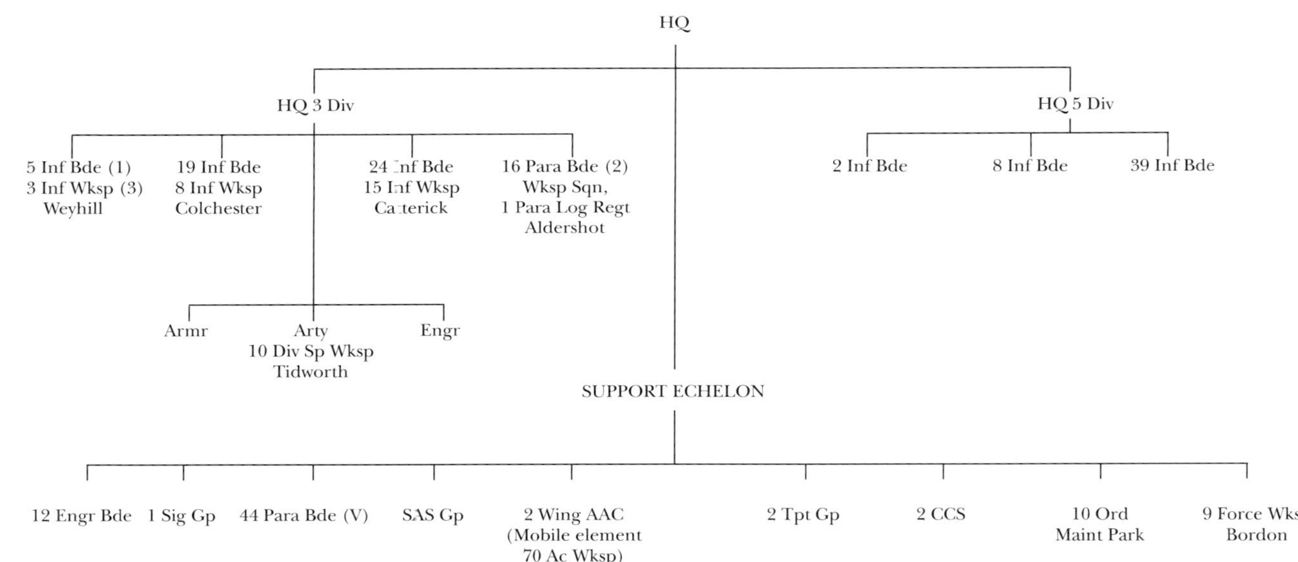

Notes:

(1) By 1970 the infantry brigades of 3rd Division had been redesignated 'airportable brigades'.
(2) By 1970 16 Para Bde was under operational command of HQ Army Strategic Command.
(3) By 1970–71 the infantry workshops had been redesignated field workshops (airportable).

Annex B

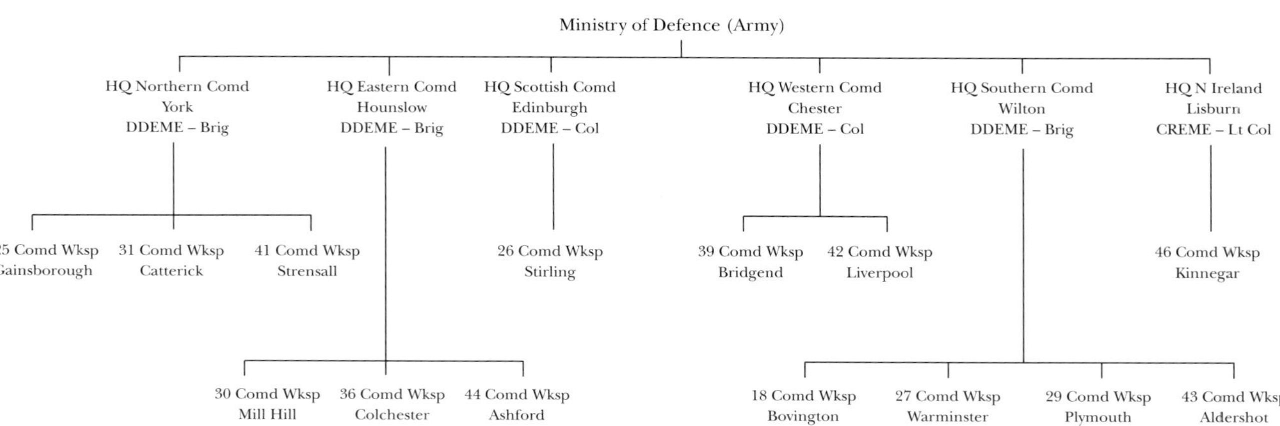

Notes:

(1) Some workshops had detachments — eight in all.
(2) There were also three field repair cells set up by central workshops to support commands.
(3) This organization was the start point for the EME 2 study described on page 37.

Annex C

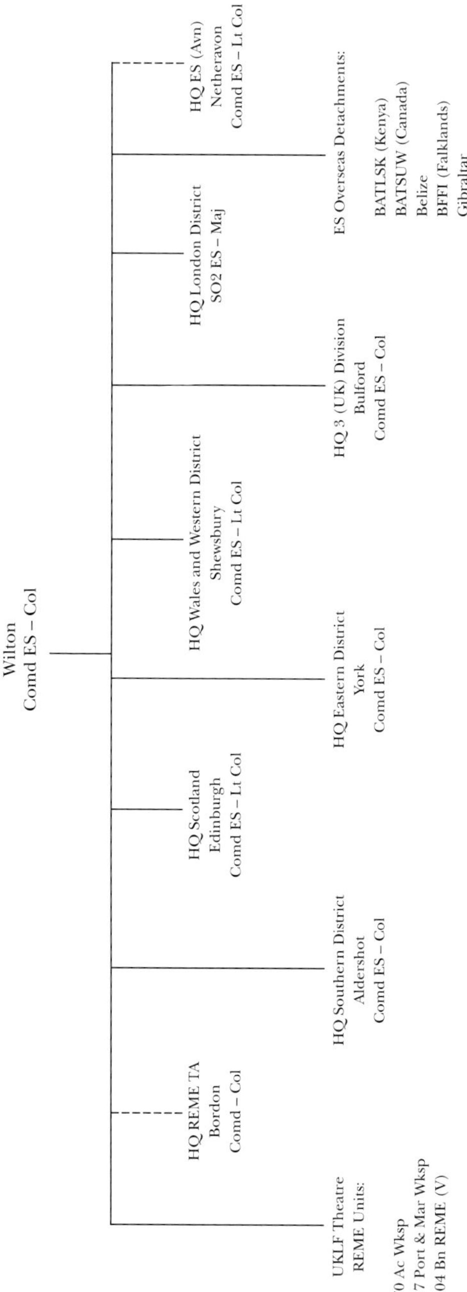
EQUIPMENT SUPPORT ORGANIZATION
UNITED KINGDOM LAND FORCES – APRIL 1992
POST LOGISTIC SUPPORT REVIEW
HQ UKLF
Wilton
Comd ES – Col
UKLF Theatre
REME Units:
70 Ac Wksp
17 Port & Mar Wksp
104 Bn REME (V)
HQ REME TA
Bordon
Comd – Col
HQ Southern District
Aldershot
Comd ES – Col
HQ Scotland
Edinburgh
Comd ES – Lt Col
HQ Eastern District
York
Comd ES – Col
HQ Wales and Western District
Shewsbury
Comd ES – Lt Col
HQ 3 (UK) Division
Bulford
Comd ES – Col
HQ London District
SO2 ES – Maj
ES Overseas Detachments:
BATLSK (Kenya)
BATSUW (Canada)
Belize
BFFI (Falklands)
Gibraltar
HQ ES (Avn)
Netheravon
Comd ES – Lt Col

CHAPTER 8

REME IN THE RESERVE ARMY

Introduction · General Organization and Roles · Servicewomen in the TA · Training – General · Collective Training · REME TA Units · TA in Operation GRANBY · Regimental Matters

INTRODUCTION

The Territorial Army (TA) was established in 1908 to provide volunteers raised locally on a county basis, as a trained reserve for the Regular Army. It was embodied in the Regular Army during both World Wars and was formed again after the Second World War when in 1947 REME TA units became part of the Order of Battle.

In 1967 the Territorial Army and the Army Emergency Reserve were amalgamated to form the Territorial and Army Volunteer Reserve (T&AVR), redesignated TAVR in 1971. This produced a much smaller Reserve Army, but one that was totally integrated within the Order of Battle of the Regular Army. When published in 1969, Volume I of 'Craftsmen of the Army' took the story of REME in the Reserve Army two years into the time following the 1967 reorganization. The picture in 1969 was of a well-motivated Reserve, with high standards and a wide range of strengths.

The role of REME in the Reserve Army from 1967 was the support of

UK-based forces under Army Strategic Command, or of the British Army of the Rhine, until 1972 when United Kingdom Land Forces replaced Strategic Command and the UK geographic commands. Reinforcement of BAOR was to become an ever more important role throughout the Seventies and Eighties in support of our NATO commitment, and in 1979 the TAVR reverted to the title Territorial Army. Many of the same types of REME unit as were in the Regular Army were represented in the Reserve Army, and the TA soldiers provided the same trades and skills within those units, and were trained accordingly.

The T&AVR consisted of two major elements; Independent Units and Sponsored Units:

- Independent Units had their own TA Centres (previously known as Drill Halls), held their own AFG 1098 equipment tables, and trained at weekends and drill nights. The minimum commitment was for a fifteen-day camp and twelve days out-of-camp training each year. These units carried out their own recruiting to their established strength and trained their own soldiers to meet the requirement of their role, recruit, trade and SNCO courses being conducted centrally at Bordon. A number of REME Regular Senior NCO Permanent Staff Instructors (PSIs) and sometimes Regular Officers ensured a standard of training compatible with the Regular Army
- Sponsored Units originated between the wars as a Supplementary Reserve of technical experts both commissioned and non-commissioned. They were reintroduced as the Supplementary Reserve (SR) in 1950 and converted into the Army Emergency Reserve (AER) in 1952. Sponsored Units worked on the assumption that there are many people who are profitably employed in civilian life who have the technical skills which an army would need in war. These units were centrally recruited from their base at Bordon, by a Central Volunteer Headquarters (CVHQ) REME. Only those with a technical skill required by REME, who would be given the requisite military training with a centralized Recruit Course, could be recruited. As the technical skills were already present, the training commitment was for a fifteen-day camp and two weekends each year. This reduced commitment enabled the CVHQ to recruit country-wide, and soldiers travelled to wherever their training was to take place.

There was a continuing desire in all ranks of REME TA to gain as much military training as possible, and to the same high standards as were evident in REME of the Regular Army. The REME Reserves had grown up alongside their Regular counterparts, shared training, and had many experiences in common. Indeed, many Territorials played a part in the early formation of the Corps in 1942. Major General M J H Bruce, one of the founders of the Corps and the first Director of Mechanical Maintenance, was a pre-war Territorial, and many others were drawn in because of the need for maintenance of the new Radar technology: one of these was Major Hexell Lewis, who continued in the TA until retiring as Honorary Colonel for Sponsored Units REME TA.

Further, many members of the SR (and AER members in particular) had served very closely with the Regular Army on various training and operational attachments. They were extremely proud of their ability to mobilize within their ranks, at short notice, a large number of volunteers with civilian technical expertise and the required military training.

Notwithstanding the various changes in the title of the TA, the volunteer soldier has always been characterized by the tremendous enthusiasm he has brought to his soldiering. To retain that loyalty and enthusiasm, those responsible for REME TA have always been conscious of the need to ensure that TA training was not only rewarding but also fun. That theme is well illustrated by what has been written over the years, and how well they have succeeded can be judged from the healthy state of REME TA today.

1971 was the 21st anniversary of the re-formation of the Supplementary Reserve which soon became the AER and eventually the TAVR. Colonel Gordon Higgs, who was in the AER, recalled in an article how in the Fifties the calling up of the 'Z' reserve soldiers of the 1939–45 war for fifteen days' service swelled the numbers of the Supplementary Reserve, and started an esprit de corps built on wartime comradeship which lasted into the Seventies. Many National Service officers and soldiers were 'bitten with the bug' and served with the Volunteers. The change of name to AER and their new role cut the numbers but sharpened their role. Colonel Higgs also wrote:

'We all enjoyed staying up all night on schemes, chasing over the countryside, and even swimming in the sea at first light when doing assault landings and watermanship training. Oh what happy days! In 1971 we have a Reserve Army renamed again – the Territorial Army Volunteer Reserve. It is still enthusiastic and capable of carrying out any emergency. Its old slogan, "We must be prepared to go away tomorrow" is just as relevant today.'

Colonel Hexell Lewis, Honorary Colonel TAVR REME (Sponsored Units) wrote in the 1973 Annual Newsletter:

'Today the TAVR is better trained, more efficient and more effectively equipped than ever was its 1939 predecessor and its morale is high. Yet it is having difficulty in finding and keeping the men it needs. I sometimes wonder whether this is because it has also become too serious in its need to be proficient and has lost the sense of fun which the pre-war TA had. It was this determination to enjoy every

minute spent in the company of their fellow men, to eat and drink and laugh together, to laugh for pure joy or to laugh at their own misfortunes, which characterized the old TA. When we turn our thoughts to the problems of recruiting should we not also think of ways and means whereby we can increase the opportunities for having fun in the TAVR?'

These two themes of recruiting and having fun were emphasized two years later by Colonel Denis Filer, Colonel TAVR, representing both Independent and Sponsored REME units – a total of seventy-seven units with some 4,500 part-time 'professionals'. His final message was: 'Let us try to improve our recruitment, our performance, and our efficiency, and above all let us enjoy and have fun in what we are doing'.

In 1976 Colonel Stuart Blackford in his Christmas message referred to the watershed when war and National Service experience in the Reserve Army had ended and how they had crossed it in the past year. He said that emphasis had been made in the previous three years on the need to enjoy reserve service, and that working hard and playing hard were the two faces of the same coin – that coin was the unit and the two faces were efficiency and high morale.

This chapter describes the organization, roles and training of REME in the Reserve Army from the formation of the T&AVR in 1967, and gives examples of the experiences of some typical units over the years until the beginning of the Nineties.

GENERAL ORGANIZATION AND ROLES

The organization of REME in the TA, which had evolved over the years as defence policy changed, mirrored that of the Regular Army. Armourers and vehicle mechanics were attached to TA infantry battalions, with LADs and regimental workshops supporting armoured reconnaissance, artillery, engineer, signals and transport units at first line. There were second-line field workshops for the BAOR Communications Zone, recovery companies, reclamation platoons, port workshops and NATO workshops, to support various formations which made up the Order of Battle.

In the Seventies there were over fifty LADs, regimental and squadron workshops and more than twenty workshops and recovery companies. Some of the second-line units were Independent, and some were Sponsored by Central Volunteer Headquarters (CVHQ), which was commanded by a Colonel of the Regular Army. The Reserve Army exercised control of professional matters through TAVR lieutenant colonels in Districts known as ADEMEs(V).

By 1984 the roles of the TA overall, which had been refined over many years, were:

Central Volunteer Headquarters REME

- To complete the Army Order of Battle for NATO assigned forces.
- To assist in maintaining the security of the UK Base.
- To provide the framework for any further expansion of the Reserves.

During the Eighties the teeth-arm units of the TA with a NATO or BAOR role were re-armed to Regular Army scales of weapons, greatly increasing the REME support task of repair and maintenance, and affecting organization and training within REME units. Commanders Maintenance in the UK Districts were helped with this addition to their TA support responsibilities by a TA SO1 Maintenance (previously known as ADEME(V)). There was also an SO1(V) Maintenance in 2nd Infantry Division.

In 1982 CVHQ REME was reorganized into HQ REME TA with a Brigadier in command, but by 1988 the appointment reverted to Colonel. Sponsored units in 1982 had an establishment of seventy-three officers and over 1,500 soldiers, with a recruited strength of 85% of this establishment. For REME Independent units at this time there was a total establishment of ninety-five officers and over 2,500 soldiers. The recruited strength was 87% of establishment, which was high by TA standards.

In 1984 REME Regular Army strength was 13,000 and REME TA strength had increased to 5,000 (Independent Units 3,250 and

Sponsored Units 1,750). By 1988 most REME TA units also had at least one WRAC member, when four years earlier there had been none. Most of these were recruited as clerks, cooks or drivers, but vehicle mechanics were also beginning to appear.

Effect of Options for Change

The revised role of the TA in 1991 after the Options for Change studies was:

- To complete the mobilized Army Order of Battle primarily with formed units and sub-units. The priority role was reinforcement of the newly formed ACE Rapid Reaction Corps (ARRC).
- To contribute to the Military Home Defence of the UK Base.
- To provide the basis for expansion to cater for the unexpected.

The REME TA role was to provide:

- Second-line units – in the form of new REME TA battalions.
- Increments to Regular Army Workshops.
- First-line workshops, LADs and attached tradesmen.

In order to keep a coherent command structure across the Districts, it was decided to have three REME battalions for the ARRC and one battalion as UKLF Reserve. With a total strength of 3,000 all ranks, these would reinforce existing Regular workshops and provide first-line support. Their place in the Field Army order of battle may be seen in Annex B to Chapter 13 – REME Regimental Activities. The three REME TA functions remained: repair, recovery and reclamation. The latter involved controlled salvage of usable spares and major assemblies, and not just cannibalization.

SERVICEWOMEN IN REME TA

The role of women in REME is covered in Chapter 13 and the increasing participation of women in engineering has been watched with interest in the TA. Until the early Eighties servicewomen (other than the Army's nursing corps, the QARANC) were restricted to employment with the WRAC in administrative appointments in the base areas. However, in view of the increasing difficulty of attracting suitable male volunteers into the TA, the changing attitudes in civilian life (the equal opportunities initiative) and individual aspirations, all TA units were asked to consider the wider employment of volunteer servicewomen. The result was that TA major units, particularly those with a Home Defence role, were permitted to recruit women. In true volunteer tradition three suitably qualified graduate engineers were attracted into REME TA units on the expectation of being REME and not WRAC officers. During the discussions which preceded the eventual change from WRAC to individual Arms and Services, the individuals themselves were always quite clear on the subject. They had joined REME TA and were proud to act and dress accordingly. By 1990 female officers were an accepted part of the overall TA scene and REME units were beginning to attract and retain suitably qualified and motivated young women into the artisan as well as administrative trades.

The Women's Royal Army Corps was disbanded on 6 April 1992 and all members transferred to the Corps with which they served. This was a milestone for the volunteer servicewoman, since firstly, with very few exceptions, all REME trades (in keeping with developments in the Regular Army) were opened up to servicewomen. Secondly, in that April, with the demise of the WRAC, all volunteer servicewomen serving in REME units rebadged into their parent Corps, though it must be admitted many had already worn REME not WRAC cap badges with the tacit approval of their local commanders. Those women not serving in REME trades, for example pay clerks and cooks, were transferred either to the Adjutant General's Corps which was formed on 6 April 1992 (which included the RAPC and clerks) or to the Royal Logistic Corps in April 1993 (which included the amalgamation of the RCT, RAOC and ACC).

Finally, with the closure of the WRAC centre at Guildford in December 1992 three servicewomen attended the first integrated Recruits Course sponsored by HQ REME TA. All three passed this robust introduction to military life and won the respect and admiration of both the Directing Staff and their male colleagues for their determination and willingness to participate in the full range of activities on equal terms.

TRAINING – GENERAL

Training for most units was generally organized on a three-year cycle of individual, military and functional training, and examples of the form that this training took are given in later paragraphs under Collective Training. Apart from individual training within units, officers attended courses at the REME Officers School or were attached to Regular HQs and units in BAOR or the UK Mobile Force (UKMF), whilst each year about 1,000 REME TAVR soldiers passed through SEME and SEE on trade courses.

National Service ended in 1963, and from the mid-Sixties to the mid-Seventies REME TA changed from a force manned and officered by those who had seen active service, or had knowledge gained in post-Second World War actions, to that of a force composed of a new generation without such experience. Individual experience latterly was

limited to those who had service in the TA or Army Cadet Force, and perhaps a few ex-Regular soldiers. It was particularly important therefore that the Permanent Staff Instructors posted to REME TA units from the Regular Army were very high-grade artificers, as they had to provide the practical experience to help make up, in some degree, for the lack of service experience within units. This was certainly achieved, generally by making early appointments for those with promising careers.

An annual exercise was held at Arborfield for all TA officers and warrant officers, enabling the annual TA Officers' Dinner to be held at West Court and the Warrant Officers' Dinner to be held in the Corps Sergeants' Mess during the period.

COLLECTIVE TRAINING

Examples of collective training in a variety of units are given in the paragraphs that follow. These give an indication of the wide range of training undertaken under a variety of conditions, with some in overseas stations.

215 Port Workshop (V) in the Gulf 1969

Twenty-two members of 215 Port Workshop stood in the cold drizzle outside Swindon railway station early in the morning of 20 April 1969. Their pale faces showed their anxiety as the RAF transport took their personal luggage and tool boxes away, hopefully to reappear in Bahrein. A good lunch at RAF Brize Norton cheered them up and that afternoon they were off in a VC10 arriving at RAF Muharraq, Bahrein, just after midnight. They stepped out of the VC10 into what seemed like an open oven door. They were welcomed by the Garrison Workshop and before long discovered that their personal baggage had arrived, but there were no tool boxes.

After a few hours' sleep most of them flew to Sharjah in an RAF Argosy where they were welcomed by Major Ray Varley, OC 1 Infantry Workshop. He had arranged for part of his light B vehicle shop to be made available to 215 Port Workshop to operate as an independent minor unit with support from 1 Infantry Workshop and its RAOC Stores Section. The work was already there and they started on it the next day at 90°F in the shade with high humidity, the missing tool boxes having arrived by direct flight to Sharjah from the UK.

The Recovery Section was soon backloading vehicles from 1st Battalion, The Cheshire Regiment, urgently required for an exercise, over the ten miles to Dubai port. There they were loaded onto a MEXEFLOTE and prepared for a sea passage to Bahrain. The vehicle repair section under Staff Sergeant Hardy was kept busy with repairs to nine SAS modified Land Rovers also required for an exercise. The Recovery Section under Sergeant Fisher was kept so busy with their backloading that they were forced to sleep under the stars. At the weekend they visited the gold and silver shops in Dubai, saw all the sights and enjoyed the unit's new luxurious open-air swimming pool. They played a football match which they won – with some help from guest players.

The next week started with plenty of vehicle repair work which highlighted the toll the desert took on steering and suspension units. One day they went out for a desert familiarization exercise, consisting of a 100-mile round trip in the Sharjah hinterland. They were equipped with a Land Rover, three 3 ton vehicles and a signals vehicle. Their long-distance drivers were staggered by the condition of the desert tracks and the concentration required, which brought home to all the problems of map-reading and navigation in the desert.

At a social evening which followed the desert exercise ASM Smith was presented with an engraved silver tankard in recognition of his long service with the Reserve Army and 215 Port Workshop. Soon they were on their way back to the cold and damp of Brize Norton. It was on the way home that Sergeant Jones found out that 'stockings footless' had their uses – they fitted a whisky bottle perfectly!

UK – Stanford Training Area

An insight into TAVR training in 1972 was given by Second Lieutenant Chris Rogers REME (V), writing in the 1972 TAVR REME Annual Newsletter. He related how he arrived one Saturday at West Tofts Camp, Stanford, to meet a bunch of strangers halfway through their two weeks' training. Four of the REME units involved in training there were 209 RCZ Workshop (V), 29 Engineer Brigade Workshop (V), 17 Port Regiment RCT Workshop (V) and his own unit, 271 Telecommunications Workshop (V), which were divided into three groups for training – 17 Port and 271 Telecommunications Workshops having combined to form one group. Early on Monday morning they moved off on Exercise Greensward V. The three groups were to be hostile to each other and to move as workshops from location to location rather like musical chairs. Patrols were sent out to reconnoitre, infiltrate and ambush each other's positions. What made the exercise more confusing was that the training area at that time of year was very crowded, so there was always the chance of coming accidentally across an infantry regiment who did not seem to treat their prisoners at all well. Some REME senior ranks soon suffered! The whole exercise was conducted without radios, which cannot have helped to reduce the confusion; it ended a day early because of a railway strike which 'gave me time to catch up on some much-needed sleep and press my trousers before going off to Arborfield'.

There he attended the two weeks' Newly Commissioned Officers Course where he described the Stanford training as 'good fun'. He went on to say, 'One does need a peculiar sense of fun to appreciate wandering around in the pouring rain at four in the morning wearing a respirator. Everybody else knew what to do and things usually went as planned. The senior ranks were very helpful and were always willing to assist. The course at Arborfield was very good. The instructors were all polished and gave good lectures and training sessions.' Twenty years later Major Chris Rogers was still serving as OC 160 Transport Regiment Workshop (V).

BAOR

Reserve Army units had been going to BAOR for many years to practise their role of support to the British forces in Germany. In 1977–78, for example, it was planned that seven Sponsored REME units would train in BAOR. One of these was 201 Field Workshop (Force Troops) (V) which went to Detmold for two weeks in June 1977 for functional training.

Exercise CRUSADER 80

This exercise in the autumn of 1980 was said at the time to be the biggest and most realistic to be launched by the British Army since the formation of NATO. It had three parts: SQUARE LEG, which was to practise the home defence in Britain and the movement of 10,000 Regular and 20,000 TA reinforcements to BAOR; JOG TROT, which was a rehearsal of the setting-up of the lines of communication across north-west Europe; and SPEARPOINT, which was committing the reinforcements as part of 1st British Corps against a massive attack. The whole exercise involved more than 63,000 British troops with the TA making up one-third of the BAOR war establishment. The experiences of the REME TA units taking part were mixed. For some there was a heavy workload, which kept them fully occupied, whilst for others work at their trades was limited. For all, however, the experience of moving to BAOR and becoming part of, and working within, the overall force under simulated operational conditions, was invaluable.

Among those units involved:

- 201 RCZ Workshop (V) was given the task of inspecting over 800 vehicles at Forward Vehicle Depot Recklinghausen, and returned to the Depot after Exercise CRUSADER 80. Two inspection teams, each of thirteen men, completed their annual camp by working twenty-four hours a day on eight-hour shifts, employed mainly on Bedford RL and Land Rover vehicles, until the task was finished.

- 30 Engineer Group Workshop (V) took part in Exercise SPEARPOINT, 13–28 September, after arriving at Sennelager. Their exercise was memorable for the amount of time spent in full NBC kit. No 2 Section went off to join 125 Field Support Squadron RE where they enjoyed a mixture of REME work and night attacks on their site.

- 216 Port Workshop (V) stayed in UK and went to Colchester to serve convoys passing through en route to BAOR: only one convoy vehicle failed to cross the Channel. The workshop also manned a recovery post at the port of Harwich.

- 227 Reclamation Platoon (V) set off for Shorncliffe and then boarded a Sealink ferry to the continent. Eventually they set up in their Exercise SPEARPOINT location outside a small factory where they enjoyed plenty of work, standing-to, sleepless nights and air and ground attacks.

- 260 Ambulance Workshop (V) met at Grantham, moved to Colchester and Harwich and landed at Zeebrugge. From there they drove to Munster where they divided into two troops to manage the

211 RCZ Workshop REME (V) Annual Camp, 1988

twenty-four-hour workload. They had enough work to do, made two moves and became used to wearing their NBC suits for days on end. One village made them particularly welcome, even making breakfast for the recovery crews one morning. They returned on the ferry from Zeebrugge to Immingham.

- 211 RCZ Workshop (V) collected their kit from Willich and deployed to a staging area at Leuth with detachments on autobahns and at barracks. The recovery mechanics had 'luxurious' Scammell Crusaders, but there was little work for them due to the convoys assembling and departing with such efficiency, and the reliability of their vehicles.

EXERCISE KEYSTONE 82

Pressures on the Armed Services in the early Eighties led to the decision to withdraw one of the four divisions in BAOR back to the UK and to increase the proportion of TA units in that division. Before activating the plan, it was decided to try out the concept known as GDP 83, and in the Autumn of 1982 Exercise KEYSTONE was mounted. A large number of TA units were earmarked to take part and simulate parts of a new, largely Territorial, Division. The new 2nd Infantry Division would mobilize in the UK, move to the RCZ for Annual Camp in BAOR, exercise, and then return to UK. It was realized at the start that a far greater degree of integration would be required between units playing unfamiliar roles, and between Territorials and Regulars at all levels, and allowance was made for the considerable diversity of planning required.

REME TA was well represented, with both 133 Corps Troops Workshop and 124 Recovery Company playing active parts. Ninety Specialist soldiers from 201 RCZ Workshop (V) joined 15 Field Workshop at Munster, and two MRGs were formed, 15A being nearly all

Regular and 15B being mostly TA. The usual sharing of skills between Regular and Territorial was apparent to all concerned and both MRGs were soon working at full efficiency. The support system was thoroughly tested and major assemblies were flown in from UK overnight. The arrival at dawn over Herford of much-needed gearboxes underslung from a helicopter was a sight never to be forgotten! In the event KEYSTONE 82 was extremely successful, valuable lessons were learned and 2nd Infantry Division became largely TA-manned, with its headquarters at York.

The success of this exercise led to a reorganization of REME TA to meet the new demand, with a TA Commander Maintenance for 2nd Division, a strong Specialist increment for 15 Field Workshop, and first-line REME tradesmen in all units. It also brought a feeling of 'being wanted' and a genuine desire to match Regular standards at all levels.

Exercise LIONHEART

201 RCZ Workshop (V), nearly 300 strong, was the biggest REME workshop in the TA. It offered all ranks some experience of regimental life, as its size justified a lieutenant colonel in command and an RSM. It provided good experience for junior officers, a challenge to its commanding officer and a problem to the planners: should it be employed on mobilization as one unit or split into smaller repair units? In 1984 it took part in Exercise LIONHEART which was said to be the biggest exercise of its kind since 1945, even bigger than CRUSADER 80. The road and ferry journey from Bordon to West Germany was a fight against fatigue, sea sickness and boredom, added to the demand of driving on the right. Nevertheless, the Workshop had successfully mobilized at Bordon and thirty hours later was concentrated in its allotted area in Germany. It had been an excellent training experience.

201 RCZ Workshop REME (V) crossing the Rhine

227 Reclamation Platoon (V) also took part in Exercise LIONHEART attached to 6 Armoured Workshop in the field at Bodenwerder, on the River Weser. They drove from Bordon to Dover early one Sunday morning and sailed on the ferry to Zeebrugge. From there they drove in convoy through the night across Belgium to the Rhine and on to Sennelager, arriving early on Tuesday morning. Their first task involved work on two AEC vehicles – one good vehicle with a ruined engine and

one ruined vehicle with a good engine. Many other jobs on Land Rovers and salvage jobs in a vehicle park followed, including an engine removal under NBC conditions.

In 1988, as a result of experience gained on the BAOR exercises, the BAOR RCZ units were reorganized to provide two new units, 215 Recovery Company (V) and 224 Reclamation Platoon (V).

Overseas Attachments

In 1989–90 twenty-two volunteers from the Specialist Units REME TA took part in longer than normal overseas attachments to Regular Army units, as far away as Cyprus and the Falkland Islands. Between March 1988 and February 1990 volunteers served in the Falkland Islands for four-week periods with the Falkland Islands Workshop, RAF Mount Pleasant, where they helped to reduce a backlog of B vehicle work. Most volunteers had trips in RAF helicopters and Hercules aircraft and on RN patrol boats too. Seven volunteers served for up to five weeks in Cyprus, including five from 3 Field Workshop TA Increment; they took part in Exercise LION SUN in February and March 1990. In August five volunteers from an LAD went to 16 Belize Field Workshop for two weeks (in addition to their annual camp) where they worked at their trades helping the unit prepare for Periodic REME Examination. The social life in their spare time was reported to be very good, and included visiting the cays, small islands off the coast with white sand and palm trees, and the biggest reef in the world except for Australia's Great Barrier Reef.

Adventurous Training

A frequent theme in REME TA Training Directives, in letters between HQs and units and in memoirs of TA service, was the necessity to make the best use of the very limited time available for training and the need to make training enjoyable and interesting for the Volunteers. In addition to military and trade training, orienteering and adventurous training became popular and were encouraged – not only as part of the search for good officers and NCOs but as a method of developing their leadership capabilities.

Exercise Welsh Rocks (how to put spark into young TAVR REME officers) will always remind those who took part of Colonel Dennis Franks – in the Seventies their Commander at Bordon. 'Right! You've got fourteen days with me on this exercise and even if you don't enjoy it you will at least remember it.' How right he was! Away they went, collected their bicycles and tents and set up their camp on Broxhead Common ready for parade at 1600 hours for sword drill. After tea there were lecturettes – five minutes from each officer on 'My Life History'.

Next day (Sunday) at 0630 hours twelve young officers paraded for PT, a run and a swim. They cycled to breakfast, cycled to the ranges, fired weapons all morning, stripped and cleaned their weapons all afternoon and then they drilled again. After tea there were swimming tests and drill, and in the evening more lecturettes. They soon knew each others' life stories and all about their civilian jobs.

On Monday 'Sir' was there again with his PT after which he said that they would cycle to Marchwood on their Sandhurst bone-crusher cycles. They undertook map-reading and initiative tests on their forty-five mile ride. They got there just in time for supper and were then turned out for a relaxing game of croquet. They were up at dawn for PT again and then to Stokes Bay for sailing and canoeing. 'Sir takes fiendish delight in getting us to capsize in our canoes.' After tea there was the 17 Port Regiment assault course, a real 'gut-shatterer' and ten-minute lecturettes after supper – they could choose their own subject. 'Sir said some of us lacked spark.'

Next day they were blindfolded and dropped in pairs in the New Forest and told to map-read a course round ten map references back to Marchwood – the shortest route was twenty miles. The following day they cycled to Calshot for dry skiing, rock climbing, track cycling and archery – the track cycling included a 'wall of death' at the end of which they had to pedal hard to stay on the wall. Next day they cycled to board an RCT boat to the Isle of Wight to plan an attack on Carisbrooke Castle using 13th century weapons, seize an airport and blow up a TV station on Chillingford Down!

On the Saturday they left their bikes behind them (gladly) and went by train to Capel Curig Camp in Snowdonia in time for a recovery exercise on Sunday with 119 Recovery Company (V) near Prestatyn – anchor pins galore! The next two days were spent either canoeing with 'Sir' to an island off the Lleyn Peninsula or on rock-climbing and hill-walking in Snowdonia. Then there was a day to help the National Trust chain-ganging 180 buckets of stone conglomerate up a mountainside to form a path – by the end of that day they claimed their arms were as long as an orang-utan's!

On Thursday and Friday they went on the expeditions again with the parties switched round. The rough sea this time gave the canoeists something to remember while the rock climbers 'enjoyed' the sleet and the rain in the mountains. So ended fourteen days of hard mental and physical graft doing many things they had never done before. 'I reckon Sir had a real ball with we young lads and I reckon he knows us all a hell of a lot better!' wrote one who claimed 'we had just got that wee bit extra spark'.

Adventurous Training approved activities were free fall parachuting, sub-aqua diving, gliding, off-shore sailing and mountain activities (including canoeing and skiing). An outstanding example of such an activity resulted in Captain Pat Gunson REME (V) receiving the Rory Cape Award for his performance on the 1976 Army Mountaineering

Expedition to Mount Everest. He played a leading part in the preparation for the expedition and was prominent in raising funds. He was a member of the advance party in Nepal, setting up the Base Camp at 17,800 feet before taking part in the hazardous task of finding and perfecting a safe way through the Khumbu ice-fall. He was chosen as a member of the second Summit team.

While the first team pair were on their way to the summit Pat Gunson and his partner Lieutenant John P Scott, Parachute Regiment, climbed to 27,600 feet (Camp 6). That night the first team failed to return. The next morning Pat Gunson and John Scott set out from Camp 6 and two hours later they found the two members of the first team preparing to leave their bivouac on the South-East Ridge at 28,000 feet. Both were severely frost bitten and very weak. Gunson and his partner gave up their own summit attempt to support the other two men down to Camp 5 and safety.

Annual Competitions

Before the reorganization of the Reserve Army in 1966–67 the old 56th (London) Division and 54th (East Anglian) Division had some very good competitions for their REME TA units and attached tradesmen, particularly Exercises Snatch Block, Holdfast and Fine Finish. In the case of 56th (London) Division REME there was an association with the Worshipful Company of Turners through Colonel Randal Steward TD who was a member of the Court and Honorary Colonel of 23rd (Southern) Corps REME TA. This association and competition involvement, however, lapsed when the two divisions were amalgamated, but was reinstated in the early Sixties. The competitions were an exercise in repair and manufacture, which subsequently became a test of a forward repair team and tactical recovery, with a skill at arms finale which sorted out those who knew how to handle their kit quickly when under pressure. In the early days some workshops worked at night using machinery lorry lights as if they were on a peacetime construction site rather than in a wartime tactical setting. Eventually, though, they reached such a standard of concealment that their own CREME could scarcely find them when working at night.

Exercise Southern Craftsman

The revival of a link with the Turners Company resulted in the first competition called Southern Craftsman, held at Bordon in 1970. The Master attended and presented the Turners Company Shield to 133 Infantry Workshop (Airportable) (V). The importance of the association with the livery company was that it brought together the Independent units of the whole of Southern Command to see how well they could perform and to learn from each other. The overall aim was to raise the efficiency of units so that at the end of Annual Camp they would be fit for their wartime role.

Exercise Southern Craftsman 71st (Yeomanry) Signal Regiment LAD REME (V)

A notable winner over the years was 133 Infantry Workshop (V), which had been at Gillingham in Kent in the Fifties and in 1967 had become 133 Infantry Workshop (Airportable) (V) (its soldiers belonging to the Special Army Volunteer Reserve, receiving higher bounties). The Workshop supported a UK peacekeeping force of six battalions with six identical sections. In 1969 its role was transferred to the Regular Army, but it remained airportable until it became 133 Field Workshop (Corps Troops) (V) in the early Seventies. In 1967 it had soldiers from as far afield as Coventry, Liverpool and Maidstone. For several years up to the start of the Nineties the Workshop was the outright winner of Southern Craftsman, although always closely challenged.

The exercise was expanded in 1984 to include assessments for military and trade skills. The Turners Company prize was still presented personally by the Master who in 1983 was Major General Sir Leslie Tyler and in 1984, and again in 1988, was Major General Sir Leonard Atkinson – both former Directors of the Corps.

The 1992 Exercise Southern Craftsman was sponsored by Commander Equipment Support Southern District, Colonel Rob Lucas, for Independent REME TA units in South East, London and Eastern Districts. REME TA tradesmen attached to other units such as infantry battalions were encouraged to take part and so was one Specialist team. 1992 was the final year for 118 Recovery Company (V) taking part in this exercise, as in 1993 REME units in Eastern District would instead take part in the Warcop Trophy. The aim of the Exercise in 1992 was to test the standards of Independent TA units in repair, recovery, manufacture, military skills and fitness. There was a limit of two senior ranks in each team. The exercise began at Longmoor Training Camp at 0700 hours Saturday 25 April when the competitors faced repair tasks, manufacturing tasks and first aid tests; they were also assessed for deployment, defence and administration in the field and tested for NBC and recovery. On the Sunday eight of the team had to be ready by 0700 hours to start the five-mile march and falling-plate shooting phases, leaving the remaining two members to guard their vehicles. Each team of eight had thirty plates to knock down, each man having ten rounds to fire.

There were ten trophies to be won and eighteen teams took part, including 9 Field Workshop (V), 133 Corps Troops Workshop (V), Cambridge, London and Oxford University OTCs, 118 Recovery Company (V) and several LADs and fitter sections. There was a regimental dinner on the Saturday evening and the prize-giving on Sunday morning was timed to allow those taking part to get to the Albert Hall in time for the Corps 50th anniversary Band Concert. The overall winner which received the Turners Company Shield was 9 Field Workshop (V), later to become 128 Reclamation Company (V).

Recovery on the Warcop Trophy 1988

Warcop Trophy

A similar type of competition was the Warcop Trophy which was the brainchild of Brigadier Meyrick Neilson, DDEME Northern Command at York in the Sixties. Taking its name from Warcop Camp training area, it was competed for by all the REME TA workshops in 49 and 50 Divisions and by the Corps and Army Troops TA in Northern Command.

1974 saw nineteen teams each of eleven men arrive at Bellerby Camp on the Catterick Training Area in mid-October, from REME TAVR units in North East and Eastern Districts. Under the eyes of Colonel Alan Cradduck, CREME of the two districts, they were prepared to shoot, run, drive, get wet and generally show that their team was the best. After a documentation inspection of their vehicles and equipment to find out who looked after their equipment best and four tick-test theory papers they were off to the deployment area. Soon they were sending their 4 tonners to driving tests, recovery vehicles to recovery tasks and Land Rovers all over the training area.

Those left in their deployment areas had to undertake two rather difficult manufacturing tasks as well as the usual domestic tasks such as cooking.

After dark there was briefing and inspection for the night-march teams, who enjoyed the benefits of the moonlight and full tool boxes as they faced the surprises provided by the DS on the dark training area. The check points were thick with visiting dignitaries, commanding officers, DS and others who certainly enjoyed the night march – perhaps more so than the competitors.

On the Sunday morning the recovery crews started their tasks at 0630 hours, thus waking up everyone else, including the shooting teams who were on the range at 0800 hours. The 4 tonners and motorcycles went off to Gandale for their cross-country driving. It became increasingly clear that the overall results would depend on the driving. The Queen's Own Yeomanry LAD (V) and 219 Squadron RCT Workshop (V) were the leading contestants. The results came in only ten minutes before the prize-giving which kept up the suspense to the end. The Queen's Own Yeomanry LAD was narrowly beaten by 219 Squadron RCT Workshop which won the Warcop Trophy and Shield. It was a very good effort by QOY LAD, especially as it was only formed in 1971, had no team in 1972, came bottom in 1973 and now was second overall of nineteen teams in 1974, winning the Tactics and First Aid Cups. Much of the competition depended on Lieutenant Colonel Alan Wilkinson ADEME (V), and most of the administration was the job of 124 Recovery Company (V) which had 400 Sunday dinners to cook.

The trophy was affected by a number of changes in the geographical boundaries of the districts over the years. Then in 1979 the competition was enlarged to include Regular REME units in accordance with the 'One Army Concept'; after the first trial year most of the trophies were won, not surprisingly, by the Regulars. In 1988 the competition rules were changed so that although the Regular and TA teams competed together, only the TA units were eligible to win the individual stand trophies and the Warcop Trophy itself. The Regular units competed for the National Breakdown Foden Recovery Trophy.

Exercise Scottish Bluebell

Another competition, Scottish Bluebell, was started in 1975 and was usually held at Stirling Training Camp (familiarly known as Drip Camp). This was CREME Scotland's annual test of military and engineering skills for his TA and Regular units. Up to eighteen teams competed, including the university teams from Scotland and Northern Ireland.

Exercise Western Approaches

Exercise Western Approaches, the Wales and Western competition, attracted nineteen teams for the 1992 exercise held in May at Nesscliff Training Camp and Swynnerton Training Area, from a Friday evening to midday Sunday; the teams included the OTCs of Birmingham University and the University of Wales, 119 Recovery Company (V), 126

Reclamation Company (V) and several regimental workshops, LADs and squadron fitter sections. The exercise, which was sponsored by Lieutenant Colonel Hamish Harvey, Commander Equipment Support Wales and Western District, was to be the last occasion on which South West District units could take part, for in 1993 they would be eligible for the Southern Craftsman competition. The aim of the exercise was to test REME TA units in military and trade skills. Each team consisted of an officer or warrant officer as team leader and eleven men.

The exercise started at Nesscliff Training Camp with a test of dress, vehicle documentation and an orders group. This was followed by a night convoy drive to Swynnerton Training Camp, where they were required to clear mines and booby traps, treat casualties and recover a vehicle. There then followed map-reading, NBC tests and an urban patrol. After a test of communications ability they had to repair a chainsaw and a Land Rover. Stamina and agility were tested by carrying their own rifles over the assault course, having stripped a replica 25 pounder gun which had to be taken with the team and assembled again after the course. The shooting test was on a 30 metre range in an ambush situation.

Exercise Western Approaches 1986
157 Transport Regiment Workshop REME (V)

There followed a military assessment of the teams' tactical locations with special emphasis on concealment and defence. On the Saturday two members of each team had nearly twelve hours in which to show their team's ability to innovate, when they designed and manufactured an 'unusual item'. The teams' stamina was further tested by a competitive stretcher race, followed on Sunday morning by an orienteering test of their initiative and map-reading skills.

The prize for the overall winning team was the Western Approaches Trophy and there were nine other trophies for the various event winners.

The winner in 1992 was The Royal Monmouthshire RE (Militia) Workshop (V). On the Saturday night there was a 'smoker' to celebrate the Corps' 50th anniversary, each team putting on a short act.

Nijmegen Marches

Over the years REME TA took an active part in the Nijmegen Marches. These marches started in 1909 and took place every year except in wartime. By 1969 there were 17,000 marchers with at least 7,000 military from various NATO countries. The marches were spread over a four-day period and covered a hundred miles. One record shows that the T&AVR team in 1969 included Lieutenant D Tinkler REME (V), 204 Engineer Support Workshop (V) and fifteen T&AVR REME soldiers, who took part weighed down with packs and weapons. Despite the many miles marched in training, blisters grew from small to large and painful. On the final day after passing the last checkpoint all the British teams joined up with the Pipe Band of the Gordon Highlanders and marched into Nijmegen to be greeted by 100,000 spectators. Lieutenant Tinkler, WO2 V S R Hartley, Sgt A E B Hewitt and several members of the team went back in 1970, and after completing the march won a handsome team medal. Many other REME units took part over the years, raising considerable sums for charity.

REME TERRITORIAL ARMY UNITS

Introduction

REME TA units have histories and roles every bit as diverse as their Regular Army counterparts. Some can trace their history back to the predecessors of the Corps and have strong allegiances to towns or counties where they have existed with various titles and roles for many years. All have the same strong bond of belonging to the Corps and pride in the contribution that they make to the Army as a whole.

Understandably, the effectiveness of their voluntary service is achieved with some differences in motivation and attitude to those found in the Regular Army. Many of these traits have served to enhance the enthusiasm and skills which individuals have brought into the Corps. In the paragraphs that follow examples of the wide-ranging attributes of differing units are given in a selection of unit activities which typify the role and aspirations of all those in REME TA. To chronicle the history and activities of all REME TA units would require a volume in itself. The following paragraphs are therefore no more than an illustration of the diversity of those units.

133 Corps Troops Workshop REME (V) recovering an Argosy aircraft with a Foden. Sergeant Homewood (left) and Staff Sergeant Harris

133 Corps Troops Workshop (V)

This workshop traces its history back to 1942 when 133 Infantry Brigade Workshop served in the Middle East with the Eighth Army, supporting 133 (Kent) Infantry Brigade; it was disbanded at the end of the war. The unit was reformed in Guildford in 1947 as 133 Infantry Brigade Workshop TA under command of CREME 44th (HC) Infantry Division TA, and it stayed there until it moved to Gillingham in 1951 when it became 133 (Kent and Sussex) Infantry Workshop TA.

In 1958 'Sussex' was dropped from its title and three years later it was amalgamated with 458 Light Anti-Aircraft Workshop (V). In 1967 it was redesignated 133 Infantry Workshop (Airportable) (V) with a parachute-trained platoon in Coventry and a headquarters in Maidstone. In 1973 its name changed to 133 Corps Troops Workshop (V). Seven years later its Coventry platoon was reformed as an independent reclamation platoon and a replacement platoon was raised at Deal. After a further seven years WRAC were recruited for the first time into certain dual-role posts. By 1989, when Major Bryan Vousden was OC, the HQ, 1 and 3 Platoons and the RAOC Stores Platoon were at Boxley Road, Maidstone and 2 Platoon was at Deal. The workshop then had a BAOR role and took part in Exercises CRUSADER 80, LIONHEART 84, KEYSTONE 87 and FULL TIDE 90. They also won the Turners Shield and Exercise Southern Craftsman.

In April 1992 the unit moved to its new TA Centre in Rowcroft Barracks, Ashford, which was opened by Major General James Johnston (late REME), the Director General Army Manning and Recruiting, and the Deal detachment closed. The unit was to become part of the new 103 Battalion REME (V), providing repair support to TA units in 3rd (UK) Division as part of the ARRC.

8 Army Recovery Company (V)

8 Army Recovery Company had its headquarters in Carlisle with sections in Perth, Workington, Gateshead, South Yorkshire, Scunthorpe, Grantham and Parkstone near Bournemouth. It provided a good example of the capabilities of the early post-war TA units, in an unusual recovery operation. The four South Yorkshire sections were commanded by Captains Bell and Walker, and the three Scunthorpe sections by Captains Hinchcliffe and Holmes; all seven sections were administered by Captain G E Mayers based at the TA Centre Wath-on-Dearne. Every Friday he visited his parish to pay his permanent staff and on this particular occasion in September 1953 he arrived at Scunthorpe the day after an accident at the Scunthorpe steelworks.

He was taken to see the accident site at which he saw an excellent opportunity to practice 'real live' recovery. Four slag ladles, each containing twenty tons of molten slag, had run off the end of the line at the top of the slag bank dragging their saddle-tank locomotive with them; fortunately the driver and his shunter escaped from the locomotive just in time. The wreckage was down the bank about 150 yards from the Scunthorpe – Grimsby road. Captain Hinchcliffe, who was an electrical engineer at the steel works, realized that the accident was an acute embarrassment to the works. The biggest mobile crane at the works was not able to lift the slag ladles even when empty and the nearest suitable crane belonged to British Rail at Doncaster. Its use would require a mile of rail track to be built round the base of the slag bank to get it to the site. An official request for help was soon made to the TA, and the sections which were due to exercise at 2 Command Workshop at Gainsborough that weekend were diverted to the TA Centre at Scunthorpe, complete with rations and blankets from that Workshop. The rations went to the steelworks canteen which provided three hot meals a day.

The steelworks started work on a rail track to receive the recovered equipment, attached stays to the locomotive's buffer plates so that tackles could be attached and built a temporary bridge over a large water main to give access to the site. The South Yorkshire and Scunthorpe sections had one Scammell 6 × 6 heavy recovery vehicle, two Diamond Ts and one 10 ton Albion gun tractor. With their assistance over the first weekend two ladle cars and one ladle were recovered after breaking up the slag, in which the ladles and locomotive were partly immersed, with crowbars and picks – it was like solidified lava. By the Tuesday night the permanent staff, helped by TA volunteers, recovered the remaining two cars and three ladles. The rest of the week was spent planning the recovery of the locomotive which was on its side halfway down the bank.

On the Friday the TA returned with one Class VI Cromwell, two D8 tractors, two 10 ton Albion gun tractors, five Diamond Ts and three

Scammell 6 × 6 heavy recovery vehicles. Captain Mayers briefed his men and on Saturday the vehicles and tackles were put in position. The over-riding requirement was that the locomotive, on a fifty-degree slope, should not be damaged – one band of men, coal miners, spent most of Saturday afternoon driving in anchor spikes. The two D8s were placed side by side on top of the bank with a tackle attached to the locomotive's rear buffer plate to prevent it sliding further down the slope; the steel company made special track anchors for the D8s which in turn were anchored to the two Albion gun tractors which had been ballasted to 18 tons and anchored to steel rails driven into the top of the slag bank. Two of the Scammells on top of the bank were to pull the locomotive onto its wheels with tackles attached to a special frame fixed to it; they were anchored to the Class VI Cromwell. Two Diamond Ts, anchored to another Diamond T, had check tackles attached also to the special frame. Early on the Sunday morning, each group of vehicles was under command of a TA officer with a PSI, all under the overall control of Captain Mayers. The whole layout was checked, and the slack taken up, and after a few problems had been overcome the locomotive was safely on its rails by 1400 hours. The triumphant gang had a late lunch in the works canteen with beer supplied by the traffic department manager – now the happiest man in Scunthorpe.

In those days TA fuel was still rationed, and when it was realized that the units involved had used nearly nine months' ration on two weekend exercises the fat was in the fire. The temperature was raised further when an MP asked a question in the House of Commons about work alleged to have been performed for private interests by troops under training. To everyone's eventual great relief the Minister disposed of it all in one sentence: 'The Army always keeps an eye open for the difficult jobs which can be tackled by military equipment and which are unlikely to have an overwhelming appeal to the civilian contractor.' The full story was published in the REME Magazine of June 1955. Two years later Captain Mayers was awarded the MBE for his service whilst with the TA.

Northern Ireland

Until 1967 there was a major REME TA unit in Northern Ireland – 107 (Ulster) Infantry Workshop REME (TA) which was raised in 1947. Captain Sam Lecky was its Regular Army Adjutant at one time. He later became a Major General and Honorary Colonel of Queen's University OTC, which had a REME section.

After 1967 REME TA remained active, keen and well recruited in Northern Ireland with LADs and unit workshops attached to The Royal Yeomanry (North Irish Horse) (V), 74 (Antrim Artillery) Engineer Regiment (V), 40th (Ulster) Signal Regiment (V) and 152 (Ulster) Ambulance Regiment RCT (V).

118 Recovery Company (V)

118 Army Recovery Company (V) was formed as part of the 1967 reorganization. It took over the role of recovery from 8 Army Recovery Company, based at Mexborough, Yorkshire. The founder members of the Company came from 148 Infantry Workshop (V) at Derby, 104 Medium Workshop (Cambridge), 566 and 595 Squadrons RCT (Northampton and Leicester) (V), together with men from Royal Engineers and attached tradesmen from disbanded infantry and yeomanry units.

The first officer commanding was Major Keith Chell, reverting to his origins as a REME officer on transfer from 595 Squadron RCT. He was followed by Major Ricky Gill from 566 Squadron who later became Honorary Colonel REME (V) East and then South, and Major Godfrey Linnett from 595 Squadron who became Colonel REME TA in 1983 and later the Deputy Commander of 2 Infantry Brigade. Major Tony Bethell, who then succeeded in command, came from the disbanded 148 Infantry Workshop (V). The Company Headquarters and two platoons were at Northampton, two platoons at Corby and one at Leicester. In 1977 the title of the unit changed to 118 Recovery Company RCZ and its role became the provision of second-line recovery support in the Rear Combat Zone and clearance of the MSRs in the NATO role; a year later RCZ was removed from its title. In 1992 it lost its independent status and became part of 102 Battalion REME (V).

Over the years its training followed the normal REME TA pattern for its role. It was also able to provide recovery aid to the civil police and help to charitable organizations, and took part in displays, fetes and carnivals. As a result of its long connection and service to the community, the Freedom of the Borough of Northampton was granted to the Company in 1983.

124 Recovery Company (Tyne Electrical Engineers) (V)

The unit traces its history back to a volunteer Royal Engineers unit formed in Jarrow on the River Tyne in 1884. Lieutenant Colonel Charles Mark Palmer, a leading North-East industrialist, was given permission to form a volunteer submarine mining company for the defence of the Tyne with sea mines remotely detonated by shore patrols. In 1895 they were the first to use an electric searchlight, powered by their steam generator set, to illuminate a defence sea minefield. In 1907 with the Haldane Reforms, which included the formation of the Territorial Army, the Royal Navy took over sea mining and the unit was renamed The Tyne Division, The Royal Engineers (V) Electrical Engineers, their role being to operate searchlights. In the 1914–18 war their searchlights were adapted to the anti-aircraft role and they saw service in many places. By 1939 they had expanded into two distinct units – a Sapper Company and a Searchlight Battalion RE. 37 Searchlight Regiment went to France with the British Expeditionary Force in 1939 and after Dunkirk became part of Anti-Aircraft Command for the rest of the 1939–45 war. The CO, Lieutenant Colonel E J Parnall, joined the Tynes in 1917; he was a Sapper, then a Gunner and in 1942 a founder officer in REME.

After the Second World War the Tyne Electrical Engineers were reformed; 86 (Field) AGRA Workshop REME (TA) emerged principally due to Lieutenant Colonel F L Turnbull, a pre-war Sapper Tyne officer, rebadged RAOC in 1939 and REME in 1942. This was the first REME unit among the Tynes.

The TA suffered similar turbulence to that of the Regular Army throughout the Fifties and Sixties until the formation of the Territorial and Army Volunteer Reserve in 1967. Out of five units in the north there emerged, on 1 April 1967, 124 Recovery Company (TEE) REME (V). The new unit had its HQ and two platoons in Newton Aycliffe and two platoons in Debdon Gardens, Newcastle. The first OC was Major Mike Coleman, and Second Lieutenant Trevor Harris (who came with Major Coleman) later commanded the unit. In August 1970 the Officer Commanding was upgraded to the rank of lieutenant colonel. Captain Bill Ellington who had joined from 34th (Northern) Signal Regiment LAD (V) as 2IC in November 1969, taken over as OC and promoted to Major in April 1970, became a lieutenant colonel in August – a meteoric rise!

From the late Sixties the unit's role was to reinforce 1 Field Workshop in Bielefeld, and so its equipment was stocked at Bielefeld and Moenchengladbach. In July 1974 Lieutenant Colonel Jimmy Martin, a Regular officer, took command and in September 208 all ranks went to BAOR for annual camp, to practise its role. By this time also SOPs had been introduced in the unit for this role, and effective training in operating with them was able to take place.

For a year in 1978–79 the unit had the well-known Corps cricketer (and later Editor of 'The Craftsman') Captain Peter Beeken as Training Officer. In 1979 also, command of the unit reverted to TAVR hands when the 2IC, Major Trevor Harris, was promoted in time to take the unit to camp at Barry Budden in Scotland. At this camp, after the middle Sunday traditional Company parade and annual photograph had been completed, the CSM asked the CO to return to the saluting dais to take the salute for a second time: to demonstrate what might have happened. On to the

124 Recovery Company REME (V) parade as ordered – without trousers!

parade ground, perfectly in step, marched the whole company properly dressed except for their trousers! When writing Part 1 Orders the Assistant Adjutant (the Padre in another role) had forgotten to include this necessary item of dress.

The unit was very much complete in all respects when in 1980 it took part in Exercise CRUSADER 80 in BAOR, drawing all its war equipment and all its stored vehicles in BAOR for the first time. The build-up towards this exercise helped recruitment and raised morale, with more than 80% of the unit taking part.

In July 1982 Lieutenant Colonel Peter Watson, a Regular Officer, took over command. (In 1991 he became the Commander HQ REME TA at Bordon). A few weeks later the unit went to camp in BAOR for Exercise KEYSTONE 82 in the Sennelager area, where they took part in a logistic trial of a new command and operational system in the Corps Rear Area. Much amusement was caused by 10th (TA) Battalion, The Parachute Regiment which attacked the unit by creeping up on the cooks' trailer and inflicting considerable damage, believing it to be the Command Post. This amusement soon evaporated when the umpires accidentally betrayed the Command Post position, which the 'Paras' then attacked successfully.

In 1984 the Company's main training effort was its participation in Exercise LIONHEART in BAOR. The efficiency of the deployment was illustrated by 121 Platoon which was deployed with all its equipment on the River Weser bridges and crossing points thirty-six hours after reporting in at Newton Aycliffe.

The 1985 camp took place at Stirling Training Camp for military training, and in the Cairngorms in the north of Scotland where initiative and leadership training was arranged. That year the Company was awarded the prestigious Fairclough Trophy, the North of England TAVRA award to the Volunteer unit which had done most for public relations in the previous year.

In April 1986 the new TA Centre, now named 'The Aycliffe Armoury', was formally opened by Sir Michael Straker, Chairman of Aycliffe and Peterlee Development Corporation in the presence of Major General John Boyne, DGEME. The company won the best TA Team Trophy at Commander Maintenance's annual Skill at Arms competition led by CSM Brian Keenan, and 15 Infantry Brigade Minor Units Championship led by Lieutenant Trevor Jones. In the following spring the first of the Foden wheeled recovery vehicles arrived with many more to come – sixteen in England and sixteen in BAOR. That year a prominent local industrialist, Mr D F Howard, Director General of the Tyne and Wear Passenger Executive, was appointed as the Company's Honorary Colonel. Colonel Howard had served as a Regular Officer in REME for thirteen years.

In 1988 ASM R B Abbott became the first TA soldier to join as a

Craftsman and become an ASM in the primary trade of recovery mechanic, whilst in July Lieutenant Colonel Peter Major, after three years in command, handed over to Major Tom Gillanders, the 2IC, who was promoted to Lieutenant Colonel. After six years the Commanding Officer was once more a TA officer.

In October 1990 the Company went for its camp to 12th Air Defence Regiment Workshop in Dortmund, a few weeks after Iraq had invaded Kuwait. Several members of the unit went to the camp with their father's words ringing in their ears: 'Don't forget, I went to camp in August 1939 and didn't get back until 1945!' During the second week in Dortmund teams of vehicle mechanics and electricians were sent to various places in BAOR to use their skills to prepare equipments to be sent to the Gulf for Operation GRANBY. The Company was granted the Freedom of Great Aycliffe in 1988.

The Queen's Own Yeomanry LAD (V)

This LAD, supporting squadrons at Ayr, Chester, Cramlington and York was based at Fenham Barracks, Newcastle upon Tyne from the time of its formation under the command of Captain T Harris in 1971. Its strength rose from fifty-one to eighty-one over the period of this volume, during which a rapid succession of LAD commanders was underpinned by the longer tours of its ASMs.

3 ton Albion 6 × 4

SARACENs and SALADINs were initially issued as the main equipments for the Regiment; twenty years later they possessed FOX armoured cars and SPARTAN APCs. The LAD was issued with a 1952 Vehicle Auto Repair Shop 3 ton Albion 6 × 4 with a maximum speed of about 25 mph! Problems of spares and how to keep up with the regiment on the autobahn on exercises in BAOR led to attempts to exchange it for something more modern and a wish from the REME Museum to procure the old Albion! In 1978 their Albion was added to the Museum's Historical Vehicle collection. The establishment was amended in view of the geographic spread and complexity of the unit's equipment to include a technical Permanent Staff Administration Officer (PSAO): Captain Ian Heath was appointed in 1987 to ensure co-ordination and continuity.

From April 1992 the Duke of Westminster commanded the Regiment in its role of armoured reconnaissance, with the Northumberland Hussars as Headquarter Squadron at Newcastle, the Yorkshire Yeomanry squadron at York, the Ayrshire Yeomanry at Ayr, the Cheshire Yeomanry at Chester and the Northumberland Hussars at Cramlington.

9 Field Workshop

This workshop traced its history from 9 Infantry Brigade Workshop in 3rd Division in the Second World War. 9 Field Workshop was reformed in 1977 as part of the reorganization of 5 Field Force, with its HQ at Bordon. The workshop supported various exercises in BAOR and in Norway in the years 1978–83, when its operational strength was increased by attaching Sponsored TA soldiers.

By 1978 9 Field Workshop consisted of 156 TAVR soldiers and forty-six Regular. In September of that year, in pouring rain, Regular and TAVR came together for the first time as a complete unit on exercise in Schleswig Holstein near the German-Danish border. Three barns in a small village were allotted to them. The first few days were spent on concentrated military training and getting used to working in field conditions. They then took part in a NATO exercise involving British, German, Danish and American forces, during which 6 Field Force, under attack from Orange Forces, withdrew to the north from their forward defensive positions, but later they counter-attacked. The Workshop completed repairs on more than 100 equipments, including the vehicles of the Royal Irish Rangers who were the enemy, and spent a short, hot and sweaty time working in NBC kit and respirators. Half the unit was out on detachment on the MSR for more than 24 hours.

Major Alistair Flett, appointed Honorary Colonel REME (V) Scotland in January 1987, recalled that it frequently rained so hard that they thought Schleswig Holstein would sink. However, they had a particularly happy relationship with the local farmers, in whose barns they lived, and kept dry for some of the time.

In the early Eighties 9 Field Workshop's role was changed to provide the REME maintenance element of the Logistic Support Group of UKMF(L), together with 119 Recovery Company (V). In 1986 the unit began to be made up of Regulars, Independent TA and Specialist TA soldiers as it moved to Hilsea, leaving most of the vehicles and equipment at Bordon as the TA Centre did not have enough room.

In 1987 9 Field Workshop, now located at the TA Centre in Hilsea Portsmouth (the home of pre-war Ordnance Mechanical Engineers), changed from Regular to Territorial Army. This was a welcome addition to the Corps on the south coast where there had previously been no REME TA unit. It started with a strong Regular element with a platoon of Specialist soldiers with the required trade skills, then gradually built up its Independent strength as its Regular and Specialist elements were phased out. This was the first time in the Corps' history that such a transfer from the Regular Army to the TA had taken place. Its location in the Southampton – Portsmouth area proved ideal for recruiting technical manpower.

Regular soldiers from the workshop were detached to the Falkland Islands and to Kenya. Their first major exercise as a TA workshop was Exercise BOLD GUARD in Germany in 1986. This was one of a series of 'BOLD' exercises designed to exercise the UKMF(L) in its role of reinforcing NATO's Northern Flank. This was followed in 1988 by Exercise BOLD GROUSE in Denmark when many more TA soldiers took part, including a detachment from 17 Port and Maritime Workshop. In July 1990 the rebuilt TA Centre and Technical Training Wing was opened by Major General Dennis Shaw, DGEME. The annual camp that year had to take place at Catterick and Eskmeals when Exercise BOLD GUARD 90 in Germany was cancelled.

The unit's annual camp for 1991 was reduced to ten days for that year and small detachments of experienced TA soldiers to support the Regular units became the norm. Deployments in 1990–92 included Belize, Canada, Germany, Jersey and Norway. At the end of that year 9 Field Workshop was recruited up to 75% of establishment. 85% of the unit personnel were classified fit for role, including ten women, having started only five years earlier with half a dozen Independent TA recruits and half a dozen Specialist TA who lived in the Portsmouth area.

Following Options for Change the Workshop was in April 1993 to be redesignated 128 Reclamation Company (V) in support of 3rd (UK) Division once more, as part of 103 Battalion REME (V), after a short but happy history as 9 Field Workshop (V).

Craftsman Barry Fogg, left, and Corporal John Hewitt in Norway with their snow-capped Scammell EKA

119 Recovery Company (V)

119 Recovery Company (V) was based at the TA Centre Prestatyn, Clwyd, under the command of Major John Stephens who took over in 1986 from Major Douglas Hardie who was appointed SO1 Maint (V) West the same year. In addition to first aid, NBC, recovery and vehicle mechanic training, initiative training courses for potential artificers and senior NCOs were held at Calshot on the Solent, Snowdonia and the Cairngorm National Parks. Survival training was

held to follow up a survival exercise on Dartmoor during annual camp.

The Company had a regular requirement to provide recovery support for the AMF(L) exercise in Norway each spring over a 6–7 week period which was achieved by rotating the crews every two weeks; this was a popular exercise, as well as being a considerable test of individual skills for those involved. In 1986 the unit was up to 95% of its establishment and was running selection weekends three or four times a year.

In September 1986 the unit took part in Exercise BOLD GUARD in Schleswig Holstein; 86% of the unit attended and earned a glowing report in a newspaper from Tracey Cardwell, the reporter who went with them. In the annual REME TA South West District Skills Competition, Exercise Western Approaches held at Swynnerton in April, the unit's teams were placed first and second out of sixteen teams competing. Their shooting skill was demonstrated when they won the South West District Small Bore competition.

The new Foden recovery vehicles increased the training requirement; in 1987 the recovery mechanics went to Ripon in mid-summer for a two-week basic and upgrading course which was run for all REME TA units in UK. The rest of the unit went to Barry Buddon in Scotland in September for a week on the ranges and a week in the Highlands map-reading and orienteering. The unit won the Welsh Cup for football twice in a few years.

A similar pattern of training took place in the next few years with trade, military and adventure training taking place at various places such as Strensal, Yorkshire, Snowdonia, Lake District and the Brecon Beacons. Volunteers also went to Belize and the British Army Training Unit, Suffield, in Canada. In 1990 camp was divided between Scarborough and Garelochhead when Exercise BOLD GUARD 90 in Schleswig Holstein was cancelled. Following Options for Change the unit, whose strength in the early Nineties was a 104 officers and soldiers, was to form the recovery company of a REME battalion with a repair workshop in Manchester, a reclamation company in the Midlands and the recovery company in Prestatyn.

Among their many good deeds for outside organizations 119 Recovery Company helped to build an adventure playground for underprivileged children in Rhyl, using their lifting and bulldozing capacity. The unit was granted the Freedom of Prestatyn and marched through the town with the REME Staff Band in September 1992.

Duke of Lancaster's Own Yeomanry LAD (V)

The Duke of Lancaster's Own Yeomanry LAD was at Chorley, Lancashire. At the beginning of the Nineties the Regiment's role was as a Home Defence reconnaissance regiment with a headquarters and three squadrons. The LAD was then under AQMS J Rimmer, who had under command eight vehicle mechanics, three vehicle electricians and three armourers. Over the years the Regiment had many different roles – cavalry, medium regiment RA, armoured regiment RAC, reconnaissance regiment and infantry battalion, with all the consequential changes in the LAD. The Regiment had served in the South African War 1900–02, France and Flanders 1915–18, and North West Europe 1944–45 by when it had its REME LAD. In 1989 HM The Queen, their Colonel in Chief, presented a new Guidon to the Regiment. At the start of 1992 the main vehicle in the Regiment was the Land Rover, with some Bedford 4 tonners; the Regiment was, however, to be reduced to one squadron.

THE TA IN OPERATION GRANBY

Both Individual REME TA soldiers and units were involved in Operation GRANBY in the UK, and some former members of the TA joined the Regular Army on full-time normal engagements, subsequently serving in the Gulf. Lance Corporal F C Evans, a former TA soldier with 119 (Holywell) Recovery Company (V) at Prestatyn, was killed in action whilst serving with the 16th/5th The Queen's Royal Lancers, and this incident is described in Chapter 12.

Several TA units were involved in the UK outloading plans and undertook lengthy and onerous commitments driving vehicles, with REME TA providing their first line support. Some individuals made themselves available for additional commitments in operational headquarters: one such volunteer was Sergeant Hugh Ashton REME (V), who was awarded a formal Commander's Commendation in the Operation GRANBY awards for his valuable work as Chief Clerk in the Land Logistics element of the Joint Force Headquarters, RAF High Wycombe.

Following Operation GRANBY an enormous amount of work was generated by the requirement to restore vehicles and equipment to a usable state in BAOR and UK. A series of Annual Camps was mounted for Specialist Units, entitled 'Golden Chain', whereby TA effort was effectively employed on this essential task.

REGIMENTAL MATTERS

Local Affiliations with Cadet Forces

An early example of REME rebadging was a battalion of Army Cadet Force in Yorkshire which was given REME badges in the late Fifties. The cadet companies were attached to TA Centres occupied by the pre-1967–68 Army Recovery Company TA which used to examine the cadets for their certificates. Other examples of Cadet Force detachments being similarly rebadged were the Newton Aycliffe ACF Detachment, when 124 Recovery Company (V) was formed as a REME unit in 1967, Reading

School CCF in 1977 in a ceremony reviewed by Brigadier Pat Lee, and the ACF detachment of the Piggott School at Wargrave, where Brigadier Tony Palmer presented each cadet with a REME badge in 1982.

In 1983 closer affiliations were made between REME TA units and ACF Detachments sharing the same TA Centre. This included rebadging some ACF units to REME so making a closer esprit de corps within TA Centres and providing a potential feed to junior TA entry. An example was the Leicestershire and Northamptonshire ACF, which was rebadged REME on 15 May 1983 at a ceremony undertaken by the Honorary Colonel REME (V), Brigadier Arthur Reading. This was held at the TA Centre at Corby with 118 Recovery Company (V), which only three weeks earlier had been granted the Freedom of the Borough of Northampton.

The old Glen Parva Barracks at Wigston, so long the Leicester home of the REME Manning and Record Office, was converted to TA and ACF use in the late Eighties. It provided accommodation for the Leicester detachment of 118 Recovery Company REME (V) and was opened by the Lord Lieutenant of Leicestershire.

118 Recovery Company REME (V) Freedom of Northampton 23 April 1983

Freedoms

1983 was the 75th anniversary of the Territorial Army. For the first time REME TA was represented at the Honorary Townspeople parade in Wokingham by combined Independent and Sponsored soldiers from Recruit Course Number 74. In that same year 118 Recovery Company (V) was granted the Freedom of the Borough of Northampton on 23 April.

Trumpeters from the REME Staff Band sounded a fanfare before the opening speeches at the Northampton Guildhall, when the Freedom Scroll was presented by the Mayor, Councillor R W Harris, to the Officer Commanding, Major Pat Dean. The Representative Colonel

Commandant, Major General R F Vincent, presented an inscribed silver salver to the Borough and read out a message from the Colonel in Chief, Prince Philip, which included the words: 'This gesture is a well-deserved recognition of the service given to 118 Recovery Company by so many public-spirited citizens of Northampton, Corby and the surrounding areas. The occasion also marks the 75th anniversary of the Territorial Army and this will be appreciated by all TA units in the area'. After the ceremony four officers and eighty-three soldiers, led by the REME Staff Band, marched through the town with bayonets fixed, the Mayor taking the salute outside the Guildhall.

119 Light Platoon was adopted by Holywell Urban District Council North Wales in July 1965 and, in December 1976, 119 Recovery Company (V) was adopted by Holywell Town Council. Later, on 12 September 1992, the Company – now renamed 119 (Holywell) Recovery Company (V) – received the Freedom of Prestatyn. The Mayor of Prestatyn, accompanied by the Representative Colonel Commandant, Major General Dennis Shaw, inspected the parade, watched by Lieutenant Colonel Sir William Gladstone, Lord Lieutenant of Clwyd. The town gave the unit an illuminated scroll and the Corps gave the town an Elizabethan alms dish. The REME Staff Band played both the National and Welsh Anthems before the parade marched through the streets of Prestatyn back to the TA Centre.

124 Recovery Company (V) was formed on 1 April 1967 in Newton Aycliffe, County Durham, and in October 1987 the Town Council offered the Freedom of Great Aycliffe to the Company. Saturday 21 May 1988 was chosen for the ceremony and to celebrate the unit's 21st anniversary. The parade marched on in two guards of sixty men in the presence of the Mayor, Councillor Mrs Wray, the DGEME, Major General Dennis Shaw, and the GOC North East District, Major General D M Naylor. The Mayor presented the Company with a handsome illuminated vellum scroll and the DGEME presented the town with a silver salver. The CO, Lieutenant Colonel Peter Major, led the march past of No 1 Guard, the band of 34th (Northern) Signal Regiment (V) followed and then the Newcastle Guard drove past led by their mascot, a 1951 Scammell Mark 1. This was followed by twenty-six Foden recovery vehicles and more than thirty other vehicles. Many of the unit's vehicles were held in Germany so they were lent vehicles by 118 Recovery Company (V), 15 Field Workshop and The Queen's Own Yeomanry LAD (V). After the parade the town held a civic lunch for all those on parade and the unit held a party in the evening. Eight founder-members of the unit had served continuously from 1967 to 1988. In 1992 the Freedom was exercised again, in celebration of the 50th Anniversary of the Corps.

The Colonel in Chief with TA officers dining at West Court 6 December 1979

The Colonel in Chief's Dinner with REME TA

It was agreed by the Corps that one of the visits of the Colonel in Chief, Prince Philip, Duke of Edinburgh, should take the form of a dinner at West Court with the Reserve Army officers of the Corps. This was held on Thursday 6 December 1979. Planning was co-ordinated by Brigadier Joe Rayment, CEME UKLF at the time. It was self-evident that applications to attend would far exceed the capacity of the Mess, so Districts and Sponsored Units were given allocations based on their current strengths. Except for a small number of Regular Officers in key appointments, all who attended were TA.

It was thought important to involve TA NCOs and soldiers as far as possible, so volunteers were sought to help with security and to guard the entrance to the Mess. A highlight of the music at the Dinner, in addition to the excellence of the Corps Band, was the solo performance on the pipes by RSM D McDowell of 201 Field Workshop (V), later commented on by the Colonel in Chief in his letter of thanks.

To commemorate this unique event in the history of REME TA, a silver figure of a bandmaster was presented to the Mess, and also a painting by Ken Howard of a REME TA workshop in the field; both had suitably inscribed plaques attached.

Honorary Colonels (V)

In 1987 Colonel Pat Kearney TD was appointed REME Honorary

Colonel (V) Northern Ireland – the first such appointment in the Province. By 1991 there were four geographic Honorary Colonels (V), plus one for 124 Recovery Company and one for Specialist Units. A complete list of Honorary Colonels is given at Annex B to this chapter.

In September 1988 the Honorary Colonel REME (V) East, Brigadier Arthur Reading, celebrated his 50th year of association with the TA and Regular Army when he was invited by the Commander REME TA, Colonel Chris Derbyshire, to review a ceremonial parade of TA soldiers at Louisburg Barracks, Bordon. In 1938, during the Munich crisis, he had joined the TA as a Gunner in 52 AA Brigade in Acton, London. The Honorary Colonel then was Lord Nuffield, famed as the founder of Morris Motors, and for his philanthropic activities which included the Nuffield Trust, of great benefit to the Services.

The Gardiner Trophy

In July 1985 'The Craftsman' reported the sad death of Colonel Derek Gardiner, aged 56. He was a man who had been very active in REME Reserve Army for most of his life, eventually reaching the appointment of Colonel REME TA, and being the sponsored representative on the Council of TAVRAs, representing units throughout the Army. He had been awarded both the ERD for his time in the AER, and the TD for his Territorial Army service. He was highly regarded for the contribution that he made to the TA, and for his unfailing sense of humour. He set high standards for volunteer military service and those who knew him ensured that they were met.

Mrs Norma Gardiner provided a magnificent silver cup to REME TA in memory of her husband, with the instructions that it should be presented each year to 'The best REME TA Unit in the United Kingdom'. The winners were:

1985 212 (Highland) Ambulance Squadron RCT Workshop (V)
1986 71st (Yeomanry) Signal Regiment LAD (V)
1987 103 (Lancashire Artillery Volunteers) Air Defence Regiment LAD (V)
1988 The Royal Yeomanry LAD (V)
1989 223 Squadron RCT Workshop (V)
1990 105 (Scottish) Air Defence Regiment LAD (V)
1992 225 (Queen's Own Lowland Yeomanry) Squadron RCT (V)
1993 128 Reclamation Company (V)
1994 146 Workshop Company (V)
1995 127 Workshop Company (V)

The Broxhead Club

The Broxhead Club, which takes its name from Broxhead House at Bordon (the original home of HQ REME TA), was formed to enable the serving officers of the REME Reserve, both Sponsored and Independent, to maintain their interest in and association with the Corps as well as an annual gathering of old friends after their retirement from active duty.

Its Fifth Annual Dinner was held in the SEME Officers' Mess at Bordon in October 1980, with thirty-four members present. The President was Colonel John Holman and the senior guest was Major General Sir Leonard Atkinson. The next morning the Chairman of the Club presented a teak garden seat to the SEME Mess to mark the long association the Club members had enjoyed for more years than many of them cared to count. In 1992 the Club was still flourishing, with exactly 100 members, and looking forward to maintaining its popularity.

Annex A

SECOND-LINE REME TA UNITS AFTER 'OPTIONS FOR CHANGE' 1991–1992

Independent Battalions

101 Battalion REME (V), Chorley (Wales and Western District)

- 119 Recovery Company (V), Prestatyn
- 126 Reclamation Company (V), Coventry
- 127 Workshop Company (V), Manchester

102 Battalion REME (V), Newton Aycliffe (Eastern District)

- 118 Recovery Company (V), Northampton
- 124 Recovery Company (V), Newton Aycliffe
- 146 Workshop Company (V), Rotherham
- 186 Workshop Company (V), Newcastle
- 218 Port Platoon (V), (Specialist)
- 219 Port Platoon (V), (Specialist)

103 Battalion REME (V), Redhill (Southern District)

- 128 Reclamation Company (V), Portsmouth
- 133 Workshop Company (V), Ashford
- 150 Recovery Company (V), Redhill

Specialist Battalion

104 Battalion (V)

- 201 Workshop Company (V)
- 209 Workshop Company (V)
- 210 Port Company (V)

Regular Army TA Increments

- 1st (UK) Armoured Division: 1, 2 and 3 Battalions REME
- 3rd (UK) Division: 6 Battalion REME
- 17 Port and Maritime Workshop, Marchwood

REME (V) Independent Battalion Specialist Platoons

Each Company of 101, 102, and 103 Battalions REME (V) has a Specialist platoon as an integral part of its establishment.

Annex B

HONORARY COLONELS IN REME TA

Date of Appointment	*Name*	*Area of Responsibility*
1 Apr 67	Col W E I Armstrong OBE TD DL	Western Command/ Northern Ireland
1 Apr 67	Col E C W Huson TD ERD	Sponsored Units
19 Jul 68	Col G Higgs ERD	Sponsored Units
1 Apr 70	Brig L C Libby MBE	Southern Command
1 Apr 70	Col R Hirst TD JP	Northern Command/ Scotland
1 Apr 71	Col H A Lewis MBE TD	Sponsored Units
1 Apr 73	Brig A E P Joy MBE	South
1 Apr 73	Col J A Ireland TD	North and East
1 Apr 73	Col W E I Armstrong OBE TD DL	West
1 Apr 74	Col S Blackford TD	Sponsored Units
1 Apr 77	Col D H Wheatcroft TD	Sponsored Units
1 Apr 78	Brig A G Cradduck	North
1 Apr 78	Col D E Filer TD	West
1 Apr 78	Col D A Gardiner ERD TD ADC	East
1 Feb 79	Col S J Cox	Scotland/Northern Ireland
1 Apr 80	Col J H Bowen TD	Sponsored Units
1 Apr 81	Brig A W Reading OBE MC TD	East
1 Apr 81	Col A F Wilkinson TD	North
1 Apr 82	Col M J Coleman TD	Scotland/Northern Ireland
1 Apr 83	Col B Giles TD	Sponsored Units
1 Apr 86	Brig G A Atkinson	Specialist Units
30 Jan 87	Col A M Flett TD	Scotland
30 Jan 87	Col P Kearney TD JP DL	Northern Ireland
1 Apr 87	Col P A Fitzgerald OBE TD	West
1 Apr 87	Col D F Howard CBE	124 Recovery Company (V)
1 Oct 88	Col R A Gill TD JP DL	East
1 Apr 89	Col C Boswell CBE TD	Specialist Units
1 Apr 89	Col P G Bennett TD	North
1 Apr 92	Col P G Bennett TD	West
1 Apr 92	Col R A Gill JP DL	South
3 Feb 93	Col D F Howard CBE	102 Battalion REME (V)
1 Apr 93	Lt Col A Rae TD	Scotland
1 Apr 93	Col I B Currier TD	101 Battalion REME (V)
1 Apr 94	Maj Gen C Tyler CB	South
1 Apr 94	Col G O Linnett TD	103 Battalion REME (V)
1 Apr 95	Col M W Whyman TD DL	Specialist Units
1 Apr 95	Lt Col G B Matthews	Northern Ireland

CHAPTER 9

OVERSEAS

Introduction · Far East · Middle East · Africa · Mediterranean · Rest of the World

INTRODUCTION

The complete withdrawal from many stations overseas, and the reduction of the British presence in others, began after the Second World War, and much of the coverage of these events is included in the first volume. We left India in the Forties, Egypt in the Fifties and Aden, Malaysia and Singapore in the Sixties and Seventies. The process was to be continued in the Nineties with the reduction of forces in Germany and the planned withdrawal from Hong Kong in 1997. The gap left by the loss of valuable military experience, previously obtained from service abroad, has since been filled by overseas training exercises, the provision of teams for training foreign and Commonwealth armies, and the encouragement of adventurous training.

This chapter is concerned with areas where the Corps served in garrisons remaining after the Sixties, some of which were still to be evacuated or reduced. There were also new or revived areas of activity in which the Corps served, including the Falklands and the Gulf, and the campaign to recapture the Falklands and the military operations of the Gulf War are described in Chapters 11 and 12 respectively. In 1990–91 amongst those garrisons remaining there were still 163 REME serving in Hong Kong, 138 in Cyprus, 88 in the Falklands and 102 in Belize. Lesser numbers were serving in the Suffield training area in Canada and in Gibraltar. The largest Corps representation outside UK still remained BAOR, to which Chapter 6 is devoted. There were soldiers on Loan Service in more than ten locations including the Antarctic, Brunei, Kuwait, Oman, the United Arab Emirates and Zimbabwe where, overall, some seventy REME officers and soldiers were serving. The largest of these numerically was Kuwait where there were more than thirty REME on Loan Service when Iraq invaded that country on 2 August 1990. Their experiences and those of their families is described in this chapter.

In the early Nineties the Corps supported from central funds over one hundred officers and nearly one thousand soldiers annually on adventurous training exercises. These involved canoeing, climbing, sailing, trekking, taking part in sub-aqua and many other such pursuits. Countries throughout the world added appeal as well as challenge to the projects, which included such adventures as a Hovercraft expedition up the River Yangtze in China. There were many other adventurous training projects both funded and organized by individual Corps units. Leadership, initiative and personal skills, which this type of training developed in individual REME soldiers, proved to be of the utmost value in war as was demonstrated in the Falklands in 1982 and in the Gulf in 1990–91.

FAR EAST

Far East Land Forces

FARELF, with its HQ in Singapore, had responsibility for a vast area from Mauritius to Hong Kong. In 1967 a Supplementary Defence White Paper was published on the policy for withdrawal from the Far East in the period 1973–76. In 1968 it was announced that the withdrawal was to be accelerated with all units withdrawn by the end of 1971. HQ Land Forces Hong Kong was to become independent of HQ FARELF on 1 April 1970. Further changes to the policy in 1969 and 1970 resulted eventually in a three-nation ANZUK force – 28 ANZUK Brigade – being formed on 1 September 1971. The British Army contribution included ninety-eight REME personnel.

The Command was involved in a series of incidents between 1968–1971. In Mauritius in 1968 law and order had to maintained in the face of communal disorders. In 1969 Singapore and Malaysia had severe floods resulting from 18 inches of rain in 24 hours, whilst in Pakistan in 1970 there was a tidal wave and cyclone. Widespread flooding in Malaysia in 1971 and the evacuation of British Nationals from Pakistan following a rift between East and West Pakistan also required involvement. For all the operations REME provided the appropriate element.

REME strength in FARELF ran down from some 3,500 in 1968 to 1,800 by mid-1970 when Seremban, Kluang and Terendak Camp in Malaya were abandoned, and during the first months of 1971 various REME units were put under the control or command of 40 Command Workshop REME in Singapore. At the same time the ANZ part of the proposed ANZUK Workshop was given accommodation in 40 Command Workshop. From July to September 1971 other ANZUK units began to form up and, with help from REME, drew their equipment. By July 1971 REME strength had fallen to 470, and by the end of that year the Corps had all left, except for the British contingent in the ANZUK force which remained in Singapore until 1975, when ANZUK was disbanded.

REME Administrative Unit FARELF

One of the best-known REME units in the Far East was the REME Administrative Unit FARELF which became the home for REME soldiers of 40 Base Workshop, REME Training Centre, Singapore District Workshop, and some units of other arms and services. It provided a temporary home for those in transit through Singapore; it administered Army Schools, married quarters estates and much else. It was well known for the performances staged at the Rowcroft Theatre until it closed in June 1971; it housed the very hospitable REME Officers' Mess until January 1965, the REME Sergeants' Mess and the Junior Ranks' 'Rundown Club', both of which closed in October 1971. The last OC was Major Bill Boazman who disbanded the unit in that same month.

Hong Kong

In April 1970 Headquarters Land Forces Hong Kong was now independent of HQ FARELF. The Headquarters Queen's Gurkha Engineers and a Gurkha Transport Regiment were transferred from Malaya to Hong Kong that year. HQ 48 Gurkha Infantry Brigade was in Sek Kong and HQ 51 Infantry Brigade in Kowloon. 50 Command Workshop set up a small Technical Services Cell and a training centre for Gurkha armourers and vehicle mechanics as well as a civilian apprentice training scheme. By 1979 the Army presence had been reduced to a Gurkha Field Force (with one British infantry battalion and three Gurkha battalions, Engineers and a Transport Regiment) and the Support Troops. During the Seventies many barracks and military areas were given up, such as nineteen hectares in Victoria Barracks in March 1979 when the HQ BFHK moved into a new tower block in the naval base, HMS *Tamar*, which on 4 March 1979 was opened by HRH The Prince of Wales. The first REME to move into the workshop there were ASM C Vickers, Staff Sergeant L J Soper and Sgt B J Ellis, and on 24 February the Sergeants' Mess held a memorable Ladies' Dinner Night in Victoria Barracks to commemorate the move.

50 Command Workshop made its mark in 1974 when it was the first REME unit to win the Wilkinson Sword of Peace Award, having been second in several previous years. The Award was presented annually to a unit from each of the Armed Forces in recognition of outstanding efforts by British units in fostering good relations in the territories in which they were stationed. The units were selected each year by the Ministry of Defence on recommendations made to them by the Admiralty, Army and Royal Air Force Boards. The 1974 presentation was made by Field Marshal Sir Michael Carver, Chief of the Defence Staff and Colonel Commandant of REME, to the OC, Major Chris Nobbs, at a special luncheon at Cutlers Hall in the City of London.

Corporal Wells REME, middle, and Corporal Parkes RAOC, right, lay the last tile

The workshop had carried out a sustained campaign of Community Relations projects designed to benefit all sections of the Chinese population in the crowded Sham Shui Po district of Kowloon, where the workshop was stationed. The work involved all members of the unit and many of their families who carried out fifty-five community projects. One was the design and manufacture of a special wheelchair for post-operative children at the John F Kennedy Centre Children's Hospital; another was to 'adopt' the Sea Cadets of the local training ship and teach them to build sailing dinghies. A third involved two junior NCOs who gave up their evenings and weekends to lay over 14,000 square feet of nylon floor tiles on the concrete floors of the Morning Hill School for Mentally Handicapped Children. The concrete floors had proved dangerous for those children who were subject to frequent falls.

Lance Corporal Morris refits a generator in the Castle Peak area

On 1 March 1984 50 Command Workshop changed its name to 50 Hong Kong Workshop. Throughout that year it moved from Sham Shui Po Camp, the former Japanese prisoner-of-war camp, where it had been since 1946, to Malaya Lines, Sek Kong, in the New Territories. The Calibration Section had already moved to Gun Club Hill Barracks in Kowloon some years earlier due to the disturbance caused by the building of the Mass Transit Railway under the camp. In February 1983 the Vehicle Repair Section had moved into the new Kowloon detachment buildings in Osborne Barracks. The main workshop had employed sixty-five British military staff, eighteen Hong Kong soldiers and 200 local civilians. It was responsible for the field and intermediate repair of Army equipment, less Royal Signals telecommunications equipment, and also certain equipments belonging to the Royal Navy and Royal Air Force. The main Workshop had been the last and only military unit in Sham Shui Po which was one of the most densely populated areas of Kowloon and under the direct flight path for Kai Tak airport. Later, in 1989, the site at Sham Shui Po became a camp for the influx of Vietnamese Boat People.

To mark the completion of the move, in December 1984 sixty-two British, Chinese and Gurkha runners carried the Wilkinson Sword of Peace the sixteen miles from Sham Shui Po, to Sek Kong. The new workshop was purpose-built next to and incorporating the Sek Kong Detachment of 50 Hong Kong Workshop, which had a strength of thirty-five military and forty-five local civilians supporting the Gurkha Field Force (later 48 Gurkha Infantry Brigade). In April 1985 Major General John Boyne officially opened the new Workshop. The OC at the time, Major Mike Crabbe, described the preparations for the opening:

'If you want to open a new unit anywhere you must have an Opening Ceremony. In Hong Kong this becomes complicated because of the different races and customs. 50 Hong Kong workshop was no exception and with British, Chinese and Gurkha soldiers, three Opening Cermonies were required. 'There is no problem with the British ceremony: you invite a General, he makes a speech and cuts a ribbon. Luckily Major General John Boyne, then Vice Adjutant General, was due to be in Hong Kong in the early spring of 1985 so we had a General. The Chinese ceremony is a little more complicated. You need a lion dance, some joss-sticks to burn and some offerings to the Gods. With over 200 Chinese civilians this was easily organized. The Gurkha ceremony was much more complicated. They insisted on a live sacrifice in the new Workshop buildings to banish the evil spirits.

'As with all good planning I took advice very early and six months before the event consulted my most senior Gurkha. He said, "No problem sahib, my cousin is the goatherd at 2nd Gurkha Rifles and we will buy a goat from him. It is best to buy it now because you buy it by the pound and it will grow to a full-size goat in the next six months. Just before the ceremony we will move it to the Gurkha Depot next door in preparation." Problem number one solved, we bought a goat. Sometime before the ceremony the Gurkha Holy Man visited to do his recce. Problem number two reared its head when we discovered that the appointed day was not a goat-killing day in the Gurkha calendar. The problem was overcome by negotiating that the sacrifice should take place on the day before the actual ceremony and, to the relief of all the families, we were able to substitute a much more palatable ceremony in the form of Gurkha music and dancing.

'Everything then went well until the morning of the day before the ceremony when the Gurkha Colour Sergeant came to my office to inform me that the goat was dead! He explained that they had moved it from the Battalion to the Depot the previous evening, but the local grass must have been too much for it and in the morning they found it dead. I did not panic, I simply asked him what we do now. "Buy another goat sahib," he replied. We were too close to the ceremony to make other arrangements and I am convinced to this day that we bought the same goat twice!. Eventually the ceremony went off without a hitch, except for the goat which was in no position to complain anyway and the junior Gurkha had carried out the ritual of decapitation in the approved manner.'

On 13 December 1989 50 Hong Kong Workshop almost stopped Hong Kong when a Scammell EKA caught fire in the Lion Rock Tunnel, which was the busiest tunnel connecting north and south of mainland Hong Kong. The workshop cleared the tunnel and the incident was reported fairly on TV and in the Chinese press; one benefit was that it enabled the Transport Department to get better fire-fighting equipment and more funds for tunnel safety.

In 1990 five REME technicians trained in medical and dental equipment were posted to the strength of the British Military Hospital in Kowloon. A Kowloon detachment of the workshop was used for recovery south of the Lion Rock Tunnel. A General Purpose Thermal Imaging

Repair Facility (known as Hong Kong GPTIRF) was installed that year to give speedier repairs of thermal imaging equipment used on the border, which until then had to be backloaded to the UK for repair. In August 1990, the end of twenty years of apprentice training, recognized as one of the best training schemes in Hong Kong, was marked by the presentation of certificates to locally employed Chinese civilians at the end of their training.

Early in 1970 Hong Kong Support Squadron RE LAD was formed, following the transfer of a pool of C vehicles and plant from Singapore; it became the Queen's Gurkha Engineers LAD in 1976 and was disbanded in 1978 when the repair of C vehicles became the sole responsibility of 50 Command Workshop. The number of REME units and men became less throughout the Seventies, years in which the Corps supported exercises in Brunei, Fiji, Australia and New Zealand.

The Army Air Corps in the Far East was centralized in 1969 when various flights, troops and Gurkha air platoons were amalgamated, resulting in the re-formation of 656 (Independent) Squadron AAC in October 1969. One Gurkha air platoon, based with the Gurkha battalion at Seria in Brunei, remained as an air platoon for a while and then became C Flight of 656 Squadron, Brunei Detachment 660 Squadron AAC in 1978, and then C Flight of 660 Squadron in 1979.

The reorganization and increase in unit size required the squadron to move to the former RAF airfield at Sek Kong. In the spring of 1970 the SIOUX helicopters were supplemented by Mark 1 SCOUTs. The last SIOUX was flown in Hong Kong towards the end of 1974 and was replaced by the GAZELLE. By the end of 1975 the GAZELLEs had been found unsuitable for Hong Kong, and they were returned to UK, leaving a squadron of SCOUTs. The SIOUX helicopters were flown in Brunei until 1977, said to be the last in the AAC, when they changed to SCOUTs.

660 Squadron from 1978 performed observation, reconnaissance, liaison and troop-lifting roles on the Chinese-Hong Kong border, and

supported the Army on exercises. In 1979, 1981 and 1982 it was heavily involved in stemming the flood of illegal immigrants from China. In 1984 it had twelve SCOUTs and eighty men, including REME; of these, two SCOUTs and eighteen men were based in Seria, Brunei, with its Light Aid Detachment under a succession of REME Artificer Staff Sergeants.

The Composite Ordnance Depot (HK) Workshop, which was commanded by an officer from 1966 until 1979 and by an ASM from 1980, had to cope with a typhoon in 1973 which damaged vehicles in stock and flooded the workshop to a depth of one foot. Other tasks were as varied as refurbishing beds for the Vietnamese Boat People in 1982, and preparing ambulances to train Gurkha drivers in 1990 before they moved to the UK and the Gulf in support of the United Nations.

Brunei

The Sultanate of Brunei Darussalam is situated on the north-west coast of the island of Borneo where it enjoys a humid tropical climate. It became a British Protectorate in 1906, but following independence the UK became responsible only for help in the event of external aggression. A Gurkha battalion with attached tradesmen had been there since 1962; throughout the period covered by this volume five battalions of the four Gurkha rifle regiments served there in rotation on two- or three-year tours. The Garrison, which included a small REME workshop, was responsible for jungle warfare training and hosted exercises mainly for units from Hong Kong. The Workshop, under an ASM, some 2,000 miles away from the nearest REME officer, provided support for a Gurkha battalion and a Gurkha transport regiment. ASM A Beedall was the Warrant Officer in Charge in 1980 when the Garrison Workshop news in 'The Craftsman' magazine said, 'This is our first contribution since 1814 and nothing much has happened since then. All in all, quite a pleasant little place'.

The Royal Brunei Malay Regiment

In the early Seventies, with the expansion of the Royal Brunei Malay Regiment, it was decided to establish Loan Service REME with responsibility for all the repair agencies in the Regiment. Major Brian Woods arrived as Force Electrical and Mechanical Engineer in 1974 with an Artificer Vehicle and an Artificer Weapons. Next year Artificers Telecommunications and Instruments arrived and a second Artificer Vehicle. The first OC RBMR Workshop, Captain Mike Couture, arrived in 1975 and in 1977 work started to build a new Force Workshop which was to be commanded by a REME loan service major. Major Cliff Squires served in the Regiment, later The Royal Brunei Armed Forces, from

1977–79 as the Force Engineering Officer. The title was later shortened to 'Force Engineer'. He was responsible to a British brigadier for engineering support to the two infantry battalions, support arms, an air wing and a naval flotilla, each with its own supporting workshop; his air experience had been a two-day course at Middle Wallop just before going to Brunei and his naval experience had not yet begun. Six months after his arrival he was chairman of an air incident inquiry when a gearbox fell out of a helicopter on landing.

About two weeks after Major Squires arrived in Brunei his Brigadier called him in and explained that their new patrol boats were to have EXOCET missiles. 'Would it not be a good idea to service these in the Integrated Weapons Complex recently developed by the Royal Navy? I want you to go to Portsmouth to have a look at it. Collect your first-class air ticket on the way out.' Major Squires pondered on the fact that the cost of the ticket was more than the new car which he had just bought on arrival in Brunei and on the advantage of a large revenue from oil.

The air and naval workshops were commanded by RAF and RN officers respectively and the Army workshop was commanded by Major Roger Jagger. The Force Engineer post was upgraded to Lieutenant Colonel, preferably with an aviation background, the first such being Lieutenant Colonel Rob Matthews.

The years 1978–1985 saw an increase in the size of the Loan Service contingent with the Royal Brunei Malay Regiment, which became the Royal Brunei Armed Forces in January 1984 when Brunei ceased to be a British protectorate. The increase reflected the growth of the equipment inventory as the Regiment was expanded, aircraft technicians being provided in 1981 to maintain newly acquired BOLKOW 105 helicopters in No 2 Squadron and radar technicians for the RAPIER missile system, as well as many single posts in technical and training appointments. The BELL helicopters dating from the Sixties and Seventies in No 1 Squadron had been supported on site by a civilian company, World Wide Helicopters, which consisted almost entirely of British expatriates, some of whom had been REME technicians. This arrangement, as for land and naval equipment, continued until 1986, when the work was taken on by the Technical Equipment Maintenance Department, a government organization. Engine and airframe overhaul was effected by contract, using facilities such as the Hong Kong Aircraft Engineering Company (HAECO, described in Chapter 4) and the Bell agency in Singapore. The Force Engineer was responsible for the equipment management and maintenance of the Army, Navy and Air Force elements of the Regiment; it was quite a challenge to be responsible for a major refit for a 37 metre patrol boat equipped with EXOCET missiles. HATs and SATs became a way of life (Harbour Acceptance Trials and Sea Acceptance Trials) as well as major servicing of BELL 212 helicopters and overhauls of wheeled APCs.

The main challenge of the post for successive Force Engineers was being project manager for equipment procurement; Lieutenant Colonel Matthews negotiated the purchase of the BOLKOW 105 helicopters and started the procurement of RAPIER. Lieutenant Colonel Mike Newby introduced the BOLKOWs into service, sold the RAPIERs to British Aerospace in exchange for a later version, negotiated the navigation and radio equipment refit of the patrol boats and started the logistic computer system. Lieutenant Colonel Brian Ross continued the RAPIER and boat projects to full introduction, progressed the computer system and started to acquire new APCs. Lieutenant Colonel Robin Joy finished the RAPIER Range project, progressed the APCs through visits to users in Oman, France and Cyprus and introduced the computer project to service, before handing over to the local officer who had been carefully trained for the job during the previous eight years. The Force Engineers were helped in their task by a group of high-calibre warrant officers.

Major John Woods arrived as Technical Training Officer in 1981 to set up new training systems for local technicians and apprentices, the latter based on the scheme used at Arborfield. After one tour the post was handed over to the local Brunei officers. Brunei officers with UK engineering degrees were recruited and technicians were trained for all three Service elements; their retention was a problem, with lucrative commercial offers always on the horizon.

Lieutenant Colonel Newby recalled flying fifty miles out to sea in a BELL helicopter flown by a local pilot, then being winched on board a 37 metre patrol boat to take part in an EXOCET firing exercise at a target boat which had been bought, and fitted with a radar reflector designed and built to represent a frigate. There were trips by boat and helicopter to uninhabited jungle areas and seventy-mile dashes down the most accident-prone road in the world on Fridays (while the locals were at prayer) to play golf at the Shell Club at Panaga in a temperature and humidity both of 85!

The British Army in Brunei

In 1986 the British workshop in Tuker Lines, Seria was opened officially by Brigadier DHA Swinburn, Director of Engineer Services (Army). The task of the Workshop was to provide unit and field repair to the Gurkha Transport Regiment, Training Team Brunei, Brunei Signal Troop, C Flight 660 Squadron AAC and garrison units including children's schools; it also gave second-line support to the LAD of the resident Gurkha Rifle Battalion in Seria. The strength of the workshop in 1991 was thirteen British soldiers, five Gurkha soldiers and seven local civilians including the RAOC Stores Section. The ASM in charge of the workshop also filled the post of Garrison Sergeant Major (GSM).

Army Aviation support to the British Army in Brunei in the Seventies and Eighties was provided by C Flight of 660 Squadron AAC which was based in Hong Kong. C Flight operated from the northern end of the town of Seria, in the south-west of Brunei, in support of the resident UK Gurkha battalion at Seria and the Training Team Brunei which provided jungle training for the whole British Army. The flight had three SIOUX helicopters up to September 1978 when they were changed for three SCOUTs operating from a concrete pan by the beach with its own small hangar. The unit had a close working relationship with the neighbouring Shell Aviation Brunei helicopters; the Shell staff were always amused and impressed by the Army operating single-engine helicopters over the unforgiving jungle canopy which was rather too high above the ground for the standard SCOUT winches. The REME team of six, commanded by a staff sergeant artificer, was helped by four Gurkha handler/drivers and locally employed storemen. The beach faced north-west only five degrees north of the equator, providing a combination of sand, high temperature and humidity requiring considerable aircraft husbandry. Second-line support was provided by HAECO, the helicopters being taken back to Hong Kong in RAF HERCULES (on 1,200 flying hours rotation).

Major General John Boyne, DGEME, toured Brunei in February 1987 with the Commander Maintenance Hong Kong, Lieutenant Colonel Tony Millington, and the GSM WO1(ASM) Graham Merrick. He met REME soldiers serving with the 1st Battalion, The 7th Duke of Edinburgh's Gurkha Rifles, Brunei Garrison Workshop and C Flight 660 Squadron AAC. Escorted by the Force Engineer, Lieutenant Colonel Robin Joy, he then toured Royal Brunei Armed Forces units, which had thirty-one REME soldiers on Loan Service. These included Bolkiah and Penanjong workshops, and 2 Squadron of the Air Wing. By 1990 there were no REME Loan Service officers but there were still fifteen soldiers: success had been achieved in training Brunei officers and soldiers to take over from REME. Forty-eight of them attended REME Training Centre courses in 1990–91.

Korea

There was no smaller detachment and no one more remote from the rest of the Corps than the one REME Sergeant Vehicle Mechanic who supported the small staff of the Commonwealth Liaison Mission (CLM) at Seoul, Korea.

The CLM was an integral part of the United Nations Command consisting of British and Australian servicemen based in the United Nations Compound in Seoul. The Command had been formed at Seoul in 1957 as the successor to the Commonwealth Division which had fought in Korea 1950–53 with such distinction. Subordinate to the Mission was a British infantry platoon from Hong Kong – one of five in the UN Honour Guard.

Sergeant Pete Elrick, second right, on the 38th parallel

REME was involved with the CLM from November 1970 when Sergeant Wilson went there on detachment from Hong Kong until November 1971. Eighteen NCOs filled the post up to 1991 when it was filled by Sergeant Pete Elrick. Their task was to maintain and repair up to field repair standard a small fleet of vehicles assigned to the CLM and the Defence Attaché; they were also responsible for all stores and accounts as the QM, and all vehicle documents, servicing and inspections as the MTO. Sergeant Chris Peerless described his time there in 1981–82 in 'The Craftsman' magazine for January 1983.

Nepal

One serving REME warrant officer provided support with his civilian tradesmen to the cantonment at Dharan, with detachments at Kathmandu and Pokhara for many years from the mid-Fifties. Visits from CREME Hong Kong and specialist inspection and repair teams could only take place during the infrequent Gurkha airlift. An important repair activity was concerned with artificial limbs for British Military Hospital, Dharan, patients and wheelchairs belonging to Gurkha pensioners and other disabled Nepalese. The arms store was just that! WO1(ASM) Ted Farrier was in charge of the Station Workshop at the British Gurkhas Nepal, Dharan, 130 miles east of Kathmandu, when on 21 August 1988 a severe earthquake, with its epicentre twenty-five miles west of Dharan, rocked the east of Nepal very early in the morning. Much of Dharan Bazaar and the hill villages was destroyed. ASM Farrier worked all day with the workshop crane or the recovery vehicle helping with the excavation and evacuation of victims in the town. Many residential buildings which were made of local poorly cured brick, with mud used as mortar, collapsed; at great risk to himself the ASM had to work at times in badly damaged, unstable buildings. He often worked alone in appalling mud and incessant rain, but by his efforts one person was pulled out alive from the wreckage of his house and thirteen bodies were recovered. Three chaotic days followed during which the ASM organized his drivers or used the crane and recovery vehicle himself. He was awarded the Queen's Commendation for Brave Conduct in the Queen's Birthday Honours 1989.

For a year from November 1989, prior to his commissioning, ASM Lance Gill served in Kathmandu as G4 Maint under an RAOC major, the SO2 G4. The station workshop at Dharan had closed just before he arrived and all that remained there was a pay office, a trekking office and a movements office. ASM Gill was responsible for the MT repair facilities in Kathmandu and Pokhara, a hundred miles to the west, which was manned by local civilians, and for the provision of local maintenance contracts for computers, office machinery and any other equipment. He was also the Equipment Manager for British Gurkhas Nepal. The only other members of the Corps whom he met were members of 50 Hong Kong Workshop taking part in 'Himalayan Bluebell', the annual Community Relations project which took place in April-May each year. The condition of various hospital equipments and lack of spares (a story heard wherever they went!) ensured that the REME tradesmen used their ingenuity to the full.

While Lieutenant Colonel Richard Heathcote, Commander Maintenance Hong Kong, was paying his annual visit to Nepal, political demonstrations and riots took place in Kathmandu: resulting in an extended curfew and a rapid change of hotels for the Colonel. After some nasty moments and confrontation by a mob, he went to stay with ASM Gill. The ASM recalls another incident during his tour when he had to visit a local hospital for a blood test for his medical board for commissioning. When he arrived he joined a long queue of women also waiting for a blood test. Eventually reaching the counter where blood samples were taken, he found to his horror a large ice cream container full of 'antiseptic fluid' and used hypodermic needles. After some argument with the 'medic', he parted with a few rupees to buy what appeared to be a new needle in a sealed bag.

MIDDLE EAST

Iran

Prior to 1979, during the rule of the Shah, the Crown Agents, through the agency of Millbank Technical Services (MTS), made a major effort to sell and support the sale of CHIEFTAIN tanks and CVR(T) SCORPION light tracked vehicles to Iran with supporting spares and ammunition. In addition to the technical training given to Iranians in the REME training schools in the UK, MTS had to provide substantial support in the field in Iran from the early Seventies, including training.

On leaving BAOR in 1975, where he had been DEME, Major General Sam Lecky became responsible under the VCGS as Director Military Assistance Office (DMAO). He fondly thought that he had also left

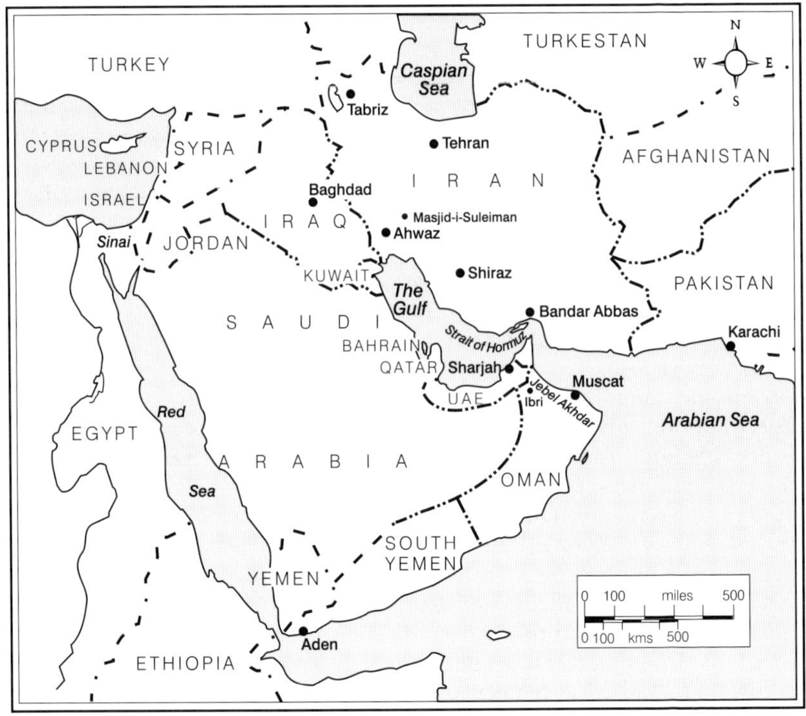

behind the CHIEFTAIN L60 engine problem and the SCORPION CVR(T) armour stress corrosion cracking, but it was not to be. Within days of taking over as DMAO he was in Iran where his Commissioning and Advisory Teams were supporting the sale of many hundreds of CHIEFTAIN tanks and 250 SCORPIONs to the Imperial Iranian Ground Forces. This became such an important project that in November 1977 he was seconded to the Diplomatic Service as Minister (Defence Supply) in the British Embassy, Tehran. He wrote:

'My wife and I landed at Mehrabad airport just as the first shots in the Iranian revolution were fired, and for the next eighteen months we watched its growth with disbelief. The disintegration of this lovely country was relentless as the daily situation became increasingly violent. On one memorable day a mob of some thousands attacked the Embassy and burned the Chancery building with us inside. Fortunately we all escaped, to ponder on the mocking of fate – it was the fifth of November! The Shah went into exile and after an exceptionally chaotic few weeks the RAF arrived on 19 February 1979 to evacuate all but a small cadre from the Embassy'.

In the mid-Seventies, soon after his retirement, Brigadier Douggie Templeton took up an appointment as Director of Support Services in Iran for MTS. Fortunately he came to the appointment with a very wide knowledge of the support problems of the CHIEFTAIN in British Army service. He was followed by Brigadier Peter Elkins who was still serving in the Corps. Support in the field by International Military Services (IMS – as MTS became when in June 1978 the Crown Agents sold it to the MOD) amounted to some 400 men, mostly ex-REME officers and artificers, but there were also a few serving REME officers on loan, dispersed throughout Iran. The tanks were received into Iran at Bandar Abbas on the Strait of Hormuz at the eastern end of the Gulf. Equipment was installed by the team at Ahwaz and handed over to the Iranian Army. At the start most support was at first line but gradually a shift of emphasis to second and third line took place. Construction of a base workshop at Dorud was well advanced; the initial design was undertaken at the REME Officers School, Arborfield, by a Senior Management Course who, as described in Chapter 5, were required to design, staff and equip a workshop for the base overhaul of a fleet of more than 750 CHIEFTAIN tanks and more than 350 SCORPION CVR(T).

The Commissioning Team, which included five REME artificers, received the first seventeen tanks at the Iranian Army Armour Centre at Shiraz, 500 miles south of Tehran, in 1971. Various problems arose, due mainly to lack of local resources. Major Bob March was sent out to Shiraz in July 1972 to find seventeen of twenty-seven tanks off the road with minor faults due to lack of spares and tools. The first Training and Instructional Team (known inevitably as TIT ONE) arrived in October 1972. By February 1974 the Commissioning Team, which had moved near to Abadan, was commissioning a company of tanks every week. The Ordnance School at Tabriz, north-west of Tehran, was another important centre where field repair training took place.

Among many potentially tactless stories it may be told that an enthusiastic officer decided one day to speed up the loading of CHIEFTAIN tanks in England by wading them out to the LST rather than wait for the MEXEFLOTE but he failed to realize that the tanks were delivered from the factory with the drain plugs removed and put in the CES pack. This initiative resulted in quick-loading two drowned tanks and many signals from Iran asking how to de-salinate CHIEFTAIN electrics!

The Technical High School at Masjid-i-Suleiman, 500 miles south-west of Tehran near Ahwaz, was set up in the mid-Seventies on the lines of the REME apprentices college at Arborfield, but it was planned to be very much larger. A combination of REME officers on loan and retired officers was employed in a school which was eventually to have 2,400 students. The first intake in September 1974 was 600 with similar intakes every six months until September 1978, which turned out to be the last. A photograph in 'The Craftsman' in January 1979 showed twenty-five serving and ex-REME staff, headed by Lieutenant Colonel Arfor Jones (Training Manager), Major Mike Dorward (Electronic Wing Adviser), Major Harry Rogers (Vehicle Wing Adviser) and Lieutenant Colonel (Retd) Don Evans (Project Manager). By January 1979 the unrest had spread and murders were taking place in many parts of the country. After two days of demonstrations and gunfire students at the School joined in, and it was closed after several students had been shot. On 15 January the IMS team were told that two RAF HERCULES aircraft would land the following day at Masjid-i-Suleiman to evacuate all dependants and most of the team.

Next morning the two HERCULES arrived from Tehran, with Major Stan Rycroft, a former member of the School staff, to pick up the party who had been escorted to the airstrip by armed soldiers. Three retired officers at the School were not evacuated, staying behind to honour the contract, including Lieutenant Colonel Don Evans. Later in the month the Iranian brigadier at the School was shot, and the three retired officers were taken in an Iranian helicopter to Tehran and put in the infamous Evin prison with Iranian generals and government officials, who were daily being selected by the revolutionary guards to be taken out and shot. The three British officers were blindfolded and moved from room to room; they thought that they too were being taken out to be shot, but, fortunately, after a few harrowing days they were released and flown back to the UK. In late January two HERCULES flew into Ahwaz to evacuate stranded members of the Chieftain Advisory Team.

After the revolution in Iran and the overthrow of the Shah's régime the new company, International Military Services, had to pay off hundreds of expatriate employees in Iran, most of whom were ex-REME, and find a new customer for their tanks. Three hundred tanks with a CHALLENGER hull and a CHIEFTAIN turret were sold to Jordan, complete with the spares, tools, test equipment, ammunition and training. The Project Manager was a retired REME Colonel, Doug Charles, who later became IMS Director of Sales and Marketing. An IMS team was set up in Amman, Jordan, with ex-REME artificers; their business grew and eventually Lieutenant Colonel John Clifton, previously a serving REME officer with the British Military Mission to the Saudi Arabian National Guard, became their manager in Amman.

IMS next turned their attention to Saudi Arabia, winning contracts for artillery and engineer equipment with all the necessary support. By the early Eighties IMS had a team of about sixty in Saudi Arabia split between the artillery and engineer schools – half of them ex-REME. The success of IMS for many years in the Middle East was at least partly due to the many REME and ex-REME men who worked for it at home and abroad.

Muscat and Oman

The Sultan's Forces comprised three battalions, the Muscat Regiment, the Northern Frontier Regiment and the Desert Regiment, with supporting arms, and the Oman Gendarmerie. The Force EME was a Major Hill who had a workshop line to overhaul Bedford and Land Rover engines.

In 1967, following his commission from Sandhurst, Second Lieutenant Nick Medlam was attached briefly to the Sultan of Muscat and Oman's Armed Forces, the country forming the eastern area of the Arabian Peninsula with a coastline stretching for a thousand miles along the Arabian Sea. Second Lieutenant Medlam was sent out at the end of his first week to Saiq in the Jebel Akhdar, a mountain range rising to over 10,000 feet without any roads up to or on the Jebel but criss-crossed with goat and donkey tracks. Saiq was a garrison fort occupied by a company of the Northern Frontier Regiment. His first task was to organize the visit of the Commander in Chief Middle East and his party, who were to stay for two days in the VIP accommodation – two mud huts. His next job was to demolish 2 inch and 3 inch mortar bombs found on the Jebel and to sort out, by years, thousands of rounds of suspect ammunition which had been handed over on relief: soldiers could not do this as they were unable to read and their counting was unreliable. His routine tasks were to administer half a company, supervise the mess and canteen and help with the training. After five weeks at Saiq he was sent to Ibri for a month where his duties were much the same, but included looking after the vehicles. This included organizing the transport for Eid al Fitr, a five-day holiday celebrating the end of Ramadan and a time for great Moslem feasting. Vehicles came in to Ibri from all the other outstations loaded with men, their kit and packs of food to be sent out to their villages.

The most interesting period he had there was in February when he commanded a half-company through its Battle Camp – battle indoctrination, demonstrations followed by section attacks with live ammunition, field firing, anti-ambush drills and half-company attacks. The march back from the battle camp was up a wadi bed for three miles, followed by a climb from 1,500 feet to 6,700 feet along a goat track. Finally there was a five-mile descent to Saiq at 6,200 feet, marching for five hours and crossing up and down seven wadis of an average depth of 300 feet.

After four unusual but enjoyable months for a REME officer, Second Lieutenant Medlam left the Sultan's Armed Forces to gain further experience on attachment to the RE at Sharjah. There is an interesting account of his experiences in the REME Journal for 1969.

Qatar

Qatar is a peninsula about 150 miles long and 50 miles wide sticking out into the Arabian gulf south of Bahrain. Qatar had a brigade group with small sea and air forces as integral parts. In 1978–79 there was a British Loan Service Team of seven under Lieutenant Colonel Gordon Barnett R SIGNALS. The team included three from the R SIGNALS and two from the Royal Navy. ASM John Todd (Local Captain) was OC Telecommunications Workshop. He made his mark when he established a new workshop with new test equipment in a portakabin. The team was there to fill specific posts until Qatar could fill them for themselves.

During John Todd's tour all the team and their wives were invited to the British Embassy to meet HM The Queen and HRH Prince Philip during their state visit. Next day they were invited to a reception on board HM Royal Yacht *Britannia.*

Kuwait

The immensely wealthy small oil state of Kuwait, the focus of the Gulf War in 1990–91, described in Chapter 12, lies at the head of the Gulf in the Middle East. It is only 17,818 square kilometres (6,880 square miles) in area and bordered by Saudi Arabia to the south and by Iraq to the north and west. Kuwait, which translated means 'little fortress', is a flat desert land, broken only by occasional low hills and shallow depressions. The elevations range from sea level in the east to nearly 1,000 feet in the south-west of the country. Significant features of the country include the Wadi Al Batin which forms the western boundary with Iraq and the Mutla Ridge which overlooks Kuwait City. The climate is semi-tropical: summer shade temperatures can reach 49°C (120°F), whereas in January, the coldest month, temperatures can drop to between –2°C and 28°C (27–85°F). The annual rainfall is up to thirty-seven centimetres, falling mainly between November and April.

The Rumaila oil fields and the islands of Bubiyan and Warbah, guarding the approaches to Kuwait, have long been the subjects of dispute with Iraq. Access to the Gulf and freedom of movement through Iraq was

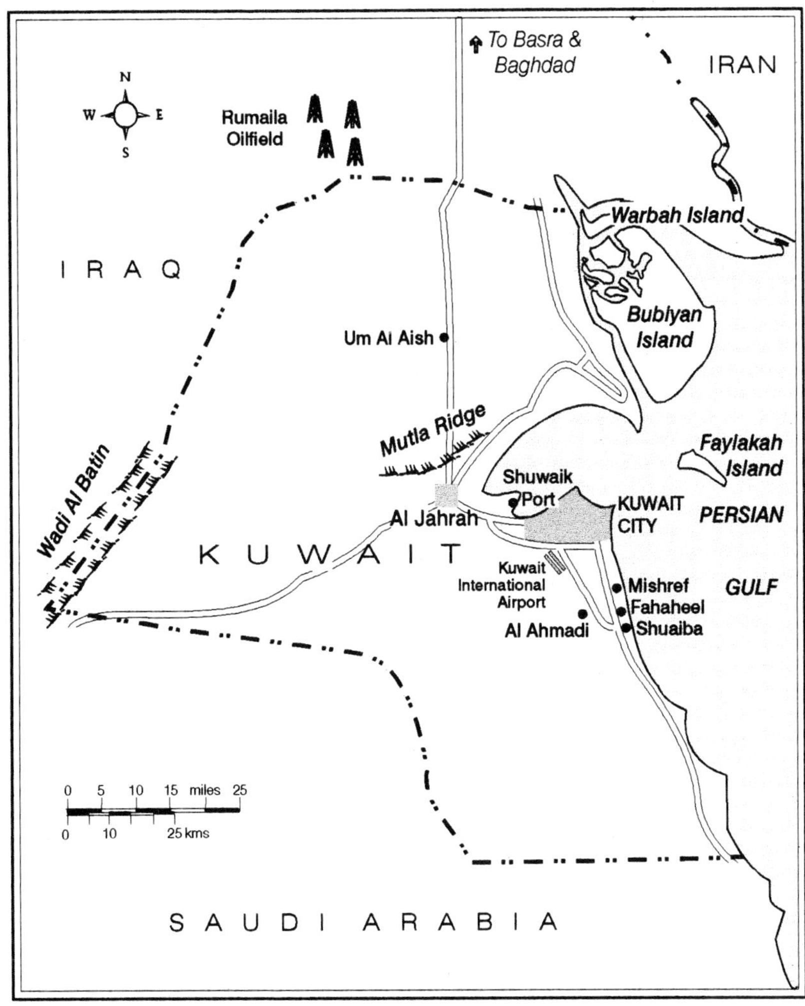

of strategic importance to Britain long before the discovery of oil in the region; the treaty accorded with Lord Curzon's policy of 'allowing no other power than England to gain influence in the Persian Gulf'. A further treaty regarding the status of Kuwait was signed with the Turks in 1913, but the outbreak of war in 1914 prevented its ratification. As a result of Kuwait's support in the war Britain declared it to be independent and a British protected state. Kuwait's independence was further guaranteed when relations with Saudi Arabia were settled in 1922 and the northern border with Iraq was agreed in 1923.

Following the Second World War, British protection of Kuwait became increasingly superfluous. Accordingly, on 19 June 1961, the British Government announced its recognition of Kuwait's independence. An exchange of Notes between the two countries terminated the treaty of 1899 and reaffirmed the British undertaking to support the Emir of Kuwait. Six days later Brigadier Kassim, the Iraqi President, announced that Kuwait was part of Iraq, his argument being that the two countries had been arbitrarily divided by Britain. The Emir appealed to Britain for assistance and a military force was quickly despatched from 24 Infantry Brigade, then based in Kenya. The Iraqis did not invade and the crisis passed. The British force was withdrawn in October 1961 and replaced by an Arab force, parts of which remained until 1963. When Kuwait's agreement with Britain ended in 1963, it was decided to establish there the Kuwait Liaison Team (KLT), made up from the British Army and the Royal Air Force. The Team's task was to provide technical training, maintenance, advice and assistance on British battle tanks and fighter aircraft sold to Kuwait.

Life in Kuwait in those days can best be summed up as 'interesting'. A common trend was for a new arrival to enjoy the novel experience for his first few months and to look forward to coming to grips with the apparent inefficiencies. This optimism could give way to frustration after about four months, with the realization that an individual was not going to change much in a system embedded in an entire culture. Most people then came to a mental accommodation of what they could best do within that system and took advantage of the many opportunities that an exotic posting offered.

All who served in Kuwait at that time will remember the free rein given to an individual style of driving cars. It was a rare and lucky person who completed his tour without a scrape or worse on his car. The Quartermasters of the Kuwaiti Army showed a similar spirit of individualism when, in the opening days of a tour, one went to draw the local uniform – not for the Kuwaitis the enforced conformity of a kit list. The new arrival was eyed by the officer-in-charge who wrote on a slip of paper what he felt the newcomer needed; no two people ever received quite the same outfit. Captain Frank Creighton, an LAD commander 1979–80, believed that he was unique when he was awarded a pair of desert boots but missed out on the black plimsolls which until then had seemed to be common currency. There was much hilarity too at the expense of a solitary officer who came out of the store with an equally solitary pillow.

Quarters for the families varied from very good to almost appalling. Another REME officer, Captain Andy Craig, moved into a flat that had been empty for a period to find pigeons nesting in the concealed lighting alcoves. He came to the rescue of Captain Creighton who was on leave in Cyprus when the Kuwaiti owner of the house returned from England and demanded his house back; the Kuwaiti Ministry of Defence gave twenty-four hours notice to the absent Creightons to move out, whereupon Captain Craig worked valiantly at packing and moving everything himself. On his return from Cyprus, Captain Creighton said that it was one of the easiest moves he ever made!

Over the years the size of the KLT fluctuated: in May 1987 it numbered six officers and fifty-one senior NCOs of whom approximately one-third were RAF. The largest single element of the Team was REME, headed by a major; there were twenty-three warrant officers and senior NCOs to cope with the 235 CHIEFTAINs, as well as ageing Vickers Main Battle Tanks. The REME Headquarters was accommodated in the Directorate of Technical Affairs (formerly the Directorate of Repair) in the area of Mishref, co-located with the CHIEFTAIN L60 Base Workshop with its single REME Adviser, the Recovery School, and the Instrument and Weapons workshop, each with its REME advisory staff.

An ASM from Mishref once said, ‘Mishref, for the uninitiated, is the mighty hub of the Kuwait military engineering machine. Situated in an attractive patch of desert, two miles from the sea, the occupants enjoy the distinct advantage of sandstorms from the west or coastal erosion from the east, depending on which direction the pollution is blowing’. A new Technical Training School was, however, rapidly approaching completion towards early 1990. This was a project which had started on the drawing board of Major Ken Robinson, who retired from the Army in Kuwait and was employed by the Kuwait Ministry of Defence. The School was to be the military showpiece of the Gulf States. A combination of SEME and SEE, it covered every trade group within the Kuwait maintenance organization. Fully equipped with the latest engineering technology, supplied by a British company, it was a most impressive technical training complex. In mid-1989 an initiative, submitted to the Kuwaitis by the British Maintenance Adviser, Major Ben Tyler (who in 1990 was appointed MBE for his work with the KLT), led to an agreement between the UK and Kuwait to increase the size of the REME element. This included six REME warrant officers to be employed as Technical Advisers to the Kuwaiti staff of the Technical Training School.

Away from Mishref, REME maintained its presence in four other far-flung areas. The furthest of these was 6 Mechanized Infantry Brigade in Um Al Aish. Located north of the Mutla Ridge the detachment was only a few miles from the Iraqi border. This location caused a few uncomfortable moments for the REME element during the Iraq/Iran conflict. Equipped with the over-age fleet of Vickers Main Battle Tanks, 9 Armoured Regiment would face the full thrust of any assault from its northern neighbour. 6 Brigade was continually at a high stage of security alert, as one of the newer members of the REME element discovered during his first inspection of a Vickers. After ‘dropping’ inside, he found to his horror it was completely ‘bombed’ up and sitting in a complete state of readiness in the shade temperatures of up to 48°C.

To the south of Kuwait was 15 Armoured Brigade, located at Shuaiba.

Lying only a short distance from the main KLT families complex in Fahaheel (IBI Camp leased from International Bechtel Incorporated and affectionately known as 'Tenko'), the three REME warrant officers had only half an hour's travelling time to their selected patch of desert. REME maintenance support was given to two CHIEFTAIN Regiments and the associated support equipments. 15 Brigade always enjoyed the enviable status of a 'showpiece brigade'; all distinguished visitors were taken there. It might also have had something to do with a relative of HH the Emir being stationed there as the Training Officer.

Further to the north-west, south of 6 Brigade, was 35 Armoured Brigade It boasted two CHIEFTAIN regiments which were supported by the REME detachment of three REME warrant officers. It was the closest brigade to Saudi Arabia and one REME warrant officer commented that the most interesting view was the traffic passing on the 'road' to Saudi Arabia.

One spring when the weather was at it best 35 Brigade went out for a two-weeks' exercise in the desert. Low mileage led to a low workload but a ripple of excitement for REME was the delivery of their first 24-hour ration pack – still on four legs and bleating. One member of REME, sleeping on top of his vehicle to avoid scorpions, awoke to discover himself about to be 'kissed' by an inquisitive camel. On the final day of the exercise a set-piece demonstration of an armoured assault was laid on for the Crown Prince. After an impressive display, the brigade was invited to a dinner in the desert, laid out in a natural depression. The tanks and other vehicles were parked on the lip of the depression and everyone walked down to their places at rows of plastic sheeting arranged in a multi-legged 'E'. Dusk gave way to a starry Arabian night with vehicles silhouetted against the sky; in dim light the soldiers sat cross-legged with their weapons cradled in their left arms as they dug into the trays of rice and goat with their right hands; together with the hubbub of conversation there was an indelible impression of an event not to have been missed.

It was at 35 Brigade that the Chieftain Technical Training Wing (CTTW) was established. In addition to the normal brigade REME establishment of three warrant officers, the CTTW employed two further REME warrant officers. The main responsibility of the CTTW was to train Kuwaiti military tradesmen in repair techniques and maintenance procedures on the CHIEFTAIN MBT. This responsibility was later transferred, together with the REME Advisers, to the new Technical Training School.

Finally, the KLT's other REME commitment was in Al Jahrah at the prestigious Armoured School. (The majority of Kuwaiti officers at the Armoured School had attended British gunnery courses at Lulworth). Prior to 1987 this detachment had been closed and the REME element withdrawn due to a Kuwaiti misunderstanding of terminology. However, this was soon clarified and a REME detachment of three warrant officers was quickly re-established. Their presence was fully appreciated by the British Armoured and Signals advisers who had exhausted all their best Arabic within a week of the detachment closing!

1987–1990 saw some interesting changes within the REME element of the KLT, now re-named British Liaison Team – Kuwait (BLT – Kuwait). In September 1989 the OC REME element undertook a radical review of the REME establishment and method of working, aiming to increase the emphasis on training local technicians, and thereby enable a possible phased reduction of REME personnel over the following 10 years. In May 1990 this review was formally presented to the Director and senior staff officers of the Directorate of Technical Affairs. Also in attendance were all workshop commanders, as well as the Commander BLT – Kuwait, Colonel B A C Duncan (late RTR). The presentation explained the need to achieve full Kuwaiti autonomy through such REME reductions, and its immediate impact on the training of local tradesmen to take over. The proposal was well received and placed the REME element in its strongest position of influence for several years. Unfortunately, no sooner had this new REME approach been implemented than Iraq invaded Kuwait.

The Iraqi invasion started in the early hours of Thursday 2 August 1990 and was spearheaded by the elite and battle-hardened Republican Guard, the most professional element of President Saddam Hussein's much-vaunted 'war machine'. Surprise was total and within four hours the invading forces had reached Kuwait City. Within twelve hours Kuwait was virtually under Iraqi control, although mopping-up operations continued for several days. The attack was well co-ordinated with tanks and mechanized infantry supported by artillery. By using Kuwait's excellent motorway network to full effect, other elements of the attacking force sped round to surround and seize the oil town of Al Ahmadi thirty kilometres to the south of Kuwait City, thereby effectively controlling the road to the Saudi Arabian border.

The Iraqi strategy appeared to be to take over military bases, surround important government buildings and occupy key installations such as water, electricity and oil plants. Kuwait International Airport was subjected to an air attack and then occupied by armoured troops of the Iraqi invasion force. The battle for Kuwait, however, had not been a complete walk-over. Elements of the Kuwaiti Army made a brave stand at Al Jahrah to the west of Kuwait City. This courageous group of Kuwaiti soldiers refused to leave their posts, despite overwhelming odds, and died in a vain attempt to halt the Iraqi onslaught. Fierce fighting was also reported around the Emir of Kuwait's two main palaces. Although the Emir escaped by helicopter to Saudi Arabia, loyal soldiers of his Emiri Guard fought to the death to save the Dasman Palace from falling into Iraqi hands. Their burned-out armoured vehicles lay around the perimeter in silent testimony to their bravery throughout the period of

Iraqi occupation. The majority of Kuwait's ruling Al Sabah family managed to escape during the night of 1-2 August. One notable exception, however, was Sheik Falid Al Sabah, the Minister of Sport. He died tragically, yet heroically, on the steps of the palace valiantly defending his home against impossible odds.

At the time of the invasion there were sixty-six members and over 150 dependants of the British Liaison Team in Kuwait. They were to find themselves embroiled in a situation which was dangerous and testing for all concerned. Fortunately, at that time all were at home with their families. The team members were housed in various locations, widely dispersed throughout Kuwait. However, the local telephone network was still operational, although the international communication lines were cut by 0900 hours on the morning of the invasion. Team members were able to contact each other, report separately on the situation and also maintain morale.

First reports painted a rather confusing picture, and sporadic fighting continued for several days throughout the Emirate. To venture out whilst fighting continued was considered most unwise, but within forty-eight hours many of Kuwait City's suburbs became quiet and almost devoid of Iraqi troops. However, the picture became more sinister when, on Friday 3 August, the Iraqis seized thirty-six members of the Team, including approximately twelve REME personnel from the main accommodation complex of IBI Camp on the outskirts of the town of Fahaheel. The men were removed and later transported to Baghdad to become members of Saddam's 'human shield', his deployment of such hostages to vulnerable targets in Iraq. The wives and children were then left to the mercy of the Iraqi military. Distressing and frantic telephone reports described an ill-disciplined rabble as running amok. Houses were reportedly broken into and looted, women were harassed and even molested. Team member's cars were 'hot wired' and raced about the complex like dodgem cars at a fairground. However, thanks to the determined efforts of the British Ambassador, Mr Michael Weston, and members of his staff, the situation was brought under control before anyone was seriously hurt.

Within 72 hours of the invasion the Republican Guard had been withdrawn and replaced by a larger but less professional Regular Army force. During the early days of the occupation these troops were openly terrified by the thought of an allied attack. Many cases were reported of Iraqi soldiers deserting, especially those located near the Kuwait/Saudi border. These were a wretched, ill-equipped and poorly led body of men. Most of the time they had to fend for themselves with regard to food and water rations. Looting became a regular pastime. Most of these unfortunate conscripts had no idea of their positions. Some are reported to have been told they were conscripted to assist in the liberation of their Moslem brothers in the 19th province of Iraq. (Kuwait had never been recognized by Saddam as an independent country.) Most of them had no real alternative but to enlist or to face execution.

One story related by Commander BLT illustrates the brutality which existed in Saddam's cruel régime. A young soldier, who had been in Kuwait for about a week, appeared to be in a daze and did not know what he was supposed to be doing. Apparently when the team of recruiters had arrived at his house about a month earlier to persuade him to enlist, he had explained that his father and elder brothers had all been killed in the war with Iran. He was the only male member of the family left and so he was responsible for looking after his mother and his four sisters. The recruiters departed, apparently satisfied, but another team came the next day. He gave them the same story, whereupon they lined up his remaining family and executed them. They then declared that his responsibilities were no longer a problem for him, so he must now enlist.

Following a BBC World Service news broadcast which informed everyone, including the Iraqi Intelligence Service, that thirty-six members of a sixty-strong British military liaison team had been taken, it was decided by the Commanding Officer, Colonel Bruce Duncan, and certain members of the team that it was desirable to move their families to a safer area.

From the outset of the invasion Colonel Duncan, his wife, two sons, two daughters and a young school friend, were completely caught up in the fighting. Within hours their house was in the midst of the Iraqi defences around Shuwaik Port. He and his family were totally cut off and it would only have been a matter of time before they were all discovered by the Iraqis. Initially, Colonel Duncan later stated, this did not appear to be a problem, but when, on 3 August, the Iraqis seized the thirty-six members of the team, their situation looked a little bleak. Several attempts were made to rescue them before the British Ambassador, Mr Michael Weston, and the Consul, Mr Larry Banks, finally succeeded in reaching them on the 7 August. Following a two-and-a-half-hour episode at the Iraqi Headquarters in Shuwaik Port, they were finally released and transported to the British Embassy. From there they were moved into a vacant Embassy staff house, which was complete with radio transmitter, located in a quiet suburb of Mishref, to the south of Kuwait City.

Meanwhile events surrounding a large complex of flats, known as 'The Marzouk Pearl', where four of the Team's officers were accommodated, took a significant turn for the worse. Iraqi troops continued to build up their coastal defences. All along Arabic Gulf Street, the main coastal road leading to Kuwait City, Russian-made T62s and artillery pieces were positioned with their muzzles pointing out over the gulf waters.

A small detachment of approximately two officers and twelve soldiers suddenly appeared in the main car park in front of the flats. It was not long before an officer, accompanied by three soldiers, entered the building. Only three British officers and their families were in the flats at the time of the invasion: Major Alex Boyd RAOC, his wife and two teenage children, Captain Colin Dunscombe AAC, his wife and two teenage children, and Major Ben Tyler REME, his wife, a two-year-old daughter and a son of only four weeks, together with a family friend who had joined them earlier for a holiday. Major Rick Stocks RCT and his family were on leave in Cyprus.

A knock at the door of his flat was the first Major Tyler knew of Iraqis in the building. The door was opened by his wife Miriam carrying the baby, a deliberate move playing on Arab uncertainty in dealing with Western women. However, the Iraqis had been planning this invasion for some considerable time and their intelligence system was well informed. Asking for 'Major Ben Tyler', the Iraqi Officer and his escort entered the flat, followed by the Manager of the Marzouk Pearl who was full of apologies as if the electricity system had failed. After asking numerous questions concerning Major Tyler's employment with the Kuwaiti MOD (Major Tyler informed them he was a mechanical engineer, never admitting to being in the military), the officer searched the flat for any sight of military clothing or equipment (which had all been hidden a few hours previously). Having satisfied himself there was nothing more he could do, he left and went upstairs to visit the other flats. Major Boyd and Captain Dunscombe were promptly arrested and taken away. It was later learned that they were held in the Scandinavian Airlines System (SAS) Hotel where they were 'interviewed' by the Iraqis. Following their interview they were transported, along with other British personnel, to Baghdad where they were deployed as Saddam Hussein's 'human shields' to protect his military installations throughout Iraq. They, along with all the British hostages in Iraq, were released before Christmas when Saddam Hussein realized that the hostage card had been played to the full.

It was at this stage, particularly after hearing reports that Iraqi troops were taking cars from the car park and driving them into the Gulf (in an attempt to prevent a beach landing by an allied invasion force), that the remaining British families in the Marzouk Pearl decided to move location. Captain Dale Millar, the newly installed REME Training Adviser, whose wife and baby were enjoying a short holiday in England, arrived on the planned day to assist the two families whose husbands had been 'lifted'. Their cars were loaded to capacity with personal items of sentimental value, clothing and most importantly, provisions. The families were moved to another vacant British Embassy staff house in the suburbs of Mishref – not far away from where Colonel Duncan and family were staying. The three families found a fourth family there, Squadron Leader John Stirling, his wife and two teenage sons. Finally, with some difficulty, all fifteen persons were safely ensconced in the three-bedroom villa.

From day one, life was conducted in a military manner. Squadron Leader Stirling was elected overall Commander, Captain Millar was responsible for all security matters and Major Tyler was elected quartermaster, responsible for food, drink and anything else that nobody did! Their wives, in addition to trying to maintain a semblance of home, took their turn on the telephone rota, maintaining a log of all calls in and out.

Each Kuwait suburb was a self-contained residential area, complete with its own Co-op, medical centre and schools. The Co-op was very similar to Co-operative stores found in Britain. Other shops, usually a bakery, a general hardware shop which sold electrical items, and a motor vehicle shop which sold mechanical components to fit most Japanese and American cars, were located around the main Co-operative. The main building and often the most imposing was the inevitable mosque and this too was situated near the shopping area.

All citizens in Kuwait had to carry a civilian identity card, which included one's address. This became a problem when shopping at the Mishref Co-op. Initially, when food stocks were plenty, identity cards were not required, but as the Iraqi occupation continued and food stocks dropped Co-op managers soon decided to serve only those card-holders whose address was shown as Mishref. To make matters worse, the Iraqis introduced their hostage policy. On 16 August all British personnel were ordered to report to the Regency Palace Hotel, whilst other Westerners were ordered to report to various other hotels. After numerous discussions on the telephone with other Britons, expatriates as well as military, it was decided to lie low.

Amongst the British expatriates was Lieutenant Colonel Denis Redmond, who, having retired from REME in 1972, was now managing director of the Ford franchise in Kuwait. At the time of the invasion he was living in a flat at Salmiya, some two miles from the centre of the city, which initially was a scene of violent battle. He too decided to stay hidden, though changing his accommodation more than once to evade capture, including staying with civilian friends at Mishref. He suffered the same problems and harrowing experiences as the serving members of the Corps and their families, and his survival was also made possible by the help he received from the Kuwait armed resistance movement. He was successful in evading capture until 6 December, when he was evacuated with other foreigners and hostages then released by Saddam. His full story was told in the REME Journal for 1991.

Although life for the four families in Mishref was restricted, to say the least, it was made more bearable by the way they were looked after by their Kuwaiti and Palestinian neighbours. Mishref was divided into six areas and each area had its own local 'vigilante' group of Kuwaitis and Palestinians which patrolled the area to protect it from looters and to warn residents of infiltration by the 'Mukhabaraat' (Iraqi secret police). In addition to conducting security patrols, these vigilante groups carried out refuse disposal and resupply of foodstuffs to the Co-ops; they brought fresh water to those houses not connected to the main supply and also co-ordinated medical care for the residents of the area. One of the main responsibilities they accepted was to support any Westerners trapped in their areas: as far as they were concerned, Westerners were guests in their country whose welfare became their chief responsibility. This responsibility extended so far as to provide money to each household, usually amounting to 100 Kuwaiti dinars (approximately £200) per week of their own money to be used to purchase basic household essentials. All members of these local vigilante groups risked certain death at the hands of the Iraqis if they were discovered either sheltering or aiding Westerners. There were many stories of individual heroism and bravery by both Palestinians and Kuwaitis, each an object lesson in all that is best in the Islamic religion.

Gradually the life style in Mishref became more and more restricted. Initially Team members were able to move around within the area, even visiting other Westerners, especially in the heat of the early afternoon when the Iraqi soldiers were resting. However, towards the end of August, about the same time that Iraq announced the closure of Western embassies, warnings were received from members of the local vigilante groups that the 'Mukhabaraat' had begun to infiltrate Mishref. Team members, along with other Westerners and their families, were advised to stay in the houses, reduce any unnecessary noise, close shutters and draw curtains.

On 16 August the British Embassy had been reduced to a skeleton staff and the Iraqis agreed to provide a military escort for the evacuating staff all the way to Baghdad. They also agreed to allow all the BLT dependants whose husbands had been seized on 3 August to travel with the convoy. It was learned later that, although all had arrived in Baghdad, their journey had been a nightmare of twenty-six hours. They had driven some 400 miles in private cars belonging to team members which had been organized by Captain Millar. The drive through the intense August heat, when many were forced to switch off the air-conditioning to conserve fuel, took its toll, and some of the children on arrival had to be taken to the Iraqi hospital suffering from heat exhaustion. Captain Millar had earlier risked capture by the Iraqis when driving round in an Embassy CD plated car on his 'morale boost' tours to various areas where Team members were located.

On 24 August Iraq formerly announced that Kuwait had been annexed and was to be known as the nineteenth province of Iraq. At the same time it was declared that all Western embassies in the new province were, with immediate effect, null and void.

At the beginning of September the good news was announced over the BBC World Service (a life-saving programme listened to by all the Westerners), that all women and children were free to leave Kuwait and Iraq.

Already a large number of the Team's dependants were hostages in Iraq, having travelled to Baghdad with the Embassy convoy on the 16 August. Now it was the turn of the remaining families to make the hazardous journey to Baghdad. Monday 3 September was a busy day for the Team's families, and detailed plans were made to transport dependants to the rendezvous located outside the Sultan Centre, a huge American hypermarket on Arabic Gulf Street. From there, coaches organized by the British Ambassador in Iraq would transport them to Baghdad, escorted by the Iraqi military to ensure their 'safety'. In the early hours of 4 September from the various locations scattered throughout the Salmiyah and Mishref areas, families were either transported by local residents or walked to the rendezvous, to commence their journey to freedom. Following what later was described as a horrifying twenty-hour ordeal, everyone arrived in Baghdad. From there they were eventually flown to the UK and safety. The trauma for the families did not end there but rather increased, as husbands and fathers were still trapped, either hiding somewhere in Kuwait or held hostage somewhere in Iraq.

Following the release of the women and children on 4 September the Iraqi military appeared to intensify their search operations for Westerners in Kuwait. A possible reason for this activity was that they had not been prepared for such large numbers of dependants who emerged from hiding to take advantage of the British-sponsored convoy to Baghdad. From this they obviously deduced that a high number of men still remained in hiding, somewhere in Kuwait. Search teams were usually about twelve to fifteen strong and comprised a mixture of Republican Guard, Mukhabaraat and conscripts. These search teams would normally arrive in an area without warning, completely seal it off and then start a house-to-house search. Any residence found locked would be forcibly entered, the occupants, if any, were either arrested or harassed and the house, if empty, was systematically looted.

As the weeks wore on Team members found the greatest enemy to be boredom, which detracted from maintaining a high state of alert. Days and sometimes weeks would pass without an Iraqi search, but then without warning soldiers and vehicles would be all around a house. No one could afford to be complacent. Early-morning watches were organized and 'escape' plans continually practised in an attempt to keep alert and avoid being 'lifted'. There was, however, one indication that a raid was being planned for an area. Since the Iraqi occupation, most of the services, water, electricity and telephones, had continued to function. This did much to keep spirits high, particularly the telephone service which was constantly used by Team members to exchange reports of Iraqi movement and pass on other items of news. When a raid was imminent telephone lines were cut off, effectively preventing it being forecast to other occupants within the area. However, it was soon realized that when the lines were off, a raid was on: these were anxious moments. When a search by Iraqi soldiers was being carried out they could be seen in the streets, in the gardens, or even heard banging on doors or attempting to break open window shutters. Team members could only think of the future and remaining free minute by minute, until the danger had passed. Existing under such stressful and trying conditions called for a strong sense of self-discipline. Daily programmes were organized: meal times, telephone calls and, in particular, physical exercise periods were programmed and strictly adhered to.

It was considered vitally important to Team members for everyone to keep in contact by telephone on a regular basis. Each sub-area had its own designated British Area Warden whose responsibility was to maintain contact within the main area and with the British Embassy. It was an accepted fact that the telephone system was insecure. A risk also existed of informers, or of the Mukhabaraat dialling telephone numbers at random to find out if a 'foreigner' answered. To overcome this a code was devised and introduced by Squadron Leader Stirling: to make contact the number would be dialled and the telephone allowed to ring three times before the receiver was replaced and then the number immediately redialled. This system proved very successful and was adopted, not only by the British expatriates, but also by the local vigilante committee members. When answering the telephone Team members would either wait for the caller to speak and identify themselves or respond initially in Arabic.

During these intense days it was inevitable that members of the Team would eventually be located by the Iraqi 'hit teams' as they became known. Group by group, Team members were either 'fingered' by informers and 'lifted' or were just unfortunate enough not to evade capture. Once 'captured', the Iraqis would transport them to the SAS Hotel where the captives were able to take advantage of most of the Hotel's facilities, albeit under constant supervision by Iraqi guards. When sufficient numbers had been lifted, they would be transported to Baghdad to join other Western hostages.

At this time the BBC World Service introduced the programme 'Gulf Link'. The programme was dedicated to sending messages from home to all those, husbands, fathers and sons, who were trapped in Iraq and Kuwait. This fifteen-minute programme was a wonderful boost to individual morale. So popular was it that the programme, which was transmitted at 1945 hours Kuwait time with a repeat programme at 0730 hours the following morning, was extended to thirty minutes and eventually to forty-five minutes. Messages provided a tremendous boost to one particular group of BLT members. A British family who had escaped by vehicle across the desert to Saudi Arabia in the early days informed anybody living in or near a certain house that they would find, hidden away in the attic, a large supply of provisions, which the family had pre-positioned. It just so happened that two REME ASMs and two RAF sergeants were listening to the programme in that very house. Not only did they find the tinned food, they also discovered, as a bonus, twelve bottles of home-made wine. It was two days before any sensible telephone messages were received from that particular group!

By mid-October only eleven members of the Team, together with Colonel Duncan's two sons, Alex and Rory, remained in hiding in Kuwait. The other fifty-five servicemen and one dependant had been transported to strategic military sites in Iraq as part of Saddam's 'human shield'.

A few days later tragedy struck Colonel Duncan's family. On the evening of 22 October, having survived three days of intensive searches by the Iraqis, Colonel Duncan received a telephone call from the British Ambassador in Kuwait informing him that Mr Edward Heath, who was in Baghdad negotiating the release of certain hostages had secured the release of Alex and Rory. They were required to give themselves up to the Iraqi authorities at the Regency Palace Hotel. They would then be transported to Baghdad in time to fly to England as part of Mr Heath's 'hostage release package' on the evening of the 23 October. The night move to the Hotel went as planned and after being 'interviewed' by the Iraqi Mukhabaraat the two boys were collected by an Iraqi driver to be taken to the Kuwait International Airport. During the drive to the airport they were involved in an accident. In the prevailing circumstances all traffic discipline had been lost and few traffic lights functioned. The accident killed Colonel Duncan's eldest son Alex and four other people. The younger son Rory and the driver of the vehicle survived, although both were seriously injured.

It was eight hours later that Colonel Duncan was informed of the accident. The Iraqis had refused to allow the Ambassador or the Consul to visit the Al-Sabbah hospital where both boys had been taken, so it was agreed that Colonel Duncan should come out of hiding, give himself up and demand that the Iraqis take him to the hospital. Two days later they were flown to Baghdad. After Colonel Duncan left, Major Tyler assumed 'command' of the remaining seven BLT members. These became known as the 'Kuwait Eight' who had succeeded in evading capture by the Iraqis in Kuwait for over four months.

At 1450 hours on the 6 December, the American News Programme CNN announced that Saddam Hussein had decided to release all foreign hostages, which was confirmed twenty minutes later on the BBC World Service. Caution was the keyword and it was two days before some of the British Team members emerged from hiding to venture out onto the streets. In the town of Al Ahmadi, WO2 Simon Evans REME had spent nearly a fortnight trapped with two RAF Team members in the attic of a bungalow occupied by a detachment of the Iraqi security forces, before this freedom came.

Three days later, with the help of the Kuwaitis, a coach was hired to drive the hostages from Mishref to the Kuwait International Airport, where they met up with all the other British hostages. Pandemonium reigned; the armed Iraqi troops still surrounding the airport appeared to be completely dazed and confused by the number of 'survivors'. Eventually everyone boarded the Iraqi aircraft and were flown to Baghdad. There they were met by the British Ambassador, Mr Harold Walker, and his staff who provided food, cigarettes, bottles of whisky and, most important, personal mail. There was a mood of euphoria which continued throughout the flight home later that evening.

So ended a most traumatic experience for all members of the Kuwait Liaison Team and other foreigners who suffered similarly. For those people life would never be quite the same. For the Kuwaitis and those foreigners unable to leave, the liberation of Kuwait was still two long months away.

Members of the Team returned to the fold of their respective services where, once again, they wore the traditional colours of khaki and blue. For their wives and children, following the colours had never been expected to be quite so traumatic. They had all been caught up in the midst of an unpredictable and hostile situation and were powerless to do anything about it. Wives, sons and daughters, especially those whose husbands were seized in early August, responded magnificently to the challenge of the situation and there were many courageous acts by those who survived the long dark days of the Iraqi occupation. Until 2 August 1990, when the Iraqis invaded, the British Liaison Team Kuwait had helped the Kuwait Armed Forces for more than twenty-six years without major problems. Much goodwill had been forged, friendships established and, despite the form of its ending, there had been satisfaction of a job well done. The Corps was proud to continue to exercise its role in the area as part of the victorious Allied Force that was to drive the Iraqis from Kuwait in February 1991.

The British Military Mission to the Saudi Arabian National Guard

The British Military Mission to the Saudi Arabian National Guard was formed in 1963 but it was not until 1970 that the first REME officer, Lieutenant Colonel 'Tuck' Townsend, was posted to the new appointment of Vehicle Adviser which he held until 1976. Long service with the Mission became usual in the Seventies to meet the wishes of the National Guard, always provided that the officer was liked and had earned their respect: this could take a long time. In 1985 Lieutenant Colonel John Clifton retired from the Army to take up a post in Jordan; he was relieved by Lieutenant Colonel Cliff Squires who was promoted in 1987 into the post of Deputy Senior British Adviser and Senior Logistics Adviser.

In Colonel Squires' time the British Military Mission had eight members headed by a Brigadier, compared with about forty officers from the US Army with their very many instructors. On exercises the RAOC adviser and the Colonel would travel around the desert in distinctive white Land Rovers to emphasize their neutrality. During the hot afternoons they would seek out the Bedu tents in search of tea, approaching with care and stopping some hundred metres away to allow the flurry of women and children racing into the tents to subside. If no man emerged they would move on, but normally they would be lucky; having seen their National Guard uniform they would be welcomed enthusiastically. After dissuading their host from killing a goat and making a feast they would be plied with cups of hot sweet tea and pumped for news – an important desert commodity. After an hour of straining their limited Arabic to the full the officers would say their farewells, with cola and oranges for the children, and then all the men would line up for a photograph. Refreshed, the two officers would rejoin the exercise and provide further logistical advice.

Colonel Barry Hodgkiss arrived in Saudi Arabia in June 1990, prior to the Iraqi invasion of Kuwait. In late 1991 Colonel Squires was appointed Defence Attaché in Kuwait.

Sinai Peninsula

A force designated the UN Multinational Force and Observers (MFO) was set up in 1982 to ensure that neither Egypt nor Israel exceeded the force levels permitted in the demilitarized and limited force zones of the Sinai Peninsula, following the Yom Kippur war of 1973 and the peace treaty of 1979 brought about by President Carter of the United States.

The UK contingent to the MFO was a headquarters company of thirty-eight providing administrative, clerical and logistical support. There were two REME posts, that of Staff Officer Automotive Support and Maintenance filled once in every eighteen months by a REME captain for a six-month tour, and a corporal clerk in Force HQ. Life in this force was described by Captain Brian McCall in the 1988 REME Journal.

AFRICA

The Gambia

The West African Republic of Gambia, the smallest independent state in Africa and formerly a British protectorate, comprises the lower valley of the River Gambia and is surrounded on three sides by Senegal. The Corps contributed a member of the British Army Training Team (BATT) and on its initial formation in 1984 Major (QM) Ken Wright was appointed. Its task was to assist in the recruiting and training of the

Gambian National Army, for which both the British and French governments were to provide equipment. He was joined by two company sergeant majors, one each from the Grenadier Guards and the Black Watch, but the fourth permanent member of the Team, a Major in the Royal Irish Rangers to command BATT, was not initially available; a captain from the KOSB was sent out to give temporary assistance.

The camp at which they were to be based, and eventually to train recruits, was near Yundum airport, the international airport some twenty miles outside Banjul (formerly Bathurst), the capital of The Gambia. As a start to the recruiting the BATT announced on Radio Gambia that they would recruit at 0830 hours one morning and said what qualities they were looking for. When the team went to the sports field to see who had responded, there were 900 candidates from whom they selected fifty.

Soon the BATT had intakes of sixty, training on the Common Military Syllabus, plus Junior NCO Cadres and Continuation Training. By early 1985 they had held an Officer Selection Board, and in November they held the first inaugural passing out parade and the official opening ceremony of Yundum Camp, performed by His Excellency Alhaji Sir Dawda Kairaba Jawara GCMG, President of the Republic of The Gambia. The parade was commanded by three officer cadets. The contingent took part in the Independence Day parade and for three months provided the ceremonial Guard of Honour at the airport when Heads of State arrived or departed. Among many social events which Major Wright and his wife attended was one at the British High Commissioner's residence on 11 March 1985 to meet REME's Colonel in Chief HRH Prince Philip, who was visiting The Gambia as President of the World Wild Life Fund. REME representation on BATT continued with Captain Trevor Stewart and Major John Payne until late 1991; the Team was withdrawn the following year.

Southern Rhodesia – Operation AGILA

Rhodesia had been self-governing since 1923, but in 1965 its government led by Ian Smith made a Unilateral Declaration of Independence (UDI): an illegal act which resulted in the external imposition of sanctions, and an armed rebellion led by Joshua Nkomo and Robert Mugabe based on their 1976 Patriotic Front coalition; their associated guerrilla armies, ZIPRA and ZANLA, however, did not integrate. Not until the end of 1979 was a cease-fire agreed, following talks in Lancaster House, London. The guerrillas were to stand down and move to assembly points for disarming. The pre-UDI constitution was to be restored and free elections were to be held: effectively marking the end of opposition to black majority rule. Independence would then be granted by Britain. The period of restoration following December 1979, prior to the elections in February 1980, was a particularly dangerous and critical time with the two groups of guerrillas coming to the assembly points, and mutual suspicion leading to ambush, attacks on villages and use of mines. Armed members of the Patriotic Front sometimes had to be persuaded to go to their assembly points.

In ensuring the safe birth of the new Zimbabwe a 1,300-strong Commonwealth Liaison and Monitoring Organization (CLAMOR) played an important role. Operation AGILA, in which REME was heavily involved, was mounted to send CLAMOR to Southern Rhodesia. Troops were deployed over two weeks at Christmas 1979 and the operation continued until 20 March 1980, following the elections.

The REME support was found from: FEME 7 Field Force, a detachment of 8 Field Workshop, 656 Squadron AAC LAD under a FEME (Aircraft), a detachment of 70 Aircraft Workshop, four REME soldiers from 3 Flight AAC and one REME soldier from 22 Engineer Regiment Workshop. Vehicle mechanics from 8 Field Force units deployed singly with each Commissioner, Monitoring and Border Crossing Team. During the two weeks before deployment a total of eighty-four Land Rovers had been fully mineplated by 18 and 27 Command Workshops and 34 Central Workshop. The REME military and civilian workforce worked long hours in order to meet the deadlines set and to solve the many technical problems.

Zimbabwe – British Military Advisory and Training Team (BMATT)

After the establishment of the Republic of Zimbabwe in April 1980 the Zimbabwe National Army (ZNA) was formed from the former Rhodesian Army and the two guerrilla armies. Colonel John Tinkler was the REME member of a UK Logistics Team, whose report included a recommendation that a team should be formed to advise the newly created army and help it in implementing their proposals. The resulting Logistics Team was established in 1981 under Lieutenant Colonel Keith Steel REME, to provide a broad spectrum of logistics advice and basic technical training to the ZNA. The main training effort was to produce vehicle mechanics, but some armourers and electricians were also trained.

Staff Sergeant R S McMillan was in Zimbabwe in 1980–81 as part of the BMATT. He described his time in the trade training school:

'It was interesting, culturally as well as technically and militarily. It was mind-boggling to be part of such a change. When I took over in the technical training school there were six apprentices who had been recruited by the Rhodesian Army after exhaustive tests: they were six out of two hundred who had sat a test for a South African university. After a few weeks I split my day up between theory in the mornings and practical in the afternoons. I taught them everything from electronic theory to how to put air in a tyre. Their writing was beautiful but I soon began to tell whether they had really understood or if they were reciting parrot fashion. On

the practical side we built a Land Rover from the chassis up, reboring the engine, making the brake pipes and the clips to fit the pipe neatly to the chassis. They were a fantastic bunch, eager to learn, but if something went wrong they would soon say, "It was him, Staff". While I was there Nkomo made a bid for power – it was unsuccessful.'

CGS talks with a Zimbabwe student, Sergeant Neil looking on

Young mechanics joined a mobile repair team run by Sergeant Priddice which gave supervised experience and much-needed roving support; he was awarded the BEM in 1982 for his work in Zimbabwe. The BMATT Logistics Team was disbanded the following year under Lieutenant Colonel Trevor Courtnell, but reformed in 1985, including Major Bill Harrison working in Army Headquarters. Lieutenant Colonel Charles Morgan, SO1 Log BMATT, developed a plan in 1988 which aimed to overhaul the logistics system to give better support to the ZNA. As a result the Team was enlarged in 1989 from two to eight officers, including Major Mal Davison who was placed in the Base Workshop as an adviser. A Logistics School was opened in the same year to teach and become a centre of expertise.

From 1987 BMATT was involved in the training of infantry companies of the Mozambique Army, which were deployed later on the Limpopo Railway Line. In 1989, as the Mozambique Training Team increased in size, it held, instead of borrowing, its own vehicles and equipment which led to the need for two REME Sergeant Vehicle Mechanics who ran what was said to have been probably the best and one of the most remote repair facilities in Africa – in a purpose-built LAD.

Namibia

Namibia is on the west coast of Africa with Angola to the north and the Republic of South Africa to the south. To monitor its transition to independence (ultimately achieved in 1990) a three-battalion force was formed, the United Nations Transitional Assistance Group (UNTAG).

From 30th Signal Regiment an UNTAG Signal Squadron was formed, its vehicles fitted with mine plates and painted white by 27 District Workshop at Warminster. NCOs from the LAD joined the advance party and flew out to Windhoek, the capital of Namibia, in March 1989 in a United States Air Force C5 aircraft, taking twelve Land Rovers, trailers and hundreds of pounds of kit with them. Two NCOs followed by sea in an American merchant ship at the end of April, bringing the rest of their vehicles; the main party flew out to arrive about the same time. Their task was to keep the vehicles on the road or track, often hundreds of miles from Windhoek and based at ten different places, while second-line support was provided by the Canadians in Windhoek. The Force returned to the UK in early 1990, and at Warminster they recall repainting the vehicles to their normal green, only to receive a fresh demand for buff livery to suit deployment to the Gulf – even before at least one had been returned to the Regiment.

MEDITERRANEAN

Cyprus

On Monday 15 July 1974 there was a major development in Cyprus when a coup took place in Nicosia to overthrow the government of Archbishop Makarios. This was organized by mainland Greek army officers of the Greek Cypriot National Guard who installed Nicos Sampson (a Greek

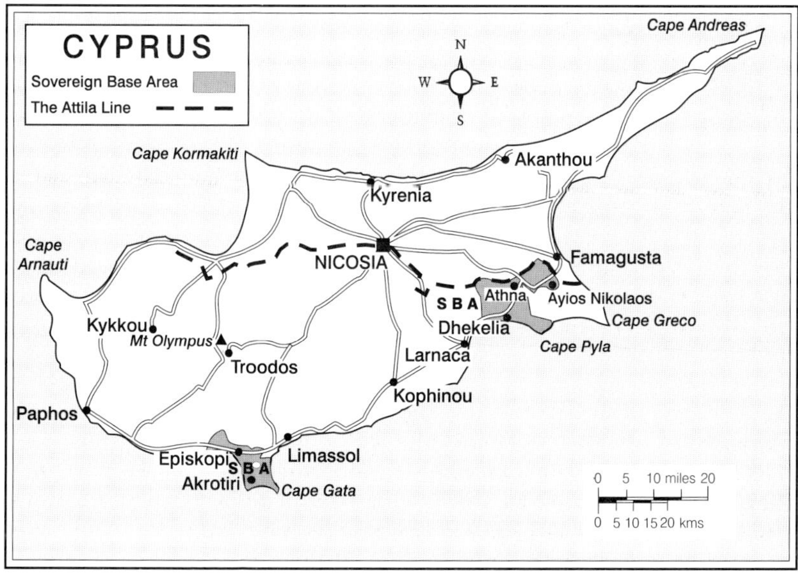

Cypriot extremist) as a puppet head of government. There was fighting between the various Cypriot factions but the Greek Cypriot National Guard became the ruling force.

The two sovereign base areas – Western (WSBA) and Eastern (ESBA) – at Akrotiri and Dhekelia, in the south of Cyprus, lay about 60 miles apart and were connected by main roads which ran through them; these were controlled by the Cypriots. On 15 July all the Famagusta, Larnaca and Limassol residents working in the SBAs were stranded at work and worried about what might be happening to their families in the dormitory towns. The appearance of armed 'uniformed' para-military groups was not reassuring, but it was possible for the Famagusta and Larnaca residents to return home that night. The Limassol residents were unable to return home because their convoy encountered many heavily armed Makarios supporters. On 20 July a Turkish invasion took place in the area of Kyrenia in the north, setting off inter-communal violence and the disappearance of local civilian labourers – some never to return. It was decided to evacuate Service families from the dormitory towns, and REME recovery crews from both SBAs accompanied the stream of cars and lorries from Limassol to the WSBA, towing in some forty cars suffering from overheating in the very hot weather. Famagusta came under air attack when the convoy was forming up; port facilities were damaged and the NAAFI burned out. ASM 'Mac' McPhail of 10 Port Squadron Workshop rescued his wife and family, together with his shrapnel-torn EMERs; his summary of defects (infantry weapons) had a bullet hole, complete with bullet, lodged within: it is in the REME Museum archives. REME recovery support was required also for a large-scale evacuation of British and foreign nationals, many of them tourists, from Kyrenia and Nicosia, because of the Turkish action there.

Turkish villages outside the invasion area were attacked and refugees began to arrive in Episkopi, including Sergeant Osman who, on compassionate leave from Northern Ireland, was at a village near Limassol. When he was rescued by the RSM of the 2nd Battalion, Coldstream Guards from a group of Turkish civilian prisoners he did not know what had happened to his family. Eventually he found them and was evacuated to the UK, but in the meantime he was in great demand as an interpreter.

At the end of the month, when a cease-fire was arranged, families were gradually returned to the dormitory towns, although things were far from normal. A Turkish refugee camp with thousands of Turkish Cypriots had been established in the main recreation area of Episkopi. In mid-August cease-fire violations took place and the Turkish army occupied parts of Nicosia and Famagusta. The families were again evacuated from all dormitory areas and it was decided to send all those from Famagusta, Larnaca and Limassol back to the UK. Before the 1974 coup d'état and invasion the REME units in Cyprus were:

Episkopi	HQ REME Recovery Team (attached RAF Workshop, Episkopi)
Dhekelia	16th/5th The Queen's Royal Lancers Squadron LAD 62 (NE) Support Squadron RE Workshop 7 Transport Squadron RCT Workshop 48 Command Workshop
Famagusta	10 Port Squadron RCT Workshop

Individual reinforcements were sent out to Cyprus under existing emergency plans. 48 Command Workshop lost civilian workers during the emergency and men from 8 Field Workshop (Airportable) were brought in to help, after its recall from the leave it was enjoying on return from a tour in Ulster: a platoon was despatched from Colchester, joining a few of its tradesmen who were already in Cyprus on adventurous training organized by HQ 19 Airportable Brigade which, fortuitously, was in skeleton form in Cyprus running a two-battalion TA exercise. The Brigade HQ was brought up to strength and, with reinforcing units including 3 Field Workshop (Airportable) from Weyhill, was based in the WSBA; the Workshop being in the RAF Workshop at Episkopi. C Squadron 4th/7th Royal Dragoon Guards with SWINGFIRE, B Squadron The Royal Horse Guards and A Squadron 16th/5th The Queen's Royal Lancers with SCORPIONs were welcome reinforcements, at first producing only a few additional REME problems.

The simple plan produced for REME support during this period was that 48 Command Workshop would support the ESBA, whilst 3 Field Workshop plus the Recovery Team would support the WSBA. It was fortunate that only a short time before the coup REME had completed overhauling field bakery trailers, water trailers and water trucks, all of which were soon in great demand. The HQ REME staff became part of Q Ops where they worked before or after a shift in HQ REME. CREME ran the office and was also PMC NEARELF Officers' Mess, which became so full that it required a tented compound, although lacking staff.

During their stay in Cyprus 3 Field Workshop in WSBA repaired thirteen A vehicles, 116 B vehicles, forty-seven pieces of plant and machinery and 123 telecommunications equipments, putting in over 2,000 productive man-hours on this task. 48 Command Workshop in the ESBA repaired many A vehicles, B vehicles and specialist vehicles with the priority switching from one category to another as operational requirements changed. At the start every possible SARACEN, SALADIN and FERRET was wanted 'yesterday'; most of those in the workshop were already stripped down at the start of the emergency. The artificers and vehicle mechanics worked long hours to repair them where they had been left by the departed Cypriot Civilian Staff. At the British Military Hospital the top priority was for ventilators and blood micro-systems which had been stripped down for overhaul. Priority Two was for extension leads for emergency casualty stations, emergency lighting and anything else that REME could do.

By Friday of the first week things had returned more or less to normal, with some of the civilians returning to work. On Saturday 20 July the Turkish invasion began and priority was given to the repair of B vehicles to carry people and their luggage. Vehicles of every size, shape and make were pressed into service – many of them being made roadworthy in 48 Command Workshop, which was helped by the men from 19 Airportable Brigade and 8 Field Workshop from the UK, and 62 (NE) Support Squadron RE Workshop which generously lent men it could ill afford to lose. When the Turks pushed on to Famagusta the work with refugee camps required more trucks, including those for water and sewage.

Engine change on an RAF Regiment Scorpion

Production next turned to specialist and A vehicles, including the newly arrived SCORPIONs. A fully laden sewage truck came into the workshop which the RCT could not unload because of a mechanical fault; someone left the top hatch open and someone else who was driving it stopped suddenly just in front of Sergeant McKay. The reader is left to guess the rest. The Telecommunications Section, down to half its strength, repaired everything in the workshop and made ready for issue all the dozens of sets held in stock in the Ordnance Depot.

Many other duties required men for family convoys, refugee duties and getting everything possible out of Famagusta where the main NAAFI store and warehouse was. In mid-August several thousand refugees poured into a tented camp set up in Athna Forest in ESBA. Four NCOs from the Instrument Section and others were busy at the start with beds and tents. A field bakery, laundry and medical centre were set up. Sergeant Bob Clifford served his home-made soup for seven hours in a lightly wooded forest about three-quarters of a mile square, full of distressed refugees, their vehicles and personal possessions; Corporal Brooks cut 300 oil drums to meet an urgent need.

In addition to this, REME soldiers and their wives helped to run various garrison organizations such as the Civilian and Military Reception Centres. Two NCOs, Sergeant Bob Scott and Corporal 'Dicky' Bird, were sector wardens in Larnaca during the evacuation of Service families, whilst the recovery crews continued to accompany the convoys from Kyrenia, Limassol and Nicosia into the SBAs. An unusual task carried out by AQMS Ian Turk, Sergeant Bill Glenn and Corporal Bird was that of moving 500 cars, abandoned in the SBA without keys but with steering locks, to a vehicle park.

In three weeks the Turks gained control of nearly 40% of the island, occupying the north, including Kyrenia, Famagusta, the chief port, and the northern part of Nicosia, the capital. Eventually a buffer zone was created between the two communities, with the United Nations Force in Cyprus (UNFICYP) – which had been set up in 1964 – providing a peacekeeping force. The boundary now created, known as the Attila Line, incorporated the 'Green Line' which had divided Nicosia ever since 1964. In 1975 a Turkish Federated State of Cyprus was declared, but this was not recognized by the British Government.

In 1983 the Turkish sector made a unilateral declaration of independence proclaiming a 'Turkish Republic of Northern Cyprus'. All efforts to unite the island again were still unsuccessful in 1991. The declaration was condemned by the UN Security Council and only recognized by Turkey. Britain retained the two Sovereign Base Areas dating from the early Sixties and, despite the division of the communities since 1974, Greek Cypriots, Turkish Cypriots and Armenian Cypriots continued to work in the UNFICYP Workshop and the ESBA Workshop at Dhekelia. Many crossed the 'border' daily and worked together in harmony.

The UNFICYP Workshop at Nicosia had a small REME element of two officers and twenty-nine soldiers commanded by a major, who was also Force EME, to control the local civilian workforce. The ASM and a handful of artificers were on two-year tours, with fitters from the RCT Transport Squadron and tradesmen, on six-month roulement tours. They maintained an ancient fleet of UN 'white' vehicles. Vehicles used for administrative purposes were gradually replaced by indigenous vehicles having local maintenance contracts with the suppliers.

The size of the British garrison steadily reduced over the years and this prompted several rationalization studies, the most far-reaching of which, in 1989, combined HQ Land Forces Cyprus and Air Headquarters into a joint HQ British Forces Cyprus with command alternating between the Army and the RAF. At the same time most single-service administrative units were merged with their counterparts – 48 Cyprus

Workshop (Akrotiri) becoming part of the Joint Maintenance Unit (JMU). The HQ REME staff branch became Maintenance Branch with an injection of RAF personnel and the assumption of technical responsibility for several RAF units in addition to those Army and Joint units previously covered.

CREME had already changed his title to Commander Maintenance in 1982 in common with other theatres: he now became DACOS (Maint), losing command of the Workshop, but retaining REME Technical Services and the Cyprus Calibration Centre. Further reorganization gave him the added responsibility of Works for 18 months until, in 1992, he became DACOS ES.

48 Command Workshop at Akrotiri underwent several changes of title, first to 48 Cyprus Workshop (Akrotiri) and then Force Workshop as part of the JMU in August 1989. The REME major was under command of an RAF wing commander and the airfield tradesmen all remained RAF. The workshop supported all units on the island with three officers, twenty-one soldiers and 150 local civilians.

The detachment of 48 Command Workshop at Dhekelia changed its name to 48 Cyprus Workshop (Dhekelia) and then became an independent command with the formation of the JMU, with the new title of ESBA Workshop. It had one officer, fifteen soldiers and sixty civilians. It supported all units in the ESBA and provided an in-depth repair service for the island fleet of FERRET scout cars which were stripped down to their bare metal and rebuilt, so extending the service life of those excellent little vehicles which were so well suited to their role in Cyprus.

REME aircraft technicians continued to provide first-line support to UNFICYP Flight and 16 Flight AAC, but the eventual replacement of the old ALOUETTE helicopters with GAZELLEs saw the demise of the Aircraft Servicing Increment at Akrotiri. Major General Gunther Greindl (Austrian Army), the Commander UNFICYP, visited the UNFICYP Flight Army Air Corps in 1986 and presented AQMS Fenwick with the Hutchins Flight Safety Trophy for 1985. During August 1986 a main rotor gearbox on an ALOUETTE helicopter failed during the Flight Commander's last operational flight in Cyprus; it was recovered by a WESSEX helicopter, the only known aerial recovery of an ALOUETTE at that time.

Gibraltar

Gibraltar is a small peninsula on the southern coast of Spain at the narrow entrance and exit to the Mediterranean Sea known as the Straits of Gibraltar. It is nearly three miles long and half-a-mile wide, rising to a height of 1,400 feet. It was captured in 1704 and ceded to Britain by the Treaty of Utrecht in 1713.

Captain Carl Mann recalled in 1991 the time he spent in Gibraltar as a Corporal telecommunications technician in 1968–69:

'I flew to Gibraltar in December 1968 with the 2nd Battalion, The Royal Anglian Regiment who were then stationed in Normandy Barracks, Felixstowe. We were on a nine-month emergency tour to support the resident battalion in its defence of the Rock against General Franco's overtures. We were accommodated with the RAF at North Front and our duties were essentially manning the border and the Rock observation posts. There were no REME officers, only attached tradesmen; we had five armourers and vehicle mechanics in addition to myself; the resident Battalion had much the same and the RE Squadron also had a few REME fitters.

'8 (Surveillance) Troop from 94th Locating Regiment in Celle (BAOR) manned the radar on the Mole at North Front. They were supported by an artificer radar and one or two radar technicians. My Battalion was supported by the RN dockyard. Over the previous eighteen months, with the help of the resident battalion telecommunications sergeant, the RN Inspector of Radio had demanded an incredible amount of test equipment and spares; the radio support was superb except for one thing – no personnel. It became the norm to send in the AF G1045 job indent from the battalion on Mondays, Tuesdays and Fridays and then spend Wednesdays and Thursdays carrying out the required repairs in the RN dockyard radio section. By far the biggest workload apart from A41 radios was the prototype Infra Red Intruder System (IRIS) which was installed along the border every night. The reason the Inspector of Radio in Gibraltar had built up such an impressive supply of spares was that he told one of his local technicians to demand the spares to support all the radios. He faithfully demanded every item as listed in the parts lists, including the first item – which was always the complete equipment. They all arrived and were written off by the Dockyard. This was a telecommunications technician's dream come true: brand-new test equipment, plenty of spares and no artificers.

'Until 1970, when the border crossing at La Linea was completely closed, General Franco still allowed Spanish male workers into the Rock, although females had been stopped. He expected the Rock's services to be completely disrupted: but the Gibraltar authorities recruited Moroccan labour at much less cost. In the meantime the Army manned various services – our Battalion provided drivers and manned the bakery. The ferry to Algeciras was still running despite the closed border, and cruise ships still called at Gibraltar making it a bustling and prosperous place.'

ASM John Feast was posted from 70 Aircraft Workshop at Middle Wallop to Gibraltar as Fortress EME (FEME) 1979–81, having volunteered in view of the prevailing surplus of aircraft artificers. The political situation with Spain was tense, the border was closed and residents had a sense of siege. A referendum had been held a few years earlier, when the very few residents who voted to join Spain were offered free suitcases by a local shop. The Army task was the security of the Rock, and the Army Commander was Deputy Fortress Commander under the Governor. The resident infantry battalion was supported by several minor but important units.

The role of the FEME was to advise Fortress HQ on all equipment matters and give all REME men direction and support. Most second-line and some third-line support was provided by the Royal Naval Dockyard; much of ASM Feast's time was spent in liaison with the Royal Navy and departments in the Dockyard. Most key posts were UK-based Ministry of Defence employees, with Gibraltarians and Moroccans making up the labour force. Sergeant Hind, telecommunications technician, was employed in the Dockyard Telecommunications Workshop. The resident infantry battalion, the 2nd Battalion, The Light Infantry, had Staff Sergeant Tommy Hughes and two other armourers, and Sergeant Brian Probert with five more vehicle mechanics. The RA Surveillance Troop had a Sergeant Radar Technician Mick Pickering, whilst the Gibraltar Regiment had Sergeant Gun Fitter Kev Wyle.

The equipment in Gibraltar at that time ranged in age from the then modern CLANSMAN radios to FERRET scout cars to the BOFORS guns operated by the Gibraltar Regiment. The biggest headache was none of these – it was the golf-ball typewriter used by the Governor's Personal Assistant. Unusual equipments included three special Land Rovers each carrying a Decca Radar, used by the RA Surveillance Troop to monitor the land and sea borders; one of those was the subject of an interesting accident report and inquiry after it had been found that a Land Rover with its radar in the scanning position would not pass through a narrow tunnel in the Rock. The Naval Dockyard not only carried out an excellent repair to the radar and to the Land Rover box body but helped with the design and manufacture of a modification to prevent another accident. During his second year ASM Feast was presiding member of the Fortress Sergeants' Mess which had a prime site just off the main street. Being host to visiting ships companies was an enjoyable part of the job; the invitations back to the ships could be dangerous – soldiers had been known to wake up in Cyprus or Portsmouth!

A REME radar technician, Sergeant R W Osgathorpe, served with 8 Surveillance Troop RA in Gibraltar 1985–87. They had four Radars No 17 Mark 1, three of which were mounted in Land Rovers; the fourth was housed in a permanent observation post, half-way up the north face of the Rock. There was also a modern Decca marine radar in the observation post, on trial as a replacement for the other ageing radars. The trial proving successful, three mobile versions were ordered and arrived for in-inspection before Sergeant Osgathorpe went home. The main task was to observe the land and sea borders with Spain, especially for small vessels at night which might be smuggling drugs or other goods. The mobile radars were also used at Europa Point for range safety when The Gibraltar Regiment fired Light Guns and mortars, the British resident infantry battalion fired mortars and MILAN, and visiting infantry companies fired mortars. The radars were used continually for training and were moved around the Rock, setting up and monitoring shipping; they were always accompanied by the REME radar technician.

One of the tasks given to the radar technician was to research and photograph the old 9.2 inch gun (O'Hara's) which sat on the top of the Rock. This was done with the help of The Gibraltar Regiment which was responsible for the gun, the RAF who provided a photographer and the Royal Navy who provided a LYNX helicopter. In 1935 O'Hara's Battery had been reconstructed to take a 9.2 inch BL Mark X gun on a Mark VII mounting, and it was fully manned during the Munich crisis in 1938 and during the Second World War 1939–45. Captain Solomon Levy described in 'The Gibraltar Regiment 50th Anniversary Journal' how he was in command of the 9.2 inch guns from 1960 until they ceased firing them in 1973, because of the damage caused to property in the town by the noise and vibration. He related that it was always exciting, especially when they fired more than one gun; on several occasions they fired O'Hara's, Lord Airey's and Spur Batteries together.

In 1986 the radar technician became responsible for advising on all military electronic and instrument equipments for the Army not covered by the telecommunications technician in the Dockyard. At that time there were nine REME with the infantry battalion in Lathbury Barracks led by a weapons staff sergeant, and a telecommunications technician on a two-year exchange with the Royal Navy. There was also a sergeant gun fitter with the Gibraltar Regiment, who looked after their guns and the 9.2 inch gun at O'Hara's Battery.

Sergeant Geordie Hudson and eleven men from 2 Field Regiment Workshop went to Gibraltar in June 1987 for two weeks to restore the

Sergeant Wylie, Gun Fitter, explains the working of the gun to a visiting party

9.2 inch gun belonging to Lord Airey's Battery which in 1934 had been put in position on top of the Rock by a visiting team from the RA and the resident RE. No longer were there three 9.2 inch guns on the site, that from Spur Battery having been removed to the Imperial War Museum. Sergeant Hudson had already spent many hours of his spare time restoring that in O'Hara's Battery during his earlier tour in Gibraltar. The guns were capable of firing a 380 pound shell to North Africa, having a range of 29,600 yards. They weighed more than 200 tons, the barrel alone weighing 28 tons. After the visiting team had restored the gun, they played host to visitors, including the Gibraltar Tourist Information Officer who said that he had fired the guns during the Second World War.

In February 1962 discussions took place with a working party from the Ministry of Defence on the hand over of the REME task in Gibraltar to the Royal Navy. Firm directions were received in December after which responsibilities were gradually handed over to HM Dockyard, 55 Garrison Workshop disbanding at the end of August 1963. After completion of the run-down programme military and civilian tradesmen attached to remaining units only carried out repairs, adjustments and minor component replacement within the limits of their resources: normal maintenance procedures were adopted. This arrangement was still in force in 1991, when further reductions in the force levels were made with the departure of the UK resident infantry battalion. ASM R S McMillan remained as WO Maintenance at Fortress HQ, together with four REME posts in the Gibraltar Regiment. ASM McMillan had been one of only three WOs1 in Fortress Gibraltar, and he had presided over the Fortress Sergeants' Mess which was housed in a fine old building on Governor's Parade in the centre of the town. After three IRA terrorists were shot dead in March 1988 in Gibraltar the 'Fortress Sergeants' Mess' sign was removed and the shutters kept closed which, with other necessary security measures, had a dampening effect on mess life.

The Gibraltar Regiment, before the departure of the resident infantry battalion, was a mixed TA regiment consisting of a Light Gun battery, air defence troop, infantry company and a permanent cadre HQ company. Their vehicle mechanics were REME trained to Class 1 standard, but wore the Gibraltar Regiment cap badge. At the beginning of the Nineties there was still a sergeant telecommunications technician working in the Naval Base civilian radio workshop on CLANSMAN radios, and a sergeant radar technician who doubled up as the WO Maintenance's technical clerk when he was not employed on the Surveillance Troop radars.

After the departure of the resident infantry battalion the Gibraltar Regiment took on a new role as infantry, with a Regular HQ company and infantry company and two TA infantry companies. The REME soldiers were reduced as the local tradesmen filled posts.

The Workshop, Holdfast Camp, Belize

THE REST OF THE WORLD

Belize

The former British colony called British Honduras was renamed Belize in 1973 and became independent in 1981. British troops remained there because of a long-running dispute with Guatemala to the south and west, which in the middle Seventies raised an old issue claiming that part of Belize City was rightly theirs, that they needed access to it and were going to secure it. The strength of British troops on six-month roulement tours was brought to an appropriate level to protect Belize, including two infantry battalions.

REME support was split between three locations under an ASM who ran the main Force Troops Workshop in Airport Camp alongside Belize International Airport. The other two sites were Holdfast Camp near the border town of San Ignacio, west of Belize City, and Rideau Camp close to Punta Gorda and the southern border. There were about ninety REME soldiers in Belize in the Seventies, including those with a squadron of Royal Engineers and a flight of the Army Air Corps; except for the REME soldiers attached to the two infantry battalions they were trickle-posted. Many tradesmen found that their trade skills were fully tested: 'repair by repair', i.e. extemporized repair, was sometimes required because of the adverse and harsh conditions in the jungle areas. Several REME tradesmen extended their tours for an extra six months as a result of job satisfaction. For relaxation there was also the attraction of swimming amongst the fish and coral of the second largest coral reef in the world, and fishing along the reef for barracuda.

Towards the end of the Eighties a Force Electrical and Mechanical Engineer (FEME) was appointed as an adviser on the staff of the Commander British Forces Belize on a six months tour.

Holdfast Camp was eighty miles from Belize City over a rough road, whilst Rideau Camp in the south could often only be reached in the rainy season by air or sea using very old Ramped Powered Lighters. Recovery of vehicles was frequently required due to the harsh ground which led to many accidents, often in most inaccessible parts of the jungle or on narrow wooden bridges. There were two AEC medium recovery vehicles in Airport Camp, a Bedford light recovery in Holdfast Camp and a unique 6 × 4 diesel Scammell in Rideau Camp – known as 'Swampy', by far the oldest recovery vehicle in use at that time; it could cross most of the wooden bridges in the south, whereas the larger AEC vehicles could not.

Scorpion engine change, Belize

An unusual recovery task was provided by an RAF VC10 which had rolled off the runway at Belize International Airport putting the airport out of service. The nose wheel was sunk well into the swamp 65 feet off the runway and the port main undercarriage bogey was just off the runway and sunk in too. The workshop duty crew arrived with their AEC recovery vehicle and Captain Graham Hughes and Staff Sergeant Steve Wiseman (an artificer vehicles) worked out how to get the aircraft back on the runway. The Sappers and the RCT prepared the route out of the mud with shovels, sandbags and Pierced Steel Plank. Safety ropes were fixed across the winch rope to prevent it kicking up and damaging the aircraft, a wise precaution since the first pull snapped the rope. The AEC compound pull gave 60 tons, the Sappers' Allis Chalmers gave 12 tons pull and a second Allis Chalmers was dug in as a ground anchor for the AEC. Four Bedford 4 tonners were used as dead-weight anchors. Four hours after the RAF called for help the VC10 was back on the runway without a scratch, ready to taxi back to the terminal for engineering checks. Two hours later it had picked up its passengers and taken off for Brize Norton.

A second recovery task took much longer when a Bedford truck hung half over a sheer drop near an outstation known as Mountain Pine Ridge. It could not be recovered for three weeks because of torrential rain and low cloud. Finally, a SCORPION CVR(T) from Holdfast Camp and an AEC recovery vehicle from Airport Camp performed a delicate balancing act to prevent the Bedford disappearing altogether, and returned it to its owners.

17 Port and Maritime Workshop at Marchwood, Southampton, had a long-standing commitment in Belize from the Seventies to the Nineties in support of Army vessels. Army Ramped Powered Lighters (RPL) were sent to Belize in the mid-Seventies to provide sea transport of stores to the troops defending the borders; they could carry many more supplies than the locally based helicopters were able to do up to that time. Two RPLs used on this operation were supplemented by a harbour launch used to ferry men in the harbour areas of Belize City. At the start a steel launch was used, but this was replaced by a Landing Craft Vehicle and Personnel Mark 4 (LCVP).

17 Port and Maritime Workshop provided a senior rank (usually the vessel inspector) to supervise the local labour working on the six-monthly overhaul and repair of the Army vessels. The work took about six weeks, slipping the RPLs and craning the harbour launch from the water to carry out routine maintenance on the underwater section of the hulls. This often included renewing propeller shafts, bearings and seals and fitting new propellers due to damage caused by operating in shallow inshore waters. In the early years the RPLs were slipped at the British Sugar Industries complex 80 miles from Belize City on a muddy river bank under primitive working conditions. The course to be navigated was uncharted, the RPL having to follow a local tug pulling a string of sugar barges. In some places the water was shallow and the RPL would touch the bottom. From 1979 the detachments to Belize were changed and carried out by a complete military team from Marchwood of shipwrights, electricians and fitter turners; the RCT vessel crews worked with the REME tradesmen to complete the team. In 1983 the trade training section of the workshop at Marchwood became involved in the vessel repairs, the Class 2-1 Upgrader Shipwright course being included in the team – giving them some useful practical on-the-job training. This practice continued over the years with the Staff Sergeant trade instructor forming part of the team and supervising the students.

In 1984 a new slipping facility was built in Belize City for the Belize Defence Force. This slip provided better working conditions and a better facility close to 16 Belize Field Workshop, which helped with administrative and technical support. The REME and RCT team worked to marine engineering standards laid down in Naval Engineering Standards, Naval Books of Reference and EMERs. With the military team Maritime Branch REME sent a civilian officer, who carried out a technical inspection of the vessels to ensure that they were seaworthy before he issued a Certificate of Survey and Certificate of Seaworthiness. The Maritime Workshop team always had a heavy load in Belize due to the vessels being used in difficult shallow waterways. The sub-tropical climate was very demanding and provided some very worthwhile technical experience for the marine tradesmen over the years. The RPLs were aged craft, basic in design and less complicated than their replacements, whilst the LCVP was constructed in marine alloy which required inert gas welding when hull repairs were needed.

Other Places

In addition to the stations mentioned already, REME officers and soldiers have served all over the world in out of the way places, for example Hanoi, Ulan Bator in Mongolia and Beijing (or Peking in former times). Sergeant Steve Johnson's experiences are but one example and are described below. He had been trained originally as a Turner at the Army Apprentices School, Arborfield in 1946. His Army service ended at SEME in May 1985, and he then became a civilian estate warden at Arborfield.

In 1953–1955 he was posted to Korea and Japan, where he saw the result of the atom bomb dropped at Hiroshima in 1945. In 1958, as a member of 2 Special Engineer Regiment Workshop, he took part in Operation GRAPPLE, the testing of Great Britain's nuclear weapons at Christmas Island in the Pacific Ocean, 1,200 miles south of Hawaii; he was stationed there for a year.

In July 1970 Sergeant Johnson joined 63 Carrier Borne Ground Liaison Section on board the 50,000 ton aircraft carrier HMS *Eagle*, the Royal Navy's largest warship at that time with a crew of 2,600. The Army section, under a Gunner major, formed a Forward Air Controller section to go ashore and talk the ship's aircraft onto their targets. After a work-up in the Channel and off Scotland they were off Gibraltar in January 1971 for their operational inspection. Visits followed to the south of France and Malta where 53 Command Workshop won their football match 2–1. The ship then returned to Gibraltar and Plymouth.

After taking on BUCCANEERs and four other types of aircraft, the ship headed south on 26 May 1971 and crossed the equator on 8 June. The football team were landed on Ascension Island by SEA KINGs and soon after they moved on to Cape Town where they 'anchored' at the end of the High Street under Table Mountain. Having left Cape Town they joined the Far East Fleet and gave a flying display at Mauritius. After crossing the Indian Ocean to Penang, Sergeant Johnson went ashore to work for the BUCCANEERs and SEA VIXEN on the Song Song bombing range, and subsequently had an enjoyable break ashore at Singapore.

On 20 July they started their journey to Australia and, after passing Java and Sumatra, fire broke out on board. Standing at emergency stations on the flight deck they realized what a long way it was down to the sea, and felt reassured to have their escort HMS *Glamorgan* alongside. (HMS *Glamorgan*, a destroyer, later played an important part in the Falklands operation in 1982 until it was hit by an EXOCET missile a few days before the cease-fire; thirteen of the crew were killed and the ship was seriously damaged.) After heading back to Singapore to put two injured firefighters ashore, they were soon sailing south again, passing

Perth and sailing through the Great Australian Bight to Sydney, where they docked near the Opera House and had many enjoyable runs ashore during August. Rough weather after leaving Sydney prevented training exercises being held on the way to New Zealand, but their five days at Wellington were very enjoyable – Maori dancing and singing, wining and dining with the hospitable New Zealanders. On the way back they visited Fremantle in Western Australia and returned to Singapore. After exercises in Subic Bay in the Philippines and a typhoon they headed north for Hong Kong where the ship provided a Royal Guard for a visit by Princess Anne. Returning past Singapore they provided aircraft for the final steam-past of the Far East Fleet. At Song Song their BUCCANEERs and Australian MYSTÈREs shot up the targets on the range. Next they had a week's flying and sailed to the Gulf to cover the withdrawal of British Land Forces, where they had a period of intense flying operations. They then headed south, arriving at Durban on 22 December, having been at sea for fifty-six days, where they stayed until 4 January. They were greatly impressed by the South African people's hospitality and the performance of the Zulu dancers. On the way home they called at Simonstown and Ascension Island and then speeded up to sail to Malta. This was followed by a day at Gibraltar before arriving back at Plymouth on 26 January 1972, eight months after leaving on 26 May 1971.

CHAPTER 10

NORTHERN IRELAND 1968–1992

Historical background · The Violence begins · Initial REME organization 1969–70 · Increasing REME build-up 1971–72 · The years of the Troubles 1973–92 · Casualties, Honours and Awards · Deployment of Field Workshops · Conclusion

HISTORICAL BACKGROUND

No description of the part played by REME in the overall role of the British Army in Northern Ireland from 1968–1992 can usefully start without some introduction to the complex political and religious background that bedevils the troubled Province. The problems of Northern Ireland and the troubles stemming from them started with armed conflicts over religious differences three centuries earlier. These historical events have been actively remembered, and celebrated or denounced, by those with opposing religious and political interests ever since.

In the 17th Century, during the reign of James I, the system of plantations was developed. The possessions of the Earls of Tyrone and Tyrconnel were confiscated and the lands of Ulster were apportioned to Scottish and English settlers, or planters as they were then called, who were mainly Presbyterian. These settlers prospered and owned most of the land by the end of the century. In 1641 the dispossessed Irish Catholic population in Ulster rebelled. Many Protestants were killed or driven from their property and stories circulated in England of atrocities and massacre, no doubt growing in the telling. Oliver Cromwell went to Ireland with his Army in 1649 to suppress the uprising, capturing Drogheda and Wexford during his campaign, with savage slaughter. This is never forgotten by either Catholics or Protestants in Ireland.

Another event, still persistently and actively remembered some three hundred years later, is the victory in 1690 of King William of Orange and the Protestants over the former King James II and the Catholics at the Boyne in 1689, following the Catholic siege of Londonderry. After the Battle of the Boyne, King James was driven out of Ireland for ever. This event is not only remembered but also celebrated annually by the controversial marches of the Protestant Orange Order, which had been established in 1795 to maintain the political and religious ascendancy of the Protestants in Northern Ireland.

Continuing troubles in Ireland, and political campaigns for Home Rule over the years, eventually led to the partition of Ireland in 1921 with the setting up of the Irish Free State. It was renamed Eire in 1937. The passing of the Republic of Ireland Act by the British Parliament followed in 1948. In 1949 it became the Republic of Ireland and left the Commonwealth. Six of the nine counties of the ancient Province of Ulster formed Northern Ireland – still popularly called Ulster – and remained within the United Kingdom. This partition did not, however, solve the overall problem of the strong religious differences within Northern Ireland, and the wishes generally of the Republican Catholics on the one hand, to have a united Ireland governed from Dublin, and the Loyalist Protestants on the other, to keep Ulster as part of the UK. The suspicions, antagonisms and discriminations that resulted were to manifest themselves at various times throughout the years that followed in communal discord and bouts of violence. In 1968, however, the situation began to deteriorate and, from a relatively peaceful garrison situation, the British Army was to become embroiled in operations against terrorism in the Province. REME was to play its full part in this action which, as this chapter tells, tested all the skills of members of the Corps, both as technicians and as soldiers. They were to pass these tests in a manner of which they can be justifiably proud.

Throughout this chapter brief details of the most heinous acts of terrorism and important political activities are given to update the background and as a continuous reminder of the sort of incidents that have perpetuated the troubles. Most of these events have not directly involved

REME except unfortunately when casualties have been suffered by members of the Corps, but the resulting actions by the forces of law and order have almost invariably affected the deployment, organization or workload of REME in the Province.

THE VIOLENCE BEGINS

In 1968 the Northern Ireland Civil Rights Association (NICRA) began a campaign, with widespread support from elements of the Catholic population, of non-violent direct action against alleged discrimination in their everyday affairs. At Londonderry on 5 October 1968 a NICRA demonstration and march was banned by the Government of Northern Ireland because it was expected to clash with an Orange March on the same day. The NICRA march took place despite the ban and the Royal Ulster Constabulary (RUC) set up a cordon, which was followed by a riot in which policemen and civilians were injured. Another riot occurred that night in Londonderry.

Various incidents followed, but the 'Troubles' really began in August 1969 with the annual march of The Protestant Apprentice Boys of Derry. The Catholics in the Bogside area of Londonderry built a barricade and established 'Free Derry' as a 'No-Go' area. The RUC moved in between the opposing factions and the struggle went on all that night and next day. Stones and bottles were thrown at the hard-pressed police. Some inhabitants of the Bogside threw petrol bombs and the police retaliated with tear gas when necessary, but lost control of the situation. The RUC were supported by their Reservists, the B Specials, who were particularly unpopular with the Catholic community. It was not long after reports of trouble in other towns that the official request for the Army to come to the aid of the civil power was made and troops were sent to Londonderry to help restore law and order.

A Company, 1st Battalion, The Prince of Wales's Own Regiment of Yorkshire took over from the Police in the Londonderry city centre at 1700 hours on 14 August. Next day troops took up positions along the 'Peace Line' established between the Catholics and Protestants in Belfast, where much damage had been done by the rioters. The Army's task started well and had been welcomed by the local Catholics who appreciated the Army replacing the B Specials to protect both elements of the whole community from each other. Alas, this acceptance was not to last. At the end of 1969 there were 7,000 troops in Northern Ireland compared with 3,000 at the beginning of the year.

In Belfast and Londonderry corrugated iron walls had been built by the Army to strengthen the 'Peace Line'. In London the Government issued a report into the causes and nature of the violence and civil disturbances. Amongst the things it recommended was the disbandment of the B Specials who would be replaced by the Ulster Defence Regiment (UDR), a part-time, non-sectarian, locally recruited regiment under the command of the GOC. This produced much bitterness amongst the Protestants and a great deal of trouble in Belfast. The UDR began recruiting on 1 January and started operations on 31 March 1970.

In 1970 the strength of the UDR grew to 4,000 and the number of troops grew to 9,000 as the sectarian 'marching season' approached. In June and July severe rioting in Belfast and Londonderry was followed by the Army announcing that it intended to use water cannon and rubber bullets against unruly mobs. The scene was set for the continuance of violence and a strengthening British Army presence. Their task was not to be an easy one. The terrorism was to continue to be fanned by the intransigence of the opposing Protestant Loyalists and Catholic Republican political parties towards any settlement of the problem.

A campaign of terrorism then began against the British people, the Government, the Northern Ireland Protestant community and all the forces of law and order, mounted by Republican terrorist groups, of which there were a number. These militants stemmed from the Irish Republican Army (IRA); a proscribed organization within which there had long been violent internal differences. These resulted in the splitting up of the organization into an official wing and various offshoots each with divergent power aims. The most prominent was the Provisional Irish Republican Army (PIRA or Provisionals, which was formed in 1970) whose aim was to drive the British from Northern Ireland by military means. Two other prominent groupings were the Irish National Liberation Army (INLA) and the Irish Peoples Liberation Organization. There was frequent feuding between the groups, resulting in killings amongst themselves. Although Republican, and therefore generally deemed to be Catholic, they were by no means supported by the majority of Catholics, either in Northern Ireland or the Republic of Ireland. Sinn Fein, the political wing of the IRA, was supported by many Republicans as a political party dedicated to the political and economic independence of a united Ireland. The extent of its links with the IRA, however, had long been a matter of conjecture and concern for the British Government and led to its exclusion from political discussions on the future of Northern Ireland.

For more than twenty years the IRA's terrorist activities had been conducted principally within Northern Ireland and the United Kingdom. But, seeking greater international impact, attacks were mounted on Government and British military targets within Western

Europe. Although there were various Republican terrorist groups, for simplicity they will all be referred to in this chapter under the generic term of PIRA or Provisionals, except in those cases where there has been a specific admission of a terrorist act by another group.

The terrorism was not entirely one-sided. There were Protestant Loyalist groups of terrorists such as the Ulster Volunteer Force, the Ulster Freedom Fighters and the Ulster Defence Association which had diametrically opposite views on unification with the Republic. They were formed on the pretext of protecting the Protestant population, but exacerbated the inter-communal difficulties with attacks on known members of the IRA and of the Catholic community they suspected of aiding the IRA. As always in such conditions, many innocent people of both religious denominations who only wanted to live peaceably were caught up in these terrorist activities. With both the Republican and Loyalist terrorist groups, sectarian and tit for tat killings were commonplace and raised tensions, militating against political settlement. Additionally much intimidation, extortion and crime was directed against the general public by all terrorist groups to raise funds and gain support.

INITIAL REME ORGANIZATION 1960–1970

At the beginning of 1969 REME in Northern Ireland was organized to support Lisburn Garrison units, three resident infantry battalions and local TAVR and CCF units. The senior REME officer was Lieutenant Colonel John Nuttman who wore the two hats of CREME and OC 46 Command Workshop (a largely civilianized workshop at Kinnegar near Holywood). An early task for the Workshop in 1969 occurred when the Army had to guard Key Points which required special lighting and various other devices. The lighting and other devices were designed by Major Reg Pearce, 2IC CREME, and made by the Workshop. The top priority for 46 Command Workshop in 1969, however, was to produce vehicle protection kits. Hinged metal grills were produced for all military vehicles to protect windscreens against missiles thrown at them. Another urgent task on which artificers worked round the clock was the design and manufacture of the prototype wooden knife rest barrier. Hundreds were then produced by the Workshop. Armoured skirts for SARACEN APCs, mobile kitchens and security lights for dangerous street corners were among countless jobs worked on with enthusiasm by the civilian tradesmen in the Command Workshop.

To increase REME second-line support when the troubles started and to provide a 24-hour service, 15 Infantry Workshop (Airportable) was sent from Plymouth. Major David Morrison's Workshop was spread between Plymouth and France when the order to move came, but he was able to send the Spearhead Platoon by air from Lyneham on 19 August 69 to Ballykelly to support 24 Infantry Brigade. They worked alongside the Brigade LAD and 701 Mobile Servicing and Repair Detachment (Army Aviation) in an RAF hangar. The rest of the Workshop except the rear party reached Belfast on 24 August in LSL *Sir Geraint* and set up in an aircraft hangar on a disused airfield at Long Kesh. There they remained until December. They had under command twenty-seven civilian tradesmen who formed the Long Kesh detachment of 46 Command Workshop and took on the task of manufacturing items required by the troops on the streets such as rifle racks, searchlight tripods and grapnels. The latter were designed by Major Pearce and were used for pulling down barricades. There was a variety of such devices employed throughout the Province, either manufactured or adapted. One LAD in 1969 had an Austin 1 ton truck fitted with two 11 inch Naval signalling lamps which proved to be very useful for lighting up the barricades as the troops dismantled them, and was in great demand.

15 Field Workshop returned to Plymouth in December but went back to Northern Ireland in July 1970 commanded by Major Chris Nitsch. He had his HQ and a platoon at Long Kesh, as well as a detachment from 10 Field Workshop, with a platoon at Londonderry and one at the Royal Naval Aircraft Yard at Sydenham, two miles east of Belfast, where they were housed in a disused cinema. They were kept particularly busy manufacturing items needed by the troops on the streets. One example was the production of masses of metal spikes which were used to seal unapproved roads across the border in an attempt to block IRA escape routes. A more normal task concerned the Commer vehicles, at that time still a well-known British commercial make, which had been used to carry RUC water cannons in the Londonderry riots in 1969. By 1970 they needed refurbishing for the anticipated peak in troubles which in August could stem from sectarian marches. As was so often the case, spares were scarce and improvisation, for which there was no lack of expertise, was the key to success.

INCREASING REME BUILD-UP 1971–72

In 1971 Mr Brian Faulkner became the Prime Minister of Northern Ireland and soon announced an amnesty for people holding illegal weapons. This produced 2,000 weapons and 100,000 rounds of ammunition. Despite this gesture, increasing violence led to severe riots throughout the Province in July. At 0400 hours on 9 August a major operation was mounted throughout the Province to round up suspected terrorists, 300 of whom were arrested and taken for interrogation. In the Catholic areas the women and children in their traditional way announced the arrival of the troops by banging on dustbin lids. Seventy suspects were released within forty-eight hours, but the remainder were detained at HMS *Maidstone* used as a prison ship in Belfast Harbour, or in the Crumlin Road Prison. Internment, which became a matter of great controversy and bitterness, had begun, and the initial effect was some reduction in violence, but this was short-lived. However, in September force levels could be reduced: 15 Field Workshop returned to Plymouth and the platoon at Londonderry was withdrawn and relocated at Sydenham.

The system of sending REME units to Northern Ireland, now being rationally developed, was either for a normal unit tour with accompanying families to the supposedly quieter parts of the Province or for a roulement tour of four months to the trouble spots. Initially, these latter tours were of six months duration for workshops, and the families were left behind in UK or Germany. In BAOR the operation to provide units for a roulement tour was known as Operation BANNER. Training beforehand and leave afterwards usually meant that the units were away from their normal role in support of NATO in Germany for about seven months. The commitments in Northern Ireland did not have much effect on BAOR in 1969 and 1970: it was not until 1971 onwards that BAOR began to play an important role in Northern Ireland, which will unfold in this chapter. The impact within BAOR of the provision of the initial, then increased support, is described in Chapter 6.

By 1971 it was clear that, because of the workload, it was impractical for CREME NI to command 46 Command Workshop. The joint appointment of CREME/OC 46 Command Workshop was therefore split, Lieutenant Colonel Rodney McMurray taking command of the Workshop and Lieutenant Colonel Chris Watson being appointed CREME. HQ REME officer strength was increased, including their first Aircraft Engineer, and 46 Command Workshop received thirty-three soldiers to build up its strength to six officers, eighty soldiers and 350 civilians.

Early in 1971 several attacks were made on vehicles with Claymore mines and this produced a request for HQ REME to find a protective device for vehicles. Major Pearce, who had been testing the ballistic properties of Glass Fibre Reinforced Plastic (GRP), designed a bolt-on kit for a Land Rover. RN Dockyard Chatham used his drawings to manufacture a prototype which was sent for trials to Northern Ireland, where it was subjected to Thompson sub-machine gun fire, nail bombs and rock bombardment. The GRP protection was a success and was put into production throughout Britain at REME command and central workshops, at RN dockyards and at RAF St Athan. One workshop worked a continuous shift system seven days a week to produce more than 2,400 kits for twelve different types of vehicle by the end of 1972. The GRP resin gave off vapour that irritated the eyes and disturbed breathing, and a special working bay, housing multiple extraction and air circulation fans, was constructed to overcome the problem.

Major Reg Pearce with a Land Rover fitted with GRP

A platoon from 8 Field Workshop arrived in the Province in January 1971 with twenty-five soldiers and was based at the RN Aircraft Yard, Sydenham, to support 39 Infantry Brigade. Three weeks later reinforcements increased its strength to fifty-seven. In six months it logged over 10,000 man-hours on over 700 jobs. There was always flexibility in providing support, and in August a Sydenham-based platoon from 9 Field Workshop moved to Drumahoe to support the Brigade in Londonderry for the operation to round up terrorist suspects for internment.

The Parachute Squadron RAC Workshop completed its third emergency tour in Northern Ireland in 1972 and it too was heavily involved in the situation following internment. It had arrived at Aldergrove a few days before the start of this operation in 1971 and soon had a team of REME recovery and vehicle mechanics in the Lower Falls area of Belfast. They supported the troops of old Ferret scout cars which were engaged with various infantry battalions clearing barricades and hijacked vehicles. The Ferrets took enormous punishment from sniper-fire, petrol bombs, stones, bottles and paint intended to obscure the periscopes of closed-down vehicles. They looked bizarre with multi-coloured paint patches. The REME soldiers frequently manned road blocks and searched vehicles for suspects between bouts of hectic activity on vehicle repairs.

An example of a regimental LAD on a four-month tour was 25th Light

Regiment RA LAD which arrived in July 1971 and was based at a disused factory just outside Belfast. The battery sections were in various places including a bus station, a TA Centre and at Andersonstown. Most of the LAD soldiers worked at their trade but some were employed guarding key points, including a police station, a bus station and a gas works. After the introduction of internment the LAD mounted a security guard on a hospital where injured terrorists were being treated and detained, a task which was very popular with the REME soldiers, thanks to the good food and pretty nurses! However, two of the Gunner batteries supplemented by riflemen found from their LAD had a less attractive job guarding Crumlin jail and HMS *Maidstone*, the prison ship. By November, when the LAD returned to their home base, most of the soldiers had run the whole gamut of experience in Northern Ireland – bombing, shooting, stone-throwing and abuse on the streets, as well as the excitement and dangers of house searches, bomb searches, raiding and arrest of wanted men, vehicle road blocks and ambushes. They had done their job well both as tradesmen and as soldiers and had gained much from their experiences.

3 Field Workshop arrived in the same month to set up at Long Kesh, Sydenham and Ballykelly and from that time onwards the UKLF field workshops came complete except for a small rear party. Major Graham Staniforth, who commanded 3 Field Workshop (Airportable) in 1971, recalled later:

'3 Field Workshop arrived in Northern Ireland on the morning of Sunday 15 August 1971. On arrival at Sydenham the vehicles on the park making up the workload were found to be not only without any documentation or register, but mixed up haphazardly with a large number of red buses which had been parked there to prevent them being used as barricades or destroyed. It was very much like one of the paper exercises which was carried out at the REME Officers School where you were told that a workshop moved onto a Backloading Point and opened for work, except those exercises never had the buses as part of the problem.'

There was always plenty of work, much of which was physically demanding. On one occasion Corporal Langford, one of the Workshop's athletes, was on his back underneath a Humber 1 ton APC known as the 'Pig' in far from ideal conditions using a short-hafted sledge hammer to remove a seized component. He was restricted for space, working hard and watched by several members of the Parachute Regiment having a break from their patrolling and interested in his obvious exertions. One of them understandingly said, 'I wouldn't have your job', or words to that effect. Corporal Langford paused, eyed the speaker suspiciously and looked doubtfully at all their riot gear and equipment. Then, being a pragmatic and good-tempered NCO, he replied, 'Don't worry, you are not going to get it, because I don't want yours either.'

Some LADs in Ulster were attached to units serving a full two-year tour, whilst others were there for only a four-month emergency tour. LADs as an integral part of the regiments tended to get much involved in the day-to-day operational activities of their parent unit. In 1971–72 Captain Phil Murphy and many of his LAD served with two successive regiments in Ulster, 17st/21st Lancers and 16th/5th The Queen's Royal Lancers who were on two-year tours. The regiments were responsible for patrolling within County Fermanagh and most of County Tyrone, which was about a fifth of the entire area of the Province and included over half of the border with the Irish Republic. Each regiment carried out this task with three armoured car squadrons and an air squadron of six SIOUX helicopters. They had in support an infantry company on a four-month tour. During those years the FERRET scout cars ran about 1,000 miles per month, the SARACENs about 600 miles and the air squadron flew some 270 hours per month – a very high rate of usage.

Based in Omagh, the LAD was forty-five miles from the nearest second-line REME workshop. All the LAD were required to take their turn at guard duties, including the protection of isolated border police stations. At times of maximum alert, when the whole regiment stood-to, every spare tradesman took his place as a member of an assault troop trained in riot drill, vehicle and boat patrols and searches, including detailed vehicle search teams at road blocks.

As the LAD was on a two-year tour it could not neglect annual training, resulting at times in as many as eight men being away on courses at the same time. The remainder just had to work harder to cope with the work load. Although the regimental vehicles were running very high mileages, by insisting on a high standard of three-monthly A vehicle inspections and by keeping B vehicle inspections in REME hands, the vehicle repair load was kept under control. The 'old fashioned' annual HQ REME examination gave the regiment a good spring clean, which proved invaluable during the busy summer season of the troublesome sectarian marches.

To provide a twenty-four hour recovery service at about thirty minutes call-out, the LAD centralized recovery and formed three five-man crews, two on duty and one off duty. Each recovery vehicle was escorted by an armoured Land Rover in radio contact with the operations room. Each crew had a recovery mechanic, a driver and a vehicle mechanic, with the remaining two being any trade from HQ LAD. On average the recovery crews did about thirty-five jobs, covering 2,500 miles, each month. For tasks in very sensitive border areas the crews were escorted and protected by armoured cars. Such tasks were often at police request, to recover blown-up or burnt-out civilian vehicles.

Captain Murphy wrote in the REME Journal in 1973 that the LAD learned four important lessons in those two years.

- That the efficiency of the LAD depended above all on the soldiers themselves. The emergency drew out the very best from them and the real and obvious purpose of their employment raised their morale. This helped to overcome the effects of the poor living and working conditions, the hard work and frequent separation from their families.
- Because they were in Northern Ireland for two years it was necessary for them to pace themselves, spending proper time on routine servicing and inspections.
- The emphasis was for centralized repair and recovery. Although small detachments were occasionally deployed, they had well-organized fast-moving recovery teams primarily designed for road work and a vehicle mechanic was always included in the team.
- The importance of getting everyone in the LAD thinking, making suggestions and taking a lively interest in supporting the parent unit. Visiting other people with similar problems and comparing notes paid dividends and one was never too proud to learn.

Field workshops too had their share of operational activity, particularly when recovery work was involved. REME recovery mechanics from field workshops based at Sydenham carried out more than 300 recovery tasks in a six-month tour in 1971, of which riot damage proved the most exciting. An incident on 5 March 1971 showed how hectic things could be. A recovery crew was first called to the Falls Road in Belfast, not high in the charts as the best place to be, where there was an urgent need to remove a double-decker bus being used as a barricade. When this had been cleared they were sent on to Leeson Street to remove a hijacked petrol tanker which was full of fuel. It was obviously an unattractive vehicle to work on in that area, as shots were being fired and petrol bombs thrown. The recovery crew removed the tanker very smartly. They were duly relieved that by their next call-out a decision had been made to issue them with 'flak jackets'!

In October 1971 the British Government decided to expand the UDR from 6,000 to 10,000 and increase the Regular Army in the Province to 14,000. Many civilians, UDR, RUC and soldiers were killed in 1971 with hundreds of houses destroyed, usually by fire. There were more than 1,500 bomb and 1,700 shooting incidents reported that year – many times more than in 1969 and 1970 combined.

1972

The year started with eight separate bomb explosions in Belfast early on New Year's Day. By now many of the Catholic population no longer looked upon the Army as their protectors, the IRA propaganda machine having portrayed the troops as brutal oppressors. In the course of 1972 103 regular soldiers were killed, as well as UDR, RUC and more than 300 civilians. On Sunday 30 January violence broke out in Londonderry when the Northern Ireland Civil Rights Association held a large march, with several thousand people taking part. One company of 1st Battalion, The Parachute Regiment was sent in towards the end of the march to arrest the rioting hooligans who had separated from the mass of marchers. The soldiers came under fire from the Rossville Flats and returned fire, during which thirteen civilians were killed and as many injured. This day became known as 'Bloody Sunday' and was followed by predictable allegations against the Army. On 2 February, in Dublin, a mob burned the British Embassy to the ground and three weeks later the IRA blew up HQ 16 Parachute Brigade Officers' Mess in Aldershot, killing seven civilians.

In March the British Government in London decided that the Stormont Government of Northern Ireland could no longer control the situation and imposed direct rule from Westminster. Mr Faulkner and his Government resigned in protest and on 25 March Mr William Whitelaw arrived to take over as Secretary of State in the new Northern Ireland Office. By 7 April there were 775 people interned in Long Kesh and

Magilligan – HMS *Maidstone* no longer being used. Mr Whitelaw released forty-seven internees that day as the start of his new policy to abolish internment.

8 Field Workshop was the roulement field workshop from February to June. The main part of the Workshop was based at Sydenham, with platoon-sized detachments at Long Kesh to support 3 Infantry Brigade and at Ballykelly to support 8 Infantry Brigade which, at that time, had no BEME: with many consequent equipment problems. The workload in Northern Ireland proved to be much greater than in the Workshop's home location in Colchester and, apart from all its normal tasks, the Workshop now provided a Special Search Team trained to strip down a suspect vehicle in a search for arms or explosives. This was an example of the many means of combating terrorism in which REME was involved; the necessary techniques that were adopted took many forms, both of an offensive and defensive nature. Apart from the REME units based in the Province taking local action in meeting such needs, those in the Corps back in UK were also very much involved in developing equipment and techniques to help units on the ground.

Lieutenant Colonel Chris Tyler, then an AQMG in the MOD Directorate of Equipment Management, participated in one such significant contribution. He recalls the beginning in 1972 of what was to become a major REME project for both UK and Northern Ireland:

'One day, having nothing else to do and with the in-tray absolutely empty, I went to see the Col Q in case he needed any help with his B Vehicle fleet! He was on the phone and he motioned me towards an armchair, signalling that I should take notes. The phone call ended and with it the planning was under way for Op BRACELET, the up-armouring of all the Humber Pigs – and for Op KREMLIN, the corresponding programme for SARACEN APCs. For good measure, we also started planning for the long-awaited Op MOTORMAN, the clearance of the "no-go" areas. This operation totally depended on putting CENTURION AVREs into Londonderry to smash the barriers into which concrete had been poured. Getting the AVREs there from BAOR was an operation comparable to getting the first tanks into battle in the First World War.'

The up-armouring had become a vital requirement when in 1972 the armour of the 'Pig' was penetrated by high-velocity armour-piercing small arms ammunition fired by the PIRA. 'Pigs' were an important element in helping to combat violence in Northern Ireland, and were used for a wide range of tasks, including troop-carrying, transporting bomb-disposal teams and as ambulances. Adequate protection for the occupants was essential and it was decided that these vehicles should be up-armoured. The implications of this decision were considerable and REME's involvement in the task was to be both substantial and impressive.

Humber 1 ton 4 × 4 'Pig'

When it was learned that British industry was unable to up-armour these vehicles within the time required by the Ministry of Defence, the Military Vehicles and Engineering Establishment (MVEE) was made responsible for designing the extra armour required and REME was given the job of fitting it. The requirement was for the completion of about half the 'Pig' fleet in 1972. Most of the REME static workshops in the UK took part in this programme which included assembling appliqué armour in six main areas of the vehicle: front visor and surround, side doors, roof plates, internal side plates, front scuttle and rear doors. Three visor blocks provided vision to the rear and sides, and a firing flap or 'Barn Door' was fitted at the rear.

A major problem in up-armouring was to keep the weight increase as small as possible, since the 'Pig' was already marginally overweight for some components, and these had to be improved as part of the programme. Extremely hard imported steel plate with a Brinell number of 500, compared with 350 for normal armour, was therefore used, but even with this armour the extra weight was 3,400 pounds. The up-armouring kits contained over 800 components, more than 400 of which were manufactured by REME workshops and required the production of some 300 drawings. The cost of the steel plates was about £1,000 per set at 1972 prices and 400 man-hours were required to fit them to each 'Pig'.

The Chief Production Engineer at Technical Group REME was given the task of planning and co-ordinating the whole activity. Colonel Reg Tibble worked almost full time on this project from the summer until late December 1972, assisted by a major and a vehicle artificer. A team drawn up at short notice from the central workshops was set up at MVEE to work closely with their design staff and with 6 Maintenance Advisory Group (MAG) and Vehicles Branch of Technical Group. Their task was to act as production advisers to the MVEE designers, to collect design information and to recommend how the task should be carried out. A major factor in planning was the realization that plasma arc cutting would be needed. By late July an outline plan had been made. The main parts of the first phase, consisting of collecting information and working preparations were:

- 38 Central Workshop at Chilwell was to reproduce the drawings and distribute them, design and manufacture the jigs and fixtures for those workshops which were to fit the kits, and write the Process Plan.
- 34 Central Workshop at Donnington was to plan the manufacture of ancillary items, mainly of mild steel, and install and bring into operation in-house cutting facilities for the armour plate.
- Other workshops, 8 Field, 18 and 42 Command, and 32 Central, were to carry out in-house training in and familiarization with the process. 8 Field Workshop, recently returned from a tour in Northern Ireland, had to move from Colchester to Marchington in Staffordshire to be closer to the other workshops in the Midlands.

The second phase was to implement the plans. The Process Plan which had been written by 38 Central Workshop had four main stages. The first was to receive and cut the armour plate to size. Initially this was done by a contractor alone, but later some of the cutting was carried out at 34 Central Workshop. For cutting the plates some 150 drawings were involved. When cut, the plates were sent as kits to 34 and 38 Central Workshops. The second stage was the fabrication of the armour plate, mild steel and other items. These were kept by 38 Central Workshop for the third stage, which was fitting to the 'Pigs'. 34 Central Workshop distributed their fabricated kits to 8 Field Workshop, 18 and 42 Command Workshops, and 32 Central Workshop. The 'Pigs' had to be prepared for fitting by the removal of unwanted parts and body projections. The fourth stage was to carry out certain reliability modifications which were essential in a vehicle which was about twenty years old and marginally overloaded before adding the armour. The rear-wheel drive shafts were replaced and the hub carrier, which was weak, was replaced by a stronger one. The torsion bars were also adjusted for extra weight. The up-armoured 'Pigs' on their way back to Northern Ireland went to the Contract Repair Workshop at Liverpool for certain other modifications.

The appliqué armour plate used for the task was an abrasion-resistant steel which had not been used for a production run in a REME workshop and required new techniques for cutting, welding and drilling the plate. Cutting was done by a plasma arc in which a very high temperature, high velocity arc was formed between a central tungsten electrode in the torch and the metal to be cut. The plasma gas and the arc were constricted by being forced through a small orifice in the torch nozzle, concentrating on a small area of the metal which was melted instantly by the intense heat. The molten metal was blown away by the jet-like stream, giving a high-speed, high quality clean cut ready for use. The heat-affected zone was very narrow, a most important requirement to avoid degrading the quality of the armour plate, and a rigid welding specification was issued by MVEE for fabrication. Metal Inert Gas (MIG) welding using carbon dioxide as a shield was employed. Drilling the armour plate was a problem at first as cutting or blowing holes in the plate using the plasma torch did not produce a good enough finish. The problem was solved by using special drills provided by the steel manufacturers.

On Friday 21 July there were twenty-two bomb explosions in one hour in Belfast city centre, killing nine people and injuring about 130, for which the PIRA admitted responsibility. There were also explosions in Londonderry and elsewhere. By 27 July there were four brigades in Northern Ireland making a total of 21,000 troops. On 31 July the long-planned Operation MOTORMAN removed the barricades to the so-called 'No-Go' areas in Londonderry and Belfast. In Londonderry four CENTURION AVREs from BAOR with large bulldozer blades on the front were used to demolish the barricades. These vehicles had been brought to the Province in great secrecy – landing from LCUs from HMS *Fearless*, at night on a specially constructed slipway in Fort George. Their presence surprised not only the local population but also most of the troops involved in the operation!

While the 'Pig' up-armouring programme was going on there was an acute shortage of APCs. It was decided to take crash action in July to provide 230 more SARACENs for the RCT, many of which came from sales dumps and were painted desert yellow and modified for hot climates. Their impending arrival led to the establishment in that same month of the Northern Ireland Saracen Workshop in four large airportable shelters at the Royal Naval Air Yard, Sydenham. The total strength of the workshop was forty-eight, increasing to eighty-seven in August, backed up by a small RAOC Stores Section. Detachments were sent from Sydenham to Ballykinler and Londonderry.

In October the first up-armoured Mark 2 Humber 'Pig' was issued by 34 Central Workshop and by April 1973 another 442 had followed. Operation BRACELET had been successfully completed. It had been a complex and costly operation, but the skills, dedication and co-operation of all concerned had produced a greatly improved vehicle, well suited to its role and meeting the major requirement to protect lives. Later there were to be further improvements to 'Pigs' in a package of modifications including seat harnesses, front visors and vision blocks. These were to be the subject of Operation BRACELET 2 which was contracted out to a civilian workshop in Liverpool. Between September 1973 and July 1974 all 443 'Pigs' were modified. As a consequence of Operation BRACELET the added weight of the 'Pigs' contributed to a sharp rise in the rate of wheel station failure from about twenty-five a week to about 100 in June 1973. Vehicles Branch had already been given the task of finding a solution to the high failure rate of Chobham joints used in the wheel stations. After trials using Tracta joints it was decided to fit Birfield joints, and their fitting between June and November 1974 reduced the failure rate to sixty per week, then to thirty and finally to nil. Other projects undertaken solely within Northern Ireland were also in the pipeline: 46 Command Workshop early in 1972 produced 700 roof hatches for Land Rovers, and forty-eight vehicles were provided with sleeping accommodation. By October the Workshop was ready to start the routine overhaul of 100 'Pigs', which would require 350 man-hours per vehicle.

The number of helicopters in the Province increased during 1972. In February the Army Air Corps had six SIOUX at both Omagh and Long Kesh and six SIOUX and five SCOUTs at Aldergrove, but by November four SCOUTs and six SIOUX were added from BAOR. REME manpower was increased to provide the additional support needed. As with vehicles, additional fittings to helicopters to help in the search for terrorists were always being examined and a useful fitting installed by REME was the NITESUN aerial searchlight, with its four-million candlepower lamp.

Amongst the incidents that occurred was the abduction on 12 October of two soldiers from 15 Field Workshop by Protestant rioters. They were disarmed and held by the rioters, but after a worrying ten hours were released. Sadly, however, four REME soldiers were killed in Ulster during the year. The casualties among REME soldiers were not limited to those engaged in their normal trades, as many volunteered for tasks during which they became more vulnerable to terrorist activities. Regrettably, on such a task, on 14 August 1972, Craftsman Brian Hope from the 19th Field Regiment RA LAD in Dortmund, who had volunteered to go to Ulster as an infantryman, was killed instantly by a mine laid by the PIRA.

THE YEARS OF THE TROUBLES 1973–1992

1973–1975

In a White Paper early in 1973 Mr Whitelaw proposed a Northern Ireland Assembly Power Sharing Executive, with Mr Brian Faulkner as its Chairman. Following this, the British Prime Minister, Mr Edward Heath, held the 'Sunningdale Talks' between the UK and Irish Republic Governments which led to a new system of devolved government being set up from 31 December 1973. During 1973 the Army took up a 'lower profile' approach and the IRA moved its area of operations to the border areas with the Republic, especially Armagh. Army strength was reduced by four infantry battalions and the use of 'Pigs' and SARACENs was scaled down as patrols were switched to Land Rovers. But despite this lessening show of strength there was no reciprocation by the terrorists and incidents continued. During the year sixty-six soldiers and 130 civilians were killed in more than 5,000 reported shooting incidents and over 1,500 bomb explosions. Four unarmed NCOs were lured to what they believed to be a normal party in a Belfast house, by women acting for the IRA, where gunmen appeared and murdered three of them, severely wounding the fourth.

After the up-armouring of 'Pigs' was completed, SARACENs were sent back to Britain for more armour to be put on them in command and central workshops under Operation KREMLIN 1. Alvis Ltd made the modification kits which converted Marks 2 and 3 SARACENs to Marks 5 and 6. Extra armoured plates up to 14mm thick were welded to the body and hull and armoured visors were fitted for the driver and observer, taking 750 man-hours per vehicle at a cost of nearly £6,000 at 1973 prices. The first ten vehicles were back in Ireland in June 1973, and the programme of 217 upgrades completed in August 1974: a great achievement in view of the Government-imposed three-day week resulting from an electrical power crisis. Following severe damage to an armoured vehicle from an RPG 7 in December 1972, protection against these anti-tank rocket propelled grenades was provided for in the Operation KREMLIN 2 programme. This started in May 1973, but when the first two kits arrived, these required local modification to overcome fitting problems. The kits were sent to Long Kesh where a platoon of 3 Field Workshop, the roulement field workshop, modified the kits to fit all marks of SARACEN. By June 1974 the roulement Workshop had modified 107 kits.

The new CREME Northern Ireland, Lieutenant Colonel Tony Baxter, was appointed in 1973. In the same year Lisburn Garrison LAD was also formed, and the Northern Ireland Saracen Workshop was renamed APC Workshop (Northern Ireland) in recognition of the amount of time spent working on 'Pigs'. The APC Workshop had a mixed force of soldiers from several REME units which were serving tours of four months, six months, eighteen months and two years. It was based at the Royal Naval Air Yard, Sydenham (later moving to purpose built accommodation at Moscow Camp) with detachments at Ballykinler and

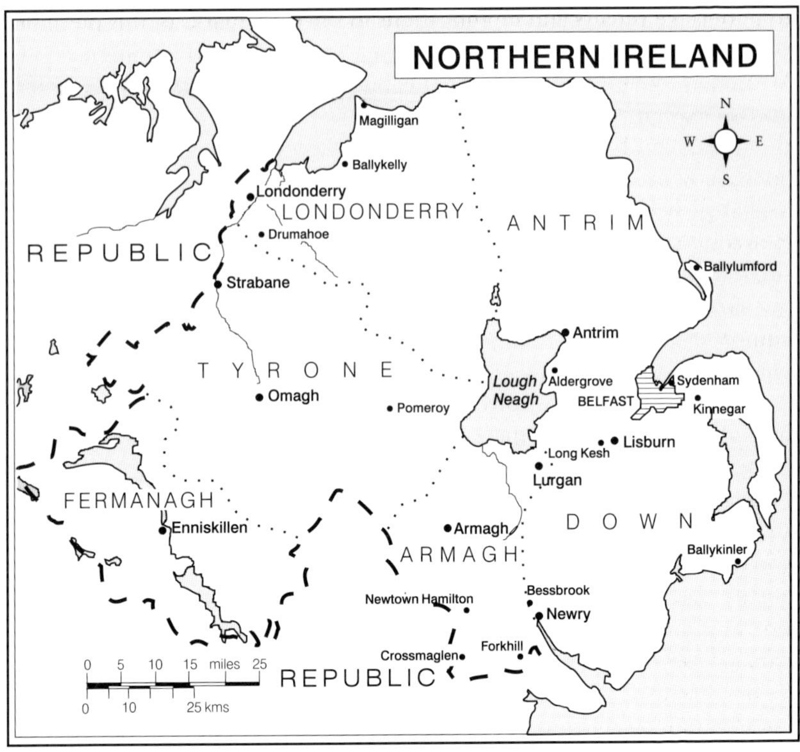

Londonderry. The Ballykinler detachment of twenty-eight soldiers was further divided into penny packets throughout 3 Infantry Brigade area including Armagh, Bessbrook, Crossmaglen, Forkhill and Newton Hamilton. These detachments were often working under very poor and difficult conditions and Crossmaglen and Forkhill could only be reached by helicopter because of the threat from culvert mines. Later they were to be faced with a new problem with the 'Pigs', which fortunately did not produce the same difficulties, now overcome, as those encountered with the Chobham and Tracta joints. Half-shaft failures were increasing, amounting to some ten a month. But, as they were easy and cheap to replace compared with a wheel station, it was decided to leave the shafts as they were rather than strengthen them and risk overloading the recently fitted Birfield joints.

An important and interesting piece of equipment with which REME was concerned both in Northern Ireland and UK from 1973 was the WHEELBARROW. This was a miniature tracked vehicle designed for use by Bomb Disposal Teams, 3 Field Workshop was the first REME workshop to undertake repairs and modifications to the early marks of this piece of equipment in the Province. Previously they had been undertaken at MVEE in England until a specialist team of REME fitters was able to take on this task in August. By 1982, nine years later, the Mark 7B WHEELBARROW had been introduced. Although at first it was regarded as an 'electronic menace' it led the way to a very successful Mark 8 in 1990. The Mark 8 was not a direct development of the Mark 7B, but was a new RARDE design, commissioned and assembled by 34 Base Workshop with sub-assemblies from sub-contractors. 34 Base Workshop then provided a fast field repair service as well as major overhaul and base repair. These equipments continued to provide a most valuable contribution in the controlled destruction of terrorist bombs.

The new system of devolved government which had been introduced in Northern Ireland at the end of 1973 was soon in difficulties. The Protestant Loyalist reaction to power-sharing and the attempt to set up a Council of Ireland to develop North-South relations led to a general strike called by the Ulster Workers Council. This strike closed the main power station at Ballylumford, prevented sewage works from operating, cut off food supplies and severely disrupted the economic life of the Province. The Northern Ireland Executive and Assembly collapsed, and from 28 May 1974 direct rule from London was reinstated.

In March 1974 8 Field Workshop took over the repair of Stornophone commercial radios from the manufacturers and reduced the 'down time' from two months to one day. This was only one example of the increasingly technical nature of REME's task, brought about by the need to employ complex electronic equipment in the fight against the terrorists. The extra load required to support the force in the Province was reflected in increased REME strength, which by mid-1974 had risen to 803 officers and soldiers and forty-four civilians. Even so, the nature of the specialized tasks meant that workshops and LADs were hard-pressed to meet all the requirements. The fact that they did so was a measure of the dedication and technical skills of all those involved.

15 Field Workshop arrived in the Province in May 1974 for a six-month tour. One unique task was to set up a specialist repair bay for the infantry battalions' explosive detector. Apart from this specialist requirement there was a steady increase in the routine workload during the tour, which the Workshop took in its stride. When it was subsequently replaced by 10 Field Workshop, which returned to Northern Ireland on roulement in November 1974, all ranks could look back with considerable satisfaction on their achievements.

During 1974 PIRA hijacked a Post Office van and captured some mail which identified firms which had worked for Contract Repair Branch.

This incident resulted in a threatening IRA letter being received saying that the CRB employees should cease to support the Army or face IRA reprisals. One named employee was posted from Ulster immediately, but the remainder as well as the contractors continued to give sterling support despite the dangers. One contractor provided a mobile inspection, servicing and repair organization for the UDR. Threats and 'soft' targets such as terrorist action against Government employees and contractors were continuing hazards and many took great personal risks in giving loyal service to the Army, not the least those employed by REME.

Not all incidents affecting civilian employees were quite so dramatic, but were nevertheless unfortunate. The RAOC Vehicle Sub Depot at Long Kesh had to be moved to Kinnegar to make room for an enlarged Maze Prison, and this also required the 46 Command Workshop detachment there to move. The soldiers went first, leaving the civilians to follow later. Regrettably, half of the civilian staff declined to move. This was not only a loss to REME of their skills and experience, which could be ill-afforded, but was certainly disadvantageous for them as well, after all the valuable service that they had given.

On a happier note was the arrival in the Autumn of the first WRAC member of HQ REME staff – Lance Corporal Helen Chant. This was indicative of the recruiting into the Corps of many more women, who were later to be REME-badged.

The PIRA announced a truce over the 1974 Christmas period but in 1975 they then directed their terror towards civilians rather than the Army. The number of soldiers killed fell as a result. For the fourth year running the number of IRA terrorists killed also fell, but civilians killed went up for the third year running. The release of people detained under the Special Powers Act which had begun in 1972 was completed in December 1975 and internment without trial ceased.

The new CREME, Lieutenant Colonel Andrew MacLauchlan, who arrived in January 1975, decided that improvements could be made to the way REME functioned in the Province. He reviewed the overall REME manpower required and proposed establishing a Northern Ireland Roulement Workshop (NIRW) to replace the APC Workshop and the roulement Field Workshop. The APC Workshop had had more than 100 APCs removed from its load, and the manpower cuts that followed reduced its strength to one officer and sixty-four tradesmen, drawn from twelve different units. They had worked under considerable pressure, but it was rewarding and their morale was high despite cramped sleeping accommodation and awful working conditions. The AFG 1198 equipment for the new Workshop would be held in Ulster and soldiers on roulement would only be required to be flown in with their personal kit. First-line REME support to APCs would be provided by RCT squadron workshop elements under command of NIRW.

A Northern Ireland Electronic Workshop (NIEW) manned by eight REME technicians on a two-year tour would be set up to provide expert support for the ever-growing quantity of electronic equipment. This electronic equipment included Pye Pocketfones, which were becoming old and less repairable, and Explosive Detectors which were issued without spares and were sensitive to rough handling and dirt contamination. They were also often waiting for the central control unit which could only be repaired by the manufacturer. The new organization was to help remedy this and provide a more rapid service for users.

Lieutenant Colonel Michael Bagnall-Oakeley, who commanded 46 Command Workshop from May 1975 to May 1978, recalled those days:

'The civilians were one-third Catholic and two-thirds Protestant. Every Ulster person knew exactly from which side of the sectarian divide every other person came, yet there was almost no trouble within the workshop. Looking back, there were ample opportunities to ferment trouble in and around the MOD site, yet it didn't happen. My worst period was six months of anonymous false bomb warnings. These had to be taken seriously, and it meant turning everyone out in all weathers whilst buildings, stores and vehicles were searched. Nothing was ever found and the waste of production time was serious.

'Employees saved throughout the year towards a Christmas Party for about thirty elderly people. Everyone was keen to help. I remember a particularly shaky old man who seemed to have slopped his tea everywhere. Leaning over, I emptied and dried his saucer, got him a fresh cup of tea and put the cup back on the saucer, feeling that a good job was done. His companion fixed me with a withering eye and announced that his friend always drank his tea out of his saucer!'

10 Field Workshop departed for Tidworth in May 1975, after its last six-month tour in Ulster. 3 Field Workshop, commanded by Major Gerry Quirke, replaced it. An important addition to the Workshop's range of test equipment was the Schlumberger 4010 Test Kit which was issued towards the end of the year. This speeded up the testing of commercial radios and reduced turn-round times, a matter which was always of concern in trying to give better service to units. Unfortunately, the year ended with an incident typical of the uncertainties of serving in Northern Ireland, with the sad death of Craftsman McInnes, 42nd Heavy Regiment Workshop. He was on sentry duty overlooking the Old City of Londonderry when a 20 pound bomb exploded on the roof of the sentry post killing him instantly.

1976–1978

In April 1976 Special Category status was ended for convicted terrorists who were no longer to enjoy treatment as 'political prisoners', but were put in normal cells in the newly constructed blocks in the Maze Prison (known as H Blocks because of their shape), formerly called Long Kesh. The prime responsibility for law and order passed to the RUC, with the Army acting in support of police operations. It was to be an even more violent year.

CREME's proposals, made in 1975, for a reorganization of REME in the Province took effect on 1 April 1976 when 8 Field Workshop from UKLF, with Major Arthur Soar in command, became the first Northern Ireland Roulement Workshop. At the same time the APC Workshop disbanded and the Northern Ireland Electronic Workshop, under an ASM, opened for work at Long Kesh on 20 April.

15 Field Workshop returned from Catterick to Ulster in May 1976 and was to be the last field workshop to complete a six-month tour. The Workshop took the opportunity to commission a painting by the artist Ken Howard to show the workshop's activities in its various locations in Northern Ireland. The original was hung in 15 Field Workshop Sergeants' Mess but many copies of what became known as the Roulement Workshop painting are displayed in REME units around the world. One activity, perhaps regrettably not included in the picture, was that of a very unusual recovery task which caught the headlines in September 1976. A crowd of teenagers in Londonderry attacked a

pregnant donkey, which in panic fell over the edge of the wharf loading platform into the mud on the banks of the River Foyle, where it became firmly stuck. To wild applause from the assembled crowd, it was winched to safety by a recovery team from 15 Field Workshop only minutes before it would have drowned.

In November 1976 11 Field Workshop arrived in Northern Ireland to replace 15 Field Workshop and was the first workshop from BAOR to form the NIRW and the first to serve a four-month tour. There was always a variety of jobs requiring different techniques. Thirty of the ubiquitous 'Pigs' were fitted with water cannons whilst a further thirty-five were fitted to carry projecting side panels to protect advancing infantry, thus earning the title of 'Flying Pigs'. A major programme to fit Land Rovers with an anti-roll bar for protection against culvert mines had also been started in August. The Equipment Explosive Detector and aged Pye Pocketfone continued to be problems but the new pocket radio, the Stornophone CQP 863, raised hopes of better availability, but this was counterbalanced by an inadequate spares backing.

In January 1977 the GOC and the Chief Constable issued a joint RUC/Army directive called 'The Way Ahead'. The policy placed the emphasis on bringing terrorists before the courts and securing their conviction, while the Army was to maintain a low profile acting in support of the RUC. The effect of this policy was that the number of bombing and shooting incidents was cut to half that of the previous year with a big reduction in the number of civilian and RUC deaths. Unfortunately the Army and UDR combined total of deaths remained the same as the year before.

The helicopter squadrons were of major importance to the efforts of the Security Forces, in achieving rapid reaction to terrorist activity and speedy and safe transport of troops in areas where road movement was vulnerable to mining. In 1977 there were three AAC squadrons in Ulster, with one resident squadron at Omagh supporting the Armoured Reconnaissance Regiment and two roulement Squadrons. Each had its own REME tradesmen, who were supported at second line by REME technicians from 70 Aircraft Workshop on a four-month tour at Aldergrove. The Aircraft Engineer, Major Bob Tonks, who had been based at HQ REME in Lisburn, later moved to Aldergrove, where he was nearer to the technicians and the aircraft.

Of contrasting activity to the work on aircraft were the special requirements that arose at frequent intervals and invariably required emergency action by the command or field workshops. A typical example occurred at the end of 1977 and early in 1978 when there was a national firemen's strike. The very old 'Green Goddess' fire engines were taken out of store in England and some were sent to Ulster, where their use in combating terrorist fire bomb attacks could have been vital. They were checked over one weekend at 46 Command Workshop, where multi-way connectors had to be made rapidly because the fire hydrants in Ulster were not compatible with the hoses on the 'Green Goddesses'. 3 Field Workshop, which was once again the roulement workshop, also fitted many of these veterans with blue flashing lights and two-tone horns.

In 1978 there was a reduction in deaths for the Army, UDR, RUC and civilian population, with more bombs but fewer shooting incidents. There was also a substantial reduction in the number of terrorists charged with offences. The force levels were reduced to 13,000 Regular and 7,700 UDR. One of the bomb incidents at Comber, County Down, in February killed twelve innocent civilians and the next day a fire bomb caused £500,000 worth of damage in the Ulster Bus Depot at Londonderry.

Recovery work provided a change of environment from the more routine work of the workshop or LAD, but could prove hazardous, not only because of the terrorists, but also the site conditions. Bogs, for instance, were not ideal places from which to recover vehicles and equipments which seemed to find their way into them with unerring accuracy. However, as a feature of the terrain in Northern Ireland, they were testing places for recovery teams on numerous occasions. Three of the many incidents which took place over the years involving the recovery of valuable equipment show the extent of the problem. The first was carried out by 1 Corps Troops Workshop in 1978 to rescue a R SIGNALS rebroadcasting station Bedford truck which had taken a short cut across the mountains near Ballykelly and had become hopelessly bogged down in peat and mud. The Workshop AEC recovery vehicle could not get within 300 metres of the casualty because of the ground. The Bedford Light recovery vehicle was sent out with a crew of two and during their efforts to haul the casualty to the top of the hill they themselves became bogged, the crews having to camp out overnight. At 0600 hours next morning Sergeant Spiers was flown to the scene through murky weather and after fruitless effort he radioed for more help. The AEC recovery

Saracen recovery

returned with Lieutenant Andrew McGregor, together with Corporal Paine in a Bedford winch truck borrowed from an infantry battalion. They brought with them thirty pieces of trackway from the Sappers which proved invaluable. To get to the casualty was a feat in itself, the track being narrow, steep and twisting, presenting a problem even to a Land Rover. The Sappers' trackway was put down, the Bedford rebroadcasting station truck was dug out and the winch truck put into place. After many hours of digging to secure the winch truck, the recovery vehicles working together pulled the casualty, which by now was sinking in the mud and listing perilously, towards firm ground.

A task which took even longer involved retrieving an AEC and a Coles Crane from a bog near Castlerock. Another AEC and a Muirhill Tractor were used for the job which took eight days to complete with the help of the Sappers, who had to rebuild a causeway in the process. In an earlier incident the REME recovery section at Shackleton Barracks, Ballykelly, helped to recover a £41,000 excavator submerged in a peat bog near Bellaghy. Once again the Sappers lent a helping hand with a bulldozer and with two REME AEC recovery vehicles the excavator was brought to safety. This particular task was not made easier by the fact that time was of the essence and the recovery had to continue in the hours of darkness or the equipment would have sunk out of sight.

1979–1984

In May 1979, soon after Mr Airey Neave MP had been murdered by a bomb fixed to his car which exploded as he drove out of the House of Commons underground car park, Mrs Margaret Thatcher became Britain's first woman Prime Minister. The Irish National Liberation Army (INLA) claimed responsibility for murdering Mr Neave, who was Mrs Thatcher's good friend and trusted adviser. In August the PIRA claimed responsibility for the murder of The Earl Mountbatten and two young boys, blown up on their boat as they left for a holiday fishing trip off the Irish coast near Mullaghmore, County Sligo. A PIRA ambush later that day at Warren Point in County Down killed eighteen soldiers. Such was the widespread violence perpetrated by the terrorists. Despite this, the background routine work which was an essential element in combating such activities went on unrelentingly. Some provided essential light relief on which the British soldier thrives in time of adversity.

Major Tony Millington, commanding 8 Field Workshop on a roulement tour in Northern Ireland in 1979, later wrote:

'We had the immense good fortune in having the services of a Company Sergeant Major who had recently transferred to the REME regimental duty roll from the

Grenadier Guards and, perhaps to be expected, he was able to balance his outstanding professionalism with a keen sense of humour. His timing was brilliant and I suspect that we, in the Workshop Headquarters in Belfast, will all remember to the ends of our service the morning when, with a characteristic crashing of boots, he reported to the effect that "the men are happy, Sir," but added the polite enquiry "permission to go outside and muck 'em about a bit!" '

The DGEME, Major General Homan, was able to make two informative and encouraging visits to units in Northern Ireland during his tour, in 1978 and 1979, and exceptionally the situation also allowed the REME Staff Band to visit in both these years. The Band was able to carry out engagements in Londonderry and Craigavon where they had a memorable march through the streets of the town, followed by lunch with the Lord Mayor. Such visits were an important part of the policy to continue Regimental activities in the Province as much as possible and help break up the more tedious routine that inevitably existed for a lot of the time. They also helped to cement the good relationship that existed with the bulk of the population.

In 1980 more troops were removed from Northern Ireland, and outside the hard Republican areas the RUC and UDR took on more regular patrols, with the RUC strength being increased by 1,000. There was a reduction in bombing and shooting incidents for the second year running, with many fewer Regular soldiers being killed than in the previous year. The RUC suffered fewer casualties than for ten years, but civilian deaths remained at the 1978–79 levels. The number of terrorists charged with offences was the lowest since 1972.

The tasks for REME continued unabated, but there were problems brought about by the sheer old age of equipment and these were less easy to solve than many others. 'Pigs' now fell into this category and spares were in short supply. Assemblies which should have been replaced were having to be repaired instead and huge backlogs built up whilst replacements were awaited from manufacturers. Being able to anticipate such problems was an essential requirement, even if all could not be readily solved, and much could be achieved in this respect by BEMEs. Although the 'double hatting' of appointments had sometimes to be abandoned when the pressure became too great, it could be advantageous. One such example was when Major Bob Stringer, OC 46 Command Workshop Detachment in Ballykelly, additionally took on the responsibilities of BEME 8 Infantry Brigade. This enabled him to manage both first- and second-line resources and anticipate potential problems within both brigade units and the Workshop.

Evidence of the increasing technology used in the fight against terrorism was the move to Aldergrove and expansion of the Northern Ireland Electronic Workshop (NIEW) and the posting in of its first OC, Lieutenant Brian Glossop. At HQ REME Lieutenant Colonel Peter Glass took over as CREME but, by 1 January 1982, the title was changed to Commander Maintenance, adopted throughout the Corps. Change also affected other staffs in Headquarters Northern Ireland: Colonel Dennis Shaw, having been appointed Colonel AQ, had his appointment changed to Assistant Chief of Staff G1/G4. He was later awarded the CBE for his work whilst in this arduous and testing appointment.

Early in 1981 the IRA started a hunger strike in the Maze Prison in an attempt to get political status for Republican prisoners. Ten hunger strikers died during the summer; one was Bobby Sands who was elected as the Member of Parliament in Westminster for Fermanagh and South Tyrone while he was on hunger strike, but he died shortly after being elected. The deaths and the funerals were followed by riots. PIRA began a series of sectarian murders, including that of the Reverend Robert Bradford, the Official Unionist Party MP for Belfast South, who was murdered in November 1981 in a Community Centre, together with a community worker.

Fitting shields to the 'Pigs'

7 Armoured Workshop from Fallingbostel in BAOR was the roulement workshop from April to September 1981. The workshop continued the conversion of 'Pigs' to 'Flying Pigs' with their shield-like wings to protect troops sheltering behind them. The 'Flying Pigs' which they produced, like most of the equipment which they repaired, came out of the Workshop with stencilled Red Rats on them – the famous 7 Armoured Brigade Desert Rat from Western Desert days in the Second World War. The unit evidently found Northern Ireland summer weather somewhat inclement after Germany, and one of the soldiers wrote in the first edition of their unit magazine, 'We have been here for thirty-two days now and it's only rained twice, the first time for fourteen days and the second time for seventeen days!' Whilst 7 Armoured Workshop was, amongst many other things, gaining experience of the Ulster weather and converting the 'Pigs', NIRW and 46 Command Workshop were fitting high-velocity weapon-protection kits to the ¾ ton Land Rovers, now to be known as 'Piglets'. This programme was completed in May, and was another step

forward in providing adequate protection for those who travelled in the more sensitive areas.

By September the situation was judged to be right to reduce the number of brigades in the Province and 3 Infantry Brigade was disbanded, leaving 8 and 39 Infantry Brigades on the ground with an adjustment of responsibilities which involved changes for REME. 39 Infantry Brigade now had more of the border with the Republic to look after and Aldergrove became part of 8 Infantry Brigade area. The result was a more even division of work between the two BEMEs and both posts were downgraded from Major to Captain. Major Jeremy Bethell and Major Simon Thompson were posted from their respective brigades soon after and replaced by Captain David Major in 8 Infantry Brigade and Captain Hamish McNinch in 39 Infantry Brigade. Subsequently there were also some small changes in the distribution of REME units and NIRW moved from Sydenham to Kinnegar in December 1982. By making NIRW a platoon of 46 Command Workshop a reduction in administrative staff became possible. Later, the armoured reconnaissance regiment at Omagh was replaced by an infantry battalion, and the regiment's LAD left with them.

The IRA turned their attention to England again in July 1982 with bombs in Regents Park and Hyde Park, killing Royal Green Jacket bandsmen and members of the Household Cavalry. The civilian population of Ulster, though, did not escape and shortly before Christmas 1982 INLA placed a bomb which went off without warning in a discothèque at Ballykelly killing seventeen people and injuring many more.

After thirteen years the force level was now 10,700 Regular and 7,200 UDR, which was about half the number of soldiers in 1972 (the worst year so far for shooting incidents, bombs and soldiers killed). The Regular Army was generally used in the hard Republican areas such as the border with the Republic, Londonderry and West Belfast, with the UDR taking up the role of first-line support to the RUC outside the 'hard areas'. Sadly, amongst those casualties at this time was Sergeant M D Burbridge REME serving with 8 Infantry Brigade Headquarters and Signal Squadron who was ambushed by the PIRA and killed in a van in which he was returning to barracks.

1983 was notable for the reduction in the numbers of soldiers and civilians killed. In September, though, thirty-eight Republicans made a mass escape from the Maze prison, much to the embarrassment of the authorities, many of them still being free a year later. Despite the overall reduction there were still some appalling incidents. In November the INLA fired on the congregation of the Pentecostal Gospel Hall in Darkley, County Armagh, murdering three and wounding several others, whilst in London a bomb outside Harrods killed six and injured many members of the public in December.

Earlier, in March, Sergeant George Johnson, a Telecommunications Technician, was travelling in a Humber 'Pig' to an outstation to inspect some equipment. As the vehicle came near Fort Pegasus in Belfast an RPG hit the vehicle, exploding and seriously injuring him. He was unconscious for two weeks in the intensive care unit of the Royal Victoria Hospital. After being told that he would never walk again due to the serious damage to his leg he showed tremendous courage and determination and returned to work instructing students at the SEE Arborfield. Following this RPG attack several 'Pigs' were provided with 'KREMLIN' mesh to protect them against this sort of action and a hole was cut in the top to improve their sentry capability. 46 Command Workshop designed and manufactured the kits, completing this modification quickly and efficiently.

Despite the volume of work, time was found within REME units for more pleasant activities. The Mayor of Wokingham, Councillor David Ireland (a former REME National Service man), visited the Province in October. A previous Mayor, Mrs Fergusson-Kelly, had also visited two years earlier. The main purpose of Councillor Ireland's visit was to present the Wokingham Cup to the Northern Ireland Roulement Workshop. It was an award for the REME unit in Ulster which had contributed most to local community and welfare projects. At this time it was 4 Armoured Workshop from Detmold and the cup was accepted by the Officer Commanding, Major Jeremy Ravn. Individuals too took part in activities which contrasted with their daily routine and were encouraged to use their own initiative. Corporal David Wilkinson, a radar technician from NIEW, joined a free fall parachuting expedition to North Carolina, USA, which had been organized by an officer in the Headquarters. Some seventy jumps were achieved by members of the expedition in two weeks and this exhilarating sport provided the participants with an excellent break from the demanding routine of Northern Ireland.

In November 1983 it was again found possible to merge the appointment of Commander Maintenance with that of the CO of 46 Command Workshop, which had been the situation much earlier with the then CREME. Lieutenant Colonel Mervyn Lemon, Commander Maintenance, thus took command of 46 Command Workshop which later, in March 1984, was renamed 46 Northern Ireland Workshop. There was a further force reduction to six resident and two roulement infantry battalions and eleven UDR battalions. Roulement battalions had about sixteen REME soldiers employed on repairs with more REME officers and soldiers often deployed as infantry or watchkeepers. In keeping with the overall force

Craftsman Armer, part of a search cordon

reductions, the total REME strength in Northern Ireland in 1983 was reduced to about 470 officers and soldiers. Importantly though, they still received high priority for manpower, equipment and spares backing.

In 1984 the PIRA turned its attacks once more onto the security forces and away from the previous year's sectarian attacks. Bomb and shooting incidents fell, as did RUC and civilian deaths, but the number of terrorists killed was the highest since 1981. In October, however, the PIRA achieved world-wide notoriety by their unsuccessful attempt to kill the Prime Minister, Mrs Thatcher, and other members of her Cabinet in the Grand Hotel, Brighton, during the Conservative Party Conference. A large bomb was detonated in the hotel, killing five people and seriously injuring many more.

REME telecommunications technicians were withdrawn from all infantry battalions in 1984, despite the extra electronic equipment held by battalions in the Province. NIEW gradually increased its strength, taking on commercial radio repair from NIRW and the UDR and employing a total of thirty-seven technicians. NIRW was disbanded in October 1984, being replaced by an Emergency Platoon of individual REME soldiers on trickle postings who were trained at Ballykinler instead of doing pre-Northern Ireland training in BAOR or UK.

1985–1987

The main political event in 1985 was the Anglo-Irish Agreement made in November by the Prime Ministers of the UK and the Irish Republic, Mrs Margaret Thatcher and Dr Garret FitzGerald, following a conference at Hillsborough. The aim was to provide a framework for closer co-operation between the two states to solve legal, political and security problems, to build up mutual confidence and trust, but to leave executive authority in Northern Ireland to the British Government. The Loyalists claimed that the agreement was a betrayal by Westminster and started a disobedience campaign with large rallies, widespread display of the slogan 'Ulster Says No', a one-day strike, clashes with the RUC and a fire-bombing campaign on the homes of RUC families.

Earlier in 1985 there had been a sustained campaign of violence against the security forces, particularly the RUC and UDR, and in February there was a devastating mortar attack by the PIRA against the RUC station at Newry, in which nine were killed. This increased violence placed a greater strain on the Army in their support of the RUC, as its strength had been reduced earlier. The SPEARHEAD battalion was therefore sent out from UK to help, neither the first nor the last time that this situation was to arise. REME support continued to be under pressure, but no problems arose that could not be dealt with effectively by what was now an organization that could withstand such changes in work tempo.

It was important, though, for morale that there should be acceptable breaks in the constant drive to achieve the highest standard of support for units. Such breaks were provided in various ways. Visits to the Corps in the Province by senior officers was one. These in themselves generated variations to activities and interests within units, gave encouragement and sharpened up thinking. All sport and other outside activities were positively encouraged to help break the inevitable routine of serving in Northern Ireland. One of these escapes from routine, and certainly there could not be a more complete change, was achieved by Sergeant Ellis and some of the members of the LAD of 1st Battalion, The Royal Regiment of Fusiliers in Ballykelly who organized an expedition to Kenya. There they helped Mr George Adamson, whose work with lions (together with his wife Joy) was chronicled in the film 'Born Free', to cut a new road into the bush. This worthwhile project was achieved with little outside help and a lot of initiative from Sergeant Ellis.

The DGEME, Major General Tony Palmer, made a second visit to the Province, and this time fared better with his travel arrangements: on a previous occasion he was not met at the right airport, causing red faces all-round, but undoubtedly sharpening up thinking! This time he arrived and was met correctly, setting the scene for a stimulating tour. He was able to visit a number of workshops and LADs and was reassured by all those he met of the high quality of support being provided for the Army by the Corps in Northern Ireland.

Despite the setback at Long Kesh in 1974 described earlier, when movement to new areas by civilian employees was not accepted, civilian recruitment continued to be positive and of considerable importance to the Corps. Training of new recruits made a real contribution to the employment prospects of the local population. This training of new recruits for the civilian element of the workshops continued to flourish and the REME Civilian Apprentice of the Year in 1985 was won by Mr Steven Henderson, a final-year apprentice of 46 Northern Ireland Workshop, who was awarded a shield and a presentation gift. His ultimate aim was to gain an MOD Bursary to attend RMCS at Shrivenham.

The New Year of 1986 started tragically for the RUC when a Radio Controlled Improvised Explosive Device exploded in the town of Newry, killing two policemen. Additional protection for vulnerable RUC stations had to be found by the Army. The SPEARHEAD Battalion proved to be insufficient and an extra battalion was sent from UK. However, the existing REME cover in the Province was well able to take on their extra load.

Second-line aircraft support up until now had been provided by detachments from 70 and 71 Aircraft Workshops, but in 1986 the Northern Ireland Regiment AAC Workshop was formed. This took in 70 Aircraft Workshop detachment, Beaver Flight and 665 Squadron AAC LAD, under Major Bernie Guignard, who was also SO2 (Aviation) Headquarters Northern Ireland. The roulement troops for this workshop were now trickle-posted which provided better continuity. 655 Squadron AAC LAD in Ballykelly remained independent because of the role of the Squadron and its distance from the Workshop.

Amongst new equipment being introduced at this time which was of special significance to REME was the latest commercial radio system by Plessey – COUGARNET. This did not add to REME's normal maintenance commitment as the system was to be fully contract-supported. However, it did bring about a change from REME's traditional maintenance role to that of monitoring the effectiveness of the equipment and its civilian support, a role thought to increase in the future.

Technicians at work

HRH Prince Philip visited the Grenadier Guards at Ballykelly in his capacity as their Colonel in November. On the day of the visit Lieutenant Colonel Andy Platt, Commander Maintenance, received a telephone call telling him that the Prince, as REME's Colonel in Chief, had expressed a wish to meet forty members of the Corps of all ranks, that afternoon. A representative group from every unit was hurriedly assembled in the

Officers' Mess Annex at Lisburn. Over a cup of tea, the Prince met and talked informally to everyone present and congratulated them on the significant contribution of the Corps to the Army's role in the Province. The Colonel in Chief spent nearly an hour with the party who were clearly hugely appreciative that he had taken time to be with them and encourage them in their efforts.

Three soldiers from NIEW were awarded honours for their services in Northern Ireland at the end of 1985. Sergeant Robertson gained the British Empire Medal and Sergeants Bacon and Lowrie the GOC's Commendation. The DGEME, Major General Boyne, was able to present these awards when he visited in February 1986. He was also able to visit Corps units further afield than was normally possible, as a helicopter was made available for his journeys from 655 Squadron AAC. The REME Staff Band was also fortuitously on its first visit to the Province for four years, and the DGEME attended a variety of functions where they played. The Band stayed on for ten days and gave a number of outside concerts, including one in Belfast City Centre, and at a charity event for the Bangor Lifeboat Society. As a result of the latter performance, which was greatly appreciated, a party from the Band was invited out on the Lifeboat in a Force 8 gale – a little Ulster humour perhaps?

In 1987 about one-third of the civilian-pattern vehicle fleet in the Province, which had been a feature for many years, was composed of standard military vehicles painted in non-standard colours. The preponderance of Vauxhall Cavaliers of whatever colour in areas like Lisburn made it highly likely that any Cavalier belonged to the Army. All the Austin Metros were the basic model without any personal frills and only the Army had diesel-engined Ford Escorts. This made it easy for the terrorists to identify military vehicle targets. It was decided to plug this possible loophole in the Army's security, and by April 1989 all standard military cars had been replaced by civilian-pattern cars and action had also been taken to civilianize certain other military vehicles. At the same time all remaining vans, trucks, coaches and ambulances were inspected and 46 Northern Ireland Workshop began the heavy programme of repainting and 'de-militarization'. The days of the purple 4 tonner and pink Land Rover were over. Trucks and vans were stripped and rebuilt to civilian-pattern specifications. Dropside vehicles became flatbeds, military-pattern lights were replaced and towing hooks removed.

Despite this special surge in activity, the now routine work on the GRP armoured Land Rover fleet, the 'Pig' fleet and the Armoured Patrol Vehicle continued at a higher rate than for some years. An unfortunate effect of the GRP armour was that it increased corrosion, especially of the chassis and bulkhead areas. The old-fashioned 'Pigs', with their sturdy suspension and body construction, showed great resilience despite the many additions which made them 50% heavier than their design weight. Land Rovers, however, were having to be rebuilt from the chassis up and, owing to problems with procurement of new diesel-engined Land Rovers, the irreplaceable ageing vehicles had to have what were previously regarded as uneconomic repairs. The REME soldier element of 46 Northern Ireland Workshop was kept very busy repairing high-priority equipment and on tasks which included special projects. An unusual experience in the Workshop was that of a civilian employee being stung by a scorpion in a vehicle tarpaulin sent in for repair after a TA exercise in Gibraltar! The scorpion was subsequently preserved in a resin block in the unit trophy room.

1988–1992

In 1987 the IRA had detonated a bomb during a Remembrance Day Parade at Enniskillen, killing and injuring many people and earning world-wide condemnation for this atrocity. The bad publicity for the Republican cause and the 1988–90 anniversaries (twenty years since the deployment of troops on the streets in 1969, 300 years since the Glorious Revolution, the Siege of Londonderry and the Battle of the Boyne) may have been the reasons for the upsurge of violence in 1988 and 1989, which during 1988 reached levels akin to the late Seventies. The Garda in the Republic found a large quantities of explosives and weapons in a hide on the Donegal Coast. Substantial quantities of weapons and ammunition were also recovered from under floor hides in Belfast and two large shipments of arms were caught in vehicle check points. In March 1988 three terrorists were shot dead in Gibraltar. There was widespread disorder at two IRA funerals, at one of which two Corporals in the R SIGNALS who accidently arrived on the scene in a vehicle were murdered by a mob. An under-vehicle device killed six soldiers in Lisburn and in August a roadside bomb killed eight soldiers and injured many more in a coach in which they had been returning from leave to their unit in Omagh. There were many other bomb attacks in Northern Ireland, in addition to attacks on Army and Royal Air Force men and barracks in England, Germany and Holland.

The response of the Security Forces in Northern Ireland in 1988 was rapid and varied, but the main reorganization was the reforming of 3 Infantry Brigade which from 1 July became responsible for the border area, with its HQ at Armagh. The first SO3 Maintenance (originally titled BEME) of the re-formed brigade was Captain Bobby Haslam, recently commissioned after a tour as ASM of the Northern Ireland Electronic Workshop. By the spring of 1989 the total security force strength in

Northern Ireland was almost 31,000, including Regular Army 10,500, UDR 6,200 (including part-time) and the RUC 12,900 (including part-time). There were 433 REME, 166 of them on roulement tours.

PIRA had no conscience about whom they attacked: anyone connected to the Security Forces, man, woman or child, could be a target. In an especially callous attack in Dortmund, Germany, the wife of Staff Sergeant Hazell REME was shot dead at the wheel of her car as she returned home at night in September 1989. Also in September the IRA bombed the Royal Marines School of Music at Deal in Kent. Eleven Royal Marines bandsmen died and twenty-two were injured in this attack.

Much new equipment was issued during the two years 1987–89, including the SA 80 in place of the SLR rifle, and more aircraft, including the new LYNX Mark 7 and the ISLANDER twin-engined monoplane. In January 1988 Major Bernie Guignard commanding the Northern Ireland Regiment AAC Workshop reported with great satisfaction that one of his crews had exchanged a LYNX main rotor gearbox by

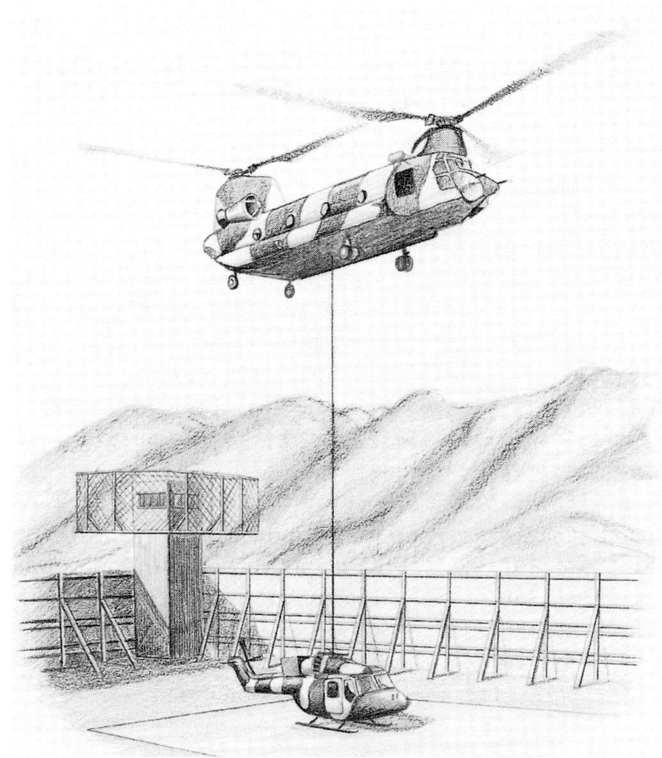

night in appalling weather in a very dangerous place in a field close to the border. In mid-1988 another LYNX helicopter had to be recovered by a CHINOOK helicopter after making a forced landing when coming under heavy terrorist fire in South Armagh. High rates of flying and changes in role and payload placed enormous pressure on the Aircraft Workshop. Both Major Guignard and ASM Phil Hall were awarded the MBE for their work.

In 1990 PIRA stepped up their campaign of murdering policemen in Ireland and also prominent citizens, soldiers and others in England and on the continent. Two Australian holiday-makers in Holland, mistaken for British Servicemen, were shot dead in the centre of Roermond, but such mistakes did not concern PIRA in their efforts to gain publicity for their murderous campaign. In London the Carlton Club was bombed and Mr Ian Gow MP, former Treasury Minister and outspoken opponent of the IRA, was killed outside his home in Sussex by a car bomb. Also a victim, Air Chief Marshal Sir Peter Terry, the former Governor of Gibraltar when the IRA members were shot there in March 1988, was shot and severely injured at his home in Staffordshire.

As this chapter closed in 1992 there was no sign of any abatement in the activity of the terrorists. Within Northern Ireland, in 1991 the campaign of murdering policemen had intensified, whilst elsewhere, in Britain and on the Continent others not directly connected with the troubles in the Province were killed or wounded in cold blood. There were many tit-for-tat killings by both Republican and Loyalist terrorist groups. At the end of 1991 and into January there were concerted fire-bomb attacks on shops in the centre of Belfast and elsewhere, and much damage was caused. In January eight Protestant construction employees of a civilian firm engaged in contract building work at Lisanelly, Omagh, were killed in their van by a roadside bomb at Teebane Cross whilst returning home.

There was nevertheless little change in the role of the Army. Within the political restraints imposed in an endeavour to find a peaceful solution with co-operation from the Republic and the political parties in Northern Ireland, the role was very much one of containment, whilst an ever-elusive political solution was sought. In December 1991 the SPEARHEAD Battalion was again sent to the Province, whilst readjustments to the dispositions of the RUC and the Army were made to give greater protection to Belfast. However, they returned again to UK before Christmas, only to be recalled in greater strength in January 1992 as the violence again increased. Further efforts continued to be made to restart the Anglo-Irish talks, which had again foundered because the Ulster politicians failed to agree amongst themselves on the way forward.

During all this turbulence the role and strength of REME in Ulster remained unaffected and it continued to provide the full maintenance service that it had done throughout.

CASUALTIES

There were unfortunately REME soldiers who died in Northern Ireland as the result of terrorist activity, road traffic accidents, drowning and other causes. The names of those who lost their lives due to terrorist activity are listed at Annex A to this chapter; many more were injured.

HONOURS AND AWARDS

The names of those given honours and awards for service in Northern Ireland are listed at Annex B to this chapter.

DEPLOYMENT OF REME FIELD WORKSHOPS

A list of field workshops which served in Northern Ireland from 1969 is attached at Annex C.

CONCLUSION

At the start of the Nineties Army life in Northern Ireland was little different from the earlier years. The Corps operated a well-tried system of REME support and Northern Ireland enjoyed high priority within the Army to meet its needs without the peacetime constraints experienced elsewhere. The change from a REME point of view was the steady increase in very sophisticated equipment to combat terrorism, details of which cannot be recorded here for security reasons. Many interesting aspects of the Corps activities in recent years are therefore unrecorded in this chapter.

Northern Ireland has always placed high demands on the military and technical skills of the REME soldiers in order to respond effectively and quickly to the constantly and sometimes very rapidly changing operational situation. The need was often to repair or modify new and unfamiliar equipments working from first principles. An unfortunate fact was that equipment courses were not possible within the available time for such a variety of equipment. This situation was very similar to that experienced in the Falklands War in 1982. The conditions in both operations required the REME soldier to face sudden danger, to live and work for long hours in often cramped or cold and wet places and to rely on his own initiative, basic skill and determination. This was a very different situation to changing spare parts in a well-equipped workshop in UK or BAOR. Both the Falklands and Northern Ireland required REME to support what were basically tough 'infantry' campaigns fought with light, technically sophisticated scales of equipment in highly contrasting but formidable operating conditions. In both cases REME officers and soldiers responded magnificently. The young men of REME in Northern Ireland had indeed been 'keeping an eye on the ball – the fitness for operations of the Army's equipment', as called for by Major General Peter Girling in his Epilogue to Volume 1.

This was recognized by the most senior Army Commanders in the Province in the Seventies and Eighties as the two following quotations show. Lieutenant General Sir David House GCB CBE MC, GOC Northern Ireland August 1975 to November 1977, wrote in his foreword to 'Ulster and the REME Contribution 1969–76' in the REME Journal for 1978:

'I know that the REME contribution has been made possible by the hard work and application of thousands of the Corps' officers, soldiers and civilians serving both in the Province and elsewhere. They have every reason to be proud of the achievements described. They have played a very significant part in the overall efforts of the Security Forces to restore law and order in the Province.'

Ten years later Major General A S Jeapes OBE MC, Commander Land Forces Northern Ireland 1985–87, wrote:

'All units in the Province know that they are all fighting the same enemy and working towards the same ends. Nowhere do I see this more clearly than amongst REME. The Northern Ireland campaign becomes evermore technically sophisticated. Indeed, some of the equipment is amongst the most sophisticated of its type in the world and, because it is scarce, when it breaks down it needs urgent work to get it back into the line as soon as possible. Men's lives may depend upon the outcome. But it is the day-to-day repair, the improvisation, the ingenuity and the sheer dogged hard work of the mechanics behind the scenes and in the bases dotted around the Province that enables the Infantry and the Engineers to respond with confidence in their weaponry, vehicles, aircraft and equipment. We have come a

long way in the last ten years and I should like to pay tribute to all those REME men and women who have taken such an important part in the campaign. But there is still a long way to go, and much will be required of the REME yet.'

Annex A

RANKS AND NAMES OF REME SOLDIERS WHO LOST THEIR LIVES IN NORTHERN IRELAND 1969–92 FROM TERRORIST ACTIVITY

Sergeant M D Burbridge	8 Infantry Brigade Headquarters and Signal Squadron.
Lance Corporal C Harker	2nd Battalion, Scots Guards
Craftsman B D Hope	19th Field Regiment RA LAD REME
Craftsman C N McInnes	42nd Heavy Regiment RA Workshop REME
Lance Corporal D Moon	664 Squadron AAC LAD REME
Sergeant S C Reid	664 Squadron AAC LAD REME
Sergeant M E Seldon	16th Light Air Defence Regiment RA Workshop REME

Annex B

HONOURS AND AWARDS IN NORTHERN IRELAND 1969–1995

CBE
1983 Colonel D Shaw
1992 Colonel P V R Besgrove

OBE
1971 Lieutenant Colonel J C D Nuttman
1990 Lieutenant Colonel A D Ball

MBE
1972 Major R L Pearce
1973 Major J F Hill
1975 Major B F Ross
1976 Major F J R Kent
1986 Major B I H Kitchener
1988 Warrant Officer Class 1 P A Hall
1989 Major B E Guignard
1991 Major S J Tetlow
1993 Lieutenant Colonel H H McNinch
1994 Captain M Savage
1995 Major P H K Miller
1995 Major P D Phillips

QGM
1981 Sergeant R Ward
1982 Lance Corporal B McClay
1993 Corporal C G Tierney
1995 Warrant Officer Class 2 R W Wells BEM

BEM
1977 Staff Sergeant S C Coward
1978 Staff Sergeant P W Collins
1981 A/Warrant Officer Class 2 K J Eaton
1981 Staff Sergeant J Walkden
1984 Sergeant S J Hunt
1985 Sergeant M Robertson
1990 Sergeant A J Arnold
1990 A/Warrant Officer Class 2 D A Atkins
1990 Staff Sergeant J A Lewthwaite
1991 Staff Sergeant I P Roberts
1991 Sergeant L M Stratford

Queen's Commendation for Valuable Services in the Air
1986 Warrant Officer Class 2 M G Ashton
1987 Warrant Officer Class 1 J Wright

Queen's Commendation for Valuable Service
1996 Sergeant N C Kerr

Mentioned in Despatches
1972 Sergeant S G Ward
1973 Staff Sergeant A L Colton
1973 Major R I C Macpherson
1973 Captain D Moore BEM
1973 Captain M H Roberts
1973 Sergeant D M Whitehead
1977 Lieutenant Colonel C R Parrish
1978 Corporal J E Hope
1978 Staff Sergeant P C O'Keefe
1978 Warrant Officer Class 1 G M Wright
1979 Lieutenant D W Chattin
1979 A/Major K Johnson
1979 A/Staff Sergeant R McKenzie
1979 Staff Sergeant A J Morris
1979 Warrant Officer Class 2 V R Tetlow
1980 Captain D M Arthur
1980 Major A J Potter
1980 Major R J Shields
1980 Lieutenant Colonel N McC Smithson
1981 Corporal D L Preston
1981 Warrant Officer Class 2 R S Smith
1982 Captain S J S Cameron
1982 Staff Sergeant R F J McGrath
1986 Captain S T Aungiers WRAC
1986 Lieutenant Colonel M D Lemon
1986 Sergeant M D Whitfield
1987 Major B I H Kitchener
1988 Warrant Officer Class 1 R W Haslam
1988 Corporal R H Williams
1991 Lance Corporal D Orr
1992 Corporal S G Cook
1993 A/Warrant Officer Class 2 A Burton
1993 Captain P G Mitchell
1993 Major D R Prowse
1993 Sergeant N A Vincent

Note: dates quoted generally refer to the date of publication in 'The London Gazette'

Annex C

SECOND-LINE REME SUPPORT IN NORTHERN IRELAND FROM 1969

The following UKLF workshops went as complete units to Northern Ireland, eighteen times in all, between 1969 and 1976:

3 Field Workshop
8 Field Workshop
9 Field Workshop
10 Field Workshop
15 Field Workshop

The system continued for the next eight years, with units from BAOR now included as well as from UKLF. The following workshops all came to Northern Ireland, some deployed as many as four times, between 1976 and 1984:

3 Field Workshop
5 Field Workshop
8 Field Workshop
10 Field Workshop
11 Field Workshop
15 Field Workshop
4 Armoured Workshop
5 Armoured Workshop
7 Armoured Workshop
12 Armoured Workshop
1 Corps Troops Workshop

From 1984 complete workshops were no longer deployed, following the creation of the Northern Ireland Roulement Workshop, which was made up of individual soldiers on emergency tours found from units in both BAOR and UKLF. In 1989 roulement of units was stopped and replaced by an emergency platoon attached to 46 Northern Ireland Workshop, manned by soldiers 'trickle-posted' on four-month tours.

CHAPTER 11

REME IN THE FALKLANDS

Introduction · REME Preparations in the UK ·
The Journey to Ascension Island · Ascension Island ·
Outline of Operations · The Falklands Landing · The Campaign ·
The Surrender and Immediate Aftermath ·
Casualties · The REME Lessons · Post-War

INTRODUCTION

The British Falkland Islands which were invaded by the Forces of Argentina in April 1982 are some 8,000 miles from the UK and 400 from Argentina. They consist of two main islands, East and West, each of more than 2,000 square miles. Their terrain is mainly moorland, rocks and peat bog and they have a harsh climate with wind, rain and cold predominating. Before the 1982 invasion by Argentina about 1,800 people, almost all of British descent, lived on the Islands and were mainly concerned with raising and tending more than half a million sheep.

Argentina had been in dispute with Great Britain over the Falklands since the 19th Century. In 1964 she took the dispute to the United Nations, which referred the problem back to the two parties, resulting in inconclusive discussions which lasted up to 1982. At the end of March 1982 Lord Carrington, Foreign Secretary, told the House of Lords that the dispute had become potentially dangerous and on 1 April the British

Ambassador to the United Nations said that an Argentine naval force was sailing towards the Falklands and it was thought that invasion was imminent. It was confirmed in London on 2 April that Argentine forces had invaded the Islands and captured the Governor, Mr Rex Hunt, and the small garrison of Royal Marines. It was reported that 5,000 Argentines had landed. This was followed on 4 April by Argentine forces seizing British South Georgia, 1,000 miles to the East of the Falklands. South Georgia was defended by a small detachment of Royal Marines, which put up a stout resistance before being overwhelmed and captured.

The House of Commons held an emergency debate on Saturday 3 April, which was their first Saturday meeting since the Suez Canal crisis of 1956, and the Prime Minister, Mrs Thatcher, announced that a task force was to be sent to the South Atlantic. This set in action Operation CORPORATE, (the code name for the task force), and with it the formidable and complex logistic effort required for its dispatch. The next day The Queen signed an Order in Council at the Court at Windsor Castle to requisition British merchant ships to carry the force. About fifty ships, known as Ships Taken Up From Trade (STUFT), were involved and were converted with remarkable speed. Many of the conversions included helicopter platforms, naval communications, extra fuel and water facilities and additional life rafts.

In the event Operation CORPORATE was to develop from the hazardous naval operation required to convey the Task Force to the Falklands, into a land campaign with minimum air cover, carried out under extraordinarily difficult conditions, both military and climatic. It required all the skills, courage and endurance of the British Solider to achieve the land victory. In this effort there was the full co-ordinated support from the onset of the Royal Navy, the Merchant Navy and the Royal Air Force. The Land Forces consisted of 3 Commando Brigade and 5 Infantry Brigade, with supporting Arms and Services. An Orbat, including details of the essential REME elements, is given at Annex A to this chapter.

The first ships of the Task Force commanded by Rear Admiral 'Sandy' Woodward (later Admiral Sir John) sailed from Portsmouth on 5 April, including the aircraft carriers HMS *Invincible* and HMS *Hermes.* These were followed on 9 April by the P & O cruise liner *Canberra* from Southampton. These departures were scenes of immense emotion and enthusiasm with military bands playing on the quayside, crowds of cheering people, flags waving and fond farewells from families and friends. The TV cameras were there to show scenes to the nation that night which many would remember all their lives. The Task Force eventually included more than one hundred ships carrying nearly 30,000 men and women.

Both Houses of Parliament were recalled from their Easter recess on 14 April to hear Mrs Thatcher say that Britain was looking for a peaceful solution but would use military strength if necessary. On 29 April Argentina, despite long negotiations and international condemnation of their invasion, rejected President Reagan's proposals for a settlement. Between 2 and 4 May the prestigious Cunard Liner *Queen Elizabeth II (QE2)* and four other ships were requisitioned to provide additional capacity for a force that was now likely to be involved in a full offensive operation. The *QE2* sailed from Southampton on 12 May taking 5 Infantry Brigade to join up with 3 Commando Brigade in the South Atlantic.

The sea-borne landings on the Islands were to be fiercely opposed from the air. There were to be damaging attacks on RN ships and aircraft, civilian vessels and the Army ashore. Defence and self-preservation from these attacks were to become part of the daily routine. REME's role in the campaign as it developed emphasized the value of personal initiative and a high standard of technical and military training. Although tanks, which normally require substantial REME support in the field, were not used in the campaign, the high-technology and sophisticated equipment that was deployed was nevertheless to prove equally formidable to maintain. This was not only because of intensive operational usage, but also because of the fragmented nature of the operations, lack of ground communications and local facilities, and the potential effect of the climate. Completion of many of the tasks depended on individual effort and the fact that the weapons and equipment were to be kept operational despite the adverse conditions was to show the ability of the Corps at its best in responding to the exceptional challenges that it faced in this campaign.

This chapter tells of the vital part played by REME from the onset of Operation CORPORATE to its successful conclusion ten weeks later. It starts with the initial preparations by those who were part of the Force and by those in the UK Base who launched it. It traces the activities during the 8,000-mile voyage and the support given to the operations from the initial landings to the final surrender. Finally it outlines the work after the surrender in the reclamation and restoration of equipment used in the campaign and the setting-up of a static workshop organization.

REME PREPARATIONS IN THE UK

The essential logistic preparations to enable REME to give effective support to the Task Force that was being assembled were carried out at great speed, as the situation demanded, despite the complexities and difficulties that had to be overcome. The complications were inevitable because of the very nature of the operation, and the necessity to plan from scratch, since there was no existing MOD contingency plan for the Falkland Islands. The speed of mounting, long lines of communication, limited shipping space, and loading priorities were overall problems. More specifically from the equipment management point of view, the high-technology nature of much of the equipment, the spares backing and time and place of availability, and the repair facilities, all contributed to the complexity of the problems facing REME. How these factors affected REME's preparations and how all concerned responded so well in finding the best possible solutions under the circumstances are described in the following paragraphs.

3 Commando Brigade

Headquarters Commando Forces Royal Marines received a signal on the morning of 2 April telling them that Argentina had invaded the Falkland Islands and that a Task Force would sail to the South Atlantic.

The staffs of both HQ 3 Commando Brigade and the Commodore Amphibious Warfare were in Denmark that morning and many of their troops, both teeth arm and logistic support, were on leave after a three-month exercise in Norway. One unit was even as far afield as Brunei on jungle training. Units and ships were given three days' notice to move and recall orders were issued. Existing plans based on NATO tasks did not cover the South Atlantic and fresh plans had to be made for the potential operation. Next day 3 Commando Brigade was put at four hours' notice to move and 3rd Battalion, The Parachute Regiment Group was also assigned to the Brigade. The BEME of 3 Commando Brigade was Captain Trevor Wilkins who was very much involved from the beginning. The embarkation order was received on 4 April and the move of men and stores began. Within three days the main elements of the Brigade and their stores had been loaded onto ships. The urgency of the loading left insufficient time to consider more than the means of providing basic REME support and shipping space was so limited that many of the REME elements were separated from their dependencies. Speed was of the essence and, contrary to normal procedures, there was little opportunity to load stores in the correct order of priority for discharge. Later, during the landing phase, the inability to unload specific requirements when needed, which this situation created, led to great difficulties.

A good example of a REME unit totally engrossed in the complexities of this stage of the operation was the LAD of 29th Commando Regiment RA. At the beginning of April it had about fifty men divided between the batteries of the Regiment which were based in Arbroath, Plymouth and Poole, all of them having volunteered for Commando Forces. The OC, Captain Paul Musgrove, had been with the LAD for more than two years. The ASM, WO 1 Peter Watson, had been there eighteen months, but some of the REME soldiers had been there for up to five years. They were all very fit and well-trained militarily, as well as having great expertise in the repair of their 105 mm Light Guns and CYMBELINE Radar. 79

Battery was returning from three months in Norway and 148 Battery was, as usual, spread around the fleet. At 0600 hours on Friday 2 April the Adjutant of the Regiment phoned Captain Musgrove telling him to report to Regimental HQ at the Royal Citadel in Plymouth immediately. At that instant, being summoned by the Adjutant at such an hour, it did momentarily cause him to wonder whether there had been any celebration in the NAAFI the previous evening which had led to misdemeanours by members of the LAD – perish the thought! His mind was quickly put to rest on that score, however, but his presence was required for something that was to occupy all his attention for some time to come and it was certainly to be no party for him or his men.

Captain Musgrove wrote later that the rest of the morning after he had received the initial news was very unreal. There were rumours that the whole Brigade was going South but nobody really believed this. A briefing and the news at lunchtime changed all that. Seven weeks' preparation including the voyage time to the Falklands followed, during which the LAD completed its most important task – the preparation of the Regiment's equipment for war. On Saturday 3 April, the number of LAD vehicles permitted to go was reduced one by one from the original loading manifests, as priorities changed. This happened as the size of the force to be sent was increased, and a corresponding reduction in the available space on the ships for each unit had to be made. The LAD now faced the distinct possibility of being unable to retain sufficient space in which to load all the essential equipment and spares it needed for maintaining its parent Regiment. The pressure was on, as much of this kit still had to be acquired by fair means or foul: help had to be sought and found.

As part of the LAD's acquisitive efforts, 4th Field Regiment RA was, for instance, persuaded to part with a FACE computer and radar parts necessary to get the major electronic equipment of 29th Commando Regiment RA up to 100% availability. The LAD also got many other spare parts out of the maintenance system which until the Thursday, had not been available to a lowly LAD without an operation in sight. Now there was one very much in sight; mountains started to be moved, but the problems were only just beginning. Many of the Regiments' Volvo BV202E tracked towing vehicles were still in Norway or on their way home. However, they were able to take those belonging to the AMF(L), but which required modification to tow the Light Guns. 17 Port and Maritime Workshop at Marchwood helped them out with this task over the weekend after a telephone call to the home of AQMS Eddie Lamb of the Workshop, an old friend of the OC. Saturday afternoon 3 April saw a continuation of the shuffle of equipment on and off the vehicles, as the planners revised and updated their plans as to which units would be going, on how many ships and on which ones.

On the Sunday the LAD zeroed weapons, tested respirators and checked again that everything they could possibly need was on the two Electronic Repair Vehicles, the FAMTO 4 tonner and the Recovery Vehicle. The choice of what to load on the vehicles had been difficult, but Captain Musgrove decided that all eventualities should be catered for, including the possible repair of requisitioned vehicles at a future destination. Spares, tools and circuit diagrams, acquired legally and illegally, to carry out every repair that they were capable of, were therefore taken, down to discrete chips on the electronic side and to manufacturing cam followers on the mechanical side.

On Monday 5 April at 0730 hours they drove their vehicles to Devonport Dockyard and at 1600 hours that afternoon, after a morning spent on final checks and preparations for a long sea voyage, the Regiment in Plymouth boarded its ship. Lance Corporal Vic Edwards wrote:

'The Commando Brigade was going to war and if that was the case, then Plymouth would see it off as well as she could. After an appeal on the local radio station, videos, books and games flooded in fast enough to provide us with sixty feature films and a paperback library worthy of any ship.'

The LSL *Sir Geraint,* which was to be the home for the voyage of the HQ element of the LAD (LAD Main), slipped at 1800 hours and went alongside another berth at 1810 hours. After dinner there was a short reprieve and they all went home! LAD Main and 79 Battery Fitter Section eventually left at 1900 hours on Tuesday 6 April, lining the decks for the benefit of two policemen in a car and a few families who braved the rain to see them off.

In another unit, the Commando Logistic Regiment Workshop Squadron, many men were still hoping on Friday 2 April to have some of their three weeks' leave which was due to start that afternoon, but it was not to be. By the end of that busy day a hundred men were preparing to sail with the Task Force by loading equipment and stores. Work went on all the weekend repairing or modifying equipment and putting GPMG mounts on the tracked Volvo BV202Es. Early on Monday 5 April they went to Marchwood Military Port to embark in LSL *Sir Lancelot.* The OC, Major Les Short, was OC Embarked Forces. Their send-off from Marchwood did not quite match the wild enthusiasm of the main Task Force leaving Plymouth the day before. The onlookers, (it is said) consisted of one lady, two dockers and a dog! Nevertheless, it was still appreciated.

On 1 April A Flight 3 Commando Brigade Air Squadron which had been on stand-by for SPEARPOINT duties was mobilized. The remainder of the Squadron was told emphatically that it would not go. Captain Larry Rotchell was OC LAD at the time. Needless to say on 2 April (his wedding anniversary) the remainder was mobilized! The logistic con-

Loading at Marchwood

tainers with the bulk of the Squadron's arctic equipment were still on their way back from Norway where the Scout Flight had been deployed from January to March. These containers were cross-decked at Plymouth just before the Squadron sailed but in the event were not available to be opened until midway through the conflict. Between 2 and 6 April, when they sailed, the amount of work and speed of execution were phenomenal. The Commando Brigade was very restricted by manpower and vehicle space on the vessels, resulting in the GAZELLE flights being reduced from four to three aircraft each, one Land Rover (the RM Command Post Vehicle) and a REME trailer. The remaining GAZELLEs were heavily cannibalized to provide spares. The two Utility SCOUTs were swapped for Anti-Tank SCOUTs (making six) and much equipment was flown in from Northern Ireland to support the operation. The Aircraft Maintenance Groups's ten men came from 70 Aircraft Workshop at Middle Wallop and were commanded by Staff Sergeant Briggs. Staff Sergeant Elliott was sent off with a Land Rover and trailer round UK to find and acquire, from various sources, anything connected with Battle Damage Repair and came back just in time for the sailing with his vehicle loaded to the limit. Before they left, one of the soldiers' wives asked her husband to ring her when he arrived on the Islands, believing like some others at the time that the Falklands were near the Shetlands off northern Scotland! However, to be fair to the wives, it was found initially that, perhaps with some good reason, many of the soldiers were also as vague as to the whereabouts of the Falklands.

A vital part of the air defence for the Force on landing, was to be provided by the RAPIERs of 12th Air Defence Regiment. At this time RAPIER was at the in-service engineering design state known as Field Standard A, the latest part of which was the progressive introduction of line-of-sight target tracking by radar (DN 181) to augment the existing manual tracking mode. Following on from this and still in development was an enhanced-performance Field Standard B 1, but not likely to appear in the field before 1984. Whilst REME was the overall RAPIER equipment manager, the weapon system support was a joint effort with the RAOC, and RAF whose procedures were adopted for the individual tracking of equipments and spares down to sub-assembly level (known as black boxes or Line Replaceable Units). Even smaller spares were treated individually if they were considered vital. RAOC managed the supply, routing repairable items via 35 Central Workshop or the manufacturers, British Aircraft Corporation.

Until Operation CORPORATE the Army and RAF units in BAOR had the priority for RAPIER logistic support. This new operational commitment to Operation CORPORATE had to be met by T (Shah Sujah's Troop) and 9 Batteries of 12th Air Defence Regiment RA at Kirton in Lindsey (Humberside) with 63 Squadron RAF from Germany. It was envisaged that a sizeable war reserve plus repair pool of major and minor spares would be necessary and these were rapidly assembled by transferring assets from Germany and cannibalizing RAPIER Fire Units in the Royal School of Artillery (used for training) and the remaining sub-units of 12th Air Defence Regiment. Overall therefore, the deployment of RAPIER for Operation CORPORATE was a matter of some complexity, but a very welcome addition to the Force, as was soon to be proved.

Staff Sergeant Nesmith, a Radar Artificer, with sixteen men under his command from 12th Air Defence Regiment Workshop, was responsible for the REME support to twelve RAPIER missile launchers of T Battery. Within twenty minutes of departing on Easter leave on Friday 2 April he was called back to be told that T Battery was going to the South Atlantic leaving at 0600 hours Sunday 4 April. There was no shipping space for the usual vehicles, so twenty tons of RAPIER stores were off-loaded from the vehicles and re-loaded onto pallets. His first-line optical repair vehicle, essential to the repair of optical trackers, had to be left behind. He was told that his support vehicles and equipment would deploy with the second wave and arrive immediately after the beachhead was secured. They arrived four weeks later! He was in some ignorance of all the problems that were yet to confront him, but was already concerned at the way in which his essential equipment and spares backing had been distributed or shut out.

The effect of these loading problems on RAPIER, with the dispersal of equipment and vehicles between vessels, was considerable. The stowage subsequently made it virtually impossible to carry out any maintenance on RAPIER during the voyage, to operate it, or prevent dampness setting in.

Later, during the assault landings at San Carlos, these overall conditions were to make the time into action lengthy. Furthermore, at that stage T Battery still had no second-line support, nor any immediate spares supply. Although between two and two-and-a-half batteries-worth of LRUs were sent in the first wave of ships to leave UK, not all of these arrived with the RAPIERs, as they had been off-loaded and left at Ascension Island during the cross-decking process which took place there. The fact that Staff Sergeant Nesmith and his team subsequently managed to support the RAPIERs so effectively once ashore, says a great deal for their training and their resoluteness in adversity.

5 Infantry Brigade

656 Squadron AAC was warned just before its Easter block leave on 8 April that it might become involved if the situation grew worse. On 15 April it was warned to supply three SCOUT aircraft to support 2nd Battalion, The Parachute Regiment Group, which was being deployed with 3 Commando Brigade, the date of departure being set for 22 April. There was much activity in the Squadron's LAD to nominate the technicians, prepare the aircraft, tools, freight and publications and equip the men with special kit. On 22 April one artificer and five technicians, backed by an FRT of three technicians from 70 Aircraft Workshop, and a SCOUT helicopter detachment from 1 Aircraft Support Unit RAOC, boarded the MV *Europic Ferry* at Southampton. Half the LAD was recalled from leave to help with these preparations. When the remainder came back on 20 April they were told that the Squadron was to become part of 5 Infantry Brigade, which was to follow 3 Commando Brigade to act as a Garrison Force when the Islands had been retaken. The Squadron and LAD build-up began in earnest. An O Group in Aldershot had discussed the concept of operations to cater for the then unlikely event of 5 Infantry Brigade being involved in the retaking of the Islands. Six SCOUT and six GAZELLE helicopters were to be deployed; light scales would be taken; all movement would be by Support Helicopter and resupply would be by sea from Ascension Island.

To prepare the Brigade, Exercise WELSH FALCON was held in Wales from 24 April. The Squadron returned early from the exercise to receive aircraft with more comprehensive modifications. These were to cater for flotation gear and folding main rotor heads for GAZELLEs and transponders and radar altimeters for both SCOUT and GAZELLE helicopters. The Squadron was also to be given aircraft on which major components had at least 200 hours' life remaining. On 9 May six GAZELLEs were loaded on MV *Nordic Ferry* and three SCOUTs on MV *Baltic Ferry*, together with the crews, technicians and freight, and sailed on the same day. The remainder of the Squadron and the LAD sailed to the South Atlantic on the *QE2* on 12 May.

70 Aircraft Workshop provided second-line support for helicopters of 3 Commando Brigade Air Squadron and 656 Squadron AAC of 5 Infantry Brigade – a total of twelve SCOUTs and fifteen GAZELLEs. An AMG with RAOC support was attached to each squadron LAD commanded by a Staff Sergeant Aircraft Artificer with one SCOUT and one GAZELLE FRT. The AMG attached to the Commando Brigade Air Squadron was deployed at twenty hours' notice, having only recently come back from supporting the same squadron on two exercises in Norway. The AMGs deployed with their full SOP scales except for items refused loading for lack of shipping space, such as Bedford cargo trucks, aircraft jacks and tentage. Some 9,000 man-hours' work was recorded at 70 Aircraft Workshop for modifications and servicing to aircraft for the Falklands, including fitting transponders, altimeters, armour and flotation equipment to GAZELLEs. The main workshop worked round the clock for a long period. Two supervising artificers, Staff Sergeants Fenwick and Taylor, were awarded the BEM for their part in this vital activity and the Workshop was awarded the Director Army Air Corps Commendation at a formal parade in August 1983 – the first time this award had been given to a unit.

Thirty 105mm Light Guns were employed in the Falklands, of which eighteen belonged to 29th Commando Regiment RA of 3 Commando Brigade and twelve to 4th Field Regiment RA of 5 Infantry Brigade. The OC of the LAD of 4th Field Regiment was Captain Norman Gould. He and his LAD spent from Monday 5 April until the deadline on the Thursday night in their preparations for supporting their Regiment in the Falklands. It was an exacting time. Lists were made and remade, stores were demanded and obtained, equipment was repaired, documentation was sorted out and even a list of lists was prepared. The EME listed his attributes and decided to find time to get married, which he did! On Friday nothing happened and two weeks went by in great expectations, but apart from several parades, in full kit, including one at the railway station, still nothing really happened. Then on 26 April 29 Battery and its four-man REME fitter section with 2nd Battalion, The Parachute Regiment sailed from Portsmouth in the P & O ferry *Norland*. The rest of the regiment, except 88 Battery which was in Belize, went to Sennybridge in Wales to train in helicopter operations.

Meanwhile, other REME units were facing different problems and taking their own particular measures to overcome them. One such unit was 10 Field Workshop at Bordon. This unit only officially became part of 5 Infantry Brigade on 1 April 1982. Its new establishment was in draft only and its manpower, vehicles and equipment did not reflect its new commitment. The RAOC Stores Platoon lacked men and vehicles, as well as being inadequately and incorrectly scaled. On 2 April the new unit paraded for the Brigade Commander who explained its new role with the Brigade and said that they must be ready to go anywhere in the world at short notice. This was very soon to be proved. After lunch the soldiers went off for a long weekend but that evening the OC, Major Tony Ball, had to start to recall them. There followed six days of great activity. The Brigade went to Sennybridge for Exercise WELSH FALCON for which the Workshop borrowed the MRG stores account and some men from 3 Field Workshop. The Brigade quickly converted from LARKSPUR to CLANSMAN radios which kept the Telecommunications Section busy with all that was involved. By the end of the exercise the Workshop received its order to deploy for embarkation with less vehicles than required to carry its stores and equipment, just as other units had already experienced. This necessitated palletizing their unit equipment and RAOC stores, including a complete workshop scale of second-line spares that had just been received, and the pallets were loaded on vessels separately.

Seventeen men went with vehicles, trailers and freight to the RO-RO Ships *Baltic Ferry* and *Nordic Ferry*. The speed of movement precluded the equipment being loaded tactically, and whatever arrived at the docks first went into the ship first (mainly combat supplies), and whatever arrived last went in last (mainly unit equipment and stores). Pallets were stacked three or four high to get them in at all, rather than in tactical order. The men were split between *Nordic Ferry* (five), *Baltic Ferry* (twelve), *QE2* (forty-seven), RO-RO *St Edmund* (fifteen follow-up) and fifteen flew to Ascension Island to join the *QE2*. The unit party for the *QE2* had a good send-off from Bordon early in the morning of 12 May and sailed away that afternoon. Overhead there were helicopters and small aircraft and in the water there was a fleet of small boats to accompany them as they started their 8,000-mile journey South. Few expected the pleasure of a voyage on the *QE2* in their lifetime, but the opportunity now presented was nevertheless justifiably viewed with some misgivings!

The REME Directorate, UK Static Workshops and Industry

Whilst the formations to be involved in the operation, 3 Commando Brigade and 5 Infantry Brigade were making their more visible preparations; there was tremendous activity taking place in the background to support them. A wide range of organizations within the UK, both military and civilian, participated in these preparations, which were pursued with the utmost vigour and enthusiasm. Not the least of these was the DGEME and his Staff at the REME Directorate. Colonel Geoff Pearce served in the REME Directorate at Andover in those hectic and stirring days when the main task of the EME branches, 5, 7, 8, and 9, was to ensure that the UK static workshops could provide all the support necessary to meet the urgent demands from units and ordnance depots for the Force. He remembers the great sense of purpose, throughout the Directorate, of putting into practice what for many had only ever been done before as an exercise.

An operations room was set up at Andover on a twenty-four hour, seven-day week basis and manned by staff, mostly of the rank of Major, from the various directorates of LE(A). A crucial task for REME was obtaining the necessary spares and test equipment. This requirement was achieved with outstanding help from almost all parts of industry, regardless of overtime costs. One difficulty that was encountered was the attitude of some of the Teeth Arms towards test equipment and spares. They would not, or could not, make room for the second-line test equipment for RAPIER systems, and paid the price in poor availability and high spares usage later. There was great difficulty in persuading the Royal Marines to take the MILAN firing-post test equipment and a few less missiles, but fortunately that point was won.

HQ DGEME EME 9 ensured that the required aircraft spares were available to sail with the Task Force, including the vital Battle Damage Repair Kits which had been developed by Aircraft Branch REME. They also made sure that reserve SCOUTs and GAZELLEs were made ready by the RNAY Wroughton should they be required to replace battle casualties. As a result of this, replacements for the two GAZELLEs subsequently lost on D Day were immediately available and ready for shipping when the news of their loss was received.

Brigadier Geoffrey Atkinson was DEE 2 at Andover in 1982. He remembers that the support from industry was immediate and magnificent. There were numerous examples of individuals, sometimes from very small firms, driving to the southern ports over Bank Holiday weekend in order to supply vital pieces of equipment to embarking formations about to sail. There was never any argument about who would pay or when the bill would be met. All was taken on trust and the paperwork sorted out later.

Amongst the workshops and ordnance depots, Chilwell and Donnington met the demands for vehicles, weapons and electronic equipment, including such items as snipers' rifles and mine-detectors, whilst Old Dalby dealt with BLOWPIPE, the hand-held ground-to-air missile launcher. The CLANSMAN range of radios was the responsibility of Newark. Extra funds were authorized for contract repair to speed availability of any indispensable items. An essential task was to find those that could be repaired to meet Priority 1 demands, assemble them for repair as quickly as possible, then return them to ordnance depots for issue. Despite all these efforts, some items could not be provided before the

Task Force sailed, and had to be flown out to Ascension Island to be married up with units when they reached there.

The command workshops' contribution to the preparations for their dependant units was considerable. As well as routine tasks, special equipment was speedily designed and manufactured. 27 Command Workshop at Warminster carried out a number of these tasks, of which the following are examples:

- Design and manufacture of Louch Poles to which GPMGs were fitted for low-level air defence.
- Manufacture of field lighting sets and the boxes in which to pack them. This required the spinning of sheet aluminium to produce reflectors for the lamps.
- Design, manufacture and fitting of armoured protection sets for helicopter seats.
- Design and manufacture of transit boxes for helicopter rotor blades.
- Fitting winterization kits to various vehicles belonging to units of 3 Commando Brigade.

The Production Manager in 27 Command Workshop at the time was Lieutenant Colonel Bob Millar, Royal Australian Electrical and Mechanical Engineers, who later became their Director General.

43 Command Workshop at Aldershot was given the task of winterizing the Land Rovers of 5 Infantry Brigade and of converting many of them to command-post vehicles. Many rough-terrain trolleys were also manufactured. These were light enough to manhandle, but could also be towed behind Land Rovers. Other special items manufactured were dismountable operating tables, huge canopies for mobile tactical headquarters and the furniture to go in them. Some of the latter items were lost in the Container Ship MV *Atlantic Conveyor* which was sunk during the landings, with much other valuable cargo, including CHINOOK helicopters.

Once the Task Force had sailed it was necessary to look at the back-up stocks in UK for the future support of the Force. RAOC stock levels held in their depots had to be restored as swiftly as possible with such items as printed circuit boards and other electronic components. To this end the Corps looked at a whole range of equipment that had been declared Beyond Economic Repair before the emergency, and repaired whatever was possible. RAPIER air defence components, LRUs and black box spares were obtained from the RAF and all other available sources. Items for base repair started to be returned by air from the Falklands even before the end of April, and fast repair loops were set up. These were to continue well beyond the subsequent cease-fire on 14 June.

THE JOURNEY TO ASCENSION ISLAND

3 Commando Brigade

Lance Corporal Edwards, 29th Commando Regiment RA LAD, on LSL *Sir Geraint* wrote at the time:

'Once out of Plymouth Sound the sea began to get choppy, around Force 8, which immediately had its effect on some of the lads. The ship's captain filled us with some alarm when he indicated that he expected to lose at least half of the vehicles and guns when we reached the vicinity of the Falkland Islands! Immediately everyone fled with chains in tow to doubly lash down everything and anything.'

The daily life varied depending on the ship. On the LSLs there was little room for much activity requiring space, four hundred men being accommodated in a very small flat-bottomed ship. On HMS *Fearless* there were fewer troops, but space was so scarce that the decks were carpeted with 10-man ration packs. The *Canberra* was relatively palatial, but filled to capacity with Paras – a daunting prospect for any outsider!

On all ships training started by the middle of the week. On the *Sir Geraint* the LAD's first instruction was on how to be an effective Damage Control Party, as the LSL's crew was insufficiently manned for the task under war-zone conditions. The LAD manned watches with the ship's engineers to help if there should be any unforeseen occurrence. On Friday 9 April the reality struck Captain Paul Musgrove when he discovered that not only was the ship darkened but they were running without any navigation lights. There were other less disturbing realities too. The water shortage on board all the LSLs had an effect in different ways. The LAD Main on the *Sir Geraint* maintained a dignified sense of decorum and continued to shave and wash! Those of the LAD on the *Sir Percivale* joined that ship's attempt to rekindle the Commando spirit of independence by starting a beard-growing competition. The CO turned a blind eye to the scruffy bunch of 'Black 8 Battery' et al.

The technicians and artificers occupied themselves finding out how the BOFORS 40mm gun-control equipment was designed to work, servicing the ship's emergency breathing apparatus, calibrating instruments and repairing telecommunications equipment, SATCOM and small arms. There was training in first aid, and on every weapon that they could lay their hands on, just in case they had to pick one up and use it in an emergency. Keeping fit was essential but difficult with so little space and PT was limited in scope but nevertheless energetic. By the end of the second week on board they were starting to get on each other's nerves and bored with training on a ship where the largest free space measured 20 metres by 3 metres. Sergeant Stew Mead wrote that after three weeks at sea they were only half way – perhaps a blinding glimpse of the obvious, but summing up the frustrations that all felt in their cooped-up situation. It made a welcome break when they were told to waterproof their vehicles in preparation for an amphibious landing. The Commando Logistic Regiment Workshop Squadron started an intense programme which helped to keep everyone busy but the lack of space and frequent use of helicopters on the flight deck of LSL *Sir Lancelot* limited what could be done as they sailed further South.

The Commando Brigade Air Squadron LAD with Captain Larry Rotchell and ASM Barry Marshall was as usual divided into flight sections and the squadron echelon: forty-two personnel in all, plus ten from the AMG. The aircraft, the men, their vehicles and equipment were loaded into four different ships. During the voyage South they were told that they would put into Ascension Island. Full benefit was obtained from this by sending many signals back to demand additional spares and Equipment Health Monitoring data. On the voyage they heard that the SNEB rocket system had been obtained for the GAZELLE helicopters and dispatched to Ascension Island. Extensive anti-corrosion measures were carried out on the aircraft during the forty-five days at sea. While in the tropics the LAD sections rigged up a device on their ships to collect condensation formed by the air-conditioning units, to alleviate a shortage of fresh water on board. The three 656 Squadron AAC SCOUT helicopters travelling in MV *Europic Ferry* to support 2nd Battalion, The Parachute Regiment Group were on the deck, so they were covered with a rather unsightly treacle-like preserving fluid PX28 which prevented any corrosion. However, all three SCOUTs were flown during the voyage which provided both interest and experience.

Depending on the types of unit occupying any particular vessel, so the activities on board with which the REME personnel became involved took on different objectives. 59 Independent Commando Squadron RE Workshop went aboard LSL *Sir Galahad* on Monday 5 April and sailed next day. On the voyage they were all involved in Royal Engineer trade training such as mine and minefield clearance, house clearance, and making and detecting booby traps. Waterproofing the Land Rovers completed the vehicle preparations for a landing. At Ascension Island they were transferred to LSL *Sir Lancelot* for which, as events turned out, they had cause to be grateful.

5 Infantry Brigade

4th Field Regiment RA left Aldershot for the South Atlantic in the second week of May. The Gunners sailed in style on the *QE2* and left on 12 May, but the REME fitters of 97 Battery, the EME and five other REME personnel travelled less luxuriously on the RO-RO ships, *Nordic Ferry* and *Baltic Ferry*. These sailed from Southampton on 9 May with equipment and combat supplies, which unfortunately, as already related, were not tactically loaded.

36 Engineer Regiment Workshop fared better than the Gunner fitters

and the main party left Southampton on 12 May aboard the *QE2* with 5 Infantry Brigade. All aboard the *QE2* were kept busy on the voyage South with training, including helicopter drill, and the only changes to routine were the two short stops at Freetown and Ascension Island. The ASM and one craftsman did not have the same opportunity for luxury travel and sailed in the *Nordic Ferry*, the ASM being appointed ship's RSM. The balance of the unit was to follow when the Falkland Islands were recovered.

The aircraft of 656 Squadron AAC in the *Baltic Ferry* and *Nordic Ferry* were below deck and only light preservation with PX24 was necessary. The deck area on the ships was large enough to work on the helicopters in comfort and the lighting was good. Tasks carried out included fitting GAZELLE flotation gear and floor armour, as well as anticipated scheduled work on the six GAZELLEs and three SCOUTs. The REME personnel on these vessels had a distinct advantage over those travelling in the LSLs, as not only was there more space generally, but they were able to carry out many more of the essential tasks on their own unit's equipment. This had the added advantage of alleviating some of the boredom of the long voyage. It was also a bonus for the AMGs (from 70 Aircraft Workshop) which were required to help their LADs to maintain aircraft operating from the decks of various ships en route to the Falklands. In addition to floor armour for the helicopters the fitting of SNEB rockets was done whilst still at sea, during the stop at Ascension Island and on landing on the Falklands. Stores and men were of necessity split between ships, and some aircraft major assemblies in ships' holds were unfortunately inaccessible during the voyage and for several days after the arrival at the islands.

10 Field Workshop travelling on the *QE2* carried out a wide range of military training on the way. Some repairs to telecommunications equipment and small arms which had suffered from the training were carried out thanks to having two airportable trailers loaded on board. With the help of the ship's engineers they designed and jointly made two Browning 0.50 inch machine-gun air-defence mountings for the ship. They also fitted Turner winches to the Brigade Signal Squadron Land Rovers. The Ferries stopped for two days at Ascension Island, which allowed time for intense repacking and reorganizing on board, but the *QE2* only stopped briefly.

Major Tony Ball recalled later that as the *QE2* left Southampton work on the helicopter flight deck was incomplete, so the construction crew stayed aboard until Ascension Island. The flight deck had been sited over the rear-deck swimming pool which had been drained, but contained a number of cans of grey paint for the flight deck once completed. One of his artificers, well known for his 'leg pulls', started a rumour that the ship was to be painted battleship grey 'en route' and the paint was there to prove it. The subject was discussed at some length on successive days at the daily Brigade Commander's conference with COs and OCs, arguments developing over unit areas of responsibility, manpower availability and so on to achieve such a demanding task. The Captain confirmed eventually that he had established that it was only a rumour, much to the relief of not only the unit commanders, but also the *QE2* crew who were convinced they would have to repaint the ship in Cunard colours on the return journey.

ASCENSION ISLAND

The arrival of the shipping at Ascension Island was the start of feverish action to remedy as many as possible of the defects in loading and distribution of personnel and stores resulting from the rapid departure from UK. Personnel and stores that had followed on by air to Ascension Island also had to be married up with those already on the vessels. Although the REME elements of the Force had had varying degrees of success on the voyage in preparing equipment, depending on the facilities available on board, there was much more to be done. Hoped-for follow-up spares and equipment also had to be retrieved from the airfield on the Island. The next few paragraphs give but brief examples of this all-important activity.

Transferring stores at Ascension Island

3 Commando Brigade

By Wednesday 21 April, 29th Commando Regiment RA LAD had been at anchor for three days busy cross-decking between ships to get everything in its right place for operations. Captain Paul Musgrove's diary described the scene:

'The view in front of me, as I sit on the "Gangway Fire Equipment Locker," is of black and brown lava trails flowing down from a green mountain until they butt against the sea like ice from an iceberg. The scene would be tranquil were it not for the continuous whack-whack of the SEA KINGs and WESSEX blades, as they motor about the fleet, like airborne 4 tonners. Our good ship seems to be the centre

of attention at the moment with one helicopter on the forward spot, one on the rear and one hovering and waiting patiently. The other four LSLs and civilian ships are also getting their fair share of attention, with MEXEFLOTEs, Rigid Raiders, lifeboats and GEMINIs moving about the water in sympathy, it seems, with the players above it. This act seems to have come on this afternoon as if the Government has suddenly said, "Go now, and make it fast." Their act gets faster as more and more aircraft fill the air, a type 21 or is it a 42, comes in from the Atlantic, a VC10 and then a C130 HERCULES draw in to land at Wideawake airstrip. If this is the overture it should be one hell of a show!'

Whilst at Ascension Island, there were changes made, not only in the allocation of individuals and equipment to ships but also complete units. On board the LSL *Sir Geraint* for instance they received an Electronic Warfare Troop and a Satellite Communications Troop. Of the equipment, two thermal imaging devices were also loaded. These were very rare at that time, and nobody really knew what to do with them, so they were given to the LAD to investigate. When the LAD found out how to use them everybody else wanted them back! They proved to be of great value in helping to keep the ship on station in the convoy during electronic silence and coming into San Carlos Water later in the operation. The Commando Logistic Regiment Workshop Squadron was also dispersed, and divided between LSLs *Sir Galahad* and *Sir Percivale.* There was now plenty to do and the vehicle mechanics waterproofed all the vehicles whilst the telecommunications technicians repaired CLANSMAN radios. More men joined them, having been flown out to Ascension from Brize Norton.

The 3 Commando Brigade Air Squadron LAD at Ascension Island was very busy modifying aircraft, fitting the SNEB rocket system and carrying out range work with SNEB and SS11 missiles. Many spares which had been demanded en route were picked up. The cross-decking of stores, equipment, vehicles and men to carry out maintenance was complicated by a perceived threat from Argentine Special Forces. Eventually the unit echelon moved to the ill-fated *Sir Galahad,* with C Flight already embarked, and Brunei Flight split between *Sir Tristram* and HMS *Fearless.* The AMG was split between *Sir Galahad* (GAZELLE FRT) and *Sir Tristram* (SCOUT FRT). Ascension Island had one more twist to its tail recalled by Captain Larry Rotchell:

'The Task Force was setting sail and one of our GAZELLEs took its last pressure refuel from Wideawake airfield. This (we discovered later) dislodged the fuel contents gauge float and caused an incorrect reading on the fuel gauge. As a result the aircraft took off towards the Fleet with the minimum of fuel on board. Half-way between the shore and the Fleet the aircraft ran out of fuel! Superb flying by the pilot (Sergeant Congdon AAC) enabled the aircraft to make a forced landing on the beach near Georgetown. I was despatched with a "down bird" team to assess the

damage and if possible recover the GAZELLE. With the sun setting and the Task Force disappearing over the horizon we watched a SEA KING lift the GAZELLE away to Sir Geraint, but we remained on the beach! At the eleventh hour the OC Squadron, Major Peter Cameron RM, flew his SCOUT to rescue us and, overweight, we flew to join our comrades.'

All that could be done at that stage at Ascension, had been done, and the fleet sailed for the operations that were to recapture the Falklands.

OUTLINE OF OPERATIONS

On 25 April the Royal Marines recaptured the island of South Georgia. On 21 May 3 Commando Brigade made its landings from San Carlos Water onto the beaches of the NW coast of East Falkland. 45 Commando RM landed at Ajax Bay – Red Beach; 3rd Battalion, The Parachute Regiment at Port San Carlos – Green Beach; and 2nd Battalion, The Parachute Regiment, followed by 40 Commando RM at San Carlos Settlement – Blue Beach. 42 Commando RM, initially held embarked as a reserve, landed later on the same day at Green Beach. The next five days were spent in consolidating a firm bridgehead, establishing air defences, and sending out patrols and observation posts. Fortunately, the Argentine aircraft did not attack the landing forces while they were still at sea, but from mid-morning on 21 May they became very active attacking naval ships protecting our shipping in San Carlos Water. Heavy losses were inflicted on the Argentine aircraft, but the Royal Navy too had serious casualties amongst their ships on the first day.

On 27 May the breakout from the bridgehead took place. 3rd Battalion, The Parachute Regiment advanced to Teal Inlet and on to Estancia, whilst 45 Commando took Douglas Settlement. In the South, with a company of 42 Commando in reserve and with only three 105mm guns of 29th Commando Regiment RA in support, 2nd Battalion, The Parachute Regiment headed out to attack Darwin and Goose Green in the south-west. In the subsequent attack on Goose Green the Commanding Officer of 2nd Battalion, The Parachute Regiment, Lieutenant Colonel H Jones, won a posthumous Victoria Cross, and the surrender of the Argentine forces there was a great blow to the morale of the remainder of their forces on the Islands. Sergeant I J McKay of 3rd Battalion, The Parachute Regiment was also awarded a posthumous Victoria Cross for a platoon action during the night attack on an enemy battalion position on Mount Longdon, an important objective in the battle for Port Stanley.

On 1 June, 5 Infantry Brigade began to disembark at San Carlos and on 2 June 2nd Battalion, The Parachute Regiment moved to Bluff Cove in the south-east. On 6 June the 2nd Battalion, Scots Guards landed at Fitzroy, but on 8 June the 1st Battalion, Welsh Guards suffered many

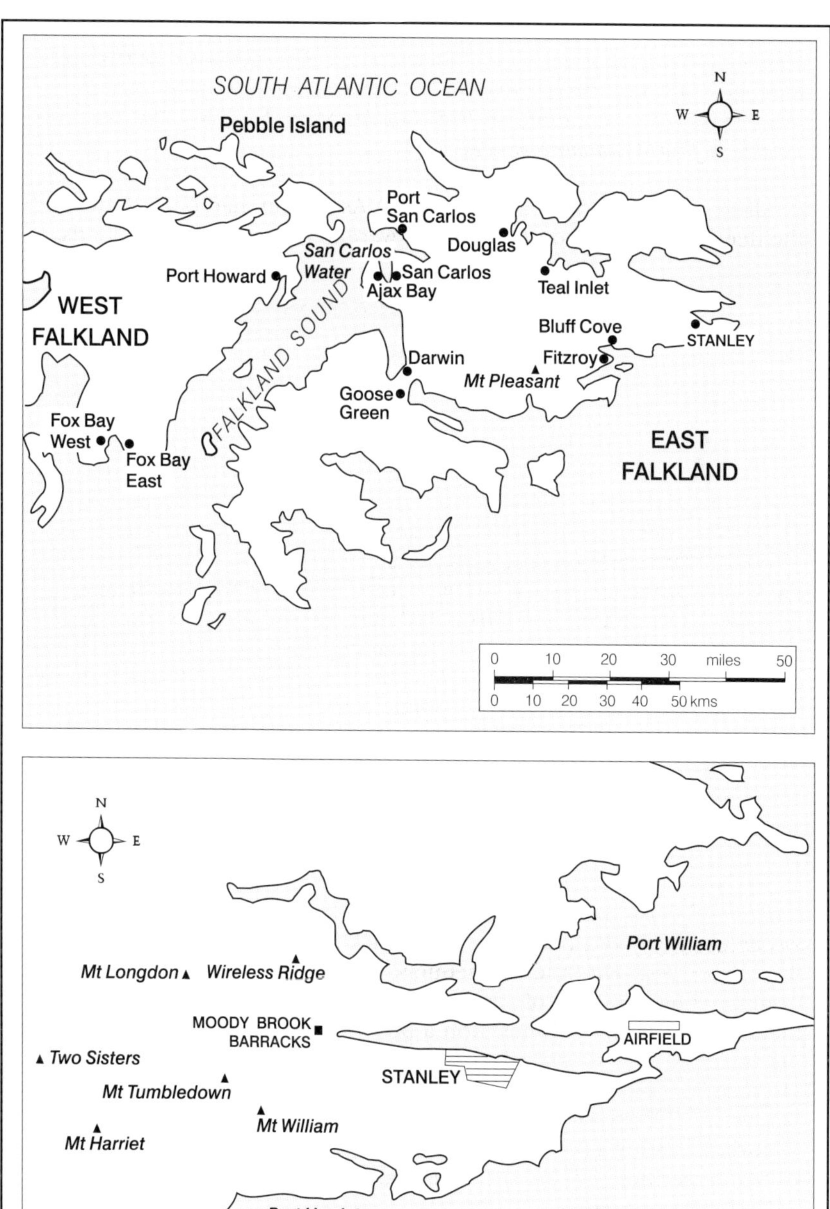
SOUTH ATLANTIC OCEAN
N
W
E
S
Pebble Island
Port
San Carlos
Douglas
San Carlos
Water
San Carlos
Ajax Bay
Port Howard
Teal Inlet
WEST
FALKLAND
FALKLAND SOUND
Bluff Cove
STANLEY
Fitzroy
Darwin
Mt Pleasant
Goose
Green
Fox Bay
West
Fox Bay
East
EAST
FALKLAND
0 10 20 30 miles 50
0 10 20 30 40 50 kms
N
W
E
S
Port William
Mt Longdon
Wireless Ridge
MOODY BROOK
BARRACKS
AIRFIELD
Two Sisters
STANLEY
Mt Tumbledown
Mt William
Mt Harriet
Port Harriet
0 1 2 3 miles 5
0 1 2 3 4 5 kms

casualties when the LSLs *Sir Galahad* and *Sir Tristram* were bombed at Fitzroy. By now, though, 3 Commando Brigade was in the mountains west of Stanley. Over the period 12–14 June the Commando Brigade captured Mount Longdon, Two Sisters and Wireless Ridge. 5 Infantry Brigade captured Mount Tumbledown and Mount William, the enemy fleeing from Sapper Hill just south-west of Stanley. On 14 June the Argentines surrendered at Port Stanley.

THE FALKLANDS LANDING

3 Commando Brigade

Aboard LSL *Sir Geraint*, after the journey from Ascension Island, D Day, 21 May, started sometime before dawn with a large pre-battle breakfast. The ships were darkened, the bridges out of bounds to all embarked troops and the doors to the outside world closed and guarded. Only those on look-out on the 'monkey islands', the deck above the LSL bridges and the forecastle, could see and hear what was going on. The remainder ate, checked their kit or remained closed up at their Damage Control Party locations. The first move of troops ashore were the Commandos and Parachute Battalions who were transported in surface craft. 29th Commando Regiment RA LAD operated in its four parts: LAD Main and three battery fitter sections.

Drawing 1: REME soldiers repair Rapier on a ridge overlooking San Carlos waters.

The first job of LAD Main under the control of ASM Watson was to unload, from the LSL *Sir Geraint*, the RAPIER ground-to-air missile detachments which were required for defence against Argentine MIRAGE and SKYHAWK aircraft. Everything was to be flown off by helicopter. The RAPIERs, for reasons unknown to the LAD, were in the hold below the guns of 79 (Kirkee) Commando Battery, the ammunition and various other vehicles. This did not make things easier. The first three elements of the overall fly-off were all from the *Sir Geraint*, so the initial positioning of men and stores on the correct flight deck was crucial. At 1100 hours the first three helicopters arrived. The procedure, followed all day on all the LSLs, was for a hovering helicopter 'taxi rank' to form off the port quarter of the ship. The RN SEA KINGs from the rank would then come in singly and land on the stern deck to pick up their internal load. Having completed that, they would move off down the port side of the ship, hover over the forward deck and pick up the underslung load. All would work smoothly provided the helicopter picked up the matching load from each deck and went to the correct LZ indicated to the pilot on a large blackboard! Staff Sergeant Fazakerley had rehearsed and then orchestrated a team to direct personnel loading on the stern deck, whilst the ASM had three teams on the forward deck for the underslung loads. The OC LAD sat in a little office in the bowels of the ship with his finger on the pulse, and matched personnel to equipment, having communications to both decks and the bridge.

The first air attacks came in as the ASM and his teams were opening the hatches and the ships' cranes were starting to lift the RAPIERs. The unloading was successful despite continuous air attacks near the ship and 79 Commando Battery and T Air Defence Battery of the Regiment were safely disembarked. LAD Main spent the first five days on the LSL which they regarded as probably the most dangerous place of any in the Regiment! Once the LAD moved ashore it became a primary task to set up local defence and protection from air and ground attack. The first few days were taken up with digging shelter trenches with overhead cover, and the improvement and camouflage of defensive positions became a continuous task. At the time the defensive positions around San Carlos were of great importance as counter-attacks could be expected. For a few days the Workshop Squadron of Commando Logistic Regiment was defending the Ajax Bay complex and the LAD Main was one of the very few sub-units between Stanley and the Brigade HQ at San Carlos. In some ways it felt to them very much like peacetime on Dartmoor, including the rain, but with the important difference that they dug for real and made sure that overhead cover was as much as the reinforcing material could support. They wrote afterwards, 'If you ask any of us what you should never forget to take with you, the answer will be a shovel or pick for each and every man whatever his rank or station'.

Some parts of LAD Main were working individually at their trade at dispersed sites. Corporal Farrell, a radar technician, made a tour of the anchorage, care of the RM Raiding Squadron:

'I was taken by Rigid Raider to my first port of call where I spent a day and a half running between my repair work and a trench. In the end I opted for staying with the broken kit otherwise I would never have finished. After disposing of various bits of electronic kit and sending a couple of generators back to the remainder of the Radar Section, I managed to hitch a ride on a chopper to my next job. This involved repairing a starter cable in a generator. To my amazement the operators of the kit wouldn't let me start until I had a cup of coffee. Great stuff!'

After finishing the final job, he was contemplating getting back to the LAD when the Argentine Air Force bombed them. He decided to hang on until the morning! Captain Musgrove wrote that the air attack Corporal Farrell refers to was on 27 May when the LAD Main and the Regimental HQ had their own air attacks, which were much too close for comfort. SKYHAWKs came in at last light on hitherto unused routes. The first pair hit Blue Beach at San Carlos just after the ASM had told the LAD that they had probably seen the last of the Argentine Air Force. The LAD were not impressed by the ASM's intelligence sources!

Early on 21 May in darkness and radio silence LSLs *Sir Galahad* and *Sir Percivale* arrived in San Carlos Water with Commando Logistic Regiment Workshop Squadron on board. 40 and 45 Commandos RM, and 2nd and 3rd Battalions, The Parachute Regiment were already ashore. The vessels dropped anchor at 0600 hours without incident, but by 1130 hours the first air attacks started and went on all week in daylight hours. Sitting on top of 350 tons of ammunition as well as petrol and other dangerous cargo still on board the ship during these attacks was a chilling experience. On 23 May HMS *Antelope* was bombed and later exploded, sinking next morning. Many accounts have been written elsewhere of the damage to our ships, the near misses and the bombs that did not explode. 3 Advanced Workshop Detachment from *Sir Percivale*, and the Workshop Troop from HMS *Intrepid* in their infantry defence role, went to the Base Maintenance Area (BMA) at Ajax Bay across the water from San Carlos. On 24 May, while the rest of the Commando Logistic Squadron was still on board, *Sir Galahad* was hit by

Sir Galahad,
Sergeant D Ryall nearest the camera

MIRAGE cannon fire, followed by an attack by SKYHAWKs with 1,000 pound bombs. One of the NCOs had the unusual experience of seeing a bomb bounce over the boat in which he was travelling and lodge in the bows of *Sir Galahad*, fortunately without exploding. The *Sir Lancelot* suffered a similar experience, but again a bomb did not explode.

After evacuating *Sir Galahad* with its unexploded bomb and spending the night in HMS *Intrepid* the men and their equipment were brought ashore and moved to the BMA at Ajax Bay where they concentrated on building bunkers to protect themselves against the daily air attacks. On 27 May two SKYHAWKs attacked the BMA, killing and wounding several men, and two bombs landed in the roof of the old refrigeration plant which was being used as a field hospital. Happily they did not explode. Ammunition in a dump nearby, however, did explode when it caught fire and explosions continued for some time afterwards.

When 45 Commando RM moved forward the Workshop Squadron was given the task of defence company for the BMA as well as their usual repair task. The Oversnow Troop vehicle mechanics went forward with the fighting troops to keep the Volvo BV202Es going. These vehicles proved to be the work-horses of the operation as there were few roads and the going was difficult everywhere. The telecommunications technicians worked long hours in the BMA, which made a welcome change from wet trenches, while the Control Equipment Technicians tried their hand at repairing thermal imagers, naval night vision equipment and rigging up lights for the prisoner-of-war compound. Others guarded prisoners, dug graves and buried the dead.

Wessex and Gazelle in support of ground troops

All the aircraft were fully serviceable when 3 Commando Brigade Air Squadron LAD arrived at San Carlos Water at dawn on 21 May. The GAZELLEs lifted off to carry out reconnaissance. At 1100 hours one GAZELLE from C flight limped back on board riddled with bullet holes and the other two from the flight were reported overdue. Sadly, the two missing aircraft had been seen shot down in the first half-hour of flying with the loss of three lives, but within two hours the bullet-riddled aircraft was flying again. *Sir Galahad* and *Sir Lancelot*, after their hits on 24 May, were subsequently beached, after the embarked troops had been evacuated. Tools and equipment were left on board. The AMG with 3 Commando Brigade went ashore to two different locations. In the next few days the bombs on the LSLs were disarmed and the stores brought ashore. Eight days later the AMG came together for the first time on Blue Beach and, after another eight days, their vehicles and heavy aircraft spares came ashore.

The Mobile Stores Detachment remained on board at first but after the air attacks it was moved with some difficulty to San Carlos settlement where it was to remain with the AMG for the remainder of the operation. Most first-line maintenance had to be done at night using very low intensity red light. Second-line work was usually done by day as lights, understandably, were not permitted at night.

5 Infantry Brigade

Near South Georgia most of the Force HQ and Brigade HQ cross-decked to HMS *Antrim* – a County Class Destroyer. At one time in the area, *QE2* was reported to have one hundred icebergs on her radar screen during a period of very poor visibility.

4th Field Regiment RA LAD had travelled in flat-bottomed ferries which rolled so much in the South Atlantic that military training was severely limited; they reported that the ships recorded an angle of 35 degrees of roll. The soldiers were understandably relieved to land at San Carlos on 1 June but their relief was short-lived. Appalling weather and the active Argentine Air Force saw to that.

On 21 May the 2nd Battalion, The Parachute Regiment Group SCOUT helicopters from 656 Squadron AAC with their REME support went ashore onto Sussex Mountain a few miles south of San Carlos settlement where they operated until the remainder of the Squadron arrived. For some inexplicable reason the MSD for SCOUTs was unloaded at Ajax Bay across the water some eight miles from Sussex Mountain!

The balance of 5 Infantry Brigade and the remainder of 656 Squadron AAC arrived at San Carlos on 2 June. The next day they were ashore operating from the area of San Carlos Bay. The LAD was one mile south of San Carlos settlement living in shell scrapes on a hill side in a very wet area called Clam Valley with the aircraft parked 150 metres away along the edge of a stream. The SCOUT Flight from MV *Baltic Ferry* joined the three SCOUTs in 2nd Battalion, The Parachute Regiment Group on Sussex Mountain but left on board the MSD. There it stayed, much to the inconvenience of the LAD, until 26 June. It was encouraging though, that all the aircraft had arrived in the Falklands without any signs of corrosion or damage.

36 Engineer Regiment Workshop sailed on in the *QE2* to South Georgia with its glaciers and icebergs. There they transferred in a choppy sea to RFA *Stromness* with its cargo of explosives, missiles and shells and had a five-day rough voyage to San Carlos Water. They arrived in darkness, but at sunrise 'It was like sailing down a loch in Scotland with green rolling hills all round and a strong wind howling from the west,' as one of them described it later. They disembarked and a few hours later were digging like moles on a gentle slope overlooking the bay. Next morning they found that they were right under the flights down 'Bomb Alley' which led to more furious digging. This proved well-justified later when there were numerous air attack warnings. They had the satisfaction of seeing an enemy CANBERRA and SKYHAWK destroyed. For three days they waited for their stores to be unloaded and, once these were received, they were able four days later to set off for Stanley.

10 Field Workshop travelled on to Grytviken Harbour, South Georgia, where, in bitter cold and with mist hiding the ice-covered glaciers, they began cross-decking to the *Norland*, *Stromness* and *Canberra*. The ferries meanwhile had gone direct to San Carlos from Ascension Island. By now

the Workshop had men and equipment aboard six ships. Two days from San Carlos Major Tony Ball received a signal to say that he was to provide fifty men from a complement of fifty-four on board the RFA *Stromness* for possible prisoner-of-war guard duties. After a sharp exchange of signals the order was suspended but not cancelled. The main body of 10 Field Workshop arrived on shore two hours before last light on 3 June with their bergens, large packs and weapons. They trudged up the hill to find a vacant area.

Their digging tools were stowed with their vehicles so they began to dig with bayonets and mess tins, but more progress was made when the Royal Marines lent them their tools. By dark they had shell scrapes and next day in driving rain they completed trenches and sangars with overhead cover.

The next five days were a strain on the soldiers who were concentrating on survival in appalling weather with little opportunity to do anything else to take their minds off it. Some soldiers showed the strain but others went from strength to strength, bringing out the importance of a man's character. The value also of having personal picks and shovels to help provide self-protection and thus a boost to morale, was demonstrated yet again.

HQ 5 Infantry Brigade moved off to Darwin leaving unit echelons and logistic units behind. The prisoner-of-war guard commitment was reduced to one officer and twenty men who went off in *Norland.* The rest of the Workshop, except those still in the ferries and the 'follow-up' party, went down to the edge of San Carlos settlement and dug in again around a former stable. Major Tony Ball had been nominated OC Blue Beach Support Area which was set up in one end of a hut with Workshop Headquarters. With their own operators and radios and a radio from the Brigade Signals Squadron they staffed a miniature Brigade Rear Headquarters with links forward to Brigade Headquarters, and sideways/rearwards to other beaches and Force Headquarters in HMS *Fearless,* who exercised the overall direction of the logistic effort. The ships in the area rarely stayed for more than one day and changed around at night. The second-in-command of the Workshop concentrated on the complicated task of trying to get some of the Workshop's equipment out of whichever ship held it, was anchored in the area and able to disgorge its cargo.

29th Commando Regiment RA gun position

THE CAMPAIGN

3 Commando Brigade

79 (Kirkee) Commando Battery RA of 29th Commando Regiment RA claim that they were the first ashore and fired the first rounds from British Army 105mm Light Guns in war. The REME fitters were split up because their tracked Volvos could not be flown forward and had to drive across country to catch up with the guns carried by helicopter. The Volvos proved invaluable, in awful conditions, supporting 2nd Battalion, The Parachute Regiment at Goose Green, pulling guns about on the gun positions and carrying packs, food and ammunition. A good indication of the conditions that existed at the time and how problems were overcome by improvisation and sheer perseverance of the sort needed in war is given in a report six months later in 'The Craftsman' of December 1982, from Staff Sergeant Dick Horlor, an Artificer Weapon:

'It is difficult to describe how one decides priorities when arriving on a gun position which is under almost constant air attack. For instance, at San Carlos my first priority was to find or construct some overhead cover but then there was the other priority of helping the BSM set up an ammo supply dump. The real priority though was to maintain the guns.'

The first gun of the Battery to fire failed, because two balancing springs fractured. Repair was vital. However, there were no spare springs, so Staff Sergeant Horlor's next step was to attempt to weld the fractures. But having no welding kit, he had to fly back to LSL *Sir Geraint* where facilities were available. The ships were 1,000 metres away in San Carlos Water and were the main target for MIRAGE and SKYHAWK attacks, so one did not go aboard without good reason, even for the pleasure of getting out of the rain! It took two attempt by Staff Sergeant Horlor to weld the springs amidst the crump of bombs dropping alongside and heard above the noise of the ship's clattering twin diesels. Three or four MIRAGEs were attacking and at least two were shot down as he got into a GEMINI craft to go ashore again. He was not very reassured by the Bosun who cheerfully told him that he had been strafed on an earlier trip! The springs were fitted, but failed again. Unable to get another helicopter, he went down to Blue Beach in a Volvo where the LAD was now ashore. They fortunately found a rare civilian garage where Staff Sergeant Horlor arc-welded support brackets onto the springs to prevent them spiralling out when compressed. They left as two SKYHAWKs dropped parachute bombs near the garage. The repairs were a success and, although the springs fractured again, the brackets kept them in line and the gun went on to fire 370 rounds mainly at high charge without failure. Staff Sergeant Horlor was awarded the BEM a year later.

3 Commando Brigade Air Squadron flights and part of the unit echelon moved north-east to Teal Inlet and Mount Kent, four miles west

Sea King recovers Gazelle

of Two Sisters, to keep up with the advancing Marines. The AMG remained behind due to the size of their stores and vehicles. At Mount Kent Argentine bombing damaged two helicopters. Captain Larry Rotchell went with a 'down bird team' and discovered that they were repairable, but that one, a GAZELLE from 656 Squadron AAC had been too severely damaged for repair on the spot. They therefore lifted it back by SEA KING, for repair at 656 Squadron's echelon close to the Commando Squadron's AMG, which was a good example of the evacuation system working to perfection.

After the Goose Green action the AMG commandeered a garage, enabling some night work to be done. Routine aircraft servicing was done, mainly lubrication and examination tasks, when conditions allowed. The garage was also being used as a 'drying-out' station for 40 Commando's foot patrols. Contingency servicing was considered, but the schedules were not to hand, so the servicing depended on professional assessment of the requirement. The governing factor was not the five hours flying per day per aircraft but the need to keep all aircraft on standby when not flying. Damage due to hostile action and wire strikes ranged from bullet holes and shrapnel damage to broken aerials and pitot heads. Bullet holes were covered with masking tape, canopies were stitched, patched and in one case covered with polythene. Each aircraft had its own crew throughout, who became very familiar with the damage repair to the aircraft.

A non-pressurized fuel pipe was repaired with a 'compo' ration tin, sealant and two jubilee clips. Stripping of the GAZELLEs which crashed on D Day produced valuable spares to supplement the FAACO holdings. Corporal Corrigan, an Avionics Technician, earned his Mention in Despatches by discovering a fault one night which, had it not been remedied, could have led next day to the catastrophic failure of half the tail rotor blades on their own SCOUTs and perhaps the loss of many others. The SCOUT Flight was not without its casualties, though, and lost one aircraft and its pilot, shot down by a PUCARA in the fighting for Goose Green.

On landing at San Carlos 59 Independent Squadron RE Workshop moved into a garage at Port San Carlos. A seized Muirhill engine was given a battleworthy overhaul and restored to life on five pistons and a filed-out main journal bearing. The top priority was to keep the plant vehicles and the CET working. Some men of the unit were still on *Sir Lancelot* on 24 May when the 1,000 pound bomb hit the ship but failed to explode and were evacuated with others on board, as described earlier. Some idea of the life of a junior REME NCO can be gained from Lance Corporal Weatherston with 1 Troop who wrote in 'The Craftsman' for December 1982:

'After a week or so at San Carlos we moved up to Teal Inlet on HMS Fearless, disembarking at 0300 hours onto a LCU, to go ashore where we rejoined most of the squadron. We spent a further seven days at Teal Inlet digging trenches, "stagging" on and generally enjoying ourselves (!) before moving on to Bluff Cove to give RE support to the Welsh Guards. We set off towards Port Stanley in one big long winding snake-like convoy, with heavily laden bergens and carrying bangalore torpedoes, with my section up front. After some time an explosion was heard. A Royal Marine had stepped on a mine, followed by another a few minutes later. Our troop then cleared a safe lane through the minefield. Once through, we dug in at the base of a hill, only to find that it was still occupied by Argentine troops. So back we went to our original positions, this time around the minefield. That afternoon we once again advanced on Sapper Hill, the Argies retreating (or should I say running away) to Port Stanley. After a thoroughly miserable night on Sapper Hill we then moved into Port Stanley.'

The Commando Logistic Regiment Workshop Squadron repair load remained fairly constant throughout the campaign. It had a heavy defence task, but their shift system enabled tradesmen to be available when necessary. More than 1,500 jobs were successfully undertaken during the campaign.

Forward Repair Teams of 12th Air Defence Regiment Workshop were deployed with their Troop Headquarters, all movement by day being by helicopter, air raids permitting, and on foot at night. The teams, consisting of two technicians and a vehicle mechanic deployed over a wide area during the campaign to Teal Inlet, Fitzroy and Port San Carlos, with a fourth team in reserve at San Carlos settlement. Manhandling RAPIER spares weighing 120 pounds over rugged ground at night through sometimes trigger-happy positions was not a pleasant task. At times they had to use copper telephone cable to replace high-frequency transmission leads on the launcher, remove printed circuit boards to short out links to keep the system firing and, on one occasion, they straightened the precision-machined missile-launching beam with a crowbar. This RAPIER killed a SKYHAWK next day.

The absence of close second-line support for the RAPIER missile battery during the campaign denied the battery support in its hour of greatest need. The two box-body repair vehicles needed to repair the faulty black boxes were sent out from UK but off-loaded at Ascension Island. With hindsight this was clearly a wrong decision, but at the time other factors affected what was a shipping priority decision. The result was that black boxes had to be flown out from the UK and dropped by parachute. Some were lost in this process and others were lost when the Container Ship *Atlantic Conveyor* was sunk on 25 May.

5 Infantry Brigade

After landing at San Carlos the gun batteries and the fitters of 4th Field Regiment RA disappeared over several hills. After five days of uncertainty, LAD Main and Regimental A2 Echelon went on board the LSLs *Sir Tristram* and *Sir Galahad* to move round the coast to an unknown destination. On the morning of 7 June all six of the LAD arrived at Fitzroy in *Sir Tristram* and landed as quickly as possible to seize an empty sheep shed. Trenches were dug twice as deep and twice as quickly as on any exercise and very soon the EME, four SNCOs and a Corporal from the LAD were helping the RQMS load artillery ammunition into nets for transport to the guns. On 8 June while still loading ammunition the LAD witnessed the air attack on *Sir Galahad* and *Sir Tristram*, only some 400 yards away. Immediately after a bomb hit the *Sir Galahad* it burned fiercely amidships with massive flames and black smoke rising into the sky. The tragedy of the conflagration and subsequent loss of *Sir Galahad* in this attack resulted in fifty-one men dead and forty-six injured. Thirty-three of those killed were from the 1st Battalion, Welsh Guards including two REME soldiers, Craftsman M W Rollins and Lance Corporal A R Streatfield, attached to the Battalion. In the evacuation of the survivors to the shore there were many individual acts of bravery. The Gunners' LAD was among the first to help the survivors, one of whom was their own Pay Sergeant who had been kept at San Carlos on the LSL for an extra day – a day that he would always remember.

Ammunition loading continued, together with occasional repairs to radios and generators as well as vehicles. The REME workload at the gun positions was much the same, the fitters keeping the guns and other equipment in battleworthy condition as they fired round the clock throughout the campaign. The six-man gun crews were increased to eight, using the Quartermaster's staff, REME and ACC soldiers, so that two four-man crews could work a 24-hour shift system. At the time of the surrender on 14 June all the Regiment's guns, radios and CYMBELINE mortar location radars were fully operational. REME had done its job.

Escape from Sir Galahad. Craftsman Owen (facing shore line), Lance Corporal Howarth (on right), Staff Sergeant Balchin (in blanket)

656 Squadron AAC remained in San Carlos Bay until 5/6 June when they deployed to four locations, the SCOUT Flight, GAZELLE Flight and Squadron HQ going to Darwin/Goose Green area, the unit echelon moving into San Carlos settlement for security and defence reasons. One GAZELLE was lost on 6 June, shot down by an Argentine missile. The AMG remained with the echelon to do the SNEB rocket modifications, working all through the night to complete one GAZELLE each night. The SNEB equipment had not been fitted earlier because it arrived too late to sail from UK in MV *Nordic Ferry* and had to be loaded into *QE2* where there was no opportunity to cross-deck it at Ascension Island. The rocket pods were still painted white and showed up glaringly, but fortunately the LAD had some tins of aircraft paint which were used to camouflage them successfully.

Once HQ 5 Infantry Brigade was established at Fitzroy after its move from Darwin, SCOUT Flight, GAZELLE Flight and Squadron HQ started to move to Fitzroy and were established by 10 June. At no time during the operation was 656 Squadron AAC LAD able to find covered accommodation for the aircraft, although after leaving San Carlos a cow shed and a pigsty for men to sleep in were discovered at Fitzroy. The ability and the performance of the technicians had been impressive, despite the difficult working conditions produced by the harsh climate and constant threat from air attacks. It was clear that the Corps had selected the right sort of men to be technicians and trained them thoroughly. The sterling quality of the artificers and NCOs had been evident to all.

The thorough preparation of the aircraft by the LAD and their second-line support had been a tremendous help on arrival in the Falklands. Flexible servicing was stretched to the limit and contingency servicing was introduced to cope with the aircraft detached to other units without technical cover for two or three days at a time. The clerks, drivers, storemen and vehicle mechanics became good infantrymen and trench diggers, making up the GAZELLE and SCOUT Defence Sections with the Squadron men. They found out that the best places for defence are often the worst to dig in, being hard clay or rock or both. On 12 June the GAZELLE Defence Section joined the RMP at the covered sheep pens to act as a prisoner-of-war guard and search team. The job of the searchers was to strip the prisoner, search all his clothing for anything that could be used as a weapon, find any useful intelligence material and get his number, rank, name, and regiment. 3,000 prisoners were processed here in a week.

By mid-June, when the Argentine Army surrendered at Port Stanley, 10 Field Workshop had received on shore some tentage and cooking equipment, and some repair vehicles to provide limited repair ability, but no spares. The latter only began to arrive shortly before they left San Carlos for Port Stanley on 24 June. Repair teams had been sent forward to Goose Green and Fitzroy to repair vehicles and office machinery and the photocopier repair technician became the most widely travelled man in the Workshop. Cannibalization and battlefield repair was the most frequent work. EAGER BEAVER forklift repairs were given priority due to scarcity, lack of spares and the pounding they received.

THE SURRENDER AND IMMEDIATE AFTERMATH

3 Commando Brigade

For REME, in particular, the period immediately after the surrender was one of gathering together of resources, which had been spread so widely during the campaign, establishing firm locations from which to work with the greatest effectiveness, and assessing the state of weapons and equipment of the Force. For the Force generally, finding suitable shelter for personnel and achieving some degree of comfort was of prime importance after the gruelling campaign.

Captain Larry Rotchell of 3 Commando Brigade Air Squadron LAD went with Brunei Flight to Stanley to establish a Forward Operating Base on the cricket pitch next to Government House. The aircraft continued to support the Commando Brigade but were in a very sorry state by peacetime standards. Soon after their arrival, a converted container ship sailed into Stanley bringing two GAZELLEs sent out from the UK to replace the aircraft lost on D Day. Captain Rotchell went aboard and met the RN Aircraft Engineering Officer who gave him a cup of coffee and told him with regret that one of the two GAZELLEs had suffered storm damage on the trip South. He had, as a result, restricted it to a maximum of 70 knots forward flight by an entry in the MOD Form 700. He was somewhat taken aback when Captain Rotchell inspected the aircraft and the small hole in the canopy bubble that caused the restriction and told him that this one aircraft had more perspex on it than the rest of his fleet put together! Shortly after the surrender most of the Squadron embarked in *Canberra*, with the remainder in the P & O Ferry *Elk*, with the aircraft, to return to UK.

Members of 70 Aircraft Workshop repair a Gazelle

656 Squadron AAC remained in the Fitzroy area until 2 July when they moved to the Beaver Seaplane hangar in Port Stanley with the LAD and AMG which became the home of 70 Aircraft Workshop Falklands Detachment. It was known in 1982 as the 'Planetarium' because of the number of bullet and shrapnel holes in it. Here they stayed until early August when they handed over to 657 Squadron AAC. It was not until six weeks after the surrender that any technical spares arrived through the system for 4th Field Regiment RA LAD, although many of these had been in the theatre for eight weeks. This was very frustrating. Personal comfort, too, took longer to achieve than everyone had hoped: water was scarce, fresh food did not appear until three weeks after the surrender and the soldiers were constantly wet and cold. Despite these discomforts, morale was high with the knowledge of a job well done. Some fared rather better for accommodation, and a week after the surrender the Commando Logistic Regiment Workshop Squadron moved to Stanley where most men were put into houses, thanks to the hospitality of the islanders. The whole town, however, was strewn with vehicles, clothing, weapons, ammunition, rubbish, filth and excrement and cleaning-up became of great importance, and everyone was involved.

5 Infantry Brigade

36 Engineer Regiment Workshop arrived at Stanley on 16 June. The burnt-out plant workshop next to Stanley Power House was chosen as the workshop site. It took four days to remove the rubbish and human filth, not to mention booby-traps and live grenades. Before long, repaired captured equipment was being issued to the Regiment. Heavy plant and

recovery equipment were soon completely serviceable, a boulder road was built to get a Combat Engineer Tractor out of a bog and the welders and electricians were kept very busy working in appalling conditions. Improvisation was essential, as there was no lifting equipment. The Workshop ably supported the task of the Regiment, which was to restore Stanley Airport, extend the runway by 200 feet, repair roads and buildings and erect a hutted camp.

On arrival at Port Stanley on 24 June the 10 Field Workshop task was to set up a Garrison Field Workshop. This was no easy task, as its equipment was still embarked on various ships and there was no suitable repair accommodation, but it was achieved. There was a huge recovery and repair load caused by everyone driving his own private captured enemy vehicle. However, the end of their time in the Falklands was in sight and men no longer required were returned to UK in mid-July leaving on the MV *St Edmund.* The main body flew out on 9 August after the arrival of the Advance Party of 2 Field Workshop.

Immediately after the surrender a high priority was to establish RAPIER air defence positions on remote hilltop sites surrounding Port Stanley. The point of major overhaul was fast approaching for all the RAPIER generator sets which had been, and still were, in constant use since landing. Major Tony Ball signalled back for more generators. The reply from LE(A) said that there were no generators available, but gave him authority to adapt the power supply to use the local mains grid! Generators requiring base repair were shipped back to 35 Central Workshop at Old Dalby, where the local purchase of automotive spares and use of outside contractors to rewind alternators was pushed to the limit. Another signal in response to an urgent vehicle spares demand suggested he made use of local purchase. This was felt to be somewhat unrealistic in a country where there was no real garage, only a handful of local vehicles, every farmer his own mechanic and the nearest source of supply in normal times was Buenos Aires! The rate of wear and demand for spark plugs, interestingly, far exceeded the expectation of the staff in the UK, but this was a minor problem compared to some. In spite of such difficulties, complete overhauls of generators were carried out in 10 Field Workshop (and later in 2 Field Workshop) in support of the detachment from 12th Air Defence Regiment Workshop. For this sort of task spare crankshafts and other parts were sent out from the UK, but were always in short supply.

CASUALTIES

There were 255 fatal casualties in the Falklands Operation CORPORATE, of which 122 were in the Army, four being REME, and 777 were wounded. The four REME soldiers who lost their lives in the Falklands Campaign were:

Corporal J Newton – 22nd Special Air Service Regiment
Craftsman M W Rollins – 1st Battalion, Welsh Guards
Craftsman A Shaw – 3rd Battalion, The Parachute Regiment
Lance Corporal A R Streatfield – 1st Battalion, Welsh Guards

THE REME LESSONS

The campaign to recapture the Falklands was not one for which contingency plans had existed and many lessons were learnt. For REME some of the main lessons learnt, or re-learnt, were:

- REME tradesmen need to be, and were in this campaign, well-versed in the first principles of their trade.
- Any REME unit must be flexible in its organization and resources so that, when mobilized, it can respond effectively to the confusion and unexpected events of war.
- An adequate provision of repair equipment, tools and spares must be made for a theatre of operations, if the proper level of REME support is to be maintained throughout a campaign. In the Falklands campaign, although there was some lack of availability of these essential requirements, REME support was maintained, despite the operating conditions and high intensity of usage of units' equipment. However, the duration of the land operations was short, and there could well have been shortages of fit equipment in units if the operations had become prolonged, and the inadequate REME resources exhausted.
- The repair and manufacturing capacity of REME UK static workshops was essential to mounting the operation successfully at short notice.
- With extended lines of communication, it is essential that the need for a channel for the fast recovery of repairable components is recognized and established from the onset of a campaign.
- Tactical loading of equipment and stores in ships is necessary, and freight must be accompanied by appropriate personnel, if REME units are to function efficiently on arrival in a theatre of operations.
- Electronic repair vehicles are an important component of the RAPIER air defence system and should not be divorced from the battery and its firing equipment.
- Unserviceable equipment soon becomes cannibalized if it is neither guarded nor recovered.
- Uncontrolled cannibalization may lead to the loss of much useful captured enemy equipment.
- Fitness and determination are essentials without which trade skills are of little value.

- The ability to make effective use of personal weapons, and of tools to dig for protection, is essential.

POST-WAR

The members of 2 Field Workshop met for the first time for a briefing by Major Nigel Ford on 22 July 1982 at the Training Battalion and Depot REME at Arborfield. It was formed from members of the Corps serving in the UK and was to be a part of the Falkland Islands Logistic Battalion (FILOG), taking over the role of Garrison Workshop from 10 Field Workshop which had been in the Falklands during the campaign since the beginning of June. The Advance Party, under Captain White and ASM Culverhouse, left Arborfield on 2 August for RAF Brize Norton and flew via Dakar in Senegal to Ascension Island. There they transferred into a HERCULES transport for the final stage to RAF Stanley, arriving on 3 August.

2 Field Workshop at Moody Brook

On 4 August they were taken to 10 Field Workshop at Moody Brook, three miles from Stanley at the western end of the harbour where the old Port Stanley Pumping Station formed the main workshop building. There were also two large galvanized sheds, one for the vehicle repair workshop and one for the RAOC Stores Section. 10 Field Workshop main party went home on 9 August, the first group of 2 Field Workshop main party arriving by HERCULES on 14 August, having had to return to Ascension Island when over Port Stanley, due to the weather being too bad to land! The second group came by sea in the MV *Norland* arriving on 20 August, but the weather was too bad for them to land. The whole Workshop was not complete at Moody Brook until 24 August. On 4 September Staff Sergeant Lewis and Private Cuthbertson RAOC left by sea to provide support for the 1st Battalion, Queen's Own Highlanders (Seaforth and Camerons) on roulement in South Georgia.

The Workshop's first task at Moody Brook was to clean out Argentine rubbish and turn the shell-damaged remains of the old Royal Marines barracks into domestic accommodation and clear up the debris of the war. By the time winter was turning into spring all were in their permanent locations. Working conditions had been greatly improved and, to quote the Chief Clerk, Sergeant Childs, the Workshop was well and truly producing the goods. Several members of the Workshop were billeted with local families and others were living in an engineering works in Stanley. A main workshop task in clearing up the debris of war became that of recovering abandoned equipments, particularly including those of Argentine origin, such as 105mm pack howitzers, 155mm field guns and various anti-aircraft guns, and moving them to Moody Brook. These had to be cleared by EOD personnel before being lifted by helicopter or towed.

Before 2 Field Workshop left UK for the Falklands the REME Benevolent Fund provided money for some home comforts, including a television set and a video recorder to allow REME soldiers to watch films in their off-duty hours. The staff at HQ REME Training Centre thought they might be able to help by recording selected television programmes and sending the cassettes to the soldiers 'down South'. They persuaded the REME Benevolent Fund to hire a compatible video recorder and to buy three dozen blank cassettes so that recordings could be made. Each night, seven days a week, three hours of UK TV programmes were recorded: Match of the Day, Rugby Special, The Two Ronnies, News at Ten etc. The selection varied. Next morning the cassette went into a Jiffy Bag and was posted off. After about three weeks the cassettes began to come back from the Falklands with cryptic comments on little pieces of paper asking for variations in the selection. This service proved incredibly popular and only the REME soldiers had this constant stream of up-to-date TV from home. 2 Field Workshop became a popular place to visit.

In December 1982 Brigadier Derrick Ballard, DEE 1, was able to visit the Falklands, the first senior REME officer to do so, to assess the maintenance situation and the extent of the equipment problems. There were a number of weaknesses clearly requiring remedial action, particularly in respect of RAPIER, B vehicle serviceability, and RE equipment. Brigadier Ballard examined these equipment support problems under the prevailing conditions and recommended action to assist the transition from an immediate post-campaign situation, with all its attendant difficulties, to a normal equipment engineering system. Although a start had been made on these essential processes, the situation was not one for instant solution. Much still had to be brought into line, from overall support from the UK base, down to improved user maintenance, before a state of normality could and would be achieved. Brigadier Ballard was greatly heartened by the praise for the work of the Corps which he received from all those that he visited, and the high morale of everyone in the Corps, working under what were still far from settled conditions.

At the time of DEE 1's visit RAPIER was still fulfilling an essential role in the air defence of the Islands and REME support for the system was still at a high workload level requiring adequate spares backing. The Fire

Units were spread over a distance of some thirty kilometres, positioned on ridges surrounding San Carlos Water. To support these equipments, REME technicians and vehicle mechanics of 12th Air Defence Regiment Workshop were based in one of two central locations either side of the Water. In the event of a failure of an equipment, personnel and Line Replaceable Units would ideally be transported to the site by helicopter. Failing this, which was often the case, personnel had to walk to the site, and the required spares would be flown in later once the fault was diagnosed; it was not uncommon for the REME tradesmen to walk in excess of twenty kilometres a day if the faults occurred outside the helicopter tasking period. The LRUs would be repaired by 2 Field Workshop.

The RAPIER generator, the maintenance of which had given cause for concern, was not designed to run for twenty-four hours a day, but had in fact performed very well over the previous three months, some engines running for at least 1,700 hours without change. It was considered at the time that with realistic spares backing from UK and the second-line support now provided from 2 Field Workshop, the generator would continue to prove effective. During the three months up until December eighteen engine changes had been carried out to generators by 2 Field Workshop, by then firmly established with an engine overhaul unit. Sealing the equipment against the elements, maintenance and the improvement of operational performance continued to be problems.

Brigadier Ballard had no reason to doubt that, overall, most REME engineering headaches were caused by shortage of spare parts. This was exacerbated by difficulty in identifying some spares if they did not have a NATO Stock Number. This was particularly the case for the Royal Engineers who had commercial equipment sent out to the Falklands in some haste. They were probably the worst off for spares provision. Approximately a quarter of their vital equipment, which was the most heavily used on the Island and suffered rapid wear and tear, was unserviceable through lack of available spares at the time of Brigadier Ballard's visit. It was a time when the help which they had from the Corps was most needed, and appreciated.

Ascension Island continued as the site for cargo transhipment to and from the Falklands, and the identification and the correct priority for delivery of items by sea or air was still a problem. The presence of a REME officer there was recommended, if only to find the third of the RAPIER spares which had failed to arrive at the Falklands!

Support to the Royal Engineers 1983

37 Engineer Regiment Workshop REME was based at RAF Stanley, five miles from Stanley itself, in two Rubb frame tents 30 metres long and 10 metres wide, plus several ISO containers. The Royal Engineers had up to 1,200 men and 400 major items of plant. Their tasks included setting up radar on East Falkland, supporting the infantry in South Georgia; build-

ing camps throughout the Islands, building groynes and access roads for floating accommodation barges called Coastels; building roads and heliports; maintaining RAF Stanley; and erecting Rubb Shelters. The building-related tasks were urgent because all the Services had to be provided with proper accommodation by the start of the winter in May 1983.

The previous pressure to lay a runway in forty-two days for the RAF PHANTOMs at RAF Stanley had left worn-out equipment. An attitude had developed that equipment could be sacrificed to complete a task on time. Much of the equipment had been used in the quarry where the quartzite rock was extremely abrasive and very hard. The rock dust, when mixed with water, produced a very destructive grinding paste, so that running gear could fail in a week instead of lasting for the life of the equipment. The thick peat mud on most work sites and lack of wash-down facilities made servicing and preventative maintenance almost impossible. This resulted in a greater workload for REME, with long working hours to achieve only a taskworthy standard and needed crisis management to complete tasks on time. The plant requiring base repair was sent back to UK by sea, and was inspected at the port of arrival, usually Southampton, by a representative from the REME Directorate. He then assessed the extent of the repairs needed and made immediate arrangements for them to be carried out. This task was to continue for two years after the end of the campaign.

The Workshop staff were always very well aware of the urgency of their work. They were visited by the Commander British Forces Falkland Islands, the CRE, the CO and up to eight squadron commanders from the Sappers, who nearly always asked, 'When will the equipment be ready?' Sometimes excessive eagerness led to the equipment being taken away before repairs were completed! The Royal Engineers had Haulamatic and Volvo dump trucks; Terex and Allis bucket loaders; Terex and Caterpillar bulldozer face shovels; rock crushers and all the usual field support plant equipment, as well as Italian mobile cement mixers; mini-excavators, new to the Army, and combat support boats. Several new equipments arrived without spares, special tools or technical information. It took a detailed stock check lasting many weeks to establish what spares remained in the Falklands from the spares sent out for Operation CORPORATE in 1982. Although spares were demanded from UK on Priority 1 it could take seven to ten days to fly them out direct to Stanley or three to six weeks if they flew to Ascension Island and then came on by sea.

Perhaps the most vital of all the equipments were the two trains of rock crushers, each made up with a primary and secondary crusher, known as Val and Rose. These two required the expertise of the electricians and control equipment technicians and were liable to electrical failure at the most awkward times. There was always a lack of spares, but an old plant left behind by the contractors who built Stanley Airfield in

1976 was a useful source, including a three-phase motor which was rebuilt. The supply of stone was so vital that even a small breakdown in the equipment in the supply chain caused a crisis and often a whole sapper squadron was needed for rock production for the crushers and loaders. The Haulamatic dump trucks which took the crushed stones to the work sites had to be cannibalized to keep the others going, five producing six weeks of spares for the remaining twenty-eight. The Workshop policy was repair by repair and nothing was thrown away. Argentine vehicles and equipments were stripped and rubbish tips searched for suitable bits.

There was a continuous demand for welding and the Workshop provided a 24-hour duty welder, but the Workshop Double-Bug petrol-powered welding sets could not stand up to the continuous demand, so two diesel-powered Oerlikon electric welders were bought and proved to be very good.

Manufacturing parts kept one or two men fully occupied, although obtaining stocks of the correct size of metal was nearly impossible. There was a real need for a skilled fitter-turner which was not met until the arrival of a senior NCO armourer who produced excellent work on the lathe. The junior soldiers coped well and had been well trained, but those who did best were those who had a good understanding of the principles, some previous practical experience and were keen to improve their knowledge. Captain Stephen Matthews wrote in the 1984 REME Journal that 'The asset of which we can be proudest is our soldiers, who have been prepared to work long hours in the most terrible weather and conditions to see the job through'.

Recovery of a Combat Engineer Tractor

1983–1984

In September 1983 Lieutenant Colonel John Woodall was posted to Headquarters British Forces Falkland Islands. His charter was to:

- Stabilize the RAPIER Air Defence Missile System at a high level of availability and to ensure that an alleged surplus of RAPIER spares and facilities was returned to the UK.
- Improve inter-service co-operation and prevent duplication.

- Improve general serviceability of all Army equipment.
- Act as Maintenance Adviser to the Commander.
- Advise on future REME establishments and manning.

On arrival in September 1983 he found it difficult to believe the poor state of the equipment. As he wrote in the 1985 REME Journal he had seen a somewhat similar situation in Guyana in 1980 but he had never expected to see the British Army get itself into such a state. It was not altogether surprising, perhaps, in view of the operations in 1982, the urgent and enormous task facing the Sappers in 1983, adverse terrain and climate, lack of dry windproof accommodation, too few spares and lack of special tools. There were poor facilities for maintenance, widespread uncontrolled cannibalization, abuse and overloading of generators and vehicles, and a lack of even basic maintenance, often due to units having too much equipment and too few men.

There were exceptions to this unsatisfactory state. Weapons were generally well maintained. Army LYNX and GAZELLE helicopters were flying many more hours each month than in BAOR, despite the GAZELLEs having been used in the 1982 operations: thorough regular servicing was producing high rates of availability. REME technicians in the Falklands were also helped by frequent visits from experienced aircraft engineers and a continual flow of technical information from the UK. CLANSMAN radios gave little trouble despite the lack of the full range of test equipment to check that they were fully up to specification. To restore the overall situation to normal high peacetime standards Lieutenant Colonel Woodall recommended that all cannibalization be stopped except for certain carefully controlled UK-authorized exceptions. He started a campaign to stop abusing equipment, to carry out regular routine REME inspections, to withdraw surplus equipment from units, to use correct REME workshop procedures and to have proper handover/takeovers, using Periodic REME Examination reports, before departure of units or posting of the OC in trickle-posted units. The reason these measures had not been taken earlier was almost certainly because each previous Maintenance Adviser had also had a full-time job as a workshop commander.

1984–1989

Until 1986 the AAC Squadron and its REME support were on roulement, but in February of that year the AAC Squadron Falkland Islands and its REME Workshop had been formed with men from 657 Squadron AAC and its LAD REME. Trickle-posting from the UK and BAOR was then introduced. At the end of December 1986 the SCOUT helicopters went into 'mothballs' but the GAZELLEs kept flying until 31 May 1987, when AAC Squadron Falkland Islands ceased operational flying and dis-

2 Field Workshop on Tin Strip

banded. This ended five years of postwar flying, and Captain Steven Moult and AQMS Mitch Roberts completed the disbanding of the Workshop.

In May 1984 2 Field Workshop left Moody Brook, moving to 'Tin Strip' on the new Canache military area, and on 1 April 1987 as part of the reorganization they changed their title to Joint Force Workshop (JFW) having moved up to Mount Pleasant Airport some weeks earlier. During the period July 1982 to March 1987 2 Field Workshop had fourteen OCs and thirteen 2ICs. They had made many friends among the Islanders during those years. Major Terry Fraser was the last OC 2 Field Workshop and the first OC JFW. The authorized manpower was one officer and fifty-six soldiers when it was set up in its excellent accommodation and was reduced to one officer and thirty-two soldiers in 1989.

Up to January 1989 the JFW provided second-line support to the many dependent units but mainly to MTSS (RAF) who gave servicing and first-line support to the RAF Mount Pleasant vehicles. In January 1989 JFW and MTSS amalgamated and, after moving, the unit was renamed MT Workshop. The Workshop included part of a Mechanical Engineering (Ground) Squadron RAF, but the whole workshop was commanded by REME officers, the first being Captain Alan Bailey. An interesting part of their work was keeping serviceable the airfield support vehicles such as fire-fighting vehicles, refuellers with trailers, cranes, snow-clearing and de-icing vehicles.

From 1983 until 1987 the Falkland Islands Field Squadron Workshop had been at Stanley, living in floating Coastel accommodation, with Rubb shelters, Portakabins, ISO containers and 'tin shacks' to work in. In 1987 it moved to new accommodation at Mount Pleasant. In 1989 it had thirty mixed RE, RAOC and REME tradesmen working in a purpose-built workshop looking after engineer plant and vehicles, some of it away in South Georgia.

Much had happened in the ten years since 2 April 1982 when the REME elements for Operation CORPORATE were gathering their resources together for what was to prove an immensely tough and testing time for them over the next ten weeks. The now stabilized Garrison in the Falklands with its well-appointed workshop carrying out its routine tasks gives little indication of what has gone before or what the future will be. Perhaps it is sufficient to say that it has a proud inheritance in which

REME played a full and vital role and will continue to do so, whatever the future holds.

Annex A

OPERATION CORPORATE: OUTLINE ORDER OF BATTLE

The Land Forces in the Falklands Campaign included:

3 Commando Brigade

40, 42, and 45 Commandos RM
3 Commando Brigade Air Squadron (Gazelle & Scout Helicopters) and LAD
Commando Logistic Regiment RM (including Workshop Squadron RM)
29th Commando Regiment RA (105mm Light Guns) and LAD
29 Battery, 4th Field Regiment RA (105mm Light Guns) and LAD Section
T Battery 12th Air Defence Regiment RA (Rapier Missiles) and Workshop Section
59 Independent Commando Squadron RE and Workshop
2nd and 3rd Battalions, The Parachute Regiment
AMG from 70 Aircraft Workshop

5 Infantry Brigade

HQ 4th Field Regiment RA and LAD
97 Battery, 4th Field Regiment RA (105mm Light Guns) and LAD Section
36 Engineer Regiment and Workshop
2nd Battalion, Scots Guards
1st Battalion, Welsh Guards
1st Battalion, The 7th Duke of Edinburgh's Own Gurkha Rifles
656 Squadron AAC (Gazelle and Scout Helicopters) and LAD
10 Field Workshop
AMG from 70 Aircraft Workshop

Both Brigades, with their attached troops, had the usual complement of attached REME tradesmen.

CHAPTER 12

OPERATION GRANBY – REME IN THE GULF WAR

Introduction · Composition of the British Land Force in the Gulf · UN Preparations in Saudi Arabia · Logistic Support in UK – JHQ · Logistic Support in UK – HQ DGEME · REME Support in Cyprus · REME Build-Up and Responsibilities in Saudi Arabia – GRANBY 1 · The Changing REME Situation on Implementation of GRANBY 1.5 · The Start of the Air War · 1st (British) Armoured Division – Approach March and Final Preparations · The Land War – General Narrative · The Land War – REME Activities · The Cease-Fire and After · REME Casualties · Honours and Awards · Citations · REME Lessons and Conclusions · Tributes

INTRODUCTION

The British Land Force elements for Operation GRANBY were found mainly from within BAOR's Order of Battle and the preparations involved for their mounting have accordingly already been described in Chapter 6 – BAOR. This chapter takes up the narrative from there and includes the preparations and mounting of those REME elements sent

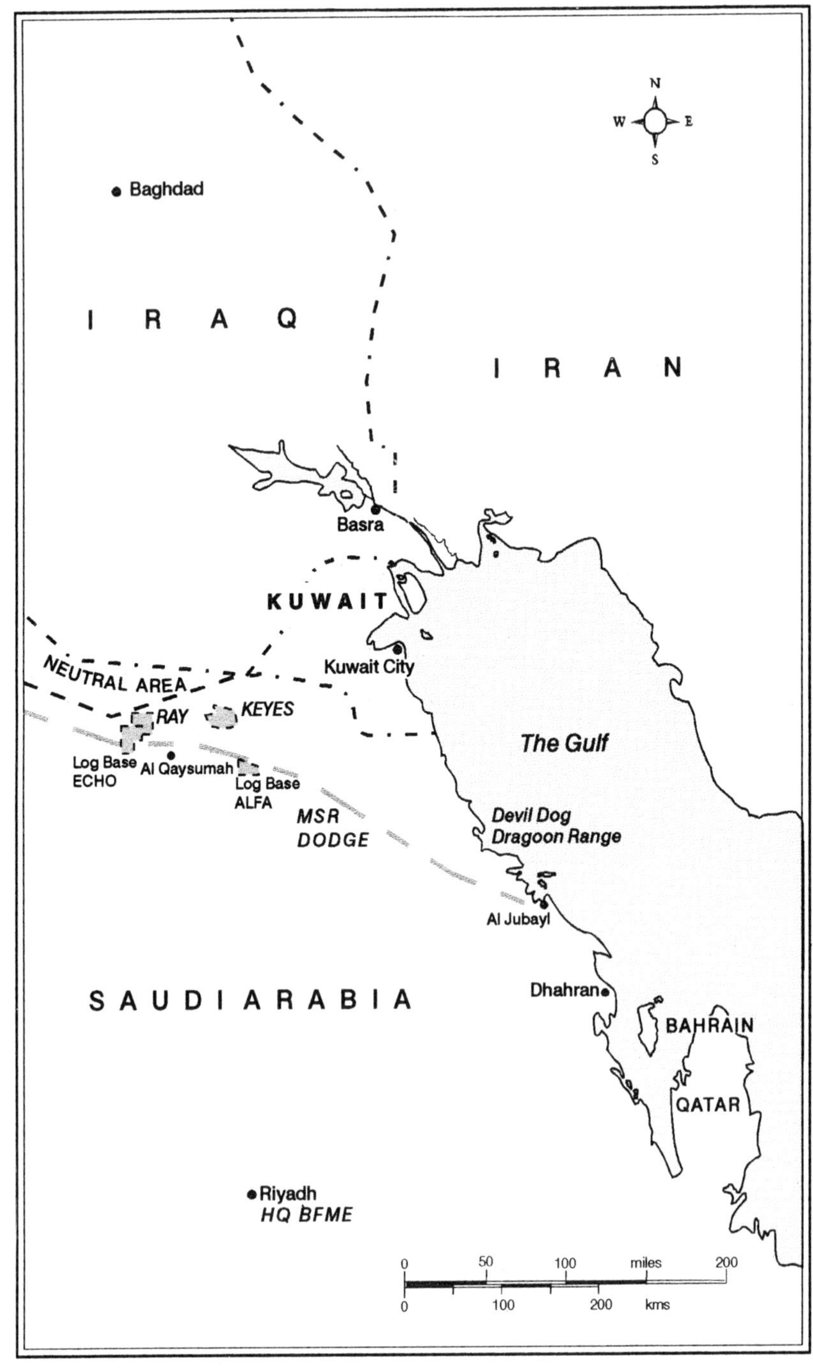
N
W
E
S
Baghdad
I R A Q
I R A N
Basra
KUWAIT
Kuwait City
NEUTRAL AREA
RAY
KEYES
Log Base
ECHO
Al Qaysumah
Log Base
ALFA
MSR
DODGE
The Gulf
Devil Dog
Dragoon Range
Al Jubayl
Dhahran
SAUDI ARABIA
BAHRAIN
QATAR
Riyadh
HQ BFME
0
50
100
miles
200
0
100
200
kms

from UK, the considerable involvement of UK-based organizations and the tasks of workshop units in Cyprus. It describes the arrival and activities of the REME element of the Force in Saudi Arabia from October 1990 until the land war was won on 28 February 1991 and ends with an account of REME's part in the clearing-up processes after the cease-fire. Although in the event only four day's land fighting proved necessary to defeat a seemingly formidable enemy, this was the largest conventional warfare operation mounted by the British since the Second World War. The codename Operation GRANBY was applied to all the forces provided by UK for operations against Iraq.

The operations in the Gulf, to which the UK Force contributed under GRANBY, were mounted in August 1990 under a United Nations Mandate. They consisted of an allied coalition of land, sea and air forces, acting in response to the occupation of Kuwait in July 1990 by Iraqi forces, under the leadership of Saddam Hussein. This act of aggression by Iraq had followed long disagreements between the two countries, centred on oil production, finance and territorial claims. The largest elements of the coalition Land Force were provided by the United States, Saudi Arabia and Great Britain, with the United States predominating and having overall command of the operation. Together with the other contributing nations, including France, Egypt, Syria, Kuwait and United Arab Emirates, they were established as a coalition in the Gulf Area as a result of United Nations Resolution 661, of August 1990. The United States were the first to send their forces to the Gulf and they established a presence there by 7 August. Their Commander, General Norman Schwarzkopf, was to become the Joint Commander of all the Coalition Forces, whilst Lieutenant General Prince Khalid bin Sultan of Saudi Arabia was the Commander in Chief. The initial aim of the Coalition was to prevent any further aggression in the Gulf area, particularly against Saudi Arabia, but was to develop into full-scale operations against Iraq, to carry out the Security Council's ultimate resolution. This increased the aim of the Coalition Force to securing the complete unconditional withdrawal of Iraq forces from Kuwait; restoring the legitimate government of Kuwait; re-establishing peace and security in the Gulf; and upholding the authority of the United Nations.

The British Land Force provided from BAOR was mounted in two phases – GRANBY 1 in October 1990, followed by GRANBY 1.5 in December. GRANBY 1 consisted of 7 Armoured Brigade Group and a Force Maintenance Area, whilst GRANBY 1.5 consisted of HQ 1st (British) Armoured Division, 4 Armoured Brigade, and a full range of supporting arms and services. More details are given in Chapter 6, and the Order of Battle is at Annex A to this Chapter. The part played by REME within the British Force from the very outset was considerable. Both the strengths and weaknesses within the support system were to be fully and practically evaluated under intense pressure. The results were also to vindicate, if there remained doubters, the validity of the continuing insistence of the Corps on the need for total equipment management. Much of the strength, convincingly proved by the achievements, lay in the skills and dedication of those on the ground responsible for the initial preparation and support of the Force in combat. The weaknesses, largely due to the inherent unreliability of some equipment, and lack of resources to support it, were to a great extent overcome by the ability of the Corps to meet the challenges that these deficiencies presented, and in this they were helped by Industry and many others in the Services who responded so willingly.

Apart from those directly involved in GRANBY, there were some in the Corps who were swept, unexpectedly, into the war situation in the Gulf. Those affected were some thirty REME officers and senior ranks, many with their families, who were in Kuwait serving with the Kuwait Liaison Team. When Iraq invaded Kuwait, the families became hostages, and the men became part of Saddam's 'Human Shield' to protect military targets in Iraq, after the families had been released. All were fortunately released by Christmas and their experiences in Kuwait are related in Chapter 9.

COMPOSITION OF THE BRITISH LAND FORCE IN THE GULF

Command

JHQ for all British operations in the Gulf was established at High Wycombe under the Joint Commander of Operation GRANBY, Air Chief Marshal Sir Patrick Hine, the UK Operations Centre being set up in the RAF Strike Command Primary War Headquarters bunker. On 1 October 1990 British Forces Arabian Peninsula changed their name to British Forces Middle East (BFME), with the Headquarters located in Riyadh, and on 6 October, Lieutenant General Sir Peter de la Billière assumed command. He was later to have at HQ BFME, as his Commander Maintenance, Colonel Peter Gibson, who would be the senior REME representative in the Gulf. The scene was now set for the arrival of the main British Land Forces despatched from BAOR, and amongst the first to arrive was the REME element of the Force Maintenance Area (FMA), described below.

7 Armoured Brigade Group

In addition to RN and RAF units already in the area, which were increased in August and again in September 1990, the Government had announced on 14 September that a Land Force consisting of 7 Armoured Brigade Group, commanded by Brigadier Patrick Cordingley, would move from BAOR to the Gulf. The Brigade would have 9,500 men; 117 CHALLENGER tanks; 101 WARRIOR infantry fighting vehicles; an armoured reconnaissance squadron; and twenty-eight M109 self-propelled guns – all backed up by their War Maintenance Reserves. It would have the support of two engineer regiments; two transport regiments; two ordnance battalions; two armoured workshops; and other specialist units. The mounting and despatch of the supporting REME elements of the Brigade in BAOR and their despatch to the Gulf is covered in Chapter 6. By late October the Brigade had completed its move to the Gulf where it soon began live firing and other training; by mid-November they were declared operationally ready.

Force Maintenance Area

The FMA, which had been established in BAOR to provide third- and fourth-line logistic support in the Gulf for 7 Armoured Brigade Group, of which it was initially part, was despatched from BAOR in early October and formed up at Al Jubayl. Subsequently, when the British Force expanded to divisional strength on GRANBY 1.5, the FMA was placed under command of HQ 1st (British) Armoured Division. When the division deployed command was changed to HQ BFME and the tasks of Colonel Peter Gibson, Commander Maintenance, are described later in this chapter. The senior REME representative on the Staff of the FMA was Lieutenant Colonel Alastair Campbell, the SO1 Maint/E Man, who described the maintenance and equipment management implications of its mounting and despatch from BAOR in Chapter 6. He continues his account of the REME activities in the FMA later in this chapter, having arrived at Al Jubayl with the pre-advance party at the beginning of October.

1st (British) Armoured Division

The UK Government announced on 22 November that it would implement GRANBY 1.5 by sending HQ 1st (British) Armoured Division commanded by Major General Rupert Smith (later to be a Colonel Commandant REME), with 4 Armoured Brigade commanded by Brigadier Christopher Hammerbeck, from BAOR, and additional ground troops to increase the UK Land Force to a division in strength, with all necessary backing. 1st (British) Armoured Division was to be operationally ready by the end of January 1991. The division, including 7 Armoured Brigade, had 28,000 men and women, 176 CHALLENGERs, 316 WARRIORs, 79 M109 and M110 self-propelled guns, plus their War Maintenance Reserves. In addition it had an armoured reconnaissance regiment; sixteen Multiple Launch Rocket Systems (MLRS); a RAPIER composite air defence regiment; two JAVELIN air defence batteries; three engineer regiments; anti-tank helicopters; five transport regiments; two ordnance battalions; three armoured workshops and other specialist units. Giving medical support there would be four field hospitals with a total of 1,600 beds. The division had the air support of RN SEA KING, and RAF CHINOOK and PUMA helicopters. The mounting and despatch of the REME elements, starting in December, is again covered in Chapter 6.

UN PREPARATIONS IN SAUDI ARABIA

UN Forces in Saudi Arabia continued the build-up of their resources during the autumn of 1990 and that winter, preparing themselves for a possible Iraqi attack perhaps using chemical or biological weapons and SCUD ballistic missiles. Saddam Hussein reinforced his troops in Kuwait and gave no sign of any intention to withdraw. Civilians from Western Countries were seized as hostages and some were placed at key military sites as human shields. Some expatriates managed to avoid capture and went to ground with the help of Kuwaiti friends. A retired REME Lieutenant Colonel, Denis Redmond, the managing director of the Ford franchise in Kuwait, was among those who successfully survived in this way. His experiences were recounted in the 1991 REME Journal. The Iraqis also put great pressure on Western diplomatic staffs who had remained in Kuwait City and their forces intimidated the civil population there with killings, torture and looting.

The Multi-National Maritime Force, taking action against shipping under Security Council Resolution (SCR) 665 to enforce sanctions laid down in SCR 661, included thirteen countries, with ships from Argentina, Australia, Belgium, Canada, Denmark, France, Greece, Italy, Netherlands, Norway, Spain, UK and USA, plus certain Gulf states. These naval forces, followed by air and land forces as the build-up in the area continued, were involved in a series of large-scale exercises to practise possible future operations, with the allies paying particular attention to operating under chemical and biological attack.

By January 1991 it was estimated that Iraq had more than 600,000 men in forty divisions, with some 400 tanks and over 3,000 artillery guns deployed in Kuwait and South-East Iraq. They had built a defensive barrier round Kuwait consisting of minefields, sand walls, razor wire fences and oil-filled ditches. With an estimated further twenty divisions with 1,000 tanks and 1,000 guns in Central and Northern areas, the Iraqi forces totalled more than a million ground troops, and seemingly presented formidable opposition and deadly potential.

LOGISTIC SUPPORT IN UK – JHQ

In the Joint Headquarters at RAF High Wycombe the Land Logistics Staff was headed by Brigadier Simon Firth, an Infantry officer, whose senior maintenance staff officer was Lieutenant Colonel Richard Peregrine. The latter headed the Maintenance/Equipment Management Cell which included one or two majors and a captain night watchkeeper during critical periods. JHQ, as far as logistics were concerned, could be said in broad terms to be responsible for pulling the UK end of GRANBY logistics together, trying to foresee requirements and organizing the sending of resources forward.

The tasks of the Maintenance Cell were summarized by the SO1:

- Firstly, and most stressful, was to brief upwards. As they were next down the chain from Ministers and MOD, and equipment matters were in very high profile, there had to be an instant response to an endless string of questions. This sometimes proved difficult and five impossible questions before breakfast were definitely not good for the digestion! Briefs included explaining and interpreting technical matters and this was particularly important to avoid misinterpretations of complex technical detail by those at the top. Every effort was made to answer questions, without involving and overwhelming those on the ground in the Gulf with seemingly limitless interrogations. It was not always easy in this respect, because of our hierarchical and democratically accountable system.
- Secondly to provide Maintenance and Equipment Management input to the planners. It seemed to the Cell that everyone was making plans the whole time, and the important thing was to avoid anyone making up their own version of a maintenance plan without an input! It was vital to ensure that the right information was disseminated, both up and down, on the Maintenance net, and this necessitated our fingers being kept on the pulse the whole time.
- Thirdly to keep in frequent touch with the FMA to try and identify its problems and requirements and route them back to those in UK or BAOR who were best able to help. In this JHQ received superb help on the REME net from BAOR and LE(A) and their staffs at all levels.

There was no doubt that the great importance of logistics was taken very seriously by those in high places at JHQ, particularly in those matters affecting equipment. The interest in sustainability, and the provision of resources to enable it to be achieved when required, was at a high level; it is discussed later in this chapter when considering the implications of achieving adequate support in the field.

LOGISTIC SUPPORT IN UK – HQ DGEME

General

The problems that confronted the Equipment Managers at HQ DGEME at Andover once Operation GRANBY was put into effect were many and varied, and to overcome them required the utmost co-operation between LE(A), the Procurement Executive, Industry, and many Service organizations. Because involvement in land operations in the Gulf were never envisaged, most of the arrangements for the deployment of the Force had to be hastily devized. Equipment with units in BAOR and reinforcing units in UK was unbalanced, both in disposition and condition, and consequently so was its overall support requirement. This was not only because of shortages, but because the requirement now was to operate equipment under very different conditions from those for which it was intended. Some of the resulting problems for which solutions had to be found, and co-ordinated across the wide range of agencies that helped in solving them, are considered in the following paragraphs.

Electronics

One of the greatest difficulties facing the equipment managers at HQ DGEME concerned with electronic systems equipment was not always knowing what required supporting and where. Units in BAOR preparing for deployment borrowed quantities of equipment from other similar units not then involved, in order to enhance their operational holdings and to provide ad hoc repair pools. For example, units of 7 Armoured Brigade Group deployed with far more than their unit entitlement of the Chemical Agent Monitor (CAM), so depleting depot stocks and other unit holdings. It then became impossible for the Equipment Manager to meet the operational requirements from existing stocks for GRANBY 1.5. To trace equipment, a census throughout the UK and BAOR had to take place during the turbulent period of out-loading and unit training. Sufficient CAMs were recovered but only 60% were serviceable and fit for immediate redeployment. The contractor could not meet the replacement demand so special repair programmes were set up at the Chemical Defence Establishment, Porton, and at 34 Base Workshop. Another example concerned the Royal Artillery who, at the start of GRANBY 1, were to deploy one regiment but eventually, by GRANBY 1.5, deployed five. The initial regiment borrowed FACE items from four other regiments and the RA Gunnery Training Establishment to make an additional in-theatre repair pool, but unfortunately HQ DGEME was not aware of the distribution of much of this equipment.

The complete CLANSMAN radio repair pool had to be reissued because the equipment sent from BAOR could not be traced to its ultimate recipients. A similar situation was repeated throughout the electronic area and affected critical systems such as PTARMIGAN. Cannibalization added to the equipment managers' problems. In order to provide spares to support the two RAPIER batteries deployed on GRANBY 1.5 it was necessary for the rest of the BAOR fleet to be cannibalized, but this was often without the knowledge of the equipment manager at LE(A). BAOR also had to strip major assemblies from their Tracked RAPIER fleet for in-theatre support for the 150 M548 tracked cargo carriers which were leased from the Americans.

Many Urgent Operational Requirement items were bought off the shelf with, inevitably in an emergency, little or no consideration for their logistic support; although invaluable to the users, they proved a nightmare for equipment managers. As a result of the lack of back-up for many of the systems purchased, contract support for spares and repair had to be hastily arranged. A subsequent post-GRANBY review revealed that there had been over 750 such individual items costing £440M. These included computers, commercial marine satellite systems and the highly successful Global Positioning System, which provided a quick solution to the problem of navigating across featureless desert with inadequate maps.

An example of contractual involvement in the preparations was the sending of a British Aerospace team to Dortmund to work with the REME technicians and conduct overall systems tests on the RAPIER fleet for GRANBY 1.5. Plessey and Cooltech provided engineers to install air-conditioning into PTARMIGAN switches before they deployed on GRANBY 1, and later sent a team to the Gulf to continue the work. General Dynamics provided contract support for Hummel VHF jammer vehicles and Fuchs NBC reconnaissance vehicles in the Gulf, in view of REME's total lack of experience of these equipments.

Typical of the help provided by other units and establishments concerned the intercept troop equipment which was normally based on 1 tonne vehicles. R SIGNALS, helped by REME Technical Services and 23 Base Workshop in BAOR, designed and made prototype installations for this equipment, to be installed in the tracked FV432. The kits were manufactured and sent out to the Gulf and fitted to twelve FV432. Similarly, the Royal Signals and Radar Establishment, Malvern, and the Royal School of Signals developed and built the interconnecting boxes, whilst 43 District Workshop made the brackets needed to install the highly successful secure speech system for VHF Combat Net Radio.

An indication of the enormous extent of the support provided for electronic equipment is given by two examples. CLANSMAN radios operating in a benign electronic environment had up to 30% surplus to unit entitlement, three times the normal war maintenance reserve and repair pool stocks, and a spares scaling equivalent to three months' tri-service global usage. RAPIER was deployed with at least three times its normal spares scaling and double its normal support. It was to achieve a peak availability of 96% and maintained an average availability well above its EMPS target during the later stages of the campaign.

Mechanical Systems

Mechanical systems equipment managers at the LE(A) faced similar difficulties to the electronic equipment managers. Their overall task in the preparatory phase of mounting GRANBY was to identify what was needed and whether the requirement was for complete equipments or support items and assemblies. It was then a matter of finding out whether BAOR could provide the items, whether they were available from UKLF, or which contractors could provide them in time. It needed very close co-operation between the equipment managers in Andover and in BAOR to produce what was needed.

There was an immense amount of cannibalization of the A vehicle fleet remaining in BAOR to produce assemblies that were required as a result of the high sustainability needed in the Gulf. Because of the anticipated conditions, a low durability of equipment had to be assumed, and this added to the number of assemblies required. Cannibalization was the only course open at the time. Many assemblies in the peacetime repair pool that would normally meet this requirement were now unfit; they were in pieces, through lack of funds for spares to repair them. LE(A) had to arrange to buy more than a million pounds worth of packing cases for these cannibalized assemblies, as well as buying many new engines and gearboxes from the contractors.

Arrangements were made in the UK with the project managers and prime contractors to obtain several long-needed modifications for the A Vehicle fleet. These modifications had been developed for some time but there had been no funds to buy them. Now they became available and were sent to the Gulf and fitted to the vehicles on the quayside in Al Jubayl. CHALLENGER and WARRIOR up-armouring also produced significant control problems for the equipment managers, in planning and tracking the movement of hundreds of vehicle armour sets which were sent to the Gulf and, after trials, were fitted in the desert.

The vehicles sent direct from UK, which included twenty-three CHALLENGER tanks, WARRIORs, and a number of CVR(T), were prepared in 18 Base Workshop and 27 District Workshop. The Workshops, as well as Vehicles and Weapons Branch, proved and documented all the modifications very thoroughly before allowing the contractors to go ahead en masse. Important improvements were made in the build standard and spares for the TN37 gearbox, as the result of detailed discussions between equipment managers, project managers, contractors, Vehicles and Weapons Branch and 23 Base Workshop. This was followed by direct delivery of spares from the manufacturer to 23 Base Workshop in BAOR, which enabled it to reduce its large pile of unfit assemblies and to base repair about 30% of the cannibalized assemblies before they were sent out to the Gulf.

REME support for the operation from UK was hampered by lack of efficient dedicated Equipment Management communications and Information Technology links between the UK and the Gulf. When, for example, the QMG asked DGEME to track all 548 CHALLENGER CV12 engines, including those fitted in the tanks, the equipment managers had great difficulty because the engines were then en route between BAOR, UK, contractors and the Gulf. Information Technology links would have made the task of tracing such movement much swifter and more accurate.

Although most of the problems concerned A Vehicles, arrangements also had to be made for the provision and support of specialist B vehicles not available from BAOR. In Aldershot 27 Regiment RCT was warned in November to move to the Gulf to provide third-line support for GRANBY 1.5. One of the squadrons, 7 Squadron, had just returned with its REME support from BAOR, where it had been detached to assist with the out-loading for GRANBY 1. For this new task in the Gulf the Regiment was issued with fifty-four 14 tonne and twenty-four new design All Wheel Drive (AWD) fuel tankers instead of their standard establishment 8 tonne vehicles. The Workshop to accompany the Regiment was formed from the three independent workshops of 7, 8 and 66 Squadrons and thirty-eight tradesmen from twelve units throughout the UK. They made a combined Workshop of one officer and ninety soldiers under the command of Captain Jim McDonald. In the next few weeks the new vehicles were received and an extensive training programme carried out, including driver training for the AWD tankers. The Workshop worked a twenty-four hour series of shifts over ten days to bring the vehicles up to standard before embarkation. From 1–14 December 350 prime movers and trailers moved to Marchwood Military Port for shipping to Al Jubayl, accompanied by maintenance parties. The main body of the Regiment followed by air at the end of the month.

Tyre Changing Facility

In an area where the terrain and mileages involved would impose much wear and tear on tyres, an anticipated major problem was to change them rapidly. The problem was exacerbated by the size and wheel-handling difficulties of the new ranges of vehicles such as DROPS, and steps were taken to produce an answer. On 7 September 1990 11 MAG received a telephone call from HQ DGEME at 0935 hours asking it to consider the feasibility of building an independent tyre changing facility for the Gulf. This was to be based on the DROPS Rack, and to be capable of changing tyres up to the size of those fitted to the DROPS vehicles. An answer, with the cost of non-standard items and time required to

Tyre changing facility designed by 11 MAG

produce two facilities, was required by 1200 hours that day! The reply given at 1200 hours confirmed that the idea was feasible and that each rack would cost about £10,000 and take 11 MAG two weeks to build.

Each rack required a 16/24 kW generator to power the compressor to inflate tyres and tubes and to provide air for both the large and small tyre-changing equipment. These, together with a tyre-inflation safety cage, made up the equipment capable of dealing with wheels up to sixty inch diameter. The order for production to start was given on 20 September, and by 4 October (the original deadline) the two facilities were complete and had been tested. Two operators arrived from BAOR on 7 October for training on a two day course and on 11 October the two racks were sent to Marchwood for shipping to the Gulf, where they were soon in full use. Two more were ordered for 1st (British) Armoured Division and delivered to Marchwood on 12 December. How this was done and who did it was described in the 1991 REME Journal.

Aircraft

Twenty-three LYNX Mark 7 helicopters and twenty-three GAZELLEs (including five of each as reserves) from the AAC, with their REME support, were sent to the Gulf. Eighteen LYNX were fitted with the TOW anti-tank system and a further five were fitted with an improved system. One ISLANDER and one AGUSTA A109 were also sent. AAC involvement in the operation was only decided at a late stage in the planning, with the result that funding for some of the necessary modifications was not authorized until four weeks before the aircraft deployed. Modifications had to be designed and developed in-house at no cost. The Gem engine fitted to the LYNX proved to be the most demanding of the engines and major assemblies deployed to the Gulf. Repair was centralized in 70 Aircraft Workshop, Middle Wallop, to husband assets of the seven modules comprising the engine. The Workshop replaced unfit modules to produce, after test, an operational engine; the defective modules were then repaired by Rolls Royce and the Royal Navy.

There were two major aircraft equipment support tasks during the mounting phase of GRANBY:

- First, the identification, selection and preparation of suitable aircraft and reserve assets including assemblies and spares. This resulted in many transfers of aircraft, equipment and assemblies from unit to unit in UK and in BAOR. Six LYNX of the remaining fleet were grounded to provide spare assemblies. These preparations were not helped by the fact that at about the same time, for operational reasons, the already high Northern Ireland flying rate was increased, placing an additional strain on resources.
- The second and largest task was to design, develop, test, clear and manufacture the various modifications needed to meet

enhanced operational capability and interoperability requirements. All the modifications had to be produced to full airworthiness standards. This was not easy in view of the involvement of such geographically and philosophically disparate organizations as Aerospatiale in France, Trimble Navigation (USA) and the Aircraft and Armament Experimental Establishment at Boscombe Down. All the design and development work was carried out in the UK, but the majority of the modification sets were sent to the Gulf for embodiment because of the lack of time available in BAOR before deployment. The major part of the staffing and planning of the activities in the mounting phase was carried out by HQ DAAC and EME 9, but the wealth of detailed engineering work and a sizeable share of the planning was done by Aircraft Branch.

REME SUPPORT IN CYPRUS

HQ British Forces Cyprus

Lieutenant Colonel Stuart Cameron was DACOS G4 Maint HQ British Forces Cyprus in the summer of 1990, when events in the Gulf raised the security state in the island to levels not seen since the Turkish invasion in 1974. Land and air forces were put on a high state of readiness to protect and operate the airfield at Akrotiri. The Maintenance Branch helped to man the Joint Operations Centre Logistic Cell, co-ordinating the engineering effort needed to maintain the high usage rates of most land equipment. It also found itself responsible for the maintenance of three RN vessels.

Both the Force Workshop at Akrotiri and the Eastern Sovereign Base Area Workshop at Dhekelia were involved in preparations on the ground. Although the workshop at Dhekelia spent many hundreds of extra man-hours in support of the local infantry battalion and 62 (Cyprus) Support Squadron RE, most of the burden fell on the Force Workshop which was at the centre of operational activity.

Force Workshop, Akrotiri

From 2 August 1990 Major Andy Philp and ASM Lynch found that they had an enormous increase in their workload at Akrotiri. RAF Akrotiri, about half-way between UK and the Gulf, was an important staging post for transport aircraft, tanker support and transit sorties during GRANBY. The air traffic passing through over the period was equivalent to nearly ten years at the normal peacetime rate. For this flow of aircraft the airfield was continuously open, and there was therefore much greater use of the airfield support vehicles which were maintained by the Force Workshop.

At the start of GRANBY the Workshop was reinforced by thirteen RAF MT technicians, much needed for the additional load, which included extra mechanical handling equipment and airfield equipment – mainly unique single equipments requiring close support from the fitters to keep them serviceable. One such vehicle was the low-profile tug used for moving TRISTAR aircraft. It was flown to Akrotiri in a BELFAST and a HERCULES aircraft, assembled over the weekend under the close supervision of the workshop officer and was operational on the Monday morning. REME warrant officers were employed additionally in the air weapons storage facility, the role of which had expanded dramatically.

Other parts of the Workshop were faced with an equally wide range of additional loads. The Electronic Repair Section repaired CLANSMAN radios for 34 Squadron RAF who were deployed in the Gulf whilst, in contrast, the A & G Section produced nine kilometres of dunnage to move cargo onwards to the Gulf and various ramps to help with the evacuation of stretchers out of any aircraft landing at Akrotiri. Perhaps surprisingly, the tradesmen in greatest demand were the RAF carpenters. These tradesmen were required to make wooden supports to enable huge quantities of weapons ex-UK to be stored efficiently in the limited space available: work requiring an enormous amount of wood and many man-hours. The REME element of the Workshop also contributed to the military duties of the Station, a REME sergeant being second-in-command of the RAF Akrotiri Station Guard Force for most of the Gulf War and other members of the Workshop providing part of the guard.

REME BUILD-UP AND RESPONSIBILITIES IN SAUDI ARABIA – GRANBY 1

GRANBY 1 – General

The first individual REME soldier to arrive in the Gulf under GRANBY 1 was Lance Corporal M N James, who was attached to 30th Signal Regiment from 21 August. He was followed on 2 October by the first REME officer to arrive, Major Cliff Coward, who filled the post of SO2 J4 Maint in the Joint HQ of British Forces Middle East, then being established at Riyadh. Thereafter REME individuals and units arrived in a steady if not always adequate stream, the first providing the REME element of the FMA. HQ FMA was established under GRANBY 1 at Al Jubayl by mid-October, and with its full range of affiliated logistic units was ready to receive men and equipment of the Force arriving by sea and air, and to maintain it. Its first major task was to use all its facilities to reunite personnel with their equipment, which would then be brought up to a fit state for deployment and training after required modifications. As described in Chapter 6, the REME element in the HQ FMA was headed by Lieutenant Colonel Alastair Campbell, joined initially by Majors Paul Marsden, Steve Colling, Bob Mears and Sergeant Taff Hollis. Their task was to control first- and second-line REME support within the FMA and to provide Equipment Management advice and control for Theatre forces. On 21 December the HQ FMA received the welcome addition of three Maintenance staff officers and three warrant officers expert in A vehicles, guided weapons, artillery, electronics and turret systems.

Initially, for GRANBY 1, the FMA equipment support was to be provided by MRG 7B from 7 Armoured Workshop and later, after GRANBY 1.5, by 6 Armoured Workshop. Their activities are described later in this chapter. In the narrative there is, however, an inevitable overlapping of activities and time scale, between those elements which arrived under GRANBY 1 and those arriving under GRANBY 1.5. Where it is clearer to do so, the overall activity of a unit is included in its first mention in the chapter. Where operational timings are of greater importance, the unit may be included more than once in appropriate phases of activity.

Force Maintenance Area

The organization of the Maintenance and Equipment Management Staff in the HQ FMA at its peak is shown at Annex B, and amounted to forty-five REME, plus up to thirty UK contractors' representatives. Lieutenant Colonel Campbell emphasized, in his description of the functions of the HQ, the necessity of HQ FMA REME staff being double-hatted to cover both Maintenance and Equipment Management responsibilities. The FMA Maintenance Operations function, which was not critical in the early stages, was carried out by HQ 7 Armoured Workshop on their arrival, and continued whilst it remained within the FMA. On the Workshop's deployment, the Maintenance Cell in HQ FMA took over. Double-hatting worked well despite adverse comments from the FMA Workshop, and it was absolutely necessary that Equipment Management had the authority to task FMA Maintenance resources. The Maintenance and Equipment Management functions were widely overlapping at the critical stage and could not sensibly have been separated at FMA level.

Equipment Management co-ordinated the Quayside Modifications Programme, for which armoured vehicle crews from regiments and their LADs, and teams from 7 Armoured Workshop were joined in strength by engineers from a number of UK civilian contractors. The civilian element of the teams had been authorized by MOD on 11 October to help carry out the modifications to CHALLENGERs and WARRIORs under Lieutenant Colonel Campbell's control. The Vickers Defence Systems team of fifteen arrived on 17 October and teams from other contractors swiftly followed. The programme for CHALLENGERs was supervised by 7 Armoured Workshop and was carried out in a large dockside warehouse, which had been earmarked for the purpose on the original reconnaissance described in Chapter 6. A similar but smaller programme was carried out for WARRIORs.

A total of fourteen modifications, including vital air filtration improvements, were completed on each of 221 CHALLENGERs. All assemblies and systems were thoroughly inspected and repaired or replaced if necessary. The knowledge of the specialist engineers from Vickers Defence Systems, Perkins, David Brown Gear Transmissions, Barr and Stroud and Marconi was passed on to the CHALLENGER crews and the REME personnel involved. Similarly, action was taken by the GKN representatives for WARRIOR, and modified air filter seals were an important modification fitted by REME technicians with GKN supervision. Land Rover also sent out representatives to check their vehicles, which were widely used by the Force.

In the desert civilian contractors worked with units to improve their operating and maintenance skills, and the crews and LADs learned much from the contractor's experience with their vehicles. During later firing practices specialist contractors also helped crews and technicians to improve their diagnostic and repair skills. Crew run-up and checking procedures for turret systems were well rehearsed, reported faults were quickly rectified, and confidence in equipment grew considerably. Later, as larger training exercises took place which tested the equipment even more thoroughly, there were more visits from representatives of UK contractors. These included the Siemens Plessey team with eight civilians and four military, and Mr Boxall. the Chairman and Chief Executive of Vickers Defence Systems who had made his first visit to gauge effects of the modification programme on CHALLENGER performance on 30 October and then returned to meet the tank crews and engineers maintaining CHALLENGERs and ARRV. Mr Kenneth Smith, of Aircraft Porous Media Europe, visited to advise mainly on air filter fits to LYNX and GAZELLE helicopters, but also covering CHALLENGER and WARRIOR, whilst Mr James of Westland Helicopters and Mr Raynsford of Rolls Royce advised 4 Regiment AAC Workshop and MRG 71 Aircraft Workshop.

Equipment Management staff worked closely and continuously with the operational staff, especially giving advice and predictions of equipment sustainability in terms of kilometres per equipment and MDBF (Mean Distance Between Failure) for major assemblies such as power packs, engines and gearboxes for CHALLENGERs and WARRIORs. At one point in November they briefed a 'fourteen star' meeting at Riyadh on CHALLENGER sustainability predictions. Additionally, formation commanders were briefed weekly by Lieutenant Colonel Campbell on critical equipment sustainability and enhancement, until a few days before ground operations began on 24 February 1991.

One of the problems that arose with some FMA units arriving in the Theatre, which was of considerable staff concern, was the manpower restriction on unit strengths imposed by MOD. In the jargon of the day they were 'manpower capped' before leaving BAOR or UK. This resulted in units drastically reducing their supporting REME manpower in favour of their own specialists. Several units for example, especially TA units and small sub-units with only attached REME tradesmen, were left without the necessary REME manpower to provide adequate first-line support. This support deficiency had to be met by spreading the load between other units and placed an additional strain on REME tradesmen whose units were already fully committed. Typical of this situation was that of 33 General Hospital in Al Jubayl which arrived with only one vehicle mechanic, Craftsman Reynolds, to provide first-line support for its fleet of ambulances, buses and its 10 kVA and 40 kVA generators providing power for the hospital. 205 (Scottish) General Hospital (V) in Bahrain similarly had only one TA corporal vehicle mechanic, Corporal Alan Grey, who had to lean on the RAF Station for help. The Armoured Delivery Squadron which later formed the basis of the Armoured Delivery Group fared no better and arrived in the Gulf with only one vehicle mechanic. This was a Corporal Speed who, after only a short time, was affectionately called ASM by all the unit staff from OC to trooper as he became the centre of excellence on all manner of tracked vehicles. The Vehicle Company of 6 Ordnance Battalion, which held and maintained hundreds of War Maintenance Reserve vehicles from hire cars to FV430 and M109, had only five fitters. The other companies of 6 Ordnance Battalion had similar problems. There was a further complication in that some units had also deployed without adequate tools, block scales or technical publications.

The solution to these support deficiencies was that sub-units and detachments in the Al Jubayl area without, or with inadequate, REME support were put on the dependency of HQ FMA and its Signal Squadron LAD. Most of these attached tradesmen worked eighteen hours a day, seven days a week without complaint, and produced excellent results despite poor accommodation, lack of tools and a shortage of spares. It was a problem still requiring constant supervision when Major Eric Hollingsworth arrived at HQ FMA in early January as BEME and took over the responsibility for organizing this support. MRG 6 later gave help in the short term with loans of men and by taking on some of the longer repairs. The arrival of Major Tim Scarlett and his REME Battle Casualty Replacements (BCRs), albeit not until January, enabled a pool of REME tradesmen to be formed who provided BCRs, a reclamation platoon of thirty, and tradesmen to fill key posts in FMA units.

HQ FMA initially produced an area recovery plan for the Al Jubayl area and south to Riyadh and Bahrain. Later, when the Forward Force Maintenance Area (FFMA) was established and 1st Armoured Division moved north to its Divisional Assembly Area at KEYES, the main supply routes (MSR) DODGE and HORSE were included in the plan, making a responsibility for 800 kilometres of roads. There were only six second-line recovery vehicles at MRG 6 and limited access to 10 and 27 Regiments RCT recovery vehicles; it was a demanding task. To provide communications and to limit travelling time, recovery vehicles were placed with RMP detachments at the critical Traffic Control Points on the MSRs. 'Flying fitters' were sent when recovery vehicle assets were exhausted or only minor repairs were required. Volunteers were normally eager and plentiful, as it was a means of escape for a few hours from day-to-day routine. But early one morning a Casualty Report came in for help with a broken-down refrigerated mortuary vehicle. Volunteers were backward in coming forward until it was confirmed that it was unloaded!

7 Armoured Workshop
The preparation for the move of the Workshop from BAOR to the Gulf is dealt with in some detail in Chapter 6. The personnel of the Workshop were complete at Al Jubayl by 23 October, at a strength of 595 all ranks, under command of Lieutenant Colonel Rod Croucher. For the first three weeks the whole Workshop was based in the dock area, whilst vehicles and equipment were received from the ships. In fact, the first ship to arrive from BAOR contained mainly vehicles for the Workshop, and MRG 7A, once complete, moved into a quayside warehouse ready to begin work on its first task of modifications to CHALLENGERs and WARRIORs when they arrived. The temperature in the warehouse during the modification programme rose to 120°F during the day and

Challenger modification for the Gulf War

working conditions were highly uncomfortable. Nevertheless, the CHALLENGER programme went extremely smoothly and there were no major hitches apart from the rather late discovery that an essential part of the air filtration ducting – a blue hose – had been removed from the vehicles. After a massive search sufficient hoses were recovered from various sources and the panic was over. Testing and repairing of power packs received from the cannibalization of vehicles in BAOR was carried out at the same time and was a lengthy task, but the overall modification period was useful in providing acclimatization for most of the Workshop. Personal fitness was very important and helped greatly in the process of acclimatization, but fitness training during this period was not easy as for much of the time everyone was working twelve-hour shifts. Other personal training had also to be fitted in whenever possible, including first aid, NBC, desert driving, navigation, and health and hygiene.

Once the CHALLENGERs and WARRIORs had been modified they were sent out in squadron and company groups to the 7 Armoured Brigade training area 50 kilometres north of Al Jubayl for training, followed by live firing. Some problems occurred on WARRIOR engines which required in-depth investigation and advice from the engine manufacturer, Perkins, whose representatives were now in the Gulf. Subsequently a programme of health checks and air filter modifications for 324 WARRIORs was carried out. FRG 7 provided initial support for the Brigade training, and the optronics platoon from MRG 7B also went out to the training area to support live-firing exercises. Contractor support, as well as REME support, was provided for the important live-firing period 5–10 November. The remainder of MRG 7B remained in the port to provide equipment support to units still arriving, many at first without their own LADs or regimental workshops. Following the work-up exercises, the MOD authorized funds for the purchase of seventy-three CHALLENGER engines and twenty-nine gearboxes, which was good news following

MRG 7B lifting a Warrior turret

relatively low reliability experienced during exercises. Early on, JHQ in UK had used greater reliability figures in calculating the sustainability of CHALLENGERs than were experienced under actual conditions. As a result, on 5 December a Maintenance Branch brief on CHALLENGER sustainability, using updated figures, was produced for the Joint Commander.

In mid-December MRGs 7A and 7B were exchanged to allow 7B to gain experience of desert operations and problems. Subsequently, after the arrival of 4 Armoured Brigade units on GRANBY 1.5, 7 Armoured Workshop found itself carrying out another modification programme as well as continuing to provide support to training. MRG 7B was in the desert with 7 Armoured Brigade, and MRG 7A was located in the port area in 'Container City' – an old grain storage area surrounded by ISO containers.

All the support to the initial training of 4 Armoured Brigade was provided by 7 Armoured Workshop which was therefore supporting two extra WARRIOR battalions and one extra CHALLENGER regiment as well as 7 Armoured Brigade, which was still training. By mid-January there were nearly one hundred vehicles awaiting major repair by MRG 7B; during one week at that time the optronics platoon accepted over 1,000 tasks. Some tradesmen worked shifts of up to twenty hours a day. However, this situation was soon alleviated when 11 Armoured Workshop, which had arrived in Al Jubayl in December, was able to deploy FRG 6 to Devil Dog Dragoon Range 100 kilometres north to support 4 Armoured Brigade, with which it remained.

10 Regiment RCT Workshop

10 Regiment RCT, with the addition of 16 Squadron from 7 Tank Transporter Regiment RCT, equipped with twenty-three Scammell COMMANDER tank transporters and 12 Squadron from 8 Regiment RCT equipped with sixty DROPS vehicles, became an RCT Group. The Group Workshop was commanded initially by Captain Dennis Prowse and, from December 1990, by Captain Jim Chadwick; they were supported throughout by ASM Bill Collings. With a strength of over 100 it faced the considerable task of supporting a wide range of vehicles under what were to prove exceptionally arduous conditions: how well this was achieved would soon be demonstrated. The advance party of the Regiment had left Germany for the Gulf on 19 October 1990, and the remainder followed soon afterwards. 16 Squadron was located in the dock area of Al Jubayl with its tank transporters, and the remainder of the Regiment, together with the Workshop, was set up in Baldrick Lines, a tented camp. As well as the heavy support load within the Regiment, the Workshop helped some of the small units and echelons in the Al Jubayl area which, as described earlier, were deficient of their own REME support. It also provided recovery within the area assigned by BEME FMA.

Within 10 Regiment, the main task of 9 Squadron, equipped with the new AWD tankers, was refuelling and replenishment of the Bulk Fuel Installations and providing the FMA fuel point. 12 Squadron was the first unit equipped with DROPS and in its first eight weeks moved 6 million litres of water, 1,500 ISO containers and 7,000 tons of ammunition. On 2 November, two Leyland DAF engineers arrived on a visit to examine DROPS vehicles employed by the Regiment in the Gulf, one of whom remained behind indefinitely to give technical support. His time was not wasted, as on 27 November serious defects were discovered on the vehicles when the flat racks started to bend. This defect could have put the bulk distribution of fuel and water with DROPS at risk, with serious effects on the overall logistic support of the division. Propeller shaft failures on nineteen vehicles also threatened off-road capability. The manufacturer's representatives resolved the problem by allowing ten-thousandths of an inch end float, and the local purchase and issue of a grease-gun for frequent use on each vehicle. The harsh terrain also caused both DROPS tanks and AWD tankers to suffer weld cracks, but this was contained by frequent inspection and repairs by unit welders.

17 Squadron carried over 16,000 tons of ammunition in its 8 tonne and 14 tonne vehicles in the first few weeks. 16 Tank Transporter Squadron was busy from the first day moving armour from MRG 7B in the port area, after completion of desertization, to the brigade exercise locations in the desert. All these tasks had been supported by the Workshop, and when Captain Chadwick arrived the scene changed to an even more intensive period of activity. By then the Workshop considered themselves old hands, and most of the teething problems with equipment were known and the cures well understood. 16 Squadron, together with its REME element, reverted to command of 7 Tank Transporter Regiment RCT on Christmas Day, when the remainder of that Regiment arrived at Al Jubayl. Early in January 1991 17 Squadron of 10 Regiment RCT, including fitters and recovery crews, moved to an area halfway up MSR DODGE in support of the Regiment and other users. On 20 January the whole Regiment moved to the FFMA to provide support to 1st Armoured Division. 9 Squadron with its REME element moved west from the FFMA to Log Base ECHO on 15 February 1991, and eventually became the forward squadron of the Regiment, following the division into Iraq and Kuwait.

7 Tank Transporter Regiment RCT Workshop

On 18 October 1990 7 Tank Transporter Regiment Workshop sent ASM Chedzoy and fourteen REME tradesmen, known as the 'Desert Detachment', to support twenty Scammell COMMANDER tank transporters and three solo tractor units of 16 Tank Transporter Squadron in the Gulf; they were to be attached to 10 Regiment RCT Group until the remainder of the Regiment was sent out. These vehicles had been loaded at Bremerhaven on 28 September 1990 as part of GRANBY 1, and the Detachment's work soon grew when 7 Armoured Brigade began training in the desert. In the nine weeks to Christmas 1990 the transporters carried more than 2,000 armoured vehicles over a distance exceeding 250,000 kilometres, and the Workshop maintained 98% availability of Scammell COMMANDERs throughout this period.

The remainder of 7 Tank Transporter Regiment RCT started to arrive at Al Jubayl at Christmas, joined from the UK by extra men and vehicles from 414 Tank Transporter Unit at Bulford. In early January *Atlantic Conveyor II*, successor to the ill-fated ship sunk in the Falklands campaign in 1982, landed several hundred vehicles including the final Scammell COMMANDERs: these built up the Regiment to seventy-two trains and ten solo tractor units. The arrival of Major David Clutson and more REME and RAOC soldiers brought the Workshop up to a strength of one officer and fifty-three soldiers.

From mid-January the Regiment had a three-week task to move 1st Armoured Division more than 300 kilometres north-west along MSRs DODGE and HORSE, creating much activity within the Workshop with many new problems not encountered in BAOR. After only one trip up MSR HORSE – a forty-five kilometres, 'cross country nightmare' connecting DODGE to KEYES – the Workshop was busy developing 'Rattle Damage Repairs' to overcome the destructive effects of the surface of the desert route. However, the Scammell COMMANDERs, as well as the Foden recovery vehicle, proved to be very good in the conditions under which they operated. Only twice did the Workshop fail to produce a minimum availability of 85 per cent: on both occasions during the post-war recovery phase.

The Regiment moved back to Al Jubayl on 7 March, except for elements of 12 Squadron and fitters who helped to outload the FFMA. The final REME packet returned from the Gulf on 24 March. RCT statistics show that the Regiment covered 2.7 million kilometres during the operation, carrying more than 7,700 armoured vehicles, including United States Army tanks and artillery. Its Workshop completed 13,000 man-hours of work, including eighty-seven major assembly changes, fifty-four of them CV12 engines which were sent back to BAOR and turned round quickly by 23 Base Workshop in Wetter, a not inconsiderable achievement by all concerned.

27 Regiment RCT Workshop

After a few days acclimatizing in Baldrick Lines, 27 Regiment RCT, which arrived from UK in late December, deployed to various parts of Al Jubayl, and its Workshop brought the equipment up to standard and provided REME support to B echelons in the area. Just before the start of the air war the Regiment moved to a quarry on the outskirts of Al Jubayl, from which the squadrons and their integral REME support were tasked at a variety of locations between Al Jubayl and the FFMA. 27 Regiment took on the re-supply of the FFMA from Al Jubayl – a loop of 700 kilometres, for which the support given by its Workshop proved fully adequate. On 24 February 1991 the forward squadron of 27 Regiment RCT followed the battle through the breach into Iraq. By the cease-fire on 28 February the Regiment and the Workshop were spread over an area from the Divisional Harbour area north of Kuwait City and south to Al Jubayl. Most of the Regiment left the Gulf on 9 April 1991, having brought back stores and ammunition from various desert locations to the port area of Al Jubayl for backloading by sea. A depleted 66 Squadron with its REME fitters remained in Al Jubayl until June, helping to clear up. The Regiment's vehicles covered over 4 million kilometres during the Gulf operation with their task vehicles maintaining an availability of around 95%, a figure which indicates the excellent support provided by the Workshop.

THE CHANGING REME SITUATION ON IMPLEMENTATION OF GRANBY 1.5

GRANBY 1.5 – General

The events leading up to the dispatch of 1st (British) Armoured Division from BAOR in December 1990 under GRANBY 1.5 have been described in Chapter 6. The division was placed under the tactical control of the US Marine Corps. There was a considerable increase in REME units and personnel as a result of the Force in the Gulf being brought up to divisional strength, with a full divisional slice of supporting arms and logistic units. By mid-January the REME strength in the Theatre was 3,436 all ranks. A total of 2,611 A vehicles and 12,069 B and C vehicles had been brought into the Theatre and became their support responsibility. In addition, there was the mixed armament of four RA regiments, R SIGNALS equipments, and forty-six AAC helicopters of the AAC regiment, with each regiment requiring its own specialized support.

All the elements of the Force dispatched separately to the Gulf under GRANBY 1 and 1.5 were now merging to become an integrated Force. In REME's case three armoured workshops and an aircraft workshop were now on the ground and were allocated to their specific operational tasks, spread between the FMA, FFMA and forward with the division. Commander Maintenance 1st Armoured Division had now arrived with his HQ, and assumed responsibility for REME support of the whole division; Regimental workshops and LADs were complete and married up with their respective units. The overall REME support for the Force was now in place. Examples of the activities of REME staff at headquarters, workshops and LADs and their tasks across the whole spectrum of unit support are given in the following paragraphs.

Headquarters British Forces Middle East

In Riyadh the REME element of HQ BFME was being assembled, and on 15 December Lieutenant Colonel Ken Postgate arrived to fill the senior maintenance appointment, quickly followed by Major John Plumb as his Aviation specialist. Sadly, on 20 December the Corps was to have its first casualty of the war when Major Andrew Burch died as the result of a road accident. He was serving in the G4 branch of HQ BFME and had been driving back on his own from a reconnaissance of the area for the FFMA adjacent to the American Logistics Base ALFA, some 350 kilometres north-west of Al Jubayl.

On Christmas Eve Colonel Peter Gibson arrived at the Headquarters to be Commander Maintenance Middle East, and joined up with those of his staff who had already arrived. As with the other Heads of Services at HQ BFME there was some doubt about their titles, and whether they should be designated Staff or Commanders. In the event they agreed jointly to call themselves by their appropriate Commander titles to avoid confusion in their contacts with BAOR where the title 'Commander' was standard. Colonel Gibson was also faced with some problems of communication, both in personal visits and transmissions of information. Visits were inhibited by the distance between Riyadh and Al Jubayl, which was about five hours drive by car, and it was not easy to keep in personal touch with the FMA and forward, by visiting. Other means of communication were affected both by the nature of the command chain and the means of disseminating information. Until early January the FMA was theoretically under command of HQ 1st (British) Armoured Division, although it had been working direct to HQ BFME for some time. There was undoubtedly uncertainty over the command chain for REME, but fortunately, despite aggravations, this was not allowed to impede the effectiveness of the support provided. He described his communications back to JHQ High Wycombe and to LE(A) Andover as appalling and, on the REME net, it was often easier for those Headquarters to deal direct with the FMA. This often meant that he was left out of the information loop, which could be somewhat tedious to say the least.

The roles of Commander Maintenance were never clearly defined by HQ BFME, but fell into place and, in the event, proved operable. There were four main roles defined by Colonel Gibson:

- To brief Commander British Forces Middle East on equipment sustainability, so that he in turn could confidently assure General Schwarzkopf that our equipment could cope with whatever the Americans asked of us. This required constant access to up-to-date reliability and usage data, which was in fact not always readily available.
- To provide sufficient equipment information to JHQ UK to

allow briefing of senior officers and Ministers, without their having to badger the FMA or the division for information.

- To lay down priorities for the use of rear area resources, and to fight for additional manpower and equipment that was essential for success.
- To assist Supply (RAOC) in dealing with spare parts and assembly problems, and in getting those items forward to the division.

HQ REME 1st (British) Armoured Division

The Commander Maintenance 1st Armoured Division, Lieutenant Colonel Andy Ashley, arrived in the Gulf with his Headquarters in December, and the REME strength in the division quickly built up to 2,500 all ranks. It was to prove of great benefit having in place those REME from the division who had arrived under GRANBY 1, and had been involved with the initial support problems on the ground. The knowledge and experience which they had gained helped to pave the way more smoothly for the support plan, now to be implemented for the whole division.

As previously mentioned, operational and functional command and control arrangements affecting REME were perhaps not perfect, and were to keep everybody on their toes for the rest of the campaign. The FMA for instance initially formed part of 7 Armoured Brigade Group and later, until early in January, was under command of 1st Armoured Division. It then passed to direct control of BFME in early January, once forward deployment of stocks started and the FFMA was established. For Lieutenant Colonel Ashley this unexpected change meant that he no longer had responsibility for 6 Armoured Workshop – MRG 6, which from early January was supporting the FMA at Al Jubayl, and for other REME elements within the FMA and, later, the FFMA.

On arrival in the Theatre, of greatest concern to Lieutenant Colonel Ashley was undoubtedly the reliability and sustainability of equipment, and of particular importance were engines of CHALLENGER and WARRIOR. He was not alone in his concern. Indications from first training reports were that the average lives of these engines were far lower than had been predicted and that the trend was downward. It was clear to him from the outset that the critical factor in achieving sustainability was the availability of complete power packs to replace failed engines. Coupled with this was the ability to rebuild rapidly the power packs that had been exchanged. Current experience suggested that more power packs would fail, based on a battlefield day of 60 kilometres, than could be rebuilt in time, and the stocks would steadily reduce. It was critical therefore to have a sufficient stock of power packs in the first place to keep pace with these failures. All stops were pulled out to obtain sufficient stocks, and the efforts of all those involved have been described in Chapter 6 and earlier in this chapter.

The quayside modification programme for CHALLENGER and WARRIOR started on the arrival of 7 Armoured Brigade at Al Jubayl, to help improve engine reliability in the desert conditions, continued with the arrival of the remainder of the division. The next consideration for Commander Maintenance was the up-armouring programme. Once the need had been established within MOD, there was intense activity in UK to provide the necessary fitments by all those concerned, and dispatch them to the Gulf. However, it was still necessary to carry out trials in the desert to assess the effect that the additional weight of three tonnes of extra armour would have on the performance of the vehicles concerned – CHALLENGER, WARRIOR and some RE C Vehicles. There was no argument about the benefits of ballistic protection, but at this stage, with engines failing often and at a steadily increasing rate, it was clearly unacceptable to have vehicles providing safety for the crews, but mechanically unable to reach their objective. To resolve this dilemma, all the factors had to be considered and the right balance achieved. A trial of a number of CHALLENGERs and WARRIORs that had already been modified and up-armoured under the programme controlled by E Man FMA was carried out in the desert by the division.

The trial looked at the speed and agility of the vehicles, both separately and in simulated combined assaults, fuel consumption, maintenance and recovery, as well as their ability to cope with bridging equipment and loading on to tank transporters. Unfortunately, there was insufficient track mileage to be able to assess the extra load on engines and general spares, but certainly the extra weight did not appear to make the operation of the vehicles significantly worse. The fitting of the armour to vehicles, both in camp and in the desert was also trialled and, at the end of the trials, the GOC 1st Armoured Division accepted the overall implications of up-armouring and the ability of unit crews and REME in the regiments to carry it out in the field. The whole programme of up-armouring was then drawn up by the Commander Maintenance and the divisional staff, and fitting was completed in the desert by unit crews and REME, directed by two specialist ASMs from Vehicles and Weapons Branch.

A programme of health checks and air filter modifications for 324 WARRIORs was implemented on 3 January. Later, when the WARRIOR CV8 engine life was dropping seriously, it was essential to increase quickly the number of replacement engines available in the Gulf. The repair time incurred by sending them back to Europe was twelve weeks, but examination in the Gulf revealed that the damage caused by dust and sand to the turbochargers, pistons and liners could be put right quite quickly if the spares and facilities were available. After taking advice from GKN, Perkins and Vickers Defence Systems, an extended second-line repair facility for CV8 engines was established in a Rubb Shelter on tarmac at Al Jubayl, which 6 Armoured Workshop MRG 6 operated from their arrival. By 24 February about twenty CV8 had been repaired; a total of thirty-six engines were completed in two months. They also repaired a CV12 engine for a Scammell and two for CHALLENGER tanks.

Establishment of the Forward Force Maintenance Area (FFMA)

Whilst elements of 1st Armoured Division were still arriving in the Theatre and beginning to train, plans were being made to establish the FFMA to support the division in offensive operations. By the end of December these plans were issued and the move forward of stocks to the FFMA started on 3 January. Elements of HQ FMA and units had begun to deploy forward on 1 January, to control and receive the incoming stocks. One essential REME element was the deployment of recovery vehicles at the traffic control posts. The FFMA was to be established on the edge of the American Logistics Base ALFA which consisted of a large rectangle of desert defended by berms and wire fences, just south of the Tapline road – MSR DODGE – some 350 kilometres from Al Jubayl. 1st Armoured Division Assembly Area KEYES was later to be some 50 kilometres further north-west, on the north side of MSR DODGE. By this time 6 Armoured Workshop (MRG 6) was established as the FMA workshop and was split between Al Jubayl and the FFMA now being established. In mid-January Major Hollingsworth, the BEME, Captain Bob Bone and a small staff moved north to set up the Maintenance/Equipment Management cell in HQ FFMA. Within 24 hours of setting up the HQ a warning sign for drivers appeared outside – 'DANGER OLD PEOPLE CROSSING'. The sign remained in place throughout the campaign. On 30 January 71 Aircraft Workshop MRG, less a small detachment, was also deployed forward to the FFMA.

On 8 January 150 M548s, the 6 ton tracked cargo vehicles, arrived on loan from the US Army. They were to be deployed to 1st Armoured Division to carry ammunition and packed fuel, as it was feared that the 8 tonne wheeled vehicles would be unable to cope with the difficult desert going. M548s were allocated direct to armoured, artillery and infantry regiments of the division and were supported by their LADs.

Workshops

Few visitors from outside the Theatre were encouraged, as units had no time to look after them during an intensive programme of preparation and training. Those who were accepted by HQ BFME were those whose presence was particularly desirable to aid the efforts of those involved in the campaign; the Prime Minister, John Major, was amongst this number. He arrived at Al Jubayl on 8 January and visited 7 Armoured Workshop in the FMA, the only logistic unit to be visited. The effect of this visit on the members of the Workshop, and the impression which he himself gave, are best summed up in the following extract from General Sir Peter de la Billière's book 'Storm Command' in which he describes the visit to BFME:

'The effect of the visit was first class, in every way: a potent morale-booster for the troops, but the same also for John Major himself. He soon realized, it seemed to me, that servicemen are quite different from a politician's normal constituents: a disciplined, high-grade group of people, both intellectually and in terms of manners, loyalty and their place in society. I think he was agreeably surprised by the complete absence of hostility and by the degree of friendship which he found, in the desert, at sea and on the air bases. His own performance was extremely impressive. He came over as someone totally committed to the servicemen. With good, plain talk, rather than high rhetoric, he put across the message that in the United Kingdom fifty million people were behind them and he fired them up to do the job of evicting Saddam as best they could. Not many official visitors provoke the members of a REME workshop to throw their caps in the air and cheer. John Major did and nobody forgot it.'

From its arrival in January the MRG of 6 Armoured Workshop under Major Mike Lower was deployed in the Force Maintenance Area. Their task in the Gulf often changed, but was mainly concerned with B Vehicles and, in particular, those of the units in the FMA. One rewarding task was the reclamation of parts from crashed vehicles, a useful source of spares for Land Rovers, 4, 8 and 16 tonne trucks. Some Land Rover engines were even rebuilt. Apart from work on B Vehicles, there were also some thirty soldiers employed on the dockside modification programme for CHALLENGER and WARRIOR. Later two- or three-man teams were provided to help the division with the up-armouring.

At work with the Coles Crane Field Medium

6 Armoured Workshop started work in Al Jubayl on a temporary site with a large shed and tarmac car park. By 14 January it had moved to a more extensive site on the southern side of the port, surrounded by ISO containers stacked two rows high. This had been occupied previously by

MRG 7A from 7 Armoured Workshop, which had now moved up into the desert. They had left behind an 'In Park' of FMA vehicles, and a steady flow of repair was maintained to the end. On 20 January, after the FFMA had been set up 350 kilometres along the MSR, the 2IC, Captain William Kelly, and a detachment joined it there. In Al Jubayl the Workshop had started in-depth repairs of CV8 engines, replacing pistons, rings and liners, provided that the crankshaft bearings were satisfactory. The contractors team from GKN and Perkins helped with advice for this work.

Power Pack repair

As the load built up at the FFMA it became necessary to send the main Workshop forward. On 10 February it moved the 350 kilometres from Al Jubayl to a triangular piece of desert with sides 500 metres long, inside the FFMA boundary, and was open for work the next day. It was said that most soldiers preferred it to 'Container City' at Al Jubayl, but certainly they had little time to dwell on any discomforts. Here they were fully involved working on the overspill from the division as well as the FFMA vehicles. MRGs 7A and 11, from 7 and 11 Armoured Workshops, left about 120 equipments behind them as they moved forward with the division to KEYES and the Forward Assembly Area RAY. Once again the 2IC went forward with recovery mechanics to supervise the backloading, on transport provided by Saudi Arabia, 120 kilometres back to the FFMA.

A Reclamation Platoon of one officer and thirty soldiers was formed from Battle Casualty Replacements and sent forward to MRG 7B with the division on 13 February. They arrived with tool boxes only, and though useful they would have been even more so had they had their own vehicles and equipment.

When the MRG of 71 Aircraft Workshop deployed to support 4 Regiment AAC it was limited to one officer and eighty-four soldiers, administered and co-located with 4 Regiment AAC. They were soon busy with Urgent Operational Requirement modifications. The potential problems of having 71 MRG and the Regimental Workshop both in the same site were avoided by co-locating 71 MRG and 12th Air Defence Regiment Workshop. In order that the Regiment could meet its flying training requirements only five aircraft of each type could be worked on at a time, and at that stage a team from Alan Mann Helicopters was also carrying out modifications to the aircraft. However, even after deployment forward to the FFMA and KEYES, it was still necessary to embody modifications, as additional kits arrived in the Theatre and were sent forward.

FRG 6, commanded by Captain Mark Munday of 11 Armoured Workshop, had similar experiences to others flying out to Al Jubayl and living in Blackadder tented camp. However, in mid-January it moved 100 kilometres to Devil Dog Dragoon Range to support its battle groups from 4 Armoured Brigade, when everyone could feel really involved. At the end of January it moved north to the Divisional Assembly Area KEYES for further training, and by mid-February the FRG had moved about 100 kilometres west to assembly area RAY. On 16 February the final MDBF and sustainability calculations were made with very encouraging results. WARRIOR air filters had been carefully fitted and checked and modifications were reported to be working well. Four days later the CHALLENGER and WARRIOR up-armouring programme was completed.

On 23 February the MRG of 71 Aircraft Workshop at RAY sent a detachment to KEYES, and on the same day a Back Loading Point was established in RAY to enable 1st Armoured Division MRGs to backload damaged equipments. On 25 February there were about 120 equipments which took five days to clear 100 kilometres back to the FFMA.

Regimental Workshops and LADs

Major David Johnson, ASM R J Love and 175 soldiers of 12th Air Defence Regiment Workshop, including twenty-three detached from 22nd Air Defence Regiment Workshop, arrived in Saudi Arabia at the beginning of January. The Regiment and the Workshop were operational almost immediately, in view of the perceived Iraqi air threat, and went through the whole gamut of experiences which were very much part of desert learning. Predominant were acclimatization and sand; losing tools in it, getting vehicles bogged down in it, particularly after rain, and recovering vehicles from it.

On arrival in Saudi Arabia 4 Regiment AAC Workshop's home at Al Jubayl was an empty grain depot with hard-standing for the helicopters, which reduced the serious wear of operating in the desert. The aircrew started an intensive flying programme, resulting in some equally intensive maintenance. At that time the workshop had only four sets of LYNX sand filters – without which the engine life was less than twenty flying hours; tail rotor and main rotor blades eroded rapidly, the main rotor tip caps melting through friction caused by the sand; sand also got into the main and tail rotor heads causing leaks. The contractor's working party from Alan Mann Helicopters arrived on 27 December to begin modifications on LYNX helicopters; two days later serious erosion of blade tip caps on LYNX was discovered. By 1 January five LYNX had failed their Power Performance Index Test after 20–25 flying hours in the Theatre, through erosion of compressor blades. As a result 70 Aircraft Workshop at Middle Wallop began 24-hour manning of their GEM engine repair facility on 4 January, ready to receive backloaded engines, whilst CO 4 Regiment AAC put a flying restriction on LYNX to preserve engine life. Because of all the extra work needed on the aircraft in addition to normal maintenance, the Workshop was unable to go into the desert until 25 January, when it moved to KEYES. Four weeks were spent there, the least interesting part of its tour in the Gulf because the flying rate had to be kept to a minimum to conserve assets. To ensure sustainability extra spares had to be carried forward, and the workshop borrowed an Atlas crane and a 1 tonne truck from 71 Aircraft Workshop to help carry them when they moved forward into RAY prior to the advance into Iraq and Kuwait.

Servicing a Lynx Mark 9

The main body of the 14th/20th King's Hussars, including most of the LAD, left BAOR for Saudi Arabia on 20 December. After eighteen hours, with a stop in Cyprus, they were soon in Al Jubayl at Blackadder Camp, overlooked by a minaret with its frequent calls to prayer. Christmas Day morning was spent in Hangar 5 modifying the Regiment's CHALLENGER tanks, which had awaited their arrival, and lifting the power packs to check for damage. The LAD was soon adjusting to the new field conditions. The sand was all-pervading and would get into everything, however hard the efforts to keep it out and, early on, the heat in the middle of the day made it very difficult to work outside in the sun. Soon, though, they were to move north with a progressive increase in work, and every day brought more confidence. After a slow hot move to the Devil Dog Dragoon Range, 120 kilometres in three hours, they parked in a defensive circle and prepared for a flood of work; instead they had a downpour of rain for several days with heavily laden vehicles sinking into the quagmire. Nevertheless, the training became more intense and the recovery mechanics worked round the clock getting vehicles out of the *sabkhas* – unstable salt flats – with satellite navigation proving its worth in a desolate landscape. The LAD moved forward with its Regiment and Captain Paul Jaques, ASM Terry Ashton and the rest of the LAD were all impressed by the sight of the concentration areas for 1st Armoured Division. There they could see all the lines of repair needed to maintain the division, the LAD in each unit, the FRG in each brigade and the three MRGs in the divisional area. This was all brought together when they started to practise crossing the breach at night into the minefields of the Iraqi defences. There were masses of light sticks of different colours to be seen, with hundreds of CHALLENGERs, WARRIORs and other vehicles following single red lights in front and blue lights to the right. In the background there were the sights and sounds of the faraway air bombardment on the Iraqi lines.

On arrival in the Gulf the 1st Battalion, The Royal Scots EME, Captain Martin Court, worked from Battle Group HQ, helped by Staff Sergeant Jim Cowie and a team of three. The ASM was back at A2 echelon, producing spares apparently from nowhere. Half of A Company fitter section under Staff Sergeant Tim Bennet spent Christmas at Blackadder Camp preparing their WARRIORs for the desert, including stringent inspections of turbochargers. The other half-section, who had spent Christmas in BAOR, arrived on 28 December, in time for exercises in the desert sand. There was consternation and not a few expletives when the deceptive *sabkhas*, with what appeared to be hard motorable surfaces, soon claimed the complete fitter section, two Bedford trucks laden with ammunition and a Foden recovery vehicle, in the clutches of the hidden soft sand. Fortunately help was at hand, and no doubt the incident provided a fund of leg-pulls. B Company Fitter Section under Staff Sergeant Chadwick went into the desert for training two days later, testing weapons, practising navigation by day and night, exercising communications and the recovery of A Company Fitter Section. Soon they went north to start battle group training, when they learned that FV432s could not keep up with the companies in long moves: fortunately the fitter section had satellite navigation in their vehicles.

The first three weeks after arriving in Al Jubayl were busy, too, for the Queen's Company, 1st Battalion, Grenadier Guards, with teething problems on the Company's vehicles, followed by up-armouring modifications. Desert training was followed by the eight-hour drive north. An FV432 which had been sprayed and packed to the roof with all the equipment spares the ASM could find in BAOR had been left loaded on the rail flats in BAOR; it did not turn up in Saudi Arabia until the section was about to move to the north. It was eventually found at the docks in Al Jubayl stripped of all its equipment.

Most of 3rd Battalion, The Royal Regiment of Fusiliers LAD arrived in Al Jubayl during the period 13 – 22 December, with their vehicles arriving soon afterwards. The latter needed much attention after the long sea journey, whilst the WARRIORs went through their desert modifications. The LAD had a fifteen-point check list with much 'pack in, pack out' and running to the GKN advisory team. Letters from home asked about the heat, but it was in fact very cold at night and sometimes not very warm by day. They, too, were soon familiar with satellite navigation aids and avoidance of the *sabkhas*. On 19 January there were live-firing battle runs followed by brigade training, and on 26 January they left the Devil Dog Dragoon Range and moved 350 kilometres to the KEYES concentration area. This was a long and difficult drive along a road packed with convoys moving west in cold, driving rain. The first night at KEYES the ground was frozen and there was frost on 'bivi-bags' in the morning, in stark contrast to the heat experienced in Al Jubayl. On 14 February they moved to RAY, where the fitter sections were given a substantial spares pack in anticipation of the most likely first-line repair tasks in the first stages of the operation; however, many of these spares were used before they even left RAY. They were also issued with maintenance free batteries for WARRIOR which overcame the shortage of distilled water and electrolyte.

The plan for the ground operations of 1st Armoured Division included the setting up of an Armoured Delivery Group (ADG) equipped with War Maintenance Reserve vehicles manned by Battle Casualty Replacements. Its role was to follow the armoured brigades, ready to provide battle replacements when needed. 1st Battalion, Queen's Own Highlanders LAD had been allocated to support the ADG. On arrival at Al Jubayl they were faced with five days' constant work to put the Regiment's vehicles back into shape – they had been stripped of parts before they were found on the vehicle park. This was followed by an epic journey to the FFMA, mostly along the crowded MSR DODGE which was littered with crashed pick-ups, overturned trucks and tankers. After several days in the FFMA they moved to RAY; here they eventually found their patch of desert, totally barren except for three dead sheep. Next morning Captain Alex Tucker and his men awoke, not to an empty desert, but to three squadrons of CHALLENGERs, three companies of WARRIORs, a battery of guns and MLRS and a squadron of Sappers. The ADG had arrived!

The REME Staff Band

On 11 January the REME Staff Band, under the Director of Music, Captain Len Tyler, arrived in the Gulf to be employed in a medical role.

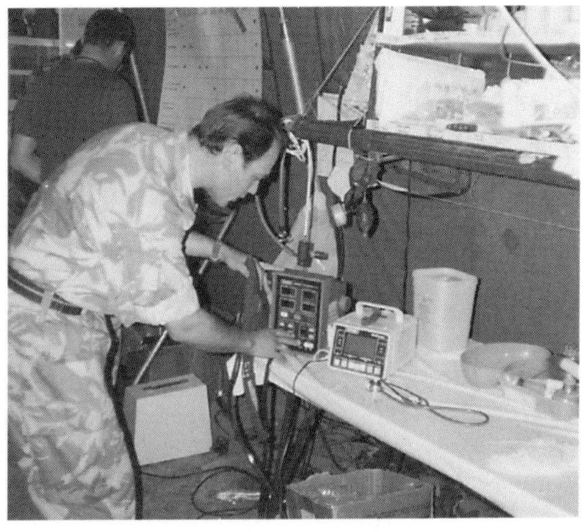
Staff Sergeant Gillatt preparing equipment in 22 Field Hospital

Captain Tyler had just taken over as Director of Music and had not yet even had the opportunity to conduct the Band. They were based in Baldrick Lines, Al Jubayl, having travelled from Arborfield via the Duchess of Kent Military Hospital, Catterick, where they had consolidated the medical training which they had carried out before Christmas. Also at Catterick they met the other reinforcements for 22 Field Hospital, some of whom were NHS doctors and nurses in the TA, some reservists with medical service, and the band of The Royal Highland Fusiliers. Sergeant Long of the Staff Band was instrumental in keeping those back in Arborfield informed of the Band's progress by sending regular reports of their activities, which were well received.

They arrived in Al Jubayl after 27 hours travelling, in time to take part in an NBC exercise. The next day they were building walls of sandbags, a duty performed by all regardless of age, rank or sex. Their task was to work in the casualty decontamination centre and at the helicopter landing site, transferring patients to and from aircraft and ambulances. Captain Tyler was responsible for designing and developing the Helicopter Landing Sites and for training the site teams. On Thursday 17 January they awoke to sirens wailing, horns blowing and the nearby mosques praying to Allah at full volume. It was a full NBC alert and the air war had begun. The civilian camp workers, somewhat understandably, disappeared like the mist, leaving the Band to their sandbagging and other fatigues which had to be done; hard work on a hot day in NBC suits.

The Band moved into the desert on 23 January to Al Qaysumah, a flat, featureless area of desert with no air-raid alarms or calls to prayer, but, instead, an artillery range. There they practised stretcher drills with a PUMA, a SEA KING and a CHINOOK twin-rotor helicopter. Those in the casualty decontamination centre, Staff Sergeant Chris Gillatt and Drum Major Marcus Gibbons, were working on resuscitation. In the meantime the hospital, which was just a collection of tents when they arrived, was filled out with operating theatres with eight tables, four wards with fifty

The REME Staff Band off-loading a casualty

beds each and all the hospital departments, including a laundry and hot showers. The weather was at times very cold, falling to −10°C., but as it became warmer there were sandstorms, flash floods and spectacular thunder and lightning. The Sappers built the helicopter landing pad, which resembled a giant piece of green parquet flooring and a twelve foot wall of sand round the camp. Exercises continued with and without helicopters, and in and out of NBC kit, including one in a sandstorm as six PUMAs arrived one after another in very poor visibility. One exercise which involved hundreds of 'volunteer patients' and dozens of helicopters went on from mid-morning until late at night.

When the ground war began on 24 February the first patients began to come in by air and were mainly Iraqi prisoners. Four days later a thick black cloud from the burning oil wells enveloped the area and it was still pitch dark at 0900 hours, although it should have become light at 0530 hours. Eventually it became light enough for the helicopters to operate, the start to a busy day as they queued up to land. Most of the Iraqi patients were delighted when they found that they did not have to pay for their food. The Band's task was soon to be completed though, to the great satisfaction of all concerned, and grateful acceptance that they had fortunately little of the task to do for which they were deployed. By early March they were dismantling the hospital and packing it into containers for shipment back to UK.

THE START OF THE AIR WAR

On 29 November 1990 the Security Council adopted Resolution 678 which gave Iraq one final opportunity to comply with SCR 660 of 2 August. It authorized member states to use 'all necessary means' to uphold and implement SCR 660 and all subsequent relevant resolutions if Iraq had not complied by 15 January 1991. Offensive air action was planned by the Allies in the Gulf, as the first stage in forcing compliance on Iraq in the event of failure to withdraw from Kuwait under the terms of this Resolution. Many weeks of planning and preparation took place for the complex and highly technical aggressive action which would be implemented in the event of Iraq's failure to respond to the UN requirement. Iraq took no steps to comply and the Allied political decision was made that the air war would start at 0001 hours Greenwich Mean Time on 17 January.

The Allied Air Forces began their air attacks on Iraq with American F-117 stealth bombers, and TOMAHAWK cruise missiles fired from surface ships and submarines, attacking command and control and air defence centres. They were followed by Allied aircraft attacking various targets: twenty RAF TORNADO aircraft attacked airfields on the first night. The aim was to establish air superiority and to destroy the enemy's command and control system and communications; to destroy their nuclear, chemical and biological warfare resources; and then to begin the attrition of their ground forces from the air, to enable the UN armies to liberate Kuwait quickly with minimum casualties to our own troops. One immediate effect on the British Force was that the UK civilian contractors helping with equipment management asked for evacuation of their men, most of whom flew home on 18 January. However, some from GKN, Alan Mann Helicopters and Perkins remained behind in Saudi Arabia and continued their work.

Naval forces began operations to gain control of the sea in the northern Gulf, particularly so that ships' guns were able to reach shore targets and also as part of the deception plan to pose to Iraq the threat of an Allied amphibious landing. The air operations, averaging 2,500 sorties per day, continued by day and night for thirty-eight days before the land war began on 24 February. Precision-guided bombs employing thermal imaging and laser devices were used; TOMAHAWK computer-programmed cruise missiles were launched from US ships at targets as far away as Baghdad and became familiar sights to television viewers world-wide. RAF VICTOR, VC10 and TRISTAR tanker aircraft played an important role from the very first night when the RAF TORNADOs were refuelled in the air in radio silence just before reaching the Iraq border.

The Iraqis made little use of their air force either in attack or defence. Nearly a quarter of their air force flew defensively to Iran, probably to conserve their assets for the ground war. RAF TORNADO reconnaissance aircraft were used to look for SCUD missile launchers which had fired at Saudi Arabia on 18 January and subsequently at Haifa and Tel Aviv in Israel. As a result a great Allied effort was made to find and destroy the launchers so that Israel would not be provoked into retaliation, with the risk of splitting the Coalition if this should lead to a 'Holy War'. The American PATRIOT missiles proved to be a very effective defence against SCUD, both in Israel and Saudi Arabia where they shot down missiles aimed at Riyadh and Dhahran. About forty SCUDs were fired at Israel and the same number at Saudi Arabia. The prime operational task for the UK Special Forces specified by General Schwarzkopf was to counter the threat of Iraqi SCUD missiles, a task which developed into the largest UK Special Forces operation since 1945.

1ST (BRITISH) ARMOURED DIVISION – APPROACH MARCH AND FINAL PREPARATIONS

General

1st Armoured Division was to be switched from the tactical control of the US Marine Corps in the east to the 7th (US) Corps which was to move to the west. On 14 January 1991 the division began secretly to move from its training area north of Al Jubayl to the Divisional concentration area, KEYES, thirty-five kilometres east of Hafar Al Batin in the 7th (US) Corps area. Much of this movement by individual units has already been described earlier in the chapter. This was a move of over 200 kilometres:

requiring the tanks to go on transporters and including the units and stores of the Forward Maintenance Area, all in secrecy.

The divisional REME workshops had a very busy time in KEYES. They had to improve their desert skills and their NBC training, build up stocks of spares ready for the expected land fighting and take part in the Divisional Commander's exercises, during which they motored many miles. RHQ 7 Armoured Workshop controlled all second-line workshop production in the three MRGs.

On 26 January tactical control of 1st Armoured Division was transferred formally from the US Marine Corps to 7th (US) Corps, and on 31 January the division was declared ready for offensive operations. Between 14–16 February it advanced to its final assembly area, RAY, north west of Hafar Al Batin. 12th Air Defence Regiment RAPIER missiles were deployed to cover the Forward Assembly Area and 2 Squadron 14th Signal Regiment (Electronic Warfare) also deployed. The operation aimed to outflank the main Iraqi forces in Kuwait, pushing north into eastern Iraq before engaging the Republican Guard armoured and mechanized divisions to the north and north-west of Kuwait. The Iraqis were to be deceived into expecting the Allies to attack southern Kuwait and make an amphibious landing from the sea. Four days of major artillery fire and various deception measures took place before the main ground offensive was launched.

REME Activities in Support

All three MRGs set up for work in RAY. MRG 7A was earmarked as the initial MRG to support the Divisional Reconstitution Group, which would provide for rapid reconstitution of an armoured brigade after a heavy battle; in the event this did not occur. MRGs 7B and 11 did most of the production work in RAY, consisting largely of run-ups and final tests on the latest batch of power packs received from BAOR. On one particular day there were more than 100 power packs in various states of repair on the ground in MRG 7B. The 120 vehicles of the MRG were sited about 100 metres apart in an area of flat and featureless desert, more than a one-kilometre square – very different from the more familiar German village locations in BAOR.

THE LAND WAR – GENERAL NARRATIVE

The first British ground troops in action were 32nd and 39th Heavy Regiments RA who, on 18 February in preliminary operations, started to fire on enemy positions with their M110 self-propelled guns and the new Multiple Launch Rocket System. The main ground offensive started at 0100 hours (GMT) 24 February by which time part of HQ 1st Armoured Division had co-located with Tactical Headquarters 1st (US) Mechanized Infantry Division. At that time it was reported that 97% of the

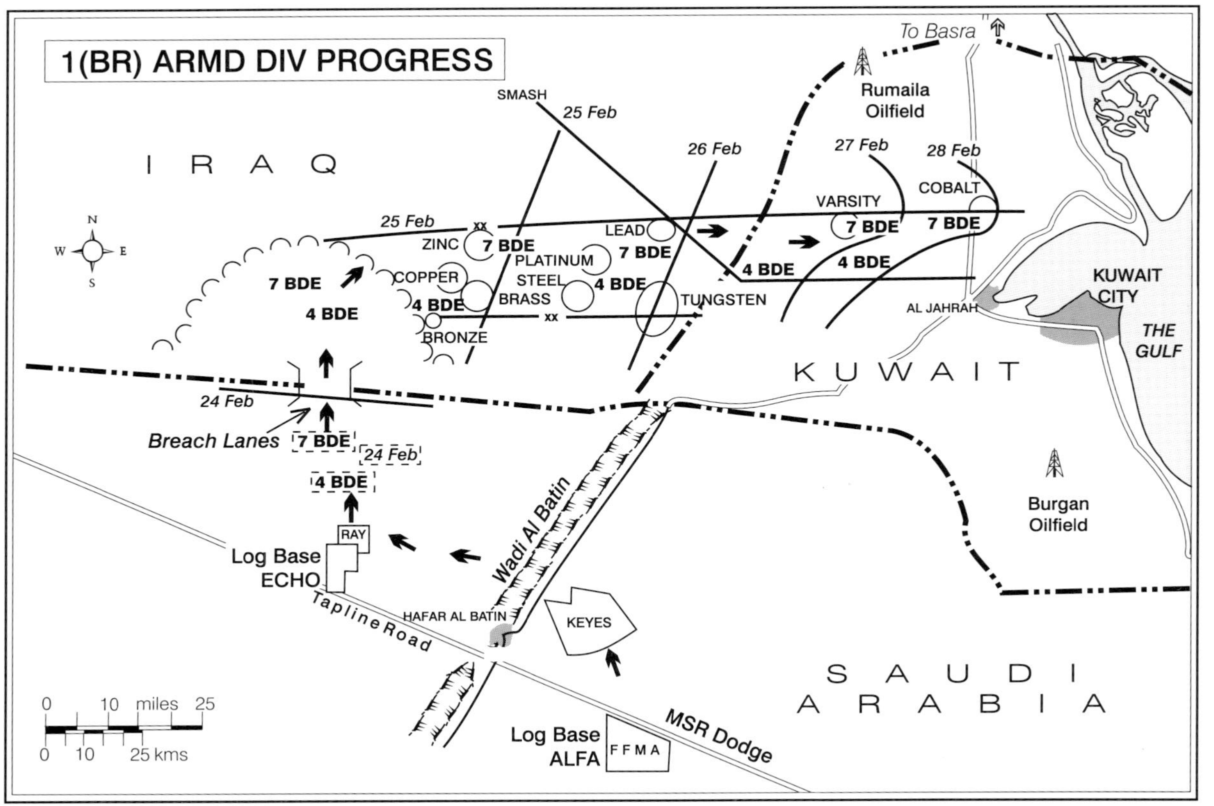
1(BR) ARMD DIV PROGRESS
I R A Q
K U W A I T
S A U D I
A R A B I A
KUWAIT CITY
THE GULF
To Basra
Rumaila Oilfield
Burgan Oilfield
AL JAHRAH
SMASH
25 Feb
26 Feb
27 Feb
28 Feb
VARSITY
COBALT
LEAD
ZINC
PLATINUM
COPPER
STEEL
BRASS
BRONZE
TUNGSTEN
7 BDE
4 BDE
24 Feb
Breach Lanes
RAY
Log Base ECHO
Wadi Al Batin
HAFAR AL BATIN
KEYES
Tapline Road
MSR Dodge
Log Base ALFA
F F M A
N
E
S
W
0 10 miles 25
0 10 25 kms

CHALLENGER tanks, 98% of the WARRIOR infantry fighting vehicles and M109 guns and 90% of the LYNX helicopters were serviceable and ready for action.

Naval gunfire and amphibious moves from the east and frontal ground attacks in southern Kuwait all aimed to distract Iraqi attention from the main land attack from the west into eastern Iraq. The 18th (US) Airborne Corps on the left flank advanced more quickly than expected, and 1st (US) Mechanized Division started to breach the enemy positions throughout the afternoon and the remainder of 24 February. 1st Armoured Division was at two hours' notice to move, once sixteen lanes had been cleared through enemy minefields in front of their Forward Assembly Area.

On the left of the divisional assault 16th/5th The Queen's Royal Lancers, with 32nd and 39th Heavy Regiments RA providing fire support from the breach area, crossed into Iraq at 0200 hours 25 February, followed by the Queen's Royal Irish Hussars and the rest of 7 Armoured Brigade at 1145 hours. Contact was made with the enemy at 1630 hours, when they attacked and destroyed a major Iraqi communication site. 1st Battalion, The Staffordshire Regiment fought through this position, clearing trenches and bunkers, and defeated an enemy counter-attack with tank support. By 2000 hours 7 Armoured Brigade had secured COPPER NORTH, their first objective, which was littered with burning and destroyed tanks.

To the right of the line of attack, 4 Armoured Brigade, supported by 2nd Field Regiment RA, advanced towards BRONZE, their first objective, where they met enemy armour, infantry and artillery. Destroying twelve tanks, other vehicles and guns, they occupied BRONZE by 0200 hours 26 February. During this period Corporal Mark Griffiths of 414 Tank Transporter Unit RCT Workshop saved a stores vehicle carrying dangerous cargo from destruction by fire, and was awarded the Queen's Gallantry Medal. The citation is quoted later in this chapter.

By daybreak 7 Armoured Brigade had destroyed many tanks, with help from 4 Regiment AAC anti-tank helicopters, and secured objective ZINC. 4 Armoured Brigade, on their way to capture COPPER SOUTH, destroyed more enemy and captured many prisoners, including two Iraqi divisional commanders. 1st Battalion, The Royal Scots, supported by the 14th/20th King's Hussars, had destroyed many tanks and guns and captured enemy positions at BRONZE. Moving to the next objectives, The Queen's Royal Irish Hussars Battle Group led the attack on PLATINUM during the afternoon, while, on the right, 4 Armoured Brigade's next objective STEEL was attacked by the 3rd Battalion, The Royal Regiment of Fusiliers, capturing it by 1530 hours and destroying three artillery battalions on the way. Large numbers of enemy surrendered and the Brigade prepared to capture TUNGSTEN that night. By 0430 hours on 27 February they had done so.

On the night of 27–28 February 7 Armoured Brigade was ordered to move rapidly eastward to Mutla Ridge north of Kuwait City. Objective COBALT was secured by 0500 hours 28 February, thus cutting the Basra road. President Bush had announced on 27 February that all offensive action by the Coalition Forces would cease at 0500 hours (GMT) on 28 February. Logistic re-supply was maintained despite the swift advance of 290 kilometres in 66 hours. The division had destroyed the best part of three Iraqi armoured divisions and taken more than 7,000 prisoners; and was ordered to destroy all enemy equipment within the areas that it now occupied. REME had helped ensure that over 95% of the armoured vehicle fleet crossed the finishing line, for although seventy-four CHALLENGER power packs had to be changed during the battle, the REME support had been so excellent that only one tank was out of action at the end.

The end of the land battle was well summed up in his Despatch of 28 June 1991 by Air Chief Marshal Sir Patrick Hine, the Joint Force Commander:

'The daily needs of 1st (British) Armoured Division were of the same order as those of the whole of 21st Army Group in the early part of Operation OVERLORD, the D Day landings in 1944. I believe that 1st (British) Armoured Division was probably the best prepared and supported force ever fielded by the British Army.'

British Army casualties were fortunately very light during the land campaign, with fifteen killed and forty-three wounded, including two REME NCOs killed by the enemy. During the whole operation forty-seven British were killed: nine before hostilities, twenty-four in action, ten during the hostilities but not in action, and four after hostilities. Twelve were taken as prisoners of war.

THE LAND WAR – REME ACTIVITIES

The divisional operational plan had been to move from RAY to a staging area and then to cross the breach in the enemy's defences before reaching Iraqi territory. The orders were very detailed and had been carefully rehearsed. The overall disposition of REME support was made to sustain the division for as long as would prove necessary to overcome Iraqi resistance. In the event the Iraqis were neither as determined nor in the strength which had been expected and battle support was only required for the 100 hours of fighting, when the aim had been achieved and the Basra road cut.

Commander Maintenance 1st Armoured Division decided that to support the armoured breakthrough of the Iraqi obstacles on G Day – the start of the land war – it was necessary to place CHALLENGER ARRVs on each lane in the breach of the Iraqi lines because the US Army

ARVs could not move CHALLENGER tanks. Power packs were placed for lifting by RAF CHINOOK helicopters to support the advance. Thereafter, BEMEs were made responsible for the allocation of Forward Repair Teams as the situation required. The experiences of some of those involved in this support are given in the paragraphs that follow.

On G Day, 24 February, 4 Armoured Brigade was to move from RAY along eight routes, four wheeled and four tracked, to form staging areas: Equipment Collecting Points (ECPs) being set up 200 metres west of each. The area of the breach was covered by five CHALLENGER ARRVs and five Foden recovery vehicles from FRG 7 and the other second-line workshops, thus allowing BEME 4 Armoured Brigade, Major David Keymer, to use his complete FRG resources (including four extra CHALLENGER ARRVs) in direct support of his Brigade. Self-help recovery, with like towing like, was to be used whenever possible, whilst he allocated FRG assets to battle group EMEs according to the size and composition of their group. The rest of the FRG moved into Iraq as a Brigade unit under his direction. Equipment casualties were recovered forward to ECPs where inspection and repairs were carried out. 4 Armoured Brigade advanced into Iraq with some speed, so rapid assembly changes were essential: the longest time in an ECP was six hours. Over the 100 hours the Brigade moved nearly 300 kilometres and, although speed of movement was a problem, the main part of the FRG was able to put twelve vehicles back on the road during the move.

Huge groups of prisoners guarded by one or two men, and even left unguarded, sometimes decided to go back to their trenches and take up their weapons again. Small arms and support weapon fire was heard well behind the fighting echelons and FRG 6 was involved in some incidents of firing from isolated pockets of the enemy. Mines and unexploded bomblets too were a constant hazard, especially at night or in driving rain or sandstorms. ECPs tended to be on or near recently cleared enemy positions which added spice and a need for prudence. On 27 February the advance halted for a few hours before continuing into Kuwait and developing into a final charge towards Kuwait City. On 28 February FRG 6 moved into the Brigade Administrative Area about 30 kilometres north of Kuwait City. That night many men had their first real sleep for four days after the most intensive and exciting period of their lives, for most of them, had ended. FRG 6 had set up sixteen ECPs since arriving in Saudi Arabia and completed 130 power pack or engine replacements; sixty major assembly replacements; and fifty-four logged recovery tasks. Captain Tony McWatters summed up his time with REME in 'The RAEME Craftsman' magazine in November 1991 as 'exciting, challenging, rewarding, tedious and boring – with everything that goes between. The REME soldier is so much like his RAEME counterpart it is uncanny!' AQMS Mick Fishwick of the FRG was awarded the MBE for his part in the campaign.

FRG 7, supporting 7 Armoured Brigade, was commanded by Captain John Ellis. It had two officers, 130 soldiers and sixty-four vehicles. In February additional vehicles were gratefully received. These were six CHALLENGER ARRVs plus ten more power pack carriers, destined to

FRG 7 arrive in Kuwait City

play a vital part in the FRG's tasks, particularly as the approach march to the Iraqi defence line created a need for power pack changes before entering the breaches. On 26 February Captain Ellis was concerned to maintain control of his FRG, when FRT tasks were mounting rapidly and the stock of packs and major assemblies dwindling accordingly. At the same time the speed of the advance meant that FRG vehicles which had stopped to carry out their support tasks were soon out of radio operating range. The battle groups had amazing speed and mobility, and keeping in touch and informing everyone of by-passed positions and minefields was a major worry. At first light on 27 February CHINOOK helicopters brought up more power packs and an ECP was ordered to be set up 40 kilometres to the rear, to collect any remaining vehicles to prevent them being taken by the Iraqis; those left behind were not seen until 2 March. However, the CHALLENGER ARRVs had nearly run out of fuel and a major effort was needed to set up the ECP, refuel the ARRVs and move the power packs and administrative vehicles. This was made more difficult since no one knew what by-passed enemy might do. At this stage 7 Armoured Brigade RCT Squadron and the FRG were separated from the Brigade Administrative Area in the approach to the Wadi Al Batin before entering Kuwait, and at that time an incident occurred for which Lance Corporal Kevin Reid, who was attached to the air defence battery providing flank protection, won the Military Medal. This is described later in the Honours and Awards section of this chapter.

By the time the FRG reached its cease-fire location north of Kuwait City it was split into four parts along some 240 kilometres of the line of march. Their route was plotted using GPS satellite navigation devices and sent back wherever possible by secure transmission modules which were issued to the CHALLENGER ARRV crews and OC FRG. On the night of 27 February, prior to the final assault, the last of twenty-two CHALLENGER power packs was fitted and the recovery mechanics blew many tracks while recovering numerous CHALLENGERs which had fallen into enemy bunkers.

On 2 March, two days after the cease-fire, the rear elements of the FRG arrived and the first 100% check of men and vehicles could be held. The CHALLENGER ARRVs had proved to be very effective: they were fast, mobile and good for towing. Although they did not leave the breach until 4 Armoured Brigade had passed through on 25 February, the ARRVs still caught up with the FRG the next day. Nearly 1,000 Casualty Reports were received by the FRG during the whole of Operation GRANBY, of which sixty-five were received and dealt with during the 100 hours of the actual war. Its vehicles travelled some 450 kilometres during this latter period and proved reliable and effective under arduous operating conditions. The CHINOOK helicopters used to bring up power packs and major assemblies enabled more rapid support, and contributed to the achievement of more than 90% of the CHALLENGERs and 95% of the WARRIORs finishing the war battleworthy. Recovery of Iraqi vehicles afterwards was a more taxing task than recovery of our own during the war.

7 Armoured Workshop had very little work for the MRGs during the battle because of the speed of movement but, as already described, the FRGs were in constant demand. Transport problems were experienced with the movement of fit power packs forward to the FRG and dead packs back to the MRG, but the CHINOOK helicopters proved invaluable for this task when the use of road transport was not feasible. The Workshop had formed up in a staging area north of RAY with the

Captain Pat Nulty leads MRG 7B

balance of 1st Armoured Division, and crossed into Iraq as part of the Divisional Rear Area. The MRGs moved three times across south-east Iraq, but it was only after the cease-fire that MRG 7B set up for work to clear an enormous ECP.

14th/20th King's Hussars LAD moved through the breach on the night of 24 February, finding it much easier than during training, as they were not closed down and not wearing respirators. The war itself was a firework display a few kilometres away, and there were hundreds of prisoners to be processed before going back to prisoner-of-war camps. The Iraqi positions were deserted except for shattered tanks, artillery and trucks which littered the desert sand. Collecting prisoners consisted of waiting for large groups of Iraqi soldiers waving white flags to walk towards them; they were quite cheerful when given food and water. The cease-fire was soon announced and the LAD moved east nearer to Kuwait City.

For A Company Fitter Section of 1st Battalion, The Royal Scots LAD the land war passed quickly with less work than expected, proving that proper preparation paid off. The real work started after the cease-fire when the recovery mechanics were especially busy with a variety of Iraqi T72 and T55 tanks and artillery pieces, as were the other recovery mechanics in the LAD. The Foden recovery vehicle was eventually named 'The Royal Scots Train' after it had five vehicles on tow for one move. The experience of B Company Fitters was similar, with the satellite navigation system proving invaluable, especially during the many moves at night. During the fighting B Company section was mainly occupied with control of the many prisoners. Similarly, the LAD fitter section of the Queen's Company, Grenadier Guards, which was in the 14th/20th King's Hussars Battle Group at the beginning of the breaching operation, was called on to secure the prisoners and deliver them to the appropriate collection point, when the Company reached its objective.

Sergeant Chris Murphy, a fitter with the Mortar Platoon, summed up his experiences:

'In the weeks leading up to G Day many a long day and night was spent repairing or changing major assemblies and a multitude of other 'fix-its', by the crew working in many different skills other than our own trade. A lot of hard work was completed and our powers of improvisation were tested to the limit. It was a challenge that was met successfully and no one was found wanting. All in all it was a rewarding experience tinged with sadness, disbelief, and sobering sights and thoughts.'

3rd Battalion, The Royal Regiment of Fusiliers LAD crossed the Iraqi border on 25 February and ended the war north-west of Kuwait City. An extract from an account by Captain Richard Welsh, commanding the LAD, gives a good idea of a day in the life of an infantry battalion LAD:

'As dawn broke on 26 February we pushed through objective COPPER, which was littered with burning Iraqi armour, and pressed on towards our next objectives,

BRASS and STEEL. At 1400 hours the WARRIORs and CHALLENGERs stormed forward, overwhelming all enemy resistance.

'The Battle Group finally stopped on the northern edge of objective STEEL to replenish from A echelon. This gave the sections time to make some running repairs and for me to update fitter section reports. I was pleasantly surprised to find that, apart from one of A Company's WARRIORs (which had been waiting for spares for a week and was being towed), the only other vehicle under tow was an FV432 from Battle Group HQ. By 0400 hours on the 27th TUNGSTEN was cleared and the Battalion moved into the Wadi Al Batin to reorganize. Our orders were then to prepare to move east and block the Kuwait – Basra highway. The equipment state still looked good. A Company still required their WARRIOR spares, but they had a WARRIOR pack which our resident FRT was fitting. C Company's FERRET Scout car had an engine fire and had burnt out. A SCIMITAR and FV432 ambulance required new engines and the FV432 from Battle Group HQ was still having starting problems. Worried that A1 echelon fitter section might run out of towing hooks, I ordered the SCIMITAR and ambulance to be dropped at the nearby ECP located with the FRG. Meanwhile Corporal Kitchen and his crew from A1 echelon fitter section managed to catch themselves some very willing Iraqi prisoners whom they brought back to the RSM.'

The views later expressed by A Company Fitter Section were that: 'The Gulf had been the ideal conflict, if there is such a thing, for REME to be involved in; ten weeks of vehicle preparation followed by three days of war involvement.'

Most of 4 Regiment AAC Workshop's time during the ground war was spent on the move. After each long drive the squadron fitter sections would have up to thirty-six aircraft requiring servicing. When they paused after crossing into Iraq, the AWD managed an engine change in six hours, the best timing of their thirty-eight engine changes made since arriving in the Theatre. A satisfying factor was that it was also an engine change made under operational conditions requiring ground runs, rigging checks and air tests completed by a four-man team; the aircraft itself had destroyed two T55 tanks and three BMP tracked APCs the day before.

When G Day arrived half the Armoured Delivery Group (1st Battalion, Queen's Own Highlanders LAD) moved forward and the other half remained in RAY. Those going forward spent much of their time perching at 45°C on the back of a tank transporter, bumping and rattling over endless tracts of desert and eventually to the quarries north of Kuwait City. Back at RAY, hours stretched into days of pouring rain and sandstorms before they moved back to the FFMA, where the Foden was in constant use moving captured Iraqi vehicles.

In his account of the war, 'Storm Command', General Sir Peter de la Billière paid this tribute to REME's contribution:

'If a vehicle broke down, it was repaired immediately: the power packs of tanks, which were the engine and gearbox combined and weighed six tons, were replaced in the field within a matter of hours. The Division as a whole achieved a remarkable standard of mobility. No praise is too high for the efforts of the REME , whose technicians made a major contribution to the British military effort through their expertise and dedication.'

THE CEASE-FIRE AND AFTER

Offensive action ceased at 0500 hours GMT on 28 February with 7 Armoured Brigade on objective COBALT astride the Basra road. The rest of the division followed in column immediately behind, to consolidate on this key objective. In the four days since the land war started, the whole division had advanced over 300 kilometres, and had been, as planned, supported continuously and effectively by all its REME elements.

MRG 7B having cleared the ECP in Iraq, mentioned above, began their next major task of recovering from Iraq all unfit British vehicles and equipment, whatever their state. This was done, firstly, to ensure that all men and equipment were accounted for and, secondly, to prevent Iraq using any of the very few destroyed British vehicles for propaganda purposes. This major operation was controlled by the Headquarters of 7 Armoured Workshop and required close co-ordination with both brigades and almost every unit deployed. Three workshop Land Rovers suffered mine damage during the four days required to complete this task, which was demanding and sometimes dangerous. All the Workshop's Foden recovery vehicles were used and some of the CHALLENGER ARRVs from the FRG. Their other major task was to recover captured Iraqi equipment. On 3 March MRG 7B finally set up north-west of Kuwait City overlooking the oil wells set on fire by the Iraqis.

On 3 March Coalition and Iraqi Commanders met to discuss the formal cease-fire, and this came into effect on 11 April. British units, however, began to go home during the second week of March. A battle group based on 2nd Battalion, The Royal Anglian Regiment remained in Kuwait with a squadron of RAF TORNADOs based in Saudi Arabia and a few REME personnel remained to help with the return of equipment.

After the cease-fire a reclamation platoon of Theatre reserves was attached to 6 Armoured Workshop to reclaim Land Rovers. The detachment set up another reclamation platoon to return fit and repairable items from all types of equipment to RAOC. The 'In Park' was backloaded to Al Jubayl as quickly as possible and it was not unusual to see fifteen transporters arrive at a time. The Workshop's own seven DROPS vehicles worked round the clock moving equipment along the MSR.

Major Keymer, BEME 4 Armoured Brigade, returned to Iraq for

several days in early March with 39 Squadron RE and, with four CHALLENGER ARRVs and twelve WARRIOR recovery or repair variants from his Brigade, he set out to recover or destroy Iraqi equipment. They recovered fifty-five vehicles: T55, BRDM, a few SAM Support Vehicles, Type 531 and many MTLB. One WARRIOR repair vehicle towed five MTLB and one towed gun in line astern for more than eighty kilometres. The T55, weighing more than 35 tonnes, was more of a problem, however, particularly off the road in sandy conditions. Even the CHALLENGER ARRV could not tow it for any length of time and there were many minor problems with the T55 recovery over a period of five days. There was by now a lack of low-loaders and tank-transporters, and these were sorely missed.

HQ FMA informed 6 Armoured Workshop on 6 March that they were to form the Logistic Support Group (LSG) Workshop in Al Jubayl. Inspection of all M548 tracked cargo vehicles received from 1st Armoured Division began on 10 March prior to handing them back to the US Army in a serviceable condition. By 28 March 111 had been inspected and 27 District Workshop in UK was nominated to refurbish them.

On 14 March 6 Armoured Workshop started to move back to Al Jubayl and was complete there by 15 March. A small detachment of vehicle mechanics was left with the FFMA while Logistic Bases ECHO and ALFA were outloaded. On 30 March one officer and twelve men were deployed to Kuwait to take over two FRTs from 11 Armoured Workshop, to support the single battle group remaining there. In Al Jubayl some 3,000 B vehicles of returning units were parked in the Convoy Marshalling Area prior to loading in ships, and these required an inspection of brakes, lights and steering by the Workshop. Eventually Major Mike Lower and his workshop returned to BAOR, leaving 5 Armoured Workshop to carry on.

The MRG of 71 Aircraft Workshop, which had been divided between RAY and KEYES since 23 February, was concentrated in area KEYES on 1 March. The cease-fire took place the day after 4 Regiment AAC Workshop moved into Kuwait, but they remained busy for another month as the Workshop had many tasks before they could return to Al Jubayl. Aircraft had to be inspected and serviced and prepared for loading into HERCULES and GALAXY C5s at Dhahran. The last aircraft returned to Germany on 25 March with the rear party.

A Logistic Support Group (Middle East) Workshop was formed in Soest, BAOR in order to relieve the LSG Workshop set up in Al Jubayl by 6 Armoured Workshop. The new LSG(ME) Workshop under Major Tony Anthistle, with ASM Shirley and 146 men from twenty-six different units, was the last REME unit to be sent out to the Gulf as the result of GRANBY. In replacing 6 Armoured Workshop its task was to support the units of the Logistic Support Group, which had now been formed, in and around Jubayl, to process and backload vehicles and equipment to BAOR. It also provided a FRG to 2nd Battalion, The Royal Anglian Battle Group in Kuwait and duty recovery wherever needed. It was disbanded in August when the last vehicles had been shipped.

REME SOLDIERS KILLED DURING OPERATION GRANBY

Major A J Burch
Sergeant M J Dowling MM
Lance Corporal F C Evans

HONOURS AND AWARDS

Commander of the Order of the British Empire
Brigadier M S Heath – Commander Maintenance BAOR

Officer of the Order of the British Empire
Lieutenant Colonel N J L Osborne – HQ DGEME

Member of the Order of the British Empire
Major R Brotheridge – Vehicles and Weapons Branch
Major C J Cromack RAEME – 7 Armoured Workshop
WO2 M A Fishwick – 11 Armoured Workshop
WO1 S Hammond – 14th Signal Regiment (Electronic Warfare) LAD
Major C J Lewis – HQ DGEME
Captain P S Milbourn – HQ REME (Aviation) UK
Major D Millar – Late of BLT Kuwait
WO2 C W Randall – Maintenance SSG, LE(A)
Major A E Topp – HQ DGEME

Military Medal
Sergeant Michael James Dowling – 16th/5th The Queen's Royal Lancers LAD
Lance Corporal Kevin Melvin Simon Reid – 22nd Air Defence Regiment Workshop

The Queen's Gallantry Medal
Corporal Mark Robert Griffiths – 414 Tank Transporter Unit RCT Workshop

British Empire Medal
Staff Sergeant S Bateman – 7 Armoured Workshop
Staff Sergeant A L Flower – 1st Battalion, The Staffordshire Regiment LAD
Corporal J O Hawker – 5 Armoured Workshop

Staff Sergeant D Morrison – 6 Armoured Workshop
Staff Sergeant L Murray – 4 Armoured Workshop
Staff Sergeant K Robinson – 21 Engineer Regiment Workshop
Corporal E S Russell – 213 Transport Squadron Workshop (V)
Sergeant K J Salter – The Queen's Royal Irish Hussars LAD
Corporal R J Speed – RAC Sales Team
Staff Sergeant G S Stewart – 39th Heavy Regiment Workshop
Staff Sergeant B C Talbot – 3 Regiment AAC Workshop
Staff Sergeant R W Wells – The Royal Scots Dragoon Guards LAD

There were also five officers and soldiers Mentioned in Despatches, and twenty Commendations.

Bronze Star Medal USA
Captain P W Jaques – 14th/20th King's Hussars LAD
Sergeant P E Burfield – 201 Signal Squadron

Army Commendation Medal USA
Corporal C T Bell – 12 Armoured Workshop

CITATIONS

Sergeant M J Dowling MM
Sergeant Dowling was employed as the REME Fitter Sergeant attached to C Squadron, 16th/5th The Queen's Royal Lancers for their deployment on Operation GRANBY.

On the morning of 26 February 1991, Sergeant Dowling was commanding one of the two M548 logistic load-carrying vehicles grouped with C Squadron. The Squadron was deployed in a screen to prevent reinforcement of the Regimental objective (Objective LEAD) from the north.

At approximately 1100 hours, while the Squadron was in close contact with the enemy, the two M548s came under enemy tank fire. While trying to evade the enemy the rear M548 broke down. Sergeant Dowling moved quickly to take the crew off the broken-down vehicle. Shortly after this his M548 was engaged by enemy tank fire again. While ordering his driver to make best speed to avoid the enemy fire, and with total disregard for his own safety, Sergeant Dowling leaned out of the cab of the M548 and engaged the tank with his personal weapon in order to try to kill the enemy commander who was engaging with his 12.7 mm machine gun. Next to him, Lance Corporal Evans, one of the rescued crewmen, was mortally wounded. Sergeant Dowling continued to engage the enemy tank until he, too, was killed by enemy fire. This was a selfless act of outstanding bravery.

('The Daily Telegraph' reported that HM The Queen had a private meeting in the State Dining Room at Buckingham Palace where she presented the Military Medal to Mrs Teresa Dowling, her son Jamie and her mother-in-law Mrs Kathleen Dowling).

Lance Corporal K M S Reid MM

On the morning of 27 February 1991 7th Armoured Brigade resumed its bold outflanking manoeuvre deep into Iraqi territory. As the leading battle groups advanced towards the Kuwait border, 10 (Assaye) Air Defence Battery was given the vital task of defending the supporting logistic units.

At 1445 hours, as the Battery was approaching the Wadi Al Batin, the JAVELIN detachments of A Troop came under accurate tank fire. Almost immediately, a SPARTAN vehicle received a direct hit and burst into flames. Although the driver and operator managed to escape, the vehicle commander, Bombardier York, was trapped and unable to release himself. Lance Corporal Reid was near the vehicle when it had been hit and could see that Bombardier York required immediate assistance. With total disregard for his own safety, Lance Corporal Reid immediately went to Bombardier York's assistance and tried to free him. Throughout, Lance Corporal Reid and the vehicle were under accurate tank fire, and a second SPARTAN only three metres away was hit and set on fire.

Although his first attempt to free Bombardier York failed, he ignored the rapidly growing flames and fought on to release him. Despite intense danger to his own life, Lance Corporal Reid managed to drag Bombardier York from the vehicle and, using his own hands, extinguished Bombardier York's burning clothes. He then dragged Bombardier York out of the line of fire and arranged for his evacuation. Only then did Lance Corporal Reid have his own burns attended to.

Throughout this incident, Lance Corporal Reid acted with exemplary courage, speed and calmness in the most dangerous of circumstances.

Rather than seek cover, and under fire, he risked the flames and exploding ammunition to free his comrade. Bombardier York himself said, as he was awaiting evacuation, that without Lance Corporal Reid he would have certainly burnt to death. Lance Corporal Reid's was a selfless action of conspicuous gallantry.

Corporal M R Griffiths QGM
On 26 February, at about 1200 hours, Corporal Griffiths's vehicle was in a convoy of tank transporters moving northwards into Iraq carrying vital replacement armour through the border breach. He was following directly behind the stores vehicle of B Troop when smoke started to come from inside the canopy. The vehicle was brought to a halt, but the fire spread quickly through the stores inside, which included four jerrycans of fuel, the Troop's reserve of ammunition, 66 mm anti-tank rockets and L2 hand grenades. In spite of the ferocity of the blaze and the dangerous cargo, Corporal Griffiths leapt into the vehicle and returned time and again to try and recover equipment and stores, until finally he had to retire for his own safety.

As the conflagration partially subsided Corporal Griffiths continued to play the most prominent part in tackling the remaining areas still alight. To accomplish this he climbed onto the vehicle with a shovel and began to jettison burning stores.

Through his personal endeavours, and the practical demonstration of the highest standard of leadership, Corporal Griffiths saved the vehicle in question from being totally destroyed by the fire and enabled it to continue throughout the operation. His behaviour throughout this incident and the personal courage he displayed, as we advanced into Iraq are in the highest traditions of his Corps and the British Army.

REME LESSONS OF OPERATION GRANBY AND CONCLUSIONS

The war in the Gulf brought out many lessons for the Corps. They have to be considered against a background of a campaign which in many ways produced unique demands on equipment and the support requirement. Our Land Forces, largely drawn from BAOR, were thrust into a situation with equipment and an overall logistic support system largely designed for a European war, neither adequate nor compatible for what was instantly required for totally different operating conditions and extended lines of communication. This had a profound effect on the means of achieving effective equipment support to meet this situation. Although many of the deficiencies were fully recognized prior to the Gulf War, the means of rectifying them was not simple in a difficult financial climate. However, much had already been achieved in the overall improvement of equipment management, and the Gulf War was to emphasize the need to continue to pursue that goal. What has gone before in this chapter, and in Chapter 6, has illustrated the inadequate standards of some of our equipment and its back-up under the changed operating conditions, but, most importantly, it has also told the encouraging story of how the equipment support provided for the Force met the operational requirement in spite of initial deficiencies.

The lessons of Operation GRANBY, as seen at HQ DGEME at the Logistic Executive (Army) in Andover, covered a wide range of Corps activities applicable to all types of operations, but there were some now mentioned that were particularly cogent to the specific character of the operations in the Gulf. Of these, some arose from the necessarily hasty mounting of the operation and the essential modifications required to equipment to meet different operating conditions. In this respect experience showed that there was a particular need for contractors' modifications to be proved by REME before production and delivery. There was also a need for a war maintenance reserve of engines, major assemblies, of line replaceable units, and of centrally repairable modules, and better packaging was required for all these items. The operations also showed that deep second-line repair could be appropriate where there are long lines of communication and dusty conditions, and once again the importance of good equipment husbandry was demonstrated. However, without the provision of efficient and dedicated equipment management communications and information technology links in the overall equipment management chain, the overall effectiveness of the system would have been seriously handicapped. How essential such communications are was convincingly proved.

Repair by Repair
Spares shortages and operational emergencies often required 'Repair by Repair'. This requirement had been experienced in the Falklands and at times in Northern Ireland. REME artificers and senior NCOs responded well, improvising and working hard to complete repairs. Younger tradesmen knew little of these 'fixing' skills; training in such skills remains necessary.

Air-Conditioning
Air-conditioning units were fitted to many key communications installations to enhance equipment performance. They were inspected and maintained by a contractor from Howden on whom we were almost totally reliant because of lack of REME expertise in this field.

Power Packs
Much time and effort was spent inspecting and running-up complete power packs sent from BAOR to establish their condition. Their documentation, packaging and general state varied widely. Too many

power packs failed soon after fitting, which may have been caused by fitting 'part-used' packs. A fresh look at quality control and fault diagnosis was needed. The alternative of assembling packs from engines and major assemblies received separately was made difficult and slow because peripherals were poorly preserved, damaged in transit, or often incomplete.

Engines and Major Assemblies
Some assemblies backloaded for repair had been mutilated during cannibalization; others had air, oil way and hydraulic system components exposed to the elements. This was a waste of resources and seldom necessary for operational reasons. Standards of engineering practice needed to be raised.

Reclamation
Much more reclamation work than expected had to be carried out on both A and B Vehicles. This work was often done by tradesmen other than vehicle mechanics who were very busy with repairs. They did well.

Recovery
Management of FMA recovery resources was difficult with such a large area of responsibility, embracing extended and congested main supply routes. Recovery vehicle radio communications proved unworkable. Casualty reports were generally completed poorly with incorrect grid references or none at all. It required all the 6 Armoured Workshop MRG recovery and spare load-carriers, plus fifteen low-loaders specially diverted from other tasks by the Staff, to clear the Back Loading Point when 1st Armoured Division made its final move to its Assembly Area. It took five days to backload about 120 equipments over 100 kilometres of road and desert track to the FFMA workshop site.

Equipment Management Predictions
Initial calculations of Mean Distances Between Failures made in BAOR based on performance data from British Army Training Unit Suffield in Canada proved to be reasonably accurate. Sustainability predictions deduced from these figures were confirmed by early results on GRANBY. When the trend showed under-performance, engines and major assemblies had to be released from operational reserves to allow training to continue, or when the figures became critically low the GOC reduced training mileages to preserve the operational reserve. As the work-up training was nearly completed, the figures for CHALLENGER and WARRIOR showed marked improvement and this allowed the GOC to increase mileages allowed for the final training exercises. It was thought that the improved figures were due to easier going on the terrain used for later exercises and better preventative maintenance as crews and

LADs gained experience and knowledge. The GOC required regular, properly supervised squadron, battery and company maintenance days during training, which were attended by Vickers and GKN contractors and, by this time, the WARRIOR air filtration modifications were fully effective.

Contractors

The technical advice and the help received from the UK contractors were of great value to equipment managers, to the crews using the equipment and to the REME personnel maintaining it. After the quayside modifications at Al Jubayl and health monitoring had been completed, the presence of the contractors' engineers in the desert with the users and REME was of great help in improving equipment husbandry and reporting of faults. As a result, LADs were trained in fault diagnosis and rectification in a systematic manner.

TRIBUTES

The Corps provided support to an operation that was mounted at short notice far away from the UK and BAOR. Everyone had to take seriously and prepare for an air and NBC threat that did not materialize. When the land war began it was one of the most rapid advances which had ever been achieved and may never happen again, but it lasted only four days. That REME officers and soldiers did their job well was confirmed by the letters from the Colonel in Chief and from the Quartermaster General.

The Colonel in Chief, HRH The Prince Philip, wrote on 28 February 1991 to the DGEME:

'The splendid news arrived this morning that hostilities had ceased in the Gulf War. That this war has been brought to a successful conclusion in such a short time and at such a small cost in casualties is largely due to the very high state of training, expertise and morale of the units involved and I would be very grateful if you could find some way of conveying my admiration and congratulations to all the members of the Corps who took part in this campaign.

'I realize of course that the Corps is serving all the units engaged, but it so happens that I was able to get to Germany only yesterday to visit regimental wives and I had the opportunity to call on the wives of the Field Workshops at Münster and Fallingbostel. They were all in great form and much relieved that the end was in sight. I imagine that their relief, and that of all Corps wives, has since turned to celebration and to the happy prospect of the return of their husbands.'

Extracts from a letter of congratulations from the Quartermaster General, Lieutenant General Sir Edward Jones KCB CBE, to Major General D Shaw CB CBE, DGEME on 8 March 1991.

'I believe that circumstances are now sufficiently clear for me to write to you to express my deep appreciation and thanks for what has been achieved by members of your Corps during Op GRANBY. . . . It was not until 17th September that an announcement was made of the Government's intention to commit ground forces in support of the Alliance. There was no contingency plan on which to base our deployment and special-to-theatre stores had largely been disposed of.

'What has been achieved in the intervening months in support of Op GRANBY. . . has been by any standards remarkable. It has underlined the professionalism and resilience of the Army at every level. The commitment and determination to overcome the inevitable multiplicity of problems has been wholly praiseworthy. Persistence, innovation, ingenuity and sheer bloody-mindedness have all played their part. I could not begin to detail every facet of this remarkable operation from the up-armouring of tanks and APCs to the distribution of Christmas puddings and Valentine cards. It would be impractical and invidious.

'That all of this has proved possible reflects the highest praise on everyone who has been involved. The range is formidable. Pride of place must go to the units deployed in the desert, but that should not in any way obscure the critical role played by others. I refer to soldiers and civilians, men and women, who have manned the distribution and supply chain, working seven days a week, including Christmas, to ensure that the needs of the men on the ground were met. I refer to those in workshops and in industry who broke all records to provide the fighting man with the tools to finish the job. . . . Wherever and however men and women of the logistic services, whether Regular, Territorial Army or individual reservist, have contributed to Op GRANBY they can be proud of a job well done. . . . I would be grateful if you would pass on as appropriate my message of thanks and great pride to all who serve in your Corps.'

General Sir Peter de la Billière KCB KBE DSO MC, Commander British Forces Middle East, wrote later:

'The first REME tradesman arrived in Saudi Arabia less than one month after Iraq had invaded Kuwait. From that day on, through the peak of activity, when 3,700 REME soldiers were deployed in the Theatre, until the departure of the last man with the Logistic Support Group in July 1991, the Corps was intimately involved in the preparation and modification of equipment for desert warfare, repair support during the land war itself and the recovery of the Force to Europe. Without the splendid commitment and the high level of technical skill demonstrated by all the tradesmen, technicians and officers deployed within the 1st Armoured Division, the Force Maintenance Area and the Force Headquarters – not forgetting those soldiers and civilians remaining in Europe who provided unstinting support at a distance – tired vehicles and other vital equipment would

have ground to a halt; the logistic stocks could not have been out-loaded and the Division could not have completed its training successfully, let alone taken part so effectively in Operation DESERT STORM. Thanks to the dedicated support of the REME soldiers at all levels, especially those serving within the forward Battle Groups, and those who gave their lives, the Division was able to advance 290 kilometres in sixty-six hours with remarkably few equipment casualties against a numerically superior enemy. There can be no doubt that the support provided by REME played a vital role in keeping the British Force rolling inexorably towards the final victory.'

Annex A

OPERATION GRANBY: ARMY ORDER OF BATTLE

HQ 1st (British) Armoured Division

HQ 4 Armoured Brigade
14th/20th King's Hussars
1st Battalion, The Royal Scots (The Royal Regiment)
3rd Battalion, The Royal Regiment of Fusiliers
2nd Field Regiment Royal Artillery
23 Engineer Regiment

HQ 7 Armoured Brigade
The Royal Scots Dragoon Guards (Carabiniers and Greys)
The Queen's Royal Irish Hussars
1st Battalion, The Staffordshire Regiment (The Prince of Wales's)
40th Field Regiment Royal Artillery
21 Engineer Regiment

Divisional Troops
16th/5th The Queen's Royal Lancers
12th Air Defence Regiment Royal Artillery
26th Field Regiment Royal Artillery
32nd Heavy Regiment Royal Artillery
39th Heavy Regiment Royal Artillery
32 Armoured Engineer Regiment
1st (British) Armoured Division HQ and Signal Regiment
4 Regiment Army Air Corps

Second/Third Line Support
39 Engineer Regiment
1 Armoured Division Transport Regiment
4 Armoured Division Transport Regiment
7 Tank Transporter Regiment
10 Regiment Royal Corps of Transport
27 Regiment Royal Corps of Transport
1 Armoured Field Ambulance
5 Armoured Field Ambulance
22 Field Ambulance
24 (Airmobile) Field Ambulance
32 Field Hospital
3 Ordnance Battalion
5 Ordnance Battalion
6 Ordnance Battalion
6 Armoured Workshop
7 Armoured Workshop
11 Armoured Workshop
71 Aircraft Workshop

187 (Tancred) Company Royal Pioneer Corps
518 Company Royal Pioneer Corps
908 Pioneer Labour Support Unit
Army War Graves Service Royal Pioneer Corps

Prisoner of War Guard Force

1st Battalion, Coldstream Guards
1st Battalion, The Royal Highland Fusiliers (Princess Margaret's Own Glasgow and Ayrshire Regiment)
1st Battalion, The King's Own Scottish Borderers

Theatre Troops

30th Signal Regiment
22nd Special Air Service Regiment

REME units who provided significant individual reinforcements or battle casualty replacements

4 Armoured Workshop
5 Armoured Workshop
12 Armoured Workshop
20 Electronics Workshop
1 Corps Troops Workshop

Note:
Additional sub-units were involved in the operation as part of other units or formations.

Annex B

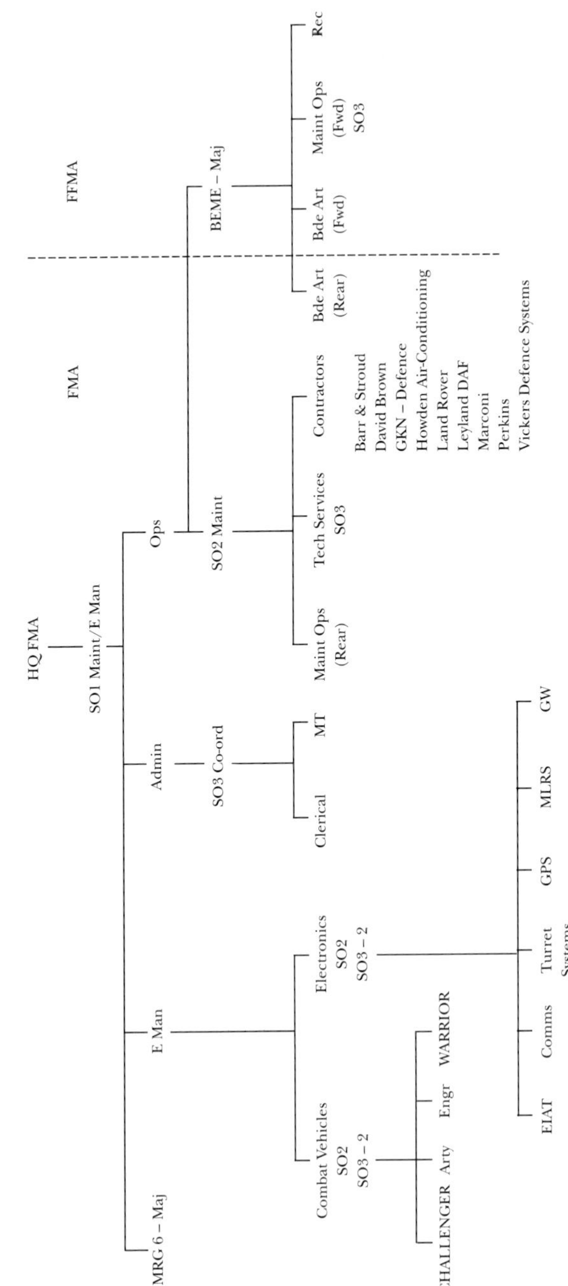
HQ FMA MAINTENANCE AND EQUIPMENT MANAGEMENT STAFF
FMA
FFMA
HQ FMA
SO1 Maint/E Man
MRG 6 – Maj
E Man
Admin
Ops
SO3 Co-ord
SO2 Maint
BEME – Maj
Combat Vehicles SO2 SO3 – 2
Electronics SO2 SO3 – 2
Clerical
MT
Maint Ops (Rear)
Tech Services SO3
Contractors
Bde Art (Rear)
Bde Art (Fwd)
Maint Ops (Fwd) SO3
Rec
Barr & Stroud
David Brown
GKN – Defence
Howden Air-Conditioning
Land Rover
Leyland DAF
Marconi
Perkins
Vickers Defence Systems
CHALLENGER
Arty
Engr
WARRIOR
EIAT
Comms
Turret Systems
GPS
MLRS
GW
Peak Manning: 13 officers 32 soldiers
20 February 1991

CHAPTER 13

REME REGIMENTAL ACTIVITIES

INTRODUCTION

There is a brief account in Volume 1 of the way in which REME regimental activities and organizations began after the end of the Second World War. In this volume, covering as it does major post-war development of the Corps and its duties and responsibilities world-wide, it is fitting that the regimental activities of the Corps should now be considered in greater detail. These wide-ranging activities, and the management of the associated organizations built up to support them, have been developed in parallel to all the technical advances of the Corps and reflect the changes in logistic responsibility that have taken place. They are essential to the life of the Corps and an indication of its strength in the role that it has to play in a rapidly changing Army. They affect all members of the

Corps in some way, wherever they may be, in their military duties, in their recreation or in aiding their welfare both when serving and retired. As such they cover a wide spectrum and some facets inevitably encroach on matters already touched on in lesser detail in earlier chapters in this volume.

This chapter describes the regimental system within the Corps starting with its Head – The Colonel in Chief, a member of the Royal Family – and the organizations from which flow all the Corps' activities other than the performance of its technical duties. Examples of regimental activities which are more pertinent to a particular part of the organization are given with the description of that part, whilst the remainder are shown under their own headings.

THE COLONEL IN CHIEF

Field Marshal His Royal Highness The Prince Philip, Duke of Edinburgh, KG, KT, OM, GBE, AC, QSO became Colonel in Chief and Head of the Corps in July 1969, when he was appointed by Her Majesty The Queen to succeed Her Royal Highness The Princess Marina, Duchess of Kent, who had died in August 1968. Prince Philip soon began a series of many visits to the Corps, at home and abroad, which have been a tremendous source of encouragement and pride to members of the Corps, and a number of these are described in other chapters. A further selection is given below.

On 19 March 1976 Prince Philip visited the REME units at Middle Wallop and presented Wings to the pilots graduating from an Army Pilots Course, including Staff Sergeant P Harrison, a Vehicle Artificer. Prince Philip saw the SIOUX helicopter XT154 which he himself flew for the award of his Army Wings in 1965.

A visit of quite another sort took place on 27 April 1978 when the Colonel in Chief opened Rowcroft Barracks, the new home of the Training Battalion and Depot REME at Arborfield. The day began with Prince Philip, attended by Major General Vincent Metcalfe, the Representative Colonel Commandant, inspecting a Passing Out Parade of Recruits and presenting prizes. This was followed by the unveiling of a plaque and a tour of the barracks, during which he saw one of the new barrack blocks built with eight-men rooms, cleverly designed to give each man some degree of privacy. General Metcalfe recalls, 'The Colonel in Chief was impressed and, on leaving the room, paused to study a plan of the layout pinned to the wall. None of us could make head or tail of it but it did not puzzle the Colonel in Chief for long. "It's upside down," he

Prince Philip unveils the plaque – Commanding Officer Lieutenant Colonel Chris Derbyshire

told us!' Later he went to meet the senior ranks assembled in the new Sergeants' Mess where he signed the Visitors' Book.

During the years 1971–75 Captain Andrew Platt filled an appointment as Extra Equerry in Prince Philip's Household. In 1989 he recalled those days:

'I had an office in Buckingham Palace where I would work for one day per fortnight on programme planning and I took my turn accompanying HRH on duty. When I was out with him, my responsibilities were to liaise with the organization he was visiting, to brief him on the programme and then make sure we kept to it, to the minute. There was the potential for a major disaster unless all the details were checked. The Household staff were very efficient and quite familiar with Prince Philip's very busy routine. However, it was one of the Equerry's jobs to make sure that cars had been arranged. There were spine-chilling stories, probably apocryphal, about previous Equerries discovering, too late, that their arrangements were not properly tied up and having to explain to Prince Philip that the dignified exit in a limousine in ten minutes' time was not possible. I was very careful to avoid this pitfall, and it fortunately never happened to me.

'Prince Philip was very professional about his job, working at a standing desk late into the night after his last engagement, preparing hand-written notes for his speeches. He would frequently have four functions a day, which also put a strain on his Equerries, particularly when a quick change was required. He would be assisted by his staff to change into any form of dress in about five minutes. We could only keep up by handing over to another Equerry who was already appropriately dressed and waiting in the wings.

'I was very pleasantly surprised to be selected for the appointment in the first place, especially after a disastrous interview with General Peter Girling. It was my first visit to his headquarters in First Avenue House and I had been summoned to be interviewed by DEME(A), but not told what for. I felt like putting blotting paper in the seat of my pants and going to see the Headmaster. Not surprisingly I had difficulty in finding the building, the entrance of which was behind the

Government Book Shop, so I arrived five minutes late. But as I was not the first victim to be called in it was not serious. However, the first thing General Girling asked me was, "Did I arrive on time?" I, truthfully, said that I had been late, whereupon he was quite cross. But my big mistake, when explaining why, was to say that I had not expected to find my Director's Office at the back of the Government Book Shop!

'I attended with Prince Philip a dinner at West Court and also a passing out parade at the Apprentices College, by which time I was serving as Adjutant at the Training Battalion and Depot. I spent many hours talking with him in the back of motor cars and helicopters, and appreciated his essential understanding of the Corps and his great interest in what we were doing. He was always full of good sound fatherly advice to a young REME captain, particularly about sailing, a great passion of his. I found it to be a most interesting appointment.'

Prince Philip has been a most assiduous Colonel in Chief ever since he accepted the appointment in 1969 and has taken a very close interest in the Corps' activities. Apart from the many military aspects with which he was involved, he has been keenly concerned with social events and was instrumental in the Corps being able from time to time to hold receptions at St James's Palace.

THE COLONELS COMMANDANT

Colonels Commandant are appointed by Her Majesty The Queen on the recommendation of the Representative Colonel Commandant and with the concurrence of the Colonel in Chief. The appointments are honorary and do not form part of the normal chain of command. Most Colonels Commandant appointed to the Corps, but not all, are selected from Major Generals late REME on retirement from the Active List or as soon after as there is a vacancy. There are normally five Colonels Commandant each serving for five years, one of whom is the Representative Colonel Commandant for one year.

The main responsibilities of Colonels Commandant include collectively guarding the Corps' traditions, fostering esprit de corps, fostering civilian connections and regimental associations, advice within the Corps on regimental matters, control of or advice on regimental matters such as charities, funds, properties, museums and memorials and, finally, maintenance of good will and liaison between all parts of the Corps, including the TA and Cadets. The Representative Colonel Commandant during his tenure is the senior regimental representative of the Corps. He exercises many of these functions by being Chairman of the REME

Corps Committee and of the Trustees of the REME Central Charitable Trust, President of the REME Institution, the REME Association and the REME Rifle Association, Chairman of the REME Institution Committee and of the REME Museum Trustees. He attends many Corps functions and visits units at home and abroad during his year in office. The Representative Colonel Commandant is the link between the Corps and the Colonel in Chief and receives him when he visits the Corps. The Honorary Colonels of the REME TA are another important group of men with whom the Representative Colonel Commandant must keep closely in touch.

Directors of the Corps have always become a Colonel Commandant, whilst distinguished senior officers from other regiments or corps have also been selected. Field Marshal The Lord Carver (two terms) 1966–76, General Sir Hugh Beach 1976–81, Field Marshal Sir Richard Vincent 1981–87, General Sir Jeremy Blacker 1987–92 and Lieutenant General Sir Rupert Smith from 1992, are officers who have given REME the benefit of their wide experience in the Army during the period covered by this book. At the time of his appointment Field Marshal Carver was Director of Army Staff Duties and was later to be Chief of the Defence Staff. General Sir Hugh Beach became Master General of the Ordnance a year after his appointment. Field Marshal Sir Richard Vincent, who became Chief of the Defence Staff in 1991–92 and then Chairman of the North Atlantic Military Committee 1993–96, and General Sir Jeremy Blacker were both Commandants of the Royal Military College of Science at Shrivenham when they were appointed, whilst Lieutenant General Sir Rupert Smith had commanded 1st (British) Armoured Division in the Gulf War.

Field Marshal Carver was particularly well known to REME soldiers, having been an enthusiastic dinghy sailor with the Corps for many years. Informality on these occasions was much appreciated. In 1989 he recalled in a letter:

'I was crewing in a REME v RAOC contest at Stokes Bay in 1969 or 1970 and the embarrassed referee, an RAOC brigadier, presiding over an objection raised by a member of an RAOC crew (actually himself in the RCT!), had to choose between the word of that lance corporal and of the GOC-in-C Southern Command, which I was at the time, who was responsible for commenting on his annual confidential report! Not surprisingly, he (correctly) rejected the objection in our favour.'

It is the Representative Colonel Commandant that serving members of the Corps are most likely to meet. His activities and visits are regularly recorded in 'The Craftsman'. The Colonels Commandant from 1966 are listed at the Appendix at the end of this volume. It is true to say that the Corps as a whole receives great benefit from the advice and wide experience of these distinguished men who give so much of their time in its service.

REGIMENTAL HEADQUARTERS

Before 1990 Regimental matters had been looked after by a variety of agencies, the Corps Secretariat being largely responsible for arranging and supporting the Corps committees, running the Museum, the Association and the Institution, 'The Craftsman' magazine and administering benevolence. The very absorbing task of running the family matters of REME was done by otherwise busy individuals, such as DEME (Organization & Training) at Andover, Commandant REME Training Centre and his staff, and the Commandant REME Officers School. This had always been an uncomfortable arrangement and the conflicting priorities were hard to balance. REME, in line with all other cap badges in the Army, needed a focus for Regimental matters. This was more than ever necessary with the formation of the Equipment Support Organization, to counteract the dilution of REME with the many other cap badges in it, which, inevitably, provided even less time for DGES(A) and his staff to become involved in Corps matters. There were also to be more responsibilities for the newly forming REME Training Group, which gave the Commandant the same problem.

In 1990 work was started to provide a focus for REME's domestic affairs by the preparation of a DGEME's Policy Committee Paper, proposing the formation of a Regimental Headquarters. The paper, written by Lieutenant Colonel Charles Morgan, considered two options to enable the Recruiting Staff, Secretariat, Museum, Band and Publications, to be centralized under a Regimental Colonel. The first option was to make the Commandant of the Officers School, a colonel, the Regimental Colonel in a double-hatted role. The second was to make the Chief Instructor of the Officers School at lieutenant colonel rank its commanding officer. The Commandant of the Officers School would then become available to be exclusively Regimental Colonel. The paper was taken on 12 October 1990 and the double-hatted option was adopted, and implemented in April 1991.

The resulting organization, under Colonel Andy Platt as the first Regimental Colonel, managed to survive the aftermath of the Gulf War and the very busy Corps 50th Anniversary programme in 1992. But it was clear that in practice the double-hatted option of running the School, the Regimental Headquarters and attending some twenty-three committees, was too heavy a burden. However, the concept of a Regimental Colonel was thoroughly sound, providing the Corps Secretary with direction, and the involvement of a serving officer below the rank of brigadier in the wide range of Regimental matters. It also greatly improved the Corps' interface with the rest of the Army. Consequently the Army Establishments Committee ultimately agreed to maintain the Colonel's post of Commandant of the Officers School and to provide an additional colonel for the dedicated post of Regimental Colonel. This was to take effect from December 1993.

THE CORPS SECRETARIAT REME

The Corps Secretariat celebrated its 30th anniversary in 1990. It had provided a service to the whole of the Corps, whether serving or retired, Regular or TA, and their dependants. In 1959 Brigadier Leonard Atkinson, then Commandant of REME Training Centre, proposed that the Corps' domestic regimental activities be centralized. They had grown up independently in the new Corps and relied on serving officers working voluntarily or on people paid from Corps funds. Accounting was carried out by Glyn Mills, the Corps' bankers. The establishment of a Corps Secretariat from April 1960 was approved, to be set up at Moat House, Arborfield where it remained for 21 years. The staff included a Corps Secretary (RO2) to be Editor of the Magazine and Journal and Secretary of the Sports Association, an Assistant Secretary (RO3) for the REME Association and Benevolent Fund, a second Assistant Secretary (RO3) for the Officers' Club and Headquarters Officers' Mess and an Accountant (RO3). This staff enabled a reduction to be made of almost 100% in Corps funds expense and a reduction from more than seven mis-employed men to one GD soldier to look after Moat House and 'half a soldier' as magazine photographer. The first Corps Secretary was Brigadier James Orr who took post on 10 October 1960. Lieutenant Colonel Wilkinson – known as 'Wilkie' to so many REME officers – ran West Court so efficiently for many years as Secretary, that it was decided not to transfer his duties to the Secretariat. The Association, Benevolent Fund and Museum were already in the capable hands of Lieutenant Colonel Bill Johnston, where they remained.

After the retirement of Lieutenant Colonel Wilkinson one of the Corps Assistant Secretaries became Mess Secretary of West Court as well as Deputy Editor of 'The Craftsman' and Secretary of the Central Unit Funds (Closed Units). These Funds, although now a component part of the Central Charitable Trust, are an important source of finance to assist unit and Mess activities throughout the Corps.

The Officers' Club became the REME Institution in 1962 and from 1966 to 1974 the Corps Recruiting Liaison Officer was on the Secretariat establishment. In 1968 the Corps Secretary became Curator of the Museum when Lieutenant Colonel Johnston retired and in 1978 he became the permanent Secretary of the Corps Committee, in place of the Staff Officer to DGEME.

At the end of 1981 the Secretariat moved from Moat House to new premises in Isaac Newton Road. The Museum, subject to a complete redesign of the displays and layouts, was not transferred to the new premises until later, with its formal opening by Major General John Homan in March 1985. As the Museum expanded a Deputy Curator, paid from Corps Funds, had been added in 1983, the post being taken up by WO1 Brian Baxter, a keen military vehicles enthusiast, on his retirement. The new museum with its modern displays, largely the concept of Mr Baxter, attracted about five thousand visitors each year. Also in 1983, the Corps Treasurer was converted from an RO3 to a civilian Executive Officer, Miss Penny Spooner.

In 1987 a new post of Deputy Corps Secretary was created, also paid from Corps funds, and Lieutenant Colonel Larry Le Var took up the appointment with particular responsibilities for the Museum as Curator in place of Brigadier Martyn Clark, the Corps Secretary. He also became Secretary of the REME Memorial Scholarship Fund, a responsibility transferred from SEME.

In 1989 the Corps Secretariat, responsible to DGEME and administered by HQ REME Training Centre, had three Retired Officers, six clerks, two part-time typists and a curatorial assistant for the Museum paid for from public funds, plus a Deputy Corps Secretary, a Deputy Curator and part-time Association sales staff paid from Corps Funds.

The essence of the Secretariat's work in the Seventies and Eighties was maintaining contact with past and present members of the Corps and their families, arranging reunions, making financial grants to units and individuals, helping the bereaved, spreading news of the Corps and maintaining Corps history.

Mr Tony Wheddon BEM, so well known to generations of REME officers as Mess Steward at West Court, finally retired from the sales staff of the Association in August 1989 at the age 74 after 43 years service in Arborfield.

The following have served as Corps Secretaries since the formation of the Secretariat in 1960:

1960 Brigadier James Orr CBE
1962 Brigadier Norman Molony
1973 Brigadier Tom Garner MBE
1983 Brigadier Martyn Clark
1995 Colonel David Axson

THE REME CENTRAL CHARITABLE TRUST

The REME Central Charitable Trust was set up in December 1986 to promote the efficiency of REME, foster esprit de corps and to provide relief for members or former members of REME or their dependants who are in need. It exists as the all-embracing amalgam of Corps funds, the only exception being that the REME Association has remained separate because of the diverse nature of its membership and of possible doubts in its eligibility for full participation in the benefits available from the CCT. The REME CCT Fund, which had its first full year of operation in 1988, received most of the Corps income, which allowed the Trustees to be flexible in directing the income to where it was most needed. A high percentage of covenanted subscriptions from soldiers to give an enhanced income was expected and achieved with over 98% of the Corps agreeing to subscribe to the Fund in the first year. The Trustees are the members of the Corps Committee, the Custodian Trustee being the Trustee Division of The Royal Bank of Scotland.

Historically the accumulating wealth of the Corps had been concentrated in the Benevolent Fund, and its use for causes beyond the overriding central matters of welfare had stretched the bounds of its trust deed, inhibiting the freedom of the trustees to do whatever was good for the Corps. In early 1984 discussions centred round this dilemma, noting the practice of sister Corps and indeed the almost universal practice of covenanting for all ranks' subscriptions: the substantial tax rebate scheme that REME had long implemented, but only amongst its officers. Further discussion in the Corps Committee was strongly reinforced by Brigadier Mike Gardner's report in the series of routine quinquennial reviews of Corps funds. His 'radical approach' was paralleled by a paper prepared by Brigadier Andrew MacLauchlan, Commandant of REME Training Centre, and his successor Brigadier John Till. The motivation was to make the wealth of the Benevolent Fund, which was accumulating a surplus, more widely available to other Corps funds and also to maximize tax efficiency. Thus in 1984 there commenced serious studies of the options, conducted by Brigadier Till and his staff and, in 1985, a detailed study commissioned from a recently

The REME Corps Committee in 1989
Brigadier M W Clark, Colonel B R Cooper, Brigadier M H Carey, Major General J Boyne, Major General D Shaw, Brigadier M T A Lord, Brigadier J A Graham

retired officer – Brigadier Terry White. His report provided detailed recommendations on organization, procedures, committee membership and implementation, and was taken by the Corps Committee in October 1985. The Committee unanimously agreed to set up a Central Charitable Trust.

There followed eighteen months of intensive work, particularly involving Major Peter Gange, in studying covenanting aspects, and the setting up of a covenanting team at the Corps Secretariat under Major Richard Crowson. Some 15,000 forms were despatched, complete with a packet of scripts and vufoils to enable the concept to be presented to all ranks in their units. The imminence of the project also gave impetus to the introduction of computer assistance to the Corps Secretariat's activities, and secured authority for the employment of the Deputy Corps Secretary. A Trust Deed providing substantial flexibility for supporting esprit de corps as well as the continuing benevolence assistance was drafted, and on 1 December 1986 was signed by the members of the Corps Committee, each donating a £1 coin in initiating the CCT's Fund. In April 1987 the CCT became fully operational, and all trustees and managing committees of principal Corps activities transferred their assets to the central fund and thereafter became bidders upon the CCT fund in its annual budgetary process. The covenanting exercise had succeeded in securing initial acceptance throughout the Corps, and subscriptions thereafter produced the anticipated benefit through income tax rebate. Soldiers continued to subscribe 50% of one day's net basic pay, whilst officers' subscriptions were set at 150% – a slight reduction against the total of their two former separate contributions of

120% covenanted and, to the Officers' Mess, 60% uncovenanted.

At this stage the officers of the WRAC permanently employed by the Corps had to continue paying their own dues centrally to the WRAC, a situation that lasted until they were re-badged REME in 1990. Until that time they received their REME benefits 'for free'. These benefits, for all ranks of the Corps from the establishment of the CCT, were the free provision of 'The Craftsman', (distributed on a pro-rata basis to units), the cessation of unit sports subscriptions, increased support to the Corps Sergeants' Mess from the subscriptions of sergeants and above, and a substantial increase in the ability to make grants for Corps projects ranging from individuals up to Corps level. At the same time more money was to be made available to those in need. The concept of a group insurance scheme covering off-duty injuries was considered but not pursued.

With a new balance achieved in Corps committees, and in particular in the setting-up of the CCT Trustees and their subordinate Finance Committee, the Corps Secretary was able to work in his role as Financial Secretary in implementing many of Brigadier White's concepts, developing an annual budgetary system, and a five-year Long Term Costing, which for the first time gave the senior Corps committees an ability to have a strategic view of their financial affairs. The Trustees were able, with their very wide discretionary powers, to ensure that monies were effectively allocated in line with the priorities of the Corps as a whole. Over the following years there were few changes to the original plan. Care was taken to ensure that funds allocated by the CCT to the REME Institution and the HQ Officers' Mess did not exceed that which was formerly subscribed by officers direct to those organizations – so protecting the position of all ranks' contributions. A significant effect of the setting up of the CCT was that its Trustees dealt thereafter with all Corps financial business, less the REME Association's affairs, which remained under the supervision of the Corps Committee. This, with the same membership as the CCT, was thus left to concentrate on all other, non-monetary, regimental business.

REME BENEVOLENCE

The REME Benevolent Fund

Major General Rowcroft, as DME, had inaugurated the REME Benevolent Fund on 7 July 1945: its principal purposes, enshrined in the trust deed, were to give charitable assistance to present or past members of the Corps or their dependants, and 'maintaining or increasing the efficiency and esprit de corps' of REME. From that day on there were never any doubts in ensuring support wherever it was needed without favour, as a result of close and even-handed assessments of true need. By the end of 1992 over 900 applications a year were being received, of which only about 4% came from serving soldiers. Rather more than half of all applicants received grants after investigation – usually through the agency of SSAFA – and subsequent committee consideration. The Executive Committee, under senior officer chairmanship and with one further officer, consisted otherwise of five warrant officers: a group of experienced soldiers who would not be considered a 'soft touch' but who would, nevertheless, authorize grants appropriate to the cases presented.

Benevolence was most frequently realized in monetary terms, and from General Rowcroft's original gift of 15 shillings (75 modern pence) the available assets of the Fund built up to exceed one million pounds by 1987, when it was brought under the financial wing of the CCT. Such successful achievement of a sound capital base was primarily the result of encouraging all ranks to subscribe annually at least one half of a day's pay. At the same time the Army Benevolent Fund (ABF), pursuing similar aims across the service as a whole, was partially dependent upon annual grants from individual regimental trusts in making major grants on their behalf, as well as supporting case-work organizations such as SSAFA. In 1966 the ABF had urged Army Regiments and Corps to secure from all ranks a full day's pay per annum to their own funds, and so to ensure a continuing source of income. An all-out drive within REME was mounted during 1970–73 with Lieutenant Colonel Freddie Parsons, as Secretary of the REME Benevolent Fund, touring major units of the Corps in BAOR and UK and spreading the gospel. The low 52% of the Corps subscribing in 1969 rose by 1984 to 96%. With such annual support thereafter being maintained, actuarial advice confirmed that a half-day's pay scheme was sufficient for the REME Fund's future demands, and so it remained. Within this it proved possible for the Fund to grant annually to the ABF sums which in later years rose to the order of £65,000, after first satisfying the needs of its domestic benevolence. The ABF routinely co-operated in the larger-scale grants needed by Corps members, thus effectively returning some of that annual grant, which otherwise was REME's contribution to Army-wide benevolence. The strength of some 165,000 REME servicemen during the Second World War, together with their spouses, were, by the Eighties and early Nineties, at least in their sixties. The load on the Fund was expected to rise accordingly and only taper off during the final years of the century.

Regular grants were made to those in hospital, including the residents of the Royal Star and Garter Home and the in-pensioners of The Royal Hospital, Chelsea. At Christmas time all of these would be visited by Corps representatives with monetary gifts and cards bearing the good wishes of the Corps. Apart from individual grants, the Fund also gave support to other charitable causes, primarily those of a Service nature. The largest item of expenditure ever incurred by the Fund was that involved in the purchase of the REME Hotel at Wertach, a significant act for the benefit of the 'REME family', described later in this chapter.

The REME Memorial Scholarship Fund

Bearing a close relationship to the Benevolent Fund, the REME Memorial Scholarship Fund had been founded in July 1955, with an obligation to make grants by way of charitable assistance for education above elementary level and for professional, technical or industrial apprenticeship fees, or for maintenance during such education or apprenticeship, to sons and daughters of present and past members of the Corps. In practice priority was normally given to those children who had lost one or both parents, and preference given towards those taking their GCSEs and A levels. In conjunction with the ABF, the Fund has successfully supported many educational needs through bursaries, albeit on a relatively small scale: for instance, during the academic year 1991–92 the Fund made awards to seven recipients and arranged a further two bursaries through the ABF.

THE REME INSTITUTION

The origins of the REME Institution, the body corporate of all those who hold or who have held a commission in the Corps, were described in the first volume. Its aims continued unaltered throughout the period covered by this volume, but differed in emphasis. Gradually the number of sports that it subsidized reduced, generally related to the social trend that fewer activities were considered to be 'officer only', leaving only those that maintained a number of fixtures for officers alone. By 1993 all sports were to be assisted wholly by the REME Sports Association.

Latterly, increasing assistance was being given towards the recruiting of officers as competition between the engineering corps intensified, reaching a stage when the Committee felt constrained to limit its assistance to no more than 15% of its annual expenditure. Meanwhile, the embrace of the Corps towards potential commissioning candidates was enhanced by giving free membership of the Institution to undergraduate cadets and bursars.

The Technical Sub-Committee of the Institution, set up in 1969 to further its standing in the profession of engineering, became more and more active in advising and assisting both officers and artificers in securing membership of their relevant civilian professional institutions, and encouraging their active involvement. At the close of the period of this volume a number of Institution-sponsored annual lectures were being planned by the Sub-Committee. These were headed by The REME Institution Lecture to be given annually by a prominent member of the national profession.

Membership remained in the region of 2,500, but was enhanced during the Eighties by inviting the widows of deceased officers to continue their contacts with the Corps through a special class of Institution membership. Finally, in 1990, the recognition that wartime and National Service had brought into temporary contact with REME many men who later achieved national eminence in their professions led to the creation of a category of Distinguished Honorary Membership. In that year an initial invitation to eleven such gentlemen brought a warm response, generally renewing fond memories of their membership of REME – but also a wish to contribute in these later years in one way or another to the Corps' benefit.

In addition to the continuing production of the annual REME Journal, the need to change printers afforded the opportunity to improve the Officers List, as mentioned later in this chapter. By 1987 the Institution was, in common with other Corps organizations, swept up financially into the CCT. Subscriptions thereafter were made to the CCT and the Institution received its funds in response to an annual bid against the CCT budget; such change did not, however, restrict the continuing activities of the Institution.

The Institution continued to award prizes to young officers, including the restored DGEME's sword for the best REME officer cadet of his year, and to run its traditional social events. The demand for places at the annual Retired Officers' Dinner invariably exceeded capacity, particularly following the introduction by Brigadier Martyn Clark of the practice of celebrating the achievement of fifty years of holding a commission – and, on occasion, by some few achieving sixty years! On one occasion, such a senior celebrant had to leave dinner quite promptly; his urge, no less for all his years, was to be on the boundary for his county's cricket match early on the next day.

'Judnick'

'Judnick' is a property owned by the REME Institution, the second house used for many years as the residence for the Mess Steward of the Headquarters Officers' Mess. After the plan to renovate the Coachman's house at West Court had proved not possible, 'Westonbirt' was bought in 1955 by the Mess for £2,350, providing rent-free accommodation in nearby Reading Road for the Steward – at that time Mr Tony Wheddon. Subsequently, he moved into 'Judnick' when it was purchased in February 1966 from Mr and Mrs Caddy, leaving 'Westonbirt' to be rented by the Ministry of Defence as a hiring until it was sold two years later for £5,000. Its unusual name commemorates the two Caddy children, Judy and Nicholas, whose parents had moved from Tidworth to Arborfield under the patronage of the Garrison Commander, Brigadier Tony Howard-Jones, to open up a hairdressing shop in one of the Biggs Lane huts; whilst living initially there they had built 'Judnick' for their use until they retired and moved away in 1966. 'Judnick' was a Georgian-style house built in about 1959, offering better and more comfortable accommodation than 'Westonbirt', and conveniently located in the Garrison area, only a few yards from the Headquarters. Its freehold was bought by the Institution under Major General Denis Redman's guidance for £6,000, assisted by a loan from Mess funds resulting from the sale of part of the grounds of 'Westonbirt', and was made the subject of a trust with Holt's Bank as a Custodian Trustee. The Training Centre Commandant and the Institution Secretary were appointed as a Managing Committee, and the Mess thereafter paid a nominal rent to the Institution. Following Mr Wheddon's retirement in 1980 the property was occupied by Mr David Green, his successor as Mess Steward. The property remains as a valuable asset, available for use in whatever way is thought best for the Corps' needs.

THE REME ASSOCIATION

The early days of the REME Association were mentioned briefly in the first volume, its birth being confirmed by a letter written by Major General Rowcroft to the Corps in July 1945. A general pattern of social events was developed, based upon regional branches which would seek to create and maintain the bonds of good fellowship between past and present members of the Corps. Assistance could also be given towards welfare cases and in the search for employment opportunities through their local contacts.

After the early post-war years, when there was a substantial number of civilians who had seen service with REME, there was a pronounced falling-off in numbers: from sixty-six branches (including twenty-three overseas) in 1965, to twenty-seven (four overseas) in 1970. After that the figure fluctuated between the mid-twenties and the mid-thirties, as individual initiatives prevailed. Meanwhile, recruiting into the Association continued through the enrolment of Life Members amongst all apprentice and adult recruits. Social occasions on a national scale were successfully introduced, with dinner dances supported by the Corps Band; the first was held in May 1973 at the Victory Services Club in London, and subsequent events at a wide range of locations as far apart as Morecambe, Portsmouth, Bristol and York. With increasing problems of securing suitably sized accommodation at reasonable cost, the Association ventured in 1989 to a Pontin's holiday centre at Hemsby in Norfolk. Initial suspicion of such a venture was dispelled by the experience, and all subsequent years, planned until 1995, continued in that vein – with enthusiastic acceptance of the professional entertainment, the many facilities and the simple but adequate accommodation at a price comfortably short of that for hotels. The numbers attending had risen to well over 500 by the Corps' 50th anniversary year.

In 1971, two years prior to the start of the dinner-dances, the involvement of branch delegates in an annual conference, generally with some accompanying activity, was initiated. This enhanced the exchange of activities between branches, keeping them in touch and securing a broadly democratic approach to Association business and creating a base of helpful advice to the Committee of Management. Equally valued during the period 1966–86 was the continuity afforded by the dedicated secretaries of the Association, Lieutenant Colonel Freddie Parsons and then Major Bill McDermott – both of whom carried similar responsibility for the REME Benevolent Fund.

Routine annual activities continued, such as the preparation of the REME plot in the Field of Remembrance at Westminster Abbey, and the annual commemoration at Lenham in Kent of the death of fifty-two members of 6 Guards Tank Brigade Workshop from the impact of a V1 'doodle-bug'. The creation of a common pattern of Standards and their issue to all branches gave emphasis to esprit de corps and a focus for formal occasions. In the late Seventies a sales drive was launched under Major McDermott's direction, substantially increasing the number of items offered in the Association's shop (including a caravan-based mobile facility run through the devotion of Sergeant Bridgeland at SEME) – and so enhanced its revenue. However, such financial success was eventually jeopardized in the Eighties by the problem of exhibiting Corps-badged items in a public environment increasingly sensitive to terrorist activity in the United Kingdom. The shop subsequently encountered further administrative and financial difficulties in 1992, under the burden of selling 'REME 50' souvenirs imposed on it by the Corps.

As the period covered by this volume drew to a close, the need for a radical overhaul of the Association's structure and general organization was being recognized, together with a simplification and rationalization of its shop. It was considered to be a logical aim to achieve such an overhaul before the Association reached its 50th Anniversary in 1995. Also at this time significant overall reductions in the strength of the Army, and consequently the Corps, were being implemented, and redundancy measures imposed. The Association was viewed as a valuable aid in the search for civilian job vacancies and assisting in the placement of those whose careers had been foreshortened. Its continued practical value, as well as its significant contribution to esprit de corps amongst the total REME 'family', was to be clearly demonstrated at this time.

THE REME MUSEUM

The new Museum in the Eighties

A Museum was included in Major General Bertram Rowcroft's long-term plans for the Corps written in 1942. Occasional appeals for the preservation of historic artefacts and documents were made subsequently, but it was not until 1956 that firm plans followed upon the publication of an Army Council Instruction authorizing regimental museums. The Director of Mechanical Engineering directed that the Museum would be at Arborfield. Space was set aside in Moat House and an appeal for funds was launched in the July 1957 issue of the 'REME Magazine'. The Museum opened some time afterwards, the first Curator being Lieutenant Colonel Bill Johnston. After the opening, a museum committee was formed. On the formation of the Corps Secretariat in 1960 the

Curatorship became an additional function of the Corps Secretary. One Civil Service assistant was provided. The ultimate direction of the Museum was by its Trustees, working through the Executive Committee.

The Museum continued to occupy rooms in Moat House until a new building was included in the revised garrison facilities built as part of the new Princess Marina College complex in the early Eighties. It was soon realized that the Moat House location would not accommodate all the historic material available to the Corps. A comprehensive small arms collection which originated partly in Bordon and the RAOC Armourers Training Branch at Hilsea had been built up at the Army Apprentices College in Carlisle and, when that college closed, was moved to Bordon to join other weapons which had been acquired previously. Some at Arborfield were moved to Bordon. This collection was arranged in a permanent display at SEME and opened formally in 1975. The man responsible for assembling much of the collection at Carlisle and subsequently for setting up the display at Bordon was Mr Jim Hopkins BEM.

Mr 'Noddy' McLoughlin with the 1951 Scammell Explorer

A few ex-REME vehicles were added to the Museum, but for security they were transferred to SEME, where gradually a considerable collection was built up and maintained, mostly in running order. A SEME Historic Vehicle Society was launched in 1983 to seek volunteers to assist with maintaining and displaying Museum vehicles at outside events in order to publicize the Corps and the Museum. A similar collection of electronic material had been gathered together at SEE and various attempts were made to formalize this into a museum. Some aeronautical exhibits were kept at the Aircraft Engineering Training Wing (School of Aeronautical Engineering from 1988) and a small collection representing the work of REME static workshops had been assembled at 43 District

Workshop. The SEE display was transformed into a proper museum through the perseverance of Lieutenant Colonel Mike Dorward and much of the work was carried out by Mr Eric Jefferies. This display was opened by the Representative Colonel Commandant, Major General John Boyne, early in 1990. These displays in training and working units were designed not only to preserve Corps artefacts but also to provide a teaching facility showing the progress in equipment design and repair techniques.

It became clear that the work of administering the growing collections was beyond the scope of one curatorial officer and in 1983 the Corps employed a Deputy Curator to relieve the Corps Secretary of much of the detailed running of the Museum. Mr Brian Baxter took up the post in time to be closely involved in the move from Moat House. The main Museum occupied its new premises in Isaac Newton Road, Arborfield, over a period of eighteen months and many new displays were set up. It was formally opened by Major General John Homan in March 1985. A small extension to the display area, the post-war 'Middle East Room', was later opened by Major General Dennis Shaw in March 1989.

The task of Curator devolved upon the Deputy Corps Secretary when this post was created in 1987 and the appointment was filled by Lieutenant Colonel Larry Le Var. He soon succeeded in gaining additional accommodation adjacent to the original new Secretariat and Museum complex, allowing a useful rearrangement of Secretariat departments and the provision of space, eventually, for two major additions to the Museum.

The Museum's collection of historical and technical documents was combined with another collection, then housed at the REME Officers School, under the title Corps Archives. The existing Museum staff was too small to handle properly this enlarged collection, growing week by week as new material was received. So in 1989 a Corps Archivist was engaged part-time and, with some assistance from volunteers, Major Derek Gilliam in this appointment transformed the loose collection into a properly housed and increasingly well-documented archive. This was formally opened by Major General Dennis Shaw on 26 November 1990 and was subsequently inspected and recognized by the Public Record Office as an authorized location for holding State Papers.

A parallel development was the creation of separate Pictorial Archives to combine the holdings of photographs, albums, films, prints, maps and paintings. This too provided secure storage and controlled access to an historically important collection. The Pictorial Archives were formally opened on 8 April 1992 by Major General Mike Heath, his first formal engagement after assuming the new appointment of Director General

Equipment Support (Army). Within the Pictorial Archives a semi-permanent photographic display depicts the history of Princess Marina College.

The Corps' 50th Anniversary led to much Museum activity, including a temporary exhibition 'in house' and assistance in the preparation of other exhibitions and events in UK and overseas. The main artefacts conveyed to and from Canada in the expedition, Exercise Master Craftsman, were placed on display in the Museum directly after their return. REME Historic Vehicles were much in demand, taking part in many events, including the Royal Tournament, the Edinburgh Tattoo and major vintage military vehicle rallies.

A very prestigious REME history exhibition, carried over from 1992, was staged in the Upper Waiting Hall of the House of Commons in February 1993. Sponsored by Sir Gerard Vaughan, MP for Reading East, the display was formally opened by Jonathan Aitken MP, Minister of State for Defence Procurement. It was later transferred to the Ministry of Defence Main Building, attracting much attention there. The actual preparation of this exhibition was largely the work of the Land Systems Technical Publications Authority (formerly Publications Branch REME) with co-design work and pictures provided by Judy Booth of the Museum.

During the Eighties the Museum made great progress in terms of professionalism and actively sought material to improve its ability to record Corps History and the interwoven history of military technology. Its status was further enhanced when it became one of the first military museums, after the major national establishments, to be accorded full 'registration' under the Museums and Galleries Commission's national scheme to improve museum standards.

A vital need exists to extend the Museum to enable it to house all its collections under one roof and thus increase their accessibility to the public. A previous plan, aimed at the necessary fund-raising, was shelved in the light of the then unknown outcome of Options for Change and other studies; however the expansion of the Corps Museum remained a long-term aim, particularly as new wars, reorganizations or peace-keeping operations add to the Corps' history.

PUBLICATIONS

'The Craftsman'

From October 1959 the 'REME Magazine' was re-titled 'The Craftsman'. Throughout the period covered by this volume the Corps regularly produced 'The Craftsman' monthly and The REME Institution issued 'The REME Journal' annually. In January 1964 the first coloured cover for 'The Craftsman' was a novelty: their use steadily increased and by 1992 all covers were in colour, as was the occasional centre spread. It is also of interest that in the Eighties, 'The Craftsman' was one of only three regimental magazines published monthly. A special edition in October 1992 commemorated the Jubilee year of the Corps. Meanwhile the cover price increased from 1s 6d (7.5p) in 1970 to 55p in 1992, though from 1987 the magazine was issued free to units as a benefit from the formation of the REME Central Charitable Trust. A peak circulation figure of 8,500 was reached in June 1992, though this was subsequently to drop with the reduction in size of the Army.

The REME Journal

As recorded in the previous volume, The REME Journal had been published by the REME Institution annually since 1951 (price five shillings, equal to twenty-five new pence). During the period covered by this volume there were only three editors. First was Colonel 'Jock' Tatman (1966–76), who took over from Brigadier Bill Kennett; these two had also compiled the first volume of 'Craftsmen of the Army'. Then Colonel Ian Swan, a former Royal Signals officer, as was Kennett, wielded the editorial pen until 1986 with equal success. The post then fell once more into REME hands with Colonel David Morrison, who held the post up to and including the 42nd edition – the edition commemorating REME's 50th anniversary, containing many articles of historical interest (price two pounds), and distinguished on its front cover by a coloured reproduction of Sally Gaywood's painting of the previous year's Gulf War. Only once before had the Journal carried an illustration on its front cover, when, in 1966, a photograph of West Court adorned the first Journal printed on art paper and produced in a larger size. The new size was not popular with those who appreciated uniformity in the sets on their bookshelves; nevertheless this size has been used ever since, albeit (with the above exception) only with the plain titled cover. Despite continuing attempts by the responsible committee, conscious of the Institution's aims, the trend most easily identified in reviewing the series was a falling-off in the proportion of engineering and other technical articles. Occasional dissertations on modern management techniques were professionally appropriate, but general military, historical, travel and occasionally humorous articles predominated. However, the Journal continued to be a diverse and interesting annual, as the Corps' principal publication proclaiming its professional standing.

The Officers List

In 1960 Major Arthur Reading suggested to the ADEME EME 2, Colonel 'Rupert' Sheppard, that the Corps should, like the Gunners, have an officers reference book. With the approval of their DDEME, Brigadier John Samuel, this was put in hand and the first REME Officers List was published under the auspices of the REME Institution in 1961 – despite the reluctance of many senior officers to have their service and qualifications available for general scrutiny. From its beginnings the book contained the essential details of all serving officers and the addresses of retired officers. With the passage of years the detail improved, particularly in specifying precise appointment details rather than identifying individuals only with the theatres to which they were posted. During the Eighties Brigadier Martyn Clark, as Corps Secretary and thus editor of the 'Blue Book' as it was generally known, introduced many refinements towards making it a more comprehensive document as computer assistance eased the way. Notably, from 1990, the inclusion of the 'familiar names' of both husbands and wives fulfilled his ambition to provide this much-needed information. Throughout its life the evident co-operation of AG21 (later PB21) was necessary to provide the essential Active List details, in latter days as 'camera ready' copy.

RECRUITING

The Corps Recruiting staff was part of the Corps Secretariat until August 1975, when it was transferred to HQ REME Training Centre and operated from the Training Battalion and Depot. The function of the Corps Recruiting Officer and his staff was to assist the MOD recruiting staff in the marketing of the Corps, to generate a flow of suitable recruits at the Army Recruiting Offices. The Mobile Display Team, consisting of a display mounted in trailers and caravans with an Artificer and a team of bright young Sergeants and Corporals, attended as many large shows and exhibitions as possible, particularly during the summer season. They also visited schools and assisted with the craft subjects in the National Curriculum, which not only promoted the image of the Corps, keeping it in the public eye, but also provided direct contact with potential recruits and was very popular with the schools, as a supplement to their teaching effort. They were very successful over the years in finding sufficient high-grade young men and women, with the right technical education and ability to assimilate the very demanding training they would receive in the Corps. Over the years the standards of technical education in the schools lagged behind REME's starting requirements, which was a real challenge for both the recruiters and the trainers. However, the Corps was less successful in recruiting officers, who were required to have either an engineering degree, or be qualified to read for one, to be accepted into the Corps.

It was usual for Welbeck College, the Army's sixth-form college, to provide roughly half the requirement of the Corps' Young Officer intake from RMA Sandhurst, equipped with the right A level grades to be accepted by either Cambridge University or the Royal Military College of Science at Shrivenham, to read an engineering degree. The remainder were found as undergraduates in universities all over the country, some of whom heard about REME through their University Officer Training Corps, where there were a number of REME Permanent Staff Instructors (PSIs), running REME platoons. Some were introduced by the professorial staff and career advisers, who attended a periodical Army Engineering Symposium, described in Chapter 5, which REME hosted in turn with the other Engineering Corps. The market place for graduate engineers was and is likely to remain very competitive, with industry recruiting in the same shrinking pool of candidates.

In 1983 the Corps set up a Potential Officer Course, which was designed to prepare a small number of young soldiers and ex-apprentices for commissioning into the Corps. They would have to take their chance at RCB and RMA Sandhurst, but their academic achievements, based on the BTEC awards which they had obtained, would be acceptable to the Corps. This was a very successful project and was master-minded by Major Patrick Mileham RTR, who was serving at the Army Apprentices College at the time. From this initiative the Corps discovered a rich seam of officers, many of whom graduated and became Chartered Engineers alongside their peers. The first pilot course was an unqualified success, three times as many as had been predicted passing RCB: Richard Mitchell won the Sword of Honour at RMA Sandhurst later that year, the

Graduation Day at RMCS 1987
Lieutenant Richard Mitchell, Lieutenant Alan Powell, Major Patrick Mileham, Lieutenant Paul Martin

first ex-Arborfield apprentice to do so. Four subsequently gained engineering degrees, with Alan Powell achieving a First Class Honours degree at RMCS Shrivenham. The potential officer wing also ran special Leadership Courses, which were effectively 'militarizing' courses for school leavers and university candidates. Several other courses were set up at the Royal Army Educational Corps Centre at Beaconsfield as a result of the REME pilot scheme. There was, however, still a loss to the Corps of high-grade officers who did not attain the academic requirements and consequently joined other Corps, although they wanted to stay in REME. They had been identified and trained on the Corps' Potential Officer Courses, but then lost to the rest of the Army. After numerous papers, Lieutenant Colonel Robin Tandy gained DGEME's approval for the entry qualification to be reduced to HNC, which was well within the ability of most REME soldiers and well above the minimum Army requirement for a commission. This provided the safety net to ensure that the Corps did not lose good quality officers. At the same time Lieutenant Colonel Tandy employed the first woman assistant Recruiting Liaison Officer, which greatly improved REME recruiting success at the universities, and generated much more interest from women applicants.

The Potential Officer Courses were very challenging, but great fun to run. On one occasion Lieutenant Colonel Tandy wrote:

'Towards the end of a potential officer training exercise on the Sandhurst training area, I received an urgent message to go to Brigadier John Graham's office. It seems that South East District had received complaints that a number of soldiers were being tortured and starved on the Sandhurst exercise area, and one had nearly been killed by Gurkha guards; our POs were the only ones near the area at the time. It was rare for Brigadier John Graham to show even mild concern in adversity (save for tasting an unsatisfactory wine), let alone panic. On this occasion he was at least somewhat concerned as the tabloids were being held at bay for a short period whilst an explanation was sought. It transpired that the "torture" accusation came from a woman walking a dog, who witnessed from a distance an exercise run to test recollection of senses when blindfolded. POs were led along the route where they were exposed to obstacles, smells, sounds etc. The woman had seen someone being held over a fire and also heard screams; you can imagine the scenario. The "starving" accusation resulted from a PO, who decided to use initiative in asking a Sandhurst guard for a sandwich rather than prepare and cook the unplucked chicken and raw vegetables with which he had been provided. Needless to say he was seen escaping by kukri-wielding guards, who had been especially deployed that night to protect a visiting four star general!'

It was not for this reason, but because the Corps was unable to fill the courses, that they were discontinued in 1992. There was also some Army-wide evidence that potential officer courses were coaching applicants prior to the RCB and distorting this important test. Among the many other activities run by the recruiting staff were familiarization visits where groups of ex-Welbexians and other prospective officer recruits were given a short introductory visit to the Corps. This included a briefing and a visit to both the training organization and a working REME unit. With the demise of the potential officer courses, pre-RCBs were initiated, which involved both a briefing on the Corps and some preparation for the RCB. These were conducted at Bordon on the basis of the outdoor command tasks, designed for the potential artificer selection boards. They were attended by candidates from all arms and services and produced a very useful introduction to the methods employed at RCB and also enabled our recruiting staff to make an early judgement on our potential REME candidates.

THE REME STAFF BAND

The REME Staff Band was formed on 1 October 1947 as a minor staff band and enlarged to a major staff band in 1956 with a role to provide music for important parades, which are held on a wide variety of occasions, for Corps social events for all ranks, and to help keep the Corps in the public eye as part of the overall Army programme. From 1977 the musicians had secondary roles as Heavy Goods Vehicle Drivers which they tested in BAOR on Exercise LION HEART in 1984. At the end of the Seventies the establishment of fifty-five all ranks enabled it to provide two parade bands of twenty-four musicians or a combination of a parade band, a mess band of sixteen and a dance band of six. Prestigious parades, beating retreat and massed bands at tattoos all required the maximum strength. A highlight in 1978 was the performance at the Training Battalion and Depot parade reviewed by the Colonel in Chief, Prince Philip, before he opened Rowcroft Barracks, Arborfield.

In 1978, as one of their regular periodical inspections, the Inspector and Deputy Inspector of Army Bands looked at every aspect of the Band according to a standard and system applied to all Army bands. The Deputy Inspector, who was also Director of Music at The Royal Military School of Music, Kneller Hall, as usual examined the musical ability of all sections of the band with various test pieces. The musical ability of the Band, then under the direction of Major David Snowden, was considered to be 'Outstanding'.

Sergeant Williams in REME Staff Band full dress uniform

One of the most obvious changes in the REME Staff Band was the replacement of No 1 Dress with a much smarter Full Dress. Prince Philip had written to Major General Peter Palmer in December 1974 about the proposed new dress. His comments on the shako included:

'I think I could stomach that shako if the band across the peak was made of some flat material, possibly patent leather or flat gold braid. I am also unhappy about the chin strap. I think it would look much better if it were made of "curb chain" or alternatively of patent leather.'

Field Marshal Sir Michael Carver, in a letter to General Palmer in March 1975, was more critical. He wrote:

'I am afraid that I regard the shako with horror. It seems to me an absurd form of headdress and particularly absurd for a Corps raised in the 20th century. When bands of the Household Division play in parks and elsewhere, I think they wear their normal No 2 Dress hat with a scarlet tunic. I can see no reason why REME should not do the same. I believe it would look far better than that terrible shako.'

It is not surprising that the Corps Committee decided in 1975 after further discussion to discard the shako and to accept nearly all the detailed improvements to the tunic suggested by Prince Philip. After approval by the Corps Committee, the Colonels Commandant, the Colonel in Chief and finally the Army Dress Committee in October 1978, the new Dress was adopted. It was the first new Full Dress uniform to be approved since the Twenties and was first worn on 23 January 1979 at Arborfield. The design was in the style of 1900 Full Dress including a universal pattern blue cloth helmet with brass spike ornament which perpetuated the pattern used by the RAOC, who were part of the Corps' ancestors. A collar dog pattern was used as the cap badge, the pattern of the jacket being based on that of the Royal Engineers, but the colour was that used by the RAOC.

During the Seventies and Eighties the Band made frequent visits to BAOR, including Berlin, and visited Cyprus, Hong Kong and Northern Ireland several times, giving great pleasure and a sense of pride to all members of the Corps who heard and saw them.

The first Director of Music, Captain D Plater MBE, who came to the Corps from The Royal Tank Regiment, arranged the Corps Quick March Lillibulero and Auprès de ma Blonde in 1951 which, after an amendment by Captain Oliver Birkin in 1959 to overcome the problem of bridging the two tunes, finally settled the Corps march which had been the subject of a world-wide consultation by the Corps Committee. The Slow March 'The Grand March (The Duchess of Kent)' was first performed by the Band on a ceremonial parade on 28 May 1964 when HRH The Princess Marina, Duchess of Kent, was present as Colonel in Chief. REME used an original version of the march arranged by Michael Retford published in the 1890s. The tune dated from 1843 and is said to have been composed by Queen Victoria's mother, the Duchess of Kent. The melody was similar to Scipio, the slow march of the Household Cavalry and Royal Artillery, and for many years Scipio was played instead as it was set in an easier key for wind instruments. The matter was finally put right by Captain Len Tyler, Director of Music, who transposed the original march into a more playable key, which was approved by the Corps Committee in April 1992.

The 1981 Defence cuts reduced the Band from a Major to a Minor Staff Band. The musicians were reduced from fifty to thirty-four by natural wastage and a ban on recruitment and transfers in. Despite this and the problems which it inevitably produced, the Band was again graded 'Outstanding' in 1983. Their Royal Public Duties included the Windsor Castle Guard in September 1986, the Buckingham Palace Garden Parties and the Sovereign's Parade at Sandhurst. The Band also performed at the annual Royal Marines (Portsmouth) Tattoo 1987, 1988 and 1989, the then Director of Music, Major Cliff Ross, being the Tattoo Musical Director. He was later to become the Army's Principal Director of Music at Kneller Hall.

Two interesting articles in the REME Journal in 1979 and 1980 by Major Bill Moore, Band President and Major David Snowden, Director of Music respectively, give much information which space does not permit in this volume.

In 1990 the REME Staff Band deployed to the Gulf for the start of the campaign there, and was the first military band to do so. In October 1990 it had become Army policy that the secondary role of bandsmen should change from Drivers HGV to Bandsmen Medical Assistant Class 3, and the REME Staff Band re-roled and trained prior to their departure to the Gulf. At this time also, Captain Len Tyler became Director of Music. The Band manned helicopter casualty evacuation sites for the whole of the Gulf War, which is covered in detail in Chapter 12. On their return from the Gulf in the Spring of 1991 they were thrown into preparations for the celebration of REME's 50th Anniversary.

THE HEADQUARTERS OFFICERS' MESS WEST COURT

The corporate life of officers of the Corps is promoted by the existence of the Headquarters Officers' Mess at West Court, Finchampstead, where important social functions of the Corps are held and hospitality offered. Volume 1 contains a few references to the Headquarters Officers' Mess but no account of its history. A most interesting account of West Court's early history was given by Major Dick Reed late of The Staffordshire Regiment in the 1971 REME Journal. This early eighteenth century Queen Anne House opened as the REME Headquarters Officers' Mess on 8 June 1953. The new bedroom wing, kitchen and dining room were completed in 1964 when the first of the many pictures were bought for the new anteroom, which used to be the dining room, and the five David Shepherd paintings were commissioned portraying REME activities in Borneo, the Western Desert, the Normandy Beaches, BAOR and the Radfan.

For many years the Headquarters Mess Committee had searched for a policy which would provide a theme for pictures on the walls of the Mess public rooms. Old prints and paintings of battle scenes, which normally adorn the rooms of other messes, were not appropriate for such a young corps, even if they could be afforded. So Brigadier Pat Lee and Lieutenant Colonel John Tinkler embarked on a theme of watercolours depicting local scenes, but soon it became clear that it was very expensive to maintain the standards required. The Mess Committee had had the expert advice of Mr Michael Finn, the retired Managing Director of the Reading Fine Art Gallery who had been involved with the framing and restoration of Mess pictures since the early Sixties. As Corps Art Adviser he suggested in 1983 that the Mess should purchase works of art by contemporary artists, which had been highly recommended by a small panel of eminent artists and which had been exhibited at the Royal Academy Summer Show. Through Mr Finn and Mr Laurie Bray at the Royal Academy, the Mess was extremely fortunate to acquire the assistance of Diana Armfield RA and of Bernard Dunstan RA, who were both very senior and respected members of the Royal Academy. The idea interested them that we were starting a collection, which would continue unbroken for some time and encapsulate the works of the best contemporary artists in a style which could easily be hung in our mess. This would soon become a collection of some note in the artistic world and would become a very valuable asset. The first picture was purchased under these privileged circumstances in June 1983. It was an unusual and slightly abstract painting, by Ben Levene RA, on a background of gold leaf; this caused a bit of a stir amongst the senior visitors to the mess and the selection committee members, Brigadier Terry White and Lieutenant Colonel Andy Platt, had some sharp questions to field until it became accepted. The cause was very much helped by Gordon Fraser Cards requesting permission to publish it in their new range. Work continued on the collection every year and by 1992 the Mess had purchased a total of sixteen paintings; this became a matter of some envy in Army circles from regiments and corps which had not adopted such an enlightened policy. It was proposed that a Fine Arts Committee should be formed to consolidate the experience acquired so far and to take the collection forward.

In addition it had become the custom to commission a painting of every significant campaign in which REME was involved. There were already those by David Shepherd on this theme, to which the Mess added the Falklands by Joan Wanklyn, and British Steel generously presented the Gulf by Sally Gaywood. Although not a campaign, a Ken Howard painting was also commissioned by REME TA of exercises in BAOR and this was added to the collection.

In the Eighties West Court underwent many improvements, particu-

West Court anteroom

larly in 1987–88 during the tenure of Brigadier John Till as Garrison Commander. The anteroom was transformed from the style of a London club with big leather armchairs into an elegant drawing room, the old fashioned gentlemen's lavatories became a bar and ladies lavatories were built in appropriate style. Such improvements were mainly funded by the Corps, but the Property Services Agency found funds for repairs and maintenance to the fabric of the Grade 1 listed building, which had suffered some neglect during the years of a government moratorium on spending. The terrace and rose garden walls were rebuilt in keeping with a Queen Anne house. By 1989 it could be said that West Court had never looked better nor been better equipped.

The Mess has had the benefit of many presents from retiring officers, courses at the REME Officers School and other benefactors who have given gifts of silver, glass, furniture and pictures. Many fine pieces of silver, some of which have been commissioned, have been bought by the Corps.

West Court has a well-stocked cellar. This includes a fine collection of clarets and burgundies and an outstanding selection of ports which, in 1992, still included the famous 1963 vintage. Both wine and ports are bought in shortly after fine vintages and laid down to mature. The first Corps Drinking Plan was produced in 1958 by Lieutenant Colonel Peter Girling, together with Brigadier Leonard Atkinson, each of whom later became head of the Corps. Their combined talent and expertise in the selection of fine wines, together with a very shrewd purchasing policy, set up the foundation of the plan, which is kept up-to-date by the PMC of

Mr David Green in the wine cellar

the Headquarters Officers' Mess. The many officers who have attended Corps Dinner Nights have reason to thank them for their foresight when they are privileged to taste the great burgundy and port of that period. West Court has very good storage facilities in the cellar and these are used to capacity to store the wines for use on Corps Guest Nights. In 1990 the drinking plan already included ports to see the Officers' Mess well into the twenty-first century.

Mr Tony Wheddon BEM, already mentioned, was the very capable Mess Steward at West Court from 1953 to 1980. After serving in the Rifle Brigade and being taken prisoner in the Second World War, he came to Hazebrouck Officers' Mess in 1946. The officers of the Corps owe a great debt to him for the high standards he set and maintained for twenty-seven years at West Court.

In May 1980 Mr David Green was appointed Mess Steward. He had served for a full career in REME which culminated as RQMS of the Apprentices College and included running the Officers' Mess in 7 Armoured Workshop, where his talents were recognized during a visit by the Colonel in Chief. He carried on the tradition of Mr Wheddon, and his immaculate 'front of house' organization at important functions impressed every senior visitor to the Mess. He always took great pains to get to know senior officers personally and had many interesting anecdotes to tell about West Court. He had complete recall of every presentation to the Mess and always made sure that each one appeared on the table near the retired senior officer who presented it, when he visited the Mess. He was well known throughout the Corps for many other personal touches and for the helpful advice to young officers in their first proper Mess. When a contractor took over management of the Mess in February 1989, he became the contract liaison officer and continued to give the same excellent service.

There have been many impressive and enjoyable social occasions over the years in West Court – lunches and dinners, some of them attended by members of the Royal Family, balls and informal occasions of all kinds for serving and retired members of the Corps. One such, which illustrates the Corps' historical connections with the Army before the Second World War, was the 50th anniversary reunion of the Ordnance Mechanical Engineers Course who had joined RAOC in April 1935. Seven of the twelve surviving members of that course joined seventy-eight other officers of the Corps for the Retired Officers' Dinner on 26 July 1985. One of the course, Brigadier Mike Brydges, had come all the way from Australia. In March 1985 the course had presented West Court with a Golden Willow tree which was planted by their senior member, Major General Mike Scott, who had served from 1935 until 1965 and then as a Colonel Commandant from 1968 to 1973. This tree should still be growing a century after those officers started their Army career, giving pleasure to generations of officers visiting West Court.

In June 1976, during the first Army Equipment Exhibition held at Aldershot to promote Defence Sales, Major General Hugh Macdonald-Smith, as DEME(A), together with other senior officers of the Corps, entertained several Allied Generals and their wives to dinner at West Court. The General recalled: 'The visitors were clearly much impressed with the setting and as one of them was taking his leave of me he remarked that he thought that my wife and I had a lovely house!'

THE REME CORPS SERGEANTS' MESS

The Corps Committee in 1961 agreed that there should be a focus for the warrant officers and sergeants of the Corps, and to this end designated the REME Depot Warrant Officers' and Sergeants' Mess as the REME Headquarters Sergeants' Mess. A Corps Instruction in 1967 confirmed this designation as a function of the Sergeants' Mess of the Training Battalion and Depot REME 'to provide a central mess to which all warrant officers and sergeants of the Corps belong and at which they may hold social functions and offer hospitality'. In 1977 Brigadier Pat Lee emphasized the need to re-vitalize the original concept, and secured the Corps Committee's agreement to the establishment of the Corps Headquarters Sergeants' Mess; in subsequent Corps Instructions the word 'Headquarters' was eliminated from the title. The first site of the Headquarters Sergeants' Mess was Poperinghe Barracks, Arborfield.

When Poperinghe Barracks was closed down in October 1977 the Corps Sergeants' Mess moved to the newly opened Rowcroft Barracks with the Training Battalion and Depot REME. The first Corps Sergeants' Mess Dinner Night was held in the Rowcroft Mess on 1st September 1978. The Corps Sergeants' Mess remained in Rowcroft Barracks until

the closure of the Training Battalion in December 1991. For two years the Corps Sergeants lacked a permanent home, but still continued to hold Corps functions in Arborfield, Bordon and Middle Wallop. It was planned that in November 1993 the Corps Sergeants' Mess would move to the Bailleul Sergeants' Mess and so remain in Arborfield. At that time the appointment of Corps RSM, ex-officio the Presiding Member, would be double-hatted with that of RSM The School of Electronic Engineering. The Mess has become the focal point for senior ranks of the Corps and some very fine presentations have been made to the Mess by other Corps sergeants' messes. Since 1987 mess income has been supplemented by provisions from the annual budget of the REME Central Charitable Trust Fund to which serving warrant officers and senior NCOs subscribe; a fixed percentage of their pay has gone to the Corps Sergeants' Mess which in turn has been able to make financial contributions to sergeants' messes in other REME units.

Many enjoyable social occasions such as Corps Dinner Nights, TA Regimental Dinner Nights, Corps Cocktail Parties, reunions and informal functions have been held in the Mess, in its many locations, since 1977. The Mess continues to maintain the prestige of the Corps by holding functions and dispensing hospitality at Arborfield and elsewhere.

WOMEN IN REME

Elsewhere in nearly all chapters of this volume the individual achievements of women, serving in REME alongside their male counterparts, have rightly been recorded as a natural development of the Corps' story. It is important, though, that mention should be made of the background to their integration into the Corps and the changes that have occurred both in their employment and acceptance as a full part of the family. There have been dramatic changes in the employment of women in the Army since the Seventies and the following paragraphs outline the progress in the Corps towards their full integration, when women were finally badged REME.

Since its very early days the Corps had employed women of the ATS, and later the WRAC, in technical roles, many years before the final hurdle of their becoming fully 'cap-badged'. Some, commissioned even before REME was formed, served during the war years, whilst others pursued more normal peacetime careers. Well remembered are Major Mary Smithwick (1943–64), Major 'Bunty' Sergant (1953–73) and Lieutenant Colonel Irene Anderson (1954–75), the latter after five years in the ranks. 'Bunty' Sergant (later Howard) went on to achieve distinction as President of the Women's Engineering Society, as Assistant Secretary of the Cambridge University Appointments Board, and as one of only five women achieving Fellowship of the Institution of Mechanical Engineers. ATS women serving in the ranks were employed in many trades, particularly as radar and telecommunications mechanics and including ostensibly more robust activities such as welders, vehicle mechanics and so on. We should not forget, either, the support of the non-technical women of the ATS and WRAC who carried out many administrative functions in training units and workshops. In the Nineties their place was taken by members of the Adjutant General's Corps who

Second Lieutenant Elaine Roberts receives the Sash of Honour from HRH The Duke of Kent

quite frequently were women, although the posts were not specifically annotated for women.

With the ending of National Service and, later, consonant with the advancing equality of women in all walks of national life, pressures mounted for absorbing women of the WRAC into their cap-badged specialities. After all, so many who were 'for permanent employment with REME' felt their primary loyalty to be to the Corps, despite their WRAC badge and its associated demands such as paying regimental subscriptions. They could be treated as 'honorary' but not as fully paid-up members of REME. Meanwhile, with a shortage of male recruits, a fresh group of officers began to join in the early Eighties which saw, in 1983, the integration of women into the RMA Sandhurst. In 1986 Second Lieutenant Elaine Roberts passed out with the Sash of Honour, a very unusual feat for a 'permanently employed' officer. Gradually the rules changed to catch up with the times, enabling women to have bursaries and cadetships, and to take in-Service degrees. Several serving with REME married, and continued to serve, and with new rules on maternity leave Major Gill Prowse continued after the birth of her children.

At long last, with strong advocacy by successive Directors General, fourteen women officers adopted the REME cap badge on 1 October 1990, followed on 1 March 1992 by the transfer of ninety-nine tradeswomen. Major General Dennis Shaw, as DGEME, needed, in the final push, to overcome male prejudice. However, he recalled, 'the toughest nut of all was the resistance of the hierarchy of the WRAC to re-badging. In reality this was not an issue as the women had re-badged themselves and women TA officers were actively designing a REME mess kit!' Faced with such determination by those directly affected, opposition finally crumbled.

Craftsman Kelly Thistlethwaite leads the re-badging

Problems remained in varying degrees, notably that of restricted deployment in the field force. In BAOR women were initially restricted to serve only to the rear of 1(BR) Corps, but the policy was relaxed to the extent that they were not to be employed forward of the

A2 echelon. Even then they could not in practice join Forward Repair Teams because of the possibility of their tasking forward to A1 or even F echelons. This limited the career opportunities of the vehicle mechanics, a source of great disappointment to some women who aspired to work with armour, and officers were unable to be employed as BEMEs. One significant advance in policy occurred in the late Eighties, when resistance to arming women was at last overcome. Henceforth they were more naturally integrated into units, able to defend themselves and not be a burden upon their male colleagues.

What now was the female junior 'tradesperson' to be called? Was she to be a Craftswoman? Fortunately the debate was solved in the most practical and appropriate way, retaining the age-old dignity of all those engaged in crafts – she simply (and proudly) assumed the title of Craftsman. By the end of 1992 the female strength on initial transfer had just about doubled. Initially only bandsman and recovery mechanic trades were closed to women. By 1993 all trades were open. In addition a small number were employed at Regimental Duties. Instructors at the training units found that they 'were no better or worse' than their male counterparts.

Units in the Field Force were keen to integrate their women craftsmen with the least fuss – an aim not in all cases easily achieved with rapidity, given the initial administrative problems of providing suitable accommodation in the same location. They sought to assess and employ the women on equal terms to the men, determining their tasks on the criteria of experience, vacancy and rank. In the field they were expected to play their full part in guards and duties, patrolling, watchkeeping, quick reaction force and so on, as well as exercising their trade skills. Major Stephen Tetlow, commanding 6 Armoured Workshop at that time, recalled that:

'There was little time for modesty: the women shared facilities and ate, washed, rested and worked in exactly the same conditions as the men. Those that needed privacy found it as best they could. The priorities of work and security were overriding.' He went on to comment that they took longer than the men to come to terms with the rigours of exercise life, but they did not lack mental strength, for example on adventurous training – *'the determination and will-power of the women to overcome personal fear on the cliff faces and on the white-water rapids was an example to all. On scaling a high waterfall five male technicians lacked the courage to complete the challenge: not so the women. Initial misgiving amongst the men acquiesced to acceptance and eventually individual worth won through.'*

Captain Ingrid Rolland remembers when the first women arrived in 4 Armoured Workshop, a prospect that some 'viewed with abject horror':

'The initial scepticism about their trade ability was soon displaced and one of them, Craftsman Kinghorn, achieved first place on her Class III-II upgrading course. On exercise they showed that they were capable of hard work and did not mind roughing it with the lads. The women participated fully in unit PT working within their physical limitations. The general opinion was that they not only livened the place up but offered real competition on a trade basis and were capable of making a real and useful contribution to the Workshop.'

In the Territorial Army, until the early Eighties volunteer servicewomen were restricted to employment with the WRAC in administrative appointments in the base areas. With increasing difficulty in recruiting male volunteers, and with the growth of an equal opportunities philosophy, TA units were then permitted limited recruiting of WRAC for administrative and support duties. Three suitably qualified engineers were, however, attracted into TA units as REME, not WRAC, officers. Their exact status was always the subject of some discussion, but the individuals themselves were quite clear on the subject: they had joined REME and were proud to act and dress accordingly. By 1990 women volunteer officers were an accepted part of the REME TA scene, although formal re-badging did not take place until 1 April 1991, and at working level units were beginning to attract and retain qualified and motivated young women into the technical as distinct from the administrative trades. In 1992, with very few exceptions all REME trades were opened up to servicewomen, and in April 1992 – with the demise of WRAC – all

Colonel Ian Currier and Captain Elizabeth Mantle

volunteer servicewomen in REME units rebadged into their parent Corps. It must be admitted that many had worn REME cap badges prior to that time, with the tacit approval of their local commanders.

Captain Elizabeth Mantle, one of the original graduate TA officer recruits, celebrated in 1991 both the award of the Territorial Decoration for twelve years' distinguished service almost entirely in REME units and her selection for command in the following year of 128 Reclamation Company (and associated promotion to Major). In December 1992 three servicewomen attended the first integrated Recruits Course sponsored by HQ REME TA, and in this robust introduction to military life won the respect and admiration of the directing staff and their male colleagues.

In the Regular Army the female career pattern began to merge in identity with that of the males. Captain Amanda Hudson recalls the sequence of early postings:

'After RMAS I was sent to the Training Battalion and Depot REME as the first female platoon commander. This was a job I loved, lots of running around, exercises and parades. During this time the CO insisted that all his officers wore swords on the parade square, so I did! This caused some eyebrows to be raised and eventually it was stopped. I was then posted to the RA Range in the Hebrides. Four days after I arrived one of our 8 Tonne fuel bowsers slid into a stream running into a salmon loch and broke its back – at 1400 hours on a Friday afternoon; none of the recovery vehicles was available and the road was single track surrounded by peat bog. I was tasked with sorting it out, which we did by 0100 hours. No fish died and I became the expert on pollution in the islands!'

After courses (in which the three female officers 'made a name for ourselves as the dirtiest and keenest of the officers especially on the repair and recovery exercise'), she became MTO with 6 Armoured Workshop. This was followed by a posting as the first female officer to command a Royal Artillery workshop and to be forward of the divisional rear boundary. When 49th Field Regiment returned from the Gulf the Workshop then had four or five months to get the M109 guns ready for firing camp, before the Regiment's disbandment. 'We succeeded in having all eighteen guns fit to fire on the last day. For the last round, however, the Gunners were short of manpower so only seventeen actually fired, much to the disgust of REME who had worked such long hours to achieve this'. In October 1992 she was posted to the School of Electronic Engineering as the first woman Adjutant.

By the end of the Corps' 50th anniversary year the integration of women into REME had become an accepted fact, no longer giving rise to uninformed prejudice. Their contribution was widely recognized as a valuable addition to technical manpower resources, and their presence in units as a sociable, civilizing influence. There would be no going back, although the Army as a whole had still to produce its definitive policy on the employment of women.

UNIT TITLES

Continuity in the history of REME units lies primarily in their numbering and, although units have been disbanded and later arisen in other theatres, it has been possible to inculcate pride and interest in the history of a unit through its various transformations. Numbers familiar to those in the Far East, such as 12 and 10, have reappeared in BAOR and UK respectively – although it is a matter of regret to some that the number 16, associating the Parachute Workshop with its distinguished parent brigade, has disappeared along with the brigade itself. Others, such as 7 Armoured Workshop, have successfully survived from their earliest days when they supported similarly numbered brigades. However, it is an unfortunate fact that numbers have not remained unique, and an extreme example of this was the existence during the Second World War of no less than seven units with differing roles each bearing the number 4! Nevertheless, attempts have been made to try to maintain some of the enduring numbers within the Corps' ORBAT.

In 1958 Major Arthur Reading, then in EME 2, was charged with trying to achieve a rationalization of unit numbering, a review carried out in conjunction with Major Harry Trewhella in AG21 – REME's officer manning branch. As an ex-Gunner Major Reading was well aware of the overriding importance in the Royal Artillery of the number rather than the role of a unit in recording history for posterity. As a result their recommended structure was based on numbers 1 to 20 being allocated to field force workshops, 21 to 39 to district static workshops and 40 onwards to command and base workshops. The Reserve Army would have the numbers from 100 upwards. The new structure was approved and implemented over 1959–60, not without some disputes such as the relative seniority between 1 Infantry Workshop and 1 Corps Troops Workshop: hence both retained the number 1, the only duplication after completion of the rationalization in 1959.

Whilst individual problems of unit nomenclature had subsequently been solved whenever necessary, the most comprehensive plan arose from the radical reorganizations associated with 'Options for Change' and the resulting 'Drawdown' of the Army. In supporting the plans for two United Kingdom divisions, the creation of REME field force battalions each with workshops as their sub-units offered a unique opportunity for rationalization: and for passionate arguments as to the most convincing logic that could also embrace the threads of historical associations. The titles were designed to be unambiguous and to avoid repetition of numbers; wherever possible an affiliation with the supported formation, preferably at brigade level, should be introduced.

The resulting organization produced by DGES(A)'s staff and agreed by the Corps Committee in 1992 is set out at Annex A. The title 'battalion' was preferred to 'regiment', although the nine new battalions could have little historical reference to the Corps' earlier training battalions. It did, however, prove possible to provide (for instance) 4, 7 and 20 Armoured Workshops as the close support sub-units of the battalions supporting 4, 7 and 20 Armoured Brigades. Even so, it was found impracticable to avoid duplicating the number 7: in the United Kingdom 7 Battalion was also to be formed to give aviation support to the ACE Rapid Reaction Corps (ARRC). It was thought – and hoped – that the two units would never appear in the same operation order. Duplication of the number 3 had also to be admitted: whilst being accorded to the battalion supporting 20 Armoured Brigade, the Corps Committee accepted UKLF's pleas for recognition of the uninterrupted history of 3 Field Workshop's title. The proposal to give it the number 14 was dropped, and with it the continuation of the former Berlin Workshop's dedicated number.

A similar review was undertaken of REME TA units. In order to give them a clearly separate identity, it was decided to give the battalions (V) and their sub-units three-digit numbers. Where possible the battalion numbers related to the formation supported (eg 103 Battalion REME (V) supporting 3 (UK) Division etc); the historical titles were maintained at sub-unit level within Independent units using numbers between 100 and 200 and Specialist units the numbers from 200 onwards. The new titles were to be adopted at various stages over the period 1992–95.

CEREMONIAL

REME at the Bank of England

The Bank Picquet started in 1780 after the Gordon Riots when two unsuccessful raids were made on the Bank. Originally, out of a force of 534 Horse and Foot Guards deployed to protect the City during the riots, fifty were stationed at the Bank. This Picquet, or Guard, was subsequently fixed at thirty-four from 1780–1900, after which there were several variations made in its strength until its abolition in August 1973. It was normally provided by the Brigade of Guards until the twentieth century when in later years it was mounted by a variety of units.

The Workshop Squadron REME of the 1st Parachute Logistic Regiment provided the guard for the Bank of England on 12 and 19 January 1971 when 16 Parachute Brigade had taken over public duties in London for a period from the Brigade of Guards. Captain Geoffrey Whiting led his guard of ten NCOs and soldiers to the Bank on 12 January. Lieutenant Fraser Mills commanded the guard a week later. Exercising the Guard Commander's privilege to entertain one male guest, in turn Major General Peter Girling and Brigadier Arthur Reading, was so invited. The second guard was piped out by Corporal Eric Luckman, a gun fitter whose piping skill was believed to have been developed during his time as a Carlisle apprentice.

Brigadier Arthur Reading and the 1st Parachute Logistic Regiment Guard

12th Light Air Defence Regiment Workshop REME provided the guard of twelve at the Bank of England from 15 December 1972 to 27 January 1973. Major Bill Crouch, the senior officer of the Guard, entertained CREME 3rd Division Lieutenant Colonel Tony Palmer to dinner at the Bank. This must have made a good impression, for Major General Palmer is amongst those recorded as staying to lunch with the Guard Commanders in the Officers' Flat at Windsor Castle Guard in 1986!

REME at Windsor Castle

On Tuesday 2 September 1986 REME assumed the duties of the Windsor Castle Guard from 1st Battalion, Irish Guards. The REME Staff Band led the 'New Guard' from The Royal Mews up Windsor High Street into the Castle where Lieutenant Edward Bearcroft accepted the ceremonial key to the Castle from the Irish Guards. So started a month-long tour of duty. A question from an American woman to her male companion in the watching crowd was overheard: 'Why are those guys dressed in brown uniforms and the others dressed in red uniforms?' The man replied, 'That's easy, honey. The ones in brown are the British Army, the ones in red are the Irish Army!'

Changing the Guard at Windsor Castle

A guard-mounting ceremony took place on every even day in September, the REME Staff Band leading each 'New Guard' through Windsor into the Castle. There they played for the fifty-minute ceremony watched by a large crowd and then led the 'Old Guard' back through Windsor to The Royal Mews.

The total strength of the REME Guard was four officers and ninety-three soldiers. The Guard Commanders were four subalterns, all platoon commanders at the Training Battalion. Most of the experienced soldiers were volunteers from the field force, but many others were young Craftsmen who had recently completed their basic military training. The Guard were fitted with greatcoats, ammunition boots, white gloves, white webbing and No 2 Dress uniforms, their SLRs were parkerised and fitted with matching plastic furniture for which chrome bayonets and black polished scabbards were supplied from the Tower of London. The sentries spent two hours on duty and four hours off throughout the forty-eight hours of each guard, the most popular sentry position being No 2 post by the Advance Gates to the Castle, where all the best-looking girls came to pose by the sentry for their photographs! At night the sentries undertook tactical patrols around the dark grounds of the Castle. All who saw the young REME soldiers, including RSMs past and present, agreed that they performed their ceremonial duties excellently. One night several alarms sounded indicating that there were intruders on the approaches to the Castle. Two police officers and a REME sentry, Craftsman White, went to meet the threat. Two people were arrested, searched and detained. The Castle Police Report referred to the well-disciplined demeanour of the sentry and his prompt and efficient response which made a significant contribution to the result. The Metropolitan Police sent a letter to the Training Battalion and Depot REME expressing their thanks for the valuable assistance, adding that all the officers and men had been very efficient whilst posted at the Castle and that this incident had highlighted the very real service they provided apart from their ceremonial duties.

REME at Buckingham Palace

In 1992, as recorded later in this chapter, the Corps was given the honour of providing the guard at Buckingham Palace to celebrate the 50th Anniversary of the formation of the Corps.

Honorary Townspeople of Wokingham

The tradition of granting to military units the Freedom of their associated local communities has had a long history, and many REME units have been thus honoured. They are mentioned appropriately in Chapters 6 (BAOR), 7 (UK) and 8 (TA). However, there is only one such privilege accorded to the Corps as a whole. On Saturday 21 October 1978 the Corps became Honorary Townspeople of Wokingham after thirty-six years association with the town. The former Borough Council had planned to offer the Freedom of the Borough to REME, but, although the Local Government reorganization took away that right, the status of Honorary Townspeople could still be granted: a distinctive honour and a happy description of the relationship.

There were five companies of soldiers, one each from UKLF, SEE, SEME, Training Battalion and Depot REME and Army Apprentices College, Arborfield, making up 450 troops on parade. The Town Guard from SEE formed up outside the Town Hall in front of the Old Rose Inn with the REME Staff Band where the Mayor, Mr Peter Johnson, and the Representative Colonel Commandant, General Sir Hugh Beach, inspected them. The Mayor presented an illuminated address and said, 'We have always been proud of our association with REME', and went on, 'It has always been a great satisfaction to us that so many members of the Corps have settled here upon completion of their service.' In his reply General Sir Hugh Beach concluded by reading a message from the Colonel in Chief Prince Philip in which he wrote:

'I know all members of the Corps of Royal Electrical and Mechanical Engineers very much appreciate this generous and hospitable gesture by the Mayor, Council and people of Wokingham. The men who train so hard to provide Britain's capacity to defend herself against aggression have been known to feel their efforts

are not always appreciated by their fellow citizens. Conferring the status of Honorary Townspeople of Wokingham on all members of the Corps is a wonderful encouragement to us all.'

General Sir Hugh Beach then presented the Mayor, on behalf of the Corps, with a silver salver to mark the occasion.

The Town Guard, led by the Staff Band and joined by the other companies, marched through the town with swords drawn and bayonets fixed, the Mayor taking the salute. The parade was followed by enjoyable social events in Wokingham and Arborfield. In the years following, the Corps celebrated the anniversary from time to time by providing a Town Guard in Wokingham which the Mayor inspected, followed by a column of troops marching through Wokingham with bayonets fixed and the Band playing. Typical of the nature of the relationship between the Corps and Wokingham is that in 1984 the Mayor of Wokingham, Mrs Ann Davis, after inspecting the Town Guard and taking the salute at the march past on 6 October visited the Corps in BAOR 29–31 October with her husband, going to HQ BAOR at Rheindahlen, 23 Base Workshop at Wetter and 22nd Air Defence Regiment Workshop at Dortmund where she lunched in the Junior Ranks Club with all ranks from the Workshop.

On 21 December of that same year Mrs Davis reviewed the Passing-Out Parade at the Training Battalion and Depot REME. On 15 May 1985 she returned to Arborfield with twelve Councillors, the Town Clerk and the Mace Bearer, to spend a day visiting all the units of REME Training Centre where they were given a clear view of the wide and thorough range of training provided for apprentices, recruits, artificers and officers.

RECREATION AND WINTER SPORTS FACILITIES IN SOUTHERN GERMANY

REME has always taken a prominent role in encouraging soldiers to ski and as far back as the Sixties was running winter chalets in Southern Germany which accommodated soldiers taking part in Exercise Snow Queen, a BAOR-sponsored annual series of inexpensive two-week skiing courses.

The first chalet was run by HQ REME 1st Armoured Division, nominated as the centre of excellence for Corps skiing. With increasing demand, 71 Aircraft Workshop combined with 4 Armoured Workshop to run a second hut, and successive huts were found in the Gunzesried Valley and elsewhere in the vicinity of Sonthofen in the Allgäu. They were often just converted barns, shared with cattle but, with a certain

charm, they are affectionately remembered. In due course the demand justified a permanent REME adventurous training centre, Berghaus Lieb.

REME Hotel

It was in 1982 that Brigadier David Clarke, then Commander Maintenance BAOR, first conceived the idea of producing more comfortable accommodation for past and present members of the Corps and their wives and families. He pursued his idea with characteristic vigour, securing the agreement of his fellow trustees, battling his way through the legal jungle both in Germany and in UK to emerge with the Corps as proud owners of Berghaus Urban, which became the REME Hotel in Wertach, Bavaria. Brigadier Clarke opened the Hotel in December 1982, from which time it has gone from strength to strength.

The aim of the Hotel is to provide holiday recreation, recuperation, training and other general benevolent facilities for serving and retired members of the Corps and their families. Not only has it achieved this aim with outstanding success but it has continued to improve both the amenities and the quality of service it provides to those who stay there. Improvements added over the years include a family sauna and additional showers. The Hotel also provides subsidized ski equipment for hire and cheap lift tickets for its customers.

The REME Hotel is not required to make a profit, nor is it required to show a return on the million Deutschemarks (£263,000) that it cost at the time. It is therefore able to offer accommodation at extremely advantageous rates. Nevertheless, Brigadier Graham recalls from his time as Commander Maintenance 1st Armoured Division being tasked with putting the Hotel on a sound financial footing immediately after the Corps had established ownership. He had no idea what the running costs would be, how many people would use the hotel or what to charge for accommodation. He therefore based the charge on what he felt a married Corporal with two young children could afford and fortunately the costs worked out about right. This guiding principle still remains and was a factor in deciding that the Hotel should also offer evening meals to its guests.

By 1986 more than 6,000 bed-nights a year, about three-quarters of its annual capacity, were being sold. The REME Hotel had established itself firmly on the map for summer and winter holidays and become a firm favourite with an increasing number of past and present members of the Corps.

Berghaus Lieb

As mentioned in Chapter 6, REME was able in 1988 to concentrate its Snow Queen and adventurous training resources in Gunzesried-Säge, offering throughout the year better accommodation closer to the skilifts in a less isolated location. Lieutenant Colonel David Roberts seized the opportunity to secure for the Corps a five-year lease on Berghaus Lieb, previously rented for sixteen years by RMP, and an option to buy in 1993. In the event the collapse of the Warsaw Pact, the subsequent reduction of the military presence in Germany and uncertainty about the long-term future of Exercise Snow Queen prompted the Corps not to take up the purchase option. Nevertheless, a new five-year lease was to be signed on expiry of the first, the Corps looking forward to retaining what must be one of the best-appointed and best-equipped chalets in the area for Exercise Snow Queen and adventurous training usage.

THE CORPS WEEKEND

For many years after the 1939–45 war the Corps birthday was celebrated annually in October with parades and festivities. However, the Corps Committee decided in 1955 that the custom should lapse, requiring only that units should hold one ceremonial parade each year. A Corps Week was then inaugurated and continued from that year until 1966, by when numbers attending had declined. It was felt that the majority of officers stationed in the United Kingdom no longer required such an event and, although many other Corps and Regiments continued, there then remained no REME highlight or festival in its calendar, other than the commemoration in some garrisons of the Corps' Patron Saint, St Eligius, on the Sunday nearest to 1 December.

In March 1978 the Corps Committee considered a proposal put forward by Colonel Geoffrey Pearce, in which he concluded that an annual festive occasion timed to include St Eligius Day would benefit such a widely dispersed Corps by promoting a stronger sense of identity and unity. As a young officer with the Cavalry and Guards he had been impressed by the effect of such 'get togethers' for all ranks and their families. However, whilst the proposal struck a sympathetic chord with the Committee, they recognized that December was not ideal for more sportive and spectator activities. Amongst other ideas the concept of a handicrafts exhibition was suggested, as a positive recognition of the place of craftsmanship in the Corps. A working party was the inevitable outcome, and even more inevitable was Colonel Pearce's appointment to lead it.

The outcome of the working party's recommendations was that a Corps Weekend was to be held at Arborfield in July 1979, initially deferring the concept of an all ranks' dance on the Saturday evening and a church service on the Sunday in favour of a rather shorter 'weekend'. On 13 July it started with a Handicrafts Exhibition in the SEE Gymnasium, and the REME Institution Cocktail Party and Buffet Supper at West Court which was enjoyed particularly by the retired officers and their wives. On Saturday afternoon the Apprentices College Pipes, Drums and Band marched around the Garrison on their way to the arena where the REME Free-Fall Parachute Display Team showed how to land within a few yards of the marker. General Sir Hugh Beach, the Representative Colonel Commandant, declared the fête open and hoped that it would be the first of many: in the event it was held in ten of the succeeding eleven years. The afternoon continued with the childrens' sports while others tried their luck at the many stalls and sideshows. The REME Staff Band kept everybody happy and relaxed until six teams took part in 'It's a Knock-Out' – at that time a very popular television outside games competition with plenty of water for the competitors to fall into. There followed the drawing of tickets in the raffle with, for many, splendid prizes. The afternoon ended with the Staff Band beating Retreat.

It was envisaged that the event would then be held at Bordon in the following year, where there was ample covered accommodation for an all-ranks' dance. In the event, although the first Corps weekend was voted to be a success, commitments at both Bordon and Arborfield precluded a repeat in 1980. It was held again at Arborfield in 1981 and annually thereafter until 1990, never at Bordon. Lunches were provided

Parade of REME Association Standards

in the Corps HQ Officers' and Sergeants' Messes. In addition the Training Battalion's Passing-Out Parade was held on the Saturday morning. Sadly the increasing demands of security, and the difficulties of providing manpower following the disbandment of the Training Battalion, spelled the end of Corps Weekends with the exception of the grand events planned for the Corps' 50th anniversary celebrations. Over the years the weekend variously included inter-unit sports, a parade of REME Association Standards, presentation of the Rory Cape Award, motor cycle displays, field gun competitions, musical marching and so on. Throughout this period from 1979 there was one mainstay of the whole operation: Major Dennis Knight. Apart from being secretary of the organizing committee, he saw to the engagement of arena displays, the printing of programmes and the considerable tasks of laying out the arena and erecting tentage and fencing. He was, perhaps, one of those not entirely sorry to be relieved of these responsibilities!

THE ARMED FORCES WHEELCHAIR MARATHON

In 1981 West Court was the location for the Sports Council's 'Sport in the South Awards', an occasion when Mr Philip Lewis – the disabled Chairman of Southern Region British Sports for the Disabled (BSAD) – asked the Garrison Commander, Brigadier Tony Palmer, whether REME could do something for disabled sport. This request was by no means a coincidence, for it had been set up by Captain Jim Fox who with Philip Lewis had felt that the Services could contribute to the 1981 'Year of the Disabled', their idea being a marathon event. Brigadier Palmer was keen to make a suitable and lasting contribution to the 1981 'Year of the Disabled', and had no hesitation in agreeing to run a Wheelchair Marathon later in that year. His understanding was that other such marathons had taken place at walking pace; his concept was the first to become a race. He aimed to raise money for the BSAD, and in doing so to provide a challenging fun day for able and disabled alike, encouraging connections between BSAD clubs and Service units. Mr Lewis and Brigadier Palmer obtained a tremendous response respectively from the clubs and the three Services in the Southern Region. Competing teams were formed from units matched to BSAD clubs, three servicemen and one disabled person then facing the 26 miles 385 yards between them – just short of six laps of 4.4 miles around the Garrison.

The Wheelchair Marathon

The first Armed Forces Wheelchair Marathon was run at Arborfield in September 1981, an event which involved a large number of broken wheelchairs being repaired by the stalwart efforts of REME's first and only Wheelchair LAD! Brigadier Palmer's complaint to the National Health Service about the fragility of wheelchairs was met by the response that they were not meant to be used for racing. Philip Lewis later became National Chairman of the BSAD and was then keen to spread the event to other regions. This was achieved, together with sponsorship by the Wilkinson Sword company, which provided in each Region a mounted sword for the winners and a mounted poignard (a ceremonial dagger) for the unit and club combination which raised the most money for the BSAD. The success of the event at Arborfield was such that by the fourth year there were 450 competitors, raising over £5,000 for the BSAD and attracting television coverage through the participation of Mr Jimmy Savile, the television personality and charity fund raiser. A spectator recalls the appearance that year of one disabled person who was determined to complete the marathon under his own steam. Lieutenant Colonel Bob Cooper, a noted Corps fitness enthusiast, was concerned for the man's capacity to match his aim, and decided to shadow his progress. After 300 metres his doubts were realized, and thereafter Colonel Cooper provided the motive power, without relief for the remaining twenty-six miles – enduring the smoke of a large cigar which the wheelchair occupant proceeded to smoke! In 1989 no less than £11,500 was raised, but the following year was to be the last at Arborfield, a consequence of the closure of the REME Training Battalion and dwindling resources.

The movement had spread during the Eighties to all of the ten BSAD Regions except for the South-East, raising considerable sums for the Association. But just as at Arborfield, the economies besetting the Services during the Nineties were taking their toll of such charitable activities. Unfortunately, at the time of writing no alternative had been secured to replace Arborfield, the birthplace of a most successful co-operative charitable venture.

THE 'CRAFTSMAN' LOCOMOTIVE

British Rail Class 47 Inter City Locomotive 47501, a 2,080 hp diesel electric locomotive weighing 117 tonnes, was named 'Craftsman' at Paddington Station on 22 October 1987, the formal unveiling being performed by Craftsman Andrew Netting, a student instrument technician at SEME who three years later was commissioned into the Corps. Major General John Boyne, DGEME, and many other officers and civilians

'Craftsman' is named

from REME were present, as well as the General Manager British Rail Western Region and representatives of British Rail and British Rail Engineering Ltd (BREL). The guests travelled on the Paddington to

Oxford train as far as Reading, pulled by 'Craftsman', after which they lunched at West Court where Craftsman Netting was presented with a scale model of 'Craftsman'.

Older members of the Corps will remember that Army locomotives used to be repaired at 32 Base Workshop Bicester before such work was put out to contract. As long ago as 1958 the name of 'REME' had been put on a Patriot Class locomotive as the result of a staff suggestions from a British Rail fireman, Mr John Webb, who was an enthusiastic REME TA soldier. The latest locomotive was not new when named, but had emerged from a base overhaul at Crewe. It bears on each side the name CRAFTSMAN together with the REME badge. John Webb was present at Paddington for its naming, together with Captain Lionel Campuzano, REME TA. Captain Campuzano was a BREL project engineer and had been involved with Mr Webb in the early concept of this latest naming project.

REME 50

It would require a chapter to itself to describe all the events which took place throughout 1992, in the very full and imaginative programme for REME 50. This account therefore only outlines a representative selection of the activities celebrating the Corps' 50th Anniversary.

The Colonel in Chief meets members of the REME Band

The Colonel in Chief, HRH Prince Philip, attended a Gala Concert at the Royal Albert Hall on the afternoon of Sunday 26 April. It was a spectacular occasion at which the Staff Band of the Corps was ably supported by the Staff Bands of the Royal Corps of Transport and the Royal Army Ordnance Corps, the London Philharmonic Choir and Musketeers from the Sealed Knot Society. The concert was compered by Mr Richard Baker, the well-known television announcer. Prince Philip also joined the Queen's Guard Company for their photograph at Buckingham Palace and attended the Corps Reception at St James's Palace on 29 October.

HM Tower of London. Yeoman Warders and Resident Governor, Major General C Tyler (late REME)

Ceremonial activities included undertaking Public Duties as the Queen's Guard Company, supported by the Staff Band, in February and March at Buckingham Palace, St James's Palace and the Tower of London. The photograph above shows former REME Yeoman Warders Tony Strafford (2nd left), Mike Bostock (7th) and John Sparrow (9th). During this period a Corps Reception was held at the Tower of London at which Sir David Plastow, Chairman of Vickers plc and a former REME officer, presented a fine silver model of a CHALLENGER ARRV to the Corps.

REME BAOR held a magnificent parade of men, vehicles and helicopters at Sennelager on 9 May which is fully described in Chapter 6 – BAOR. An officers' ball was also held that evening in the HQ 1(BR) Corps Officers' Mess at Bielefeld.

The largest adventurous training exercise ever held by the Corps, Exercise Master Craftsman, took place from February to October. REME crews sailed from England across the Atlantic and through the Great Lakes and back again. Exercise Maple Canoe on rivers in North Alberta and the North-West Territories in June and July and Exercise Maple Trail in July and August trekking along the Mackenzie Heritage Trail completed the activities in Canada. This exercise is described in detail in Chapter 5.

The Corps Weekend 3–4 July was the most ambitious programme ever arranged, held on a site covering twenty acres of arena, fairground, sideshows, trade stands and displays, including the REME Historic Vehicles. On the Saturday morning the War Memorial statue, created by James Butler RA, was unveiled by Major General Dennis Shaw and dedicated by the Chaplain General. It stands at a focal point in

Arborfield Garrison on the perimeter of the cricket field next to the Church, and was financed by the REME Memorial Projects Appeal. The 16th/5th The Queen's Royal Lancers Warrant Officers' and Sergeants' Mess presented the Corps with a painting of the Gulf War scene in which two REME NCOs, Sergeant Dowling MM and Lance Corporal Evans, were killed by enemy fire. In the afternoon the REME Parachute Team dropped, the Royal Marines Band (Portsmouth) and the Staff Band of the Royal Corps of Signals played and marched, the Historic Vehicles drove past and the Corps Staff Band entertained the 12–15,000 spectators who came despite poor weather.

In July the Corps provided a large static display at the Royal Tournament Earls Court which depicted the development of REME over fifty years, including past and present recovery vehicles.

Many sporting events were held to celebrate REME 50. An anniversary cricket match was played at Arborfield during the Corps Weekend between a Past XI and the Present XI, attended by a mass of past chairmen, secretaries, captains, umpires, scorers and players. The golfers held a tournament for sixty pairs at Tidworth 5–6 August and in BAOR they had already enjoyed a competition for fifty players at the Hannover Garbsen Golf Club in July. On 18 September the REME 50 BAOR Half Marathon attracted 239 runners from 31 units to Münster (Oertze). The Rugby players organized an international Rugby Festival 9–11 October with teams from RAEME, RNZEME, REME BAOR and REME UK playing at Bordon and Arborfield, followed by a dinner for 120 players at Bordon. There is more about the Festival in Chapter 14. On 5 December sixty-six runners enjoyed the REME TA Orienteering Championships held at Bordon.

ASM David Critchlow and G-REME

A Cessna 152 light aircraft based at Old Sarum was registered 'G-REME' and, piloted by ASM David Critchlow, embarked during 1992 upon a round-UK charity flight in aid of the REME Benevolent Fund. He visited eleven principal locations from Andover to Benbecula, where REME units were invited to organize raffles, with the prizewinners in each location being taken for a trip in the aircraft. Many lucky members had a new (aerial) outlook on their workshop!

On 3 October the Corps exercised its right to march through Wokingham as Honorary Townspeople with bayonets fixed and with the

Staff Band and Princess Marina College Band playing, to commemorate the close links between the Corps and the townspeople – the first time since 1988.

Many units arranged their own celebrations, a typical example being at Electronics Branch Malvern, which celebrated REME 50 with a bracing nine-mile walk over the local hills, a fifty kilometres canoe trip on the Wye and planting commemorative oak trees to start a copse of 150 English trees in the North Site, Malvern. The entrance was marked with a large rock from a quarry in the Malvern hills.

Many sporting and social events took part in the Far East which provided an enjoyable year for those in Hong Kong, Brunei, Korea and Nepal. In the Middle East at Abu Dhabi a reception was held on 1 October for all serving members of the UK armed forces in Abu Dhabi and for old comrades.

The Territorial Army celebrated REME 50 too; only three events are mentioned here. The Lord Lieutenant of Northamptonshire reviewed 118 Recovery Company (V) on its parade on 4 April 1992, led by the Staff Band, to commemorate both the 50th Anniversary of the Corps and the 25th Anniversary of the unit. Ninety soldiers with bayonets fixed marched through the streets of Northampton after the parade to exercise their right acquired in 1983 when the Company was granted the Freedom of the Borough of Northampton. They were followed by past and present recovery vehicles of the unit.

The Town Mayor of Newton Aycliffe, County Durham, inspected the parade of 124 Recovery Company (TEE) (V) who celebrated on 20 June both the Corps 50th Anniversary and their right to march through the town, having been granted the Freedom of Great Aycliffe in 1988. The seventy soldiers on parade will long remember that on a very hot day the Mayor insisted in inspecting and talking to every man and woman on parade. The final march past was accompanied by twenty Foden recovery vehicles.

The many social events held to celebrate REME 50 included the REME Association Reunion held at Pontin's Sand Bay Chalet Hotel, Weston-super-Mare, from 10–12 April. The SEME Sergeants' Mess at Bordon decided to celebrate with three functions on or as close to 1 October as possible and invitations to guests were sent out far and wide. They held a Cocktail Party on 26 September in a resplendent Physical and Recreational Training Centre decked out with flowers and a display of Corps silver from the Corps Sergeants' Mess and West Court. On 1 October 294 members sat down to a magnificent dinner, followed by toasts and speeches and Major General Mike Heath cutting a ceremonial birthday cake. Finally, a Grand Ball for 600 people was held on 3 October

Founder members of the Corps at the West Court REME 50 Dinner

with a splendid buffet supper followed by breakfast at 4.15 am.

The REME 50 Corps Ball, which was held on 12 June at West Court and attended by 500 officers and ladies, was widely regarded as a great success, and included such innovations as fairground 'dodgem cars', while the Retired Officers' Dinner had to be held in two parts to meet the demand – on 24 July at Havannah Officers' Mess, Bordon, and on 31 July at West Court. At the latter were twenty-six 'founder members' who had held commissions before 1 October 1942 and nine others who had been commissioned later that year.

Also in October a REME party gathered together by the Corps Secretary travelled to Egypt, visiting Commonwealth Graves Commission Cemeteries at Cairo, Alexandria and El Alamein, before attending on 25 October the international and national ceremonies commemorating the Battle of El Alamein. The veterans were accompanied by Major Tonie Holt, a retired REME officer whose prominent battlefield touring company provided highly experienced travel expertise.

One of the last events of 1992 was the Corps' commemoration of St Eligius on 6 December, when the Chaplain General, together with the Deputy Chaplain General and the Principal Roman Catholic Chaplain, dedicated the Memorial Chapel and four stained glass windows at St Eligius Church, Arborfield.

SAINT ELIGIUS

Saint Eligius was chosen by the Corps Committee in 1959 to be Patron Saint of REME. The original idea of having a patron saint, which so many regiments and corps as well as civilian organizations had had for many years, was to have a representative in heaven to plead their cause or to protect them from perils to which they were especially exposed. Eventually it became more usual to choose a saint who had some connection with the relevant craft or occupation, and an unblemished moral record. The Patron Saint could then be held up as an example to his protégés.

Two REME officers studied the lives of 2,400 saints, many of them in detail. A short list was prepared for approval by the Chaplain General and passed to the Corps Committee who selected St Eligius, whose statue is in the Henry VII Chapel of Westminster Abbey. St Eligius is famous in Europe where he is known as St Eloi and venerated as the patron saint of all smiths and workers in metals. He was born at Chaptelat near Limoges about 588 AD and apprenticed to a goldsmith, later working as a skilled metal worker with a remarkable talent for engraving and smithing. He made his name when commissioned to build a gold-covered portable throne adorned with jewels for Clotaire II King of France. He achieved the highest standards of his craft and displayed exceptional regard for honesty and economy using the chippings and filings of precious metal to such good effect that he was able to make two thrones, instead of one, from the material provided; it was common practice in those days for the craftsmen to keep the chippings and filings for themselves. The King rewarded him for his honesty and skill by appointing him to be Master of the Mint, and gold and silver coins bearing his name are still in existence. St Eligius became a trusted friend of the King and of his son King Dagobert. He displayed his courage when he made a dangerous journey fraught with perils to the Atlantic coast into the country of the barbarous Bretons where he negotiated a treaty as the King's representative. He showed no interest in politics or personal gain despite many offers of advancement. It was only after insisting on two years preparation as an itinerant priest that he agreed to be appointed as Bishop of Noyon and Tournai in 641, which accounts for his popularity in the Netherlands where he was painted by Rubens a thousand years later. He converted property and estates given to him by King Dagobert to found a nunnery in Paris and a monastery at Solignac in Limousin, the ruins of which still stand. Unlike many saints he was not called upon to suffer martyrdom but died in his home on 1 December 660. His body lies in the Cathedral at Noyon where he has remained ever since except for a few years from

1914 when he was moved to safety in Holland during the First World War. His Saint's Day is on 1 December.

It is clear that St Eligius was an excellent choice for Patron Saint for the REME officers and soldiers of the twentieth century. Perhaps some of those who served in the post-war campaigns would agree they needed a representative in heaven. Others would agree that the Saint's moral qualities and skill were just what the Army needed, and were displayed by many REME officers and soldiers in those campaigns in difficult circumstances. In 1979 Major General Sir Leslie Tyler, a former DEME and Colonel Commandant, was on holiday with his wife in the Limoges area. They were told by a villager that there had been a very severe drought in the village and the villagers had prayed to St Eloi to do something about it. A spring suddenly appeared in a field near the church, thus answering their prayers. The villagers put up a statue to St Eloi. A photograph of the church which contains a chapel dedicated to St Eloi, and of the statue, were published in 'The Craftsman' in November 1979 with a letter from Sir Leslie. The same year Sergeant D Fegasse had been on holiday in the Trier area of Germany where he photographed an ancient sculpture of St Eligius in the Trier Museum where he was described as the Patron Saint of farriers. Sergeant Fegasse also sent a letter and a photograph, published in 'The Craftsman'. It is strange to think of all the farriers who must have been employed at Arborfield shoeing horses in the Army Remount Depot long before anyone had ever thought of REME!

In the north porch of Wincanton Church is an unusual carving of St Eligius. On August Bank Holiday for several years a cricket match was played between REME and Wincanton for the St Eligius Cricket Cup. One wonders what he thought of this English game played in his name. This match was started by ASM Brian Glossop and continued by Major Martin Beer, a former captain of the Corps team.

The Church of St Eligius is the first multi-denominational Garrison Church in Arborfield since the Remount Depot opened in 1904. It was dedicated on Sunday 3 December 1989 by the Chaplain General in the presence of Major General Dennis Shaw, DGEME, Brigadier John Graham, Garrison Commander, their wives and many other members of the Garrison. It is perhaps appropriate that the building had started life as a reception stable for horses arriving at the Remount Depot. The Church is furnished with Victorian pews and an altar table from the closed Methodist church in Aldershot, whilst the chairs and kneelers used by officiating chaplains were made in 1947 from 400-year-old oak by 781 MT Command Workshop in Austria. During 1992 four stained glass windows were installed depicting St Eligius, the Creation, the Holy Spirit and the Carpenter's Shop, the cost of which was met by donations made by members of the Corps as a result of the REME 50 Memorial Projects Appeal, together with a grant from the REME Central Charitable Trust. The Appeal also facilitated the addition of a REME Memorial Chapel, housing the Book of Remembrance and providing an area for private prayer, and for which wooden furnishings were made and donated by several REME workshops. On St Eligius Sunday 1992 the Memorial Chapel and stained glass windows were dedicated by the Chaplain General. There is an interesting history of the Garrison Church written by Lieutenant Colonel Mike Dorward, normally to be found on sale inside the Church.

THE CORPS COLLECT

The collect with its reference to 'honest craftsmen, seeking only the good of all in peace and war' and recognizing a 'God of power and might' was written in the early Fifties by The Reverend Canon Freddie Hughes. When General Montgomery took over the Eighth Army in 1942 he had wanted a first-class chaplain and found Freddie Hughes who was then the senior chaplain of a division. He became one of the five senior officers for whom Montgomery sought War Office permission to accompany him as soon as he heard he was to leave Eighth Army in Italy in December 1943, to command 21st Army Group for the invasion of North-West Europe. The Reverend Freddie Hughes remained with Montgomery for the rest of the war. He later became Chaplain General of the Army and then Dean of Ripon, and was the father-in-law of Lieutenant Colonel Colin Broadbent who served in the Corps from 1944–76.

Canon Hughes in an address said that he had been deeply impressed by the care that was taken to provide the Corps with a collect. Many attempts were made before it was agreed what the four foundations should be on which the corporate character would be built. These were:

- The Power of God
- The Spirit of Goodwill
- The Standard of Craftsmanship
- The Example of a Royal Corps

In his address Canon Hughes went on to explain how the symbols of these four can be found in the Corps Badge. The words of the Corps Collect are:

'O God of power and might, whose all-pervading energy is the strength of nature and man, inspire, we pray Thee, us Thy servants of the Royal Electrical and Mechanical Engineers with the quickening spirit of goodwill, that as honest craftsmen, seeking only the good of all in peace or war, we may glorify Thee both in the work of our hands and in the example of our fellowship, through Jesus Christ our Lord.'

Annex A

REME FIELD ARMY ORGANIZATION POST 'OPTIONS FOR CHANGE' TO BE EFFECTIVE 31 MARCH 1995

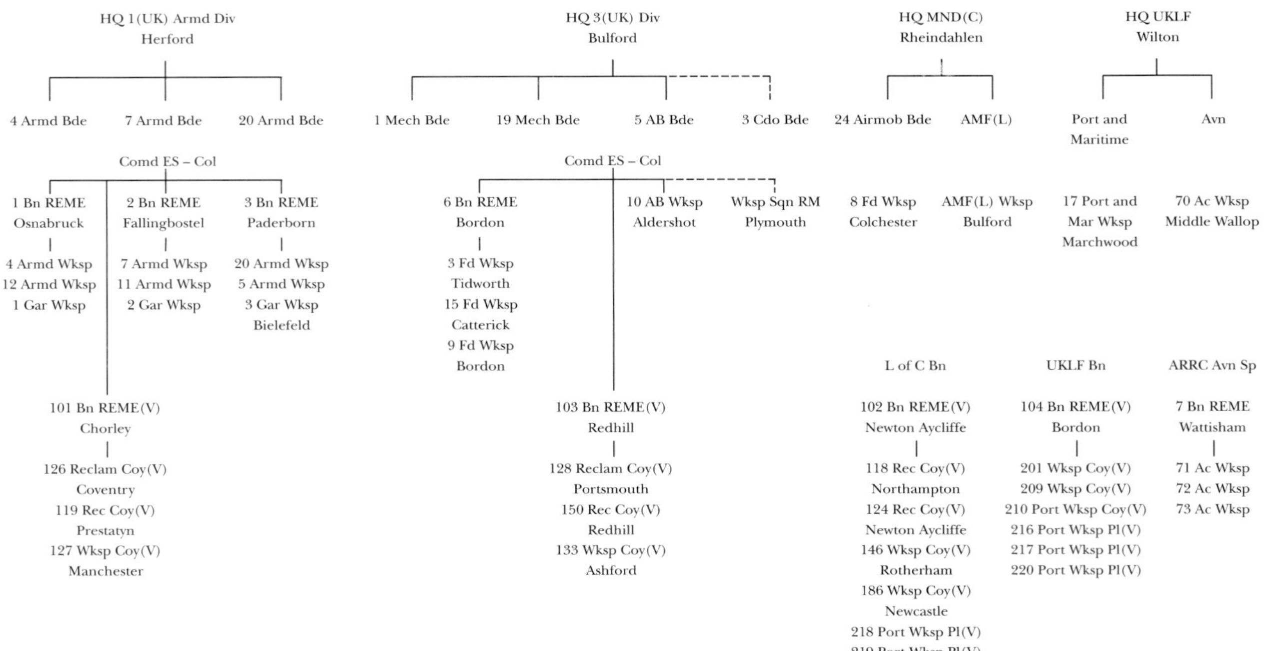

MND (C) – Multi-National Division (Central). Other nations' elements of this three-brigade division are not shown

CHAPTER 14

SPORT AND SHOOTING

INTRODUCTION

Sport in the Corps has been encouraged since the earliest days but especially since the end of the Second World War and the formation of the REME Sports Association in 1948. In 1992 this Association had a Central Committee under the Vice-President and Chairman, with six members representing districts in the UK, plus the Chairman, Treasurer and Secretary of REME BAOR. There were twenty-one sub-committees for the individual sports from association football to winter sports; the last had three Vice-Chairmen responsible for skiing (UK), skiing (BAOR) and bobsleighing.

Sport undoubtedly makes a valuable contribution to individual morale, to developing fitness, character and unit pride and, at higher levels, to pride in the Corps and the Army. There has sometimes been a conflict between the time that could be devoted to sport and the time required for military duties. Nevertheless, the achievements of REME officers and soldiers, whether playing for regiments to which they were attached, for REME units, or for representative sides at Command or Army level, have been a source of pride to all concerned and an example of what can be achieved despite very busy military duties.

The Quinquennial Review of Corps Funds in 1992 recommended, *inter alia*, greater co-ordination between the various world-wide elements of the REME Sports Association receiving Corps Funds. The value of competitive sport in helping to maintain overall morale in the Corps in a period of unprecedented change and significant redundancies was fully recognized. It was judged paramount that to assist the promotion of all sport it was necessary to maintain a high level of funding for the many activities involved. The Review expressed a wish that BAOR and other theatres should make their annual bids to the Executive Committee of the Sports Association for sports income instead of directly to the REME Central Charitable Trust. The results of Drawdown and reductions in REME overall manpower made it clear that co-ordinated world-wide control of REME Sports Association funds was necessary and possible, and steps were taken to achieve it.

The first volume dealt only minimally with sport, amounting to a single page devoted to rugby football, association football and modern pentathlon, and a similar allocation for shooting and expeditions. This chapter therefore aims to fill in some of the gaps before 1969 as well as outlining a selection of the major achievements since, all of which have been recorded in the REME Journal and 'The Craftsman' over the years.

Corps shooting was the responsibility of the REME Rifle Association, the Committee of which had representatives for Full-Bore Target Rifle, Small-Bore and Air Weapons, Target Pistol and seven district representatives for a very active and successful sport. It was responsible also for the selection and training of Corps teams for Service weapon shooting.

Women serving in the Corps have excelled in a wide range of sports with more than their 'fair share' of Army representatives. The pages of 'The Craftsman' record that more and more REME women are in teams and also taking part in adventurous training.

The following sports were all flourishing within the Corps at the beginning of the Nineties: association football, athletics, badminton, basketball, bobsleighing, canoeing, cricket, cross country running, cycling, free fall parachuting, golf, hang-gliding, hockey, judo, modern pentathlon, motor cycling, motor rallying, orienteering, rugby football, sailing and windsurfing, skiing and other winter sports, squash, swiming and water polo, tennis, and sporting expeditions. Additional sports, such as rowing and sub-aqua, are still emerging as Corps sports, and no doubt there will be others to follow with equal success to these now listed.

It is hoped that the few extracts given in this Chapter from the long story of REME team and individual successes in sports and shooting will show what a remarkable effort REME officers and soldiers made throughout the period when they were also busy keeping the famous punch in the fist of the other 90% of the Army. It characterizes determination, fitness and skill – and in, one word, 'guts'.

HIGHLIGHTS OF CORPS SPORT

Colonel Jock Tatman reviewed Corps Sport in the 1972 Journal, describing 1970–71 as a vintage year. Twenty years later one can see that, good as it undoubtedly was, it was really just one more year in the long successful record of Corps Sport. In 1980, for example, REME officers and soldiers represented the Army in fourteen sports and our country in seven.

Apart from cricket, association football, rugby football, golf, modern pentathlon, sailing and swimming, all described at greater length in this chapter, the Corps made its mark in many other less publicized sports. SEE had been Army basketball champion eight times by 1978 and started the REME Orienteering Club in 1968. Orienteering became a Corps Sport in 1974 and Captain Alan Meekings represented Great Britain in 1976. The REME Parachute Club was formed in 1968 to put on free fall displays; it carried out the parachute drops for the scenes in the film 'The Eagle has Landed'.

Adventurous training exercises are included in Chapter 5 but other equally adventurous activities belong with sport in this chapter. Over the past twenty-five years these wide-ranging activities have been carried out in every sort of terrain, both on land and water, all over the world. On land, Lieutenant Colonel John Peacock was in charge of logistics for the successful Army Mountaineering Association expedition to Everest in 1976, whilst Captain Pat Gunson, a REME TAVR officer, was one of the lead climbers. His story is in Chapter 8; only bad weather prevented him and his companion reaching the summit. Both John Peacock and Pat Gunson had been on the preparatory climb at Nuptse in 1975 and both were recipients of the Rory Cape Award. Captain Brian Daniels excelled on land and water and held the world non-stop walking record when he walked more than 220 miles in a little over 70½ hours in 1971; he was also captain of Army canoe sprint and long distance teams 1968–70. He was awarded his Army colours for canoeing in 1966 and 1968–70.

Very much on water, Sergeant Lynch took part in the London to Monte Carlo power-boat race in 1972, Warrant Officer Class 1 Dobson sailed on the *Golden Hinde* replica in 1973, and Staff Sergeant Leslie was the only member of the crew to sail in both legs of the Round the World Clipper Race in *Great Britain II* in 1975–76. Leslie also won the Rory Cape Award and skippered the HMSTY *Adventure* from Cape Town to Auckland in the Whitbread Round the World Race in 1977. The only junior rank to win the Rory Cape Award was Corporal David Inman, an internationally recognized karate exponent who, in 1981 at his own expense, travelled to Japan to train under Hirokasu Kanazawa, the chief instructor of Shotokan Karate International; at the end of his five-month stay he was graded 2nd Dan black belt and achieved referee and instructor qualifications. This was a significant achievement, particularly as karate was not a recognized Army sport at that time. The origin of the Rory Cape Award is told in Chapter 5.

ASSOCIATION FOOTBALL

Association football has probably been the most popular team game in the Army for decades. The records show that REME soccer got off to an excellent start at Arborfield in the 1945–46 season and the Base Workshops in Japan and Singapore made a vigorous start in the Far East. The Base Workshop in Japan won the British Commonwealth Base Soccer Cup in 1947. Throughout the Army until 1962 there were a number of professional footballers undertaking their National Service, and these undoubtedly provided an advantage to those units in which they were serving. Eventually, to be fair to all teams concerned in representative matches, the number of professional players was restricted.

Army Challenge Cup

The Army Challenge Cup was open to all Army units stationed in BAOR and the UK. In the thirty-six years 1946–82 REME unit teams won the Army Cup eight times, were runners-up on three other occasions and in the semi-finals five other times. Major Arthur Hall, posted to 7 Armoured Workshop in 1947, decided that a first-class soccer team was one of the best ways to boost unit morale. How well he succeeded! 7 Armoured Workshop reached the semi-final in three seasons, 1947–50, losing in 1950 to the eventual Cup winners; this unit, without any professional players, won the 1947–48 season 7th Armoured Division league and Cup, REME Rhine Army Cup and the BAOR Army Cup, but lost the Army Cup semi-final to an all-professional team from a training regiment. Lieutenant Colonel Hall later recalled that Squadron Leader Cliff Michelmore – later a prominent television broadcaster – regularly commentated on the Workshop's matches on the British Forces Network. He always commenced by announcing, 'Here I am with my favourite REME workshop . . .'

Before long Major Hall went to 4 (Armament) Training Battalion where he soon built a team around Sergeant Jack Wilkins. In 1950–51, from more than 200 entrants, the team won the 50th Army Cup final, beating the 1st Battalion, The East Yorkshire Regiment. Each team was restricted to five professionals only, under the new rules. 4 (Armament) Training Battalion repeated this success in 1956–57 and 1957–58; in the latter season HM The Queen and HRH The Duke of Edinburgh attended the Army Cup final, when Craftsman Nelson received the Cup from Her Majesty.

16 Parachute Workshop performed a very great giant-killing act in 1964 when they won the Army Cup. Although technically a minor unit, less than 150 strong, they beat the 13th/18th Royal Hussars (Queen Mary's Own) after a replay. After the amalgamation of 4 and 6 Battalions REME in 1961 to form SEME, the soccer tradition was maintained and encouraged by the Chief Instructor, Lieutenant Colonel Stan Dixon. In 1965 SEME won the Army Cup with a 6–3 victory over the Royal Highland Fusiliers. SEME won the Army Cup again in 1971 when Lieutenant Colonel Arthur Hall was CO of SEME Regiment. The ultimate Army soccer trophy came to SEME again in 1974 after a splendid season in which they won every game. Credit must go to Major Neville Cooper who for four seasons had managed the SEME team to achieve two Army Cup victories and one attendance at the semi-final. 1976 was another glorious year, when SEME scooped the Services soccer Triple Crown by taking the King's Cup (UK Army champion unit) and the Jubilee Cup (UK inter-Services champion unit), as well as the Army Cup. SEME continued to feature in the forefront of Army soccer, reaching the Army Cup final in 1977, 1981 and 1982. In the decade 1980 to 1990 SEME reached the final seven times. They defeated 28 Amphibious Engineer Regiment from Hameln to win the Cup in 1983 and, in 1984, in the first all-REME UK final, they defeated SEE after a close contest by the only goal scored. They went on to win the Army Cup, beating 45th Field Regiment RA from BAOR by the same score.

Further success was thwarted by 28th (BR) Signal Regiment in 1987 who won a replay 4–3 after an exciting 4–4 draw and by their old rivals 28 Amphibious Regiment in 1990. However, SEME gained some consolation in the 1987 season when they defeated 94th Locating Regiment RA 6–0 in the UK final and, despite being beaten in the Army final, went on to win the Jubilee Cup. They had won this trophy six times previously and their last appearance in the competition was in 1990 when they lost to RAF Brize Norton on penalties. The skill of the Corps' soccer players has been supported by the encouragement they received from all ranks. In SEME particularly the school gave enthusiastic backing to their team and the lead came from the top; all the Commandants took a keen interest in the game, none more so than Major General Alex McKay, who, when he was Commandant, made clear his view that REME's high morale and its reputation throughout the Army owed much to the Corps' sporting prowess: a close second to engineering competence. Particular credit is due to Colonel Brian Porter, Corps Soccer Chairman during the golden years from 1975–86. Major Jack Smith gave unstinted service to Corps Soccer as Secretary from 1972–85, the last ten years as a Retired Officer in SEME, where he also managed the School team.

1 Corps Troops Workshop had an astonishing and uniquely successful 1988–89 season, its achievements being regularly reported on the BAOR radio and TV service. At the time of these successes it had only 126 men. They won the BAOR Senior Craftsman's Cup beating 4 Armoured Workshop, going on to beat SEME on Bordon's Daly Ground to become REME champions. The Workshop won the 4th Armoured Division Minor Units Cup, winning the final 10–1, and was runner-up in the Division's Major Units Cup, losing 2–0 to 10 Regiment RCT which had just won the Army Cup. It went on to win the Army Minor Units Cup, which up to that year had never been won by any BAOR unit and never by any REME unit. The captain, manager and trainer was CSM Danny McCreesh, who captained and managed the BAOR Corps team and later managed the UK team, while the coach was Sergeant Brian Wilson who had represented the Corps from 1977. Several of the team players made their mark later, including Lance Corporal Henry Heard.

The Craftsman's Cup

1978 Craftsman's Cup Final UK
C Company SEME Regiment v 70 Aircraft Workshop

The Craftsman's Cup competition started in 1947–48; divided into Senior and Junior sections, the Senior was open to all REME units and the Junior to those under a hundred strong. Separate competitions were held in BAOR and UK, although a Junior competition was not started in Germany until 1981.

The UK Junior Craftsman's Cup until 1968 was dominated by 26 Command Workshop, Stirling, which reached the final five times, winning the Cup three times; by 11 Vehicle Depot Workshop which reached the final on three occasions winning on each; and by 16 Parachute Workshop which reached the final five times, including winning the Cup in each of the three seasons 1962–65. The 1981 final between 38 Engineer Regiment Workshop and the Workshop Squadron, Commando Logistic Regiment RM was a notably exciting match: at half-time the Sapper Workshop was leading 2–0, at full time the score was 2–2, and extra time produced six further goals with 38 Engineer Regiment Workshop winning 7–3.

The first fourteen seasons of the Senior Craftsman's Cup in the UK were during the era of National Service, many of those serving being professional footballers. The games were largely dominated by the training battalions, 4 (Armament) Training Battalion winning the Cup five times.

In BAOR, during the same fourteen seasons, the Senior Craftsman's Cup competition was won by 7 Armoured Workshop for the first five years and by 1(BR) Corps Troops Workshop over the following nine years. The first LAD to win the Cup was 3rd Carabiniers LAD in 1971. 1 (BR) Corps Troops Workshop, Bielefeld, was the first REME BAOR team to win both the Army Minor Units Cup and the Senior Craftsman's Cup.

The BAOR Craftsman's Cup competition always attracted many entries in both the Senior and Junior sections: it was quite usual for seventy to eighty teams to enter and produce a keenly contested competition, attracting the attention of all ranks throughout the season. In 1992, the REME 50 year, 22nd Air Defence Regiment Workshop won the Senior and 15th/19th The King's Royal Hussars LAD the Junior competitions.

Various units continued to rise into periods of supremacy: in the early Eighties SEE and Headquarters Company SEME dominated the Senior finals, while later in the decade 71 Aircraft Workshop, 1 Corps Troops Workshop and 4 Armoured Workshop (twice) recorded wins in 1987, 89, 90 and 91 respectively. In the Junior finals the competition brought glory to many units including The Royal Hussars (Prince of Wales's Own) LAD, 3rd Battalion, The Light Infantry LAD and 15th/19th The King's Royal Hussars LAD who ensured that their larger workshop brothers did not have it all their own way. 50th Missile Regiment Workshop, 38 Engineer Regiment Workshop, AMF(L) Workshop and 18 Base Workshop did, however, win the trophy during the most recent seasons. One of the most interesting units to do well in the competition was Electronics Branch REME, which reached the final for three consecutive years 1989–91, winning it in 1990. With a team mainly of officers and warrant officers, its average age was in excess of 40 years, especially when the Commanding Officer Colonel Mike Selby was playing. This was probably the first time the Chairman of Corps Football had to present a medal to himself!

Corps Representative Soccer

The first recorded representative Corps match was played on 28 September 1946 against the RASC: the result was 3–3. In those early days many Corps matches were also arranged against R SIGNALS, RAMC, RAOC, often at the Aldershot Stadium. The annual match against RAOC (and now RLC) for a cup donated in 1947 by Arthur Stambois, an industrialist who supplied vulcanizing equipment to the Army during the Second World War, continues to this day. In due course Bordon and its Daly ground became the home of Corps soccer, just as Arborfield became the home of Corps cricket, rugby and modern pentathlon.

In 1980 an annual contest between REME UK and REME BAOR began. BAOR won the first match 4–2 at Fallingbostel, during which Sergeant Tam Tervit played exceptionally well and scored a hat trick. In

1992 the REME 50 game produced an exciting, hard-fought and skilful match: BAOR went into a 3–1 lead but the UK side came back to 3–3. Neither side scored during extra time; the penalty shoot-out settled the score at 5–4, so enabling BAOR to retain the trophy which they had won more times than the UK. In 1983 this annual competition was named the 'Trussler Trophy' in memory of Sergeant Alan Trussler, who was killed after leaving a coach returning from the Army Cup final in Aldershot, in which he had played for SEME: he was a Corps, Army and Combined Services player.

The first really distinguished Corps side, after the end of National Service and the loss of professional footballers, was the 1966–67 team which won all eight matches and had six regular players in the Army team. Three of them, Corporal Douggie Aitchison, Corporal Steve Morton and Lance Corporal Joe Ramsden, each of whom rose to senior non-commissioned rank, formed the core of the notable REME teams which were supreme in Army soccer from 1969–75. There were other great REME players over this period. Three forwards from the Army Cup-winning SEME team of 1971 were also Corps and Army players: Warrant Officer Class 2 Barry Harkness, the fast and agile striker Staff Sergeant Lionel Grancourt and the very speedy Sergeant Sammy McKay (who had also been in the victorious SEME 1965 Army Cup team). Sergeant Les Chinou, too, was another Corps forward who represented the Army. Strength in the Corps team's defence was also evident, with Army representation by Corporal Brian Roberts (a 1976 Army Cup winner with SEME), Warrant Officer Class 1 Andy Miles and Warrant Officer Class 2 Bruce Menzies (also a versatile mid-field player, who played many times in the Army team). Warrant Officer Class 2 Ken Hardy was a mid-field player for the Corps and later coached the Army Youth team. Such names are just a few from the REME soccer pantheon: there are many more. During the six seasons 1969–75 the Corps team lost none of its thirty-six matches against other Corps, drawing once with the Gunners and winning five out of six matches against the Royal Air Force Training Command. The 1983 REME Journal records that in thirty-six years the Corps side played 187 matches against the Royal Air Force and other Corps sides, winning 126 and drawing nineteen.

Corps soccer was just as impressive in the Eighties. In 1983 the UK team won nine out of ten matches and the BAOR team won six out of eight. Three players represented both the Army and Combined Services: Warrant Officer Class 2 John Woodward, Lance Corporal Butler and Lance Corporal White; five others represented the Army.

The Corps team won the 1987–88 Quadrangular Cup tournament at Chatham for the first time in five years, beating RA and RE and drawing with R SIGNALS, under the captaincy of Staff Sergeant Steve Oldfield, who received the cup from Major General John Boyne. In the following season the Corps team in UK was drawn from eighteen units, with forty-three players selected. Corporal Guy Whittingham, who scored eighteen goals in fourteen matches, was voted Army and REME player of the year. The Corps won the 1989 Quadrangular tournament, beating RA and R SIGNALS and drawing with RE. The first ever REME match against the TA was played on the Daly Ground in January 1990, resulting in a draw 2–2.

In 1988 Major General Boyne donated a trophy to be played for annually between REME and its arch-rivals R SIGNALS. Unfortunately, REME up to 1992 had won the trophy only once. Corps fixtures against the Royal Air Force Support Command recommenced in 1989 and the Infantry was beaten in 1992 for the first time in three encounters. Prestigious friendlies were being played against Liverpool, Portsmouth, Reading, Halifax Town and Lincoln City, as well as local non-league teams in pre-season friendlies, together with the Dan Air/Parasol League (old Surrey Counties) which provided tough opposition prior to the annual inter-Corps quadrangular tournament.

Great Players

One of the earliest great players was a professional during National Service days: Lance Corporal Charles Thompson, the goalkeeper. He won an Army Cup medal with 4 (Armament) Training Battalion in 1950–51, and in the same season won the League medal, League Cup medal and Glasgow Cup medal with Clyde. He later played for Chelsea and won an FA Cup-winners medal with Nottingham Forest in 1959. Lance Corporal Willie Fraser, goalkeeper for Airdrieonians and Sunderland, was twice capped for Scotland in 1955; his brilliant play for 26 Command Workshop at Stirling led to their success in the Junior Craftsman's Cup in 1954. However, talent had not always been recognized prior to National Service: Craftsman Jeff Hall while playing for an unknown REME unit in 1949 was discovered, signed up by Birmingham City and went on to become a regular England player in the Fifties.

The most outstanding Army amateur player during the National Service era was Sergeant Jack Wilkins, who captained the Army team fifty times against other Services, French and Belgian Armies, Luxembourg and Scotland; he played for an FA XI against Ireland in 1950 and was skipper of the Corps side 1950–52. He led 4 (Armament) Training Battalion to be the first REME team to win the Army Cup.

The Sixties and Seventies were the golden years for Corps soccer and many outstanding players were discovered. When serving with the LAD Staff Sergeant 'Nobby' Clarkson, as captain, and Sergeant Brian Moriarty played in the 10th Royal Hussars team which won the Army Cup in 1963. Later both players were posted to SEME and reversed their roles: Moriarty achieving the distinction of captaining the team to win the Army Cup in 1965, while Clarkson played in the Cup-winning side of 1971. Warrant Officer Class 2 Steve Morton played for SEME and the

Corps from 1963–81 and for the Army and the Combined Services for over ten years from 1963. During this period he captained all these teams for a large part of the time. Sergeant Joe Ramsden, who first played soccer at school in Oxford with Morton, was an equally distinguished player, representing the Corps from 1962–76, the Army from 1965–76 and the Combined Services. His playing career was cut short by a back injury and he switched his talents to coaching the SEME and Corps teams. He was appointed Army coach in 1979.

Staff Sergeant Douggie Aitcheson has an outstanding record. Like Sergeant Moriarty he played for two different Army Cup final winning teams. He captained 39th Field Regiment RA team which won in 1978. With his earlier membership of the winning SEME team in 1965, 1971 and 1976, he now gained four Army Cup-winner's medals. Later he added two runners-up medals in 1981 and 1982, again with SEME. He played regularly for the Army from 1966–74 and for the Combined Services from 1968–74. Corporal Alan Goucher, an outstanding mid-field player, played for the Corps and the Army for ten years until he left the Army in 1977. He played regularly for the Combined Services in 1970–74 and captained the Army in 1972–74 and the Combined Services in 1971 and in 1974. Corporal Goucher won Army Cup-winner's medals with the SEME team in 1974 and 1976. Staff Sergeant Barry Tolfrey played for SEME, the Corps and the Army; later, after qualifying, he coached SEME and subsequently the Territorial Army national team.

The Army team in 1974–75 called upon ten REME players at various times: Corporal Ramsden (captain), Corporal Goucher, Corporal Aitchison, Corporal Dudley and Corporal Wilson all from SEME, Sergeant F Cartlidge of the 1st Parachute Logistic Regiment, Corporal Brown from SEE, Lance Corporal Richard Freeman and Corporal Lewis from 70 Field Workshop, and Lance Corporal A MacDonald of 9 Field Workshop.

In summary, for twelve seasons during the years 1966–81 a REME player captained the Army team: Morton 1966–72, Goucher 1972–74, Ramsden 1974–76, and Staff Sergeant John Woodward 1979–81 who also captained the Combined Services in all matches. In 1981 Staff Sergeant Woodward, Lance Corporal Tracey and Craftsman White represented the Army throughout the season, Tracey and White also representing the Combined Services in all matches. REME continued to make a substantive contribution to Service teams in the Eighties. The Corps had ten Army players in 1984–85, three of whom represented the Combined Services, and in 1987 eight Corps players played for the Army. Two of the best players to wear a Corps shirt in the late Eighties left the Army to join professional league clubs. Lance Corporal Steve Butler of SEE was bought out of the Army by Brentford, and played for Maidstone before being transferred to Watford for a reported fee exceeding £100,000, with a further move to Cambridge United. Corporal Guy Whittingham left

SEME for Portsmouth and in 1989–90 was their leading goal scorer, leading to a transfer valuation in 1992 in excess of £1 million (an offer from a Premier League side having been turned down by the club the previous year); the following season he moved to Aston Villa. The REME players who represented the Army and Combined Services in the late Eighties and early Nineties included Craftsman McGregor, Lance Corporal Tony Wright and Lance Corporal Shane Smith, while Sergeant Wood played numerous games for the Army. Craftsman 'Ginger' Burns left the Army for Reading as goalkeeper and later moved on to Airdrie .

Referees

Colonel John Punter, an Army Referee Class 1, had to wait until 1978 to take charge of an Army Cup final: a disqualification caused by SEME's frequent appearance in the final. In the event his Cup Final was drawn after extra time, providing him with a replay to referee the next day. He refereed at all levels from 1955–80, including the Royal Navy versus the Royal Air Force, and was a member of the Army FA Referees Committee for many years.

REME referees for Army Cup finals included Captain F C Green in 1948, who had to abandon the match when lightning killed two players during the replay; CSM Jack Clover in 1955 and ASM Wally Woods in 1963 – the latter having the previous year refereed the Army match against the Football Association at Roker Park, Sunderland. CSM Clover also refereed two Army matches with Everton and a Royal Navy match against the Royal Air Force. Major Peter Pittaway was the referee for the 1984–85 Army Cup final, served on the Army Referees Committee from 1980 and was its Chairman for four years, being succeeded in 1992 by Lieutenant Colonel Mike Crabbe. In a football career spanning more than thirty years, Major Pittaway had twice refereed matches between the Belgian and French Armed Forces and several Combined Services matches against top league clubs including Chelsea, Southampton and West Bromwich Albion. He was a football league linesman 1980–85, and officiated in 1983 in that capacity at a Charity Shield match between Manchester United and Liverpool and in 1984 at the UEFA Cup semi-final between Inter Milan and SV Hamburg.

Army FA Executive Committee

Major General John Boyne was Chairman of the Army FA 1984–87, in addition to serving as a member of its Executive Committee for a number of years. Brigadier Tony Hughes and Lieutenant Colonel 'Tiny' Davies (a formidable 6 feet 7 inches goalkeeper) served as members of the Army FA Executive Committee and made major contributions to Army football. Brigadier Hughes had joined the Committee in the Sixties while serving as a Lieutenant Colonel at SEME, and after eight years became Chairman for the next five of his thirteen years service on the Committee. Colonel Phil Kay was a member of the Committee

1989–91, being replaced by Colonel Selby. Major Pittaway also served on the Executive Committee 1988–92, representing the views of Army referees.

ATHLETICS

Captain Harry Whittle was the greatest REME athlete in the early days of the Corps: amongst his achievements, in 1947 he equalled the Army long jump record and was second in the 400 metres hurdles in the match between Great Britain and France. In 1948 he represented Great Britain in the London Olympic Games in the 400 metres hurdles.

Corps athletics 1983

Many outstanding Corps athletes followed, most starting their claims to fame in the annual Corps Meeting; some of them are mentioned below.

- As an Apprentice Tradesman at Chepstow, Peter Lillington came to early attention as an exceptional sprinter, becoming the Welsh Junior champion in each of the three years 1947–49, achieving 10.1 seconds over 100 yards on the turf of rugby football grounds and representing Wales Juniors. In 1952 Sergeant Lillington became the Army 100 yards champion and during 1951–53 represented the Army and Combined Services in the sprint and sprint relay teams; he was awarded their colours in these years, in which he also earned his REME rugby football colours. Running with Polytechnic Harriers he also won an Amateur Athletic Association (AAA) medal in the 4×100 yards relay. Further progress at home was cut short by posting to the Far East, where he equalled the 100 yards record of 10.0 seconds in Singapore and represented the colony each year in the Malayan Games. Later in his career he continued to give lasting support to athletics by becoming a 'three As' starter, encouraged by Lieutenant Colonel Ruarc Eraut, Corps Treasurer and AAA official.
- ASM Neville Hart-Ives won the Army individual Javelin championship twelve times between 1964–1976, winning the Inter-Services championship five times 1967–72. He represented Great Britain at Edinburgh in the International Games twice, against France in 1969 and 1971 and against Finland in 1969. His personal best was 245 feet 9 inches (74.90 metres) in 1971. In 1975 he was presented with the Army Athletics Association Senior Field Events Challenge Trophy and elected to the committee of the Army Athletics Association.
- Corporal David Bayes set an Army individual record in throwing the hammer 180 feet in 1963, and over the following thirteen years represented the Army in the Inter-Services championship. From 1963–70 he represented the Combined Services in the same event, as well as setting new Corps marks during that period.
- Staff Sergeant Alex Burdon was the Army individual discus champion in 1969–71. He represented the Army against the Germany Army in 1969 and was awarded his Army colours. He set a Corps record in 1970 with 142 feet 4 inches.
- In 1971, Captain Brian Daniels broke the existing British and World endurance walking record covering 220 miles 410 yards in 70 hours 35 minutes. Sergeant Eric Ricketts won the Army putting the shot event 1969–72 and was runner-up in 1965–68; he won the Inter-Services championship 1968 and 1970–72. He was awarded his Army colours in 1965 and his Combined Service colours in 1968. He

represented the Army against the Germany Army in 1969. Southern Counties AAA awarded him their colours in 1969.

- In the 1988 season ASM Mick Johnson won the Army Discus championship and competed regularly for the Army whilst RSM John McIllmurray won the Army Marathon championship, and again in 1989.
- Lance Corporal Paul Beaumont won the Army 400 metres and 400 metres hurdles, also in the 1988 season, and competed regularly for the Army reaching both the UK final and the Olympic trials finals at 400 metres hurdles. The following year he went on to represent England in a quadrangular match against Portugal, Spain and Wales. Corporal Beaumont was the outstanding athlete at the end of the Eighties and the early Nineties, was the Corps champion from 1989 and consistently won the Inter-Services 400 metres and 400 metres hurdles. He, together with Corporal Alvin Walker (triple jump) and Craftsman Paul Wildridge (high jump), competed regularly for the Army and Combined Services in 1990–92. In 1992 Corporal Beaumont was ranked sixth in Britain in the 400 metres hurdles.

BADMINTON

The Corps team performed well in the UK inter-Corps league from 1969–79, winning it in 1971–72, 1974–75 and 1976–77. In 1979 the competition was renamed the UK inter-Corps tournament. REME (UK) won the competition in 1983–84, 1985–86, 1990–91 and 1992–93. The Corps won the final of the inter-Corps Army competition (UK versus BAOR) in 1983–84 (UK), 1985–86 (UK), 1986–87 (BAOR), 1988–89 (BAOR), 1989–90 (BAOR), 1990–91 (UK) and 1992–93 (UK). The Corps team won the UK inter-Corps tournament and beat the BAOR champions in the Army final 1983.

Well-known players have included:

- Warrant Officer Class 2 S Dowell who played regularly for SEE and the Corps in the Sixties, becoming captain of the Corps team. He first played for the Army in 1965–66 and won his Army colours. While at the School of Artillery, Manorbier 1968–71 he represented the Army sixteen times and Pembrokeshire County team six times. He became an umpire for several county championships, the All England championships and the English National championships. In 1972 he umpired the England match against Holland. He was a committee member of the Berkshire and the Pembrokeshire County Badminton Associations for several years.
- Private Chris Fetherston, a recruit in The Training Battalion and Depot, who became an All England badminton champion in

January 1978 when he and his partner, Darrell Roebuck, won the Boys under-18 doubles at Watford. They were the first unseeded pair to win the championship, beating the No 1 seeds in the final. Craftsman Fetherston won the Army singles championship in 1980.

- ASM Alan Dixon who at the start of the Nineties was the best-known REME player in the Army team. He played in the Army team for many years and was captain on their tour of Hong Kong in 1991. Also Corporal S Everett was awarded his Army colours that year.

Warrant Office Class 2 S Dowell

AQMS Peter Tidey

BASKETBALL

The SEE basketball team were UK Army champions 1970–74 and in consequent representation of Army UK beat the BAOR champions in 1971, 72 and 73. Five of their star players were:

- Sergeant Ray Allen who was a member of the Army team in 1965, 66, 70 and 71 and of the Combined Services team 1970–71.
- Sergeant Paul Roach who was a member of the Army team 1965–66, 1969–71, Combined Services 1965–66, 1969–71, and of the England team in nine matches during 1970.
- Sergeant Mike Smith who was an Army player 1968–71, Combined Services 1969–71 and in the England training squad 1970–72.

- AQMS Peter Tidey (who captained the SEE team 1971–72) played for the Army and the Combined Services 1960–72, for England in 1966 and Great Britain in 1968.
- Sergeant Eric Ricketts who played for the Army 1969–72, Combined Services 1970–72 and England twice in 1971.

In 1981 the Corps side won ten of its thirteen matches and the newly established inter-Corps tournament. Lieutenant Roach, ASM Ricketts and ASM Smith represented the Army; Ricketts played for Wales and Craftsman Nick Emmanuel played regularly for the Army under-21 team. SEE was the Major Unit champion.

In 1986 Staff Sergeant Paul Smith, Sergeant Gary Morris and Corporal Martin Toney all represented the Army senior team, while Craftsmen Billy Reid and Dale Hinds, Apprentice Tradesmen Sergeant S T McCann, Corporal D A Leach and Lance Corporal M D Reeves all played for the Army under-21 side.

In 1987 the Army inter-Corps basketball championship was played at Aldershot between nine Corps. REME won seven of its eight matches, and lost one in which ACC beat the Corps in the last seventeen seconds with a 3-point shot when the Corps had been leading 80–78. This created a championship tie between RE and REME: under the rules, the winner of the match between them would be the champions, and because the Corps had beaten the Sappers 86–79 in their match, they were declared the overall champions.

The Corps was runner-up to the APTC in the inter-Corps competitions in 1988, 89 and 90. In 1991 REME won the trophy again and won both the UK and the BAOR championships – the first Corps to do so.

In 1991 SEE were Army finalists. Warrant Officer Class 2 Morris and Corporal Reid represented the Army and Combined Services in the years after 1987; in those years Sergeant Hinds, Corporal Ian Phippen, Corporal Duane Leach, Lance Corporal Neil Tolsen and Craftsman Carl Black all represented the Army.

In 1992 Captain Walker Nesmith was the Army Team Manager, Captain Steve Lallament was the Army Technical Secretary and at the end of 1992 Captain Trevor Stipling was to be Army Secretary; the last two were also both kept busy refereeing Army and civilian basketball.

BOBSLEIGHING

This dangerous and exhilarating sport first attracted REME teams in BAOR in the Eighties under the chairmanship of Colonel Murray Wildman. Two REME teams entered the Army two-man championships at St Moritz in the 1987–88 season. The No 1 team, Corporal Dave Bunce and Corporal Mick Ellis, came second and the No 2 team, Lance Corporal Gary Smith and Corporal West, came seventh, Lance Corporal

Smith winning the best novice driver prize. All four represented the Army at the Inter-Services championships on the notoriously difficult track at Cervinia in the shadow of the Matterhorn in Italy, where Lance Corporal Smith again won the best novice driver prize.

The following season was outstandingly successful. The Army championship was again held at Cervinia, during which Corporal Bunce and Lance Corporal Don Newell won the Army title, while Sergeants Pat Gallagher and Kev Hill at seventh place were the fastest novice crew. Corporal Bunce and Lance Corporal Newell represented the Army in the subsequent Inter-Services championships also at Cervinia. Corporal Bunce finished second overall, beating one of the 1988 Winter Olympic team and winning a prize for the fastest lauf of the day.

Army Junior Bobsleigh Championship 1988. Corporals Bunce and Ellis

Corporals Bunce, West, Smith and Lance Corporal Newell were all selected to represent Great Britain in international events. Corporal West, as brakeman to Lance Corporal Sean Olsen PARA, came fifteenth in the World Junior championships, winning the European Junior championship.

Returning again to Cervinia for the 1990 Army bobsleigh championships, REME alone had four crews – more than the Parachute Regiment, R SIGNALS and AAC with three each, while other Regiments or Corps had one team. After several days of training runs (involving some crashes, damaging both bobs and crews) the Corps was able to produce three crews on the day of the race – by that stage more than anyone else. Corporal Smith and Lance Corporal Newell came fourth, Sergeant Pat Gallagher and Lieutenant Steve Goodburn sixth, Lance Corporal Andy Tetley and Corporal 'Chappy' Chapman seventh. The top experts had spent much of the year on the international circuit, whereas Corporal Smith had not driven since the Army championships the year before! Brigadier Murray Wildman became the Director of Finance for the Army Bobsleigh Association.

CANOEING

Prior to the formation of a REME Canoe Club, enthusiastic individuals had enjoyed varied forms of canoeing, many of whom had achieved some distinction through their expertise. The earliest individual was AQMS Mike Tapscott of SEE, who was a regular at many canoeing events and gave much of his time to young Corps members. In later years as a civilian instructor in Princess Marina College he trained and entered many boys for the Devizes to Westminster canoe race and the Army canoe championships, achieving many successes in the early Seventies.

ASM Brian Daniels was another early enthusiast, being notably successful in the Sixties: he won his Army colours in the sport in 1966 and colours chevrons in each of the three years 1968–70. In the latter period he was captain of the Army canoe sprint and long distance team. He was three times a member of a 16 Parachute Brigade team which in the late Sixties represented England against France in annual events, involving a 100 kilometres race and a slalom on successive days both, unusually, with the challenge of using the same canoe. In 1969 he competed in the national surf championship and won first place as anchor man for the Army team in the relay race.

In the late Seventies the success of other individuals brought canoeing into greater prominence, and in 1977 the REME Canoe Club was established by Colonel Dennis Franks, who became its first Chairman. It soon made its mark by nearly sweeping the board at the 1979 Army championships, winning the open water, intermediate and novice competitions. This was also the year of its first official entry, and best performance so far, in the Devizes to Westminster Canoe Race. Collective enthusiasm was naturally fostered by the existence of a Corps club, whilst many talented individuals made their mark over the years, amongst whom were:

Lance Corporal John Speck in the 10,000 metres K1 at the National Championship

- Lance Corporal John Speck who, at the 1977 Inter-Services canoe championships at the National Water Sports Centre, Holme Pierrepoint, was in the winning Army team in the K1 (Kayak Single) and K4 (Kayak Four) events. In the same championships the Army also won the Long Distance event on the River Trent, when he came second in the K1 race – a great achievement. Two years later he came second in the 10,000 metres K1 at the national championship, and was in the Army crew which won the K4 event. In that year, too, at an international canoe regatta in Belgium, he triumphed over seventy competitors in the 10,000 metres Senior B event. Thus well noticed, in 1980 he joined the British team for an event in Spain, and on several other occasions in 1981 and 1983. In 1982 REME fielded nine canoeists in Army representative teams, and Lance Corporal Speck won four individual events in the Army championships and Inter-Services championships, followed by two bronze medals in the national championships. In 1984, as Sergeant Speck, he represented Great Britain in the marathon Grand Prix squad.

• Apprentice Tradesman Eric Sutherland came to attention in 1977, his first year as an apprentice, when he represented the Army in slalom and won his Army colours. By 1978 he was able to represent the Combined Services against Scotland, and in that year was awarded both his Army and Combined Services colours; the following year he became the Army slalom champion. In the same year he became Junior surf champion in the Army surf championships in Devon, in which it was reported that 'he surfed along the waves in his canoe in a most professional manner and well deserved his award'. He was, during the late Seventies, and as an adult soldier in the Eighties, the outstanding individual performer: his expertise was surf canoeing in the 'Waveski' discipline, winning the Army championships eight times in eleven years, and the European championships in 1987. In 1990 he represented Britain in the World Cup in California, finishing third in the mixed doubles, seventh in the Seniors and thirteenth in the Open. He was also active on the organizational side, as a founder member of the British Wave Ski Association (BWSA) and a member of the Army Canoe Union Executive Committee. He organized the 1989 World championships at Newquay on behalf of the BWSA and has been involved in the organization of Army and Inter-Services surf championships for many years whilst rising to warrant officer rank.

• Andrew Eaton also paddled for the Army as an Apprentice Tradesman. With AT Sutherland he competed in the 1977 Inter-Services slalom championship at Grandtully, Scotland, when the Army team beat the Royal Navy, the event overall being won by the RAF. In 1979, still an apprentice, he was runner-up in the Army slalom championships, whilst in the same event another Arborfield apprentice, Ellis, was first out of some eighty in the Novice event. In the following year Craftsman Eaton became the Army slalom champion and, together with Craftsmen Sutherland and 'Smudge' Smith, formed the winning team for REME in the inter-Corps event. In 1988, together with Sergeant Steve Pearson, he represented the Army and Combined Services in White Water events in the Canadian Doubles. His partner competed a year later in the Great

Britain open championships and was again in the Combined Services team.

• Staff Sergeants Roger Ivey and Stan Richmond were selected to represent Great Britain in the 1979 World White Water Canoeing Championships in Canada. Their class was the Canadian Double (C2), a five-metre long, eighty-centimetre wide fragile glass fibre canoe propelled with single paddles whilst kneeling. Their seemingly endless training increased with intensity under two excellent coaches, Sepp Schumacher and the West Germany team coach, Karl Knapp. They met the teams from Austria, Belgium, France, Italy and Switzerland at Bourg St Maurice, when all including Great Britain were making their selections. The finale of the selection week in May took the form of an open race between the nations' top paddlers, and it appeared that nothing was going to stop the French and Swiss. A month of intensive training ensued, including a week on the River Loisach for the German national championship. The World championship course in Canada had a dangerous stretch of water thirty metres from the start, where the paddlers dropped into a deep hole and became engulfed by returning waves – known to canoeists as 'a stopper'. This was followed by a rock face which turned the river through a right-angle, making the most difficult rapid of the course. The remainder was non-stop rapids with deep holes hidden behind small rocks, which could damage the back of a boat quite badly. Two small pools amongst the rapids gave the team a chance to get their breaths back and sprint 100 metres before the next rapid. The most physically testing part of the course was the last three kilometres to the finish, as the river suddenly opened up into a flat, very wide and shallow rapid in which the race could be won or lost. The two sergeants finished their first World championship race seventeenth out of twenty-four, and the other British C2 was fifteenth. These results were the best overall that the C2s had ever achieved. In receiving their Army colours the two Sergeants also received the ACU President's Trophy for outstanding achievement in 1979. RQMS Richmond was first in the Inter-Services championships in the Canadian Doubles, and represented the Combined Services in the Canadian Doubles slalom in an international event in which he came seventh. He was the Army and Inter-Services champion in both the Canadian Singles and Doubles White Water events in 1985. White Water racing has been well described by Staff Sergeant Ivey in the 1980 REME Journal.

Devizes to Westminster Canoe Race

In the Sixties ASM Daniels competed twice in this race, gaining a creditable time of 17 hours 35 minutes in 1967. The first official REME Canoe Club entry in the Devizes-Westminster race was made in 1979 by

Corporal Alan Larter and Lance Corporal John Hodson from Detmold. Using part of their annual leave to train and compete every day, they covered increasing distances in both Germany and England to make sure that they were physically prepared for this very hard race, as well as their mental preparedness for the gruelling 125 miles which involved seventy-six portages around locks (one of over a kilometre). Leaving Devizes at midday on Good Friday, they paddled all day and night to arrive at Westminster at 0750 hours on Saturday morning, creating their first ever REME official record time of 18 hours, 52 minutes and 14 seconds; this compared with the winners' record time of 15 hours, 34 minutes and 12 seconds. The REME pair were placed eleventh out of seventy finishing crews, some 300 having started. Amongst the Services only two Sapper crews did better than them.

In 1992 two racing K2 crews entered the race, the number two crew in their first attempt completing the course in 23 hours 26 minutes. The number one crew, Lieutenant Colonel Roger Jagger (Chairman of REME canoeing) and Lieutenant Colonel Roger Owen (Chairman of Army canoeing), was the highest placed veteran military crew with a time of 22 hours 9 minutes.

Lieutenant Colonels Roger Owen and Roger Jagger competing in the Devizes–Westminster Race

Adventurous Activities

The challenge of canoeing offers considerable scope for military adventurous activities, and has featured in many such expeditions. Exercise Southern Waters was planned to take place in South America in 1982, but had to be switched after the advent of the Falklands conflict to an expedition down the Missouri River and part of the Mississippi. Ten years later, in one of the many events to commemorate REME's fiftieth anniversary, Exercise Maple Canoe took place in Canada, as part of Exercise Master Craftsman; it is described in Chapter 5 under Adventurous Training.

Support

The centre of REME canoeing has traditionally been at Arborfield, a particularly ideal centre for training for the Devizes-Westminster race. Corps canoeing equipment has been lent to REME canoeists throughout UK and BAOR when possible. With junior REME soldiers at Princess Marina

College and some young REME officers showing an active interest, continued REME participation in the sport at all levels seems assured – particularly as a fitting complement to regular canoeing in unit adventurous training programmes. In the early Nineties REME paddlers were continuing to be represented in Army and Combined Services canoeing.

CRICKET

REME Corps cricket sprang into life in 1946 under Colonel Douglas Henchley, when the Corps team beat RAOC in a two-day match at Chilwell. In the next forty-six years there were only eight chairmen of cricket: Colonel Douglas Henchley in the Forties to 1962, Colonels Terry Aram (1963–65) and Owen Tranter (1966–69), Lieutenant Colonel Hugh Wright (1970–71) Lieutenant Colonel Peter Crooks (1972–81), Colonel George Briggs (1982–88), Lieutenant Colonel Robin Tandy (1988–90) and Colonel Nick Holland from 1991.

Most home games were played at Arborfield on the delightful ground in front of Hazebrouck Officers' Mess – a beautiful setting. For thirty-five years the changing room was a garden shed but in later years a pavilion was provided.

Fixtures

There were three matches in 1946 – two against RAOC, and one against RASC. Next year the R SIGNALS and RAMC, who were powerful forces in the days of National Service, were added and formed the core of the fixture list. In the Fifties most large corps were added, except for the Gunners, and some strong civilian clubs were included such as Hampshire 2nd XI and the Berkshire County team. With the end of National Service the best civilian fixtures had to be dropped and a new list evolved. Welbeck College was a regular fixture except from 1964–80 and the Sapper fixture was lost between 1967–81.

The most significant change took place in 1967, when two-day fixtures were reduced to a single day because of increasing difficulties in releasing Corps cricketers from their units. In 1982 the Parnaby Cup was presented by the RAOC for their annual match against REME in memory of Brigadier Alan Parnaby who was their most noted player from 1946 until he retired in 1971.

National Service Days – The Fifties

During the National Service era the standard of REME cricket was much improved by several young cricketers who played for county clubs. Four Corps players played for the Army and two became well known in cricket circles: Corporal Keith Andrew (1951–52) later became the Director of Coaching for the National Cricket Association, and Lance Corporal Phil

Sharpe (1956–57) later became an England selector, both having played for England. Craftsman Ken Graveney, the brother of Tom Graveney, was not selected for the Army, but went on to captain Gloucestershire in 1963.

The Sixties and Early Seventies

Corps cricket received a boost in the early Sixties after a special recruiting drive in the Caribbean. Several fine players from the West Indies joined the Corps and the Corps team. Sergeant 'Brad' Bradshaw and Corporal Wes Quintyne quickly earned their Corps colours and became the scourge of opposing batsmen. Three other outstanding players from the West Indies transferred to REME: Corporal Trevor Dimmick from RE, Corporal 'Chubby' Roberts from R SIGNALS and Corporal Brian Garrett from RCT. The enthusiasm and attacking cricket of the West Indian players really set Corps cricket alight; sadly, few stayed for a full career.

Great Players

ASM Peter Wood represented and captained both the Army BAOR and the British Forces Hong Kong teams. In 1983–84 he was captain and secretary of the Army team, and in 1984–85 he was captain of the British Combined Services Hong Kong team which won the Hong Kong Wimpey Sime Darby League for the first time for fourteen years. He travelled to Bangladesh to represent Hong Kong Colony in the South-East Asia World Tournament in 1984, which reached the final against Bangladesh at Dacca Stadium in front of 28,000 spectators. In November 1984 he played for Hong Kong Colony against Singapore in the three-day inter-Port game. At the end of the season he was voted Hong Kong Player of the Year 1984–85, winning the Hong Kong Bank Trophy.

Earlier, in 1981 as an AQMS, he captained the BAOR team on its tour to Barbados. In 1977, 80 and 82 he won the Rothmans Trophy, awarded each year to the most outstanding cricketer in BAOR. This trophy was won by Sergeant Bradshaw in 1970 and 1971, Corporal Roberts in 1972, Captain Bob Stranks in 1976, Corporal Steve Durston in 1987 and Sergeant Paul Woolnough in 1988.

Colonel George Briggs, who retired in 1988, had thirty-one years' association with Corps cricket. He played his first game for the Corps at Arborfield in 1957 while an undergraduate at Cambridge. In the Sixties he ran REME cricket in Aden and became the captain of the Corps team in the UK in 1965 after a long spell as secretary. He was awarded his colours in 1964. He captained the Corps side again in 1969–70 and 1975–77. He became Chairman 1982–87, playing his last full game in 1985.

Memorable Matches

Many fine matches have been played against RASC and RCT – a fixture which perhaps stirred the emotions most of all the Corps fixtures. In 1968 RCT was chasing a REME total of 98 on a wicket affected by rain; in the event they were dismissed for a record low score of 13, Corporal Bradshaw taking 7 wickets for 9 runs.

In 1956 the RAPC captain had rued his decision not to declare, prolonging their first innings to 281–9. REME struggled to score only 143 and so was forced to follow on, scoring 241 for 8: seeking a draw but leaving RAPC a token chance to win if they could score 104 runs in 35 minutes. Thirty years later RAOC placed REME in a similar situation to that which had faced RAPC, after they had scored 168 for 8. REME replied with 302 for 6 after which RAOC scored 256 for 4: leaving REME twelve overs in which to score 123 runs; after losing quick wickets REME settled for a draw.

In 1980 RAMC were all out for 30 and REME replied with 35 for 1 wicket in 9 overs. Corporal David Evans scored 32, beating RAMC almost on his own; the match was all over before lunch.

Army and Combined Services Cricket

Between 1950–88 ten REME cricketers represented the Army in matches against the Royal Navy and Royal Air Force. Three of them played for the Combined Services. Several more played for the Army under-25 team. Lance Corporal Stuart Fox and Corporal Paul Purnell regularly played for the Army in 1980 and for the Army under-25 team. In 1991 Craftsman Simon Wherry and Lance Corporal John Checkley played for the Army and Checkley also played for the Combined Services In 1992 Lieutenant Alistair Houldsworth won his Army Cap without a ball being bowled in the game against the Royal Navy!

Officials

Colonel Douglas Henchley, who gave so much service to Army cricket from 1946–63, was appointed Chairman of Army cricket in 1963 – the only REME officer ever to achieve an official post in senior Army cricket in forty-five years.

In 1982 and 1983 Major Nick Holland was manager of the Army under-25 team. In 1992, as Colonel Holland, he became Chairman of the Army Cricket Umpires and Scorers Association.

Colonel Terry Aram took up umpiring at the end of the 1939–45 war when the loss of his leg had ended his playing days. He achieved a memorable record, umpiring every Army representative match between 1949–60. He started an organization of cricket umpires in the mid-Fifties and formed the Army Cricket Umpires Association (ACUA) in 1963 and was their Chairman until 1970. Several REME umpires appeared in the first ACUA register of 1966; one of them, Sergeant Norman Dewdney, became its General Secretary several years later. Scorers, too, did not go unrecognized for their demanding task; AQMS Glyn Winterbottom, a scorer for ten years, was awarded his Corps colours in 1981 prior to his retirement.

Major Peter Beeken

Major Peter Beeken played his first match for the Corps in 1958 as a wicket keeper and batsman. In 1963 he played for the Army and the Corps in Aden, and was awarded his Corps colours in 1967. In 1970–75 he played for REME BAOR and became the secretary for the BAOR Corps XI for two years and its captain for three. He became secretary of Corps cricket in 1979 and during the Eighties captained the Corps team for six consecutive years. In 1984 he was posted to Arborfield for the first time in his career, where he became responsible for several important improvements to the Corps cricket ground. He represented the Corps in 1990, so recording the distinction of playing for the Corps in each of five decades. During his career he was secretary for eight years, captain for nine and treasurer for five.

Unit Cricket

The Craftsman's Cup for UK units was introduced in 1970 to stimulate unit cricket. A play-off was arranged between the winners of the UK Cup and the winners of the REME BAOR inter-unit competition which had existed for several years. A tour was arranged concurrently with the Cup final by adding a few Corps players to the party; these innovations were a success, encouraging unit cricket and fostering links between UK and BAOR. Although SEE had won the Craftsman's Cup nine times by the early Nineties and SEME six times, small units like 9 Field Workshop won it three times and REME Aldershot won it once to prove what small units can do together.

Army Cup

From 1946 Command competitions were the main source of competition for units. SEME beat a Commando side from Plymouth at Tidworth in 1965 in what was then considered to be the Army final. Army Major and Minor Units competitions began in the early Seventies; in 1993 SEME became the first REME unit to reach the final of the Army Major Unit competition, winning the UK final but losing to the BAOR winner. In 1986 SEME won the Army UK Major Units championship, the first time for a REME unit.

The AAC Centre team had five REME players, including the captain, when they won the Army championship in 1979. In the Minor Units competition the Training Battalion and Depot REME won the championship in 1979, and reached the final in 1981. 3 Field Workshop was in the final in 1989 and won in 1990.

BAOR

7 Armoured Workshop won the BAOR Major Units cup in 1991, whilst in the Minor Units competition REME units won five times and were runners-up six times in the 27 years from the start of the competition in 1965 up to 1992.

Corps Cricket in the Eighties

The Corps side was undefeated in 1983–85. In 1986, the year that SEME won the Army Major Units championship for the first time, ASM Wood, Sergeant Woolnough, Corporal Durston and Lance Corporal Mick Halifax all played for the Army, but the Corps side suffered its first defeat since 1982 at the hands of the RE at Chatham.

1990 Championship

CROSS COUNTRY RUNNING

This sport flourished over the years with several members of the Corps running for the Army and the Combined Services. REME (UK) and REME (BAOR) hosted the annual Corps championships in alternate years, usually held with the host Theatre championships.

To mark REME 50 in 1992, a special

event hosted by SEME was held instead of the annual Corps championships. 200 runners from twenty-five units took part, the overall REME 50 champion being Corporal Shaw, serving with 42 Survey Group RE. The Major Unit winner was SEME and the Minor Unit 7th Parachute Regiment Royal Horse Artillery LAD – their seventh successive Minor Unit title. In 1992 Craftsman McKenna represented the Army at Junior level in the Inter-Services championships; he was subsequently selected for Combined Services and later awarded his Army and Combined Services Junior colours.

FREE FALL PARACHUTING

In the early Sixties a REME/RAOC Parachute Club had been formed in Cyprus by Captain Ian Macpherson. In 1966, based on this experience, he created in the United Kingdom the REME Parachute Club. He was Secretary of the Club for the first six years, and later served a further eight years as its Chairman. He piloted his own Tiger Moth, led the Corps team on many of its public displays until well past his 50th birthday, and was honoured to become Vice-President of the Army Parachute Association from 1977–81. While he was serving in the Ministry of Defence he had qualified for High Altitude Low Opening (HALO) – 25,000 feet at night with oxygen and full equipment. He led the development of modern free fall parachute equipment, wrote the MOD instructions for adventurous parachuting, gave recruiting lectures, and encouraged many to take up the sport. From a few like-minded individuals meeting on a draughty airfield at weekends, he saw REME parachuting develop into a full-blown sponsored team winning honours in all major events around the world.

The Corps A team won the Best Corps Team Trophy in the Army championship in 1981 and 1982, and in the following year the Corps team won the Army Canopy Relative Work Event and the Best Corps Team Trophy. Three members, including Craftsman Applegate of the Territorial Army, were awarded Army colours. In 1984 the Corps team won the Army Best Corps Team Trophy for the fourth successive year; Sergeant Ames represented the Army at the World Parachute Meeting in Australia and Corporal Dyas was selected for the British team at the World Championship (Relative Work) in France.

The Corps team again won the trophy for the best Corps team in 1986. Several team members took part in the fifty way link-up over Wiltshire in 1988, a new British and European record. The team was invited to appear at two international air shows in Switzerland.

The Corps did well again at the 25th Annual Army Parachute Championship at Netheravon in August 1989. More than 130 competitors took part, including top competition teams from the armed forces of West Germany, Spain and Oman. The REME A team won two silver medals in the four-way relative work events (free fall formations) –

one in open competition and the other in British Army events, being narrowly beaten by the Red Devils full-time competition team. The REME A team consisted of Major Mike Smith, Joint Air Transport Establishment, Captain Peter Hough, Electronics Branch, Captain John Horne, SEE, and Staff Sergeant Brian Dyas, London University OTC.

Thirteen REME parachutists from the REME Parachute Club gathered for the 1990 Army Parachute Championships at Netheravon. Most of the opposing teams, which included those from The Parachute Regiment, Oman National Squad and the Spanish Army, were full-time display teams, some of whom had spent months training for the competition; the Club team was one of the very few truly amateur teams but they won several of the team awards: Corps champions, Relative Work Event – silver, Accuracy Team Event – silver, Canopy Relative Work – bronze. Second Lieutenant Jeanne Ebling, newly commissioned and only days from her first posting, won the gold Intermediate Ladies Style event award.

Pre-eminent amongst REME sports parachutists was Captain Horne, one of the best practitioners within the British Armed Forces with over 3,000 jumps to his credit by 1990. It is recorded that he was 'the catalyst to the Corps' strong free fall parachute cadre that has established REME as the leading force in Army parachuting'. He represented the Armed Forces on the British Parachute Association's senior committee, was on the Army Parachuting committee, had captained the Army Squad and was Team Leader of the REME Display Team. He was selfless in devoting time and effort particularly to training others including REME novices, and played a key part in introducing into the United Kingdom the revolutionary Accelerated Free Fall method of instruction – whereby novices exit an aircraft at 12,000 feet in free fall on their first descent. His 'outstanding leadership, courage, selfless commitment to the service of others in a highly adventurous pursuit' was quoted as exemplifying the spirit of Rory Cape when he received the Award for 1990.

GOLF

'Golf is a splendid game for the serviceman. It can be played almost anywhere. It is one of the very few sports where handicapping really works. It can very accurately compensate for age and ability, but unfortunately not for mental stupidity.' These words of Brigadier Geoffrey Walker came from his Foreword to an article on Corps golf in the REME Journal for 1990, written by Lieutenant Colonel David Hastings.

The first REME Officers' Club annual golf meeting was held at the North Hants Golf Club at Fleet in September 1946 organized by Major Eric Coulthard, the first Corps match was played in 1947 which RAOC won, and the first Corps championship was held in 1953 when the entry included four soldiers. Soldiers very soon made their mark in Corps and Army golf:

- Corporal Steven Mariner was runner-up in the Army championship in 1981 and 1982, but became the Army champion in 1984 at Rye and again in 1988 at Princes Golf Club, Sandwich, as a Staff Sergeant.
- Lance Corporal Douglas Spiller won the Army championship in 1982 at Royal Birkdale and was runner-up in 1983 at Royal Cinque Ports, Deal, and in 1988 at Princes. He was a regular member of the Army team throughout the Eighties and played in the international match against the French and Belgian Army teams in 1986–88.

Staff Sergeant Steve Mariner

Major General Dennis Shaw recalled his first outing on the Catterick Garrison Course in 1958:

'In 1958 I served in 1 Command Workshop REME in Catterick when the CO was Lieutenant Colonel Eric Coulthard. It was his flair for golf which caused me, at the end of the cricket season, to try my own hand at the game. I equipped myself with a set of George Nichols Pinsplitter irons and John Letters woods – all second-hand. Being something of a novice I, rather naively, was impressed with the lovely shiny leather grips. On my first outing to the Garrison Course the driver, whilst I was taking a practice swing, slipped from my grasp and described a parabola as it flew through the air and disappeared into the wood alongside the clubhouse. On my way to retrieve it Eric Coulthard, who was on his way to start at the tenth, greeted me with a puzzled expression as I plunged into the wood. It was an hour and a half later, as Eric was crossing from the 18th green to the first tee, that I emerged from the trees clutching my driver! He found my explanation – which was not entirely truthful – somewhat bizarre. However, he did notice the shiny grips and his tip of applying a solution of castor oil and glycerine prevented a recurrence.'

The 1988 season was the most successful on record for Corps golf: the REME A team retained the inter-Corps championship (The Royal Irish Rangers Trophy); Staff Sergeant Mariner was the Army individual champion and Corporal Spiller was runner-up; the SEE team won the Army Challenge Cup (the Army Cup in golf) at Catterick, the first REME unit to do so; and Staff Sergeant Mariner, Corporals Spiller and Stuart Scott played in the victorious British Army team in the annual international match against the French and Belgian Armies.

The Corps started the Nineties well. The ten best REME golfers went to Royal Porthcawl in May 1990 for the Army championships, in which Craftsman Rick Smart won the individual title at his first attempt and the REME A team of Captains Patrick Griffiths, Micky Bryant, Lieutenant Mark Snape and Craftsman Smart won the Royal Irish Rangers Trophy. In the following year, for the first time a REME officers team – of Major Nigel Barnard, Captains Alan Baker, Micky Bryant, Mike Cripps and Brian Smy – won the coveted Ordnance Cup at the Army Officers Golf Society Spring Meeting at Hillside, Southport. In 1992 Corporal John Maguire emerged as a new force in Army golf, becoming runner-up in the Army championship at West Lancashire at his first attempt and winning the Army 72-hole Stroke Play championship at Little Aston, narrowly beating Major Roger Crook. They were both in the victorious Army team in the international match played at Saunton.

The REME Golf Association was still thriving as 1993 approached, helped in no small measure by support from Corps sports funds to offset ever-rising green fees. There was a full fixture list with matches against other Corps, the Army Staff College, The Royal Military Academy Sandhurst and clubs such as Blackmoor, High Post and Knighton Heath, with whom the Corps has long traditional golfing links. Most matches were fully representative with officers and soldiers selected, but the REME Officers' Golfing Society also had several fixtures of its own. About 100 golfers represented the Corps each season. The officers and soldiers also ran their own seasonal meetings, the officers holding spring, summer and autumn meetings, the latter taking place at North Hants where Corps golf began in 1946, the soldiers holding spring and autumn meetings.

The Corps' oldest fixture, against RAOC for the Pioneer Cup, was still, after forty-six years, the most competitive match of the season with each Corps fielding its best team. Although RAOC won more of the matches, REME won for the last four years since the venue changed from Wentworth to Frilford Heath.

The keenest contest within the Corps was the Officers versus Soldiers match played at West Hill each October, referred to as the Annual Conflict! The largest entry of the year gathered for the end of season match at Tidworth, to contest the (sometimes aptly named) Brass Balls Trophy.

HANG-GLIDING

Captain Jim Taggart, earlier a military and free fall parachutist (and a Corps and Army athlete), took up hang-gliding in 1973. He soon became known as one of the acknowledged masters of the sport in the United Kingdom and in Europe. During five years in BAOR he inspired many to become devoted to the sport and lobbied to get hang-gliding officially recognized by the Army Sports Control Board. It was mainly due to his efforts that the Army Hang-Gliding Centre at Brecon was set up in 1981, where he was appointed Chief Instructor. His work led to it becoming the Joint Services Hang-Gliding Centre, and he was rewarded by appointment as an MBE in the New Year Honours of 1983. Sadly he was to die in a hang-gliding incident later that year: ironically after some 34,000 flights had been made from the Centre without serious mishap.

In 1986 AQMS James McMenemy was awarded the first ever Army colours for hang-gliding, being the first Army hang-glider pilot to qualify for the British Hang-Gliding Association Pilot 3 rating, and also the first to achieve the Fédération Aéronautique Internationale Silver C Award. He started flying in 1976 when the sport in the UK was in its infancy. After a tour in BAOR with Captain Taggart, he returned to the UK for his artificer course and won the RAF championship in 1982 and second place in the Army championship. To earn his International Silver C award he had to fly 75 kilometres after take-off and make an endurance flight of more than five hours. He served for three years on the council of the British Hang-Gliding Association and was a well known hang-gliding photographer. He also flew for the Army in Inter-Services competitions.

AQMS James McMenemy

At the Army Hang-Gliding Association's AGM in 1991 the President presented Sergeant Mark Lewis of 9 Regiment AAC Workshop with his

Army colours for his services to hang-gliding. He represented the Army in the Inter-Services championship and the Services at national level. In the 1991 Joint Services championship in South Wales in July he was third in the Individual Open Class.

HOCKEY

During the twenty years 1972–92 REME hockey grew to become a major sport. In the Seventies and early Eighties the Corps competed energetically for Army honours but failed to overcome the much stronger and more skilful RA, RAOC and RAPC teams. The breakthrough came in 1987 when REME won the inter-Corps championship and retained it in 1988. In the following three years semi-finals or finals were lost to RAOC and twice to RA, who had players of international standard.

In 1992 a great effort was made to win back the trophy, including games against civilian clubs to improve the commitment, fitness and skills. The inter-Corps final was played on 2 October 1992, the day after the REME's 50th anniversary, when the Corps won a very close match against the R SIGNALS.

Corps players who played for the Combined Services included Major Tochi Marwaha, Captain Julian Thomson and Corporal David Antonelli. Army players included Captain Peter Frostick, AQMS Bill George, Sergeant Robbie Wilkinson, Corporal Micky Bale and Corporal Karl Jordan. Second Lieutenant Adam Johnstone played for the Scotland under-21 team.

Corporal Antonelli in action

Major Marwaha, a great sportsman and strong driving force, was the backbone of the Corps hockey team for twenty years. He played for the Combined Services, the Army and the Corps and coached the Army hockey squad for several years.

A fitting end to this brief note of hockey in the Corps is to record that Corporals Bale, Jordan and Antonelli played for the Army team which won the Inter-Services championship for the third year in succession in March 1992, beating the Royal Air Force at Reading.

JUDO

A snapshot in time records that in 1986 Lance Corporal Morton, the coach of the SEME judo team, was the Army champion in both Under 60 Kilo and 65 Kilo classes and Combined Services champion Under 60 Kilo. He was also a member of the Army team which won the Inter-Services competition in that year and was awarded Combined Service colours in 1987. Six soldiers won bronze, silver or gold medals at the UKLF championships.

In 1992 Second Lieutenant Jim Platt was awarded a full Blue for judo at Cambridge University and subsequently a bronze medal in the British Student Championships.

LUGE

Luge was a relatively new sport in Army winter sports in the late Eighties. The 22 Kilo luge has no steering mechanism and no brake and the rider lies flat on his back, feet first, manoeuvring the small streamlined sled through corners at 70 mph by shifting his body weight. This requires courage, concentration and quick reactions, countering forces of several 'g's on tight corners. The first BAOR championships were held in 1987–88 when Captain Mark Armstrong of 71 Aircraft Workshop came second and, in the Novices Section, Corporal Keith Yandell of 20 Electronics Workshop was second and Corporal Gallagher of 71 Aircraft Workshop third. In the British Novice championship Captain Armstrong was sixth. In the 1989–90 championships Captain Armstrong emerged as Army champion. Captain Armstrong and Corporal Yandell were selected for the Army team 1988–89 and

Captain Mark Armstrong

were in the Great Britain team for the World Cup B races in Germany and Austria 1989–90. A year later they were in the senior Great Britain squad for the World Cup races. Sergeant Yandell competed in each subsequent year, and just missed selection for the 1992 Olympic Games: being third in a field of selection for a team of two. In 1992 Captain Armstrong became Secretary of the Army Luge Association and the Services representative on the Committee of the Great Britain Luge Association.

MODERN PENTATHLON

Beginnings

The first volume described how the enthusiasm of Brigadier Tony Howard-Jones, when Commandant of the REME Training Centre at Arborfield, took REME into modern pentathlon, and mentioned the early successes of Sergeant Jim Fox. The first year of Corps modern pentathlon was 1959 when the REME team came eighth in the Army championship; until then the sport had been dominated by the Cavalry. In 1961 REME won the Army team championship, taking possession of the King of the Hellenes Shield for the first of what was to be twenty-five times in thirty-one years. That team consisted of Lieutenant Stan Terrett, Corporal Jim Darby and Corporal Carl Honey. Lance Corporal Jim Fox was a member of the winning Corps team in 1962 and won the Army individual title in 1963. He later appeared in eight World Championships and four Olympic Games. His many successes included being British individual champion ten times.

The Corps team won the British team championship for the first time in 1970 – Sergeant Jim Darby, AQMS Terry Bunyard and Sergeant Jim Fox. By 1987, REME was able to celebrate winning the Army championship for the twenty-fifth time, which was also the last year of competition for Sergeant Peter Whiteside, who had been a member of the Great Britain team several times, as mentioned below.

Olympic Games

Sergeant Jim Fox took part in the Olympics in both 1964 (as a Corporal) and 1968 and together with Sergeant Jim Darby was selected for the Munich Games in 1972. In the latter Sergeant Fox finished fourth, missing his bronze medal by one shooting point. The following year he won the bronze medal in the World Championships in Mexico – the first ever for Britain. In the 1976 Olympics he was a member of the British gold medal winning team in Montreal, a fitting climax to so many years of determination, dedication and hard work.

Corporal Peter Whiteside competed in the Moscow Olympics in 1980. Staff Sergeant Bernie Moss went in 1984 to the succeeding Games in Los Angeles as both team coach and armourer, a year in which Sergeant Whiteside and Corporal Peter Hart represented Great Britain several times. Sergeant Whiteside went on to become British individual champion in 1985. Corporal Hart went to Seoul, Korea in 1988 as fourth member of the Olympic team which won the bronze medal.

Sergeant Jim Fox

World Championships

Sergeants Darby, Fox, Whiteside and Corporal Hart competed also in World Championships as did Corporal Peter Twine, Craftsman Tony Woodall and the late Corporal Steve Birley. Corporal Peter Whiteside of SEE was in the British team in the World Championships in Budapest in August 1979. He came sixteenth in this his first World Championships, ahead of his two fellow team members who came twenty-second and sixty-second. In the British Senior championships he came second, representing the Army A team which won the British team championship. They were to represent the Southern Region of Great Britain in the European Cup in Berlin in October 1979. The Corps produced fifteen international competitors between 1968 and 1992.

Officials

In 1980 and 1984 respectively Staff Sergeant Moss and Sergeant Whiteside became National Team and Centre of Excellence coaches. Staff Sergeant Moss had previously been honorary secretary of the Modern Pentathlon Association of Great Britain (MPAGB), while Corporal Peter Hart on leaving the Army in 1990 became the Association's National Development Officer. Major Terry Bunyard, an international competitor for many years and a reserve for the Munich Olympics team, was Secretary of the Army MPA 1983–92 and President of the MPAGB 1989–94, a great honour for a serving REME officer, as well as continuing as a coach to the Centre of Excellence described below. He was much involved in latter years in recruiting pentathletes, both military and civilian, and in progressing their training and pentathlon careers.

Many competitors and spectators remember the endless work and enthusiasm of Major Harry Ridout who was Secretary of REME modern pentathlon from 1966–73. His successor, Major Gordon Lyon, was given a posthumous 'Sport in the South' award by the Sports Council in 1982. Colonel Mike Selby became Chairman of the REME MPA in 1989 and of the Army MPA in 1993.

Centre of Excellence

After the Montreal Olympic Games in 1976 the Minister of Sport, Mr Denis Howell, recommended that regional committees of the Sports Council examine the possibility of setting up Centres of Excellence for various sports throughout the country, to provide the best possible training and working facilities for members of the many national squads and those talented individuals likely to become members of national squads within a year or two. The Army MPA were looking at the possibility of setting up a Modern Pentathlon Centre at Arborfield or Sandhurst for pentathletes of all three services. A proposal was submitted by Brigadier Pat Lee, Commandant REME Training Centre, and agreement was obtained. The Sports Council, Southern Region held a meeting to discuss the formation of a Committee to establish and manage the Centre of Excellence for Modern Pentathlon which was given a grant of £3,100 for the first year. The Committee had members from the MPAGB, the Bracknell Sports Centre, the Armed Services and the Sports Council. The first elected Chairman was Brigadier Pat Lee. Arborfield was selected for the Centre of Excellence because of its facilities for swimming, fencing, running and some riding. The Sports Council helped the Chairman to get a grant of £5,625 to establish a properly designed pentathlon pistol range and firing point building, which was formally opened in May 1978 by Mr Dickie Jeeps, the Chairman of the national Sports Council; on that occasion a pistol match was staged against a Great Britain team. Training took place throughout the seven days of the week under Captain Fox and Staff Sergeant Moss. Before long, young teenage potential pentathletes were coming for training at weekends and in school holidays; they produced the ladies World champions, team and individual, over the years 1978–1980 and team champions in 1981. They also produced the men's World bronze medal Junior team and Richard Phelps, the individual silver medallist in 1980 – the first time ever for Britain. Phelps later went on to become the World senior individual champion.

Leading Pentathlon Athletes

An outstanding athlete in the first twenty years of REME modern pentathlon was Staff Sergeant Jim Darby, who had joined REME in 1956. He started pentathlon training in 1957 and was soon participating at senior levels. He won his Corps colours in 1958, took part in the Swedish Invitation Pentathlon in 1960, represented Great Britain in 1961 at the Austrian Tetrathlon and won his Army colours in 1962. His subsequent career included further achievements:

- In pentathlon, he was a member of the Corps teams which won the Army championships 1961–64, and was captain of the REME team for three seasons. He was in the Army team again 1963–67. He represented Great Britain once more in 1968, at the World Championships at Warendorf, Germany in 1970, and at the Munich Olympics in 1972.
- With his particular skills in fencing, he represented the Army in 1967, and won the Inter-Services épée championship, the first time a REME fencer had achieved this. He was the Inter-Services and Army champion in 1969.
- In the Seventies he spent much time in coaching and encouraging promising young athletes.

Captain Jim Fox, an outstandingly successful pentathlete, was trained at the Army Apprentices School, Carlisle and then posted to 16 Parachute Workshop. As a Lance Corporal he started pentathlon training in 1962 and was soon representing the Corps and the Army. He was seventh in the International Pentathlon in 1963 representing Great Britain; in the same year he became British individual champion and represented Great Britain in the World Championships in Berne, Switzerland. The following year he represented the country in Hungary, Budapest and in the Tokyo Olympic Games, and in 1965 in the Eight Nations Competition at Cagliari, Sardinia, he came fourth. Over the following ten years he achieved many successes at the highest level:

- His individual skill in fencing brought him early success, becoming British Junior épée champion in 1967 and Inter-Services épée champion in 1968.
- Frequent participation in internationals took him around the world, gaining first places early on when representing the Army at Brugg, Switzerland, and in Sweden in 1966. By now a Sergeant, he represented Great Britain in Rome, Hamburg, Holland and Arborfield, his individual places being second, first, second and first.
- In World Championships he competed regularly between 1966–75, gaining his highest place in the latter year in Mexico City, when he came third and thus won the very first medal for Great Britain in that major event.
- He was a regular participant in the Olympic Games, at Tokyo

> (1964), Mexico (1968), Munich (1972) and Montreal (1976), progressing to the high achievement of fifteenth individual place at Montreal and membership of the gold medal-winning British team. In the latter year he retained, as so often before, his Inter-Services, Army and Corps individual titles.

He left the Army for a year in 1969, but soon returned to continue his achievements with the advantage of military facilities. He was appointed MBE in the New Year Honours List (Civil) for 1975 for 'services to sport'. This was followed in the same year by the UNESCO award of a Diploma of Merit in Paris, to mark the constant example of sporting spirit demonstrated during his career as a champion pentathlete. He was commissioned in 1976, setting up the Centre of Excellence as its first coaching co-ordinator. He retired as a captain seven years later. In 1979 he took part in the first ever 'Champion of Champions' event in which all disciplines were run on a single day, a precursor of the system destined to be run for the first time in the 1996 Olympics. In 1992 he continued to retain close links with the MPAGB. An interesting biography of him was written by David Hunn, an 'Observer' sports columnist, called 'Smelling of Roses'.

MOTOR CYCLING

Motor cycling as a competitive sport has naturally been centred upon Bordon over many years, although the enthusiasm of individuals – very likely gained initially at Bordon – has often been carried by them into the life of many other units.

1978 was a notable season of great success for REME motor cyclists. In the Army championship trial at Catterick Craftsman S M Newman was Best Regular Army Rider, First Class awards were won by Corporal Gwyn Barraclough, Sergeant McVee and Lance Corporal Karl Werner, and the Best Novice rider was Lance Corporal Nicholson, REME TAVR. The Welsh Two-Day International Trial in that year was one of the toughest for a long time, in which Corporals Barraclough and Porter won gold medals, and Lance Corporal Werner a silver medal. As a result they were selected to form the Army team for the 1978 Six-Day International Trial in Sweden. Described as 'the Olympics of motor cycling' this Trial was held in September, Corporal Barraclough emerging with a Silver award.

Amongst successes in the Eighties was the best competition team award won by the REME team in the 1982 Army championships, and the best Service award deriving from five rounds of the British National Enduro Championship, whilst Staff Sergeant Barry Langmead was the British national champion in the 'Expert of 250cc class'. Following the placing of the Corps team as the first Service team in the National

Enduro Championship and in the Welsh International Enduro, they were invited to enter the International Six-Day Enduro, the world championship, in 1983: they achieved seventh UK place and eighteenth in the world (and in the process beat both the Army A and B teams). A year later they were the best Service team in five National Enduro rounds, and after several years as the most successful Army team in the National they once again captured the first Service team award in 1987. Other successes were gained in the Welsh International Two-Day Enduro: in 1989 second place overall and first Service team went to the REME BAOR team, and second Service team to REME UK; the latter team again winning the best Service team award in both 1990 and 1992.

Moving into the Nineties ASM Langmead in 38 Squadron RCT Workshop, who had been successful over many years on Service machines, took part in the Welsh Two-Day Trial in 1990 as part of a BAOR team, using an issue Armstrong motor cycle. In the same Trial in 1992 a REME BAOR team successfully competed using their own civilian competition machines: Sergeant Noy of 32 Armoured Engineer Workshop, Corporal Altass of 3 RTR LAD and Corporal Gorse of 1st Battalion, The Light Infantry LAD. However, there was very little activity in the second half of that year in the aftermath of the Gulf War. In the following year it proved possible to hold BAOR championships, organized by ASM Langmead, while in UK two SEME teams secured second and third places in the Army championship trial.

Prominent Motor Cyclists

Particularly notable amongst those who provided the essential driving force in creating and maintaining enthusiasm and expertise within the Corps was AQMS Ted Johns, who had transferred into REME from R SIGNALS in 1952. He started riding in motor cycle competitions in 1961 and was the REME champion in 1972. Employed as an instructor at SEME in 1974, in his capacity as REME Motor Cycle Competition Manager he placed the Corps in the first rank of off-road motor cycling. REME was the only Corps ever to organize events to international standard, and from 1979 a British Championship

AQMS Ted Johns

Enduro round was based at Bordon. Under his guidance, the REME Enduro team was the most successful Service team for the decade 1982–92. The reputation gained enabled the Corps to obtain sponsorship from Kawasaki (UK) Ltd in the form of four motor cycles which were used in all the British championship rounds and were replaced regularly. AQMS Johns' personal successes included:

- Member of Great Britain British Vase A Team in International Six-Day Motor Cycle Trials in Poland in 1967, and the Isle of Man in 1971.
- Member of Army team on many occasions, winning First Class awards in the Scottish Six-Day Trials in 1965–67, and one gold medal and two silver medals in the Welsh Three-Day international trials in the same years.
- First Class awards in Army Motor Cycle championships four times between 1964 and 1972.
- REME champion in 1967, 1970 and 1972.

Other successful motor cyclists were AQMS Leon Green, Permanent Staff Instructor with 118 Recovery Company (V), who in 1991 represented the Army in the International Six-Day Enduro in Czechoslovakia, amongst 360 riders from twenty-one countries; Corporal Dave Braithwaite from SEME who, in 1992, represented the Army in both the Scottish Six-Day Trial and the International Six-Day Enduro in Australia, was individual runner-up in the Army championship trial in 1991 and 1992, and was awarded his Army colours; and Craftsman Bill White who won the Best Private Soldier award in the 1992 Army championship (when four other REME entrants won First Class awards).

MOTOR RALLYING

Motor rallying was organized under the auspices of the British Army Motoring Association (BAMA). Lieutenant Colonel Ted Bartlett, a retired REME officer at the Army School of Mechanical Transport at Leconfield, North Humberside, was Executive Secretary of BAMA and the Army Motor Cycling Association (AMCA) for several years. In BAOR at the end of the Sixties and the start of the Seventies BAMA kept a rally car in Bielefeld. Much of the practical expertise was to be found in enthusiastic individuals amongst whom were:

- Colonel John Skinner, whose consuming sporting interest was motor sport, stemming from the late Fifties when he was at The Royal Military College of Science, Shrivenham, from where he competed in club rallies with his 'souped up' Morris Minor. His interest and involvement developed into competing in the RAC Scottish Rally in which he twice won his class award. He also had successes in the Baltic Rally and Finnish Thousand Lakes Rally when he was BEME 20 Armoured Brigade in Detmold. He also competed in the Munich World Cup Rally, which involved crossing the Sahara Desert and fully tested his engineering ingenuity.

- Major Derek Hunter, who started his career in motor rallying in Malaya in 1963 with 17th Gurkha Signal Regiment. His first event was as navigator of a three-man crew in a 500-mile exercise involving 120 military crews starting and finishing in Seremban. The other crew members were Lance Corporal Bryan Jarvis (later body builder editor of 'Commercial Motor') and Craftsman Terry Hill, who took turns at driving and 'resting' in the back of the heaving and bucking Land Rover: they finished sixth overall and won many glittering awards. Major Hunter navigated with Sergeant Stan Watters in events in Malaya and Singapore, with Corporal Nellie Peters in Barnard Castle and Catterick in the late Sixties and with Staff Sergeant John Fox in Moenchengladbach in the mid-Seventies. He also took part in international stage rallying, such as the Scottish and Welsh rallies, the Hunsrueck and Hessen rallies in Germany, the Southern Cross in Australia and the Rothmans Cyprus International Rally.
- Captain Bernie Stevens, who was well known for his organizational flair as well as being the Services' best navigator; as AQMS at 12 Armoured Workshop he set up the Motor Sports Club, Osnabruck in 1976, ably assisted by Staff Sergeant Alan Strachan, said to be the quickest ever Land Rover driver and the aptly named Mr Martin Quick.

Scottish Rally 1978

- Major Phil Waterman, who organized events and competed for almost twenty years. He resurrected the Motor Sports Club, Herford, and gave it much needed momentum.
- Major Colin Den-McKay RAOC, who was a former REME officer and was well known in rallying circles; in Germany he won the Military Class in the prestigious ADAC

Hunsrueck Rally in 1981 with Major Hunter as co-driver.

- Sergeant Adam Davies, a rising star in the early Nineties, was at 4 Armoured Workshop at Detmold, which later became 3 Battalion REME. He took up the sport in 1984 and by 1986–88 was the undisputed Services' champion in Cyprus, competing in his own car against some of Europe's best stage rally drivers. He achieved the best-ever finish by a Service driver in the Rothmans Cyprus International Rally in 1987, and continued his rallying into the Nineties.

Driver Training Exercises

REME crews usually did very well in the BAOR driver training exercises. Exercise Magnum Spirit was a demanding 500-mile annual event, while in the UK the Army held a similar event known as Exercise Roadmaster. Although these events were strictly driver training exercises, they were regarded as an enjoyable sport by many of the participants. Each event would attract about 120 crews from all three services and other NATO forces, including Americans and Canadians. Navigator Sergeant Mick Ellicott won Magnum Spirit in three successive years 1984–86; he was the first person to do so and he had a different driver each time.

Staff Sergeant Joe Bain from 3 Field Workshop and the former REME officer, Captain Bernie Stevens RAOC (V), won Magnum Spirit in 1991 and 1992, winning in the latter year without a single penalty throughout the three-day event. Staff Sergeant Bain was equally good as a driver or navigator and was the winning driver in the Military Class of the 1990 Royal Scottish Automobile Club Scottish Rally.

ORIENTEERING

Orienteering in REME was born through the interest of Staff Sergeant Tony Wale, an instructor at SEME, who in 1963 started to participate in civilian competitions and sought its introduction as a military training activity at SEME. He went on to form the Army Orienteering Club and persuaded the Director of Army Training to recognize it as a sport: the DAT, however, deemed it to be military training.

Staff Sergeant Wale asked the Royal Marines Orienteering Club – in existence before the Army became interested – to run the first unofficial Army championships in the New Forest in 1967, a year before the British national championships were held. The fourth (and first official) Army championships were run by HQ Southern Command in the New Forest in 1970. From that first 1967 event the Army individual champion for each year to 1972 came from REME, Staff Sergeant (and latterly AQMS) Wale winning three times and AQMS Terry Bunyard, Sergeant Jim Darby and Corporal Younger once each.

From the mid-Seventies REME orienteers achieved success at all levels of the sport, with pride of place going to Captain Alan Meekings, who won the Army individual championship 1974–76 and 1978–79, this title then having been secured by members of REME eleven times in thirteen years. In 1976 Captain Meekings was selected to represent Great Britain in an international orienteering match against France and Switzerland. The event was held at Fontainebleau, France, over a course of ten miles with twenty controls and a 1,000 feet climb. The individual winner was the Swiss national champion in a time of eighty-one minutes with Captain Meekings running well to finish as the first British competitor home in a time of ninety-two minutes. The remainder of the British team achieved a creditable second place behind the Swiss team. Captain Meekings went on to consolidate his position as the Corps leading orienteer by becoming the Army individual champion in the 1976 Army individual championships held on the Deister Hills in Lower Saxony.

In 1981 Lieutenant Richard Croft was the Inter-Services individual champion; no REME runner since has won this title. In the early Eighties Major Meekings maintained his association with national level orienteering by being appointed official coach to the National Team in 1981, the same year in which he finished second in the Army championships and was selected to represent the Army team. He was joined in the Army Team that year by Captain Phil Hall, who was again selected for the Army team in 1982 along with Staff Sergeant Tim Sands and Corporal Peter Hart. Since then REME orienteers have regularly represented the Army with Lieutenant Tony Marshall, Captain David Smale, Sergeant Roger Hawkins, Corporal Paul Thwaites and Lance Corporal Craig Chapman all being selected to compete in Army colours on the Army Team tour to Sweden and in the Inter-Services championships. Furthermore, as the Eighties progressed and more women joined the Corps, they proved themselves to be equal to the men in orienteering, with Captain Gill Gibson being awarded her Army colours in 1986 and 1987 for representing the Army Ladies Team in the Inter-Services championships. Captain Mandie Hudson won the Army orienteering championship whilst still a subaltern in 1986, and represented the Army on numerous occasions from 1987 onwards. She was awarded her Army colours in 1993.

REME runners were well represented in the early championships, and SEE and SEME both won the Major Unit team title. However, such successes could not be counted on, REME not having held its own orienteering championships until 1976, when they were organized by ASM Charlie Coates of SEE, and won by 71 Aircraft Workshop. In the late Eighties the Corps established itself as the leading Arm or Service in Army orienteering. For many years the RA had dominated the Senior inter-Corps championships, until 1989 when the REME Senior Team achieved success in this prestigious event. Such was the depth of REME orienteering at the time that this success began a series of victories in both the Senior inter-Corps championships held in UK and BAOR which extended into the early Nineties.

Not to be outdone, the Corps Junior team emulated their Senior counterparts by winning the Army Junior inter-Corps championships, thus confirming Corps superiority in Army orienteering. The leading Juniors, Craftsman Neil Hall and Apprentice Tradesman Chapman, were selected to tour Sweden with the Army Senior Team in 1991.

The Princess Marina College Orienteering Team. Apprentice Tradesman Corporal Powis approaching the final control

Consistent success in Army inter-unit competition has remained elusive for REME. That said, Captain Jerry Wormington coached the 11 Armoured Workshop team to win the BAOR Minor Units championships in 1991, the same year in which the Workshop team were runners-up in the Army Minor Units championship. Also in 1991, Captain Smale led the 71 Aircraft Workshop team to victory in the 1(BR) Corps relay competition, which was organized by Captain Wormington and 11 Armoured Workshop. Between 1986–92 Princess Marina College won the Army Junior inter-unit championship seven times under the guidance of Captain Ken Williams, Staff Sergeant Hawkins and a former REME orienteering Secretary, ex-ASM Jan Belza. It also became a respected force in the British Schools championships.

As well as proving their ability in competition, Corps orienteers played an active role in the organization of Army orienteering in the Eighties, first with Lieutenant Colonel Robert Shields and subsequently Lieutenant Colonel Bob Mount acting as Chairman of the Army Orienteering Association Committee. Major Alan Meekings played his part, working as Technical Adviser to the Committee, with Captain Ken Williams who was the Army Team Manager for many years.

ROWING

Rowing is a sport demanding team work, stamina and self discipline, joining many other sports in reinforcing the qualities demanded of the professional soldier. Officers, in particular, have had opportunities to take part in competitive rowing at school, university or Shrivenham and enthusiasm to continue their indulgence as a Corps sport has surfaced from time to time. In 1987 a dozen members of REME were representing the Royal Military College of Science and they resolved to enter a REME boat in the 1988 Joint Services Regatta. In early 1988 Major Nigel Williams, as Secretary, gained official recognition from the REME Sports Association, and the REME Boat Club was born. In subsequent years his successor, Major Paul Musgrove, brought organizational enthusiasm as well as frequent participation to the sport. Major General Vic Hayward donated two silver cups that he had won in earlier years, one to be awarded annually to the most successful REME competitor in open events; the other was loaned to the Joint Services Regatta as The REME Cup for the winning Veteran Pair.

Up to 1992 members of the REME Boat Club had competed in various events, not least in challenging the Sappers in their long-held dominance of the sport. Entry of Senior Fours and Veteran Fours and Pairs in the annual RE Regatta at Reading, and the Joint Services Regatta at Peterborough, have been the principal events, but other opportunities have been taken: for instance, in Heads Races in the autumn of 1987 a REME Staff College crew was one of 500 crews, and came tenth in the Senior C class as the fastest coxed Service entry, beating a number of Cambridge college and other university crews, two RE crews, the RMCS Shrivenham crew and eight Royal Navy and Royal Air Force crews. The Reading Town Regatta and Cambridge Autumn Regatta have featured amongst other individual entries. The REME Boat Club is a member of the Amateur Rowing Association and of the Army Rowing Clubs Association, of which Major Peter Robertshaw became Secretary in 1990 and Brigadier Bob Cooper its Chairman in 1992: when plans were afoot to introduce soldiers and women towards their participation in the sport at Corps and Army levels.

Major Paul Marsden brought considerable talent to Army rowing, having joined REME as an already experienced oarsman: he had earned his Blue at Oxford as a member of the 1974 winning crew against Cambridge. However, his early postings kept him in Germany throughout the Eighties, where his rowing was confined to local European opportunities. A return to prominence occurred in 1992 at the Veterans World championships in Cologne where, in conjunction with Major Nick Holland RE, another Oxford Blue, entry into the Coxless Pairs led to their carrying off the gold medal – forging a partnership which was to prove the basis of a revival in Army rowing successes.

RUGBY FOOTBALL

The first volume described how Brigadier Leslie Tyler laid the foundations for REME rugby while he was Commandant at Arborfield. It does not report this extract from the London evening paper, 'The Star', on 9 March 1946:

'An Army side from Arborfield, composed of officers and men, has appeared amongst the big clubs. This season they have met such teams as the Kiwis, Rosslyn Park, Bedford, Devonport Services, London Irish and Rugby Town and won 22 out of their 33 matches.'

In those early days team captains Sergeant Joe Starling and Major Philip Joy were supported by such personalities as Major Joe Dobie who was General Secretary, Majors Murray Grammer and Ian Priest, Captain Peter Wildman, Lieutenants Bill Bailey and David Lister, and Second Lieutenant John Stewart; some of these were well known in the Corps for the next forty-five years. In the 1947–48 season Major Joy played several times for the Army, against the other Services and the French Army. The Garrison fielded three XVs at that time, but as the players left the Army or were posted away the Arborfield Club declined, most of the main club fixtures were dropped and after the 1950–51 season the club ceased to field a full team and concentrated on club sevens, an activity which had become very popular since the late Forties.

In 1947 a REME team reached the finals of the Middlesex Sevens but lost to London Welsh in the first round. In 1956, at the similar stage of competition, a 6–3 win over London Scottish was achieved: a notable upset for the favourites who fielded six internationals. Sadly, the REME team failed in the succeeding round, losing to Northampton. REME Arborfield won the Berkshire Sevens in 1955 and 1956.

REME Arborfield

The REME Arborfield RFC revived in the mid-Sixties with the arrival of Captain Philip Winchcombe, skipper of the Corps XV, and Major Dennis Bowen. Brigadier Geoffrey Walker, Commandant at Arborfield, was a keen supporter and in 1966–67 a regular 2nd XV played and sometimes a 3rd XV. Tours to Yorkshire and Bournemouth took place. The 1st XV won 37 of 39 matches and the annual club dinner was honoured by the presence of the RFU President, Mr Douggie Harrison. The club also won the Berkshire Cup twice during the Seventies. From this revival the Corps XV went on to win all its nine representative matches in 1968–69: scoring 230 points with only 17 against, the best result for twenty years.

During the Eighties the REME Arborfield side again went into decline as the numbers in training were reduced, more soldiers wanted to go home at weekends and the better players were encouraged to play for higher-standard civilian clubs. The final 'nail in the coffin' was the RFU's introduction of stringent rules for the registration of players. After several seasons of struggle the club was wound up in 1991.

ASM John Morgan

County Players
Many REME players have represented Berkshire since 1946 when the County first competed in the County championship. The first Berkshire team contained seven REME players, and in 1969–70 more than half the Berkshire Colts XV came from the Army Apprentices College, Arborfield. David Spawforth and Bryan Reynolds became two of the County's most capped players, both receiving the County Award of Merit. The 1992–93 County squad contained AQMS Tony Pittaway, Staff Sergeant Paul Simon and Sergeant Dave Bott. Tony Pittaway and Paul Simon had both played for Berkshire previously when stationed at Arborfield. For Hampshire Major Keith Allcock, ASM John Morgan and Staff Sergeant Bernie Byrne were perhaps the best known of REME's recent players and officials. Keith Allcock also played for Berkshire and John Morgan represented Dorset and Wiltshire.

BAOR
For many years the REME UK XV toured BAOR at Easter, including playing the REME BAOR XV for the Pegasus Trophy in what had always been a keen contest. The REME BAOR Team competed annually against other Corps for the Ellis Cup, and in 1990, having won that cup, it went on to win the inaugural Cathedral Cup as BAOR Corps champions. The 1992–93 reduction in strength in Germany left the future of the Corps and BAOR rugby in some doubt.

Corps Representative Matches
The first recorded Corps match was in the 1945–46 season at Larkhill

against the RA which the Corps won 23–8. When the Corps drew with the R SIGNALS at Leicester 6–6 in 1947–48, the replay at Northampton was lost, despite the support of thirteen bus loads of spectators from Arborfield.

During the National Service era Corps rugby flourished, able to call on such outstanding players as Second Lieutenant J S 'Ian' Swan (Scotland), Corporals Haydn Morgan (Wales and British Lions) and John Hancock (England), thereby putting the Corps in high standing throughout Services rugby. This standing was maintained into the Nineties, long after the end of National Service.

1974–75 was a very successful year for Corps rugby, the Corps team winning all its eight matches, the scores varying from 16–10 against the Royal Military Academy Sandhurst to 66–0 against the RAOC.

In the three seasons 1983–86, when the Corps teams were selected by ASM Dave Whittaker, the Corps lost only one inter-Corps match, that against the RE at Chatham. In 1984–85 there was a very successful Corps tour to the USA.

The 1987–88 season was the first time that the Corps side was undefeated in all civilian and Services matches. The coach for this period was ASM Dennis Prowse, one of the more talented Corps players and perhaps the most talented Corps coach. He also coached the Army Colts at this time, and they too were very successful. In 1988 Major Keith Allcock and Captain Dennis Prowse took a Corps side to the Hong Kong International 10s; the Corps team was runner-up which was a superb achievement.

The selection of the Corps team during the Eighties and early Nineties was under the chairmanship of three men – Captain Dai Lloyd, ASM Whittaker and Major Allcock, all of whom had been outstanding Corps players in their day.

The last battle between REME and RAOC for the Palestine Cup, before RAOC lost its identity as a separate Corps, was suitably marked in the 1992–93 season when two 'old and bold' sides took to the field representing over thirty years of Corps rugby. The success of the 'senior' REME XV in the morning was more than matched by the REME XV in the afternoon.

Inter-Corps Merit Table

The 1991–92 season saw the start of an inter-Corps merit table. REME was placed in Division 1 with the Royal Marines, RA, RE, R SIGNALS and the Infantry, and finished third in the competition. In 1992–93 it only just avoided relegation by coming fourth.

REME 50

In 1992–93 the Corps hosted teams from RAEME, RNZEME and REME BAOR in a very successful tournament to celebrate REME's fiftieth

The REME 50 Trophy

anniversary. The four teams played each other in front of large crowds over three days. Some excellent rugby was played, with RNZEME being unbeaten after a narrow victory over REME UK who finished second. The trophy, a beautiful wooden rugby ball made by 43 District Workshop, was presented by Major General Mike Heath. The final dinner was attended by almost 200 players and officials. Roger Uttley, the former England captain and coach, was the guest speaker and all three Corps contributed to the after-dinner entertainment.

Army Cups

Although the Corps has had such strong teams and so many good players no REME unit had won the Army Cup by 1993. SEE came close several times, being UK runner-up three times – most recently in 1985. In the Army Minor units competition several field workshops did well and in the Seventies the 1st Parachute Logistic Regiment very nearly won through, two-thirds of its team being REME. The same applied to 5 Airborne Brigade Logistic Battalion in the Eighties. 3 Field Workshop, under the leadership of Staff Sergeant George Raw, won the UK Minor Units final in 1983–84 beating Depot, The King's Division but was narrowly defeated by 14 Topographical Squadron RE in the final of the Army Cup. In 1993 the same Workshop won the UK Minor Units final against 24 Field Squadron RE, and then triumphed in an all-REME Army Minor Units final at Sennelager against 12 Armoured Workshop.

Combined Services and Army Team Representatives

The Army side in 1974–75 included, in various matches, Staff Sergeant Bob Collier, Staff Sergeant Keith McQuilton, Staff Sergeant John Mills, Corporal John Morgan, Corporal Brian Reynolds, Corporal David Spawforth and Craftsman Roger 'Snowy' Spurrell. Corporal John Morgan and Craftsman Spurrell were nominated for the England under-23 squad. Of these players, Staff Sergeant Mills played for the Army regularly from 1969 and for the Combined Services, including the match against Japan, in 1976; Corporal Reynolds played in the match against Japan and against Australia and the French Army in 1975; Corporal

Spawforth, one of REME's greatest players, played for the Combined Services and the Army from 1968–77 and also played for Combined Southern Counties, and captained the Army team as a lance corporal: some considered him to be the best scrum half in England, although he was never selected for his country. The team which beat Japan 23–21 in 1976 contained three other REME players: Corporal Morgan who played for England Under-21, Corporal Spawforth and Craftsman Spurrell, who played for England Under-21, Cornwall and later captained Bath.

These players were followed by Bernie Byrne (captain of the Army XV), Lieutenant Graham Morgan (who overtook Captain Dickie Moyle's long- standing record of thirteen Army caps) and Captain Brian McCall (Ireland), who, with three caps in 1984–86, became the first Army player to receive an International Cap since 1969. Captain McCall and Lieutenant Graham Morgan were also both selected for a Combined Services and British Police tour of New Zealand but McCall had to withdraw because of injury.

Between 1980–93 forty-eight members of the Corps played for International, National, Combined Services and Army teams, including under-21 and under-19 sides. Staff Sergeant Paul Simon and Corporal Geordie Watson were selected for the Army XV and awarded their Army caps in the 1992–93 season. Staff Sergeant Simon also gained his Combined Services cap. AQMS Tony Pittaway and Sergeant Dave Bott represented Berkshire and were awarded their County colours. Lieutenant Adam Griffiths played for the Scottish Colts.

Internationals

'Ian' Swan, Haydn Morgan and John Hancock have already been mentioned; Swan won seventeen caps on the wing playing for Scotland –

Captain Brian McCall in possession against Japan

a record for any Army back – whilst Haydn Morgan played for Wales twenty-seven times – a record for any Army player. A more recent REME international was Captain McCall. The Corps can be proud of their record.

Officials

Colonel Peter Crooks and Brigadier Chris Tyler were both Chairman of the Army Rugby Union. Earlier in their careers, Brigadier Tyler and Major Peter Lillington had refereed at every level other than full international, and became Chairman and Vice-Chairman respectively of the Army Rugby Referees' Society. In the early years 1951–54 Sergeant Lillington had played in the REME team and won his Corps colours.

Brigadier Crooks was one of the great figures in Corps rugby, and he was also a Corps cricketer. He was selected for an England rugby trial but was injured, and regularly played for Berkshire. He played also for Durham and the Combined Southern Counties, the Combined Services, and regularly for the Army. He was later the Army representative on the RFU.

Other senior positions were occupied at separate times by Brigadier Philip Joy as Chairman and Colonel Peter Wildman as a member of the Army Selection Committee, Brigadier Joy being also the Army representative on the RFU Committee. In more recent years, Lieutenant Graham Morgan was also on the ARU Selection Committee (1992–93) and was one of the senior XV coaches, whilst ASM Tim Pratt was Secretary of the ARU Coaching Committee and Secretary of the Hampshire Referees' Society in the same season.

Brigadier Murray Wildman became Director of ARU Marketing and Finance in 1988 when that Committee was set up, and still held the post in 1992–93, being responsible for securing sponsorship to run such a major sport. Colonel Nick Holland has been Chairman of the ARU Referees' Society from the 1992–93 season.

SAILING

The challenge and adventure associated with sailing has for a long time been recognized by the Army as a means of developing leadership, team building, resourcefulness and many other personal attributes relevant to soldiering. Thus it is considered both as a sport and an important training medium. The distinction between recreational sailing and adventurous training can sometimes become blurred, as both often take place in the same vessels and present similar challenges. As a result, the sport has been greatly enhanced by the official support which this training aspect has attracted. This is particularly evident in the sailing expeditions which are described in this chapter. The intellectual and practical challenges posed by the very different disciplines of offshore and dinghy sailing and windsurfing have proved to have been well matched by a highly numerate and skilled Corps, which has resulted in many very successful and talented REME sailors making a major impact at all levels.

An article in the 1974 REME Journal described the early moves during the Sixties to pass on the resources of the REME Officers' Sailing Club, sponsored by the REME Institution, to a REME Sailing Association, with the express purpose of extending sailing facilities to all in the Corps, serving or retired, and to civilians serving with REME. This purpose has been fully realized since the formation of the Association on 1 August 1966. While this was concerned with sailing in the United Kingdom, in BAOR, where dinghy sailing had been the principal activity, a REME Sailing Association (BAOR) was formed in 1970. In 1980 the two associations were amalgamated and renamed The REME Yacht Club. Under the Club's auspices the three main sectional activities of offshore, dinghy and windsurfing have prospered, and are described briefly in the ensuing paragraphs.

Offshore Sailing

The newly-formed REME Sailing Association wasted no time in introducing offshore sailing when, in early 1967, they bought their first offshore yacht, a new Arden 4 sloop, which was named *Thea* after the wife of the first Vice Commodore, Colonel George Preston. In 1973 a three-year-old Hustler 30, *Precedent*, was bought to replace *Thea*, and renamed *Seahorse of REME*. In turn replacement yachts were acquired: *Seahorse of REME II*, a new Contessa 32, was launched in 1981 and *Seahorse of REME III*, a new Sadler 34, was launched in 1988. A small family cruiser, a 26 foot Westerley Centaur, was also bought as a third yacht when under a year old and renamed *Craftsman*; she was still in use in the Nineties. *Thea* was kept initially at Marchwood, but from 1971 the Corps yachts were berthed at Gosport.

Similarly, in Germany the REME Sailing Association (BAOR) set to in 1970 under its Commodore, Lieutenant Colonel Geoffrey Atkinson, to secure its first offshore yacht. A Sabre 27 was bought in kit form in 1972 and built at 7 Field Workshop, Fallingbostel. Launched at Kiel in 1973, she was named *Lillibulero* and replaced in turn by *Princess Marina*, a Contessa 28, in 1979 and by *Blue Belle*, a Sadler 34, in 1988.

Major Hugh Hind skippered Army Nicholson 55s frequently in the Services Offshore Race and was Army Offshore captain for many years. Colonel Jeremy Towler, Lieutenant Colonel John Haverson, ASMs Barry Wickett and Zammit, and Staff Sergeant Nigel Rennie were among skippers who over the years won the Dolphin Trophy in the Army Sailing Association (ASA) Regatta. A REME yacht or REME crew was selected frequently to represent the Army in the Services Offshore Race. The REME Yacht Club sponsored the Army entry, a Nicholson 55, in the 1984 Trans-Atlantic Tall Ships Race.

In 1989 the School of Electronic Engineering organized Exercise CARIBBEAN SEE on behalf of the Joint Services Adventurous Training Centre (JSASTC) – as the Joint Services Sailing Centre (JSSC) had become. In this exercise a JSASTC Nicholson 55, HMSTC *Dasher*, sailed 20,000 miles with some 190 crew members, two-thirds of whom were novices. Staff Sergeant Dickie Boast master-minded the whole exercise, for which he was given the Rory Cape Award for 1989.

Fastnet Race 1991

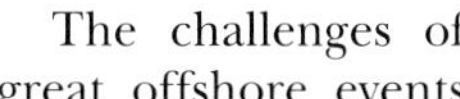

The challenges of great offshore events were accepted by the enthusiasts, whether on the world's oceans or closer to home. For instance in the Fastnet Race REME skippers and crews frequently participated over the years. In the ill-fated 1979 race Major Jeremy Gomersall skippered a JSSC Contessa 32 in hurricane-force winds, and was forced to retire. Lieutenant Colonel Towler, Major Mark Allen and Captain Terry Frazer were crew members for another JSSC entry, *Kukri* (a Nicholson 55) which retired after being damaged. In the 1983 Fastnet Race Lieutenant Colonel Towler and Staff Sergeant Miles were selected for the Army crew, while the REME Yacht Club formed the complete crew for the Army entry in the 1991 Race, skippered by the Commodore, Colonel Andy Platt. On the global scale there was the Whitbread Round the World yacht race: in 1973–74 the Services entry, *British Steel*, included Captain Ian Bye, Captain Andrew Edsor and Staff Sergeant David Leslie. As mentioned at the beginning of this chapter, Staff Sergeant Leslie was the only member of the crew to sail in both legs of the Round the World Clipper Race in *Great Britain II* in 1975–76; he also won the Rory Cape Award and skippered HMSTY *Adventure* from Cape Town to Auckland in the Whitbread Round the World Race in 1977. In 1977–78 Leslie was secretary of the selection committee for

Adventure as the Services entry, on which Captain Jim Stanyer crewed on the first leg and skippered the second leg from Cape Town to Auckland.

In 1987 Major Stanyer was one of the many who lost their lives when the cross-channel ferry *Herald of Free Enterprise* overturned near Zeebrugge. He had done so much work for the REME Yacht Club as Offshore Secretary since 1982 and had taken part in many off-shore sail training exercises, including skipper of HMSTY *Sabre* on the Nova Scotia to Liverpool leg of the 1984 Tall Ships Race. He held Army and Combined Services colours for sailing. He was 48 and still serving at the time of his death, and had been presented with the Preston Trophy for outstanding service to the offshore section of the REME Yacht Club at its AGM a few weeks earlier.

The offshore section ran an end-of-season rally in the autumn, when over a weekend the club yachts and club members with other yachts took part in a fun event on the Saturday, ending up in a suitable harbour in the Solent. A dinner in the evening was followed by a pursuit race back on the Sunday. In recent years a nautical version of 'Trivial Pursuit' type questions formed part of the Saturday test.

Dinghy Sailing

Major Bruce Burnett had a similar and equally distinguished sailing career as those of Captain Bye and Lieutenant Colonel Nick Ross, which are mentioned later. He qualified for the World Laser championship in 1973 but did not take part, going to Sandhurst instead. He captained the Cambridge University team and represented the Army and Combined Services regularly; he was the Army captain for three years when Lieutenant Colonel Ross was abroad.

Staff Sergeant C J Knight, a possible candidate for the 1976 Olympics, went on to represent Great Britain in the OK Dinghy World championship at Hanko in Finland where he was forty-ninth out of seventy-five.

Captain Bruce Burnett offering 'advice' at the Seaview Regatta

In 1972 Major Stephen Abate and Major Geoffrey Simpson (later Commodore of the REME Yacht Club) competed in the European championship of the National Hornet dinghy at Fécamp in France where they came sixth and qualified for the World championship.

In the early Nineties the pattern of sailing events which had emerged over the years was that each of the sections of the club held regattas or competitions. The dinghy section was originally based at Thorney Island Sailing Club before moving in 1970 to Stokes Bay where it held an annual regatta for many years, and subsequently at Theale, a flooded sand pit near Reading to which the fleet moved in 1979. A very popular event was the annual Seaview Regatta on the Isle of Wight when the club invaded the sleepy little village and sailed the delightful three-man Mermaid keelboats belonging to the Seaview Yacht Club.

Windsurfing

'Board sailing' was a fast-growing sport amongst the younger members and later became 'Windsurfing'. Its growth made it necessary in 1983 to form a new section with its own secretary, and by 1992 it had twenty-three boards covering all levels. This enabled training to be given from fundamentals to the very advanced and highly skilled techniques of the RYA Race Training syllabus. The REME Yacht Club windsurfers established their place from the start in high-level competitions: Apprentice Tradesman Parsons represented the Army in 1984 in the Inter-Services championships, and in 1985 Staff Sergeant Peter Priddle came 10th in that competition.

Captain Neil Curry led the Army team in the first World board sailing championships in Cornwall in 1987, when he came forty-eighth out of fifty-seven in the Heavyweight division. He was the Army Heavyweight team captain again later, and became the National Super Heavyweight champion in the 6 square metre class in 1990, the same year as Corporal Dave Tindall was the Joint Services champion and won the UK National Series in that class.

In October 1988 the Inter-Services team board sailing championship was held at Portland. Captain Curry, captain of Army board sailing, was the team manager and the Lightweight team included Corporal Tindall. After a very exciting final race the Army had won three matches, the Royal Navy two and the Royal Air Force one. Unfortunately a protest then went against the Army with one of the Heavyweight team being disqualified for touching a buoy and not re-rounding which gave the match to the Royal Air Force, so all teams finished up with two matches each. The points total was then added up, the trophy finally going to the Royal Navy. In 1990 the Army windsurfing team again included Corporal Tindall and Major Curry, together with Craftsman Nick Scott.

The Barry Trophy, awarded annually by the ASA from 1982 onwards to the young sailor who has made the most outstanding contribution to Army sailing, went in 1990 to Corporal Tindall. He had made a valuable contribution to the Army and the Corps by encouraging and training others at all levels of the sport. It was also won by Lance Corporal Scott in 1992.

The windsurfers held their own regatta at Theale and on a few occasions they ran it concurrently with the dinghy regatta with interesting results!

REME 50

With REME's 50th anniversary year in view, the REME Yacht Club obtained in 1991 a 39 foot Westerly Sealord, with a loan of £50,000 from the Central Charitable Trust. In February 1992 Mrs Frances Heath, wife of the Director General (ex-officio Admiral), named her *Master Craftsman.* The yacht later sailed to America and the Great Lakes of Canada and back to Marchwood as part of the REME 50 celebrations, sailing a course of thirteen legs. Exercise Master Craftsman is described in Chapter 5.

The REME 50 year was a most successful year for REME sailors, in addition to Exercise Master Craftsman. In offshore and dinghy sailing and in windsurfing the Corps was unbeaten and provided the bulk of the teams which represented the Army:

- The Corps swept the board at the ASA Regatta and the Services Offshore Race. ASM Wickett's Victoria 34 was first in the ASA and Staff Sergeant Rennie was second. The REME Yacht Club won the Dolphin Trophy and was chosen to represent the Army in the Inter-Services Offshore Race in which Staff Sergeant Rennie, skippering *Lambis,* won the Victoria Trophy and the Société Régates du Havre Trophy for the second yacht in Division 3. ASM Wickett skippered the successful Army yacht which won the Inter-Services competition.
- In dinghy competitions the Corps was equally impressive with Lieutenant Colonel Ross and Major Burnett as members of the Army team that won the Inter-Services Conningham Cup, the Victory Trophy and the team dinghy competition. The Corps also won the inter-Corps dinghy league.
- The REME windsurfers were the inter-Corps champions and Army Team champions. Lance Corporal Scott was the Army and Joint Services Heavyweight champion and ranked number one in the British Windsurfing Association amateur rankings; he reached the last twelve in the Olympic squad but was not chosen. He was the 'Fanatic' one-design Windsurfing Amateur World Champion in 1992. Sergeant Tindall was second overall in the Army championships, third in the Joint Services championships and Army (UK) champion.

Prominent Sailors

Captain Ian Bye was captain of the Sandhurst team in 1966 and sailed for the Army and the Combined Services, rubbing shoulders with Olympic helmsmen and national champions during these events. At Cambridge he was awarded his Half Blue and was a member of the British

Universities team when they sailed against the American Universities. He sailed for REME and the Army at keelboat regattas at Seaview, Isle of Wight and one year captained the Army team. He entered the 1971 Fastnet Race under the REME flag with a mainly REME crew, including Lieutenant Ross, and won Class III B, the Golden Dragon Trophy, and in 1973 was a member of the crew of *British Soldier*, the Army entry in the Round the World Race.

Lieutenant Colonel Nick Ross had a remarkable sailing career. He succeeded Captain Bye as captain of the Sandhurst team and was sailing for the Army before he was commissioned. At Cambridge he was awarded his sailing Half Blue and was selected to sail for the British Universities team in 1971. He sailed for the Army and REME at this time and captained the Army team for the first time in 1973 and, with some alternation with Colonel Stuart Jardine RE, he was still captain in 1992. In 1975, with Captain Bye as crew, he sailed a 470 class dinghy in the pre-Olympics in Kingston, Ontario, but did not make the team at the 1976 Games. He competed with the Combined Services team and also proved very successful in the Mermaid keelboats at Seaview, winning the coveted Gold Cup of the Association of Service Yacht Clubs three times in four years in the Eighties. In 1983 he was the Joint Service and Army board sailing champion in Division 1 boards, and remained Corps champion 1983–85; he was also BAOR champion 1988–89.

Skipper – Major Hugh Hind

In 1992 Major Hugh Hind took over as OC of the

Adventurous Training Wing and Captain of Boats of the British Kiel Yacht Club: this was the first time the post had gone to anyone other than a Sapper. Later in 1992 he was appointed Commandant of the Kiel Training Centre. He stood down that year as captain of the Army Offshore team, having won the Services Offshore Race twice and captained the Army team to victory three times in the previous six years.

Major Brian Daniels, mentioned elsewhere in connection with his canoeing and walking activities, had been a member of the crew of *Great Britain II* for the first Round the World yacht race in 1973–74, skippered by Chay Blyth with an all 16 Parachute Brigade crew. Then in 1978–79 he and his wife built a 38 foot yacht *Pegasus of Arne*, with which he competed in the International Parmelia Race from Plymouth to Fremantle via Cape Town, in commemoration of the establishment of the first settlement in Western Australia by the *Parmelia* in 1829. He took an all-REME crew of Corporals John Hands and Bill Millsop, and Lance Corporal Keyes, and gained ninth place out of the forty-two competing yachts. On the return voyage he was accompanied by AQMS Keith Smith and Staff Sergeant John Oxford. For this adventurous project Major Daniels received the 1979 Rory Cape Award.

In 1988 REME provided the captains of all three Army sailing teams: Major Hugh Hind for offshore, Major Bruce Burnett for dinghies and Captain Neil Curry for windsurfing.

SKIING

Skiing was both a sport and an adventurous training pursuit in the Army. Units organized ski exercises and courses which were run under the Snow Queen scheme in Germany. Snow Queen was an adventurous training scheme to provide opportunity for soldiers to undertake cross-country and downhill skiing in Bavaria. All manner of competitions were run by formations in BAOR and by the Army.

The REME chalet and buying the REME Hotel at Wertach are included in the BAOR Chapter 6 and Regimental Activities Chapter 13. Many soldiers learned to ski in British Troops Austria (BTA) in the late Forties; it was at Bad Gastein Austria in 1947 that the Corps won its first skiing medals. Staff Sergeant Hirst was one of those who learned to ski in BTA and Staff Sergeant Gover learned to ski there as a boy, coming out for school holidays to see his father the BTA Workshop Commander; in 1956 he represented Great Britain in the Olympic cross-country ski team, but soon after, as a result of an accident, his energies were put to teaching others to ski.

Before long the scene was set with Major Tony Giblett as BEME 7 Armoured Brigade in Soltau, Staff Sergeant Hirst at 7 Armoured Workshop in Fallingbostel and Lieutenant Colonel Fred Lindsay, CREME 1st Division in Verden, who was a keen skier. Craftsman Carey, a good runner, was posted in to 7 Armoured Workshop; he had run for

Coventry Harriers but never skied before his National Service, but after two seasons he was selected for the British National Cross-Country Ski team. In the Sixties, despite a lack of funds, and the time and expense of prolonged training in Norway, Bavaria and Austria, the REME team, based on 7 Armoured Workshop and supported by HQ REME 1st Division in Verden, acquitted themselves very well at 1st Division championships and Army championships at St Moritz and later at Oberjoch. The outstanding Corps trainer in those days was Staff Sergeant Les Sheppard who coached the REME 7 Armoured Workshop team from 1969–73.

To widen the scope of skiing from a few 'gladiators' to a sport for all, the Corps ran a series of Snow Queen huts as mentioned in Chapter 6. The first REME ski championships were held in 1977 just before Christmas in the Gunzesried Valley under the direction of the CREME 1st Division, Lieutenant Colonel Graham Staniforth. Thereafter the REME championships continued annually at Gunzesried-Säge under HQ

REME 1st Division direction, invariably successful and well supported. 1st Division remained responsible for the chalet and later the REME Hotel at Wertach which was purchased in 1982.

Great Corps Skiers

Sergeant Jeffery Stevens represented Great Britain in biathlon at the 1972 Olympic Games at Sapporo and, as a staff sergeant, at the 1976 Games at Innsbruck. Subsequently Corporal Paul Gibbins represented Great Britain in the World biathlon championship in 1980 and at the Olympic Games at Lake Placid. Staff Sergeant Dave Joseph of 12 Armoured Workshop Osnabruck qualified to take part in the 1988 World Masters Cross-Country Ski championship at Seefeld held over the 1985 Olympic and World Cup courses. The GB team met in the village square at Seefeld for the first time at the opening ceremony where each country paraded through the town behind the national flag led by a very loud Austrian band. The Finnish team won five out of six classes in the 30 kilometres classical; in the free style the Norwegians, Swiss and Germans shared the honours; in the 15 kilometres the Scandinavians won first three places in several classes. In the 3 × 10 kilometres relay the GB team of three, including Dave Joseph, finished eleventh overall over the World Cup relay course, which was a good result. Switzerland were the winners after a battle royal with Germany. On the last day the Scandinavians took the honours in the 50 kilometres classical race.

Captain Gail Tilford British Services International Ski Championships – 1989

Captain Gail Tilford from 22nd Air Defence Regiment Workshop represented the Army ladies team, for the second year, at the 1989 Portakabin British Services International Ski Championships at Megève, France, and Lieutenant Michael Johnston of 12 Armoured Workshop was in the Army men's Alpine team. He represented the Army for several years after 1989, and was eventually captain of the men's Alpine team. He was undoubtedly the best Alpine skier that REME has ever had. Competitors came from seven other countries, and from the Royal Navy and the Royal Air Force. Both the Army men's and ladies' teams won the Combinations, with congratulations from all including the Duchess of York. That evening they enjoyed the champions' champagne at the prize giving – a nine-litre bottle! In 1992 Lieutenant Janicke Tvedt came second in the Army Ladies Alpine Combination and was selected for the Army Team, coming ninth overall in the Inter-Services Alpine Combination.

The REME ski meeting had to be cancelled in 1990 due to lack of snow, and in 1991 due to Operation GRANBY in the Gulf. In 1992 the REME meeting was again held in the Gunzesried valley where many teams and individuals enjoyed a good week's skiing

Lieutenant Colonel Richard Platt

Skibobbing

Skibobbing is often seen as a minority winter sport. Several members of the Corps have shown the enthusiasm to promote the sport within the Army and shown their ability to perform at the top level of competition. Until the mid-Seventies skibobbing in the Army was dominated by the RA and RMP. Major Richard Platt, at Headquarters BAOR, took the lead in having the existing Army 'Jafca' skibobs refurbished and finding funds for new ones. By the early Eighties he and Major Len Hawkins had recruited several enthusiasts, who began to do well at the British National championships. By the end of the Eighties Lieutenant Colonel Platt had become Chairman of Army Skibobbing and President of the British Skibob Racing Club. He was the British champion several times and consistently within the top twenty placings in international competitions. His best position was 15th at the World championships at Seefeld in 1990. Lieutenant Colonel Platt introduced several members of the Corps to skibobbing and trained some up to the standard for selection into the British National team. In 1991 REME produced five of the ten men in the British National team for the World championship in Zell-am-See in Austria. Major Geoff Wright (18th), ASM Barry Langmead, AQMS Danny McGarrigle (23rd) and AQMS Dave Norman proved that they had the courage and skill to keep the Corps at the forefront of British skibobbing.

In the Eighties and the start of the Nineties members of the Corps made their mark in skibobbing. In the eleven years 1982–92 Lieutenant Colonel Platt was Army champion eight times and both Major Wright and AQMS Colin Fenwick were Army champions once each. ASM Barry Langmead, an experienced motor cyclist, came second in his first British

National championship in Austria. He gave invaluable service to the British team until his retirement, both by his expertise in skibob maintenance and as a racer where his best performance was 23rd in the World championships at Spindlemuhle in the Czech Republic in the winter of 1992. By the end of the Eighties Lieutenant Colonel Platt was running regular courses in Bavaria to teach skibobbing to the Army as a whole, which greatly improved the competitiveness and standard of racing.

SQUASH

Sergeant Heavyside
Corps Champion 1973–75

Squash is a sport principally played by many at all levels of expertise as an enjoyable challenge and aid to fitness. Until the late-Sixties it was a game principally played by officers and most Army courts belonged to officers' clubs. In the early-Sixties the REME Institution built a court at the REME Headquarters Officers' Mess, West Court. The first Corps champion was Captain Peter Todd in 1956, followed for two years by Lieutenant Colonel David Mangles. For the next thirteen years four officers shared the honours in various ranks: David Bonnor-Moris, Rob Lucas, Sam Roberts, and Ian Stark a record seven times. The first soldier to be Corps champion was Sergeant Chris Heavyside in 1973.

On a team basis it has long been played in REME, the team's successes and failures little publicized and followed only by the enthusiasts. However, as in most sports, REME on occasion has made its mark and played a full part in supporting the game at Army level. In inter-regimental activity Army squash has been organized in divisions, REME moving primarily within the second tier. Division 2 consists of up to seven teams which play each other over one weekend. The bottom team is relegated and the top team promoted to Division 1. In 1978 the Corps came top of Division 2 after beating the RAC, R SIGNALS and The Prince of Wales's Division, losing only to RCT: promotion to the senior Division resulted, but lasted only the one season. However, promotion was achieved once more nearly a decade later, in 1987, after a successful series of matches against The Queen's Division, Infantry, RAEC, RA and RAC, winning an aggregate of twenty-one games against four, the RA and Infantry being the sole winners of two games each. Sadly, the Division 1 experience once more lasted only the one season. However, in the final two years within the scope of this volume, REME broke the shackles of past history and achieved unprecedented success. In the 1990–91 season all six matches were won in Division 2 and the Corps ascended once more into the top Division. The following season's competition was played again at the Waverley Squash Club in Farnham, when REME won four of its five matches and so finished up as runner-up of Division 1 for the first time.

A REME team was also entered in the civilian Berkshire League, selecting players from those within reasonable travelling distance of Arborfield; this gave players valuable regular exposure to competitive squash, and in the two seasons 1990–92 the team won all its twenty-eight league matches – moving up one division each year to reach Division 2. The Corps side was undefeated in its season's total of thirty matches in 1990–91, and lost only two out of twenty-nine in 1991–92

At unit level the conventional Corps system of Craftsman's Cup competitions operated in both UK and BAOR for major and minor units, while Army competitions for major and minor units provided more public challenge. In the most recent years the School of Electronic Engineering and Electronics Branch became losing Army finalists in the United Kingdom, while 12 Armoured Workshop became the BAOR winner in 1990–91, but went on to lose to the Light Division Depot in the Army final. Several years earlier 4 Armoured Workshop had established a fine record: in 1986–87 it won the BAOR Major Units Cup, and then went on to beat the corresponding United Kingdom champions to win the 'Soldier' Cup, an overall success which it repeated four times in five years, the final successful season being 1988–89.

Such successes are rarely achieved without the spur of one or more particularly expert players giving a lead within their units. REME has produced its fair share of such talent, many members playing for the Army, or its restricted categories of Junior (now assimilated into Under-25), Under-25, and Veterans (over 35). In representing the Army in the Inter-Services competition Corps players have included Corporal Adam in 1978, a year in which he was awarded his Army colours; Lance Corporal Jenkins (Under-25) in 1985; Lieutenant John Ensor and Corporal Gordon Cole (Army) in the same championship – in which Cole was the best Army player – and AQMS Tony Fisher (Veterans, playing still for the Army in these championships in 1988–89); and in various of the three years 1990–92 Corporal M Evans, Craftsmen Cotton, Lawrence and Simpson (Under-25s) and Corporals Clarke and Evans (Army). In the 1990–91 Army championships Lance Corporal Clarke reached the Open final, the first REME player to have done so, and Corporal Evans won the doubles; while in the following year Craftsman Cotton became the first

REME player to secure an Army title in winning the Under-25s competition. With such players and a youthful nucleus, aided by the stiffer opposition to be encountered in the higher levels of the Berkshire League, optimism in 1992 for the future of REME squash was high.

Corps members have also made their contributions in coaching and refereeing, including in the later Eighties Staff Sergeant Parker who was the Army Junior squash coach and AQMS Arthur Bright who was in charge of Army squash coaching and a member of the Army Squash Rackets Association executive committee.

SWIMMING

Swimming was adopted as a REME sport in 1952. Over the following forty years there were many successes, with members of the Corps achieving the highest levels of Services representation. National Servicemen, as with other sports, made a notable contribution, and there was a marked drop in competition entries and standards when that era came to an end in the early Sixties. In more recent years expert leadership has been given by the chairmen. Lieutenant Colonel Andy Morton took up that position in 1981 while still the British Team Manager and continuing to be Chairman of the Army Swimming Union (ASU), of which he eventually became a Life Vice President. He had been the Assistant Great Britain Team Manager 1970–71 when in Germany, and subsequently the Great Britain Team Manager for thirteen seasons 1976–88 in which his duties took him to many countries, including all the 'Iron Curtain' except Czechoslovakia. After being prevented by Government policy from managing the team at the 1980 Moscow Olympics he went on to manage the England team at the Commonwealth Games in Brisbane in 1982, and the Great Britain team at the 3rd World Championships in Ecuador in 1982 and the Los Angeles Olympics in 1984. In 1987 he handed over Corps swimming to Lieutenant Colonel Chris Scotcher, a former Army swimmer. Lieutenant Colonel Scotcher decided that a return to days of former glory could be achieved and successfully developed the lapsed inter-Corps events. As Vice Chairman of the ASU he continued this work by establishing Masters Swimming for the three Services, whereby swimmers of all ages could compete against others within discrete five-year age brackets. Other official Army positions were taken by Major Keith Pinder (who by 1961 as a young Lance Corporal had been introduced to Combined Services and Army swimming as a 100 metres free-styler), in charge of the Army team from 1975–84 and 1988–89 and of the Combined Services on several occasions, and by Lieutenant Mick Burrows who coached the Army women for a brief period in the early Eighties. Lieutenant Colonel Scotcher and Major Pinder also became Life Vice Presidents of the ASU.

The first Corps swimming championships were held at the Aldershot

Military Pool in 1953, to coincide with the Corps athletics meeting. It was hardly surprising that a REME Training Centre team, then made up from the four training battalions in Arborfield and Bordon, should win the water polo: for the team included Craftsman Ken Fennell, an England international, and Sergeant Jim McLeod. In the previous year 4 (Armament) Training Battalion had won the Army inter-unit water polo with these two prominent players in the team, and in 1953 the unit won the Army inter-unit swimming. In 1979 the 30 metre Aldershot pool was closed for extensive repairs and the Corps championships were moved to Arborfield, where the pool was 25 metres long which meant that a new series of Corps records had to be started. Domestic facilities at the home of the Corps were better than those at Aldershot, and so it was decided to retain the swimming and water polo at Arborfield.

Unit successes could often be correlated with the movements of skilled individuals, and when Staff Sergeant McLeod was posted to 27 Command Workshop in 1957 he set about organizing a Southern Command REME swimming team; it soon won both the major cups at the Corps championships, much to the surprise of the training battalions. By 1959 he was back in 4 (Armament) Training Battalion, when five of its water polo players were in the Army team. In 1965 the REME BAOR water polo team, led by Captain McLeod at the age of 39, was dominant in beating SEME (captained by ASM Ken Burrows aged 47) by two goals. Later achievements in water polo came with Craftsman Keith Alderton representing the Army in 1984–85, and also the Combined Services water polo team in the latter year, and in 1988 as a Corporal together with Craftsman Mark Jackson, playing water polo for both Combined Services and the Army. In 1988 Corporals Coombes and Genders also represented the Army. In the following year's Corps swimming championships it was recorded that 'a vocal and knowledgeable crowd was treated to a marvellous display of skill by Sergeant Keith Alderton, captain of SEE and probably the finest water polo player the Corps has ever had, in a very physical and entertaining game'. In that year five members of the Corps swam, played water polo or both for the Army in the Inter-Services competitions.

Swimming had a strong place in the activities of the Junior Leaders Unit and the two Army Apprentices Schools at Arborfield and Carlisle, all of which took part in the Corps championships in the mid-Sixties. In those for 1966 Carlisle (newly designated as a College), coached by AQMS Penny, won all events but one; that one was the 220 yards freestyle won by Captain McLeod, an event won several times by the pentathlete Sergeant Jim Fox. In the following year Carlisle apprentices Barnes, Bowen and Inman represented the Army at both Senior and Junior levels. The Carlisle team won the Army Senior swimming championships in each of the three years 1966–68. In 1985 Princess Marina College became Army Junior champion, and three years later eight apprentices from the College swam or played water polo – or both – for the Army Juniors. 1989 was the year in which 12 Armoured Workshop, based at Osnabruck, won the Army swimming championships held at the Royal Military Academy, Sandhurst: a win decided in the final medley relay race, in the course of which the Workshop team broke the ten-year-old record by three seconds.

It will be evident from the foregoing paragraphs that REME made substantial contributions to swimming and water polo at representative levels. The strength of water polo in 4 (Armament) Training Battalion in 1959 was much enhanced by the presence of Lieutenant Morton (of the London-based Otter Club), Sergeant Mick Reeves (York City) and the Scottish international Corporal Jimmie Brownlee (Galashiels), all of whom played for Combined Services. In 1981 – a year in which the individual butterfly race was reintroduced for the first time since 1962, and the backstroke relay race was abolished – Craftsman Wheeler represented the Army in swimming, while Craftsman Anstey played goal-keeper in the Army water polo team; in 1983 six Corps members represented the Army at swimming or water polo, including the pentathletes Corporals Steve Shaw and Peter Whiteside and Lance Corporal Woodall (who were each awarded Army swimming colours), and in 1984 Sergeant Whiteside, Corporal Shaw and Craftsman Coombes were in the Army swimming team. As might be expected pentathletes have featured frequently in the annals of Corps swimming, and note might be taken here of yet another, Corporal Steve Birley, who swam for the Army and was Combined Services and Army backstroke champion for several years: he won thirteen Corps free style and backstroke records between 1968–74, a number exceeded only by Major McLeod. His greatest swimming feat perhaps was to have won the 1973 General's Challenge Cup, a sea race of 600 yards round a buoy off Southsea which for many years had been a Royal Navy preserve while Aldershot units were not eligible.

In memory of Jim McLeod, who made nineteen annual appearances for the Army and died in 1980, the REME Swimming Association established a Victor Ludorum trophy. Lieutenant Colonel McLeod had represented the Combined Services on many occasions and regularly turned out for Essex and later Hampshire. The first winner of the new trophy was Sergeant Peter Whiteside. Exceptionally, Lieutenant Colonel Scotcher was awarded the trophy in 1990 for his work in promoting swimming and water polo in the Corps and his leadership of the Training Battalion and Depot REME to become the Army Minor Unit champion in the same year.

TENNIS

Over the period of this volume a Corps focus in Lawn Tennis was maintained, a nucleus of enthusiasts ensuring that it was not simply regarded as a private diversion. Indeed, there were some significant successes in the Corps' name, such as the two years 1987-88 in which REME BAOR won the Theatre's inter-Corps tournament. The Corps team participated annually in the Army Lawn Tennis Association's summer and winter leagues. The Corps venue was originally at Bordon but since 1985 all home matches and Corps championships were held on the all-weather courts at Arborfield.

Captain Mark Jeffery

Some individual talents were particularly significant, with Captain Mark Jeffery being outstanding within the Army as a whole. He had been captain of tennis at Welbeck, Sandhurst and Shrivenham. Within the Corps he was singles champion 1973–76 and 1982–83; doubles champion 1974, 1976 and 1982. In Army tennis he was the Under-21 singles champion 1972–74; singles champion 1976, 1980 and 1982–83; men's doubles champion 1976–77 and 1981; and mixed doubles champion 1973–76 and 1978. He was the first member of REME to be Army singles champion. He was a member of the Army team for eight seasons 1975–83, and in the Combined Services team 1980–83. Such a distinguished career came to an end when in 1983 he retired from the Army, leaving a particular memory of 1976, a year in which he achieved a 'clean sweep' in Corps and Army singles and doubles competitions.

Apart from these individual successes Captain Jeffery played for the Corps team throughout his service, and in 1983 led it to its first victory in the Turpin Cup, the inter-Corps league competition. His pre-eminence should not, however, obscure the talents of others in REME, amongst whom were Sergeant Tony Tomlinson, who was the Corps singles champion in 1985 and played for the Army 1985–86; and Sergeant Barnicoat and Corporal Prys-Roberts who, whilst stationed in Detmold in 1990, became Army doubles champions.

EXPEDITIONS

It is generally accepted that most sports provide challenges both to individuals and collectively to teams; they provide inestimable military value in improving fitness and mind for the ultimate tests under operational conditions, and almost always contribute significantly to morale. Adventurous and enterprising activities have for these reasons long benefited from financial assistance, available from Corps funds and more generally from various forms of Service sponsorship. Some such activities have been based upon sports mentioned in this chapter, distinct from the types of expedition exemplified in Chapter 5. Two such occasions are described below, by way of illustrating the inventiveness of soldiers in creating their own physical and mental challenges.

Three Peaks Yacht Race

The Three Peaks Yacht Race was first held in 1977, starting in Barmouth, North Wales to celebrate The Queen's Silver Jubilee. It was the concept of Major Bill Tilman, a notable climber and explorer who had led the 1938 Everest expedition and appropriately presented 'The Daily Telegraph' silver salver to the 1977 winners. He then set off by boat to climb a mountain in Antarctica at the age of 79; after leaving South America he was never seen again. The Race involved sailing 350 miles from Barmouth to Fort William, via Caernarvon and Ravenglass, in combination with running seventy-three miles to the tops and back of Snowdon, Scafell Pikes and Ben Nevis, a combined vertical ascent of over 11,000 feet.

In 1988 this race attracted for the fourth time the Corps and Army marathon champion RSM J K McIllmurray from SEME and Lance Sergeant Jeff Shaw, a REME tradesman attached to the 2nd Battalion, Scots Guards. Their race in the 30 foot trimaran *Memic* started at Barmouth at 1730 hours on Saturday 25 June, and after sailing to Caernarvon they took three and a half hours to run the twenty-four miles up and down Snowdon (3,560 feet). They then set sail for Ravenglass in Cumbria, and only thirteen hours later were on their way to the top of Scafell Pikes (3,210 feet); they covered the thirty-two miles in five hours and fifty-seven minutes, which put their yacht into second place out of the thirty-three competing. The last sailing stage of 235 miles took them to Fort William, arriving at 1930 hours on Wednesday 29 June. They were then in fourth place: the first and second teams had finished the night before, but the third team was only eighteen minutes ahead. The run was only seventeen and a half miles, but it included getting up and down the 4,406 feet of Ben Nevis. The run went well and the REME team passed their rivals half-way up the mountain and managed to retain third place through to the welcome sight of the finishing line.

Three Peaks by Land and Air
Another way of attacking the three peaks was a record-breaking attempt made in October 1990 by a team of three runners who ran in one day from sea level at Fort William to sea level at the Menai Straits via the three summits, a LYNX helicopter transporting them to the base of each mountain. The three runners were Sergeant Brennan, Corporal O'Connor and Corporal Carney, all from 3 Commando Brigade Air Squadron LAD. After cloudy Ben Nevis they were flown in bad weather to Wasdale Head for the start up Scafell Pikes. There was thick cloud at the summit which slowed them down, as a navigating mistake would have ruined their attempt on the record. However, all went well and they got down off the mountain and back to the helicopter without incident. By the time the runners set off on their third run of the day fatigue and muscle pains had set in, challenging their grit and determination. As they arrived back at the helicopter a large crowd of well-wishers cheered them on and the LYNX landed at Caernarvon a few minutes later for a total time of 7 hours 59 minutes, breaking by twenty-three minutes the previous record set by the Manchester Police in 1984. This result could not have been achieved without the skilled flying in poor weather by Captain Peter Terrett AAC and Warrant Officer Class 2 Bayley of 629 Squadron, 9 Regiment AAC. Their efforts raised several hundred pounds for the Save the Children Fund.

SHOOTING

Seemingly in inverse order to the Corps motto 'Arte et Marte' , it has always been an official Corps precept that its members are 'soldiers first, tradesmen second'. Thus shooting has always received the attention it deserves as a basic military skill, and the quality of Corps shooting has been reflected in REME representation at Army, National and International levels.

The Army Rifle Association (ARA) aims to promote interest in small arms shooting for Service purposes, through the medium of individual and team competitions both in Service and target shooting, and the culmination of the annual Regular Army Skill at Arms Meeting (RASAM) held in July at Bisley. The Corps' early prominence in Army shooting was recorded in the first volume of 'Craftsmen of the Army' , in particular its successes at RASAM in 1953 and 1957 in the prestigious Methuen Cup, the premier award in Inter-Services shooting. REME has won that Cup twice more, in 1971 and 1973, when Captain Ray McDonald and Staff Sergeants R Adcock and V Donald were in the team of six on both occasions; ever since then the Cup has been won by Infantry teams except RE in 1979 and the Royal Marines in 1992. In that 1971 meeting Captain McDonald distinguished himself by becoming the seventh REME marksman to win the ultimate Service Rifle prize of Her Majesty

Captain Ray McDonald, winner of the Queen's Medal 1971

the Queen's Medal as Army Rifle champion. It was an appropriate mark of REME's many contributions to shooting in the Services that for RASAM 93, in marking the ARA's centenary, the Corps was designing a new Champion's Chair for the Queen's Medallist to be made by members of 43 District Workshop.

Within the Corps the REME Rifle Association has been the responsible body, chaired by the Commandant of SEME at Bordon which, as the home of armourers' training, has usually held the nucleus of shooting expertise. The Association has been responsible for running the annual Corps Skill at Arms Meeting (CORPSAM) and for sponsoring other internal competitions. Meanwhile, units have had every opportunity to compete in other shooting events organized at formation levels, all contributing to the improvement of essential military skills. Since 1956 a finely cast silver medal has been presented annually by the Worshipful Company of Armourers and Brasiers to the REME armourer who achieved the highest individual score at CORPSAM. The medal could be presented only once to any individual, so improving the chances amongst all armourers to win the coveted medal, which was frequently presented in person at CORPSAM by the Master of the Company.

Towards the end of the Sixties the REME Rifle Association Committee was searching for ways to make more economic use of the finance and manpower needed to run CORPSAM. The hire of the ranges at Bisley had become too expensive, and so the 1967 meeting was run at

Longmoor Ranges after their major refurbishment by SEME and the Ministry of Public Building and Works. Three years later CORPSAM moved to Ash Ranges near Aldershot, and continued there until 1982 when it was cancelled in order to make further savings; medals and trophies were then awarded on the results achieved at the annual ARA Bisley meeting. As it turned out that decision was overshadowed by the inception of the Falkland Islands campaign, some members of the Corps thus gaining their shooting experience for that year under Active Service conditions. In the ensuing decade the central REME Rifle Association meetings had a more chequered history.

In the 1979 Army meeting Lance Corporal 'Geordie' Hunter made a name for himself, at that time being only a Class B shot (between two and five years' service), by winning the Association Match against several hundred of the Army's best shots, and also picking up medals in the LMG and Whitehead Matches. Eight members of the Corps were in the Army 100 Rifle finals, and five in the Pistol XXX, four of whom finished in the top ten places. In the subsequent National Rifle Association (NRA) meeting Corporal Terry Buller and Lance Corporal Hunter were subsequently chosen as members of the Army VIII for the Inter-Services Service Rifle match at the NRA meeting, raising a few veterans' eyebrows, but they went on to collect their winners' medals. Lance Corporal Hunter had earlier made his mark at CORPSAM when he won the Rifle championship as a Craftsman, the first time in Corps history.

In 1983 all CORPSAMs were amalgamated into two main meetings, to be held at Bulford in May-June and at Ash (and sometimes also in Longmoor) in March-April. For REME the Joint CORPSAM was at Ash, making great savings in manpower and general effort by sharing administration with RE, RCT, RAOC, RAPC, ACC and – later – RAMC, while all effectively ran their own concurrent meetings. Each Corps then took it in turn to assume chairmanship of the Joint CORPSAM, such joint administration continuing until the seventh meeting in 1989. In 1990 REME had to pull out due to lack of manpower at Bordon to provide support, and was soon followed by RCT and RAOC. A solution for a joint central Skill at Arms meeting could not be found and in consequence REME ran a non-central competition in which units ran their own meetings and sent their scores – duly umpired by independent officers and warrant officers – back to the Secretary of the REME Rifle Association for collation and allocation of trophies. Not long after, echoing the Falklands nine years earlier, the incidence of the Gulf War made the plans temporarily redundant. CORPSAM was also cancelled in 1991, but in 1992 it proved possible once more to hold a Joint CORPSAM at Ash, all participating units being required to share in the provision of supporting manpower. With all major Corps competing, REME entered fifty-seven TA and forty-seven Regular competitors, the latter comprising teams and individuals from eleven REME units. On the

Inter-Corps champions: REME Full-Bore Target Rifle Team 1979

finals day Captain Jim Crichton, the Corps Rifle champion, led the REME team to victory in the inter-Corps rifle match.

Apart from sponsoring competitions in the core skills of rifle, machine gun and pistol, the REME Rifle Association maintained a central focus for target rifle and small-bore shooting. The ARA recognized the advanced marksmanship involved in target shooting, adding interest and raising standards to the Service's benefit. Competitions could be run as non-central postal events, such as the REME BAOR small-bore championship which included the particular demands of three-position shooting (prone, kneeling and supine). In these weapons there was no lack of expertise: in 1977 five members of the Corps were in the Army small-bore team. However, it was in target full-bore rifle that some particular successes were recorded. In October 1978 a proposal that target shooting should become an official Corps sport was made by Brigadier Martyn Clark, Chairman of the Rifle Association, and approved: since then target shooting has been eligible for the financial and other benefits stemming from membership of the REME Sports Association. The first central REME Target Rifle Meeting was held in June 1979 at Longmoor and Havannah Barracks, Bordon. Soon after, the REME team competed in the inter-Corps target rifle match at Bisley – a key event in each season since 1973. A most prodigious success was secured by the

Corps in winning that match against very strong opposition. REME held off RA, the favourites, by five points and broke the record of 736 by scoring 744 out of a possible 800. The full-bore target rifle team was captained by Major Philip Corp for this match, a responsibility accepted by him over the following fourteen seasons. Later, he became Chairman of the Army Target Shooting Sub-Committee for the eleven years 1983–93, after which he was expected to succeed to chairmanship of the main Target Shooting Committee.

In all weapons members of the Corps demonstrated their ability to rise to the highest levels and many were selected to represent the Army. In 1979 Captain John Woods, ASM Bill Smith and Staff Sergeant Alan Westlake were in the Army VIII which won the Inter-Services pistol match. In the NRA 1982 meeting Staff Sergeant Westlake and CSM Peter Walshaw were members of the victorious Army Pistol VIII team. Over the five years 1980–84 before he retired Westlake was Army Service pistol champion in each of the four years he was available and represented Great Britain on a number of occasions. In 1985 eight members of the Corps were in the RASAM Meeting Pistol XXX at Bisley, with Craftsman Lofthouse emerging as Army champion. Lofthouse also secured the top score for the Army in the subsequent Inter-Services pistol competition; sadly, he left the Service soon afterwards. CSM Walshaw and Sergeant Derek Brooks represented the Army on Exercise SHARP SHOOTER – the annual participation by a selected unit team and individuals in the Dominion of Canada Rifle Association Service Weapons and the Canadian Forces Skill at Arms Meetings, whilst in 1987 Captain Jim Dunn and ASM Jeff Chandler fired for the Army in the Inter-Services target rifle match. Captain Peter Hawkes, AQMS Dave Ward and CSM Walshaw represented the Army in various competitions. Hawkes and Ward were selected for the Great Britain pistol squad, by no means the first REME members to join representative teams at national level; as well as Staff Sergeant Westlake mentioned above, other instances were ASM Smith competing with the Great Britain pistol team in the World championships in Seoul, Korea in 1978, and Sergeant David Bright in the national small-bore rifle team.

Three names come to mind when considering outstanding shooting merit, which have brought considerable credit to the Corps' name: CSM Bill Meaker, AQMS Arthur Clarke and Lieutenant Colonel John Woods. CSM Meaker was not given space in the first volume of Corps history, so it should be recorded here that he acquired over 1,000 trophies, shot for England on many occasions and was reserve in the British pistol team for the 1948 Olympic Games. He won the Army Pistol Cup several times, and in 1951 won the All-England pistol championship. Amongst his achievements in 1947 he was the first Englishman to score a 'possible' with the .22 pistol, and in the following year he secured a World record also with .22 pistol in placing thirty successive shots in the bull at fifty yards; the

NRA target having been discontinued, that record stands to this day. After retiring in 1961 he remained as a civilian armourer at SEME until 1981.

AQMS Clarke's achievements were mainly secured after he left the Service. He had been an Apprentice Armourer 1937–41 and served in RAOC and REME until 1962, when he became a civilian instructor at SEME until 1968. During his Service he represented the Army in all weapons: pistol, SMG, small-bore, target and Service rifles. In later years he represented Scotland and Great Britain on numerous occasions and was variously captain and coach of the Great Britain Rifle Team 1985–94. He was a Queen's Prize finalist at Bisley sixteen times, and is believed to be the oldest ever finalist in 1992 at the age of 70. He was the first shooter to score a maximum 75 out of 75 at 1,200 yards in over 120 years of match rifle shooting at Wimbledon and Bisley.

In more recent decades Lieutenant Colonel Woods has been well known as a marksman, team captain, coach and committee member throughout the Services and in those Commonwealth countries where he represented the Army or England. His interest in shooting started while he was still in his school cadet force and, having joined as an apprentice gun fitter in 1953, he moved on to become an artificer before he was commissioned in 1973. Thus he served in all ranks from craftsman to lieutenant colonel, in many countries abroad from Germany to Hong Kong, and as far south as the Falkland Islands. In competitions his successes seemed endless: he was in the Army Service Rifle 100 six times and the Service Pistol XXX five times, Army target shooting champion for small-bore rifle three position in 1968, full-bore target rifle in 1975 and small-bore pistol in 1982. He won the National Pistol Association Service Pistol championship in 1978, became the national champion in Service Pistol at the NRA championships in 1979 and won the gold medal at the Commonwealth Shooting Federation meeting in 1981 for rapid fire pistol. In 1988 he was Adjutant to the winning British Army fifteen-man team participating in the Australian Army Bi-Centennial Skill at Arms Meeting, defeating the United States Army which was second, and the Australian Army. Retiring from the Army in 1991, as a member of the Great Britain Pistol Council he was appointed Team Manager for the next Nordic championship. Fittingly, he then took up the post of Assistant Secretary to the Army Rifle Association, to give many more years service to the sport he loved.

EPILOGUE

As noted in the Preface, this volume of the history of REME covers the Corps' second quarter-century, up to 1992. Like many an equipment project, it has taken rather more time and effort to produce than originally envisaged. This is not to cast any aspersions on those concerned, for, unlike an equipment, there is no scope for in-service modifications: it must be right first time. To essay a potted history of the intervening three to four years in as many pages would be idle (besides pre-empting Volume III), but a few headlines will serve to illustrate that change continues unabated.

- Land Command formed in April 1995, spanning the Field Army world-wide except for Northern Ireland, Cyprus and Hong Kong. Brigadier Andrew Figgures was the first one star Commander Equipment Support LAND succeeding Colonel Tony Millington who had, over the previous four years, developed the branch.
- REME officers and soldiers continue to serve on operations in Northern Ireland and Bosnia, and since 1992 have served also in Kuwait, Rwanda and Angola.
- The REME second-line reorganization is virtually complete, including the re-formation of 14 Field Workshop as a second General Support company for 6 Battalion REME and the formation of an additional Specialist battalion, 105 Battalion REME(V). Many units have occupied excellent new accommodation, notably 3 Battalion REME at Paderborn, 6 Battalion REME at Bordon, Catterick and Tidworth, and 7 Battalion REME at Wattisham.
- SEE and SAE have combined at Arborfield to form the School of Electronic and Aeronautical Engineering. Princess Marina College now provides an eight-month foundation course, followed by technical education and equipment training in the adult trade schools. A combined Army Apprentices College providing foundation training for tradesmen in RE, R SIGNALS, RLC and REME is to form in Rowcroft Barracks, Arborfield, starting in 1996.
- Closure of ABRO Old Dalby and ABRO Ashford by the end of 1996 will leave two strategic base workshops and five district workshops. Market-testing may further reduce the latter.
- The six equipment branches and technical authorities were formed into the Army Technical Support Agency in October 1995. The principal, Land System, elements are expected to co-locate at Chertsey in 1998. A strong uniformed REME presence will be retained.

- Army aircraft equipment support management became part of the Defence Helicopter Support Authority in April 1994, under Royal Navy control. Brigadier Rob Jones was the first tri-Service Director.
- Andover equipment support management directorates have assumed responsibility for post-design services, modifications and spares funding. The two spares provisioning and procurement divisions co-located at Telford in early 1996 and reorganized to align with Equipment Support Managers.
- In 1994 the Corps celebrated the 25th anniversary of His Royal Highness The Prince Philip becoming our Colonel in Chief.
- The REME Association celebrated its Golden Jubilee in 1995.

The relative certainties of four decades of the Cold War, focused largely on the North German Plain, are long gone. A capability-based Army, smaller in number than at any time in living memory and ever more dependent on its equipment, is faced with a wide spectrum of potential defence roles and tasks. In parallel, a plethora of government initiatives seeks to achieve more with less, through greater delegation of financial and other forms of authority, rationalization, competition and wider involvement of the private sector – as illustrated above. Such circumstances place a premium on the lively mind, the developed intellect: on the ability to think from first principles rather than cling to rule of thumb; the willingness to adopt or adapt ideas or best practice from other fields; the ability and determination to translate theory into practical achievement; the commitment to do things *better*, be it in terms of quality, time or cost – in short, on those attributes that have long been the hallmark of the true professional engineer.

Some concern has recently been expressed that the identity of REME as a corps is in danger of being weakened within the rather amorphous Equipment Support Organization. There is good reason to believe that such fears are unfounded, albeit they sound a timely note of caution. In the Epilogue to Volume 1 – well worth re-reading – Major General Peter Girling introduced the concept of equipment engineering, and said:

'The evolution of the engineering support system has been natural – the forces have been pragmatic not dogmatic.'

This has on the whole been true also of the many changes from 1969 to 1995, although the dividing line has arguably become finest most recently. Throughout these changes there has been constancy of purpose; their effect has been progressively to increase authority to match the responsibility for ***keeping fit equipment in the hands of troops***. Provided this authority is exercised wisely, the Corps should be more the master of its own destiny, not less. Moreover, Equipment Support is predominantly a staff function; the first- and second-line units within the Field Army, which now embrace 90% of the Corps' manpower, remain unequivocally REME.

And yet, within the multi-disciplinary ethos of Equipment Support, is there a risk that the influence of engineering will be diluted? A risk perhaps, and one that must be guarded against. But the very word 'risk' is one that has lately assumed a new prominence within the engineering profession. Public tolerance of accidents has reduced while legislation and litigation have increased: hence greater emphasis on safety and risk management accompanied by professional accountability. Removal of Crown immunity means that members of the Corps may be held legally liable for their decisions within the Equipment Support Organization. Still less must equipment engineering be allowed to merge into the pot-pourri of 'logistics', notwithstanding our cordial relationship with our sister corps; for to do so would be to forget the hard-learnt lessons which led to REME's formation.

The Epilogue to Volume 1 ended with the following words; they remain (subject to the inclusion of the female sex) as true as when they were written:

'*In this changing world, the Corps may look forward to the future with confidence if it goes on as it has started – engineering professionalism, a lively and flexible approach to new problems, a willingness to change methods, a continued belief in the importance of a thorough clinical knowledge of equipment, a spirit which allows every soldier to go as far as his abilities and ambitions will let him, unhindered by artificial barriers, and, above all, keeping an eye on the ball – the fitness for operations of the Army's equipment.*'

We in REME can cherish the double distinction of belonging to two old and honourable professions: the profession of arms and the engineering profession. This is encapsulated in our motto – ***Arte et Marte***. Our strength and our future lie in continuing to make a unique contribution to both.

Major General P J G Corp CB
Director General of Equipment Support (Army)

APPENDIX

COLONEL IN CHIEF AND COLONELS COMMANDANT, DIRECTORS OF THE CORPS AND OTHER GENERAL OFFICERS 1969–1996

Colonel in Chief

1969– Field Marshal His Royal Highness The Prince Philip, Duke of Edinburgh, KG KT OM GBE AC QSO

Colonels Commandant (from 1966)

1966–1976 Field Marshal The Lord Carver GCB CBE DSO MC
1967–1972 Major General Sir Leonard Atkinson KBE
1968–1973 Major General M F Scott JP
1968–1973 Major General R F Shields OBE
1969–1974 Major General A McGill CB CBE
1972–1977 Major General P H Girling CB OBE
1973–1978 Major General P G Palmer MBE
1973–1978 Major General G V Hayward
1974–1980 Major General A M McKay CB
1976–1981 General Sir Hugh Beach GBE KCB MC
1977–1982 Major General V Metcalfe
1978–1983 Major General H Macdonald-Smith CB
1978–1984 Major General D B Wood CB
1980–1986 Major General S K Lecky CB OBE
1981–1987 General Sir Richard Vincent GBE KCB DSO
1982–1988 Major General J V Homan CB
1983–1989 Major General P H Lee CB MBE
1986–1991 Major General T B Palmer CB
1987–1992 Lieutenant General Sir Jeremy Blacker KCB CBE
1988–1993 Major General J Boyne CB MBE
1989–1994 Major General C Tyler CB
1991–1995 Major General D Shaw CB CBE
1991–1996 Major General G M Hutchinson CB
1992– Lieutenant General Sir Rupert Smith KCB DSO ■ OBE QGM
1993– Major General J F J Johnston CB CBE
1994– Major General M S Heath CB CBE
1996– Major General P J G Corp CB
1996– Major General A G Sharman

Directors and Directors General of the Corps

1969–1972	Major General P H Girling CB OBE
1972–1975	Major General A M McKay CB
1975–1977	Major General H Macdonald–Smith CB
1978–1979	Major General J V Homan CB
1979–1983	Major General P H Lee CB MBE
1983–1985	Major General T B Palmer CB
1985–1988	Major General J Boyne CB MBE
1988–1991	Major General D Shaw CB CBE
1991–1993	Major General M S Heath CB CBE
1993–	Major General P J G Corp CB

Major Generals, other than Directors

1968–1971	Major General P G Palmer MBE Commandant Technical Group REME
1971–1973	Major General G V Hayward Commandant Technical Group REME
1973–1976	Major General V Metcalfe Commandant Technical Group REME 1973–74 Commander REME Support Group 1974–76
1975–1978	Major General D B Wood CB Director of Army Quartering
1975–1980	Major General S K Lecky CB OBE Director Military Assistance Office 1975–77 Minister(Defence Supply) British Embassy Teheran 1977–80
1976–1979	Major General D W R Walker Commander REME Support Group 1976–77 Director of Equipment Engineering 1977–79
1987–1989	Major General C Tyler CB Deputy Chief of Staff and Senior British Officer Headquarters Allied Forces Northern Europe
1988–1990	Major General G M Hutchinson CB Vice Master General of the Ordnance
1990–1993	Major General J F J Johnston CB CBE Director General Army Manning and Recruiting
1995–	Major General A G Sharman Director General Land Systems

GLOSSARY

AN EXPLANATION OF SOME OF THE TERMS AND ABBREVIATIONS USED IN THIS BOOK

A1 Echelon	See Echelon.
A2 Echelon	See Echelon.
A Vehicle	A tracked or wheeled armoured combat land vehicle usually designed for offensive purposes or a specialist vehicle derived from these basic designs.
AAC	Army Air Corps.
ABRO	Army Base Repair Organization. A Defence Agency launched in April 1993.
AC	Companion of the Order of Australia.
ACC	Air Control Centre or Army Catering Corps.
ACE	Allied Command Europe – the command including all NATO forces in Europe.
ACF	Assistant Chaplain to the Forces, or Army Cadet Force.
ACOS	Assistant Chief of Staff.
ACU	Air Conditioning Unit.
ADEME	Assistant Director of Electrical and Mechanical Engineering – a staff post held by a colonel or lieutenant colonel.
ADEME(V)	Assistant Director of Electrical and Mechanical Engineering (Volunteers) – a staff post held by a lieutenant colonel in the Reserve Army.
ADG	Armoured Delivery Group formed during Op GRANBY in the Gulf 1990–91 to hold reserves of crews and armoured vehicles.
ADP	Automatic Data Processing using computer systems.
AER	Army Emergency Reserve.
AESP	Army Equipment Support Publication. Replaced Electrical and Mechanical Engineering Regulations (EMERs) in 1978.
AETW	Aircraft Engineering Training Wing based at Middle Wallop. It was renamed The School of Aeronautical Engineering on 1 January 1988.
AFG1098	A table listing all the equipment required by a deployable (field force) unit. Now referred to as an Equipment Table.
AFG1198	A table listing all the equipment required by a non-deployable (static) unit.
AFV	Armoured Fighting Vehicle such as a tank or armoured personnel carrier.
AGC	Adjutant General's Corps. Formed in 1992 from RAPC, WRAC, RAOC Staff Clerks, RMP, MPSC, RAEC and ALC. In 1993 Regimental Clerks from all Arms and Services joined the Corps.

AIEFSO	Accident Investigation and Engineering Flight Safety Officer. An appointment held by a REME aircraft engineer. (previously AIFSO).
AMF(L)	Allied Command Europe Mobile Force (Land). A lightly equipped, multi-national NATO force capable of deployment mainly to its Northern and Southern flanks.
AMG	Aircraft Maintenance Group. Part of an aircraft workshop which replaced the Mobile Servicing and Repair Detachments in the late Seventies.
ANZUK	Australia, New Zealand and UK.
AOP	Air Observation Post used for directing artillery fire.
APC	Armoured Personnel Carrier used by infantry and others.
APSC	Army Personnel Selection Centre.
AQMS	Artificer Quartermaster Sergeant, an artificer in the rank of Warrant Officer Class 2; or Artisan Quartermaster Sergeant (for non-artificer stream trades).
Army Entrants	Young soldier candidates for commissioning as officers.
ARP	Army Restructuring Plan, 1974–75. One of many economy plans.
ARRC	ACE Rapid Reaction Corps, first formed in 1993. A multi-national formation.
ARROW	Automatic data processing assistance to RAOC and REME Operations in Workshops.
ARRV	Armoured Repair and Recovery Vehicle eg CHIEFTAIN ARRV (RECLAIMER), and CHALLENGER ARRV (RHINO); Armoured Recovery Vehicles with crane to lift AFV power packs.
Artificer	The most highly skilled category of tradesman; ranked from Staff Sergeant to Warrant Officer Class 1.
ARU	Army Rugby Union; or Annual Report on a Unit, a formal inspection by the chain of command on a unit to check its fitness for operations and peacetime administrative procedures.
ARV	Armoured Recovery Vehicle used by REME to recover AFVs.
ASCA	Army Scaling and Cataloguing Authority. See Scales.
ASM	Artificer Sergeant Major, an artificer in the rank of Warrant Officer Class 1; or Artisan Sergeant Major (for non-artificer stream trades).
ASV	Armoured Staff Vehicle; an armoured office AFV or truck.
AT	Apprentice Tradesman at Princess Marina College or Army Apprentices Colleges Carlisle, Chepstow or Harrogate.
ATE	Automatic Test Equipment used with electronic equipment.
ATGW	Anti-Tank Guided Weapon.
ATP	Application Test Package for electronic test equipment.
ATS	Auxiliary Territorial Service, formed for women in 1938. It became the WRAC in 1949.
Avionics	Aviation electronics and instruments in Army aircraft.
AVRE	Assault Vehicle Royal Engineers.
AWD	Advanced Workshop Detachment of a second-line workshop, or All Wheel Drive.
B Echelon	See Echelon.
B Vehicle	A tracked or wheeled land vehicle, self-propelled or towed, which is not primarily designed for offensive purposes but which may in some cases be armoured for defensive purposes.

BAC	British Aircraft Corporation; the forerunner of British Aerospace.
BAOR	British Army of the Rhine. HQ at Rheindahlen near Moenchengladbach.
BARV	Beach Armoured Recovery Vehicle. The Royal Marines took over the BARVs at Instow after Fording Trials Branch closed in December 1978.
BATES	Battlefield Artillery Target Engagement System.
BATUS	British Army Training Unit Suffield; in Canada.
BCR	Battle Casualty Replacement.
Bde	Brigade. A formation commanded by a brigadier.
BDR	Battle Damage Repair; emergency repair to keep equipment in action in the field.
Beach	A review of the selection and training of RCT, RAOC and REME officers made by Lieutenant General Sir Hugh Beach (late RE) in 1976–77.
Below the line	The income and expenditure which was not accounted for in the original budget. Also used to describe units under DGES(A)'s direct control but not part of his Headquarters' staff.
BEM	British Empire Medal.
BEME	Brigade Electrical and Mechanical Engineer. Major or captain.
BER	Beyond Economic Repair. A repair decision meaning that repair is possible but not economic; equipment is then scrapped or cannibalized.
Berm	Sand barrier for defence as used in Gulf. Literally, an edge, the space between a ditch and a parapet in fortifications.
BERR	Battlefield Equipment Reliability Return. A computer-based system.
BFHK	British Forces Hong Kong.
BFME	British Forces Middle East.
BGN	British Gurkhas Nepal.
BITE	Built-in Test Equipment.
Black Box	A discrete assembly containing electronic or electro-optical equipment, eg a Line Replaceable Unit or a Centrally Repairable Module. It is not necessarily black nor a box.
BLB	Basic Level Budget. See also IHLB, HLB and TLB.
BLOWPIPE	A shoulder-launched surface-to-air missile system.
BLR	Beyond Local Repair. A repair decision implying the intention to side-load or back-load for repair.
BLT	British Liaison Team, for example in Kuwait.
BMA	Base Maintenance Area from which logistic support (eg ammunition, petrol, oils and lubricants, spares, and rations) is provided for forward troops.
BMATT	British Military Advisory and Training Team. Deployed to such countries as Zimbabwe.
BMH	British Military Hospital.
BMM	British Military Mission, eg to the Saudi Arabian National Guard.
BMP	Russian-made tracked APC used by Iraqis in Gulf 1991.
BOWMAN	Project BOWMAN provides the successor to the CLANSMAN radio system.
BQMS	Battery Quarter Master Sergeant in the Royal Artillery in the rank of Staff Sergeant.

BR	Beyond Repair. A repair decision meaning for scrap or cannibalization. Also a military abbreviation for British.
BRDM	A 4-wheeled amphibious reconnaissance vehicle of Soviet origin with a 5-man crew. Several variants were produced.
BSM	Battery Sergeant Major in the Royal Artillery in the rank of Warrant Officer Class 2.
BTEC	Business and Technician Education Council, formerly the Technician Education Council (TEC).
BV202	An articulated tracked vehicle manufactured by Volvo. Used by British Forces in Norway and in the Falkland Islands bogs and mud in 1982. REME used the vehicle with a winch for recovery.
BV206	The Hägglund and Söner BV206 is an articulated tracked vehicle designed to transport personnel and material across snow-covered country and uncleared snow-covered roads. It was developed from the BV 202, entering the British Army on trial in 1981.
C Vehicle	A wheeled or tracked item of earth-moving equipment either self-propelled or towed; all self-mobile, self-steering, purpose-made cranes; cable-laying ploughs; all industrial and agricultural tractors and rough-terrain fork-lift tractors, excluding ware house tractors.
CADWS	Close Air Defence Weapon System.
CAE	The Chief Aircraft Engineer; a colonel (late REME).
CAESAR	Central Army Equipment Support data Analysis and Retrieval system.
CAM	Chemical Agent Monitor.
Cannibalize	To remove serviceable parts from a repairable item of equipment in order to install them on another item of equipment.
CAPSS	Computer Assistance to the Production and Stores System.
CAPTURE	Containerized Automotive Power Train Repair Equipment for repair of power packs in the field.
CA Release	Issue of a Certificate of Airworthiness that certifies an aircraft as fit to fly.
CASE	Commissioning and Support of Equipment Study in 1984 sponsored by MGO and QMG.
CB	Companion of the Order of the Bath, Counter Battery or Container Body.
CBE	Commander of the Order of the British Empire.
CCREME	Corps Commander REME. Interim title at start of the Eighties in place of DDEME 1(BR) Corps, a brigadier, prior to becoming Commander Maintenance; later Commander Equipment Support in 1992. HQ 1(BR) Corps was at Bielefeld.
CCT	REME Central Charitable Trust.
CEME	Chief Electrical and Mechanical Engineer of UKLF. The appointment was preceded by DDEME STRATCO and was held by four brigadiers between 1 April 1972 and 1 January 1982 when it became ACOS G4 Maint in HQ UKLF.
CENTREM	A Centrally Repairable Module sent back to Base or a contractor.
CENTURION	The main battle tank before CHIEFTAIN. Used in the war in Korea and in BAOR in the Fifties and Sixties. Variants still in service in the Nineties.

CES	Complete Equipment Schedule, eg accessories and tools for a vehicle.
CET	Control Equipment Technician, or Combat Engineer Tractor.
CGLI	City and Guilds of London Institute: part of Imperial College of Science and Technology, London University.
CHALLENGER	Main Battle Tank which replaced CHIEFTAIN. Used in BAOR and Gulf 1990–91.
CHARRV	Chieftain Armoured Repair and Recovery Vehicle (RECLAIMER). See ARRV.
CHIEFTAIN	Main Battle Tank which replaced CENTURION, used throughout the Seventies and Eighties. Replaced by CHALLENGER.
CHINOOK	Royal Air Force heavy-lift battlefield-support helicopters with twin contra-rotating rotors.
Chown	A study of artificer selection, training and employment led by Colonel RH Chown (late REME) in 1976.
CI	Order of the Crown of India.
CIAT	Communications Installation Advisory Team. Originally the CLANSMAN IAT. A R SIGNALS, RAOC and REME team in BAOR which installed CLANSMAN radios and PTARMIGAN area communications equipment in All Arms vehicles.
CinC	Commander in Chief, eg General Officer Commanding BAOR or UKLF.
CINCENT	Commander in Chief Allied Forces Central Europe; a NATO command.
CINCNORTH	Commander in Chief Allied Forces Northern Europe; a NATO command.
CINCSOUTH	Commander in Chief Allied Forces Southern Europe; a NATO command.
CIS	Command, Control, Communications and Information System.
CL	Commercial, as opposed to military designed vehicles.
CLAMOR	Commonwealth Liaison and Monitoring Organization in Rhodesia 1979–80.
CLANSMAN	Army combat net radio system used in the field by all arms and services. Replaced LARKSPUR in the late Seventies.
CMT	Close Monitoring Team in trials of new equipment, collecting reliability data for the Project Manager.
CODERM	Committee for Defence Reliability and Maintainability.
COFFER	Computerized Office for Field Force Enquiries and Records. An RAOC system.
Comd ES	Commander Equipment Support. The senior REME officer at the HQ of a division or similar level, in the rank of colonel or lieutenant colonel.
Comd Maint	Previous title for Comd ES. (See CREME).
Contingency Plans	Plans made for a possible emergency or operation.
CORPORAL	A surface-to-surface guided missile made in the USA and issued to the RA in BAOR in the late Fifties and early Sixties.
CORPORATE	Operation to recapture the Falkland Islands in 1982.

Corps	An operational formation of divisions and supporting arms and services commanded by a lieutenant general; or a body such as the Corps of Royal Electrical and Mechanical Engineers.
COSLOG	Chief of Staff Logistics at LE(A) Andover.
CPU	Corporate Planning Unit; the QMG's corporate planning staff.
Craftsman	A REME soldier's rank before promotion to NCO. 'The Craftsman' is the REME monthly magazine.
CRARRV	CHALLENGER Armoured Repair and Recovery Vehicle (RHINO). See ARRV.
CREME	Commander REME. The senior REME officer at the HQ of a division or similar level, in the rank of colonel or lieutenant colonel. The title was changed in the early Eighties to Commander Maintenance and then to Commander Equipment Support in 1992.
CSDE	Central Servicing Development Establishment, Royal Air Force, at Swanton Morley, Norfolk.
CSM	Company Sergeant Major, in the rank of Warrant Officer Class 2.
CSRV	Combined Sight Repair Vehicle.
CTAD	Commander Training and Arms Directors UKLF. He later became Inspector General Doctrine and Training in 1991. A central focus for all Army training except collective training.
CVHQ	Central Volunteer Headquarters. CVHQ REME (later HQ REME TA) is at Bordon, Hants.
CVR(T) or (W)	Combat Vehicle Reconnaissance (Tracked) or (Wheeled).
CYMBELINE	A mortar-locating radar operated by the RA.
DACOS	Deputy Assistant Chief of Staff. DACOS G4 Maint was the Senior REME appointment (Colonel) at HQ UKLF from 1982 when EME Branch became a logistic staff branch with the title of G4 Maint. His title changed twice, firstly to Commander Maintenance and then in 1992 to Commander Equipment Support.
DAMA	Director of Army Management Audit (replaced in 1992 by Director of Manpower Audit (DMA)).
DAR	Director of Army Recruiting.
DDEME	Deputy Director EME. A colonel or brigadier at Corps HQ or Command HQ before the title changed to Commander Maintenance, or a brigadier on DEME(A) staff before 1977.
DEE	A Director of Equipment Engineering in HQ DGEME LE(A).
DEME(A)	Director of Electrical and Mechanical Engineering (Army) until 1977. The appointment became Director General of Electrical and Mechanical Engineering in April 1977, and Director General of Equipment Support (Army) in April 1992. Major general rank and head of REME.
DESERT SABRE	The 1st (British) Armoured Division part of DESERT SWORD.
DESERT SHIELD	The early operation to defend Saudi Arabia during the Gulf War 1990–91. Op GRANBY was code name for the British operation.
DESERT STORM	The offensive operation to liberate Kuwait during the Gulf War.
DESERT SWORD	The ground force part of DESERT STORM.

DFS	Daily Flight Servicing before first flight of the day.
DGEME	Director General of Electrical and Mechanical Engineering. See DEME(A). Major general rank and head of REME.
DGES(A)	Director General of Equipment Support (Army). See DEME(A) and ESO. Major general rank and head of REME.
DGLP(A)	Director General of Logistic Policy (Army). A major general on QMG's staff. Later Chief of Staff at HQ QMG.
DIANA(DTDF)	Digital and Analogue (Digital Test and Diagnostic Facility) automatic test equipment mounted in an electronic-repair vehicle.
Div	Division. A formation made up of brigades and supporting arms and services, commanded by a major general.
Divisional Slice	Resources required to maintain one division, eg a division's 'share' of Corps or Army support.
DL	Deputy Lieutenant. One of a number of deputies, within a county, of a Lord Lieutenant.
DMA	Director of Manpower Audit. See DAMA.
DMAO	Director Military Assistance Office, a major general's appointment.
D of E Man	Director of Equipment Management on the staff of DQMG. Terminated April 1977 upon the formation of LE(A).
Downtime	Time out of action, non-effective or non-productive time.
DPC	DGEME's Policy Committee. Formed in 1988 to be the principal committee for the consideration of all policy matters within the Corps (i.e. military and technical matters as opposed to those domestic regimental matters in the province of the Corps Committee). It was superseded in April 1991 by DGEME's Senior Management Board, adding financial management matters within DGEME's Higher Level Budget.
Drawdown	Reduction of Army strength in Nineties under 'Options for Change'.
DROPS	Demountable Rack Off-loading and Pick-up System; a logistic load-carrying system mounted on trucks.
DS	Directing Staff of a school or a training exercise.
DSC	Distinguished Service Cross.
DSO	Distinguished Service Order.
DSP(A)	Director of Support Planning (Army). A brigadier responsible for initial support planning for all new Army equipment projects, on QMG's staff. Post dis-established and responsibility transferred to DGES(A)'s staff in 1992.
DUS(Army)	The Deputy Under-Secretary of State in the Ministry of Defence Army Department; Secretary to the Army Board. The post remained until 1984.
E Vehicle	A truck-mounted or trailer-mounted equipment or a static generator whose registered number must be recorded for legal or management purposes.
EAGER BEAVER	A rough-terrain fork-lift truck.
ECAB	Executive Committee of the Army Board. Deals with top policy.

Echelon — Echelons are sub-divisions formed on operations within a battle group:
- F Echelon – the headquarters, together with the fighting elements of the squadron and company groups, their fighting equipment, ambulances and fitter sections.
- A1 Echelon – those elements required for immediate support and replenishment of F Echelon, eg combat supplies, regimental aid post and some REME equipment support resources.
- A2 Echelon – the remaining administrative troops and equipments required to stay close at hand to the battle area, eg vehicles, technical stores, remainder of the LAD, which are normally grouped towards the rear of the brigade area.
- B Echelon – unit non-urgent administrative resources, normally placed well to the rear of the divisional area.

ECP — Equipment Collecting Point for equipment casualties awaiting back-loading or repair.

EFD — Early Failure Detection. Used by aircraft engineers mostly to prevent failure in service. Includes magnetic chip collection, analysis of filter debris and vibration records analysis.

EHM — Equipment Health Monitoring. Used by aircraft engineers and others to prevent failure in service.

EKA — Commercial recovery systems designed in Sweden and used on the Scammell and Foden recovery vehicles.

E&MAs — Engines and Major Assemblies such as gearboxes, final drives and steering boxes.

EMA — Ease of Maintenance Assessment by MAG during development of new equipment.

EME — Electrical and Mechanical Engineering or Engineer (a REME officer).

EMERs — Electrical & Mechanical Engineering Regulations. They included a mass of technical information. Replaced by Army Equipment Support Publications in 1978.

EMPS — Equipment Management Policy Statement issued by the General Staff for major Army equipments giving target availability required and repair policy.

EM(T) — Efficiency Medal (Territorial), awarded to TA soldiers. It does not entitle the holder to any post-nominal letters.

Engineering Branches — EME 6, EME 7, EME 8, EME 9 and EME 10 in HQ DGEME, and subsequently ES 21–52 in DGES(A)'s staff.

EOD — Explosive Ordnance Disposal. In the Army undertaken by RE and RAOC experts. Applies also to IEDs q.v.

EOM — Ease of Maintenance.

Equipment Branches — Aircraft Branch, Electronics Branch, Maritime Branch, Vehicles and Weapons Branch (and their predecessors Radar Branch, Telecommunications Branch, Fording Trials Branch and Fleet Repair Branch.)

Equipment Management — The process of controlling the allocation, repair policy, refurbishment, redesign and replacement of, and re-supply of material for an equipment throughout its service life. Later Equipment Support Management.

ERB	Executive Responsibility Budget covering all costs, both cash and non-cash, of the budget holder, typically a Commanding Officer.
ERD	Emergency Reserve Decoration. An efficiency medal awarded to AER officers.
ERV	Electronic Repair Vehicle for workshops and light aid detachments.
ES	Equipment Support; the staff and support function provided by the ESO q.v.
ESO	Equipment Support Organization. A term used to describe all those involved in the function of equipment support management of all the Army's weapons, vehicles, aircraft, vessels and technical equipments from MOD down to brigade level. DGEME became DGES(A) and functional or professional head of the ESO set up under the Logistic Support Review reorganization 1992.
ESPO	Engineering Support Planning Officer. A military staff officer or civilian concerned with the introduction of new equipment into service.
F Echelon	See Echelon.
FAACO	First Aid Aircraft Outfit providing for unit-level repairs.
FACE	Field Artillery Computing Equipment.
FAIR VALUE	A study into cuts in the QMG's department of civilian manpower in the mid-Seventies after the Defence Review of 1974.
FAMTO	First Aid Mechanical Transport Outfit. Spares held by a unit for their own transport repairs.
FANY	First Aid Nursing Yeomanry: a women's volunteer organization.
FARELF	Far East Land Forces: for example, those in Singapore, Malaya and Hong Kong.
Fast Repair Loops	A specially organized procedure for a quick turn-round in the repair of priority items.
FEMIS	First-line Equipment Management Information System.
FERRET	A light-armoured wheeled scout car used for liaison and reconnaissance.
FFMA	A Forward Force Maintenance Area for logistic support in Op GRANBY in the Gulf 1991.
FIE	Fuel Injection Equipment for diesel engines.
FILOG	The short title for the Logistic Battalion in the Falkland Islands.
Finniston	'Engineering our Future – Report of Committee of Inquiry into the Engineering Profession'. Led by Sir Montague Finniston in 1980.
First Line	The first line of repair available to the Field Force, eg Light Aid Detachment which provides immediate equipment engineering support to one or more units or a HQ. Usually integrated within the supported unit.
FLOS	First Line Operating System. A proposed ADP system.
FMA	Forward Maintenance Area, or Force Maintenance Area, as used in Op GRANBY in the Gulf 1991.
FMI	The Government's Financial Management Initiative in 1982 which required greater emphasis on value for money in the public sector.
FMIS	Financial Management Information System to monitor progress for the QMG's Corporate Plan.

FOB	Forward Operational Base.
FORWARD	Feedback of Repair Workshop and Reliability Data. An ADP system using the Data Centre at Woolwich; initiated in the Sixties, it produced its first output in 1967.
FOX	A light-armoured car also known as CVR(W), equipped with a 30mm RARDEN cannon.
FPU	Functional Planning Unit in HQ DGEME and from 1992 on the staff of DGES(A).
FRB	Fleet Repair Branch; it became Maritime Branch REME in 1977.
FRG	Forward REME Group. Responsible for forward repair and recovery in support of armoured and mechanized forces. Formed from a second-line workshop.
Frodsham	'The Provision of Engineering Officers in the Armed Forces'. Led by A F Frodsham, lately Director General Engineering Employers Federation, in 1983.
FRT	Forward Repair Team. A section of an FRG which replaces a power pack or does other repairs to vehicles and equipment in a forward area.
FRTV	Forward Repair and Test Vehicle.
FSA	Field Standard A: an improved RAPIER missile system incorporating tracker radar giving improved capability in poor weather and at night.
FSB	Field Standard B. B1 was a further improved RAPIER system to cut down the false alarm rate and give better performance. B2 was a redesigned system giving further enhanced performance, incorporating built-in test equipment (BITE).
FV430	A family of tracked vehicles; FV432 replaced the SARACEN wheeled APC. FV434 was the REME 'fitter's vehicle'.
FV600	A family of 6-wheeled reconnaissance vehicles; included Armoured Personnel Carriers (SARACEN) and armoured cars (SALADIN).
FVRDE	Fighting Vehicles Research and Development Establishment at Chertsey, Surrey; from 1970–84 known as Military Vehicles Engineering Establishment (MVEE), then Royal Armament Research and Development Establishment (Chertsey) until 1991 when it became part of the Defence Research Agency.
G1	NATO standard designation for personnel staff.
G2	NATO standard designation for intelligence and security staff.
G3	NATO standard designation for operations and training staff. Sometimes also used as an oral abbreviation of GSO3 (a captain) on the General Staff.
G4	NATO standard designation for logistics and quartering staff.
G5	NATO standard designation for civil/military co-operation staff.
GAZELLE	Helicopter used by the Army for liaison and reconnaissance.
GBE	Knight Grand Cross or Dame Grand Cross of the Order of the British Empire.
GCB	Knight Grand Cross or Dame Grand Cross of the Order of the Bath.
GCVO	Knight Grand Cross or Dame Grand Cross of the Royal Victorian Order.
GOA	Ground Observation Aid sight or Gazelle Observation Aid.

GOC	General Officer Commanding, eg District or Divisional Commander.
GPATE	General Purpose Automatic Test Equipment for electronic equipment testing.
GPMG	General Purpose Machine Gun; 7.62mm belt-fed.
GPS	Global Positioning System. A satellite-based navigation device.
GPTE	General Purpose Test Equipment for testing electronic equipment.
GPTIRF	General Purpose Thermal Imaging Repair Facility for repair of thermal imagers.
GRANBY	The British operation in the Gulf in 1990–91 as part of the American DESERT SHIELD, DESERT STORM and DESERT SWORD. GRANBY 1 was concerned with the deployment of 7 Armd Bde from BAOR and other troops up to November 1990. GRANBY 1.5 was concerned with the deployment of HQ 1(BR) Armd Div, 4 Armd Bde and other troops, raising the number of British ground troops in the Gulf from 16,000 in Nov 90 to more than 33,000 at their peak, including more than 3,800 REME.
GRAPPLE	Operation GRAPPLE: the provision of cover by the United Nations Protection Force (UNPROFOR) for the delivery of humanitarian aid in Bosnia-Hercegovina. The UK contribution was supplied in November 1992 by 1 CHESHIRE with REME support, and subsequently by units on roulement. It was also the name for the testing of British nuclear weapons at Christmas Island in 1957.
'Greenie'	Originally a nickname for Royal Navy Electrical Branch specialists who wore green material between their rank rings, carried into the Army by Fleet Air Arm personnel who transferred in 1958. Applied to REME Aircraft Technicians (Electrical, Instruments and Radio), retitled in 1972 as Avionic Technicians.
GS	General Service as applied to equipment in common Army use.
GSE	Ground Support Equipment used for support of Army aircraft. Much of it was supplied by the RAF.
GSGE	Generating Set Gasoline Engine, an electrical generator used to power towed RAPIER FS B1. Phased out of service to be replaced by diesel GSDE.
GSR	General Staff Requirement. A staff statement in broad terms of the function, main features and performance required of a proposed equipment.
GST	General Staff Target. A staff statement in broad terms where the feasibility of a proposed equipment has still to be verified.
HANWOOD	UN operation in the former Yugoslavia, setting up UN protected areas up to September 1993. The British contribution was a Field Ambulance unit deployed to Croatia, with support.
HAT	Harbour Acceptance Trial.
HAVEN	Operation HAVEN, a humanitarian operation to protect the Kurds in Northern Iraq and South-Eastern Turkey following the Gulf War in 1991.
HGV	Heavy Goods Vehicle.
HLB	Higher Level Budget, eg that held by IGDT, or DGES(A).

HMIS	Higher Management and Information System. A proposed ADP system.
HNC	Higher National Certificate.
Hotwork	Repairs such as welding and brazing of fuel tanks requiring special cleaning techniques to remove risk of explosion from residual gases.
HPPA	High Pressure Pure Air system, needed for many thermal imaging systems
HPTO	Higher Professional and Technical Officer. A civil service engineer, senior to a PTO, in the Defence Engineering Service, which was to amalgamate with the Defence Science Group in 1993 to become the Defence Engineering and Science Group.
HVM	High Velocity Missile; a Close Air Defence Weapon System.
ICL	International Computers Limited – a computer manufacturer.
IDR	In-Depth Repair, a thorough overhaul applied to B Vehicles which are not subject to base repair.
IED	Improvised Explosive Device, usually referring to terrorist-made bombs, grenades or mortar rounds.
IFCS	Improved Fire Control System for CHIEFTAIN and CHALLENGER tanks.
IFTU	Intensive Flying Trials Unit which trials a new aircraft coming into service.
IGDT	Inspector General Doctrine and Training. Formerly Commander Training and Arms Directors (CTAD) until April 1991.
IHLB	Intermediate Higher Level Budget, the level between a Basic Level Budget (BLB) and an HLB q.v.
ILS	Integrated Logistic Support. A methodology for ensuring that whole-life cycle equipment support requirements and costs are addressed during procurement. Began to be introduced for Army equipment in 1989–90.
INLA	Irish National Liberation Army.
IRA	Irish Republican Army. See also PIRA
ISD	In Service Date. The date by which a new vehicle, weapon or other equipment is due into service.
ISO	International Shipping Organization, as applied to ISO containers used in freight transportation. Also International Organization for Standardization (sic), based in Belgium.
IT	Information Technology; all systems for communicating and processing information usually based on computers.
J4	NATO standard designation for Joint Service logistics and quartering staff. The letter J may also be applied similarly to other staffs (see G1–G5).
JHQ	Joint Headquarters (could be permanently established as at Rheindahlen BAOR or temporarily to command a specific operation as at Northwood, Wilton and High Wycombe).
Job Evaluation	A method of analysing jobs to establish their relative worth for pay.
JSRMAT	Joint Services Reliability and Maintainability Advisory Team located at Stevenage, responsible for the RAPIER Missile system.
JSTU	Joint Services Trials Unit.

KBE	Knight Commander of the Order of the British Empire.
KCB	Knight Commander of the Order of the Bath.
KLT	Kuwait Liaison Team.
LAD	Light Aid Detachment REME. A first-line workshop attached to a regiment or battalion.
LAH	Light Attack Helicopter.
LANCE	A US nuclear missile system used by the British Army.
LARKSPUR	Army combat net radio system used in the field before CLANSMAN.
LBH	Light Battlefield Helicopter such as the LYNX Mark 9 which is not armed.
LCU	Landing Craft Utility to carry up to 140 men or two main battle tanks.
LE(A)	Logistic Executive (Army) at Andover, formed April 1977.
LEAN LOOK	Cuts in civilian manpower in the static workshops and elsewhere, implemented Army-wide in the mid-Seventies.
LEME	Land Electrical and Mechanical Engineers (Canada). Formerly RCEME, they became LORE (Land Ordnance Engineers) in the Sixties and LEME in the Eighties.
LHS	Load Handling System.
Log Sp	Logistic Support. Staff and support function involving supply and distribution, catering, pioneers and postal and courier services. Since 1993 the responsibility of RLC.
LRU	Line Replaceable Unit, eg a 'black box' (q.v.) or part of an equipment that must be removed for repair.
LSA	Logistic Support Analysis, part of the ILS assessment of a new equipment
LSF	Logistic Support Force. A grouping of logistic units to provide third-line support to UKMF (q.v.) from 1969–74. Principally comprised of TA units, REME resources were controlled by CREME (Force Troops), a lieutenant colonel REME (V). See also LSG.
LSG	Logistic Support Group. A grouping of logistic units to provide third-line support to a brigade group deployed on overseas contingency operations, from 1969–92. Subsidiary to LSF, the LSG task passed from UKMF to 6 Field Force at Aldershot in 1975, and subsequently to 1 Infantry Brigade, Tidworth in 1981, continuing until the LSG was superseded by the formation of the Combat Service Support Group (UK) in 1992. CSSG (UK) provides third-line support to the rear of a division, DSG (Divisional Support Group)and BSG (Brigade Support Group) providing support at the relevant levels of command. An LSG was set up in the Gulf after hostilities ended in 1991, based at Al Jubayl specifically to recover equipment.
LSR	Logistic Support Review 1990-91. The review was headed by Major General A N Carlier (late RE) and led to the concepts of ES and Log Sp, and the formation of the RLC.
LST	Landing Ship Tank used for carrying tanks and other vehicles. It can unload over beaches.

LSTPA	Land Systems Technical Publications Authority; the amalgamation of REME Publications Centre and QAD (Publications) in the mid-Eighties.
LSW	SA 80 Light Support Weapon. A 5.56mm machine gun.
LTC	Long Term Costings of the Defence Budget which is compiled in MOD every year covering the next 10-year period.
LTG	Local Tactical Grid or Logistic Task Group.
LYNX	Army twin-engined helicopter, can be armed with TOW missiles.
LZ	Landing Zone.
M548	Non-armoured, tracked, 6 ton cargo vehicle using M113 APC running gear, leased from US Army during Op GRANBY. Also the basis for tracked RAPIER and its maintenance vehicle, and the LANCE missile launcher.
M 578	American-made light, armoured, recovery vehicle used in artillery regiments. It uses the same hull and running gear as the M 110.
M Series	American tracked vehicles including self-propelled guns. The M 109 and M 110 self-propelled guns were used by 1st (British) Armoured Division in the Gulf in 1991.
MACS	Management Accountants Computer System.
MAG	Maintenance Advisory Group; part of a REME Equipment Branch concerned with the development of equipment.
Maintainability	The probability that an item can be retained in, or restored to, specification within a stated period of time under stated conditions.
MARTSU	RN Mobile Aircraft Repair, Transportation and Salvage Unit.
MATE	Multi-system Automatic Test Equipment for electronic equipment.
MBE	Member of the Order of the British Empire.
MBT	Main Battle Tank eg CHIEFTAIN or CHALLENGER.
MC	Military Cross.
McLeod	A committee led by General Sir Roderick McLeod in the Sixties to review the whole of the Army's logistic requirements and organization. It confirmed REME as the overall repair Corps and brought about the formation of the RCT, transferring various RASC functions to RAOC and RE Movement and Transportation functions to RCT.
MCV 80	Mechanized Combat Vehicle later named WARRIOR. Issued to BAOR in 1987 and first used on operations in Op GRANBY in the Gulf 1990–91. There are a number of variants, including REME repair and recovery versions. See WARRIOR.
MDBF	Mean Distance travelled Between Failures of a vehicle, engine etc.
Mellor Loop	A systems approach procedure applied to the training process, named after Brigadier J F M Mellor (late REME), Director of Technical Training in the late Sixties.
MEXE	Military Engineering Experimental Establishment at Christchurch, Dorset.
MEXEFLOTE	A raft used to carry vehicles or stores ashore. It can be connected to others in various configurations.
MGO	Master General of the Ordnance, the head of Land Systems procurement in MOD (PE).
MHD	Military Home Defence of the UK.

MIAS	Management Information and Accounting System.
MILAN	Man-portable, wire-guided anti-tank missile system.
MINIS	MINisterial Information System introduced by Mr Michael Heseltine when Secretary of State for Defence in the Eighties.
MINTECH	Ministry of Technology.
MLR	Mid-Life Refurbishment of complex, expensive B Vehicles such as recovery vehicles, fuel tankers and tank transporters, intended to bring them back to 80% of new condition.
MLRS	Multiple Launch Rocket System. An artillery system, designed in the US, first used on operations in the Gulf War 1991.
MM	Military Medal.
MMBF	Mean Mileage Between Failures.
MMLC	Medium Mobility Load Carrier. A vehicle with better cross-country mobility than a normal commercial truck, but not so mobile as some all-wheel-drive or tracked vehicles.
MND(C)	Multinational Division (Central), formed in April 1992. A three-brigade NATO formation.
MOD	Ministry of Defence.
MOD (A)	Ministry of Defence (Army); that part of the MOD responsible for the Army.
MOD (PE)	Ministry of Defence (Procurement Executive); that part of MOD responsible for procuring new equipment for the armed forces.
MOD Form 700	Aircraft Servicing Forms to record all occurrences for every aircraft.
MRG	Main Repair Group formed from a second-line workshop which also provides one or more FRGs.
MSD RAOC	Mobile Stores Detachment RAOC.
MSR	Main Supply Route, eg from FMA to forward areas in the Gulf 1991.
MSRD	Mobile Servicing and Repair Detachment, replaced in the late Seventies by the Aircraft Maintenance Group.
MSTAR	Manportable Surveillance and Target Acquisition Radar.
MTLB	A multi-purpose tracked vehicle of Soviet origin with a crew of two. Commonly used to transport ammunition and tow artillery pieces.
MTO	Motor or Mechanical Transport Officer.
MTS	Millbank Technical Services, formerly International Military Services under the Crown Agents. In 1978 it became a MOD Agency providing sales and support services to overseas countries including technical training, military vehicles, weapons and equipment. It employed many former REME officers and soldiers.
MV	Military Vigilance.
MVEE	Military Vehicles Engineering Establishment at Chertsey, Surrey (see FVRDE).
NAAFI	Navy, Army and Air Force Institutes; supplying canteens and shops for the Forces.
NARO	Naval Aircraft Repair Organization.
NATO	North Atlantic Treaty Organization. The treaty was signed 4 April 1949 by twelve nations. Greece and Turkey acceded in 1952, Western Germany in 1955 and Spain in 1982.
NBC	Nuclear, Biological and Chemical. (Protective clothing was sometimes referred to as a 'Noddy Suit').

NCO	Non-Commissioned Officer. Ranks range from Lance Corporal to Warrant Officer Class 1. See WO.
NDT	Non-Destructive Testing by means of dye penetrants, X-Ray or ultrasonics.
NIEW	Northern Ireland Electronic Workshop.
NMS	New Management Strategy introduced by Ministry of Defence in 1991, creating a hierarchical budgetary management structure. (See PROSE).
Nye	Lieutenant General Sir Archibald Nye chaired the committee which led to the separation of the Arms and Services Directors from the War Office in 1964. DEME(A) moved from Golden Cross House, off Trafalgar Square, to First Avenue House, High Holborn, London.
O GROUP	Orders Group; to which a commander at any level gives orders for an operation or task to those under command.
OBE	Officer of the Order of the British Empire.
Odling	Major General W Odling (late RA) led the Committee on the Repair of Telecommunication Equipment which reported in 1965. This led to REME taking over first-line repair of radios not operated by R SIGNALS.
OE	Operational Emergency projects. See UOR.
OLAE	Officers Long Aeronautical Engineering course.
OOA	Out Of Area. For British troops this meant operations outside the NATO area.
Options for Change	The Secretary of State for Defence, The Right Honourable Tom King, in a statement to the House of Commons in 1990, proposed overall reductions in the size of the armed forces of 20 percent, with a greater cut in the Army. In June 1991 he announced that the Army would be cut to 116,000, a reduction of 40,000 or about 25 percent.
ORBAT	Order of Battle: a list of units in a force or formation.
OR Branches	MOD branches responsible for specifying the Army's Operational Requirements for new weapons and equipments.
P Vehicle	A powered, mobile, materiel-handling equipment that is used in a warehouse or industrial environment including a tractor, trailer or hand pallet truck, whose registered number must be recorded for legal or management purposes.
PAMPAS	Personnel Administrative Microcomputer ADP System. (The second 'P' originally stood for 'Pilot').
Pay Banding	The system of grouping Army Pay by rank, skill and commitment to a stated length of service, eg 3, 6 or 9 years.
PDS	Post-Design Services. Work undertaken to ensure that modifications and minor design alterations are properly appraised and, where approved, implemented. It covers the re-design, re-development and engineering to preserve or enhance an equipment's capabilities.
PE	MOD Procurement Executive. See MOD (PE).
PEC	Panel, Electronic Circuit.
'Pig'	Humber 1 ton wheeled APC which was converted for use in Northern Ireland.

PIRA	Provisional Irish Republican Army; also known as the Provisionals or Provos.
POL	Petrol, oil and lubricants. Includes diesel fuel.
Power Pack	The specially designed power train (usually of an armoured vehicle), including engine, gearbox and cooling system which can be removed as one assembly. This design aids speed of replacement. CHIEFTAIN, CHALLENGER and WARRIOR all have power packs.
PRE	Periodic REME Examination of vehicles, weapons and equipment.
PROSE	Performance Review and Objective Setting Exercise in MOD New Management Strategy. See NMS.
PSA	Property Services Agency, responsible for Government buildings including building and maintenance of barracks and workshops.
PSAO	Permanent Staff Administrative Officer with the Territorial Army.
PSI	Permanent Staff Instructor with the Territorial Army.
PTARMIGAN	A mobile and secure area telecommunications system.
PTO	Professional and Technical Officer; a civil service engineer in the Defence Engineering Service (see HPTO).
PUMA	Royal Air Force medium-lift battlefield helicopter.
PW	Prisoner(s) of War.
PWSST	PTARMIGAN and WAVELL System Support Team.
PX24/28	Preserving fluids used to prevent corrosion of military helicopters. It was used on the voyage from UK to the Falkland Islands. PX24 was used below decks; PX28, a treacle-like fluid, was used for helicopters stored on deck.
Q Ready	The completion of all arrangements to support a new equipment in the field eg spares, test equipment tools and publications.
QGM	The Queen's Gallantry Medal
QM	Quartermaster.
QMG	Quartermaster General.
QSO	The Queen's Service Order, a New Zealand decoration.
R Equipment	An item of engineer or construction plant or an ancillary which is neither a C nor an E vehicle and whose registered number must be recorded for legal or management purposes.
RA	Royal Regiment of Artillery: the 'Gunners'. Also Royal Academician.
R SIGNALS	Royal Corps of Signals.
R&D	Research and Development.
RAEME	Royal Australian Electrical and Mechanical Engineers.
RAF	Royal Air Force.
R&M	Reliability and Maintainability.
RAMD	Reliability, Availability, Maintainability and Durability.
RAOC	Royal Army Ordnance Corps. The providers of ammunition, petrol, oil and lubricants, rations. equipment, vehicles and spare parts. (Now part of RLC).
RAPC	Royal Army Pay Corps. (Now part of AGC).
RAPIER	Surface-to-air anti-aircraft missile system. Used by the Army on operations in the Falkland Islands 1982.

RARDEN	30mm cannon fitted to FOX, SCIMITAR, FV432 and WARRIOR. Named after the Royal Armament Research and Development Establishment, Fort Halstead and the Royal Small Arms Factory, Enfield.
RASC	Royal Army Service Corps; became the Royal Corps of Transport in 1965.
Rayner Report	The 1971 White Paper 'Government Organization for Defence Procurement and Civil Aerospace' which led to setting up the Procurement Executive in the MOD. Mr Derek Rayner, a Director of Marks and Spencer, became Chief Executive MOD(PE) 1971–72.
RCB	Regular Commissions Board. It selects candidates for commissioning as Regular officers in the Army.
RCIED	Radio Controlled Improvised Explosive Device.
RCT	Royal Corps of Transport. The providers of Army transportation, other than integral unit transport. (Now part of RLC).
RCZ	Rear Combat Zone.
RD/GD	Regimental Duty/General Duty.
RE	Corps of Royal Engineers: the 'Sappers'.
RECLAIMER	The CHIEFTAIN Armoured Repair and Recovery Vehicle.
Recovery	The process of extracting a vehicle or equipment which has broken down or become disabled, and moving it to a place where it can be backloaded or repaired.
Regt	Regiment or Regimental.
Reliability	The probability that an item will continue to meet its specification over a period of time under stated conditions of maintenance.
REME	Corps of Royal Electrical and Mechanical Engineers.
REME 50	The REME 50th Anniversary celebrations in 1992.
REME Journal	The annual publication of the REME Institution.
REME Volunteer	The journal of REME TA.
Repair Pool	An additional stock of vehicles, equipments, or assemblies, procured specifically to allow for equipment undergoing lengthy overhaul.
Retrofit	Fitting a production modification to equipment already in service eg improved sighting systems to tanks.
RFA	Royal Fleet Auxiliary, comprising support ships such as oil tankers.
RFU	Rapier Fire Units or Rugby Football Union.
RHINO	The CHALLENGER Armoured Repair and Recovery Vehicle.
Rigid Raider	A small semi-rigid inflatable boat used by the Royal Marines for patrolling and landings.
RLC	Royal Logistic Corps. Formed in 1993 from RE (Postal and Courier Communications) RCT, RAOC, RPC and ACC.
RM	Royal Marines.
RMAS	Royal Military Academy Sandhurst.
RMCS	Royal Military College of Science, at Shrivenham.
RMP	Corps of Royal Military Police.
RN	Royal Navy.
RNZEME	Corps of Royal New Zealand Electrical and Mechanical Engineers.
RO-RO	Roll On-Roll Off. Ferries which allow vehicles to drive straight through the vessel to offload at the opposite end.
Roulement	The process of rotating formed units or sub-units through a temporary tour of duty, usually for a few months only.

RPG	Rocket-Propelled Grenade.
RPL	Ramped Powered Lighter; RCT vessel used in Belize, Cyprus, Falklands and elsewhere.
RQMS	Regimental Quarter Master Sergeant, in the rank of Warrant Officer Class 2.
RSA	Royal School of Artillery, Larkhill, Wiltshire.
RSM	Regimental Sergeant Major, in the rank of Warrant Officer Class 1.
RUC	Royal Ulster Constabulary.
RYO	Regular Young Officer.
SA 80	5.56mm rifle and machine gun issued to the Army in the Eighties.
SACEUR	Supreme Allied Commander Europe: a NATO appointment.
SAE	School of Aeronautical Engineering at Middle Wallop, formerly Aircraft Engineering Training Wing until I January 1988.
SAGW	Surface to Air Guided Weapon, eg RAPIER.
SAMSON	CVR(T): a light-tracked armoured recovery variant of the SCORPION family, introduced in 1980.
Sandhurst	The Royal Military Academy Sandhurst at Camberley, Surrey.
SAS	Special Air Service Regiment.
SATCOM	Satellite Communications.
SATs	Sea Acceptance Trials.
SBA	Sovereign Base Area in Cyprus under British control.
Scaling	The preparation of a scale of spare parts to support a new equipment coming into service, undertaken by the Army Scaling and Cataloguing Authority. Formed in 1990 by merging the Army Scaling Authority with the Army Cataloguing Authority.
SCIMITAR	CVR(T): a light, tracked, armoured vehicle equipped with a 30mm RARDEN cannon and issued to armoured regiments and armoured infantry battalions for reconnaissance.
SCORPION	CVR(T): a light, tracked, armoured vehicle equipped with a 76mm gun and issued to armoured regiments for reconnaissance.
SCOUT	A multi-role gas-turbine-engined Army helicopter, in service 1963–94.
SCRA	Single Channel Radio Access for entry into PTARMIGAN area communications system.
SEA KING	A helicopter used by Royal Navy to carry men or to operate against submarines.
Second Line	The second line of repair support available to units, providing a greater engineering depth and complexity than is possible at first line. Usually provided by armoured or field workshops and, latterly, REME battalions.
SECS	Superintending Engineer and Constructor of Shipping. A Civil Service grade held by the head of Maritime Branch REME, the engineering support branch responsible for the Army's own vessels.
SEE	School of Electronic Engineering at Arborfield.
SEM	Service Equipment Modifications, term used in Army Aviation support.
SEME	School of Electrical and Mechanical Engineering at Bordon.

SERCo	A support service company providing a wide range of services, and the first to provide contract training at Arborfield from 25 March 1991.
Services	Term used to differentiate the Corps such as RLC, RAMC and REME from the Arms (RAC, RA, RE, R SIGNALS, Infantry and AAC).
SES(A)	School of Equipment Support (Army) at Arborfield. Formerly the REME Officers School until 1 April 1992.
SHIR	A tank developed for Iran; one version became the CHALLENGER.
SLA	Service Level Agreement, a signed and dated agreement between two organizations within the MOD which defines their responsibilities to each other. Most frequently used in support areas.
SLATE	Second Line Automatic Test Equipment.
SNEB	French rocket system fitted to GAZELLE Army helicopters for Operation CORPORATE.
SOAP	Spectrometric Oil Analysis Programme for detecting wear in mechanisms such as engines and gearboxes.
Somerville	The Logistic Reorganization Committee headed by Major General R M Somerville (late RA), VQMG, set up in 1974 and which reported in 1975. It led to the formation of the Logistic Executive (Army) at Andover in April 1977.
SOP	Standing Operating Procedure.
SP 70	A 155 mm self-propelled gun which was being developed jointly by Britain, Germany and Italy throughout the Seventies. The project was abandoned.
SPEARHEAD	The codeword for a UK-based infantry battalion group at 72 hours' notice to deploy world-wide, with a leading company group at 24 hours' notice.
SPEARPOINT	A series of exercises in BAOR for 1(BR) Corps, named after the emblem of 1(BR) Corps.
SPTO	Senior Professional and Technical Officer; a civil service engineer in the Defence Engineering Service, senior to an HPTO q.v.
SR	Staff Requirement. Also Supplementary Reserve.
SRB	Staff Responsibility Budget. One of the two main budgetary systems introduced as part of the Government's Financial Management Initiative in 1982.
SRIM	Service Radio Installation Modification. A term adopted from the RAF, used in Army aviation support.
SS11	Nord Aviation wire-guided anti-tank missile system fitted to Army SCOUT helicopters. Fired for the first time in action in the Falkland Islands in 1982 against ground targets. Declared obsolete in 1987.
SSTE	Special to System Test Equipment.
Staff	A commander's advisers and planners who issue orders and instructions on his behalf eg Personnel (G1), Intelligence and Security (G2), Operations (G3), Logistics (G4) and Civil/Military Co-operation (G5) staffs. Under the former British system G2 and G3 were parts of the G or General Staff. G1 was A and G4 was Q. AQ thus combined the functions of A and Q.
'Stagging'	Slang for periods spent by sentries on guard eg to go on 'stag'.

Stainforth	A study of the United Kingdom Future Command Structure headed by Major General C H Stainforth (late RASC), leading to the formation of UKLF in 1972.
STALWART	An amphibious 6-wheeled load carrier with all-wheel drive; highly mobile with an armoured cab.
Star	NATO terminology referring to senior officers' ranks. For example, 'one star', a brigadier in UK or 'brigadier general' in some other armies, eg Canada; 'two star', a major general; 'three star', a lieutenant general; 'four star', a general; 'five star', a field marshal in the British Army. Red 'star plates' used to be mounted on Army staff cars, helicopters and Land Rovers to show the rank of the occupant. This practice was abolished when the security threat led to senior officers travelling in plain clothes and 'civilian' cars without Army registration plates.
STRATCO	Army Strategic Command formed on 1 April 1968 at Wilton, near Salisbury. Replaced by UKLF 1 April 1972.
STUFT	Ships Taken Up From Trade, exemplified by British merchant ships requisitioned for the Falkland Islands Operation CORPORATE in 1982.
Sustainability	The ability of a force to maintain the level of fighting power for the duration required to achieve its objectives. This requires sufficient personnel, equipment and stocks on hand, together with the ability to repair, resupply and reinforce as necessary. Equipment sustainability is governed by the number of complete equipments, repairable assemblies and spare parts critical to the support of operations that can be made available.
SWR	Static Workshop Review. An MOD review of the resources and the requirements for static workshops in the UK, conducted in 1981–84.
TA	Territorial Army; established in 1908 and reformed in 1947.
T&AVR	Territorial and Army Volunteer Reserve; formed in 1967 and became the Territorial Army Volunteer Reserve (TAVR) in 1971 and reverted to the Territorial Army (TA) in 1979.
TAVR	Territorial Army Volunteer Reserve; reverted to TA in 1979.
TD	The Efficiency Decoration (Territorial). An efficiency medal awarded to TA officers.
TEC	Technician Education Council. It became the Business and Technician Education Council.
Tech Gp REME	Technical Group REME. It became REME Support Group on 1 June 1974 and merged with the DEME(A)'s Directorate to form the Logistic Executive (Army) at Andover in April 1977. Its Headquarters was at Woolwich where it was formed on 1 April 1960.
TI	Thermal Imager or Imaging. Device that detects temperature gradients caused by radiant heat and uses this to recreate a picture of an object from its radiation.
Tickell	A REME Manpower Review Committee headed by Major General ME Tickell (late RE). Set up in 1976 to find savings in REME manpower which was likely to exceed 10% of the Army as its workload increased.

TICM	Thermal Imaging Common Module. Standard sub-assemblies used in a variety of Thermal Imaging Equipment.
TLB	Top Level Budget, eg that held by a CinC.
TLS	Tank Laser Sight.
TOGS	Thermal Observation Gunnery System. Sometimes used solely for Thermal Observation Gunnery Sight as fitted to CHIEFTAIN and CHALLENGER tanks. It uses the Thermal Imaging system.
TOPMIS	TOP Management Information System in MOD.
TOW	Tube-launched, Optically-tracked and Wire-guided US anti-tank system. Fitted to LYNX helicopters in the British Army.
TPEAT	Test Package Evaluation and Acceptance Team. Part of Electronics Branch REME which evaluated software for testing systems.
TQM	Total Quality Management. A management philosophy intended to raise and maintain the quality of management products and service provided by an organization.
TRE	Test Rig Electronic eg for CLANSMAN radios.
Trickle Posting	The system of posting individuals to and from a unit, rather than replacing the whole unit at once ('arms plotting') as practised by infantry battalions and armoured regiments etc. A REME Workshop may stay in the same place for years but its personnel will change as they are trickle posted in and out.
TTF	Truck Tanker Fuel, ie fuel tankers.
UAE	United Arab Emirates (formerly the Trucial States).
UDR	Ulster Defence Regiment; formed in 1970, locally raised and mainly part-time. (Now part of The Royal Irish Regiment).
UE	Unit Entitlement; the authorized scale of equipment holding.
UKFCSS	UK Future Command Structure Study, headed by Major General C H Stainforth (late RASC), leading to the creation of UKLF in 1972.
UKLF	United Kingdom Land Forces. Replaced Army Strategic Command on 1 April 1972 with HQ at Wilton near Salisbury. It commanded the UK-based field forces for operations overseas, and districts in the UK.
UKMF	United Kingdom Mobile Force, formed by 3rd Division with 38 Group RAF 1969–77 to reinforce NATO forces in Europe. It was the Division's primary role. Later found by 1 Infantry Brigade and the LSG.
UNFICYP	United Nations Forces in Cyprus.
UNICOM	Unit Computing. A peacetime administrative computer system for all regular and reserve units worldwide. To be introduced in the mid-Nineties for personnel, pay, finance, stores, training, mechanical transport etc.
UOR	Urgent Operational Requirement. Part of a 'fast track' procurement process to meet an urgent operational need.
V	Volunteer, as in title of TA units and appointments.
Value Engineering	A technique for getting better value from engineering repairs, eg by avoiding putting everything through a base repair programme when the complete base overhaul process is not required It later became known as 'Economic Base Repair'.

VCGS	Vice Chief of the General Staff.
VOR	Vehicle Off the Road (awaiting repair or backloading).
VQMG	Vice Quartermaster General.
WARRIOR	Armoured, tracked troop carrier for infantry battalions, equipped with a turret mounting a 30mm RARDEN cannon and a Hughes Chain Gun. First used on operations in the Gulf War in 1991.
Warsaw Pact	The Soviet Union and its allies in Eastern Europe formed the Warsaw Pact with a strong military structure which was abolished after the collapse of the Soviet Union. The largest forces facing NATO were provided by the Soviet Union, Czechoslovakia, East Germany, Hungary and Poland.
WAVELL	A computer-based battlefield command and control information system in 1(BR) Corps.
Weibull	A family of statistical distributions which is especially useful in reliability studies of early failure, random failure and wear-out failure.
WELSH FALCON	An exercise in April 1982 for the reformed 5 Infantry Brigade in Wales at Sennybridge before going to the Falkland Islands. 2nd Battalion, Scots Guards and 1st Battalion, Welsh Guards had just replaced 2nd and 3rd Battalions, The Parachute Regiment.
WEPC	Weapons Equipment Policy Committee of the Ministry of Defence.
WESSEX	Troop-carrying helicopter, operated by RN and RAF.
Wheel Station	An assembly of a vehicle road-wheel hub and supporting suspension arms and rods.
Whole to Part	A technical training system adopted at SEE, introducing a whole equipment before detailed study of its parts.
Wire Strike	Collision with power or telephone lines by low-flying aircraft/helicopters.
WMR	War Maintenance Reserve: stocks kept in peace for use in war.
WO	Warrant Officer Class 1 or 2. The most senior of the non-commissioned ranks.
WRAC	Women's Royal Army Corps, formed 1 February 1949 and disbanded 6 April 1992.
YW 531	A tracked armoured personnel carrier (Type YW 531 H) of Chinese origin, with a crew of two carrying thirteen passengers. Several variants were produced. Armed with a 12.7mm machine gun.
ZNA	Zimbabwe National Army, formed from former Rhodesian and guerrilla armies.
ZULU	ZULU Time is Greenwich Mean Time as distinct from local time. ALFA time is one hour ahead of GMT.
■	Denotes the award of a bar to a decoration or medal for valour. eg 'DSO, MC■' indicates that a Military Cross was awarded twice.

LIST OF ARTISTS

INDEX

· A rank shown against a name is, generally, the highest rank attained at the time of publication (wherever known) and may not be the rank held at the relevant time in the book.
· Committees, Exercises, Formations, Operations and Units are listed under those sections. (REME and other technical support units are listed under 'REME').
· The granting of Freedoms and equivalent honours are listed under 'Freedoms'.
· Subjects contained in the Glossary are marked thus * in addition to their page reference.
· Where an entry appears in full and abbreviated form in the book it is indexed only in abbreviated form (e.g. Quartermaster General appears as QMG).

Suffield
(BATUS)
NORTH
GIBRALTAR
ATLANTIC
PACIFIC
BELIZE
JAMAICA
GAMBIA
Equator
AMAZONAS
ASCENSION
ISLAND
SOUTH
OCEAN
ATLANTIC
FALKLAND
ISLANDS
SOUTH GEORGIA
BRITISH
ANTARCTIC
TERRITORY